# Interpersonal Relations & Professional Development

**Taken from:**

*Human Relations for Career and Personal Success: Concepts, Applications, and Skills,* Eighth Edition by Andrew J. DuBrin

*Human Relations: Interpersonal Job-Oriented Skills,* Tenth Edition by Andrew J. DuBrin

## Learning Solutions

New York   Boston   San Francisco
London   Toronto   Sydney   Tokyo   Singapore   Madrid
Mexico City   Munich   Paris   Cape Town   Hong Kong   Montreal

Cover Art: Courtesy of DigitalVision/Getty Images, Corel Professional Photos, and Eyewire/Getty Images.

Taken from:

*Human Relations for Career and Personal Success: Concepts, Applications, and Skills*, Eighth Edition
by Andrew J. DuBrin
Copyright © 2008 by Pearson Education, Inc.
Published by Prentice Hall
Upper Saddle River, New Jersey 07458

*Human Relations: Interpersonal Job-Oriented Skills*, Tenth Edition
by Andrew J. DuBrin
Copyright © 2009, 2007, 2004, 2000, 1994, 1990 by Pearson Education, Inc.
Published by Prentice Hall
Upper Saddle River, New Jersey 07458.

This special edition published in cooperation with Pearson Learning Solutions.

All trademarks, service marks, registered trademarks, and registered service marks are the property of their respective owners and are used herein for identification purposes only.

Pearson Learning Solutions, 501 Boylston Street, Suite 900, Boston, MA 02116
Pearson Education Company
www.pearsoned.com

Printed in the United States of America

2 3 4 5 6 7 8 9 10 XXXX 14 13 12 11 10

2009160727

CY

ISBN 10: 0-558-51066-3
ISBN 13: 978-0-558-51066-4

# Brief Contents

Chapter 1    Human Relations and You    2

Chapter 2    Self-Motivation and Goal Setting    32

Chapter 3    Understanding Individual Differences    62

Chapter 4    Stress Management and Personal Productivity    96

Chapter 5    Managing Conflict    136

Chapter 6    Developing Teamwork Skills    168

Chapter 7    Diversity and Cross-Cultural Competence    200

Chapter 8    Problem Solving and Creativity    234

Chapter 9    Getting Ahead in Your Career    268

Chapter 10    Job Search and Career Management Skills    298

Chapter 11    Building Self-Esteem and Self-Confidence    340

Chapter 12    Becoming an Effective Leader    368

Chapter 13    Motivating Others    402

Chapter 14    Enhancing Ethical Behavior    428

Chapter 15    Communication in the Workplace    460

# Contents

**Chapter 1**    **Human Relations and You**   **2**

What is the Nature and Importance of Human Relations?   4

How Can Studying Human Relations Help You?   6

How Do Work and Personal Life Influence Each Other?   7

In What Way Does Human Relations Begin with Self-Understanding?   10

How Did the Human Relations Movement Develop?   15

What Major Factors Influence Job Performance and Behavior?   21

**Chapter 2**    **Self-Motivation and Goal Setting**   **32**

How Do Needs and Motives Influence Motivation?   34

How Do Goals Contribute to Motivation?   41

What Are Some Self-Motivation Techniques?   47

How Do You Develop the Self-Discipline to Achieve Goals and Stay Motivated?   49

**Chapter 3**    **Understanding Individual Differences**   **62**

Personality   64

Mental Ability   74

Values As a Source of Individual Differences   83

**Chapter 4**    **Stress Management and Personal Productivity**   **96**

Understanding and Managing Stress   98

Improving Personal Productivity   110

**Chapter 5**    **Managing Conflict**   **136**

Why Does So Much Conflict Exist?   138

The Good and Bad Sides of Conflict   143

What Are Some Techniques for Resolving Conflicts?   145

What Are Some Suggestions for Managing Anger?   158

**Chapter 6**    **Developing Teamwork Skills**   **168**

Types of Teams   171

The Advantages and Disadvantages of Teams and Teamwork   176

Team Member Roles   180

Guidelines for the Interpersonal Aspects of Team Play   184

Guidelines for the Task Aspects of Team Play   189

Contents

**Chapter 7**   **Diversity and Cross-Cultural Competence**   **200**

What Are the Major Dimensions of Differences in Cultural Values?   202

What Are Some Barriers to Good Cross-Cultural Relations?   206

What Are Some Approaches to Improving Cross-Cultural Relations?   209

How Do You Overcome Cross-Cultural Communication Barriers?   219

Why Are Gender Differences in Leadership Style Regarded as Cultural Differences?   221

What Are Some of the Legal Aspects of Working in a Culturally Diverse Environment?   222

**Chapter 8**   **Problem Solving and Creativity**   **234**

What Are Some Personal Characteristics That Influence Your Problem-Solving Ability?   236

What Are the Problem-Solving and Decision-Making Steps?   240

What Do I Need to Know About Creativity in Decision Making?   245

How Do I Improve My Creativity?   252

**Chapter 9**   **Getting Ahead in Your Career**   **268**

What Are the Basics of Conducting a Job Search?   270

What Are Some Effective Career Advancement Strategies and Tactics?   277

Developing Your Networking Skills   287

**Chapter 10**   **Job Search and Career Management Skills**   **298**

Conducting a Job Search   301

The Vertical and Horizontal Career Paths   315

Career Advancement Strategies and Tactics   319

**Chapter 11**   **Building Self-Esteem and Self-Confidence**   **340**

The Meaning of Self-Esteem and Its Development and Consequences   343

Enhancing Self-Esteem   348

The Importance of Self-Confidence and Self-Efficacy   354

Techniques For Developing and Enhancing Your Self-Confidence   355

**Chapter 12**    **Becoming an Effective Leader    368**

Key Leadership Traits to Develop    371

Suggestions for Developing Charisma    380

Developing Team Leadership Skills    383

Developing Your Leadership Potential    391

**Chapter 13**    **Motivating Others    402**

Motivation Skill Based on the Principle of
"What's in it for me?"    406

Using Positive Reinforcement to Motivate Others    407

Using Recognition to Motivate Others    411

Using Expectancy Theory to Motivate Others    414

**Chapter 14**    **Enhancing Ethical Behavior    428**

Why be Concerned about Business Ethics?    430

Why We Have So Many Ethical Problems    433

Guidelines for Behaving Ethically    441

**Chapter 15**    **Communication in the Workplace    460**

What Are the Formal Channels of Communication
Within Organizations?    463

What Are the Informal Channels of Communication
Within Organizations?    465

What Are the Challenges to Interpersonal Communication Created
by Information Technology?    468

How Does One Do An Effective Job of Conducting
or Participating in a Business Meeting?    475

Chapters 1, 2, 5, 7, 8, 9, and 15 were taken from *Human Relations for Career and Personal Success: Concepts, Applications, and Skills,* Eighth Edition by Andrew J. Dubrin.

Chapters 3, 4, 6, 10, 11, 12, 13, and 14 were taken from *Human Relations: Interpersonal Job Oriented Skills,* Tenth Edition by Andrew J. Dubrin.

# 1 Human Relations and You

## Learning Objectives

## Outline

After studying the information and doing the exercises in this chapter, you should be able to:

1 Describe the nature and importance of human relations.

2 Understand how studying human relations will help you.

3 Pinpoint how work and personal life influence each other.

4 Understand how effective human relations begins with self-understanding.

5 Understand the timeline and development of the human relations movement, plus the major concepts in human relations today.

6 Understand the major factors influencing job performance and behavior.

1 What is the Nature and Importance of Human Relations? 4

2 How Can Studying Human Relations Help You? 6

3 How Do Work and Personal Life Influence Each Other? 7

4 In What Way Does Human Relations Begin with Self-Understanding? 10
General Information about Human Behavior
Informal Feedback from People
Feedback from Superiors
Feedback from Coworkers
Feedback from Self-Assessment Quizzes
Two Self-Evaluation Traps

5 How Did the Human Relations Movement Develop? 15
Scientific Management
The Hawthorne Studies
The Threat of Unionization
The Philosophy of Industrial Humanism
Theory X and Theory Y of Douglas McGregor
Relevance of the History of Human Relations to Today's Workplace
Major Concepts in Human Relations Today

6 What Major Factors Influence Job Performance and Behavior? 21

W hen David Neeleman, founder, chair, and Chief executive officer (CEO) of the highly successful airline JetBlue, was asked to describe his Golden Rule, he replied as follows:

*My grandfather ran a general store, and if a customer needed something that wasn't in stock, he did whatever it took to get the item—even running across the street to a competitor—rather than asking the customer to take her business elsewhere. He never told me, "Take care of others, and they'll take care of you"—he didn't have to. I saw it happen.*

*When I entered the aviation business, I never thought in terms of "passengers" or "tickets sold" but of "people" and "customers." It was distressing to hear airline colleagues complain about the customers—even going so far as to say how much easier it would be for them if there were fewer passengers.*

*When JetBlue started flying in February 2000, my goal was to bring humanity back to air travel. We hire nice people and train them in the skills they require to help run the airline. . . . We are all servants in the best sense of the word, which brings amazing personal and professional rewards. [1]*

The comments by the highly successful and much admired business executive David Neeleman focus on the importance of effective human relations. You have to be nice to begin with (have good human relations skills and a positive attitude), and then you have to treat your customers well (more good human relations skills.) This book presents a wide variety of suggestions and guidelines for improving your personal relationships both on and off the job. Most of them are based on systematic knowledge about human behavior.

■ **Learning Objective 1**

# What is the Nature and Importance of Human Relations?

■ **Human relations**
the art of using systematic knowledge about human behavior to improve personal, job, and career effectiveness

In the context used here, **human relations** is the art of using systematic knowledge about human behavior to improve personal, job, and career effectiveness. Human relations is far more than "being nice to people" because it applies systematic knowledge to treating people in such a way that they feel better and are more productive, such as providing a more relaxed work atmosphere to enhance worker creativity.

Similar to the field known as *organizational behavior,* human relations studies individuals and groups in organizations. Human relations, however, is essentially a less technical and more applied version of organizational behavior. In this text we make some references to research and theory, but the emphasis is on a more personal and applied approach to the subject matter.

From the standpoint of management, human relations is quite important because it contributes to **organizational effectiveness**—the extent to which an organization is productive and satisfies the demands of interested parties, such as employees, customers, and investors. Steve Kent, an equity analyst (not a human relations specialist) at Goldman Sachs & Co., made extensive observations about the importance of treating employees well (using principles of human relations). He found that treating employees with respect and paying them fairly contributes to developing an efficient and creative organization. Business firms that go the extra mile to treat employees well often derive tangible benefits, such as a high quality of customer service.

Kent notes that Starbucks Corporation is at the forefront of treating workers with respect. CEO Howard Schultz has set the tone from the top and made it clear that workers will not be neglected. For example, employees who work at least 20 hours per week are eligible for health benefits and may receive a chance to receive a stock option grant. (A stock option allows the employee to purchase stock at a specified price at a later date. So if the stock rises in price, the employee can buy it at a profit.) As a result of good human relations, Starbucks's employee turnover is low for the restaurant industry, and its customer service levels are high. [2]

■ **Organizational effectiveness**
the extent to which an organization is productive and satisfies the demands of interested parties, such as employees, customers, and investors

## Human Relations in Practice

### Growing a Technology Company by Focusing on People

When John Nix and Larry Spear founded a technology company as graduate business students, they were short on cash but big on ideas, including how to treat employees. Seven years later, as recipients of a Best Bosses award by Winning Workplaces and *Fortune Small Business*, the co-founders of Go2Call.com credit their employees for the company's ability to make money in the dot-com and telecom industries and achieve profitability at a time when many competitors failed.

At Go2Call, the company's 35 employees know exactly what they need to accomplish for the company to succeed, thanks to management's open-book philosophy, which involves sharing the company's financials with all workers at regular meetings. Staffers also have a stake in boosting the company's performance, by receiving bonuses based on profitability.

"It's the people who make the company," said Nix, recalling how his workers pulled together in 2001 to quickly launch a resellers platform, bringing the company a new revenue stream when it desperately needed it. Most of the staffers are still with the company. "Retention [of employees] has been really critical to our success," Nix said. "Our technology is complex. Our engineers have been building it for years—they understand it."

**Question:** So in what way are Nix and Spear practicing good human relations?

Source: Ann Meyer, "Firms Value Worker Morale as Asset: Employees' Ideas, Enthusiasm Can Have Effect on Bottom Line," *Chicago Tribune* on-line edition, September 26, 2005.

Why does paying more attention to the human element improve business performance? Organizational behavior professor Jeffery Pfeffer at Stanford University notes that people work harder when they have greater control over their work environment, and when they are encouraged by peer pressure from teammates. Even more advantage comes from people working smarter. People-oriented management practices enable workers to use their wisdom and receive the training they need to perform better. Another contribution to improved performance stems from eliminating positions that focus primarily on watching and controlling people. [3] The accompanying Human Relations in Practice box insert provides additional information about the payoff from company management practicing good human relations.

■ Learning Objective 2

# How Can Studying Human Relations Help You?

Another way of understanding the importance of human relations is to examine its personal benefits. A person who carefully studies human relations and incorporates its suggestions into his or her work and personal life should derive the five benefits discussed next. Knowledge itself, however, is not a guarantee of success. Because people differ greatly in learning ability, personality, and life circumstances, some will get more out of studying human relations than will others. You may, for example, be getting along well with coworkers or customers so that studying this topic seems unnecessary from your viewpoint. Or you may be so shy at this stage of your life that you are unable to capitalize on some of the suggestions for being assertive with people. You might have to work doubly hard to benefit from studying that topic. The major benefits from studying human relations are the following:

## Human Relations in Practice

### Personal Characteristics of Job Applicants Valued at Enterprise Auto

"We look for several attributes in potential employees, but, in short, Enterprise is made up of individuals who thrive on or being in charge or dream of being entrepreneurs. We look for individuals who have leadership skills and who have worked in some capacity to develop these skills. We also like to see individuals who are genuine team players, who are eager to share ideas, and who have demonstrated their enthusiasm and drive, and who have a customer service attitude."

Source: Andrew Taylor, CEO and Chairman of Enterprise Rent-A-Car, quoted in *BizEd*, July/August, 2003, p. 16.

**1. Acquiring valid information about human behavior.** To feel comfortable with people and to make a favorable impression both on and off the job, you need to understand how people think and act. Studying human relations will provide you with some basic knowledge about interpersonal relationships, such as the meaning of self-esteem, why goals work, and win–win conflict resolution. You will even learn such things as effective methods of dealing with difficult people.

**2. Developing skills in dealing with people.** People who aspire to high-level positions or enriched social lives need to be able to communicate with others, work well on a team, manage stress, and behave confidently. Relating well to diverse cultural groups is also an asset. Studying information about such topics, coupled with practicing what you learn, should help you develop such interpersonal skills. The accompanying Human Relations in Practice box insert illustrates how much employers value skills in dealing with people.

**3. Coping with job problems.** Almost everyone who holds a job inevitably runs into human relations problems. Reading about these problems and suggestions for coping with them could save you considerable inner turmoil. Among the job survival skills that you will learn about in the study of human relations are how to deal with difficult people and how to overcome what seems to be an overwhelming workload.

**4. Coping with personal problems.** We all have problems. An important difference between the effective and the ineffective person is that the effective person knows how to manage them. Among the problems studying human relations will help you cope with are self-defeating behavior, dealing with a difficult coworker, overcoming low self-confidence, and working your way out of debt.

**5. Capitalizing on opportunities.** Many readers of this book will someday spend part of their working time taking advantage of opportunities rather than solving daily problems. Every career-minded person needs a few breakthrough experiences to make life more rewarding. Toward this end, studying human relations gives you ideas for developing your career and becoming a leader.

You are invited to take the accompanying Human Relations Self-Assessment Quiz 1-1 to think through your current level of human relations effectiveness.

# How Do Work and Personal Life Influence Each Other?

■ Learning Objective 3

Most people reading this book will be doing so to improve their job effectiveness and careers. Therefore, the book centers on relationships with people in a job setting. Keep in mind that human relationships in work and personal life have much in common. Several studies have supported the close relationship between job satisfaction and life satisfaction. One such study conducted by Timothy A. Judge, psychology professor at the University of Florida, and Remus Ilies, psychology professor at Michigan State University, involved 74 university employees with administrative support positions, such as secretaries or office managers. The researchers collected reports of mood and job satisfaction at

# Human Relations Self-Assessment Quiz  1-1

## Human Relations Skills

For each of the following statements about human relations skills, indicate how strong you think you are right now. Attempt to be as objective as possible, even though most of us tend to exaggerate our skills in dealing with people. To help obtain a more objective evaluation of your capabilities, ask someone who knows you well (family member, friend, or work associate) to also rate you on these factors. Use the following scale: (1) very weak, (2) weak, (3) average, (4) strong, (5) very strong.

|  | Self-Rating | Rating by Other Person |
|---|---|---|
| 1. Listen carefully when in conversation with another person | _____ | _____ |
| 2. Smile frequently | _____ | _____ |
| 3. Tactful when criticizing others | _____ | _____ |
| 4. Comfortable in dealing with people from a different generation from myself | _____ | _____ |
| 5. Comfortable in dealing with a person from a different ethnic group from myself | _____ | _____ |
| 6. Comfortable in dealing with a person from a different race than myself | _____ | _____ |
| 7. Let my feelings be known when I disagree with another person | _____ | _____ |
| 8. Let my feelings be known when I am joyful about something | _____ | _____ |
| 9. Make a neat, well-groomed appearance | _____ | _____ |
| 10. Congratulate the winner when I lose an athletic or any other type of contest | _____ | _____ |
| 11. Concentrate on another person when in conversation instead of accepting a call on my cell phone, making use of call waiting, or responding to e-mail | _____ | _____ |
| 12. Compliment others when the person merits a compliment | _____ | _____ |
| 13. Good sense of humor | _____ | _____ |
| 14. Patient with people who do not understand what I am saying | _____ | _____ |
| 15. Cooperate with others in a team effort | _____ | _____ |
| 16. Have controllable temper | _____ | _____ |
| 17. Respected for being honest and dependable | _____ | _____ |
| 18. Hug people when the situation is appropriate | _____ | _____ |
| 19. Trusted by other people | _____ | _____ |
| 20. Motivate others to do something they hadn't thought of doing | _____ | _____ |
| **Total Score** | _____ | _____ |
| **Combined Score (self plus other)** | | _____ |

## Interpretation

1. **Self-ratings:** If your self-rating is 85 or more, and your scoring is accurate, you have exceptional human relations skills. Scores between 60 and 84 suggest moderate, or average, human relations skills. Scores of 59 and below suggest below-average human relations skills in the areas covered in this quiz.

2. **Rating by other person:** Because people tend to judge us a little more critically than we judge ourselves in human relations skills, use the following scale: 80 or more suggests exceptional human relations skills; 55 to 79 suggests moderate, or average, human relations skills; 55 and below suggests below-average human relations skills.
3. **Combined ratings:** 165 or more suggests exceptional human relations skills; 115 to 163 suggests moderate, or average, human relations skills; 114 or below suggests below-average human relations skills.

**Action plan:** Whether you scored high, low, or medium on this quiz, there is always room for improvement, just as athletes, actors, and musicians are always looking to improve their art. Scores in the bottom category suggest a more urgent need for improvement in human relations skill.

work, mood away from work, and job satisfaction. Data were collected using questionnaires posted on a Web site.

The major findings of the study were that mood influences job satisfaction, with a positive mood increasing satisfaction. The effect decreases rapidly because moods pass quickly. The researchers also found that employee's satisfaction with their jobs, measured at work, influences the mood at home. Workers who are more emotional by nature are more likely to experience these relationships, such as joy or anger, on the job spilling over to home life. A related finding was that a mood developed on the job spilled over to the home later in the day. [4] In short, this study confirmed the old cartoons about a worker who is chewed at by the boss coming home and swearing at his or her dog or kicking the furniture!

An earlier study by Judge and a colleague based on a nationwide sample supports the close relationship between job satisfaction and life satisfaction. The study also found that both job satisfaction and life satisfaction influence each other. Life satisfaction significantly influenced job satisfaction, and job satisfaction significantly influenced life satisfaction. The relationship between job and life satisfaction is particularly strong at a given time in a person's life. However, being satisfied with your job today has a smaller effect on future life satisfaction. [5]

Work and personal life influence each other in a number of specific ways. First, the satisfactions you achieve on the job contribute to your general life satisfactions. Conversely, if you suffer from chronic job dissatisfaction, your life satisfaction will begin to decline. Career disappointments have been shown to cause marital relationships to suffer. Frustrated on the job, many people start feuding with their partners and other family members.

Second, an unsatisfying job can affect physical health, primarily by creating stress and burnout. Intense job dissatisfaction may even lead to heart disease, ulcers, intestinal disorders, and skin problems. People who have high job satisfaction even tend to live longer than those who suffer from prolonged job dissatisfaction. These benefits may be attributed to better physical health and passion for life. Finding the right type of job may thus add years to a person's life.

Third, the quality of your relationships with people at work and in personal life influence each other. If you experience intense conflict in your family, you might be so upset that you will be unable to form good relationships with coworkers. Conversely, if you have a healthy, rewarding personal life, it will be easier for you to form good relationships on the job. People you meet on the job will find it pleasant to relate to a seemingly positive and untroubled person.

Personal relationships on the job also influence personal relationships off the job. Interacting harmoniously with coworkers can put one in a better mood for dealing with family and friends after hours. Crossing swords with employees and customers during working hours can make it difficult for you to feel comfortable and relaxed with people off the job.

Fourth, certain skills contribute to success in both work and personal life. For example, people who know how to deal effectively with others and get things accomplished on the job can use the same skills to enhance their personal lives. Similarly, people who are effective in dealing with friends and family members and who can organize things are likely to be effective supervisors. Can you think of other ways in which success in work and success in personal life are related to each other?

■ Learning Objective 4

# In What Way Does Human Relations Begin with Self-Understanding?

Before you can understand other people very well, and therefore practice effective human relations, you must understand yourself. All readers of this book already know something about themselves. An important starting point in learning more about yourself is self-examination. Suppose that instead of being about human relations, this book were about dancing. The reader would obviously need to know what other dancers do right and wrong. But the basic principles of dancing cannot be fully grasped unless they are seen in relation to your own style of dancing. Watching a DVD of your dancing, for example, would be helpful. You might also ask other people for comments and suggestions about your dance movements.

■ **Self-understanding**

gathering valid information about oneself; self-understanding refers to knowledge about oneself, particularly with respect to mental and emotional aspects

Similarly, to achieve **self-understanding,** you must gather valid information about yourself. (Self-understanding refers to knowledge about you, particularly with respect to mental and emotional aspects.) Every time you read a self-help book, take a personality quiz, or receive an evaluation of your work from a manager or instructor, you are gaining some self-knowledge.

■ **Self**

a complex idea generally refering to a person's total being or individuality

In achieving self-understanding, it is helpful to recognize that the **self** is a complex idea. It generally refers to a person's total being or individuality. A neuroscientist expressed wonder at the experience referred to as the self in these words:

*It is astonishing that we have a sense of self at all, that we have—that most of us have, that some of us have—come continuity of structure and function that constitutes identity, some stable traits of behavior we call a personality. Fabulous indeed, amazing for certain, that you are you and I am me.* [6]

To help clarify the meaning of the self, a distinction is sometimes made between the self a person projects to the outside world and the inner self.

The **public self** is what the person is communicating about himself or herself and what others actually perceive about the person. The **private self** is the actual person you may be. [7] A similar distinction is made between the real self and the ideal self. Many people think of themselves in terms of an ideal version of what they are really like. To avoid making continuous distinctions between the various selves throughout this text, we will use the term *self* to refer to an accurate representation of the individual.

Some scientific evidence suggests that the self is based on structures within the brain. According to the research of Joseph LeDoux at New York University, the self is the sum of the brain's individual components, or subsystems. Each subsystem has its own form of memory, along with its interactions with other subsystems. [8] Two examples of subsystems in the brain would be a center for speech and a center for hearing. The implication to recognize here is that the self could be an entity that is both psychological and biological.

Because we discuss the self in the first chapter, it does not imply that the other chapters do not deal with the self. Most of this text is geared toward using human relations knowledge for self-development and self-improvement. Throughout the text you will find questionnaires designed to improve insight. The self-knowledge emphasized here deals with psychological (such as personality traits and thinking style) rather than physical characteristics (such as height and blood pressure). Here we discuss five types of information that contribute to self-understanding, along with potential problems in self-evaluation.

## GENERAL INFORMATION ABOUT HUMAN BEHAVIOR

As you learn about people in general, you should also be gaining knowledge about yourself. Therefore, most of the information in this text is presented in a form that should be useful to you personally. Whenever general information is presented, it is your responsibility to relate such information to your particular situation. One such general cause is limited resources, that is, not everyone can have what he or she wants. See how this general principle applies to you. An example involving others is, "That's why I've been so angry with Melissa lately. She was the one given the promotion, whereas I'm stuck in the same old job."

In relating facts and observations about people in general to yourself, be careful not to misapply the information. Feedback from other people will help you avoid the pitfalls of introspection (looking into yourself).

## INFORMAL FEEDBACK FROM PEOPLE

As just implied, **feedback** is information that tells you how well you have performed. You can sometimes obtain feedback from the spontaneous comments of others or by asking them for feedback. An order-fulfillment materials-handling specialist grew one notch in self-confidence when coworkers began to call him "Net Speed." He was given this name because of the rapidity with which he processed orders. His experience illustrates that a valuable source of information for self-understanding is what the significant people in your life think of you. Although feedback of this type might make you feel uncomfortable, when it is consistent, it accurately reflects how others perceive you.

■ **Public self**
what a person communicates about himself or herself and what others actually perceive about the person

■ **Private self**
the actual person an individual may be

■ **Feedback**
information that tells one how well he or she has performed

With some ingenuity you can create informal feedback. (In this sense, the term *formal* refers to not being part of a company-sponsored program.) A student enrolled in a human relations course obtained valuable information about himself from a questionnaire he sent to 15 people. His directions were as follows:

> I am hoping that you can help me with one of the most important assignments of my life. I want to obtain a candid picture of how I am seen by others—what they think are my strengths, areas for improvement, good points, and bad points. Any other observations about me as an individual would also be welcome.
>
> Write down your thoughts on the attached questionnaire. The information that you provide me will help me develop a plan for personal improvement that I am writing for a course in human relations. Mail the form back to me in the enclosed envelope. It is not necessary for you to sign the form. If you are not concerned about being anonymous, just fill out the questionnaire on the document in the e-mail I sent you.

A few skeptics will argue that friends never give you a true picture of yourself but, rather, say flattering things about you because they value your friendship. Experience has shown, however, that if you emphasize the importance of their opinions, most people will give you a few constructive suggestions. You also have to appear sincere. Because not everyone's comments will be helpful, you may have to sample many people.

## FEEDBACK FROM SUPERIORS

Virtually all employers provide employees with formal or informal feedback on their performances. A formal method of feedback is called a *performance evaluation*. During a performance evaluation (or appraisal) your superior will convey to you what he or she thinks you are doing well and not so well. These observations become a permanent part of your human resources record. Informal feedback occurs when a superior discusses your job performance with you but does not record these observations.

The feedback obtained from superiors in this way can help you learn about yourself. For instance, if two different bosses say that you are a creative problem solver, you might conclude that you are creative. If several bosses told you that you are too impatient with other people, you might conclude that you are impatient.

## FEEDBACK FROM COWORKERS

**■ Peer evaluations**

system in which teammates contribute to an evaluation of a person's job performance

A sometimes-used practice in organizations is **peer evaluations,** a system in which teammates contribute to an evaluation of a person's job performance. Although coworkers under this system do not have total responsibility for evaluating each other, their input is taken seriously. The amount of a worker's salary increase could thus be affected by peer judgments about his or her performance. The results of peer evaluations can also be used as feedback for learning about yourself. Assume that coworkers agree on several of your strengths and needs for improvement. You can conclude that others who work closely with you generally perceive you that way.

Teammates might rate each other on performance dimensions such as cooperation with other members of the team, customer service attitude, productivity, and contributions to meetings. If several teammates rated you low in one of these dimensions, it could indicate a **developmental opportunity,** an area for growth, or weakness.

## FEEDBACK FROM SELF-ASSESSMENT QUIZZES

Many self-help books, including this one, contain questionnaires that you fill out by yourself, for yourself. The information that you pick up from these questionnaires often provides valuable clues to your preferences, values, and personal traits. Such self-examination questionnaires should not be confused with the scientifically researched test you might take in a counseling center or guidance department or when applying for a job. Another source of useful self-assessment quizzes is *www.queedom.com*, which offers a variety of tests that contribute to self-understanding, including the classical Intelligence quotient (IQ), mental toughness, risk-taking, and self-esteem among many others.

The amount of useful information gained from self-examination questionnaires depends on your candor. Because no outside judge is involved in these self-help quizzes, candor usually is not a problem. An exception is that we all have certain blind spots. Most people, for example, believe that they have considerably above-average skills in dealing with people.

As a starting point in conducting self-examination exercises, you already completed Human Relations Self-Assessment Quiz 1–1. Quiz 1-2 gives you an opportunity to write some things down about yourself.

## TWO SELF-EVALUATION TRAPS

The theme of this section of the chapter is that self-awareness is a positive force in our lives. Yet self-awareness also has two negative extremes or traps. One of these extremes is that focusing on the self can highlight shortcomings the way staring into a mirror can dramatize every blemish and wrinkle on a face. Certain situations predictably force us to engage in self-reflection and become the object of our own attention. When we talk about ourselves, answer self-quizzes, stand before an audience or camera, or watch ourselves on DVD or videotape, we become more self-aware and make comparisons to some arbitrary standard of behavior. The comparison often results in negative self-evaluation in comparison to the standard and a decrease in self-esteem as we discover that we fall short of standards. [9] Keeping the self-awareness trap in mind will help you minimize needless underevaluation, thereby benefiting from gathering feedback about yourself.

In contrast to underevaluation, it is also true that many people tend to overestimate their competence, such as thinking they deserve a bigger raise or an A in every course. A particular area in which people overestimate their competence is in the moral domain. Many people suffer from a "*holier than thou*" syndrome. A study with college students, for example, found that they consistently overrated the likelihood that they would act in generous or selfless ways. For example, in one study 84 percent of the students initially predicted that they would cooperate with their partner but in reality only 61 percent did. [10]

■ **Developmental opportunity** teammates rating one another on performance dimensions, such as cooperation with other members of the team, customer service attitude, productivity, and contribution to meetings

## Human Relations Self-Assessment Quiz    1-2

### The Written Self-Portrait

A good starting point in acquiring serious self-knowledge is to prepare a written self-portrait in the major life spheres (or aspects). In each of the following spheres, describe yourself in about 25 to 50 words. For example, under the social and interpersonal sphere, a person might write, "I'm a little timid on the surface. But those people who get to know me well understand that I'm filled with enthusiasm and joy. My relationships with people last a long time. I'm on excellent terms with all members of my family. And my significant other and I have been together for five years. We are very close emotionally and should be together for a lifetime."

**A.** Occupational and school: _____

_____

_____

**B.** Social and interpersonal: _____

_____

_____

**C.** Beliefs, values, and attitudes: _____

_____

_____

**D.** Physical description (body type, appearance, grooming): _____

_____

_____

_____

Cultural differences help explain at least some of the differences in underevaluation versus overevaluation. Several studies have shown, for example, that East Asians tend to underestimate their abilities, with an aim toward improving the self and getting along with others. North Americans are more likely to overestimate their abilities and not be so prone to look for areas of self-improvement. [11] Cultural differences are stereotypes that apply to the average individual from a culture.

The antidote to the twin self-evaluation traps is to search for honest and objective feedback from others to help you supplement your self-evaluation. Competing against peers, such as in school, sports, and contests on the job (for example, a sales contest or creative suggestion contest) can help you evaluate yourself more realistically. Next, we look more at human relations from the standpoint of the workplace rather than the individual.

# How Did the Human Relations Movement Develop?

■ Learning Objective 5

The **human relations movement** began as a concentrated effort by some managers and their advisors to become more sensitive to the needs of employees or to treat them in a more humanistic manner. In other words, employees were to be treated as human beings rather than as parts of the productive process. The human relations movement was supported directly by three different historic influences: the Hawthorne studies, the threat of unionization, and industrial humanism (see Figure 1-1). [12] Scientific management, which predated the growth of human relations in industry, contributed indirectly to the movement.

■ **Human relations movement**
movement that began as a concentrated effort by some managers and their advisors to become more sensitive to the needs of employees or to treat them in a more humanistic manner

## SCIENTIFIC MANAGEMENT

The study of management became more systematized and formal as a by-product of the Industrial Revolution that took place from the 1700s through the 1900s. Approaches to managing work and people needed to be developed to manage all the new factories that were a central part of the Industrial Revolution. The focus of **scientific management** was on the application of scientific methods to increase individual workers' productivity. Frederick W. Taylor, considered the father of scientific management, was an engineer by background. He used scientific analysis and experiments to increase worker output. Taylor's goal was to remove human variability so each worker could become essentially an interchangeable part. His model for human behavior was a machine, with inexpensive parts, each of which has a specific function. Using the principles of scientific management, a worker might assemble a

■ **Scientific management**
theory that focuses on the application of scientific methods to increase individual workers' productivity

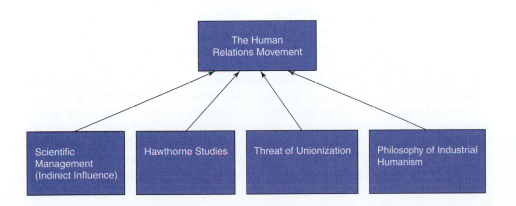

**Figure 1-1**

**Influences Supporting the Human Relations Movement**

washing machine with the least number of wasted motions and steps. United Parcel Service (UPS) relies heavily on the principles of scientific management to get the most productivity from carriers and shipping personnel, including tightly timing their deliveries.

With scientific management sounding so dehumanizing, how could the movement have contributed to good human relations? Taylor also studied problems such as fatigue and safety. He urged management to study the relationship between work breaks and the length of the workday, and productivity. He convinced some managers that work breaks and shorter workdays could increase productivity. Furthermore, scientific management proposed that workers who produced more be paid more.

Scientific management also contributed to the human relations movement by creating a backlash against what many people thought was mistreatment of workers. The industrial engineer with his or her stopwatch and clipboard, hovering over a worker measuring each tiny part of the job and the worker's movements, became a hated figure. [13] The objection to this approach called for a better way to treat people, that came to be known as the human relations movement.

## THE HAWTHORNE STUDIES

The human relations school of management is generally said to have begun in 1927 with a group of studies conducted at the Hawthorne plant of an AT&T subsidiary. These studies were prompted by an experiment carried out by the company's engineers between 1924 and 1927. Following the tradition of scientific management, these engineers were applying research methods to investigate problems of employee productivity.

Two groups were studied to determine the effects of different levels of illumination on worker performance. As prescribed by the scientific method, one group received increased illumination, whereas the other did not. A preliminary finding was that when illumination was increased, the level of performance also increased. Surprisingly to the engineers, productivity also increased when the level of illumination was decreased almost to moonlight levels. One interpretation of these findings was that the workers involved in the experiment enjoyed being the center of attention. In other words, they reacted positively because management cared about them. Such a phenomenon taking place in any work or research setting is now called the **Hawthorne effect.** [14]

■ **Hawthorne effect**
applying research methods to investigate problems of employee productivity using the scientific method; in the study, employees reacted positively because management cared about them

As a result of these preliminary investigations, a team of researchers headed by Harvard professors Elton Mayo and Fritz J. Roethlisberger conducted a series of experiments extending over a six-year period. The conclusions they reached served as the foundations for later developments in the human relations approach to management. It was found that economic incentives are less important than generally believed in influencing workers to achieve high levels of output. Also, leadership practices and work-group pressures profoundly influence employee satisfaction and performance. An example of an effective leadership practice would be coaching and encouraging workers to higher performance. The researchers noted that any factor influencing employee behavior is embedded in a social system. For example, to understand the impact of pay on performance, you have to understand the atmosphere that exists in the work group and how the leader approaches his or her job.

A major implication of the Hawthorne studies was that the old concept of an economic person motivated primarily by money had to be replaced by a more valid idea. The replacement concept was a social person, motivated by social needs, desiring rewarding on-the-job relationships, and more responsive to pressures from coworkers than to control by the boss. [15] Do you believe that workers are more concerned with social relationships than with money?

## THE THREAT OF UNIONIZATION

Labor union officials and their advocates contend that the benefits of unionization extend to many workers who themselves do not belong to unions. Management in nonunion firms will often pay employees union wages in order to offset the potential advantages of unionization. A similar set of circumstances contributed to the growth of the human relations movement. Labor unions began to grow rapidly in the United States during the late 1930s. Many employers feared that the presence of a labor union would have negative consequences for their companies. Consequently, management looked aggressively for ways to stem the tide of unionization, such as using human relations techniques to satisfy workers. [16] Their reasoning is still valid today: dissatisfied workers are much more likely to join a labor union, in hope of improving their working conditions. [17]

Today the threat of unionization is primarily in the public sector. Although unionization has declined considerablly in manufacturing, about 36 percent of government workers, including those in education, are union members compared with about 8 percent of workers in private-sector industries. In 1945 about 36 percent of the U.S. workforce was unionized, versus about 12 percent today. [18] The decline of manufacturing jobs has contributed to the decline of union membership.

## THE PHILOSOPHY OF INDUSTRIAL HUMANISM

Partly as a by-product of the Hawthorne studies, a new philosophy arose of human relations in the workplace. Elton Mayo was one of the two key figures in developing this philosophy of industrial humanism. He cautioned managers that emotional factors (such as a desire for recognition) were a more important contributor to productivity than physical and logical factors. Mayo argued vigorously that work should lead to personal satisfaction for employees.

Mary Parker Follett was another key figure in advancing the cause of industrial humanism. Her experience as a management consultant led her to believe that the key to increased productivity was to motivate employees, rather than simply ordering better job performance. The keys to both productivity and democracy, according to Follett, were cooperation, a spirit of unity, and a coordination of effort. [19]

# THEORY X AND THEORY Y OF DOUGLAS MCGREGOR

The importance of managing people through more effective methods of human relations was advanced by the writings of social psychologist Douglas McGregor. His famous position was that managers should challenge their assumptions about the nature of people. McGregor believed that too many managers assumed that people were lazy and indifferent toward work. He urged managers to be open to the possibility that under the right circumstances people are eager to perform well. If a supervisor accepts one of these extreme sets of beliefs about people, the supervisor will act differently toward them than if he or she believes the opposite. These famous assumptions that propelled the human relations movement forward are summarized as follows:

## Theory X Assumptions

1. The average person dislikes work and, therefore, will avoid it if he or she can.

2. Because of this dislike of work, most people must be coerced, controlled, directed, or threatened with punishment to get them to put forth enough effort to achieve organizational goals.

3. The average employee prefers to be directed, wishes to shirk responsibility, has relatively little ambition, and highly values job security.

## Theory Y Assumptions

1. The expenditure of physical and mental effort in work is as natural as play or rest.

2. External control and the threat of punishment are not the only means for bringing about effort toward reaching company objectives. Employees will exercise self-direction and self-control in the service of objectives to which they attach high valence.

3. Commitment to objectives is related to the rewards associated with their achievement.

4. The average person learns, under proper conditions, not only to accept but also to seek responsibility.

5. Many employees have the capacity to exercise a high degree of imagination, ingenuity, and creativity in the solution of organizational problems.

6. Under the present conditions of industrial life, the intellectual potentialities of the average person are only partially utilized. [20]

The distinction between Theory X and Theory Y has often been misinterpreted. McGregor was humanistic, but he did not mean to imply that being directive and demanding with workers is always the wrong tactic. Some people are undermotivated and dislike work. In these situations, the manager has to behave sternly toward group members to motivate them. If you are a Theory Y manager, you size up your group members to understand their attitudes toward work.

## RELEVANCE OF THE HISTORY OF HUMAN RELATIONS TO TODAY'S WORKPLACE

Many of the pioneering ideas described in the history of human relations are still relevant, partly because human nature has not undergone major changes. Most of the core ideas in the history of the human relations movement are still part of the human relations and organizational behavior curriculum today, even though they have more research substantiation and new labels. A good example is the push toward creativity and innovation based on the involvement of loads of workers, not only specialists from one department. The link to history is that Theory Y encourages empowering employees to use their ingenuity and creativity to solve organizational problems. Next is a bulleted summary of ideas from the human relations movement that still influence the practice of human relations today.

■ Many principles of scientific management are useful in making workers more productive so business firms can compete better in a global economy.

■ Ideas from the Hawthorne studies have helped managers focus on the importance of providing both congenial work surroundings and adequate compensation in order to motivate and retain workers.

■ Industrial humanism is widely practiced today in the form of looking for ways to keep workers satisfied through such methods as flexible work arrangements, family leave, and dependent care benefits.

■ Theory Y has prompted managers to think through which style of leadership works best with which employees. Specifically, a modern manager is likely to grant more freedom to employees who are well-motivated and talented. Spurred partially by Theory X, few managers today believe that being the "bull of the woods" is the best way to supervise all workers.

## MAJOR CONCEPTS IN HUMAN RELATIONS TODAY

A major purpose of this text is to provide a presentation of major concepts or themes in human relations today. Ideas already presented in this chapter, including the modern-day spinoffs from the human relations movement, are major themes in human relations. Subsequent chapters in this text deal with these plus other major concepts in human relations today. In quick overview, here are the major themes and concepts of human relations you will be studying:

■ **Self-understanding.** Practicing good human relations begins with self-understanding.

■ **Self-esteem and self-confidence.**  It helps to feel good about yourself when you are dealing with others.

■ **Self-motivation and self-discipline.**  You cannot succeed in today's world if you cannot light your own fire. Without being focused individuals usually accomplish very little.

■ **Emotional intelligence and positive attitudes.** Having technical smarts is not enough. You need to be able to understand people and have a positive, can-do attitude.

■ **Values and ethics.** Most of the greatest business flops in recent years can be attributed to warped values and low ethics.

■ **Problem solving and creativity.** All types of workplaces seek imaginative and creative employees in professional and technical positions. If you can only provide standard solutions to problems, you are in danger of being replaced by software or a handbook.

■ **Communication effectiveness.** A major requirement for success in both technical and nontechnical positions is being able to communicate effectively with other people. Organizations also have a responsibility to establish systems that enhance communication among people, including company blogs as a recent development.

■ **Getting along with others in the workplace.** When one cave-person grunted to the other, "Good job catching fish," the importance of constructive relationships with managers, coworkers, and customers began. Developing effective interpersonal relationships remains the major purpose of studying human relations and one of the major requirements for a successful workplace.

■ **Managing conflict.** Managing conflict is another major concern of human relations. Too much unresolved conflict results in such negative consequences as negative stress, strikes, and worker violence.

■ **Leadership.** The study of how to effectively lead others has become the hottest topic in human relations, organizational behavior, and management in the past decade. Effective leaders are in demand at every level of the organization from team leader to chief executive officer.

■ **Motivating others and developing teamwork.** Motivating employees to high standards of performance is still seen as a major pathway to productivity and competitiveness. At the same time, the leader must develop teamwork because business is a team sport.

■ **Diversity and cross-cultural competence.** The workplace has become increasingly diverse both domestically and in terms of working with people from other countries. Being able to work effectively with diverse individuals has become one of the major human relations competencies.

■ **Learning strategies, perception, and life-span changes.** Three significant topics in managing our life are understanding how we learn, how we make sense out of the world (perception) and how to deal with a variety of predictable challenges from adolescence to the final stages of physical life.

■ **Developing effective work habits.** A starting point in being productive is managing your work and time effectively, including overcoming the number-one form of self-defeating behavior—procrastination. Human relations emphasizes being productive as well as getting along well with others.

■ **Getting ahead in your career.** Another useful aspect of studying human relations is to strategize ways of getting the biggest return on your most important asset—you. Understanding how to become successful has become even more important as so many people's careers are threatened by moving some jobs to other countries.

■ **Managing stress and personal problems.** Staying mentally and physically healthy is a human relations issue because organizations need productive workers who are not so stressed out or distracted that they lose time from work and run up medical costs.

# What Major Factors Influence Job Performance and Behavior?

■ Learning Objective 6

Part of understanding human relations is recognizing the factors or forces that influence job performance and behavior. In overview, the performance and behavior of workers is influenced by both factors related to the employee, manager, job, and organization as discussed next and outlined in Figure 1-2. Here we present a sampling of these many factors because a comprehensive understanding

**Figure** **1-2**

**Factors Contributing to Performance and Behavior in the Workplace**

**Factors Related to the Employee**

Mental ability and education
Physical abilities
Job knowledge
Motivation and interest
Encouragement from family and friends
Distractions and personal problems
Level of stress

**Factors Related to the Organization**

Culture including ethics
Work group influences
Human resource policies

Employee Performance and Behavior

**Factors Related to the Manager**

Leadership style
Quality and quantity of communication
Feedback on performance
Quality of relationship
Favoritism

**Factors Related to the Job**

Adequate equipment, well designed for humans
Challenge and excitement within job
Adequate training and instructions

of them would encompass the study of human relations, organizational behavior, and management.

1. **Factors related to the employee.** The major influence on how a worker performs and behaves, or acts, on the job stems from his or her personal attributes. The worker's mental ability influences how quickly and accurately he or she can solve problems. Physical ability would influence some types of performance, such as the ability to stand up for long periods of time as a store manager or lift boxes as a warehouse attendant. Job knowledge is obviously important, such as a financial consultant being knowledgeable about a variety of investments. Employees who are well motivated and interested in the work are likely to perform better and behave in a more professional manner. Workers who receive encouragement from friends and family are likely to perform better. Being distracted, such as Internet surfing during the workday or experiencing heavy personal problems, can influence performance negatively. Having the right amount of stress can boost performance, whereas being overstressed can lower performance and distracting behavior such as appearing confused.

2. **Factors related to the manager.** The manager, or supervisor, is another major influence on work behavior. A manager's whose style, or approach, is warm and supportive is likely to bring out the best in many employees. However, some workers required a more directive and demanding supervisor to perform at their best. Ample communication among the manager and group members is likely to enhance performance and guide employees toward doing what is expected of them. Most workers need considerable feedback from their supervisor to stay on track and be highly motivated. A high-quality relationship between the manager and group members leads to high performance, more loyalty, and lower absenteeism. Favoritism is another key factor related to the manager. A manager who plays favorites is less likely to gain the cooperation of the entire group.

3. **Factors related to the job.** The job itself influences how well the worker might perform and behave. Given the right equipment, designed well for human use, a worker is likely to perform better, such as being less likely to have aches, pains, and wrist injuries as a result of many hours of keyboarding. A proven strategy for improving worker motivation is to give the employee an exciting, challenging job, such as the opportunity to make presentations to management about a project. Adequate training and instructions can be a big boost to job performance. For example, IBM invests annually more than $100 million in employee training and development.

4. **Factors related to the organization.** The organization as a whole can have a profound influence on the individual worker's performance and behavior. The *culture*, or atmosphere and values of a company, establishes an unwritten standard for how employees perform and behave. At Google, for example, employees are placed in an atmosphere where being creative and making suggestions is expected. And all Southwest Airlines employees know that having fun is supposed to be part of the job. The culture of the organization also influences the ethical behavior of employees, with some companies expecting honest treatment of workers and employees. Other

companies are much less ethical, and encourage tactics such as deceiving customers. The work group, as part of the organization, can influence the employee in such ways as encouraging teamwork and high productivity. Human resource policies are another notable influence on the individual. If your company offers you generous medical and dental benefits, and allows time off for family emergencies, it becomes easier to concentrate on the job.

The four factors just listed often have a combined influence on the worker. Let us take an extreme example: Jack, a well-motivated and talented assistant hotel manager, reports to a manager with whom he has a great relationship, which includes giving Jack ample feedback on his performance. Jack finds his job challenging, and his hotel has the advanced equipment necessary for success. The hotel has a friendly climate, along with generous benefits. As a result of this combination of factors, Jack is an outstanding performer who approaches his job with a high degree of professionalism.

# Concept Review and Reinforcement

## Key Terms

Human relations, 4
Organizational effectiveness, 5
Self-understanding, 10
Self, 10

Public self, 11
Private self, 11
Feedback, 11
Peer evaluations, 12

Developmental opportunity, 13
Human relations movement, 15
Scientific management, 15
Hawthorne effect, 16

## Summary and Review

Human relations is the art and practice of using systematic knowledge about human behavior to improve personal, job, and career effectiveness. From the standpoint of management, human relations is important because it contributes to organizational effectiveness. Treating employees with respect and paying them fairly contributes to developing an efficient and creative organization.

Major benefits of studying human relations include:

- Acquiring information about human behavior
- Developing skills in dealing with people
- Coping with job problems
- Coping with personal problems
- Capitalizing on opportunities

Work and personal life often influence each other in several ways, as follows:

- Mood influences job satisfaction, but the effect passes quickly.
- Job satisfaction influences the mood at home, with more emotional employees more likely to experience this relationship.
- A high level of job satisfaction tends to spill over to your personal life. Conversely, an unsatisfactory personal life could lead to negative job attitudes.

- Your job can affect physical and mental health. Severely negative job conditions may lead to a serious stress disorder, such as heart disease.
- The quality of relationships with people in work and personal life influence each other.
- Certain skills (such as the ability to listen) contribute to success in work and personal life.

To be effective in human relationships, you must first understand yourself. Five types of information that contribute to self-understanding are as follows:

- General information about human behavior
- Informal feedback from people
- Feedback from superiors
- Feedback from coworkers
- Feedback from self-examination exercises

Be aware of the self-evaluation traps of highlighting your shortcomings and unrealistically overevaluating your competence. Cultural differences help explain some of the differences in underevaluation versus overevaluation.

The human relations movement was a concentrated effort to become more sensitive to the needs of employees or to treat them in a more humanistic manner. The movement was supported directly by three historic influences along with the indirect influence of scientific management:

- Scientific management applied scientific methods to increase worker productivity.
- The Hawthorne studies showed that concern for workers can increase their performance as much or more than improving physical working conditions.
- The threat of unionization, in which (management used human relations techniques to deter workers from joining a labor union.
- The philosophy of industrial humanism, in which motivation and emotional factors are important.

Many of the pioneering ideas described in the history of human relations are still relevant, partly because human nature has not undergone major changes. An example of a pioneering idea in use is that Theory Y has prompted managers to think through which style of leadership works best with which employees.

The major concepts in human relations today are reflected in the chapter topics of this text, including understanding the self, dealing effectively with people, developing career thrust, and staying emotionally healthy.

The major factors influencing job performance and behavior are rlated to the employee, manager, job, and organization.

## Check your Understanding

1. Why do you think good human relations skills are so important for supervisors who direct the work activities of entry-level workers?
2. Give an example of a business executive, politician, athletic coach, or professor whom you think has exceptional human relations skills. On what basis did you reach your conclusion?
3. Give an example from your own experience of how work life influences personal life and vice versa.
4. How might a person improve personal life to the extent that the improvement would also enhance job performance?
5. How might a person improve his or her job or career to the extent that the improvement would actually enhance personal life?
6. Of the five sources of information about the self described in this chapter, which one do you think is likely to be the most accurate? Why?
7. How can your self-concept affect your career?
8. How might you improve your self-efficacy for a specific job that you are performing?
9. Imagine yourself as a manager or small-business owner. How might you apply the Hawthorne effect to increase the productivity of workers reporting to you?
10. In your current job, or any previous one, which set of factors had the biggest impact on your performance and behavior—those related to the employee, manager, job, or organization? How do you know?

## Web Corner

The Dale Carnegie organization has long been associated with teaching human relations effectiveness. The company stemmed from the work of Dale Carnegie who many years ago popularized the idea of "winning friends and influencing people." Visit *www.dale-carnegie.com/* to understand what type of skills Dale Carnegie teaches. Compare the course listing to subjects listed in the table of contents in this text. What similarities do you see?

### INTERNET SKILL BUILDER *The Importance of Human Relations Skills in Business*

One of the themes of this chapter and the entire book is that human relations skills are important for success in business. But what do employers really think? To find out, visit the Web sites of five of your favorite companies, such as www.apple.com or www.ge.com. Go to the employment section and search for a job that you might qualify for now or in the future. Investigate which human relations or interpersonal skills the employer mentions as a requirement, such as "Must have superior spoken communication skills." Make up a list of the human relations, or interpersonal skills, you find mentioned. What conclusion or conclusions do you reach from this exercise?

# Developing Your Human Relations Skills

*Human Relations Application Exercises*

## Applying Human Relations Exercise 1-1

### Learning about Each Other's Human Relations Skills

A constructive way of broadening your insights about human relations skills is to find out what other people perceive as their strengths in dealing with others. Toward this end, each class member comes to the front of the class, one-by-one, to make a two-minute presentation on his or her best ability in dealing with people. To help standardize the presentations, each student answers the following question: "What I do best with people is _____."

In this exercise, and all other class presentation exercises contained in the text, students are asked to share only those ideas they would be comfortable in sharing with the class. Here, for example, you might be very good at doing something with people about which you would be embarrassed to let others know.

As the other students are presenting, attempt to concentrate on them and not be so preoccupied with your presentation that you can not listen. Make note when somebody says something out of the ordinary. When the presentation is over, the class will discuss answers to the following questions:

1. What was the most frequent human relations capability mentioned?
2. To what extent do classmates appear to be exaggerating their human relations skills?
3. What omissions did you find? For example, were there any important human relations skills you thought a few students should have mentioned but were not?

## Applying Human Relations Exercise 1-2

### My Human Relations Journal

A potentially important aid in your development as a person with effective human relations skills is to maintain a journal or diary of your experiences. Make a journal entry within 24 hours after you carried out a significant human relations action, or failed to do so when the opportunity arose. You, therefore, will have entries dealing with human relations opportunities both capitalized on and missed. Here is an example: "A few of my neighbors were complaining about all the vandalism in the neighborhood. Cars were getting dented and scratched, and lamplights were being smashed. A few bricks were thrown into home windows. I volunteered to organize a neighborhood patrol. The patrol actually helped cut back on the vandalism."

Or, in contrast: "A few of my neighbors . . . windows. I thought to myself that someone else should take care of the problem. My time is too valuable." (Here, the key human relations skill the person exercised was leadership.)

Also include in your journal such entries as feedback you receive on your human relations ability, good interpersonal traits you appear to be developing, and key human relations ideas about which you read.

Review your journal monthly, and make note of any progress you think you have made in developing your human relations skills. Also consider preparing a graph of your human relations skill development. The vertical axis can represent skill level on a 1-to-100 scale, and the horizontal axis might be divided into time internals, such as calendar quarters.

## Human Relations Case Study 1-1

### *We Can't Afford Good Human Relations around Here*

Tammy Ho was happy to be hired by Bradbury Foods as a supervisor in the main food processing plant. It was apparent to her that being a supervisor so soon after graduation from career school would be a real boost to her career. After about a month on the job, Tammy began to make some critical observations about the company and its style of management.

To clarify issues in her own mind, Tammy requested a meeting with Marcus Green, plant superintendent. The meeting between Ho and Green included a conversation of this nature:

Marcus:   Have a seat, Tammy. It's nice to visit with one of our new supervisors. Particularly so when you didn't say you were facing an emergency that you and your boss couldn't handle.

Tammy:   (*nervously*) Marcus, I want to express my appreciation for your willingness to meet with me. You're right, I'm not facing an emergency, and I am not here to complain about my boss. But I do wonder about something. That's what I came here to talk to you about.

Marcus:   That's what I like to see—a young woman who takes the initiative to ask questions about things that are bothering her.

Tammy:   To be truthful, I am happy here and I'm glad I joined Bradbury Foods. But I'm curious about one thing. As you may know, I majored in business at my career college. A few of the courses I took emphasized using human relations knowledge and skills to manage people— you know, kind of psychology on the job. It seems like the way to go if you want to keep employees productive and happy.

Here at Bradbury it seems that nobody uses human relations knowledge and skills. I know that we're a successful company. But some of the management practices seem out of keeping with the times. The managers make all the decisions. Everybody else listens and carries out orders. Even professionals on the payroll have to use time recording devices for checking in and checking out. I've been here for almost two months and I haven't even heard the term "human relations" used once.

Marcus:   Oh, I get your point. You're talking about using human relations around here. I know all about that. The point you are missing, Tammy, is that human relations is for big, profitable companies. That stuff works great when business is good and profit margins are high. But around here business is so-so, and profit margins in the food business are thinner than a potato chip. Maybe someday when we get fat and profitable we can start using human relations. In the meantime, we've all got a job to do.

Tammy:   I appreciate your candid answer, Marcus. But when I was in career school, I certainly heard a different version of why companies use human relations.

### Questions

1. What is your evaluation of Marcus' contention that human relations knowledge is useful primarily when a firm is profitable?
2. To what extent should Tammy be discouraged?
3. What should Tammy do next about her concerns about the application of human relations knowledge at Bradbury?
4. Based on your experiences, how representative of most managers is Marcus's thinking?

## Human Relations Case Study 1-2

### Critical Carrie of the Claims Department

Carrie Donahoe is one of five claims examiners in a regional office of a large casualty and property insurance company. The branch is still thriving despite the insurer selling many policies on-line, and billing conducted by a centralized office. The sales group sells policies and services existing business, such as consulting with managers and business owners about upgrading their policies. The sales representatives also answer questions about policies, such as whether the policy owner is covered against a terrorist attack.

Carrie works with four other examiners, as well as her supervisor Michelle Pettigrew. The essential job of the claims examiner is to visit the site of a client with a demand for reimbursement for damages, such as a fire, flood, or industrial accident. The claims examiner then files a report with a recommendation for payment that is reviewed by the examiner's supervisor. Also, the home office reviews estimated payments beyond $15,000. Carrie has held her position for five years. She has received satisfactory performance evaluations, particularly for the accuracy and promptness of her insurance claim reports.

Carrie has frequent negative interactions with her coworkers who resent many of her suggestions and criticisms. Jim, a senior claims analyst, says his nickname for Carrie is "Ms. Pit Bull," although he has not shared this nickname with her. Asked why he refers to Carrie as a pit bull, he replied, "It's not that Carrie physically attacks people, but it's that she's so negative about so many things. I'll give you two recent examples.

"Carrie asked me to show her a sample claims report for mud damage. I e-mailed her a report. Two days later she sent me back the report, underlining six words or phrases she said were wrong. She didn't even thank me for the report.

"I came back from a two-day trip to inspect a building damaged by a runaway truck. When I returned to the office, Carrie asked me why it took me two days to investigate a simple claim."

Sharon, a junior claims examiner, says that at her best Carrie is a charming coworker. Yet at her worst, she grates on people's nerves. "Here's what I'm talking about. Last week I came to work wearing a blue skirt and a red blouse, on a day the vice president of claims was coming to visit our office. Carrie tells me that a person should never wear a red-and-blue combination for a special event. Not only is Carrie critical, her criticisms are sometimes way off base.

"Another time she told me that I should not waste my time studying for advanced certification in claims because it's a waste of time. She said that no manager in the company really cares about certification. Either you can do your job or you can't."

A human resource specialist from the home office asked Michelle Pettigrew how she was handling Carrie's personality clashes with coworkers and about her personal relationship with Carrie. Michelle said that she was mildly concerned about Carrie's personality problems but that Carrie still gets her work done. Yet Michelle did mention that several clients indicated that Carrie surprised them with some of her criticisms of their operation. She told one tool-and-die shop owner that a well-managed firm never has a serious accident. That was the company's first claim in 50 years being insured by us.

"When she's snippy with me, I just shrug it off unless it gets too personal. Then I tell Carrie that she's gone too far. For example, a week ago she told me that I don't do a good job of getting enough resources for our branch. That if I were a strong branch manager, we would have our offices refurbished by now. I told Carrie that our conversation was now over."

The human resources director said to Michelle, "I think you and I should talk about effective ways of dealing with Carrie and her problems."

## Questions

Note to student: You might want to peak ahead to the section about dealing with difficult people to give you some more ideas for case analysis here.

1. What do you recommend that Michelle Pettigrew do to improve Carrie's human relations skills in the office?

2. What is your evaluation of Michelle's approach to dealing with Carrie so far?

3. What do you recommend that Carrie's coworkers do to develop more harmonious relationships with her?

# REFERENCES

1. David Neeleman, "My Golden Rule: Never, Ever Forget That You Are a Servant," *Business* 2.0, December 2005, p. 122.
2. Steven Kent, "Happy Workers Are the Best Workers," *The Wall Street Journal*, September 6, 2005, p. A20.
3. Jeffery Pfeffer, *The Human Equation* (Boston: Harvard Business School Press, 1998), p. 59; Pfeffer, "Producing Sustainable Competitive Advantage through the Effective Management of People," *Academy of Management Executive*, November 2005, pp. 95–108.
4. Timothy A. Judge and Remus Ilies, "Affect and Job Satisfaction: A Study of Their Relationship at Work and Home," *Journal of Applied Psychology*, August 2004, pp. 661–673.
5. Timothy A. Judge and Schinichiro Watanabe, "Another Look at the Job Satisfaction–Life Satisfaction Relationship," *Journal of Applied Psychology*, December 1993, pp. 939–948.
6. A. R. Damasio, *The Feeling of What Happens: Body and Emotion in the Making of Consciousness* (New York: Harcourt Brace, 1999), p. 144.
7. C. R. Snyder, "So Many Selves," *Contemporary Psychology*, January 1988, p. 77.
8. Etienne Benson, "The Synaptic Self," *Monitor on Psychology*, November 2002, p. 40.
9. Saul Kassin, *Psychology*, 3rd ed. (Upper Saddle River, NJ: Prentice Hall, 2001), p. 74.
10. Research summarized in Tori DeAngelis, "Why We Overestimate Our Competence," *Monitor on Psychology*, February 2003, p. 61.
11. Ibid.
12. Robert Kreitner, *Management*, 5th ed. (Boston: Houghton Mifflin, 1992), pp. 51–52.
13. Edward G. Wertheim, "Historical Background of Organizational Behavior," available at *http://web.cba.neu.edu/~werthein/introd/history.htm* retrieved March 15, 2006.
14. Elton Mayo, *The Human Problems of Industrial Civilization* (New York: Viking Press, 1960).
15. James A. F. Stoner and R. Edward Freeman, *Management*, 4th ed. (Upper Saddle River, N.J.: Prentice Hall, 1989), p. 49.
16. Kreitner, *Management*, p. 50.
17. Alan B. Krueger, "Job Satisfaction Is Not Just a Matter of Dollars," *The New York Times*, available at nytimes.com, retrieved December 8, 2005.
18. "Union Members Summary," *Bureau of Labor Statistics News*, available at (*www.bls.gov/news*), retrieved January 27, 2005.
19. Kreitner, *Management*, p. 62.
20. Douglas McGregor, *The Human Side of Enterprise* (New York: McGraw-Hill, 1960), pp. 33–48.

# 2

# Self-Motivation and Goal Setting

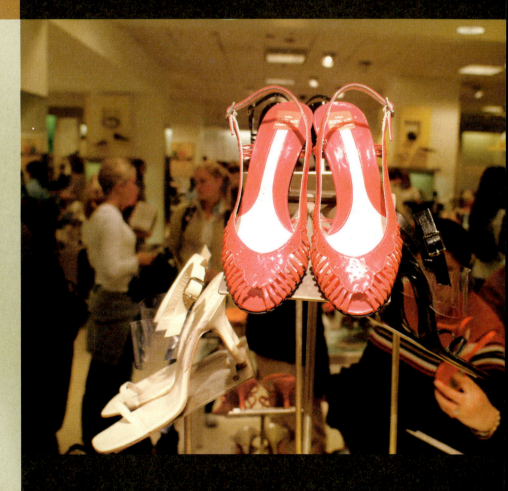

## Learning Objectives

After studying the information and doing the exercises in this chapter, you should be able to:

1 Explain how needs and motives influence motivation.

2 Identify several needs and motives that could propel you into action.

3 Pinpoint how the hierarchy of needs could explain your behavior.

4 Explain why and how goals contribute to self-motivation.

5 Describe how to set effective goals and the problems sometimes created by goals.

6 Describe several specific techniques of self-motivation.

7 Apply the self-discipline model to achieving your goals.

## Outline

1 **How Do Needs and Motives Influence Motivation?    34**
The Need Theory of Motivation
Important Needs and Motives People Attempt to Satisfy
Maslow's Need Hierarchy

2 **How Do Goals Contribute to Motivation?    41**
Advantages of Goals
The Learning and Performance Orientations toward Goals
Goal Setting on the Job
Personal Goal Setting
Action Plans to Support Goals
Guidelines for Goal Setting
Problems Sometimes Created by Goals

3 **What Are Some Self-Motivation Techniques?    47**

4 **How Do You Develop the Self-Discipline to Achieve Goals and Stay Motivated?    49**

E
lizabeth Schweitzer represents the future of retailing. When the 21-year-old was planning to graduate from the Wharton School of the University of Pennsylvania, she was not following most of her classmates to investment banking or consulting. Instead, she would be joining the executive training program at Bloomingdale's, a job that many could perceive as less financially attractive. But her goals were at least as lofty; someday she wants to be CEO of Bloomingdale's parent, Federated Department Stores Inc.

"This is a ripe time for young talent to come up in the world of retailing. And I feel lucky," said the Larchmont, New York, native, who learned the ropes of merchandising at age 13 while working at a clothing store.

Schweitzer, who took a buying internship at Bloomingdale's one summer, said that she has made many contacts in the industry through the program, which provides a strong partnership with the industry. [1]

Maybe a career in upscale retailing is not your dream, and maybe you do not aspire to become the CEO of a major business corporation. Yet Schweitzer's comments emphasize an important truth. You have to be motivated and establish goals to achieve success in your career. Strong motivation is also important for personal life. Unless you direct your energies toward specific goals, such as improving your productivity or meeting a new friend, you will accomplish very little. Knowledge of motivation and goal setting as applied to yourself, therefore, can pay substantial dividends in improving the quality of your life. Knowledge about motivation and goal setting is also important when attempting to influence others to get things accomplished. Motivating others, for example, is a major requirement of the manager's job.

Being well motivated is also important simply to meet the demands of employers. Most organizations insist on high productivity from workers at all levels. Assuming that you have the necessary skills, training, and equipment, being well motivated will enable you to achieve high productivity.

The general purpose of this chapter is to present information that can help you sustain a high level of motivation, centering on the importance of needs and goals.

## How Do Needs and Motives Influence Motivation?

■ Learning Objective 1

■ **Need**
an internal striving or urge to do something, such as a need to drink when thirsty

According to a widely accepted explanation of human behavior, people have needs and motives that propel them toward achieving certain goals. Needs and motives are closely related. A **need** is an internal striving or urge to do something, such as a need to drink when thirsty. It can be regarded as a biological or psychological requirement. Because the person is deprived in some way (such as not having enough fluid in the body), the person is motivated to take action toward a goal. In this case the goal might be simply getting something to drink.

A **motive** is an inner drive that moves a person to do something. The motive is usually based on a need or desire and results in the intention to attain an appropriate goal. Because needs and motives are so closely related, the two terms are often used interchangeably. For example, "recognition need" and "recognition motive" refer to the same thing.

■ **Motive**
an inner drive that moves a person to do something

## THE NEED THEORY OF MOTIVATION

The central idea behind need theory is that unsatisfied needs motivate us until they become satisfied. When people are dissatisfied or anxious about their present status or performance, they will try to reduce this anxiety. This need cycle is shown in Figure 2-1. Assume that you have a strong need or motive to achieve recognition. As a result, you experience tension that drives you to find some way of being recognized on the job. The action you take is to apply for a position as the team leader of your group. You reason that being appointed as team leader would provide ample recognition, particularly if the team performs well. You are appointed to the position, and for now your need for recognition is at least partially satisfied as you receive compliments from your coworkers and friends. Once you receive this partial satisfaction, two things typically happen. Either you will soon require a stronger dose of recognition, or you will begin to concentrate on another need or motive, such as achievement. In either case, the need cycle will repeat itself. You might seek another form of recognition or satisfaction of your need for power. For example, you might apply for a position as department manager or open your own business. Ideally, in this situation your boss would give you more responsibility. This could lead to more satisfaction of your recognition need and to some satisfaction of your need for achievement. (The needs mentioned so far, and others, are defined next.)

The need theory suggests that self-interest plays a key role in motivation. [2] People ask, "What's in it for me?" or "WIIFM" (pronounced *wiff'em*) before engaging in any form of behavior. In one way or another people act in a way that serves their self-interest. Even when people act in a way that helps others, they

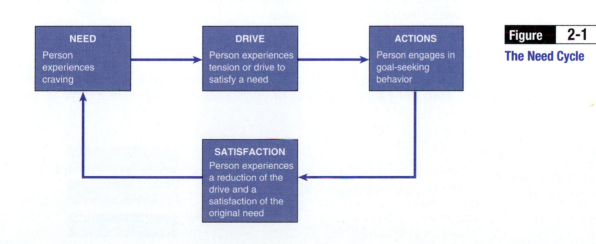

| **NEED** Person experiences craving | → | **DRIVE** Person experiences tension or drive to satisfy a need | → | **ACTIONS** Person engages in goal-seeking behavior |

**SATISFACTION** Person experiences a reduction of the drive and a satisfaction of the original need

**Figure** **2-1**

**The Need Cycle**

are doing so because helping others helps them. For example, a person may give money to poor people because this act of kindness makes him or her feel wanted and powerful.

■ Learning Objective 2

# IMPORTANT NEEDS AND MOTIVES PEOPLE ATTEMPT TO SATISFY

Work and personal life offer the opportunity to satisfy dozens of needs and motives. In this and the following section, important needs that propel people into action are described. As you read about these needs and motives, relate them to yourself. For example, ask yourself, "Am I a power-seeking person?"

## Achievement

■ Need for achievement
the desire to accomplish something difficult for its own sake

The **need for achievement** is the desire to accomplish something difficult for its own sake. People with a strong need for achievement frequently think of how to do a job better. Responsibility seeking is another characteristic of people with a high need for achievement. They are also concerned with how to progress in their careers. Workers with a high need for achievement are interested in monetary rewards primarily as feedback about how well they are achieving. They also set realistic yet moderately difficult goals, take calculated risks, and desire feedback on performance. (A moderately difficult goal challenges a person but is not so difficult as to most likely lead to failure and frustration.) In general, those who enjoy building business, activities, and programs from scratch have a strong need for achievement. Figure 2-2 outlines the preferences of workers with strong achievement needs.

## Power

People with a high power need feel compelled to control resources, such as other people and money. Successful executives typically have a high power motive and exhibit three dominant characteristics: (1) They act with vigor and determination to exert their power; (2) they invest much time in thinking about ways to alter the behavior and thinking of others, and (3) they care about their personal standing with those around them. [3] The power need can be satisfied through occupying a high-level position or by becoming a highly influential person. Or you can name skyscrapers and hotels after yourself, following the lead of Donald Trump.

## Affiliation

People with a strong affiliation need seek out close relationships with others and tend to be loyal as friends or employees. The affiliation motive is met

**Figure 2-2**

**Preferences of Workers with Strong Achievement Needs**

Workers with Strong Achievement Needs → Personal responsibility / Feedback / Moderate risks

directly through belonging to the "office gang," a term of endearment implying that your coworkers are an important part of your life. Many people prefer working in groups to individual effort because of the opportunity the former provides for socializing with others.

## Recognition

People with a strong need for recognition want to be acknowledged for their contribution and efforts. The need for recognition is so pervasive that many companies have formal recognition programs in which outstanding or long-time employees receive gifts, plaques, and jewelry inscribed with the company logo. The recognition motive can be satisfied through means such as winning contests, receiving awards, and seeing your name in print. A major reason the need for recognition is such a useful motivator is that most people think they are underappreciated (and overworked).

## Order

People with a strong need for order have the urge to put things in order. They also want to achieve arrangement, balance, neatness, and precision. The order motive can be quickly satisfied by cleaning and organizing your work or living space. Occupations offering the opportunity to satisfy the order motive almost every day include accountant, computer programmer, and paralegal.

## Risk Taking and Thrill Seeking

Some people crave constant excitement on the job and are willing to risk their lives to achieve thrills. The need to take risks and pursue thrills has grown in importance in the high-technology era. Many people work for employers, start businesses, and purchase stocks with uncertain futures. Both the search of giant payoffs and daily thrills motivate these individuals. [4] A strong craving for thrills may have some positive consequences for the organization, including willingness to perform such dangerous feats as setting explosives, capping an oil well, controlling a radiation leak, and introducing a product in a highly competitive environment. However, extreme risk takers and thrill seekers can create such problems as being involved in a disproportionate number of vehicular accidents and making imprudent investments. Take Human Relations Self-Assessment Quiz 2-1 to measure your tendency toward risk taking.

## MASLOW'S NEED HIERARCHY

The best-known categorization of needs is **Maslow's need hierarchy.** At the same time, it is the most widely used explanation of human motivation. According to psychologist Abraham H. Maslow, people strive to satisfy the following groups of needs in step-by-step order:

1. *Physiological needs* refer to bodily needs, such as the requirements for food, water, shelter, and sleep.

2. *Safety needs* refer to actual physical safety and to a feeling of being safe from both physical and emotional injury.

■ **Learning Objective 3**

■ **Maslow's need hierarchy**
the best-known categorization of needs; according to psychologist Abraham H. Maslow, people strive to satisfy the following groups of needs in step-by-step order: physiological needs, safety needs, social needs, esteem needs, and self-actualizing needs

3. *Social needs* are essentially love or belonging needs. Unlike the two previous levels of needs, they center around a person's interaction with other people.

4. *Esteem needs* represent an individual's demand to be seen as a person of worth by others—and to him- or herself.

5. *Self-actualizing needs* are the highest level of needs, including the needs for self-fulfillment and personal development. [5]

A diagram of the need hierarchy is presented in Figure 2-3. Notice the distinction between higher-level and lower-level needs. With few exceptions, higher-level needs are more difficult to satisfy. A person's needs for affiliation might be satisfied by being a member of a friendly work group. Yet to satisfy self-actualization needs, such as self-fulfillment, a person might have to develop an outstanding reputation in his or her company.

The need hierarchy implies that most people think of finding a job as a way of obtaining the necessities of life. Once these are obtained, a person may think of achieving friendship, self-esteem, and self-fulfillment on the job. When a person is generally satisfied at one level, he or she looks for satisfaction at a higher level. As Maslow describes it, a person is a "perpetually wanting animal." Very few people are totally satisfied with their lot in life, even the rich and famous.

The extent of need satisfaction is influenced by a person's job. Some construction jobs, for example, involve dangerous work in severe climates, thus frustrating both physiological and safety needs. Ordinarily there is much more opportunity for approaching self-actualization when a person occupies a prominent position, such as a top executive or famous performer. However, a person with low potential could approach self-actualization by occupying a lesser position. In the current era, workers at all levels are threatened with the frustration of security needs because so many companies reduce the number of employees to save money.

How do Maslow's needs and the other needs described in this chapter relate to self-motivation? First you have to ask yourself, "Which needs do I

**Figure  2-3**

**Maslow's Need Hierarchy**

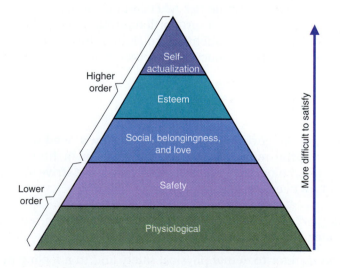

# Human Relations Self-Assessment Quiz 2-1

## The Risk-Taking Scale

Answer true or false to the following questions to obtain an approximate idea of your tendency to take risks, or your desire to do so:

|  | True | False |
|---|---|---|
| 1. I eat sushi or other raw fish. | ☐ | ☑ |
| 2. I would rather be a stock broker than an accountant. | ☐ | ☑ |
| 3. I think that amusement park roller coasters should be abolished. | ☐ | ☑ |
| 4. I enjoy doing creative work. | ☑ | ☐ |
| 5. I enjoy (or did enjoy) the excitement of looking for new dates. | ☐ | ☑ |
| 6. I don't like trying foods from other cultures. | ☑ | ☐ |
| 7. I would choose bonds over growth stocks. | ☐ | ☑ |
| 8. Friends would say that I do not like to take risks. | ☐ | ☑ |
| 9. I like to challenge people in positions of power. | ☐ | ☑ |
| 10. I don't always wear seat belts while driving. | ☐ | ☑ |
| 11. I sometimes talk on my cell phone while driving at highway speeds. | ☑ | ☐ |
| 12. I would love to be an entrepreneur (or I love being one). | ☑ | ☐ |
| 13. I purposely avoid traveling overseas. | ☑ | ☐ |
| 14. Most days are boring for me. | ☐ | ☑ |
| 15. I would like helping out in a crisis such as a product recall. | ☐ | ☑ |
| 16. On the highway, I usually drive at least 10 miles per hour beyond the speed limit. | ☑ | ☐ |
| 17. I would like to go cave exploring (or already have done so). | ☐ | ☑ |
| 18. I like to have a daily dose of simulation. | ☑ | ☐ |
| 19. I would be willing to have at least one-third of my compensation based on a bonus for good performance. | ☐ | ☑ |
| 20. I would be willing to visit a maximum security prison on a job assignment. | ☐ | ☑ |

## Scoring and Interpretation:

| | | | | |
|---|---|---|---|---|
| 1. T | 5. T | 9. T | 13. F | 17. T |
| 2. T | 6. F | 10. T | 14. F | 18. T |
| 3. F | 7. T | 11. T | 15. T | 19. T |
| 4. T | 8. F | 12. T | 16. T | 20. T |

Give yourself one point each time your answer agrees with the key. If you score 16–20, you are probably a high risk taker. 10–15: You're a moderate risk taker. 5–9: You are cautious. 0–4: You're a very low risk taker.

**Questions:** 1. How does your self-evaluation of your risk-taking tendencies compare with your score on this quiz?

2. Do you see any needs for improvement in terms of becoming more (or less) of a risk taker?

**Source:** The idea of a test about risk-taking comfort, as well as several of the statements on the quiz come from psychologist Frank Farley.

really want to satisfy?" After answering the question honestly, concentrate your efforts on an activity that will most likely satisfy that need. For instance, if you are hungry for power, strive to become a high-level manager or a business owner. If you crave self-esteem, focus your efforts on work and social activities that are well regarded by others. The point is that you will put forth substantial effort if you think the goal you attain will satisfy an important need.

Another way of understanding self-motivation as related to need satisfaction is to examine what work factors are important to you. A job satisfaction survey conducted by the Society for Human Resource Management and CNN found the factors listed in Figure 2-4 "very important" by 600 employees at a variety of companies. The list shows the order of importance of job satisfaction factors among employees as a group. [6] Two examples of how needs come into play are (4) job security and (9) opportunities to use skills/abilities. If 4 is important to you, it might reflect a strong need for security. If 9 is important to you, it might reflect a strong need for self-fulfillment.

---

The 2004 *Job Satisfaction Survey* conducted by the Society for Human Resource Management and CNN found the following factors "very important" by 600 employees at a variety of companies. The list shows the order of importance of job satisfaction factors among employees as a group.

| Rank According to Employees | Rank According to You |
|---|---|
| 1.  Benefits | |
| 2.  Compensation/pay | _____ |
| 3.  Feeling safe in the work environment | _____ |
| 4.  Job security | _____ |
| 5.  Flexibility to balance work/life issues | _____ |
| 6.  Communication between employees and senior management | _____ |
| 7.  Relationship with immediate supervisor | _____ |
| 8.  Management recognition of employee job performance | _____ |
| 9.  Opportunities to use skills/abilities | _____ |
| 10. The work itself | _____ |
| 11. Overall corporate culture | _____ |
| 12. Autonomy and independence | _____ |
| 13. Career development opportunities | _____ |
| 14. Meaningfulness of the job | _____ |
| 15. Variety of work | _____ |
| 16. Career advancement opportunities | _____ |
| 17. Contribution of work to organization's business goals | _____ |
| 18. Organization's commitment to professional development | _____ |
| 19. Job-specific training | _____ |
| 20. Relationship with coworkers | _____ |
| 21. Networking | _____ |

**Question:** Why do you think modern employees rank benefits (e.g., medical insurance and life insurance) as the most important job satisfaction factor?

**Suggestion:** Make your own ranking of the 21 factors. What big differences do you see between your ranking and the national ranking?

**Source:** Adapted from Pamela Babcock, "Find What Workers Want," *HR Magazine*, April 2005, p. 53.

**Figure   2-4**

**Ranking of Job Satisfaction Factors by 600 Employees**

# How Do Goals Contribute to Motivation?

■ Learning Objective 4

At some point in their lives, almost all successful people have established goals, attesting to the importance of goals. A **goal** is an event, circumstance, object, or condition a person strives to attain. A goal thus reflects your desire or intention to regulate your actions. Here we look at five topics to help you understand the nature of goals: (1) the advantages of goals, (2) different goal orientations, (3) goal setting on the job, (4) personal goal setting, and (5) guidelines for goal setting, as well as potential disadvantages of goals.

**■ Goal**
an event, circumstance, object, or condition a person strives to attain

## ADVANTAGES OF GOALS

Substantial research indicates that setting specific, reasonably difficult goals improves performance. One of many possible examples involves the American Pulpwood Association, which wanted to increase the productivity (employee cords per hour) of independent loggers in the southern United States. Based on goal-setting theory, Pulpwood crew supervisors assigned a specific high goal for the loggers. They also handed out tally meters to enable the workers to keep count of the number of tress they cut down. Productivity soared in comparison to those crews who were simply urged to do their best. According to professor of organizational effectiveness, Gary Latham of the Rotman School of Management, goal setting instilled purpose, challenge, and meaning into what was previously seen as a boring, tiresome, task. [7]

Goals are useful for several reasons. First, when we guide our lives with goals, we tend to focus our efforts in a consistent direction. Your conscious goals affect what you achieve. Without goals, our efforts may become scattered in many directions. We may keep trying, but we will go nowhere unless we happen to receive more than our share of luck.

Second, goal setting increases our chances for success, particularly because success can be defined as the achievement of a goal. The goals we set for accomplishing a task can serve as a standard to indicate when we have done a satisfactory job. A sales representative might set a goal of selling $300,000 worth of merchandise for the year. By November, she might close a deal that places her total sales at $310,000. With a sigh of relief she can then say, "I've done well this year."

Third, goals serve as self-motivators and energizers. People who set goals tend to be motivated because they are confident that their energy is being invested in something worthwhile. Aside from helping you become more motivated and productive, setting goals can help you achieve personal satisfaction. Most people derive a sense of satisfaction from attaining a goal that is meaningful to them.

## THE LEARNING AND PERFORMANCE ORIENTATIONS TOWARD GOALS

Another useful perspective on understanding how goals influence motivation is that goals can be aimed at either learning or hoping to perform well. [8] A learning-goal orientation means that an individual is focused on acquiring new skills and mastering new situations. For example, you might establish the goal of learning how to develop skill in making a computerized presentation package. You say to yourself, "My goal is to learn how to use PowerPoint [or similar software] so I know even more about how to apply information technology."

A performing-goal orientation is different. It is aimed at wanting to demonstrate and validate the adequacy of your competence by seeking favorable judgments about your competence. At the same time, the person wants to avoid seeking negative judgments. For example, your goal might be to make PowerPoint presentations that would highly impress whoever watched them. Your focus is on looking good and avoiding negative evaluations of your presentations.

A person's goal orientation usually affects his or her desire for feedback. People with a learning-goal orientation are more likely to seek feedback on how well they are performing. In contrast, people with a performing-goal orientation are less likely to seek feedback. If you focus too much on setting performance goals, you might have a tendency to overlook the value of feedback. Yet the feedback could help you improve your performance in the long run.

Goal orientation is also important because it can affect work performance. Attempting to master skills often leads to better results than does attempting to impress others. A study of the effects of the two different goal orientations was conducted with 167 salespeople working for a medical supplies distributor. The salespeople were paid mostly on the commission of the gross profits they generated. The researchers found that a learning-goal orientation was associated with higher sales performance. In contrast, a performing-goal orientation was unrelated to sales performance. An important implication of the study for managers and workers is that a focus on skill development, even for an experienced workforce, is likely to lead to higher performance. [9]

Another positive consequence of a mastery (or learning-goal) orientation is that it often prompts workers to develop better relationships with their supervisors. A study in a Dutch energy supply company found that workers with a mastery orientation had stronger job performance and job satisfaction than those workers with a performance orientation. The positive outcomes of stronger job performance and satisfaction appeared to take place because the workers developed better relationships with their supervisors. [10]

A recent synthesis of evidence points to a key reason why a learning- (or mastery) goal orientation is so important in today's business world. The purpose of a learning goal is to stimulate a person's imagination, to engage in discovery, and to think imaginatively. A performance goal focuses more on exerting effort to attain an objective using the knowledge one already possesses. When an effective strategy requires innovation that has yet to emerge—as is often the case—specific, high-learning goals should be set. [11] An example of a learning goal of high importance would be figuring out how to dispose of debris after a hurricane.

## GOAL SETTING ON THE JOB

Virtually all organizations have come to accept the value of goal setting in producing the results they want to achieve. In most goal-setting programs, executives at the top of the organization are supposed to plan for the future by setting goals such as "Improve profits 10 percent this year." Employees at the bottom of the organization are supposed to go along with such broad goals by setting more specific goals. An example is "I will decrease damaged merchandise by 10 percent this year. I will accomplish this by making sure that our shelving is adequate for our needs."

You participate in the goal-setting process by designing goals to fit into the overall mission of the firm. A bank teller might set a personal goal of this nature: "During rush periods, and when I feel fatigued, I will double-count all the money that I handle." In some goal-setting programs, employees are requested to set goals that will lead to their personal improvement. An auditor for the state set this goal for herself: "Within the next 12 months, I will enroll in and complete a supervisory training course in a local college." This woman aspired toward becoming a supervisor.

A sample set of work goals is shown in Figure 2-5. The service and repair shop supervisor who set these objectives took into account the requirements of his boss and the automobile dealership. Even if you set goals by yourself, they must still take into account the needs of your employer.

## PERSONAL GOAL SETTING

If you want to lead a rewarding personal life, your chances of doing so increase if you plan it. Personal goals heavily influence the formulation of career goals as well. For this reason, it is worthwhile to set personal goals in conjunction with career goals. Ideally, they should be integrated to help achieve a balance between the demands of work and personal life. For example, if your preferred style would be to live in a rural area, a career in manufacturing would be more sensible than a career in advertising. This is true because manufacturing within North American has moved mostly to rural areas, whereas advertising remains mostly in large cities.

### Types of Personal Goals

Personal goals can be subdivided into those relating to social and family life, hobbies and interests, physical and mental health, career, and finances. An example of each type follows:

*Social and family life.* "By age 30 I would like to have a spouse and two children."

---

**JOB TITLE AND BRIEF JOB DESCRIPTION**

**Manager, Service Department:**
Responsible for supervision of service department of automobile dealership. Responsible for staffing service department with appropriate personnel and for quality of service to customers. Work closely with owner of dealership to discuss unusual customer problems. Handle customer complaints about mechanical problems of cars purchased at dealership.

**Objectives for Scott Gilley**

1. By December 31 of this year, decrease by 10 percent customer demands for rework.
2. Hire two general mechanics within 45 days.
3. Hire two body specialists within 45 days.
4. Decrease by 30 percent the number of repairs returned by customers for rework.
5. Reduce by 10 percent the discrepancy between estimates and actual bills to customers.
6. Schedule at least 20 percent of our service appointments through our Web site by January 15 of next year.

**Figure 2-5**

**Form used in Automobile Dealership for Statement of Goals**

*Hobbies and interests.*  "Become a black belt in karate by age 28."

*Physical and mental health.*  "Be able to run four miles without stopping or panting for breath by April 15 of next year."

*Career.*  "Become office manager by age 28."

*Finances.*  "Within the next four years be earning $70,000 per year, adjusted for inflation."

Other categories of personal goals are possible, yet the list presented represents convenient categories for most people.

## ACTION PLANS TO SUPPORT GOALS

Ideally, reading this chapter and doing the exercises in it will start you on a life-long process of using goals to help you plan your life. But before you can capitalize on the benefits of goal setting, you need a method for translating goals into action. An **action plan** describes how you are going to reach your goal. The major reason you need an action plan for most goals is that without a method for achieving what you want, the goal is likely to slip by. If your goal were to build your own log cabin, part of your action plan would be to learn how to operate a buzz saw, to read a handbook on log cabin building, to learn how to operate a tractor, and so forth. Some goals are so difficult to reach that your action plan might encompass hundreds of separate activities. You would then have to develop separate action plans for each step of the way.

Some immediate goals do not really require an action plan. A mere statement of the goal may point to an obvious action plan. If your goal were to start painting your room, it would not be necessary to draw up a formal action plan such as "Go to hardware store; purchase paint, brush, and rollers; borrow ladder and drop cloth from Ken; put furniture in center of room"; and so on.

## GUIDELINES FOR GOAL SETTING

Goal setting is an art in the sense that some people do a better job of goal setting than others. Following are suggestions on setting effective goals—those that lead to achieving what you hoped to achieve.

### Formulate Specific Goals

A goal such as "attain success" is too vague to serve as a guide to daily action. A more useful goal would be to state specifically what you mean by success and when you expect to achieve it. For example, "I want to be the manager of customer service at a telecommunications company by January 1, 2010, and receive above-average performance reviews."

### Formulate Concise Goals

A useful goal can usually be expressed in a short, punchy statement, for example, "Decrease input errors in bank statements so that customer complaints are decreased by 25 percent by September 30 of this year." People new to goal setting typically commit the error of formulating lengthy, rambling goal statements. These lengthy goals involve so many different activities that they fail to serve as specific guides to action.

## Set Realistic as Well as Stretch Goals

A realistic goal is one that represents the right amount of challenge for the person pursuing the goal. On the one hand, easy goals are not very motivational—they may not spring you into action. On the other hand, goals that are too far beyond your capabilities may lead to frustration and despair because there is a good chance you will fail to reach them. The extent to which a goal is realistic depends on a person's capabilities. An easy goal for an experienced person might be a realistic goal for a beginner. Self-efficacy is also a factor in deciding whether a goal is realistic. The higher your self-efficacy, the more likely you are to think that a particular goal is realistic. A person with high self-efficacy for learning Chinese might say, "I think learning two new Chinese words a day is realistic."[*]

Several goals that stretch your capability might be included in your list of goals. The goal of becoming the CEO of Federated Department Stores established by the college student in the chapter opener represents an extreme stretch goal. Another type of stretch goal is striving for a noble cause. A logging supervisor may not get excited about having the crew load a certain number of felled trees on a flatbed truck. However, she might get excited about the trees being used to build homes, schools, and hospitals.

[*] The accompanying Human Relations in Practice insert provides an example of the use of stretch goals.

## Human Relations in Practice

### Technology Executive Sets Challenging Goals

The best goals are a bit of a stretch according to technology executive Margaret Heffernan. She learned this lesson more than a decade ago when a software company hired her to manage the immediate launch of some newly acquired software. A big problem, however, was that the software did not function properly. So, Heffernan and her team decided to reengineer (or reconfigure and redesign) the product in only 90 days.

"The software specialists knew they had set themselves up for a tough challenge and that reaching it was a real coup," she says. "But everyone knew that with each process we rethought, we were closer to the goal. We created energy and optimism rather than quashing it."

Source: Adapted from Margaret Heffernan, "The Morale of the Story," *Fast Company*, www.fastcompany.com, as reported in "Goals Should Challenge, Not Overwhelm," *Manager's Edge*, May 2005, p. 1.

### Set Goals for Different Time Periods

Goals are best set for different time periods, such as daily, short range, medium range, and long range. Daily goals are essentially a to-do list. Short-range goals cover the period from approximately one week to one year into the future. Finding a new job, for example, is typically a short-range goal. Medium-range goals relate to events that will take place within approximately two to five years. They concern such things as the type of education or training you plan to undertake and the next step in your career.

Long-range goals refer to events taking place five years into the future and beyond. As such, they relate to the overall lifestyle you wish to achieve, including the type of work and family situation you hope to have. Although every person should have a general idea of a desirable lifestyle, long-range goals should be flexible. You might, for example, plan to stay single until age 40. But while on vacation next summer, you might just happen to meet the right partner for you.

Short-range goals make an important contribution to attaining goals of longer duration. If a one-year work goal is to reduce mailing and shipping costs by 12 percent for the year, a good way to motivate workers is to look for a 1 percent saving per month. Progress toward a larger goal is self-rewarding.

## PROBLEMS SOMETIMES CREATED BY GOALS

Despite the many advantages of goals, they can create problems. A major problem is that *goals can create inflexibility.* People can become so focused on reaching particular goals that they fail to react to emergencies, such as neglecting a much-needed machine repair to achieve quota. Goals can also make a person inflexible with respect to missing out on opportunities. Sales representatives sometimes neglect to invest time in cultivating a prospective customer because of the pressure to make quota. Instead, the sales rep goes for the quick sale with an established customer.

Another problem is that *performance goals can sometimes detract from an interest in the task.* People with a performance-goal orientation (focusing on being judged as competent) will sometimes lose interest in the task. The loss of interest is most likely to occur when the task is difficult. [12] Assume that your primary reason for working as an information technology specialist is to perform well enough so that you can earn a high income. If carrying out your responsibilities encounters some hurdles, you may readily become discouraged with information technology as a field. However, if your orientation is primarily to advance your knowledge about a dynamic field, you will not be readily frustrated when you encounter problems. You might even look on it as a learning opportunity.

A tight focus on goals can also encourage unethical behavior and a disregard for *how* the goals are attained. A sales representative might give kickbacks simply to gain a sale, and a CEO might lay off needed workers and neglect investing in new-product research simply to make certain profit figures.

Despite the problems that can arise in goal setting, goals are valuable tools for managing your work and personal life. Used with common sense and according to the ideas presented in this chapter, they could have a major, positive impact on your life.

# What Are Some Self-Motivation Techniques?

■ **Learning Objective 6**

Many people never achieve satisfying careers and never realize their potential because of low motivation. They believe they could perform better but admit that "I'm simply not a go-getter" or "I'm simply not that motivated." Earlier we described how identifying your most important needs could enhance motivation. Here we describe six additional techniques for self-motivation.

**1. Set goals for yourself.** As shown throughout this chapter, goal setting is one of the most important techniques for self-motivation. If you set long-range goals and support them with a series of smaller goals set for shorter time spans, your motivation will increase.

**2. Find intrinsically motivating work.** A major factor in self-motivation is to find work that is fun or its own reward. Intrinsic motivation refers to the natural tendency to seek out novelty and challenges, to extend and use one's capacities, to explore, and to learn. [13] The intrinsically motivated person is involved in the task at hand, such as a technology enthusiast surfing the Web for hours at a time. Finding a job that offers you motivators in ample supply will help enhance your intrinsic motivation. For example, you might have good evidence from your past experience that the opportunity for close contact with people is a personal motivator. Find a job that involves working in a small, friendly department or team.

Based on circumstances, you may have to take whatever job you can find, or you may not be in a position to change jobs. In such a situation, try to arrange your work so you have more opportunity to experience the reward(s) that you are seeking. Assume that solving difficult problems excites you but that your job is 85 percent routine. Develop better work habits so that you can take care of the routine aspects of your job more quickly. This will give you more time to enjoy the creative aspects of your job.

**3. Get feedback on your performance.** Few people can sustain a high level of motivation without receiving information about how well they are doing. Even if you find your work challenging and exciting, you will need feedback. One reason positive feedback is valuable is that it acts as a reward. If you learn that your efforts achieved a worthwhile purpose, you will feel encouraged. For example, if a graphics display you designed was well received by company officials, you would probably want to prepare another graphics display.

Industrial psychology professors Remus Ilies of Michigan State University and Timothy A. Judge of the University of Florida conducted an experiment with management students about the effects of feedback on goal setting. The study demonstrated that participants adjusted their goals upward after receiving positive feedback and downward after negative feedback. It was also found that when the students were more emotional about the feedback, the positive and negative results were more pronounced. [14] The link here to self-motivation is that when goals are higher, motivation will be higher.

**4. Apply behavior modification to yourself.** **Behavior modification** is a system of motivation that emphasizes rewarding people for doing the right things and punishing them for doing the wrong things. Many people have used behavior

■ **Behavior modification**
system of motivation that emphasizes rewarding people for doing the right things and punishing them for doing the wrong things

modification to change their own behavior. Specific purposes include overcoming eating disorders, tobacco addiction, Internet abuse, nail biting, and procrastination. To boost your own motivation through behavior modification, you would have to first decide what specific motivated actions you want to increase (such as working 30 minutes longer each day). Second, you would have to decide on a suitable set of rewards and punishments. You may choose to use rewards only because rewards are generally better motivators than punishments.

**5. Improve your skills relevant to your goals.** The **expectancy theory of motivation** states that people will be motivated if they believe that their efforts will lead to desired outcomes. According to this theory, people hold back effort when they are not confident that their efforts will lead to accomplishments. You should, therefore, seek adequate training to ensure that you have the right abilities and skills to perform your work. The training might be provided by the employer or on your own through a course of self-study. Appropriate training gives you more confidence that you can perform the work. The training also increases your feelings of self-efficacy. [15] By recognizing your ability to mobilize your own resources to succeed, your self-confidence for the task will be elevated.

**6. Raise your level of self-expectation.** Another strategy for increasing your level of motivation is to simply expect more of yourself. If you raise your level of self-expectation, you are likely to achieve more. Because you expect to succeed, you do succeed. The net effect is the same as if you had increased your level of motivation. The technical term for improving your performance through raising your own expectations is the Galeta effect. In one experiment, for example, the self-expectations of subjects were raised in brief interviews with an organizational psychologist. The psychologist told the subjects they had high potential to succeed in the undertaking they were about to begin (a problem-solving task). The subjects who received the positive information about their potential did better than those subjects who did not receive such encouragement. [16]

High self-expectations and a positive mental attitude take a long time to develop. However, they are critically important for becoming a well-motivated person in a variety of situations.

**7. Develop a strong work ethic.** A highly effective strategy for self-motivation is to develop a strong work ethic. If you are committed to the idea that most work is valuable and that it is joyful to work hard, you will automatically become strongly motivated. A person with a weak work ethic cannot readily develop a strong one because the change requires a profound value shift. Yet if a person gives a lot of serious thought to the importance of work and follows the right role models, a work ethic can be strengthened. The shift to a strong work ethic is much like a person who has a casual attitude toward doing fine work becoming more prideful.

**8. Develop psychological hardiness.** A comprehensive approach to becoming better self-motivated would be to develop a higher degree of **psychological hardiness**—a mental state in which the individual experiences a high degree of commitment, control, and challenge. *Commitment* is a tendency to involve oneself in whatever one is doing or encounters, such as being committed to

---

■ **Expectancy theory of motivation**
people will be motivated if they believe that their efforts will lead to desired outcomes

---

"Remind yourself that you have personal power, and that you can make things happen. Erase those negative mental tapes that say 'No, I can't.'"

—E. Carol Webster, clinical psychologist, quoted in *Black Enterprise Magazine*, September 2005, p. 157.

---

■ **Psychological hardiness**
mental state in which the individual experiences a high degree of commitment, control, and challenge

developing a successful video game. *Control* is a tendency to feel and act as if one is influential, rather than helpless, in facing twists and turns in life. *Challenge* is a belief that change rather than stability is normal in life and that changes lead to growth and are not threats to security. (Moving in these three directions would involve substantial personal development.) A study with more than 600 college students demonstrated that those who scored higher on psychological hardiness tended to have stronger motivation to study and learn. [17] Psychological hardiness would also be helpful in work motivation.

# How Do You Develop the Self-Discipline to Achieve Goals and Stay Motivated?

■ **Learning Objective 7**

Another perspective on achieving goals and staying motivated is that it requires **self-discipline,** the ability to work systematically and progressively toward a goal until it is achieved. The self-disciplined person works toward achieving his or her goals without being derailed by the many distractions faced each day. Self-discipline incorporates self-motivation because it enables you to motivate yourself to achieve your goals without being nagged or prodded with deadlines. Our discussion of how to develop self-discipline follows the model shown in Figure 2-6. You will observe that the model incorporates several of the ideas about goals already discussed in this chapter. Without realizing it, you have already invested mental energy into learning the self-discipline model. To think through your own tendencies toward being self-disciplined, you are invited to take Human Relations Self-Assessment Quiz 2-2.

■ **Self-discipline**
the ability to work systematically and progressively toward a goal until it is achieved

Figure   2-6

**The Self-Discipline Model**

# Human Relations Self-Assessment Quiz   2-2

## The Self-Discipline Quiz

On the following scale, indicate the extent to which each of the following statements describes your behavior or attitude by circling one number for each: disagree strongly (DS), disagree (D), neutral (N), agree (A), agree strongly (AS). Consider asking someone who knows your behavior and attitudes well to help you respond accurately.

| | DS | D | N | A | AS |
|---|---|---|---|---|---|
| 1. I have a strong sense of purpose. | 1 | 2 | 3 | 4 | 5 |
| 2. Life is a pain when you are always chasing goals. | 5 | 4 | 3 | 2 | 1 |
| 3. My long-range plans in life are well established. | 1 | 2 | 3 | 4 | 5 |
| 4. I feel energized when I have a new goal to pursue. | 1 | 2 | 3 | 4 | 5 |
| 5. It is difficult for me to picture an event in my mind before it occurs. | 5 | 4 | 3 | 2 | 1 |
| 6. When success is near, I can almost taste, feel, and see it. | 1 | 2 | 3 | 4 | 5 |
| 7. I consult my daily planner or a to-do list almost every day. | 1 | 2 | 3 | 4 | 5 |
| 8. My days rarely turn out the way I had planned. | 5 | 4 | 3 | 2 | 1 |
| 9. What I do for a living is not (or would not be) nearly as important as the money it pays. | 5 | 4 | 3 | 2 | 1 |
| 10. Some parts of my job are as exciting to me as any hobby or pastime. | 1 | 2 | 3 | 4 | 5 |
| 11. Working 60 hours per week for even a short period of time would be out of the question for me. | 5 | 4 | 3 | 2 | 1 |
| 12. I have personally known several people who would be good role models for me. | 1 | 2 | 3 | 4 | 5 |
| 13. So far I have never read about or known anybody whose lifestyle I would like to emulate. | 5 | 4 | 3 | 2 | 1 |
| 14. My work is so demanding that it's difficult for me to concentrate fully on my personal life when I'm not working. | 5 | 4 | 3 | 2 | 1 |
| 15. When I'm involved in an important work project, I can enjoy myself fully at a sport or cultural event after hours. | 1 | 2 | 3 | 4 | 5 |
| 16. If it weren't for a few bad breaks, I would be much more successful today. | 5 | 4 | 3 | 2 | 1 |
| 17. My best helping hand is at the end of my arm. | 1 | 2 | 3 | 4 | 5 |
| 18. I get bored easily. | 5 | 4 | 3 | 2 | 1 |
| 19. Planning is difficult because life is so unpredictable. | 5 | 4 | 3 | 2 | 1 |
| 20. I feel that I'm moving forward a little bit each day toward achieving my goals. | 1 | 2 | 3 | 4 | 5 |

## Scoring and Interpretation:

Calculate your score by adding the numbers circled.

**90–100 points:**    You are a highly self-disciplined person who should be able to capitalize on your skills and talents. Studying about self-discipline might help you capitalize even further on your strong self-discipline.

**60–89 points:**    You have an average degree of self-discipline, so studying the self-discipline model could point to areas for personal improvement.

**40–59 points:** You may be experiencing problems with self-discipline. Start putting into practice the ideas contained in the self-discipline model.

**20–39 points:** If your answers are accurate, you have enough problems with self-discipline to limit achieving many of the things in life important to you. In addition to studying the self-discipline model, study about work habits and time management.

**Questions:** **1.** How does this score agree with your evaluation of your self-discipline?

**2.** Who might you use as a role model of a person with high self-discipline?

**Component 1:** *Formulate a mission statement.* Who are you? What are you trying to accomplish in life? If you understand what you are trying to accomplish in life, you have the fuel to be self-disciplined. With a mission, activities that may appear mundane to others become vital stepping-stones for you. An example would be learning Spanish grammar to help you become an international businessperson. To help formulate your mission statement, answer two questions: What are my five biggest wishes? What do I want to accomplish in my career during the next five years?

**Component 2:** *Develop role models.* An excellent method of learning how to be self-disciplined is to model your behavior after successful achievers who are obviously well disciplined. To model another person does not mean you will slavishly imitate every detail of that person's life. Instead, you will follow the general pattern of how the person operates in spheres related to your mission and goals. An ideal role model is the type of person whom you would like to become, not someone you feel you could never become.

**Component 3:** *Develop goals for each task.* Your mission must be supported by a series of specific goals that collectively will enable you to achieve your mission. Successfully completing goals eventually leads to fulfilling a mission. Each small goal achieved is a building block toward larger achievements.

**Component 4:** *Develop action plans to achieve goals.* Self-disciplined people carefully follow their action plans because they make goal attainment possible. It is helpful to chart your progress against the dates established for the subactivities.

**Component 5:** *Use visual and sensory stimulation.* A self-disciplined person relentlessly focuses on a goal and persistently pursues that goal. To accomplish this consistent focus, self-disciplined people form images of reaching their goals—they actually develop a mental image of the act of accomplishing what they want. As mysterious as it sounds, visualization helps the brain convert images into reality. The more senses you can incorporate into your visual image, the stronger its power. Imagine yourself seeing, tasting, hearing, smelling, and touching your goal. Can you imagine yourself sitting in your condo overlooking the ocean, eating a great meal to celebrate the fact that the business you founded now has 10,000 employees?

> "Nothing in the world can take the place of persistence. Persistence and determination alone are omnipotent. The slogan 'press on' has solved, and always will solve, the problems of the human race."
> — Calvin Coolidge, thirtieth president of the United States

**Component 6:** *Search for pleasure within the task.* A self-disciplined person finds joy, excitement, and intense involvement in the task at hand and, therefore, finds intrinsic motivation. Instead of focusing on the extrinsic (or external) reward, the love of the task helps the person in pursuit of the goal. An axiom of becoming wealthy is not to focus on getting rich. Instead, focus on work. If the task at hand does not thrill you, at least focus on the pleasure from the most enjoyable element within the task. A bill collector might not find the total task intrinsically motivating, but perhaps he or she enjoys developing skill in resolving conflict.

**Component 7:** *Compartmentalize spheres of life.* Self-disciplined people have a remarkable capacity to divide up (or compartmentalize) the various spheres of their lives to stay focused on what they are doing at the moment. While working, develop the knack of concentrating on work and putting aside thoughts about personal life. In the midst of social and family activities, concentrate on them rather than half thinking about work. This approach will contribute to both self-discipline and a better integration of work and family life.

**Component 8:** *Minimize excuse making.* Self-disciplined people concentrate their energies on goal accomplishment rather than making excuses for why work is not accomplished. Instead of trying to justify why they have been diverted from a goal, high-achieving, self-disciplined people circumvent potential barriers. Undisciplined people, in contrast, seem to look for excuses. If you are an excuse maker, conduct a self-audit, writing down all the reasons blocking you from achieving any current goal. Be brutally honest in challenging each one of your excuses. Ask yourself, "Is this a valid excuse, or is it simply a rationalization for my getting sidetracked?"

| Key Factor | Average Score on Factor for 325 Adults | Relationship to Self-Discipline Score |
|---|---|---|
| 1. Age | 34.7 years | Almost zero |
| 2. Years of formal education | 15.9 | Slightly positive |
| 3. Salary in U.S. dollars | $45,899 | Slightly positive |
| 4. Self-rating of career on scale of 1 to 7 | 4.9 | Quite positive |
| 5. Self-rating of goal accomplishment on scale of 1 to 7 | 5.6 | Quite positive |
| 6. Self-discipline score on scale of 20 to 100 | 76.9 | ------ |

**Figure    2-7**

**Relationship between Self-Discipline Score and Key Factors**
**Score:** Table derived from data presented in Andrew J. DuBrin, "Career-Related Correlates of Self-Discipline," *Psychological Reports*, 2001, Vol. 89, p. 109.

The belief that self-discipline contributes to goal attainment and success is about as strong as the belief that a healthy diet and exercise contribute to physical health. Nonetheless, a study conducted with 325 working adults provides reassurance about the benefits of self-discipline. The study participants completed the self-discipline questionnaire previously presented, and they also answered questions about their age, education, salary, and how they felt about their career success and goal accomplishment. As shown in Figure 2-7, positive relationships were found between being self-disciplined and education, salary, career success, and goal attainment. Self-ratings of career success and goal accomplishment were the most strongly related. [18] In conclusion, self-discipline pays. Why do you think it was found that self-discipline was positively associated with years of formal education?

# Concept Review and Reinforcement

## Key Terms

Need, 34
Motive, 35
Need for achievement, 36
Maslow's need hierarchy, 37

Goal, 41
Action plan, 44
Intrinsic motivation, 47
Behavior modification, 47

Expectancy theory of motivation, 48
Psychological hardiness, 48
Self-discipline, 49

## Summary and Review

Self-motivation is important for achieving success in work and personal life. A well-accepted explanation of human behavior is that people have needs and motives propelling them toward achieving certain goals.

- The central idea behind need theory is that unsatisfied needs motivate us until they become satisfied.
- After satisfaction of one need, the person usually pursues satisfaction of another, higher need.

Work and personal life offer the opportunity to satisfy many different needs and motives. Among the more important needs and motives are achievement, power, affiliation, recognition, and order. The need for risk taking and thrill seeking is also important for some people.

According to Maslow's need hierarchy, people have an internal need pushing them on toward self-actualization.

- Needs are arranged into a five-step ladder. Before higher-level needs are activated, certain lower-level needs must be satisfied.
- In ascending order, the groups of needs are physiological, safety, social, esteem, and self-actualization (such as self-fulfillment).

Need theory helps in self-motivation. First identify which needs you want to satisfy and then focus your efforts on an activity that will satisfy those needs.

Substantial research indicates that setting specific, reasonably difficult goals improves performance. Goals are valuable because they

- focus effort in a consistent direction
- improve your chances for success
- improve motivation and satisfaction

Goals can be aimed at either learning or performing. A learning-goal orientation means that an individual is focused on acquiring new skills and mastering new situations. A performing-goal orientation is aimed at wanting to demonstrate and validate the adequacy of your competence by seeking favorable judgments of competence. People with learning-goal orientations are more likely to

- seek feedback on how well they are performing
- have higher job performance
- improve performance and lead to skill development
- develop better relationships with their supervisors
- be innovative in solutions to problems

Goal setting is widely used on the job. Goals set by employees at lower levels in an organization are supposed to contribute to goals set at the top.

Goal setting in personal life can contribute to life satisfaction. For maximum advantage, personal goals should be integrated with career goals. Areas of life in which personal goals may be set include

- social and family
- hobbies and interests
- physical and mental health
- career
- financial

To increase their effectiveness, goals should be supported with action plans. Effective goals are

- specific and concise
- realistically challenging, yet also include stretch goals
- set for different time periods

Goals have some problems associated with them. They can create inflexibility, performing goals can detract from an interest in the task, and goals can encourage unethical behavior.

Key techniques of self-motivation include

- setting goals for yourself
- finding intrinsically motivating work

- getting feedback on your performance
- applying behavior modification to yourself
- improving your skills relevant to your job
- raising your level of self-expectation
- developing a strong work ethic
- developing psychological hardiness (a high degree of commitment, control, and challenge)

Achieving goals and staying motivated requires self-discipline. A model presented here for developing self-discipline consists of eight components:

- formulate a mission statement
- develop role models
- develop goals for each task
- develop action plans
- use visual and sensory stimulation
- search for pleasure within the task
- compartmentalize spheres of life
- minimize excuse making

A study found positive relationships between self-discipline scores and education, salary, satisfaction with career success, and satisfaction with goal attainment.

## Check your Understanding

1. How would the need theory of motivation explain the fact that shortly after accomplishing an important goal many people begin thinking about their next possible goal?
2. One of the biggest issues in labor-management relations today is that workers want employers to pay more of their health-care insurance. What does this issue tell us about the importance of satisfying the lower-level needs of workers?
3. How might having a strong need for affiliation retard a person's career advancement?
4. Identify any self-actualized person you know or have heard of and explain why you think that person is self-actualized.
5. Why does a learning-goal orientation often contribute to more peace of mind than a performing-goal orientation?

6. Why is self-motivation so important even when you have a job skill that is in high demand?
7. Give examples of two jobs in your chosen field you think are likely to be intrinsically motivating. Explain your reasoning.
8. Explain how you might be able to use the Galatea effect to improve the success you achieve in your career and personal life.
9. What sacrifices might a highly self-disciplined person have to make in contrast to a lowly self-disciplined person?
10. Ask a person who has achieved career success how much self-discipline contributed to his or her success.

## Web Corner

*Motivation: www.beginnersguide.com*

*Self-discipline: www.mindperk.com*

***INTERNET SKILL BUILDER Anchoring***

At www.InstantPower.com you will learning about the technique called *anchoring* that is designed to help you experience your most enabling emotional state any time you want. The purpose of the anchoring program is to help you go from feeling afraid, hesitant, or depressed to confident, determined, and happy. After reading about the program, you decide if it appears promising or is simply a bunch of exaggerated promises.

## Applying Human Relations Exercise 2-1

### Goal-Setting and Action Plan Worksheet

Goal setting, along with developing action plans to support the goals, is a basic success strategy. Here you are being asked to refine a process you may have already begun. Consider entering more than one goal and accompanying action plan in each category. To clarify the meaning of the following entries, we provide examples in italics of a recent graduate entering the retail field (as illustrated in the opening case to the chapter). Before writing down your goals, consult the section "Guidelines for Goal Setting." If you are not currently employed, set up hypothetical goals and action plans for a future job.

#### Long-Range Goals (beyond five years)

Work: *Ultimately become CEO of a major division of a retail company, perhaps the CEO of Bloomingdales.*

(Place your entry here.)

Action plan: *Work my way up, position by position, starting as assistant merchandising manager.*

(Place your entry here.)

Personal: *Married, with children, home ownership.*

(Place your entry here.)

Action plan: *Continue to develop relationship with my boyfriend as life partner. We will both save and invest at least 10 percent of our incomes each year.*

(Place your entry here.)

#### Medium-Range Goals (two to five years)

Work: *Become merchandising manager for one store in a large retail chain.*

(Place your entry here.)

Action plan: *Will work hard as assistant merchandising manager, listen to and act on feedback from my supervisors, take courses in human relations and merchandising management.*

(Place your entry here.)

Personal: *Continue to develop relationship with my boyfriend and marry him within three years.*

(Place your entry here.)

Action plan: *Communicate in depth with each other regularly to build relationship. We will work on not criticizing each other so often. After he proposes marriage, we will use our business skills to plan the wedding.*

(Place your entry here.)

#### Short-Range Goals (within two years)

Work: *Do an outstanding job as assistant merchandising manager this month.*

(Place your entry here.)

Action plan: *Will take care of more e-mail and other routine work when not in the store. In this way I can put more time and energy into merchandising. I will ask my supervisor for feedback from time to time so I can make adjustments to my performance.*

(Place your entry here.)

Personal: *Get further into digital photography, particularly learning how to take action shots. Will go beyond the "point-and-click" approach to photography.*

(Place your entry here.)

Action plan: *I will study the camera manual more carefully and attend one of the digital photography workshops given at my former community college.*

(Place your entry here.)

## Skill-Building Exercise 2-2

### *Need Identification among Members of Generations X and Y*

Following is a list of work preferences characteristic among members of generations X and Y (collectively people born since 1965). Identify what psychological need or needs might be reflected in each work preference. Jot down the needs right after the work preference.

- They like variety, not doing the same thing every workday.
- Part of their career goals is to face new challenges and opportunities. It's not all based on money, but on growth and learning.
- They want jobs that are cool, fun, and fulfilling.
- They believe that if they keep growing and learning then that's all the security they need. Advancing their skill set and continuous learning is their top priority.
- They have a tremendous thirst for knowledge.

- Unlike many baby boomers, who tend to work independently, members of generations X and Y like to work in a team environment.
- They prefer learning by doing and making mistakes as they go along.
- They are apt to challenge established ways of doing things, reasoning that there is always a better way.
- They want regular, frequent feedback on job performance.
- Career improvement is a blend of life and job balance.

### Questions

1. How well does the analysis presented apply to you? Do the statements fit your work preferences?

2. What needs are you (or will you be) attempting to satisfy on the job? How do you know?

**Source:** Reprinted with permission from the TemPositions Group of Companies, 420 Lexington Avenue, Suite 2100, New York, NY, 10170-0002.

## Human Relations Case Study 2-1

### *Motivating the Staff at HRPro*

Tammy Sheldon is a program manager at HRPro, a company that supplies human resource services to small and medium-size organizations, including businesses, hospitals, and a variety of nonprofit firms. The human resources services include administering payroll and employee benefits, bonus plans, and training. Sheldon is the program manager for training services, a small but growing part of client work for HRPro.

   The three members of Sheldon's staff are Christina Conway, Peter Wang, and Maria Sanchez, all of whom hold the job title of human resources

consultant. All three consultants are performing adequately, yet Sheldon has been thinking lately about enhancing their performance. Sheldon's immediate manager, the vice president of client programs, agrees that her staff has room for improvement in terms of effort and commitment. Sheldon's preliminary action plan for enhancing the motivation of her staff is to interview them to search for specific motivators.

   In Sheldon's words, "As an HR professional, I'm not naïve enough to think that a one-size-fits-all approach to motivation is going to work. I'm going to offer each member of my team a gift certificate to their favorite on-line shopping service as a reward for outstanding performance. Gifts are nice, but I want to try something a little more sophisticated." Excerpts from the interviews are as follows:

Sheldon: "Chris, what do you really want from working at HRPro? What would it take to get you to the next level of effort?"

Conway: "Thanks for asking me, Tammy. I haven't given the issue much thought yet. But off the top of my head, I would say I want your job and then to keep moving. I see a great future in human resource programs being outsourced, and I want to be part of that future. I'm 26 right now, and I can see myself as a CEO of a human resources outsourcing firm by the time I hit 35. So if I could see some clear signs of career advancement, I would put a little more pressure on the accelerator."

Sheldon: "Peter, what do you want to get out of working for HRPro? How could we get you to be even more strongly motivated?"

Wang: "I like what I see at the company, yet I'm falling into a little bit of a routine. I keep doing safety training and diversity training for clients. It's getting a little repetitious. I have to appear excited and enthused even if I've given the identical training program seven times in one month. I want to branch out, and maybe help install a bonus system for a client or two. I want to get into other aspects of HR.

"I don't want to feel like I'm finished growing as an HR professional. I'm only 31."

Sheldon: "Good morning Maria. How are you doing today? I wanted to learn a little bit more about what makes you happy and motivated. What do you hope to get out of working for HRPro? What type of work would get you even more fired up?"

Sanchez: "I thought I was pretty fired up. I think I could be more committed to the company if the company was more committed to me. I feel I am only as good as my last client assignment. Suppose the company runs out of client assignments for me. Does that mean I'm out the door?

"Stable employment is pretty important for me. I have a child, and my husband is a full-time student in a field with little prospect for high-paying work. I would like to wake up every morning and feel that my job at HRPro will be there."

## Case Questions

1. What needs are Conway, Wang, and Sanchez attempting to satisfy?
2. Make a suggestion to Sheldon and her manager for motivating Conway, Wang, and Sanchez.
3. Should Sheldon have asked each staff member exactly the same question in order to understand more clearly their potential motivators?

## Human Relations Case Study 2-2

### *How Self-Disciplined Is Gus?*

Cora, an office temporary, noticed that Gus, one on the professionals in the office where she was assigned, was constantly seated in front of the computer. One day when Gus returned from lunch, Cora engaged him in general conversation about the weather and the recent Winter Olympics games. Gus looked down at the time indicated on his cell phone, and said, "Excuse me, but I have to get back to work."

Cora commented, "Excuse me for saying so, but don't you get bored just sitting in front of the computer all day? I mean, don't you just want to take a break and get some fresh air? How much can a human being stare at a monitor all day?" Gus smiled and replied, "It may look like I'm just sitting in front of a computer monitor all day just banging the key board. But the computer is a tool that helps me accomplish something very important. I'm analyzing data to help determine how our company can make products more environmentally friendly. Our company wants to be 'green.' In this way, I'm helping to improve the world."

### Questions

1. Which elements of the self-discipline model is Gus applying?
2. To what extent might Cora have a self-discipline problem?

# REFERENCES

1. Anne D'Innocenzio, "Retail Seeking More Top Business Grads," Associated Press, February 26, 2006.

2. For a theoretical explanation of the principle of self-interest, see Dale T. Miller, "The Norm of Self-Interest," *American Psychologist,* December 1999, pp. 1053–1060.

3. David C. McClelland and Richard Boyatzis, "Leadership Motive Pattern and Long-Term Success in Management," *Journal of Applied Psychology,* December 1982, p. 737.

4. Marvin Zuckerman, "Are You a Risk Taker?" *Psychology Today,* November/December 2000, p. 53.

5. The original statement is Abraham H. Maslow, "A Theory of Human Motivation," *Psychological Review,* July 1943, pp. 370-396. See also Maslow, *Motivation and Personality* (New York: Harper & Row, 1954).

6. Pamela Babcock, "Find What Workers Want," *HR Magazine,* April 2005, p. 53.

7. Gary P. Latham, "The Motivational Benefits of Goal Setting," *Academy of Management Executive,* November 2004, pp. 126–129.

8. Don VandeWalle and Larry L. Cummings, "A Test of the Influence of Goal Orientation on the Feedback-Seeking Process," *Journal of Applied Psychology,* June 1997, pp. 390–400; VandeWalle, William L. Cron, and John W. Slocum, Jr., "The Role of Goal Orientation Following Performance Feedback," *Journal of Applied Psychology,* August 2001, pp. 629–640.

9. Don VandeWalle, Steven P. Brown, William L. Cron, and John W. Slocum, Jr., "The Influence of Goal Orientation and Self-Regulation Tactics on Sales Performance: A Longitudinal Field Test," *Journal of Applied Psychology,* April 1999, pp. 249–259.

10. Onne Janssen and Nico W. Van Yperen, "Employee Goal Orientations, The Quality of Leader–Member Exchange, and the Outcomes of Job Performance and Job Satisfaction," *Academy of Management Journal,* June 2004, pp. 368–384.

11. Gerard H. Seijts and Gary P. Latham, "Learning versus Performance Goals: When Should Each Be Used? *Academy of Management Executive,* February 2005, p. 130.

12. VandeWalle and Cummings, "A Test of the Influence of Goal Orientation," p. 392.

13. Richard M. Ryan and Edward L. Deci, "Self-Determination Theory and the Facilitation of Intrinsic Motivation, Social Development, and Well-Being," *American Psychologist,* January 2000, p. 70.

14. Remus Ilies and Timothy A. Judge, "Goal Regulation across Time: The Effects of Feedback and Affect," *Journal of Applied Psychology,* May 2005, pp. 453–467.

15. P. Christopher Earley and Terri R. Lituchy, "Delineating Goals and Efficacy: A Test of Three Models," *Journal of Applied Psychology,* February 1992, p. 96.

16. Taly Dvir, Dov Eden, and Michal Lang Banjo, "Self-Fulfilling Prophecy and Gender: Can Women Be Pygmalion and Galatea?" *Journal of Applied Psychology,* April 1995, p. 268.

17. Michael S. Cole, Hubert S. Field, and Stanley G. Harris, "Student Learning Motivation and Psychological Hardiness: Interactive Effects on Students' Reactions to a Management Class," *Academy of Management Learning and Education,* March 2004, pp. 64–85. The definition of psychological hardiness is from citations on page 66 of the same source.

18. Andrew J. DuBrin, "Career-Related Correlates of Self-Discipline," *Psychological Reports,* 2001, Vol. 89, pp. 107–110.

# 3

# Understanding Individual Differences

## Learning Objectives

After reading and studying this chapter and doing the exercises, you should be able to:

1 Make adjustments for the individual differences among people in dealing with them on the job.

2 Develop insight into how your personality, mental ability, emotional intelligence, and values differ from others.

3 Respond to personality differences among people.

4 Respond to mental ability differences among people.

5 Respond to differences in values among people.

## Outline

1 **Personality    64**
   Eight Major Personality Factors and Traits
   The Eight Factors and Traits and Job Performance
   Personality Types and Cognitive Styles
   Guidelines for Dealing with Different Personality Types

2 **Mental Ability    74**
   Components of Traditional Intelligence
   Practical Intelligence
   Multiple Intelligences
   Emotional Intelligence
   Guidelines for Relating to People of Different
   Levels and Types of Intelligence

3 **Values As a Source of Individual Differences    83**
   How Values Are Learned
   Clarifying Your Values
   The Mesh between Individual and Job Values
   Guidelines for Using Values to Enhance
   Interpersonal Relations

A t Intuit, the Mountain View, California, maker of Quicken, TurboTax, and other money-management software, CEO Steve Bennett understands that employees who are unhappy at work won't contribute their best efforts—on the job or even at home. "It will cause trouble in their personal relationships," he says. He tells his Intuit managers to create a "psychological contract" with every employee, spelling out what is expected of them, how well they are performing, and what they must do to advance.

*When he joined Intuit six years ago, Bennett found a company where employees didn't know how to handle differing emotions and opinions. They were afraid to counter one another at meetings and they couldn't make decisions without spending hours trying to reach a consensus. He subsequently urged all employees to voice their views and without fear of offending anyone.*

*"We want everyone to aim for what we call True North objectives—or better short-term as well as long-term results—and we want everyone to feel enthused and connected at work," says Bennett, who spends half his time coaching employees. "If you accept this contract and want to learn but aren't getting good results, we'll find you a job at the company where you can perform better." [1]*

■ **Individual differences**

variations in how people respond to the same situation based on personal characteristics.

The scenario that took place at Intuit illustrates how the ability to manage emotions on the job can contribute to business and individual success. One of the many topics about individuals we study in this chapter concerns emotional intelligence, or managing emotions. The major theme of this chapter deals with how people vary in a wide range of personal factors. **Individual differences** exert a profound effect on job performance and behavior. Such differences refer to variations in how people respond to the same situation based on personal characteristics. One of hundreds of possible examples is that some people can concentrate longer and harder on their work, thereby producing more and higher quality work than others.

This chapter describes several of the major sources of individual differences on the job. It also gives you the chance to measure your standing on several key dimensions of behavior and helps you develop skill in responding to individual differences. Knowing how to respond to such differences is the cornerstone of effective interpersonal relations.

■ **Learning Objective 1**

■ **Learning Objective 2**

# Personality

"We're not going to promote you to department head," said the manager to the analyst. "Although you are a great troubleshooter, you've alienated too many people in the company. You're too blunt and insensitive." As just implied, most successes and failures in people-contact jobs are attributed largely to interpersonal skills. And personality traits are important contributors to interpersonal, or human relations, skills.

**Personality** refers to persistent and enduring behavior patterns and tend to be expressed in a wide variety of situations. A person who is brash and insensitive in one situation is likely to behave similarly in many other situations. Your personality is what makes you unique. Your walk, your talk, your appearance, your speech, and your inner values and conflicts all contribute to your personality. Have you ever noticed that when you know a person well, you can identify that person by his or her footsteps even though you do not see the individual? This is true because many people have a distinctive gait.

I illustrate the importance of personality to interpersonal relations in organizations by describing eight key personality traits and personality types related to cognitive styles. In addition, you are given guidelines for dealing effectively with different personality types.

■ **Personality**
persistent and enduring behavior patterns that tend to be expressed in a variety of situations

## EIGHT MAJOR PERSONALITY FACTORS AND TRAITS

Many psychologists believe that the basic structure of human personality is represented by five broad factors, known as the Big Five: neuroticism, extraversion (the scientific spelling of *extroversion*), openness, agreeableness, and conscientiousness. This approach to understanding personality is often referred to as the Five-Factor Model. Three more key personality factors—self-monitoring of behavior, risk taking and thrill seeking, and optimism—are so important for human relations that they are considered here.

All eight factors have a substantial impact on interpersonal relations and job performance. The interpretations and meanings of these factors provide useful information because they help you pinpoint important areas for personal development. Although these factors are partially inherited, most people can improve them, providing they exert much conscious effort over a period of time. For example, it usually takes a minimum of three months of effort before a person is perceived to be more agreeable. The eight factors, shown in Figure 3-1, are described in the following list.

1. *Neuroticism* reflects emotional instability and identifies people prone to psychological distress and coping with problems in unproductive ways. Traits associated with this personality factor include being anxious, insecure, angry, embarrassed, emotional, and worried. A person of low neuroticism—or high emotional stability—is calm and confident, and usually in control.

2. *Extraversion* reflects the quantity or intensity of social interactions, the need for social stimulation, self-confidence, and competition. Traits associated with extraversion include being sociable, gregarious, assertive, talkative, and active. An outgoing person is often described as extraverted, whereas introverted persons are described as reserved, timid, and quiet.

3. *Openness* reflects the proactive seeking of experience for its own sake. Traits associated with openness include being creative, cultured, intellectually curious, broad-minded, and artistically sensitive. People who score low on this personality factor are practical, with narrow interests.

**Figure    3-1**

**Eight Personality Factors Related to Interpersonal Skills**

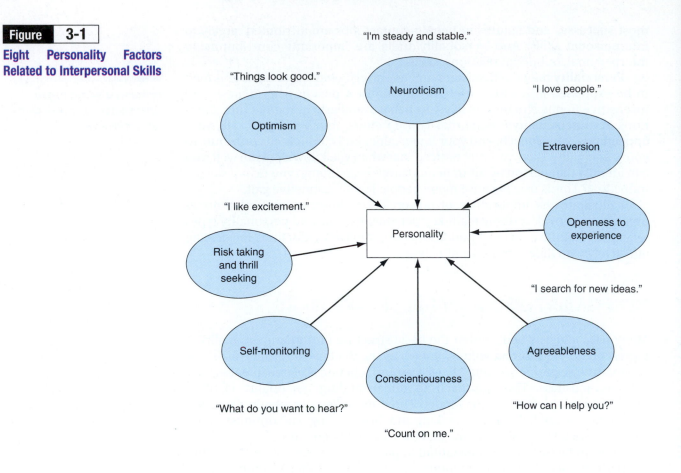

"I'm steady and stable."

"Things look good."

"I love people."

Neuroticism

Optimism

"I like excitement."

Extraversion

Personality

Risk taking and thrill seeking

Openness to experience

"I search for new ideas."

Self-monitoring

Agreeableness

Conscientiousness

"What do you want to hear?"

"How can I help you?"

"Count on me."

4. *Agreeableness* reflects the quality of one's interpersonal orientation. Traits associated with the agreeableness factor include being courteous, flexible, trusting, good-natured, cooperative, forgiving, softhearted, and tolerant. The other end of the continuum includes disagreeable, cold, and antagonistic people.

5. *Conscientiousness* reflects organization, self-restraint, persistence, and motivation toward attaining goals. Traits associated with conscientiousness include being hardworking, dependable, well organized, and thorough. The person low in conscientiousness is lazy, disorganized, and unreliable.

6. *Self-monitoring* of behavior refers to the process of observing and controlling how we are perceived by others. Self-monitoring involves three major and somewhat distinct tendencies: (1) willingness to be the *center of attention*, (2) *sensitivity* to the reactions of others, and (3) ability and willingness to *adjust* behavior to induce positive reactions in others. High self-monitors are pragmatic and even chameleonlike actors in social groups. They often say what others want to hear. Low self-monitors avoid situations that require them to adapt to outer images. In this way their outer behavior adheres to their inner values. Low self-monitoring can often lead to inflexibility. Take Self-Assessment Quiz 3-1 to measure your self-monitoring tendencies.

# Self-Assessment Quiz  3-1

## The Self-Monitoring Scale

**Directions:** The statements below concern your personal reactions to a number of different situations. No two statements are exactly alike, so consider each statement carefully before answering. If a statement is true or mostly true as applied to you, *circle the "T"* next to the question. If a statement is false or not usually true as applied to you, *circle the "F"* next to the question.

(T) (F)    **1.** I find it hard to imitate the behavior of other people.
(T) (F)    **2.** My behavior is usually an expression of my true inner feelings, attitudes, and beliefs.
(T) (F)    **3.** At parties and social gatherings, I do not attempt to do or say things that others will like.
(T) (F)    **4.** I can only argue for ideas which I already believe.
(T) (F)    **5.** I can make impromptu speeches even on topics about which I have almost no information.
(T) (F)    **6.** I guess I put on a show to impress or entertain people.
(T) (F)    **7.** When I am uncertain how to act in a social situation, I look to the behavior of others for cues.
(T) (F)    **8.** I would probably make a good actor.
(T) (F)    **9.** I rarely seek the advice of my friends to choose movies, books, or music.
(T) (F)  **10.** I sometimes appear to others to be experiencing deeper emotions than I actually am.
(T) (F)  **11.** I laugh more when I watch a comedy with others than when alone.
(T) (F)  **12.** In groups of people, I am rarely the center of attention.
(T) (F)  **13.** In different situations and with different people, I often act like very different persons.
(T) (F)  **14.** I am not particularly good at making other people like me.
(T) (F)  **15.** Even if I am not enjoying myself, I often pretend to be having a good time.
(T) (F)  **16.** I'm not always the person I appear to be.
(T) (F)  **17.** would not change my opinions (or the way I do things) in order to please someone else or win their favor.
(T) (F)  **18.** I have considered being an entertainer.
(T) (F)  **19.** In order to get along and be liked, I tend to be what people expect me to be rather than anything else.
(T) (F)  **20.** I have never been good at games like charades or improvisational acting.
(T) (F)  **21.** I have trouble changing my behavior to suit different people and different situations.
(T) (F)  **22.** At a party, I let others keep the jokes and stories going.
(T) (F)  **23.** I feel a bit awkward in company and do not show up quite as well as I should.
(T) (F)  **24.** I can look anyone in the eye and tell a lie with a straight face (if for a right end).
(T) (F)  **25.** I may deceive people by being friendly when I really dislike them.

## Scoring and Interpretation:

Give yourself one point each time your answer agrees with the key. A score that is between 0–12 would indicate that you are a relatively low self-monitor; a score that is between 13–25 would indicate that you are relatively high self-monitor.

| | | | | |
|---|---|---|---|---|
| 1. F | 6. T | 11. T | 16. T | 21. F |
| 2. F | 7. T | 12. F | 17. F | 22. F |
| 3. F | 8. T | 13. T | 18. T | 23. F |
| 4. F | 9. F | 14. F | 19. T | 24. T |
| 5. T | 10. T | 15. T | 20. F | 25. T |

**Source:** Mark Snyder, Professor of Psychology, University of Minnesota.

7. *Risk taking and thrill seeking* refer to the propensity to take risks and pursue thrills. Persons with high standing on this personality trait are sensation-seekers who pursue novel, intense, and complex sensations. They are willing to take risks for the sake of such experiences. The search for giant payoffs and daily thrills motivates people with an intense need for risk taking and thrill seeking. [2] Take Self-Assessment Quiz 3-2 to measure your propensity for risk taking and thrill seeking.

8. *Optimism* refers to a tendency to experience positive emotional states, and to typically believe that positive outcomes will be forthcoming from most activities. The other end of the scale is *pessimism*—a tendency to

## Self-Assessment Quiz  3-2

### The Risk-Taking Scale

**Directions:** Answer true or false to the following questions to obtain an approximate idea of your tendency to take risks, or your desire to do so:

|  | True | False |
|---|:---:|:---:|
| **1.** I eat sushi or other raw fish. | ❑ | ❑ |
| **2.** I think that amusement park roller coasters should be abolished. | ❑ | ❑ |
| **3.** I don't like trying foods from other cultures. | ❑ | ❑ |
| **4.** I would choose bonds over growth stocks. | ❑ | ❑ |
| **5.** I like to challenge people in positions of power. | ❑ | ❑ |
| **6.** I don't always wear a seat belt while driving. | ❑ | ❑ |
| **7.** I sometimes talk on my cell phone or send text messages while driving at highway speeds. | ❑ | ❑ |
| **8.** I would love to be an entrepreneur (or I love being one). | ❑ | ❑ |
| **9.** I would like helping out in a crisis such as a product recall. | ❑ | ❑ |
| **10.** I would like to go cave exploring (or already have done so). | ❑ | ❑ |
| **11.** I would be willing to have at least one-third of my compensation based on a bonus for good performance. | ❑ | ❑ |
| **12.** I would be willing to visit a maximum security prison on a job assignment. | ❑ | ❑ |

### Scoring and Interpretation:

Give yourself one point each time your answer agrees with the key. If you score 10–12, you are probably a high risk taker; 6–9, you are a moderate risk taker; 3–5, you are cautious; 0–2, you are a very low risk taker.

| | | | |
|---|---|---|---|
| **1.** T | **4.** F | **7.** T | **10.** T |
| **2.** F | **5.** T | **8.** T | **11.** T |
| **3.** F | **6.** T | **9.** T | **12.** T |

**Source:** The idea of a test about risk-taking comfort, as well as several of the statements on the quiz, comes from psychologist Frank Farley.

experience negative emotional states, and to typically believe that negative outcomes will be forthcoming from most activities. Optimism versus pessimism is also referred to in more technical terms as *positive affectivity versus negative affectivity*, and is considered a major personality trait. A person's tendency toward having positive affectivity (optimism) versus negative affectivity (pessimism) also influences job satisfaction. Being optimistic, as you would suspect, tends to enhance job satisfaction. [3]

Evidence for the relevance of the Five-Factor Model (traits one through five of the previous list) of personality in understanding human behavior comes from a cross-cultural study involving 7,134 individuals. The five-factor structure of the American personality was also found to hold true for German, Portuguese, Hebrew, Chinese, Korean, and Japanese samples when the personality test questions were translated into each of these languages. Based on this extensive study, it was concluded that personality structure is universal, much like the structure of the brain or the body. [4] Another look at the evidence found that extraversion, agreeableness, and conscientiousness are major personality factors in most cultures. Neuroticism and openness are more dependent on the culture and are particularly relevant in the United States. [5]

## THE EIGHT FACTORS AND TRAITS AND JOB PERFORMANCE

Depending on the job, any one of the preceding personality factors can be important for success. One explanation for personality being tied to performance is that a particular personality trait gives us a bias or positive spin to certain actions. [6] A person high in conscientiousness, for example, believes that if people are diligent they will accomplish more work and receive just rewards. Conscientiousness relates to job performance for many different occupations, and has proven to be the personality factor most consistently related to success. However, there are a few instances in which being highly conscientious can interfere with job success. If the job requires considerable spontaneity and imagination, a highly conscientious person might perform poorly because he or she dislikes breaking the rules or straying from conventional thinking. [7] For example, a conscientious advertising worker might hesitate to develop a television advertisement that depicts a woman jumping out of a building onto a United Parcel Service (UPS) delivery truck.

As explained in the previous discussion, each of the Big Five factors is composed of more narrow or specific traits. With respect to conscientiousness, the specific trait of *dependability* may be the most important contributor to job performance. [8]

Another important research finding is that extraversion is associated with success for managers and sales representatives. The explanation is that managers and salespeople are required to interact extensively with other people. [9] For people who want to advance in their careers, being a high self-monitor is important. An analysis was made of the self-monitoring personality by combining 136 studies involving 23,101 people. A major finding was that high self-monitors tend to receive better performance ratings than low self-monitors. High self-monitors were also more likely to emerge as leaders and work their way into top management positions. [10]

Another advantage to being a high self-monitor is that the individual is more likely to help out other workers, even when not required. [11] An example would be helping a worker outside your department with a currency exchange problem even though this was not your responsibility. The willingness to go beyond one's job description without a specific reward apparent is referred to as **organizational citizenship behavior.** Good organizational citizens are highly valued by employers. A recent perspective on organizational citizenship behavior is that an employee will make a short-term sacrifice that leads to long-term benefits to the organization. [12] An example would be an employee voluntarily working from home to deal with customer confusion about a product recall, which would lead to more loyal and appreciative customers.

A study with 141 customer service employees demonstrated that having low standing on the Big Five personality factors is associated with counterproductive work behavior such as (a) taking property without company permission and (b) playing a mean prank on a coworker. The customer service employees most likely to engage in these behaviors scored low on agreeableness and conscientious, and high on neuroticism. The same study showed that when employees were more satisfied with their job, they were less likely to be counterproductive. [13] Experienced workers are likely to be aware of this fact, and a scientific study like this would reinforce their observations.

A combination of personality factors will sometimes be more closely associated with job success than one factor alone. A study about personality and job performance ratings was conducted with diverse occupations, including clerical workers and wholesale appliance sales representatives. A key finding was that conscientious workers who also scored high on agreeableness performed better than conscientious workers who were less agreeable. [14] (Being agreeable toward your manager helps elevate performance evaluations!) A study with experienced pharmaceutical sales representatives found that the combination of extraversion and conscientiousness was associated with higher sales. However, being conscientious was the personality factor most closely associated with growth in sales over several years for the experienced sales representatives. [15]

Optimism and pessimism also can be linked to job performance. Optimism can be quite helpful when attempting such tasks as selling a product or service or motivating a group of people. Yet psychologist Julie Normen has gathered considerable evidence that pessimism can sometimes enhance job performance. Pessimists usually assume that something will go wrong, and will carefully prepare to prevent botches and bad luck. A pessimist, for example, will carefully back up computer files or plan for emergencies that might shut down operations. [16]

## PERSONALITY TYPES AND COGNITIVE STYLES

People go about solving problems in various ways. You may have observed, for example, that some people are more analytical and systematic while others are more intuitive. The most widely used method of classifying problem-solving

■ **Organizational citizenship behavior**
the willingness to go beyond one's job description without a specific reward apparent

styles is the Myers-Briggs Type Indicator (MBTI®). Many readers of this book will have already taken the MBTI. Modes of problem solving are referred to as **cognitive styles.** According to this method of understanding problem-solving styles, your personality traits strongly influence how you approach problems, such as being introverted gives you a preference for working with ideas. Knowledge of these cognitive styles can help you relate better to people because you can better appreciate how they make decisions.

■ **Cognitive style**
mental processes used to perceive and make judgments from situations

The MBTI is a self-report questionnaire designed to make the theory of psychological types developed by psychoanalyst Carl Jung applicable to every-day life. Jung developed the theory of psychological types, but he did not develop the measuring instrument in question. Katharine Cook Briggs and Isabel Briggs Myers are the authors of the MBTI.

More than 2 million assessments are administered to individuals annually—including many employees of Fortune 500 companies. The pur-poses of using the MBTI include team building, career exploration, conflict management, leadership development and coaching, retention, and exploring the world of work. The administrations must be given by a certified MBTI administrator. The developers of the MBTI caution that the instrument should be taken voluntarily, and should not be used in the hiring or firing process.

As measured by the MBTI instrument, four separate dichotomies direct the typical use of perception and judgment by an individual. The four dichotomies can also be considered a person's cognitive style.

1. **Extraversion–Introversion dichotomy of attitudes or orientations of energy.** Extraverts direct their energy primarily toward the outer world of people and objects. In contrast, introverts direct their energy primarily toward the inner world of experiences and ideas.

2. **Sensing–Intuition dichotomy of functions or processes of perception.** People who rely on sensing focus primarily on what can be perceived by the five pri-mary senses of vision, touch, sight, sound, and smell. People who rely on intuition focus primarily on perceiving patterns and interrelationships.

3. **Thinking–Feeling dichotomy of functions or processes of judgment.** People who rely primarily on thinking base conclusions on logical analysis and emphasize objectivity and detachment. People who rely on feelings base conclusions on personal or social values, and focus on understanding and harmony.

4. **Judging–Perceiving dichotomy of attitudes or orientations toward dealing with the outside world.** People who use the judging process prefer to use the judging processes of Thinking or Feeling because the processes lead to decisive-ness and closure. People who use one of the Perceiving processes (Sensing or Intuition) do so because they prefer the flexibility and spontaneity that results from using these processes. [17]

Combining the four types with each other results in 16 personality types, such as ISTJ people who *I* (draw energy from and pay attention to their inner world); *S* (like information that is real and factual); *T* (use logical analysis in decision making); and *J* (like a structured and planned life). Four of the per-sonality types relate directly to cognitive styles as shown in Figure 3-2. People with different cognitive styles prefer different occupations. [18]

| Figure **3-2** |
| --- |

**Four Cognitive Styles of the Myers-Briggs Typology**

| ENTP (Conceptualizer) | ISTJ (Traditionalist) | INTJ (Visionary) | ESTJ (Organizer) |
| --- | --- | --- | --- |
| Quick, ingenious, will argue either side of issue for fun, may neglect routine assignments. (Good for creative work where deadlines are not crucial.) | Serious, quiet, practical, logical, dependable. (Good for work requiring careful attention to detail such as accountant or auditor.) | Original thinking, determined to implement, skeptical, critical, independent, and high standards. (Good for major leadership role such as CEO.) | Practical, realistic, has a natural mind for business or mechanics, likes to organize and run activities. (Good for manufacturing supervisor.) |

**Note:** *I* = Introvert, *E* = Extravert, *T* = Thinking, *F* = Feeling, *S* = Sensing, *N* = Intuitive, *J* = Judging, and *P* = Perceiving.

**Source:** Modified and reproduced by special permission of the Publisher, CPP, Inc., Mountain View, CA 94043. From *Introduction to Type*, 6th ed., by Isabel Briggs Myers and Katharine D. Myers, p. 13. All rights reserved. Further reproduction is prohibited without the Publisher's written consent.

You might want to take the MBTI in an authorized center such as a counseling center to discover your type. CPP, Inc., can refer customers to the organization that can offer qualification and certification programs at http://www.cpp.com. You can also study these four types and make a tentative judgment as to whether one of them fits your problem-solving style. Recognizing your problem-solving style can help you identify work that you are likely to perform well, as detailed in Figure 3-2. For example, the ENTP cognitive type is labeled the "conceptualizer." He or she is passionate about new opportunities and dislikes routine, and is more likely to be an entrepreneur than a corporate manager. The ISTJ cognitive type is labeled the "traditionalist," and will often become an accountant or financial analyst. The INJT type is labeled the "visionary." Although a small proportion of the population, these individuals are often chief executives of business firms. One of the most common types among people in general, as well as among managers, is the ESTJ, labeled the "organizer."

Far too many people overinterpret Myers-Briggs personality types as being definitive indicators of an individual's personality, and therefore pigeonhole that person. In contrast, the founders of the MBTI caution us: "You may use type to understand and forgive yourself, but not as an excuse for doing or *not* doing anything. Type should *not* keep you from considering any career, activity, or relationship." [19]

An interpersonal skills application of understanding the Myers-Briggs personality types is to help people get along better within a work group. All the group or team members would have their types assessed using the MBTI, and all members would be made aware of each other's type or working style. Knowing your type among the 16 types, and the type of the other group members would give you some clues for working smoothly together.

To illustrate, I will use a couple of the types shown in Figure 3-2. Visualize yourself as a member of a work group. You know that Nick is a visionary (INTJ). The group has an assignment that calls for creating something new, so you consult with Nick to capitalize on his original thinking, high standards, and determination to follow through. Yet you know that you and Margot are organizers (ESJT), so you two will play a heavy role in helping translate Nick's plan into action. And you, Nick, and Margot know that Jason is a traditionalist (ISTJ), so you will have to work slowly with him to get him involved in the new project. The reason is that Jason is quiet and likes to focus on details.

## GUIDELINES FOR DEALING WITH DIFFERENT PERSONALITY TYPES

■ Learning Objective 3

A key purpose in presenting information about a sampling of various personality types is to provide guidelines for individualizing your approach to people. As a basic example, if you wanted to score points with an introvert, you would approach that person in a restrained, laid-back fashion. In contrast, a more gregarious, lighthearted approach might be more effective with an extravert. The purpose of individualizing your approach is to build a better working relationship or to establish rapport with the other person. To match your approach to dealing with a given personality type, you must first arrive at an approximate diagnosis of the individual's personality. The following suggestions are therefore restricted to readily observable aspects of personality:

1. When relating to a person who appears to be neurotic based on symptoms of worry and tension, be laid back and reassuring. Do not attempt to project your own anxiety and fears. Be a good listener. If possible, minimize the emphasis on deadlines and the dire consequences of a project's failing. Show concern and interest in the person's welfare.

2. When relating to an extraverted individual, emphasize friendliness, warmth, and a stream of chatter. Talk about people more than ideas, things, or data. Express an interest in a continuing working relationship.

3. When relating to an introverted individual, move slowly in forming a working relationship. Do not confuse quietness with a lack of interest. Tolerate moments of silence. Emphasize ideas, things, and data more heavily than people.

4. When relating to a person who is open to experience, emphasize information sharing, idea generation, and creative approaches to problems. Appeal to his or her intellect by discussing topics of substance rather than ordinary chatter and gossip.

5. When relating to a person who is closed to experience, stick closely to the facts of the situation at hand. Recognize that the person prefers to think small and deal with the here and now.

6. When relating to an agreeable person, just relax and be yourself. Reciprocate with kindness to sustain a potentially excellent working relationship.

7. When relating to a disagreeable person, be patient and tolerant. At the same time, set limits on how much mistreatment you will take. Disagreeable people sometimes secretly want others to put brakes on their antisocial behavior.

8. When relating to a conscientious person, give him or her freedom and do not nag. The person will probably honor commitments without prompting. Conscientious people are often taken for granted, so remember to acknowledge the person's dependability.

9. When relating to a person of low conscientiousness, keep close tabs on him or her, especially if you need the person's output to do your job. Do not assume that because the person has an honest face and a pleasing smile he or she will deliver as promised. Frequently follow up on your requests, and impose deadlines if you have the authority. Express deep appreciation when the person does follow through.

10. When dealing with a person whom you suspect is a high self-monitor, be cautious in thinking that the person is really in support of your position. The person could just be following his or her natural tendency to appear to please others, but not really feel that way.

11. When relating to a person with a high propensity for risk taking and thrill seeking, emphasize the risky and daring aspects of activities familiar to you. Talk about a new product introduction in a highly competitive market, stock options, investment in high-technology start-up firms, skydiving, and race car driving.

12. When relating to a person with a low propensity for risk taking and thrill seeking, emphasize the safe and secure aspects of activities familiar to you. Talk about the success of an established product in a stable market (like pencils and paper clips), investment in U.S. Treasury bonds, life insurance, camping, and gardening.

13. When dealing with a sensing-type person, emphasize facts, figures, and conventional thinking without sacrificing your own values. To convince the sensing type, emphasize logic more than emotional appeal. Focus on details more than the big picture.

14. When dealing with an intuiting-type individual, emphasize feelings, judgments, playing with ideas, imagination, and creativity. Focus more on the big picture than details.

To start putting these guidelines into practice, do the role-plays in Skill-Building Exercise 3-1. Remember that a role-player is an extemporaneous actor. Put yourself in the shoes of the character you play and visualize how he or she would act. Because you are given only the general idea of a script, use your imagination to fill in the details.

# Mental Ability

■ **Intelligence**

the capacity to acquire and apply knowledge, including solving problems

Mental ability, or intelligence, is one of the major sources of individual differences that affects job performance and behavior. **Intelligence** is the capacity to acquire and apply knowledge, including solving problems. Intelligent workers can best solve abstract problems. In an exceedingly simple job, such as packing shoes into boxes, having below-average intelligence can be an advantage because the employee is not likely to become bored.

Understanding the nature of intelligence contributes to effective interpersonal relations in the workplace. Your evaluation of a person's intelligence can influence how you relate to that person. For example, if you think a person is intelligent, you will tend to seek his or her input on a difficult problem. If you realize that different types of intelligence exist, you are more likely to appreciate people's strengths. You are thus less likely to judge others as being either good or poor problem solvers.

Four important aspects of mental ability include: (1) the components of traditional intelligence, (2) practical intelligence, (3) multiple intelligences, and (4) emotional intelligence. (This fourth type of intelligence can also be regarded as personality, not mental ability.) Knowledge of the four aspects will enrich your understanding of other workers and yourself.

## COMPONENTS OF TRADITIONAL INTELLIGENCE

Intelligence consists of more than one component. A component of intelligence is much like a separate mental aptitude. Evidence suggests that intelligence consists of a *g* (**general**) **factor** and *s* (**special**) **factors** that contribute to problem-solving ability. Scores of tests of almost any type (such as math, aptitude for spatial relations, or reading skill) are somewhat influenced by

■ *g* **(general) factor**
a factor in intelligence that contributes to the ability to perform well in many tasks

■ *s* **(special) factors**
specific components of intelligence that contribute to problem-solving ability

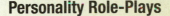

## Skill-Building Exercise 3-1

### Personality Role-Plays

**The Extravert:** One student assumes the role of a successful outside sales representative who has just signed a $3 million order for the company. The sales rep comes back to the office elated. The other student assumes the role of a member of the office support staff. He or she decides this is a splendid opportunity to build a good relationship with the triumphant sales rep. Run the role-play for about seven minutes. The people not involved in the role-play will observe and then provide feedback when the role-play is completed. (These directions regarding time, observation, and feedback also apply to the two other role-plays in this exercise and throughout the book.)

**Openness:** One student plays the role of an experienced worker in the department who is told to spend some time orienting a new co-op student or intern. It appears that this new person is open to experience. Another student plays the role of the co-op student who is open to experience and eager to be successful in this new position.

**Sensing and Intuiting Types:** One student plays the role of a sensing-type individual who is responsible for reviewing the company expense accounts. The other student plays the role of a manager in whose department many expense account abuses (such as lack of documentation and high expenses) have been uncovered. This manager is an intuitive type. The person in charge of the accounts is visiting the manager in the latter's office to discuss this problem.

the *g* factor. The *g* factor helps explain why some people perform well in so many different mental tasks. Substantial evidence has accumulated over the years indicating that workers with high intelligence tend to perform better. The relationship between *g* and job performance is likely to be strongest for those aspects of jobs that involve thinking and knowledge, such as problem solving and technical expertise. [20]

Over the years, various investigators have arrived at different special factors contributing to overall mental aptitude. The following seven factors have been identified consistently:

1. **Verbal comprehension.** The ability to understand the meaning of words and their relationship to each other and to comprehend written and spoken information.

2. **Word fluency.** The ability to use words quickly and easily, without an emphasis on verbal comprehension.

3. **Numerical acuity.** The ability to handle numbers, engage in mathematical analysis, and to do arithmetic calculations.

4. **Spatial perception.** The ability to visualize forms in space and manipulate objects mentally, particularly in three dimensions.

5. **Memory.** Having a good rote memory for symbols, words, and lists of numbers, along with other associations.

6. **Perceptual speed.** The ability to perceive visual details, to pick out similarities and differences, and to perform tasks requiring visual perception.

7. **Inductive reasoning.** The ability to discover a rule or principle and apply it in solving a problem and to make judgments and decisions that are logically sound.

Being strong in any of the preceding mental aptitudes often leads to an enjoyment of work associated with that aptitude. The reverse can also be true: enjoying a type of mental activity might lead to the development of an aptitude for the activity.

> The best measure of a person's intelligence is the type of life he or she leads.
> —David Wechsler, developer of one of the most widely used IQ tests

## PRACTICAL INTELLIGENCE

Many people, including psychologists, are concerned that the traditional way of understanding intelligence inadequately describes mental ability. An unfortunate implication of intelligence testing is that intelligence as traditionally calculated is largely the ability to perform tasks related to scholastic work. Thus, a person who scores very high on an intelligence test could follow a complicated instruction manual, but might not be street smart.

To overcome the limited idea that intelligence mostly involves the ability to solve abstract problems, the **triarchic theory of intelligence** has been proposed. See Figure 3-3. The theory holds that intelligence is composed of three different subtypes: analytical, creative, and practical. The *analytical* subtype is the traditional intelligence needed for solving difficult problems. Analytical intelligence is required to perform well in most school subjects. The *creative* subtype is the type of intelligence required for imagination and combining things in

■ **Triarchic theory of intelligence**
an explanation of mental ability holding that intelligence is composed of three different subtypes: analytical, creative, and practical

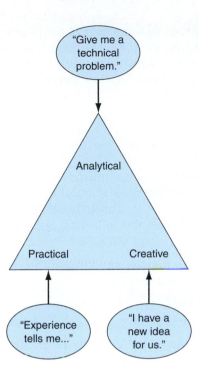

**Figure   3-3**

**The Triarchic Theory of Intelligence**

novel ways. The *practical* subtype is the type of intelligence required for adapting your environment to suit your needs. [21] The idea of practical intelligence helps explain why a person who has a difficult time getting through school can still be a successful businessperson, politician, or athlete. Practical intelligence incorporates the ideas of common sense, wisdom, and street smarts.

A person with high practical intelligence would also have good **intuition,** an experience-based way of knowing or reasoning in which the weighing and balancing of evidence are done automatically. Examples of good intuition include a merchandiser who develops a hunch that a particular style will be hot next season, a basketball coach who sees the possibilities in a gangly youngster, and a supervisor who has a hunch that a neighbor would be a great fit for her department. Intuition is also required for creative intelligence.

An important implication of practical intelligence is that experience is helpful in developing intellectual skills and judgment. At younger ages, raw intellectual ability such as required for learning information technology skills, may be strongest. However, judgment and wisdom are likely to be stronger with accumulated experience. This is why people in their forties and older are more likely to be chosen for positions such as the CEO of a large business or a commercial airline pilot. Poor judgment is *sometimes* associated with inexperience and youth. Several years ago in Amagasaki, Japan, a commuter train derailed and hit the parking garage of a nine-story building, killing 73 people and injuring 441. Investigators focused on excessive speed and a 23-year-old train conductor's lack of experience after the train jumped the track and plowed into the apartment building garage a few yards from the tracks. [22]

■ **Intuition**
an experience-based way of knowing or reasoning in which the weighing and balancing of evidence are done automatically

One major reservation some have about practical intelligence is the implication that people who are highly intelligent in the traditional sense are not practical thinkers. In truth, most executives and other high-level workers score quite well on tests of mental ability. These tests usually measure analytical intelligence.

## MULTIPLE INTELLIGENCES

■ **Multiple intelligences**
a theory of intelligence contending that people know and understand the world in distinctly different ways and learn in different ways

Another approach to understanding the diverse nature of mental ability is the theory of **multiple intelligences.** According to Howard Gardner, people know and understand the world in distinctly different ways and learn in different ways. Individuals possess the following eight intelligences, or faculties, in varying degrees:

1. **Linguistic.** Enables people to communicate through language, including reading, writing, and speaking.

2. **Logical-mathematical.** Enables individuals to see relationships between objects and solve problems, as in calculus and statistics.

3. **Musical.** Gives people the capacity to create and understand meanings made out of sounds and to enjoy different types of music.

4. **Spatial.** Enables people to perceive and manipulate images in the brain and to recreate them from memory, as is required in making graphic designs.

5. **Bodily-kinesthetic.** Enables people to use their body and perceptual and motor systems in skilled ways such as dancing, playing sports, and expressing emotion through facial expressions.

6. **Intrapersonal.** Enables people to distinguish among their own feelings and acquire accurate self-knowledge.

7. **Interpersonal.** Makes it possible for individuals to recognize and make distinctions among the feelings, motives, and intentions of others as in managing or parenting.

8. **Naturalist.** Enables individuals to differentiate among, classify, and utilize various features of the physical external environment.

Your profile of intelligences influences how you best learn and to which types of jobs you are best suited. Gardner believes it is possible to develop these separate intelligences through concentrated effort. However, any of these intelligences might fade if not put to use. [23] The components of multiple intelligences might also be perceived as different talents or abilities. Having high general problem-solving ability ($g$) would contribute to high standing on each of the eight intelligences.

The three types of intelligence mentioned so far (cognitive, practical, and multiple) all contribute to but do not guarantee our ability to think critically. Critical thinking is the process of evaluating evidence, and then based on this evaluation, making judgments and decisions. Through critical thinking, we find reasons to support or reject an argument. [24]

The various types of intelligence, particularly the cognitive type, give us the capacity to think critically. Personality factors heavily contribute to whether we choose to use these skills. For example, the personality factor of openness facilitates critical thinking because the individual enjoys gathering evidence to support or refute an idea. Also, conscientiousness also facilitates critical thinking because the individual feels compelled to gather more facts and think harder. [25]

## EMOTIONAL INTELLIGENCE

Later research has updated and expanded the idea of practical intelligence, suggesting that how effectively people use their emotions has a major impact on their success. **Emotional intelligence** refers to qualities such as understanding one's own feelings, having empathy for others, and regulating one's emotion to enhance living. A person with high emotional intelligence would be able to engage in such behaviors as sizing up people, pleasing others, and influencing them. Four key factors included in emotional intelligence are as follows [26]:

■ **Emotional intelligence**
qualities such as understanding one's own feelings, empathy for others, and the regulation of emotion to enhance living

1. **Self-awareness.** The ability to understand your moods, emotions, and needs as well as their impact on others. Self-awareness also includes using intuition to make decisions you can live with happily. A person with good self-awareness knows whether he or she is pushing other people too far. Imagine that Amanda is an assistant to the food service manager at a financial services company. Amanda believes strongly that the cafeteria should ensure that no food served on company premises contains trans fats. However, the food services manager seems lukewarm to the idea. So instead of badgering the manager, Amanda decides to fight her battle bit by bit with by presenting facts and reminders in a friendly way. Eventually the manager agrees to have a meeting on the subject with an invited nutritionist. Amanda's self-awareness has paid off.

2. **Self-management.** The ability to control one's emotions and act with honesty and integrity in a consistent and acceptable manner. The right degree of self-management helps prevent a person from throwing temper tantrums when activities do not go as planned. Effective workers do not let their occasional bad moods ruin their day. If they cannot overcome the bad mood, they let coworkers know of their problem and how long it might last. A person with low self-management would suddenly decide to drop a project because the work was frustrating.

   Imagine that Jack is an assistant to the export sales manager, and today is a big day because a company in Russia appears ready to make a giant purchase. The export sales manager says, "Today we need peak performance from everybody. If we nail down this sale, we will exceed our sales quota for the year." Unfortunately, Jack is in a grim mood. His favorite NFL team was eliminated from the playoffs the night before, and his dog has been diagnosed as having a torn abdominal muscle. Jack would like to lash out in anger against everybody he meets today, but instead he focuses his energy on getting the job done and does not let his personal problems show through.

3. **Social awareness.** Includes having empathy for others and having intuition about work problems. A team leader with social awareness, or empathy,

would be able to assess whether a team member has enough enthusiasm for a project to assign him to that project. Another facet of social awareness is the ability to interpret nonverbal communication, such as frowns and types of smiles. [27] A supervisor with social awareness, or empathy, would take into account the most likely reaction of group members before making a decision affecting them.

Imagine that Cindy has been working as an assistant purchasing manager for six months. Company policy prohibits accepting "lavish" gifts from vendors or potential vendors attempting to sell the company goods or services. Cindy has been placed in charge of purchasing all paper toweling for the company. Although most of the purchasing is made over the Internet, sales representatives still make the occasional call. The rep from the paper towel company asks Cindy if she would like an iPhone as a token gift for even considering his company. Cindy really wants an iPhone, but it is not yet in her budget. After thinking through the potential gift for five minutes, Cindy decides to refuse. Perhaps an iPhone is not really a lavish gift, but her intuition tells her it would appear to be a conflict of interest if she accepted the iPhone.

4. **Relationship management.** Includes the interpersonal skills of being able to communicate clearly and convincingly, disarm conflicts, and build strong personal bonds. Effective workers use relationship management skills to spread their enthusiasm and solve disagreements, often with kindness and humor. A worker with relationship management skills would use a method of persuasion that is likely to work well with a particular group or individual.

Much of this book is about relationship management, but here is yet another example. Donte is an information technology (IT) specialist. His assignment for the first six months is to visit users at their workplace to help them with any IT problems they might be experiencing. In discussing his role with his supervisor, Donte begins to realize that helping with technical problems is not his only job. He is an ambassador of goodwill for the IT department. He and his manager want to build a network of support for the efforts of the department. So when Donte visits the various departments he is courteous and friendly, and asks about how an IT rep could make work easier for the person in question.

Two researchers who study emotion emphasize that the idea behind emotional intelligence is that it represents a skill through which employees treat emotions as valuable information in navigating a situation.

An example follows:

*Let's say a sales manager has come up with an amazing idea that will increase corporate revenues by up to 200%, but knows that his boss tends to be irritable and short-tempered in the morning. Having emotional intelligence means that the manager will first recognize and consider this emotional fact about his boss. Despite the stunning nature of the idea—and his own excitement—he will regulate his own emotions, curb his enthusiasm, and wait until the afternoon to approach the boss. [28]*

## BACK TO THE OPENING CASE

To achieve the objectives sought by CEO Steve Bennett, most workers and managers at Intuit would have to develop their emotional intelligence. Among these competencies would be expressing their feelings explicitly in resolving conflict without throwing a tantrum, or becoming so angry that a useful solution could not be reached. Expressing en-thusiasm also requires some emotional intelligence because many people are too emotionally flat in the workplace. Enthusiasm is contagious, so it helps Intuit when workers spread their enthusiasm.

Emotional intelligence thus incorporates many of the skills and attitudes necessary to achieve effective interpersonal relations in organizations. Most of the topics in this book, such as resolving conflict, helping others develop, and possessing positive political skills, would be included in emotional intelligence. As mentioned earlier, emotional intelligence might also be regarded as a major aspect of personality rather than true intelligence. For example, if you can read the feelings of other people, aren't you just being smart?

## GUIDELINES FOR RELATING TO PEOPLE OF DIFFERENT LEVELS AND TYPES OF INTELLIGENCE

■ **Learning Objective 4**

Certainly you cannot expect to administer mental ability and emotional intelligence tests to all your work associates, gather their scores, and then relate to associates differently based on their scores. Yet it is possible to intuitively develop a sense for the mental quickness of people and the types of mental tasks they perform best. For example, managers must make judgments about mental ability in selecting people for jobs and assigning them to tasks. Following are several guidelines worth considering for enhancing your working relationships with others:

1. If you perceive another worker (your manager included) to be mentally quick, present your ideas in technical depth. Incorporate difficult words into your conversation and reports. Ask the person challenging questions.

2. If you perceive another worker to be mentally slow, present your ideas with a minimum of technical depth. Use a basic vocabulary, without going so far as to be patronizing. Ask for frequent feedback about having been clear. If you have supervisory responsibility for a person who appears to be below average in intelligence, give that person the opportunity to repeat the same type of task rather than switching assignments frequently.

3. If you perceive a work associate to relish crunching numbers, use quantitative information when attempting to persuade that person. Instead of using phrases such as "most people," say "about 65 percent of people."

4. If you perceive a work associate to have high creative intelligence, solicit his or her input on problems requiring a creative solution. Use statements such as "Here's a problem that requires a sharp, creative mind, so I've come to you."

5. If you perceive a work associate to have low emotional intelligence, explain your feelings and attitudes clearly. Make an occasional statement such as

"How I feel about his situation is quite important" to emphasize the emotional aspect. The person may not get the point of hints and indirect expressions.

To start putting these guidelines into practice, do the role-plays in Skill-Building Exercises, 3-2 and 3-3.

## Skill-Building Exercise 3-2

### Adapting to People of Different Mental Abilities

**The Mentally Sharp Coworker:**  One student plays the role of a worker who needs to learn a new software package in a hurry. This person intends to approach a particular coworker who is known for having a sharp mind. The worker wonders whether this highly intelligent person will be interested in your problem. The other person plays the role of the computer whiz who ordinarily does not like to solve problems for people that they should be able to solve themselves. The first worker meets with the second to discuss loading the software.

**The Mentally Average Team Member:**  One student plays the role of a supervisor who needs to explain to a team member how to calculate discounts for customers. To the supervisor's knowledge, the team member does not know how to calculate discounts, although it will be an important part of the team member's new job. The supervisor and the team member get together for a session on calculating discounts.

## Skill-Building Exercise 3-3

### Helping an Intellectually Challenged Worker Get Started

You are an order-fulfillment supervisor at the distribution center for a large online store. Your area of responsibility is the order fulfillment of games, toys, and sports. Part of top-level management's human resource philosophy is "give a break to those who need a break." One way of implementing this philosophy is to hire the occasional job applicant who is well below average in cognitive (traditional) intelligence. Under this program, you are assigned Jimmy, an amiable, physically able, and energetic 20-year-old who has substantially below-average problem-solving ability (such as measured by IQ). Your manager instructs you to assign Jimmy to a job you think he can handle. You decide that packing orders for video games would be a starting point. It is day one on the job, and you want to get Jimmy to feel useful right away. Jimmy also wants to feel useful, yet he is apprehensive about the situation.

Demonstrate how you will reassure Jimmy, and show him how to get started packing the box and attaching the shipping label. Another student plays the role of Jimmy.

# Values As a Source of Individual Differences

Another group of factors influencing how a person behaves on the job is that person's values and beliefs. A **value** refers to the importance a person attaches to something. Values are also tied to the enduring belief that one's mode of conduct is better than another mode of conduct. If you believe that good interpersonal relations are the most important part of your life, your humanistic values are strong. Similarly, you may think that people who are not highly concerned about interpersonal relations have poor values.

Values are closely tied in with **ethics,** or the moral choices a person makes. A person's values influence which kinds of behaviors he or she believes are ethical. Ethics convert values into action. An executive who strongly values profits might not find it unethical to raise prices higher than needed to cover additional costs. Another executive who strongly values family life might suggest that the company invest money in an on-site child care center. Ethics is such an important part of interpersonal relations in organizations that the topic receives separate mention in Chapter 14.

Differences in values among people often stem from age, or generational, differences. Workers over age 50, in general, may have different values than people who are much younger. These age differences in values have often been seen as a clash between Baby Boomers and members of Generation X and Generation Y. According to the stereotype, Boomers see Generation Xers and Yers as disrespectful of rules, not willing to pay their dues, and being disloyal to employers. Generation Xers and Yers see Boomers as worshipping hierarchy (layers of authority), being overcautious, and wanting to preserve the status quo.

Table 3-4 summarizes these stereotypes with the understanding that massive group stereotypes like these are only partially accurate because there are literally millions of exceptions. For example, many Baby Boomers are fascinated with technology, and many Generation Yers like hierarchy.

## HOW VALUES ARE LEARNED

People acquire values in the process of growing up, and many values are learned by the age of 4. One important way we acquire values is through observing others, or modeling. Models can be teachers, friends, brothers, sisters, and even public figures. If we identify with a particular person, the probability is high that we will develop some of his or her major values.

> Derek, a restaurant owner, was known for his ability to offer employment to troubled teenagers and then help them get back on their feet. Asked why he put so much effort into helping youths in trouble, he explained, "I was greatly influenced as a boy by my Uncle Clarence. I was going through troubled times—stealing from a variety store and getting drunk on beer.
>
> "Uncle Clarence took me under his wing and spent hours listening to my problems. He would take me fishing and ask if there was anything he could do to help me. Finally, I straightened out. I decided that I would be like Uncle Clarence if someday I had a chance to help young people."

■ **Value**
the importance a person attaches to something

■ **Ethics**
the moral choices a person makes. Also, what is good and bad, right and wrong, just and unjust, and what people should do

| Baby Boomers (1946–1964) | Generation X (1961–1980) | Generation Y (1981–2002) (Millennials) |
|---|---|---|
| Uses technology as necessary tool | Techno-savvy | Techno-savvy |
| Appreciates hierarchy | Teamwork very important | Teamwork very important |
| Tolerates teams but values independent work | Dislikes hierarchy | Dislikes hierarchy; prefers participation |
| Strong career orientation | Strives for work–life balance but will work long hours for now | Strives for work–life balance but will work long hours for now |
| More loyalty to organization | Loyalty to own career and profession | Loyal to own career and profession and feels entitled to career growth |
| Favors diplomacy | Candid in conversation | Ultracandid in conversation |
| Favors old economy | Appreciates old and new economy | Prefers the new economy |
| Seeks long-term employment | Will accept long-term employment if situation is right | Looks toward each company as a stepping-stone to better job in another company |
| Believes that issues should be formally discussed | Believes that feedback can be administered informally | Believes that feedback can be given informally, even on the fly |
| Somewhat willing to accept orders and suggestions | Often questions why things should be done in a certain way | Frequently asks why things should be done in a certain way, and asks loads of questions |

**Figure    3-4**

**Value Stereotypes for Several Generations of Workers**

**Source:** Several of the ideas in this table are from Robert McGarvey, "The Coming of Gen X Bosses," *Entrepreneur*, November 1999, pp. 60–64; Joanne M. Glenn, "Teaching the Net Generation," *Business Education Forum*, February 2000, pp. 6–14; Gregg Hammill, "Mixing and Managing Four Generations of Employees," *FDUMagazine Online*, Winter/Spring 2005, p. 5; Sommer Kehrli and Trudy Sopp, "Managing Generation Y: Stop Resisting and Start Embracing the Challenges Generation Y Brings to the Workplace," *HR Magazine*, May 2006, pp. 113–119.

**Note:** Disagreement exists about which age bracket fit Baby Boomers, Generation X, and Generation Y, with both professional publications and dictionaries showing slight differences.

Another major way values are learned is through the communication of attitudes. The attitudes that we hear expressed directly or indirectly help shape our values. Assume that using credit to purchase goods and services was considered an evil practice among your family and friends. You might therefore hold negative values about installment purchases. Unstated but implied attitudes may also shape your values. If important people in your life showed no enthusiasm when you talked about work accomplishments, you might not place such a high value on achieving outstanding results. If, however, your family and friends centered their lives on their careers, you might develop similar values. (Or you might rebel against such a value because it interfered with a more relaxed lifestyle.) Many key values are also learned through religion and thus become the basis for society's morals. For example, most religions emphasize treating other people fairly and kindly. To "knife somebody in the back" is considered immoral both on and off the job.

Although many core values are learned early in life, our values continue to be shaped by events later in life. The media, including the dissemination of information about popular culture, influence the values of many people throughout their lives. The aftermath of Hurricane Katrina intensified a belief in the value of helping less fortunate people. Volunteers from throughout the United States and several other countries invested time, money, and energy into helping rebuild New Orleans and several other Gulf Coast cities. Influential people, such as NBA players, were seen on television building houses for Katrina victims. Such publicity sent a message that helping people in need is a value worth considering.

The media, particularly advertisements, can also encourage the development of values that are harmful to a person intent on developing a professional career. People featured in advertisements for consumer products, including snack food, beer, and vehicles, often flaunt rudeness and gross grammar. The message comes across to many people that such behavior is associated with success.

Changes in technology can also change our values. As the world has become increasingly digitized, more and more people come to value a *digital lifestyle* as the normal way of life. Many people would not think of leaving their electronic gadgets behind when spending time away from the house, even while participating in sports or watching sports. Being part of the digital lifestyle is therefore an important value for many people of all ages.

## CLARIFYING YOUR VALUES

The values that you develop early in life are directly related to the kind of person you are and to the quality of the relationships you form. [29] Recognition of this has led to exercises designed to help people clarify and understand some of their own values. Self-Assessment Quiz 3-3 gives you an opportunity to clarify your values.

## THE MESH BETWEEN INDIVIDUAL AND JOB VALUES

Under the best of circumstances, the values of employees mesh with those required by the job. When this state of congruence exists, job performance is likely to be higher. Suppose that Jacquelyn strongly values giving people with limited formal education an opportunity to work and avoid being placed on welfare. So she takes a job as a manager of a dollar store that employs many people who would ordinarily have limited opportunity for employment. Jacquelyn is satisfied because her employer and she share a similar value.

When the demands made by the organization or a superior clash with the basic values of the individual, he or she suffers from **person–role conflict**. The individual wants to obey orders, but does not want to perform an act that seems inconsistent with his or her values. A situation such as this might occur when an employee is asked to produce a product that he or she feels is unsafe or of no value to society.

■ **Person–role conflict**
the situation that occurs when the demands made by the organization clash with the basic values of the individual

## Self-Assessment Quiz    3-3

### Clarifying Your Values

**Directions:** Rank from 1 to 20 the importance of the following values to you as a person. The most important value on the list receives a rank of 1; the least important a rank of 20. Use the space next to "Other" if the list has left out an important value in your life.

_____ Having my own place to live

_____ Having one or more children

_____ Having an interesting job and career

_____ Owning a car

_____ Having a good relationship with coworkers

_____ Having good health

_____ Sending and receiving e-mail messages, and using the Web

_____ Being able to stay in frequent contact with friends by cell phone and text messaging

_____ Watching my favorite television shows

_____ Participating in sports or other pastimes

_____ Following a sports team, athlete, music group, or other entertainer

_____ Being a religious person

_____ Helping people less fortunate than myself

_____ Loving and being loved by another person

_____ Having physical intimacy with another person

_____ Making an above-average income

_____ Being in good physical condition

_____ Being a knowledgeable, informed person

_____ Completing my formal education

_____ Other

1. Discuss and compare your ranking of these values with the person next to you.
2. Perhaps your class, assisted by your instructor, can arrive at a class average on each of these values. How does your ranking compare to the class ranking?
3. Look back at your own ranking. Does it surprise you?
4. Are there any surprises in the class ranking? Which values did you think would be highest and lowest?

A manager of a commercial weight-reduction center resigned after two years of service. The owners pleaded with her to stay, based on her excellent performance. The manager replied, "Sorry, I think my job is immoral. We sign up all these people with great expectations of losing weight permanently. Most of them do achieve short-term weight reduction. My conflict is that over 90 percent of our clientele regain the weight they lost once they go back to eating standard food. I think we are deceiving them by not telling them up front that they will most likely gain back the weight they lose."

## GUIDELINES FOR USING VALUES TO ENHANCE INTERPERSONAL RELATIONS

■ Learning Objective 5

Values are intangible and abstract, and thus not easy to manipulate to help improve your interpersonal relations on the job. Despite their vagueness, values are an important driver of interpersonal effectiveness. Ponder the following guidelines:

1. Establish the values you will use in your relationships with others on the job, and then use those values as firm guidelines in working with others. For example, following the Golden Rule, you might establish the value of treating other people as you want to be treated. You would then not lie to others to gain personal advantage, and you would not backstab your rivals.

2. Establish the values that will guide you as an employee. When you believe that your values are being compromised, express your concern to your manager in a tactful and constructive manner. You might say to your manager, "Sorry, I choose not to tell our customers that our competitor's product is inferior just to make a sale. I choose not to say this because our competitor makes a fine product. But what I will say is that our service is exceptional."

3. Remember that many values are a question of opinion, not a statement of being right versus wrong. If you believe that your values are right, and anybody who disagrees is wrong, you will have frequent conflict. For example, you may believe that the most important value top managers should have is to bring shareholders a high return on their investment. Another worker believes that profits are important, but providing jobs for as many people as possible is an equally important value. Both of you have a good point, but neither is right or wrong. So it is better to discuss these differences rather than hold grudges because of them.

4. Respect differences in values and make appropriate adjustments when the value clash is reasonable. If you are an older person, recognize that you may have to win the respect of a younger coworker rather than assume that because you are more experienced, or a manager, that respect will come automatically. [30] If you are a younger person, recognize that an older person might be looking for respect, so search for something you can respect right away, such as his or her many valuable contacts in the company.

5. Recognize that many people today are idealistic about their jobs, and want to have an impact on the lives of others. [31] In the meantime, you might feel that you need that person's cooperation to get an important task done right now, such as fulfilling a larger order. Invest a couple of minutes in helping that person understand how an ordinary task might be having an impact on the lives of others—such as earning money to feed a hungry baby at home!

## Skill-Building Exercise 3-4

### The Value-Conflict Role-Play

One student plays the role of a company CEO who makes an announcement to the group that the company must soon lay off 10 percent of the workforce to remain profitable. The CEO also points out that the company has a policy against laying off good performers. He or she then asks four of the company managers to purposely give below-average performance ratings to 10 percent of employees. In this way, laying them off will fit company policy.

Four other students play the role of the company managers who receive this directive. If such manipulation of performance evaluations clashes with your values, engage in a dialogue with your manager expressing your conflict. Remember, however, that you may not want to jeopardize your job.

Conduct this group role-play for about seven minutes, with other class members observing and being prepared to offer feedback.

To help you put these guidelines into practice, do Skill-Building Exercise 3-4. Remember, however, that being skilled at using your values requires day-by-day monitoring.

## Self-Assessment Quizzes in Overview

The several self-assessment quizzes presented in this chapter taken collectively will help you paint a verbal portrait of your personality. Self-Assessment Quiz 3-1, The Self-Monitoring Scale, gives you insight into how much you go out of your way to please others, often by telling them what they want to hear. Self-Assessment Quiz 3-2, The Risk-Taking Scale, looks at a dimension of personality that could lead you toward being adventuresome and innovative. Quite often people who are high risk takers are low self-monitors because they risk telling people what they do not want to hear, such as pointing out flaws in a company product.

Self-Assessment Quiz 3-3 gives you a chance to reflect on what is important to you. Your values are linked to the first two scales in that some people want to please others, and therefore would place a high premium on values like "helping people less fortunate than myself" and "loving and being loved by another person." Examples of strong values for a high risk taker would be "having an interesting job and career" and "making an above-average income."

# Concept Review and Reinforcement

## Key Terms

Individual differences, 64

Personality, 65

Organizational citizenship
   Behavior, 70

Cognitive style, 71

Intelligence, 74

g (general) factor, 75

s (special) factors, 75

Triarchic theory of intelligence, 76

Intuition, 77

Multiple intelligences, 78

Emotional intelligence, 79

Value, 83

Ethics, 83

Person–role conflict, 85

## Summary of Key Concepts

Individual differences are among the most important factors influencing the behavior of people in the workplace. Knowing how to respond to such differences is the cornerstone of effective interpersonal relations.

Personality is one of the major sources of individual differences. The eight major personality factors described in this chapter are neuroticism, extraversion, openness, agreeableness, conscientiousness, self-monitoring of behavior, risk taking and thrill seeking, and optimism. Depending on the job, any one of these personality factors can be important for success; they also affect interpersonal relations. Conscientiousness relates to job performance for many different occupations, and has proved to be the personality factor most consistently related to success.

Personality also influences a person's cognitive style, or modes of problem solving. According to the Myers-Briggs Type Indicator (MBTI), four separate dichotomies direct the typical use of perception and judgment by the individual: Extraversion–Introversion; Sensing–Intuition; Thinking– Feeling; and Judging–Perceiving. Combining the four types results in 16 personality types, such as a person being a conceptualizer, traditionalist, visionary, or organizer. For example, the organizer (ESTJ) scores high on extraversion, sensing, thinking, and judging.

Mental ability, or intelligence, is one of the major sources of individual differences that affect job performance and behavior. Understanding the nature of intelligence contributes to effective interpersonal relations in organizations. For example, understanding that different types of intelligence exist will help a person appreciate the strengths of people.

Intelligence consists of many components. The traditional perspective is that intelligence includes a general factor ($g$) along with special factors ($s$) that contribute to problem-solving ability. A related perspective is that intelligence consists of seven components: verbal comprehension, word fluency, numerical acuity, spatial perception, memory, perceptual speed, and inductive reasoning.

To overcome the idea that intelligence involves mostly the ability to solve abstract problems, the triarchic theory of intelligence has been proposed. According to this theory, intelligence has three subtypes: analytical, creative, and practical (street smarts included). Another approach to understanding mental ability contends that people have multiple intelligences, or faculties, including linguistic, logical-mathematical, musical, spatial, bodily-kinesthetic, intrapersonal, interpersonal, and naturalist.

Emotional intelligence refers to factors other than traditional mental ability that influence a person's success. The four components of emotional intelligence are (1) self-awareness, (2) self-management, (3) social awareness, and (4) relationship management. Emotional intelligence is a skill through which employees treat emotions as valuable information in navigating a situation.

Values and beliefs are another set of factors that influence behavior on the job, including interpersonal relations. Values are closely tied in with ethics. People acquire values in the process of growing up and modeling others, and in the process of communicating attitudes. Later, life influences such as the media also shape values. The values a person develops early in life are directly related to the kind of adult he or she becomes and to the quality of relationships formed. Values-clarification exercises help people identify their values. Person–role conflict occurs when the demands made by an organization or a superior clash with the basic values of an individual.

## Check Your Understanding

1. Why is responding to individual differences considered the cornerstone of effective interpersonal relations?
2. How can knowledge of major personality factors help a person form better interpersonal relations on the job?
3. Identify two job situations (or entire jobs) in which being pessimistic might be an asset.
4. Suppose a high self-monitoring person is attending a company-sponsored social event and that person dislikes such events. How is he or she likely to behave?
5. Identify two business occupations for which a high propensity for risk taking and thrill seeking would be an asset.
6. What kind of problems would individuals who rely on *feelings* prefer to tackle?
7. Which of the seven components of traditional intelligence represents your best mental aptitude? What is your evidence?
8. How could you use the concept of multiple intelligences to raise the self-esteem of people who did not consider themselves to be very smart?
9. Suppose a person is quite low in emotional intelligence. In what type of job is he or she the most likely to be successful?
10. How can you use information about a person's values to help you relate more effectively to him or her?

## The Web Corner

*http://myskillsprofile.com*

(This site provides many self-quizzes, including emotional intelligence, sports mental skills, and spiritual intelligence. Several of the tests are free.)

*http://www.queendom.com*

(This site provides many tests and quizzes related to cognitive factors, personality, and emotional IQ.)

*Internet Skills Builder: Boosting Your Mental Ability*
Do you want to be smarter? Thousands of specialists think they have developed intelligent ways of making people more intelligent. You will find at least one million Web sites that provide information about improving brain functioning through such methods as practice in problem solving and taking food supplements. Try out one of these sights. Evaluate the suggestions for plausibility. You might even try the exercises for a couple of weeks and observe if you become smarter. Ask somebody close to you if have become smarter. You might also see if you do better on tests with the same amount of study and classroom attentiveness.

# Developing Your Human Relations Skills

### *Capitalizing on Hidden Talent at Westmont Center*

Ginette Gagnon is the director of Westmont Center, a residential center for older persons who require assisted living, such as being served meals, help with taking baths, and supervision for taking daily medication. Many of the residents also need readily available professional health care provided by physicians or nurses. Westmont takes care of an average of 125 guests on a given month.

At a recent meeting with the Westmont board of directors, Gagnon addressed the center's most critical problem. She explained, "We are in good shape financially. Because of the aging population in the area we serve, there is a never-ending supply of people who want entrance to Westmont. I say with pride that the good reputation of our staff and our comfortable physical facilities have enhanced our reputation.

"Our biggest need is to attract staff who will stick around long enough after they are trained and experienced. You will recall that we used to emphasize hiring young people. We still hire young people, but they tend not to stay very long. Many of them see taking care of older people as a stepping-stone to other work. Our program of recruiting young retirees has worked somewhat. The older folks usually have developed nurturing skills, and that is exactly what our residents need. The big problem is that we cannot find enough retirees who want to take care of people not much older than themselves."

"Ginette, please get to the point," said Karl Adams, one of the board members.

"OK, here's what I am proposing. I would like to start a pilot program of hiring about five workers with developmental disabilities to work on our staff. Our local university has a program of preparing people with light intellectual deficiencies for the workforce. The people in the program are not college students, but individuals whose parents or guardians have enrolled them in this cooperative program between the psychology department and a community agency.

"We would assign these workers to basic jobs like baking bread and muffins, folding laundry, and bringing meals to residents. Running the dishwashing machine would be another possibility, as would be trimming bushes. We would make sure that the workers in the pilot program perform the same task everyday. McDonald's has had a program like this for years, and both the workers and the restaurants have benefited quite well."

"Hold on," said Jean Weiss. "When the word gets out that we are staffing our center with mentally unstable people, we will be in big trouble. I can imagine headlines in the newspapers and the blogs."

Ginette responded with a tone of anger. "I must say, Jean, you do not understand the meaning of an intellectual deficiency, or I am not making myself clear. A developmental disability such as having difficulty learning has nothing to do with mental instability, which refers to emotional problems. Emotional stability and IQ are not particularly related."

The discussion with the board lasted another hour. Ralph Goodwin, the chairperson of the board, concluded the meeting in these words: "I think we see advantages and disadvantages in hiring about five people with intellectual deficiencies to work at Westmont. We would be doing a social good, we would have a new source of dependable workers. Yet, we have some concerns about hiring people who might not be able to think well in emergencies. Also, maybe some of our constituents would think that we are hiring mentally unstable people."

"I am disappointed that we could not reach an approval of my plan today," said Gagnon. "However, with more study, I think the board will see the merit in my plan of hiring a group of workers who have mild intellectual deficiencies."

## Case Questions

1. What do you recommend that the board should do in terms of approving Gagnon's plan for hiring about five people with intellectual deficiencies to work at Westmont?
2. Assuming that the workers with mild intellectual deficiencies are hired, what recommendations can you make to the supervisors for their training and supervision?
3. Gagnon mentioned a few potential jobs at the center for workers with light intellectual deficiencies. What other tasks would you recommend?

## Interpersonal Relations Case 3-2

### *"We've Got to Make Our Numbers"*

Bruce Malone works as an account manager for an office-supply company with branches in most cities of the United States. The company has two lines of business, retail and commercial. Among the many products the company sells are computers and related equipment, office furniture, copy paper, and other basic office supplies.

The retail trade is served by customers walking directly into the store or ordering online. Many of the customers are small business owners or corporate employees who work at home part of their work week. The commercial trade also does some walk-in purchasing and online ordering. However, each large customer is also assigned an account manager who calls on them periodically to discuss their needs for larger purchases such as office furniture and multiple copiers and desktop computers.

Malone is meeting his sales targets for the year despite a flat economy in the city where the office supplier is located. Shortly before Thanksgiving, Malone was analyzing his sales to estimate his performance for the year. According to his projections, his total sales would be 1 percent beyond his quota, giving him a satisfactory year. Making his quota would qualify him for a year-end bonus.

The Friday after Thanksgiving, Malone received an e-mail message from his boss Lucille Whitman requesting that the two meet Monday morning before Bruce began working with his customers. At the start of the meeting, Whitman told Malone that she had something very important to discuss with him. "Bruce, we're getting a lot of heat from corporate headquarters," Whitman began. "If we don't make our numbers [attaining the sales goals] the stock price could dip big time, and the home office executives will be in trouble. Even their bonuses will be at risk."

"I've done what I can," responded Malone. "I'm going to make my quota for the year plus a little extra margin. So I guess I'm covered. There isn't much I can do about the company as a whole."

"Let me be a little more specific," replied Whitman. "The company is in trouble, so we all have to pitch in and show better numbers for the year. What we need our account managers to do is to pump up the sales figures a little. Maybe you could count as December sales a few of the purchases your customers have planned for early January. Or maybe you could ship extra-large orders at a discount, and tell your customers they can pay as late as February or March.

"You're smart, Bruce. Beef up your sales figures for the year a little because we have got to make our numbers."

"Lucille, maybe I could work extra hard to pull in a few more sales in the next four weeks. But I would feel rotten faking my sales figures for December. I'm a professional."

With an angry tone, Whitman responded, "I don't care what you call yourself; we have got to make our numbers. Get back to me soon with your plan for increasing your numbers for December."

## Case Questions

1. What type of values is Lucille Whitman demonstrating?
2. What do you recommend Bruce should have done to work his way out of the problem he was facing?
3. Is Bruce too naïve for a career in business?

## Interpersonal Skills Role-Play 3-1

### The "Making the Numbers" Conundrum

Here is an opportunity to practice dealing with the type of conflict facing Bruce Malone. One person plays Bruce, who has a follow-up conversation with Lucille Whitman about improving his December sales figures by less than straightforward means. Another student plays the role of Lucille Whitman, who is focused on the corporate demands of "making the numbers." Bruce wants to communicate clearly how uncomfortable he feels about fudging the facts, while Lucille feels enormous pressure to meet the demands of the executive group. Ideally, the two role-players will reach a solution acceptable to both sides.

# REFERENCES

1. Excerpted from Carol Hymowitz, "Business Is Personal, So Managers Need to Harness Emotions," *The Wall Street Journal*, November 13, 2006, p. B1.
2. Marvin Zuckerman, "Are You a Risk Taker?" Psychology Today, November/December 2000, p. 53.
3. Remus Ilies and Timothy A. Judge, "On the Heritability of Job Satisfaction: The Mediating Role of Personality," *Journal of Applied Psychology*, August 2003, pp. 750–759.
4. Robert R. McRae and Juri Allik, eds., *The Five-Factor Model of Personality Across Cultures* (New York: Kluwer, 2002).
5. Roger R. McRae and Paul T. Costa, Jr., "Personality Trait Structure as Human Universal," *American Psychologist,* May 1997, pp. 509–516.
6. Lawrence R. James and Michelle D. Mazerolle, *Personality in Work Organizations* (Thousand Oaks, CA: Sage, 2002).
7. "Which Traits Predict Job Performance?" APA Help Center, http://www.apahelpcenter.org/articles/article.php?id=33, accessed March 22, 2005.
8. Nicole M. Dudley, Karin A. Orvis, Justin E. Lebiecki, and José M. Cortina, "A Meta-Analytic Investigation of Conscientiousness in the Prediction of Job Performance: Examining the Intercorrelations and the Incremental Validity of Narrow Traits," *Journal of Applied Psychology*, January 2006, p. 51.
9. Gregory M. Hurtz and John J. Donovan, "Personality and Job Performance: The Big Five Revisited," *Journal of Applied Psychology*, December 2000, pp. 869–879.
10. David V. Day, Deidra J. Scheleicher, Amy L. Unckless, and Nathan J. Hiller, "Self-Monitoring Personality at Work: A Meta-Analytic Investigation of Construct Validity," *Journal of Applied Psychology*, April 2002, pp. 390–401.
11. Gerald L. Blakely, Martha C. Andrews, and Jack Fuller, "Are Chameleons Good Citizens? A Longitudinal Study of the Relationship Between Self-Monitoring and Organizational Citizenship Behavior," *Journal of Business and Psychology*, Winter 2003, pp. 131–144.
12. Jeff Joireman, Dishan Kamdar, Denise Daniels, and Blythe Duell, "Good Citizens to the End? It Depends: Empathy and Concern with Future Consequences Moderate the Impact of a Short-Term Time Horizon on Organizational Citizenship Behaviors," *Journal of Applied Psychology*, November 2006, p. 1315.
13. Michael Mount, Remus Ilies, and Erin Johnson, "Relationship of Personality Traits and Counterproductive Work Behaviors: The Mediating Effects of Job Satisfaction," *Personnel Psychology*, Autumn 2006, pp. 591-622.
14. L. A. Witt, Lisa A. Burke, Murray R. Barrick, and Michael K. Mount, "The Interactive Effects of Conscientiousness and Agreeableness on Job Performance," *Journal of Applied Psychology*, February 2002, pp. 164–169.
15. Carl J. Thoresen, Jill C. Bradley, Paul D. Bliese, and Joseph D. Thoresen, "The Big Five Personality Traits and Individual Job Performance Growth Trajectories in Maintenance and Transitional Job Stages," *Journal of Applied Psychology*, October 2004, pp. 835–853.
16. Cited in David Stipp, "A Little Worry Is Good for Business," *Fortune*, November 24, 2003, p. 68.
17. Isabel Briggs Myers, *Introduction to Type®*, 6th ed. (Mountain View, CA: CPP, Inc., 1996), p. 10. (Revised by Linda K. Kirby and Katharine D. Myers.)
18. An example of this research is John W. Slocum and Donald Hellreigel, "A Look at How Managers' Minds Work," *Business Horizons*, vol. 26, 1983, pp. 58–68.
19. Myers, *Introduction to Type®*, p. 42.
20. Brian S. Young, Winfred Arthur, Jr., and John Finch, "Predictors of Managerial Performance: More than Cognitive Ability," *Journal of Business and Psychology*, Fall 2000, pp. 53–72.
21. Robert J. Sternberg, *Beyond IQ: A Triarchic Theory of Human Intelligence* (New York: Cambridge University Press, 1985); Bridget Murray, "Sparking Interest in Psychology Class," *APA Monitor*, October 1995, p. 51.
22. "Speed, Driver's Age, Cited in Japan Crash," Associated Press, April 26, 2005.
23. Howard Gardner, *Intelligence Reframed: Multiple Intelligence in the 21st Century* (New York: Basic Books, 1999).
24. Charles G. Morris and Albert A. Maisto, *Psychology: An Introduction*, 11th ed. (Upper Saddle River, NJ: Prentice Hall, 2002), p. 11.
25. Sharon Begley, "Critical Thinking: Part Skill, Part Mindset and Totally Up To You," *The Wall Street Journal*, October 20, 2006, p. B1.
26. Daniel Goleman, Richard Boyatzis, and Annie McKee, "Primal Leadership: The Hidden Driver of Great Performance," *Harvard Business Review*, December 2001, pp. 42–51.
27. David A. Morand, "The Emotional Intelligence of Managers: Assessing the Construct Validity of a Nonverbal Measure of 'People Skills,'" *Journal of Business and Psychology*, Fall 2001, pp. 21–33.
28. Research cited in "Managing Emotions in the Workplace: Do Positive and Negative Attitudes Drive Performance?" Knowledge@Wharton (http://knowledge.wharton.upenn), April 21, 2007, p. 2.
29. David C. McClelland, "How Motives, Skills, and Values Determine What People Do," *American Psychologist*, July 1985, p. 815.
30. Jean M. Twenge, *Generation Me* (New York: The Free Press, 2006).
31. "Get Ready for 'Millennials' at Work," *Manager's Edge*, January 2006, p. 1.

# 4

# Stress Management and Personal Productivity

## Learning Objectives

## Outline

**After reading and studying this chapter and doing the exercises, you should be able to:**

1 Explain many of the symptoms and consequences of stress, including burnout.

2 Describe personality factors and job factors that contribute to stress.

3 Manage your own stress effectively.

4 Reduce any tendencies you might have toward procrastination.

5 Identify attitudes and values that will enhance your productivity.

6 Identify work habits and skills that will enhance your productivity.

7 Pinpoint potential time wasters that drain your productivity.

1 **Understanding and Managing Stress** 98
Symptoms and Consequences of Stress
Personality and Job Factors Contributing to Stress
Methods and Techniques for Stress Management

2 **Improving Personal Productivity** 110
Dealing with Procrastination
Enhancing Personal Productivity through
Attitudes and Values
Enhancing Personal Productivity through Work
Habits and Skills
Overcoming Time Wasters

K aren Behnke is CEO of Juice Beauty, a San Rafael, California, organic beauty products firm with approximately $10 million in annual sales. "Our top line is doubling, our EBITDA (earnings before interest, taxes, depreciation, and amortization) is doubling," says Behnke, 49. "We're doing very well."

*But like the rest of us, Behnke has days when life gets in the way. She recalls one chaotic workday when her husband, Howard Luria, an interventional cardiologist, was away and she needed to make an hour-long drive to Napa where her dad, who is battling a brain tumor, had gotten worse.*

*To add to the stress, Behnke was between babysitters and didn't have anyone to watch her son and daughter, ages 9 and 7, until she got back. She made hasty child-care arrangements with another mom and began making her way over the winding roads to Napa with her phone ringing nonstop. One minute, her 83-year-old mother was calling; the next minute, she was talking to a scheduled client call or speaking with one of Juice Beauty's 30 employees. Then there was the emotion involved in checking her dad into the hospital.*

*It was 9 P.M. when Behnke finally got home and put the kids to bed, but it wasn't lights out for her yet: She opened her laptop to find 120 e-mails waiting for her. "Those are the days that you think, 'Oh, my God: How am I going to do this?'" she says. "When something lands on top of my schedule, that's when it just kind of falls apart." [1]*

The small business owner just described is attempting to manage stress and juggle her schedule at the same time. In the process she is engaging in dangerous (and often against the law) multitasking as she talks on her phone while navigating a busy California highway. The urgency of the topics makes the calls even more distracting. Although this book is primarily about interpersonal skills, information about managing stress and enhancing personal productivity is relevant. Having your work under control and not being stressed out enables you to focus better on interpersonal relationships.

The first half of this chapter deals with the nature of stress and how it can be managed, whereas the second half describes various approaches to improving personal productivity. The two topics are as closely related as nutrition and health. When you effectively manage stress, you can be more productive. And when your work is under control, you avoid the heavy stress of feeling overwhelmed. A useful thought to keep in mind is that many readers of this book will become or are already **corporate athletes**, workers who engage in high-level performance for sustained periods. [2] To be a corporate athlete, you have to manage your energy and stress well, in addition to having good work habits and time management.

■ **Corporate athletes**
workers who engage in high-level performance for sustained periods

# Understanding and Managing Stress

A major challenge facing any worker who wants to stay healthy and have good interpersonal relationships is to manage stress effectively. A recent survey conducted by the American Psychological Association indicates that work is

America's No. 1 source of stress. A full 74 percent of respondents reported that work is their top stressor. [3] Although *stress* is an everyday term, a scientific definition helps clarify its meaning. **Stress** is an adaptive response that is the consequence of any action, situation, or event that places special demands on a person. Note that stress, as used here, refers to a reaction to the situation, not the situation or force itself. A **stressor** is the external or internal force that brings about the stress.

Individual differences in the perception of an event play a key role in determining what events are stressful. Giving a presentation to management, for example, is stressful for some people but not for others. Some people perceive a presentation as a threatening and uncomfortable experience, while others might perceive the same event to be an invigorating challenge.

The term *special demands* is also critical because minor adjustments, such as a pencil point that breaks, are usually not perceived as stressful. Yet piling on of minor adjustments, such as having 10 small things go wrong in one day, is stressful. This is true because stress is additive: A series of small doses of stress can create a major stress problem.

This textbook's approach to understanding stress centers on its symptoms and consequences, personality and job factors that contribute to stress, and methods and techniques for stress management. Managing stress receives more emphasis because the same techniques can be used to combat a variety of stressors.

## SYMPTOMS AND CONSEQUENCES OF STRESS

The physiological changes that take place within the body in response to stress are responsible for most stress symptoms. These physiological changes are almost identical for both positive and negative stressors. Ski racing, romantic attraction, and being downsized can make you feel about the same physically. The experience of stress helps activate hormones that prepare the body to run or fight when faced with a challenge. This battle against the stressor is referred to as the **fight-or-flight response**. It helps you deal with emergencies.

A modern explanation of the fight-or-flight response theory explains that, when faced with stress, the brain acts much like a thermostat. The brain is the organ that decides whether a situation is stressful and produces the behavioral and physiological responses. Yet, the brain's response is based on personal experience and culture. Eating seal meat would rarely be stressful for an Eskimo, yet might be for a Floridian. When outside conditions deviate from an ideal point, the thermostat sends a signal to the furnace to increase heat or air-conditioning. The brain senses stress as damage to well-being and therefore sends out a signal to the body to cope. The purpose of coping is to modify the discrepancy between the ideal (low-stress) and actual (high-stress) conditions. [4] The brain is thus a self-regulating system that helps us cope with stressors.

### Physiological Reactions

The activation of hormones when the body has to cope with a stressor produces a short-term physiological reaction. Among the most familiar reactions is an increase in heart rate, blood pressure, blood glucose, and

■ **Stress**
an adaptive response that is the consequence of any action, situation, or event that places special demands on a person

■ **Stressor**
the external or internal force that brings about stress

■ **Learning Objective 1**

■ **Fight-or-flight response**
the body's physiological and chemical battle against a stressor in which the person tries to cope with the adversity head-on or tries to flee from the scene

blood clotting. The stress hormone cortisol and other chemical responses to a stress can increase the cardiovascular function and the immune system in the short-term. To help you recognize these symptoms, try to recall your internal bodily sensations the last time you were almost in an automobile accident or heard some wonderful news. Less familiar changes are a redirection of the blood flow toward the brain and large muscle groups and a release of stored fluids from places throughout the body into the bloodstream.

If stress is continuous and accompanied by these short-term physiological changes, annoying and life-threatening conditions can occur. Damage occurs when stress levels rarely subside. Eventually the immune system is suppressed, and memory is impaired. When the immune system is impaired, the severity of many diseases and disorders increases. For example, people whose stress level is high recover more slowly from colds and injuries, and they are more susceptible to sexually transmitted diseases. [5]

A stressful life event usually leads to a high cholesterol level (of the unhealthy type) and high blood pressure. Other conditions associated with stress are cardiac disease, migraine headaches, ulcers, allergies, skin disorders, irritable bowel syndrome, and cancer. People under continuous negative stress, such as having severe family problems or having a life out of control, also age more quickly partially because of cell damage. [6] (Have you ever observed that stressed-out friends of yours appear older looking than their chronological age?) A study of 812 Swedish workers conducted over a 25-year period found that work stress doubles the risk of dying from a heart attack. Seventy-three of the workers died from cardiac disease during the study. The major type of stress studied was having high work demands with little control over the work, combined with being underpaid. [7]

Stress symptoms vary considerably from one person to another. A general behavioral symptom of intense stress is for people to exaggerate their weakest tendencies. For instance, a person with a strong temper who usually keeps cool under pressure may throw a tantrum under intense pressure. Some common stress symptoms are listed in Figure 4-1.

| Figure | 4-1 |
| --- | --- |

**A Variety of Stress Symptoms**
**Note:** Anxiety is a general sense of dread, fear, or worry not linked to a specific event, such as being anxious about your future.

| Mostly Physical and Physiological | |
| --- | --- |
| Shaking or trembling | Mouth dryness |
| Dizziness | Upper and lower back pain |
| Heart palpitations | Frequent headaches |
| Difficulty breathing | Low energy and stamina |
| Chronic fatigue | Stomach problems |
| Unexplained chest pains | Constant craving for sweets |
| Frequent teeth grinding | Increased alcohol or cigarette consumption |
| Frequent nausea | Frequent need to eliminate |

| Mostly Emotional and Behavioral | |
| --- | --- |
| Difficulty concentrating | Anxiety or depression |
| Nervousness | Forgetfulness |
| Crying | Restlessness |
| Anorexia | Frequent arguments with others |
| Declining interest in sex | Feeling high strung much of the time |
| Frequent nail biting or hair tugging | |

## Job Performance Consequences

Stress has both negative and positive consequences. **Hindrance stressors** are those stressful events and thoughts that have a negative effect on motivation and performance. Many of these have already been mentioned. In contrast, **challenge stressors** have a positive direct effect on motivation and performance. [8] The right amount of stress prepares us for meeting difficult challenges and spurs us on to peak intellectual and physical performance. An optimum level of stress exists for most people and most tasks. In general, performance tends to be best under moderate amounts of stress. If the stress is too great, people become temporarily ineffective; they may freeze or choke. Under too little stress, people may become lethargic and inattentive. Figure 4-2 depicts the relationship between stress and job performance. An exception to this relationship is that certain negative forms of stress are likely to lower performance even if the stress is moderate. For example, the stress created by an intimidating supervisor or worrying about radiation poisoning—even in moderate amounts—will not improve performance.

Job stress can also lower job performance indirectly because distressed workers are more likely to be absent from the job, thereby not accomplishing as much work. A study of 323 health service workers in the United Kingdom found that job-related psychological distress, particularly depression, was associated with more days absent and a greater number of times absent. [9] (That is, one worker could be absent only twice and miss a total of 20 days, while another worker could be absent 10 times yet miss a total of 10 days.)

The optimum amount of stress is a positive force that is the equivalent of finding excitement and challenge. Your ability to solve problems and deal with challenge is enhanced when the right amount of adrenaline flows in your blood to guide you toward peak performance. In fact, highly productive people are sometimes said to be hooked on adrenaline.

■ **Hindrance stressors**
those stressful events and thoughts that have a negative effect on motivation and performance

■ **Challenge stressors**
those stressful events and thoughts that have a positive direct effect on motivation and performance

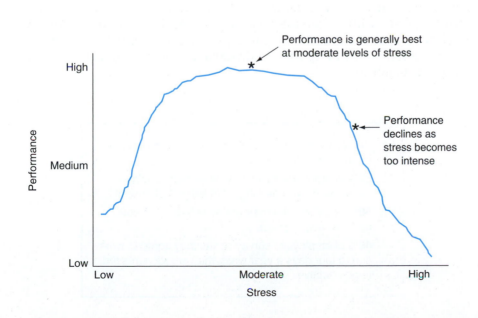

Performance is generally best at moderate levels of stress

Performance declines as stress becomes too intense

**Figure** **4-2**

**Relationship between Stress and Job Performance**

**Burnout**

a condition of emotional, mental, and physical exhaustion in response to long-term stressors

### Burnout and Stress

One of the major problems of prolonged stress is that it may lead to **burnout**, a condition of emotional, mental, and physical exhaustion in response to long-term stressors. Burnout is also referred to as work exhaustion because fatigue is usually involved. Burned-out people are often cynical. Two other examples of burnout symptoms are irritability and impatience.

Burnout is a complex phenomenon, but it often occurs when people feel out of control. Other critical factors that contribute to burnout are insufficient recognition and reward, a lack of emotional support in the workplace, or an absence of fairness. Christina Maslach observes, "When the workplace does not recognize the human side of work, then the risk of burnout grows, carrying with it a high price and hurting all the parties involved." [10]

The key feature of burnout is the distancing that occurs in response to work overload. Burnout sufferers shift into a mode of doing the minimum as a way of protecting themselves. They start leaving work early and dehumanizing their clients, patients, or customers. People experiencing burnout may do their jobs, but their heart is not in it anymore. [11]

A synthesis of dozens of studies shows that burnout often damages the physical health of workers. Partly because burnout is a consequence of stress, burnout increases the risk for cardiovascular disease as much as well-known risk factors such as smoking, an elevated body mass index, and too much bad cholesterol. Other potential links between burnout and health problems include poor health behaviors and sleep disorder. [12]

Figure 4-3 provides more insight into how job stress affects the attitudes and job performance of workers. Note that stress leads to increased absenteeism and decreased job performance.

■ Learning Objective 2

## PERSONALITY AND JOB FACTORS CONTRIBUTING TO STRESS

Workers experience stress for many different reasons, including personal predispositions, factors stemming from the job, or the combined influence of both. If a person with an extreme negative predisposition has to deal with irate customers, he or she is most likely to experience substantial stress. Here we describe a sampling of important individual and organizational factors that contribute to job stress.

**Figure    4-3**

**Job Stress Takes a Toll**

**Source:** EAP provider ComPsych's first half of 2006 StressPulse Survey, as reported in Kathryn Tyler, "Stress Management," *HR Magazine*, September 2006, p. 81.

1. Survey research shows that stress is a major issue for many employees.

2. **51%** of employees say they have "high levels of stress, with extreme fatigue/feeling out of control."

3. **50%** of employees miss one to two days of work per year due to stress.

4. **46%** of employees surveyed say they come to work one to four days a year when they are too stressed to be effective.

## Personality Factors Predisposing People toward Stress

Individuals vary considerably in their susceptibility to job stress based on their personality traits and characteristics. Four such factors are described next.

*Low Perceived Control.* A key factor in determining whether workers experience stress is how much they believe they can control a given adverse circumstance. **Perceived control** is the belief that an individual has at his or her disposal a response that can control the negative aspects of an event. A survey of over 100 studies indicated that people with a high level of perceived control had low levels of physical and psychological symptoms of stress. Conversely, people with low perceived control are more likely to experience work stress. [13]

*Low Self-Efficacy.* Self-efficacy, like perceived control, is another personal factor that influences susceptibility to stress. (Note that because self-efficacy is tied to a specific situation, it is not strictly a personality trait.) When workers have both low perceived control and low self-efficacy, the stress consequences may be much worse. However, having high self-efficacy softens the stress consequences of demanding jobs. [14]

Two studies with about 2,300 U.S. Army soldiers each showed that respondents with strong self-efficacy were less stressed out mentally and physically by long work hours and work overload. A key conclusion of the studies is that high levels of self-efficacy may help employees cope more effectively with job stressors. [15] To illustrate, an active coping method would be to reorganize an overwhelming workload so it can be performed more efficiently.

*Type A Behavior and Hostility.* A person with **Type A behavior** is demanding, impatient, and overstriving, and is therefore prone to negative stress. Type A behavior has two main components. One is the tendency to try to accomplish too many things in too little time. This leads the Type A individual to be impatient and demanding. The other component is free-floating hostility. Because of this sense of urgency and hostility, trivial things irritate these people. People with Type A behavior are aggressive and hardworking.

Type A personalities frequently have cardiac diseases, such as heart attacks and strokes, at an early age, but only certain features of the Type A personality pattern may be related to coronary heart disease. The heart attack triggers are hostility, anger, cynicism, and suspiciousness, as contrasted to impatience, ambition, and being work driven. In fact, hostility is more strongly associated with coronary heart disease in men than smoking, drinking, overeating, or high levels of bad (LDL) cholesterol. [16] A recent review of studies confirms that there is no significant association between Type A personalities and heart disease. However, there is a strong association between hostility and coronary heart disease. Hostility of the sort seen in habitual angry driving is also a heart disease risk factor. [17] Note that the heart attack triggers also make for strained interpersonal relationships.

*Negative Affectivity.* A major contributor to being stress prone is **negative affectivity**, a tendency to experience aversive emotional states. In more detail, negative affectivity is a pervasive disposition to experience emotional stress that includes feelings of nervousness, tension, and worry. The same disposition

■ **Perceived control**
the belief that an individual has at his or her disposal a response that can control the negative aspects of an event

■ **Type A behavior**
a behavior pattern in which the individual is demanding, impatient, and overstriving, and therefore prone to negative stress.

■ **Negative affectivity**
a tendency to experience aversive emotional states

also includes such emotional states as anger, scorn, revulsion, guilt, self-dissatisfaction, and sadness. [18] Such negative personalities seem to search for important discrepancies between what they would like and what exists. Poor interpersonal relationships often result from the frequent complaining of people with negative affectivity.

### Job Sources of Stress

Almost any job situation can act as a stressor for some employees, but not necessarily for others. As just described, certain personality factors make it more likely that a person will experience job stress. Furthermore, other personal life stressors may spill over into the workplace, making it more likely that a person will experience job stress. Five frequently encountered job stressors are outlined in Figure 4-4 and described in the following.

*Role Overload, Including Extreme Jobs.* Having too much work to do, **role overload**, can create negative stress in two ways. First, the person may become fatigued and thus be less able to tolerate annoyances and irritations. Second, a person subject to unreasonable work demands may feel perpetually behind schedule, a situation that is itself a powerful stressor. Downsizing often creates overload because fewer people are left to handle the same workload as before. (If work is carefully streamlined, role overload is minimized.) According to a Families and Work Institute survey, one in three American workers feels chronically overworked. People were found to be working longer and harder, yet nowadays younger workers in particular are finding ways to balance the demands by dividing their focus between the job and personal life. Many employers were found to be more flexible in helping workers achieve this balance, such as allowing flexible working hours. [19]

■ **Role overload**

having too much work to do

**Figure** **4-4**

**Five Significant Sources of Job Stress**

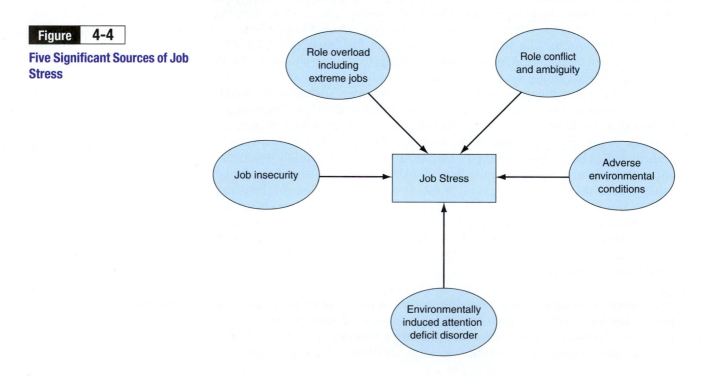

Work overload often takes the form of an **extreme job** in which the incumbent works at least 60 hours per week in a position that usually requires tight deadlines and heavy travel. Many of these jobs with long hours are found in IT and financial services fields, yet many business owners work comparable hours. The availability of work associates across the globe in different time zones facilitates extreme jobs. One financial analyst who immigrated to the United States from India reportedly works 120 hours per week, leaving only 48 hours for nonwork activities, including sleep. Although many extreme job holders experience considerable job stress, many are exalted by the excitement and the high income. [20]

■ **Extreme job**

a situation in which the incumbent works at least 60 hours per week in a position that usually requires tight deadlines and heavy travel

*Role Conflict and Role Ambiguity.* Role conflict, as an important workplace conflict, is also a major workplace stressor. People experience stress when they have to choose between two sets of expectations. Suppose an accountant is asked by her manager to state company earnings in a way that conflicts with the professional norms of accountants. If she complies with her manager, she will feel that she is betraying her profession. If she does not comply with her manager, she will enter into dispute with the manager. The woman is likely to experience job stress.

**Role ambiguity** is a condition in which the jobholder receives confusing or poorly defined expectations. Workers in many organizations are placed in situations in which they are unsure of their true responsibilities. Some workers who are placed on a self-managing work team experience role ambiguity because they are asked to solve many problems by themselves. It is less ambiguous to have the manager tell you what to do. Many people experience stress symptoms when faced with role ambiguity.

■ **Role ambiguity**

a condition in which the job holder receives confusing or poorly defined expectations

*Adverse Environmental Conditions.* A variety of adverse organizational conditions are stressors, as identified by the National Institute for Occupational Safety and Health (NIOSH). Among these adverse organizational conditions are unpleasant or dangerous physical conditions, such as crowding, noise, air pollution, or ergonomic problems. Enough polluted air within an office building can create a sick building in which a diverse range of airborne particles, vapors, molds, and gases pollute the indoor environment. The result can be headaches, nausea, and respiratory infections as well as the stress created by being physically ill. [21]

Ergonomic problems refer to a poor fit between the physical and human requirements of a job. The demands of the modern workplace contribute to the development of musculoskeletal disorders. Working at a computer monitor for prolonged periods of time can lead to adverse physical and psychological reactions. The symptoms include headaches and fatigue, along with eye problems. According to the Vision Syndrome Information Center, about 90 percent of people working on computers more than three hours a day have vision problems, with some 10 million a year seeking treatment. Common visual problems are dry eyes and blurred or double vision. Another vision-related problem is that people lean forward to scan the monitor, leading to physical problems such as back strain.

■ **Carpal tunnel syndrome**
a condition that occurs when repetitive
flexing and extension of the wrist
causes the tendons to swell, thus
trapping and pinching the median nerve

The repetitive-motion disorder most frequently associated with keyboarding and the use of optical scanners is **carpal tunnel syndrome**. The syndrome occurs when repetitive flexing and extension of the wrist causes the tendons to swell, thus trapping and pinching the median nerve. Carpal tunnel syndrome creates stress because of the pain and misery. About one in five computer users will suffer from carpal tunnel syndrome at some point. [22] The thoughts of having to permanently leave a job requiring keyboarding is another potential stressor. If ergonomic principles, such as erect posture, are incorporated into computer usage, these stress symptoms diminish.

Commuting to and from work is a major stressor for many people that could be classified as an adverse environmental condition. We emphasize *for many people* because individual differences again come into play. Some people enjoy driving, or being on a train or bus, for such reasons as the opportunity to listen to the radio or read. A study with New Jersey–to–New York commuters found that train rides of over one hour are particularly stressful for commuters. Longer commutes were associated with elevated cortisol (a stress hormone), poorer performance on a proofreading task given the study participants, and high levels of perceived commuting stress. The researcher also observed that for many workers commuting is the most stressful aspect of work. [23]

To avoid the stress of commuting in rush hour traffic, some workers leave home several hours before work, and then use the early arrival time to have breakfast, read the newspaper, or visit an athletic club near the work site. [24] Furthermore, a major reason many people work from home is to avoid the stresses associated with commuting.

*Environmentally Induced Attention Deficit Disorder.* According to psychiatrist Edward Hallowell, many people suffer from an attention deficit disorder brought on by technology and activity overload. This problem appears to be a combination of the environment and the individual who chooses to overuse IT devices. The symptoms of environmentally induced attention deficit disorder include frequently feeling rushed and impatient, being easily distracted, forgetfulness, and having little time for creative thought. In short, the person feels frazzled. A major cause of this type of attention deficit disorder is attempting to do more in less time. [25] Many of the suggestions about work habits and time management described later are useful in coping with environmentally induced attention deficit disorder.

*Job Insecurity.* Worrying about losing your job is a major stressor. Even when jobs are plentiful, having to search for another job and facing the prospect of geographic relocation are stressors for many people. Downsizing and corporate mergers (which usually result in downsizing) have contributed to job insecurity. The anticipation of layoffs among employees can increase negative stress and lower job performance. In addition, the survivors of a downsizing often experience pressure from the fear of future cuts, loss of friends, and worry about a sudden increase in workload. [26]

■ **Learning Objective 3**

## METHODS AND TECHNIQUES FOR STRESS MANAGEMENT

Unless stress is managed properly, it may lead to harmful long-term consequences, including disabling physical illness and career retardation. Managing stress refers to controlling stress by making it a constructive force in your life.

Managing thus refers to both preventing and reducing stress. However, the distinction between methods of preventing and reducing stress is not clear-cut. For example, physical exercise not only reduces stress, it also contributes to a relaxed lifestyle that helps you prevent stress.

A key principle about managing stress is that you are less likely to experience distress from stressors if you have the right resources. Having the right personality characteristics, such as high perceived control, high self-efficacy, and not being hostile, helps ward off stress. External resources to help ward off negative stress include having a network of friends who provide support, an encouraging manager, and programs for helping distressed employees. [27] Assume for example that a worker is heavily stressed from by a long rush hour commute. If the company provides flexible working hours that help decrease commuting during rush hour, the worker can experience less of a hindrance stressor.

Coping with, or managing, stress includes hundreds of activities, with substantial individual differences in which technique is effective. Running is a case in point. For many people running or jogging is an excellent method of stress reduction. Others find that running creates new stressors, such as aching knees, shin splints, dizziness from breathing in vehicle exhausts, and worrying about being hit by vehicles. In general, coping efforts involve cognitions and behaviors aimed at managing the stressor and its associated emotions. For example, you might have to decrease the troublesome elements in your job (such as role overload) and deal with the tension generated by overwork. The following subsections describe eight methods for managing stress, including a list of everyday stress busters.

## Eliminate or Modify the Stressor

The most potent method of managing stress is to eliminate or modify the stressor giving you trouble. One value of relaxation techniques and tranquilizing medication is that they calm a person enough so that he or she can deal constructively with the stressor. A helpful way to attack the cause of stress is to follow the steps in problem solving and decision making. You clarify the problem, identify the alternatives, weigh the alternatives, and select one alternative. One difficulty, however, is that your evaluation of the real problem may be inaccurate. There is always a limit to self-analysis. For example, a person might think that work overload is the stressor when the true stressor is low self-efficacy.

## Get Appropriate Physical Exercise

A moderate amount of physical exercise is a cornerstone of managing stress and achieving wellness. To manage stress, it is important to select an exercise program that is physically challenging but does not lead to overexertion and muscle and bone injury. Competitive sports, if taken too seriously, can actually increase stress. Aerobic exercises are most beneficial because they make you breathe faster and raise your heart rate. Walking is highly recommended as a stress reducer because it is inherently relaxing, and offers many of the benefits of other forms of exercise with a minimum risk of physical danger. Doing housework, yard work, and waxing a vehicle are examples of everyday forms of gentle exercise that offer the side benefits of getting tasks accomplished. A major mental and emotional benefit of physical exercise stems from endorphins produced in the thalamus portion of the brain. The endorphins are associated with a state of euphoria referred to as "runner's high." Endorphins also work like painkillers, adding to their stress-reduction value.

Millions of people seek to reduce and prevent stress through yoga, which is both physical exercise and a way of developing mental attitudes that calm the body and mind. One of yoga's many worthwhile goals is to solder a union between the mind and body, thereby achieving harmony and tranquility. Another benefit of yoga is that it helps people place aside negative thoughts that act as stressors. [28]

A caution about yoga is that too much bending too soon can lead to injured hamstring muscles and torn blood vessels.

## Rest Sufficiently

Rest offers benefits similar to those of exercise, such as stress reduction, improved concentration, improved energy, and better tolerance for frustration. Achieving proper rest is closely linked to getting proper exercise. The current interest in adult napping reflects the awareness that proper rest makes a person less stress prone and enhances productivity. A study was conducted of 23,681 healthy Greek adults over a six-year period, many of whom napped for about 30 minutes three times a week. Study participants who napped had a 37 percent lower risk of dying from a heart attack than the people who did not. A criticism offered of this study is that the people who napped may also take better care of their bodies and mind in general. [29] The connection of this study to stress management is that many heart attacks are stress induced.

A growing number of firms have napping facilities for workers, and many workers nap at their desks or in their parked vehicles during lunch breaks. Naps of about 15 minutes' duration taken during the workday are used both as energizers and as stress reducers. Napping can help a worker become more less stressed as well as more productive. A rested brain is a more effective brain. To keep the effectiveness of workday napping in perspective, workers who achieve sufficient rest during normal sleeping hours have less need for a nap during working hours. [30]

## Maintain a Healthy Diet

Another practical method of stress reduction and prevention is to maintain a well-balanced, and therefore healthy, diet. Nutritious food is valuable for physical and mental health, making it easier to cope with frustrations that are potential stressors. Some non-nutritious foods, such as those laden with caffeine or sugar, tend to enhance a person's level of stress. According to the Dietary Guidelines of the United States Department of Agriculture, a healthy diet is one that

- Emphasizes fruits, vegetables, whole grains, and fat-free or low-fat milk and milk products

- Includes lean meats, poultry, fish, beans, eggs, and nuts

- Is low in saturated fats, *trans* fats, cholesterol, salt (sodium), and added sugars

These recommendations are for the general public over two years of age. Using MyPyramid, the government personalizes a recommended diet, taking into account our age, sex, and amount of physical exercise. Consult *http://www.mypyramid.gov*, as shown in Figure 4-5.

## Build a Support Network

A **support network** is a group of people who can listen to your problems and provide emotional support. These people, or even one person, can help you through your difficult episodes. Members of your network can provide you with a sense of closeness, warmth, and acceptance that will reduce your stress. Also, the simple expedient of putting your feelings into words can be a healing experience. The way to develop this support network is to become a good listener so that the other person will reciprocate. A support network is therefore a method of stress management based squarely on effective interpersonal skills.

◼ **Support network**
a group of people who can listen to your problems and provide emotional support

## Practice Visualization and Meditation

Perhaps the most effortless and enjoyable relaxation technique for managing stress is to visualize a pleasant experience, as explained in Skill-Building Exercise 4-1. Visualization, like so many stress-reduction techniques, including meditation, requires concentration. Concentrating helps slow down basic physiological processes such as the heartbeat and dissipates stress. Forcing yourself to concentrate is also valuable because a key stress symptom is difficulty in concentrating.

Meditation is a relaxation technique used to quiet the mind, as well as to relieve stress, and is more complicated than simple visualization. A typical mediation technique proceeds as follows: Hold your back straight, and relax the body. Take three gentle breaths, breathing in and out through the nostrils. Let the respiration follow its natural flow. Your body breathes as if it was fast asleep, yet you remain vigilant. If you become distracted, simply let go of the thought and return to the breath. It is helpful to count each inhale up to 21. Each time your mind wanders, return back to one. Practice meditating about 20 minutes a day, and meditate on the spot after a stressful event or thought. [31] The breathing part of meditation is so important that is an everyday method of stress reduction itself.

Meditation is practiced by many corporate athletes (mentioned at the outset of the chapter). A. G. Lafley, the top executive at Procter & Gamble says, "I've tried to teach myself to meditate. When I travel, which is 60% of the time, I find that meditating for five, ten, or 15 minutes in a hotel room at night can be as good as a workout. Generally, I think I know myself so much better than I used to. And that has helped me stay calm and cool under fire." [32]

**The Food Groups**

Grains

Vegetables

Fruits

Milk

Meat & Beans

Oils

**Figure** **4-5**

**Dietary Guidelines for Americans, developed by the U.S. Department of Agriculture. Access the pyramid to receive your personalized set of recommendations for a healthy diet.**
**Source:** U.S. Department of Agriculture, *http://www.mypyramid. gov.*

## Skill-Building Exercise 4-1

### Visualization for Stress Reduction

A standard, easy-to-use method for reducing stress symptoms is to visualize a pleasant and calm experience. You need to concentrate carefully on your object or scene, otherwise stress reduction is unlikely to take place. If you are experiencing stress right now, try the technique. Otherwise, wait until the next time you perceive your body to be experiencing stress. In this context, visualization means to picture yourself doing something that you would like to do. Whatever fantasy suits your fancy will work, according to the advocates of this relaxation technique. Visualizations that work for some people include smiling at a loved one, floating on a cloud, caressing a baby, petting a kitten or puppy, and walking in the woods. Notice that all of these scenes are relaxing rather than exciting. What visualization would work for you?

To implement the technique, close your eyes and bring the pleasant image into focus in your mind. Think of nothing else at the moment (as in meditation). Imagine that a DVD of the pleasant experience is playing on the television screen in your brain. Breathe softly and savor the experience. Slowly return to reality, refreshed, relaxed, and ready to tackle the challenges of the day.

### Practice Everyday Methods of Stress Reduction

The simple expedient of learning how to relax is an important method of reducing the tension and anxiety brought about by both positive and negative stress. Visualization of a pleasant experience is one such method. A sample of everyday suggestions for relaxation and other methods of stress reduction are presented in Figure 4-6. If you can accomplish these, you are less likely to need tranquilizing medication to keep you calm and in control. Your stress symptoms will ordinarily return, however, if you do not eliminate and modify the stressor. If the stress is an emotional conflict you do not see or understand, assistance from a mental health professional is recommended.

Now that you have studied various methods of managing stress, reinforce your thinking by doing Skill-Building Exercise 4-2.

# Improving Personal Productivity

Achieving personal productivity is more in vogue than ever. Companies strive to operate with smaller staffs than in the past by pushing workers to achieve higher productivity. At the same time, there is a movement toward simplifying personal life by reducing clutter and cutting back on tasks that do not add much to the quality of life. **Personal productivity** refers to the amount of resources, including time, you consume to achieve a certain level of output. We approach

> **"I think the reason there are so many laptops today is that companies want to keep driving productivity out of their employees. That is our culture today."**
> —Robert McNabb of Korn/Ferry
>
> International, the executive recruiting firm, quoted in *The Wall Street Journal*, January 23, 2007, p. B3

Figure 4-6
**Stress Busters**

- Take a deep breath and exhale slowly. Inhale and your heart beats faster. Exhale and your heart beats more slowly, and slow down the cardiac muscle.[31]
- Give in to your emotions. If you are angry, disgusted, or confused, admit your feelings. Suppressing your emotions adds to stress.
- Take a brief break from the stressful situation and do something small and constructive, such as washing your car, emptying a wastebasket, or getting a haircut.
- Get a massage, because it can loosen tight muscles, improve your blood circulation, and calm you down.
- Get help with your stressful task from a coworker, supervisor, or friend.
- Concentrate intensely on reading, surfing the Internet, a sport, or a hobby. Contrary to common sense, concentration is at the heart of stress reduction.
- Have a quiet place at home and have a brief idle period there every day.
- Take a leisurely day off from your routine.
- Finish something you have started, however small. Accomplishing almost anything reduces some stress.
- Stop to smell the flowers, make friends with a young child or elderly person, or play with a kitten or puppy.
- Strive to do a good job, but not a perfect job.
- Work with your hands, doing a pleasant task.
- Find somebody or something that makes you laugh, and have a good laugh.
- Minimize drinking caffeinated or alcoholic beverages, and drink fruit juice or water instead. Grab a piece of fruit rather than a can of beer.
- Help somebody less fortunate than you. The flood of good feelings will act like endorphins.

**Figure** | **4-6**
**Stress Busters**

productivity improvement from four perspectives: (1) dealing with procrastination, (2) attitudes and values that enhance personal productivity, (3) work habits and skills that enhance personal productivity, and (4) overcoming time wasters.

■ **Personal productivity**
the amount of resources, including time, you consume to achieve a certain level of output

## DEALING WITH PROCRASTINATION

■ **Learning Objective 4**

The person who procrastinates delays action on tasks that need to de done for no good reason. **Procrastination** lowers productivity because it wastes time and many important tasks never get done. Another serious problem is that undone tasks rumble around in the back of your consciousness, thereby decreasing your concentration. Chronic procrastination can even lead to debt, divorce, and job loss. [33] Even productive people sometimes procrastinate. If these people did not procrastinate, they would be even more productive.

■ **Procrastination**
delaying action for no good reason

Many people regard procrastination as a laughable weakness, particularly because procrastinators themselves joke about the problem. Yet procrastination has been evaluated as a profound, debilitating problem, with about 20 percent of working adults identifying themselves as chronic procrastinators. [34]

Approximately 90 percent of college students report problems with overdue papers and delayed studying. About 25 percent are chronic procrastinators, and many of them drop out of school. [35] The enormity of the procrastination problem makes it worthwhile to examine methods for bringing it under control. Do Self-Assessment Quiz 4-1 to think through your own tendencies toward procrastination—and don't wait until tomorrow.

# Skill-Building Exercise 4-2

## Personal Stress-Management Action Plan

Most people face a few powerful stressors in their work and personal life, but few people take the time to clearly identify these stressors or develop an action plan for remedial action. The purpose of this exercise is to make you an exception. Here is an opportunity to inventory your stressors, think through the problems they may be causing you, and develop action plans you might take to remedy the situation. Use the form below or create one with a word processing table or a spreadsheet.

| Work or School Stressor | Symptoms This Stressor Is Creating for Me | My Action Plan to Manage This Stressor |
|---|---|---|
| 1. | | |
| 2. | | |
| 3. | | |
| Personal Life Stressor | Symptoms This Stressor Is Creating for Me | My Action Plan to Manage This Stressor |
| 1. | | |
| 2. | | |
| 3. | | |

Seven days after preparing this work sheet, observe if any of your stress symptoms have diminished. Also, identify those stressors for which only a long-term solution is possible. One student reported that a major work stressor he faced is that he wanted to work in international business, particularly business with Italian fashion companies. Yet he was experiencing stress because he had almost zero knowledge of the Italian language or culture. (By the way, can you offer this man any suggestions?)

Choose from among the following suggestions for controlling procrastination, based on those that appear to best fit your type of procrastination. A combination of techniques is likely to be the most effective.

**1. Commit to what you want in life.** According to psychology professor Timothy Psychl, if you are not committed to something you want in life, you are likely to be chronic procrastinator. The reason is that it is difficult to prioritize and take action. (See the later discussion about a personal mission and work habits.) [36]

**2. Calculate the cost of procrastination.** You can reduce procrastination by calculating its cost. You might lose out on obtaining a high-paying job you really

## Self-Assessment Quiz 4-1

### Procrastination Tendencies

**Directions:** Circle yes or no for each item.

| | | | |
|---|---|---|---|
| 1. | I usually do my best work under the pressure of deadlines. | Yes | No |
| 2. | Before starting a project, I go through such rituals as sharpening every pencil, straightening up my desk more than once, and reading and responding to all possible e-mail. | Yes | No |
| 3. | I crave the excitement of the "last-minute rush," such as researching and writing a paper right before the deadline. | Yes | No |
| 4. | I often think that if I delay something, it will go away, or the person who asked for it will forget about it. | Yes | No |
| 5. | I extensively research something before taking action, such as obtaining three different estimates before getting the brakes repaired on my car. | Yes | No |
| 6. | I have a great deal of difficulty getting started on most projects, even those I enjoy. | Yes | No |
| 7. | I keep waiting for the right time to do something, such as getting started on an important report. | Yes | No |
| 8. | I often underestimate the time needed to do a project, and say to myself, "I can do this quickly, so I'll wait until next week." | Yes | No |
| 9. | It is difficult for me to finish most projects or activities. | Yes | No |
| 10. | I have several favorite diversions or distractions that I use to keep me from doing something unpleasant, such as a difficult homework assignment. | Yes | No |

Total Yes Responses: _____

### Scoring and Interpretation

The greater the number of "yes" responses, the more likely it is that you have a serious procrastination problem. A score of 8, 9, or 10 strongly suggests that your procrastination is lowering your productivity.

want by not having your résumé and cover letter ready on time. Your cost of procrastination would include the difference in compensation between the job you do find and the one you really wanted. Another cost would be the loss of potential job satisfaction.

**3. Follow the WIFO principle, which stands for "worst in, first out."** [37] If you tackle the worst task on your list first, doing the other tasks may function like a small reward. You get to do what you dislike the least by doing first what you dislike the most. WIFO is particularly effective when faced with a number of tasks simultaneously.

**4. Break the task into manageable chunks.** To reduce procrastination, cut down a task that seems overwhelming into smaller projects that seem less formidable. If your job calls for preparing an enormous database, begin by assembling some readily available information. Then take the next step by assembling another small segment of the database—perhaps all customers whose last names begin with Z. Think of your task as pulling together a series of small databases that will fit into a master database.

**5. Make a commitment to other people.** Try to make it imperative that you get something done on time by making it a commitment to one or more other people. You might announce to coworkers that you are going to get something accomplished by a certain date. If you fail to meet this date, you are likely to feel embarrassed.

**6. Remove some clutter from your mind.** Procrastination escalates when people have many unfinished projects in the back of their mind, draining their concentration. Too much to do can freeze us into inaction. Just eliminating a few trivial items from your to-do list can give you enough mental energy to overcome procrastination on a few major tasks. Notice carefully that this approach to overcoming procrastination requires that you apply enough self-discipline to take the first step. Notice the unfortunate cycle: procrastination leads to poor concentration (as described above), and procrastination hampers concentration.

**7. Satisfy your stimulation quota in constructive ways.** If you procrastinate because you enjoy the rush of scrambling to make deadlines, find a more constructive way of using busyness to keep you humming. If you need a high level of stimulation, enrich your life with extra projects and learning new skills. The fullness of your schedule will provide you the stimulation you had been receiving from squeezing yourself to make deadlines and reach appointments on time. [38]

**8. Eliminate tangible rewards you are giving yourself for procrastinating.** If you are procrastinating through socializing with coworkers, taking a walk to obtain a beverage, surfing the Internet, or any other pleasant experience—stop rewarding yourself. Just sit alone in your work area doing nothing while procrastinating. If you remove the pleasant activities from your stalling routine, you may be able to reduce procrastination.

■ Learning Objective 5

## ENHANCING PERSONAL PRODUCTIVITY THROUGH ATTITUDES AND VALUES

Developing good work habits and time-management practices is often a matter of developing the right attitudes toward your work and toward time. If, for example, you think that your schoolwork or job is important and that time is a precious resource, you will be on your way toward developing good work habits. In this section, we describe a group of attitudes, values, and beliefs that can help a person become more productive through better use of time and improved work habits.

### Begin with a Mission and Goals

A mission, or general purpose, propels you toward being productive. Assume that a person says, "My mission is to be an outstanding professional in my field and a loving, constructive spouse and parent." The mission serves as a compass to direct your activities, such as being well organized in order to accomplish more work and be highly valued by your employer. Goals are more specific than mission statements; they support the mission statement, but the effect is the same. Being committed to a goal also propels you toward good use of time.

If you know that you can obtain the position in international business that you really want by mastering a second language, you are likely to work diligently on learning that language. Skill-Building Exercise 4-3 gives you the opportunity to establish a mission statement and supporting goals.

## Play the Inner Game of Work

Timothy Gallwey developed the inner game of tennis to help tennis players focus better on their game. Over time the inner game spread to skiing, other sports, life in general, and work. The key concept is that by removing inner obstacles such as self-criticism, you can dramatically improve your ability to focus, learn, and perform. According to Gallwey, two selves exist inside each person. Self 1 is the critical, fearful, self-doubting voice that sends out

## Skill-Building Exercise 4-3

### Using a Mission Statement and Goals to Power Work Habits

People with a well-defined mission statement and supporting goals tend to have better work habits and time management than those who do not. The following exercise is designed to help you establish a mission statement and goals so you will be energized to be more productive.

A. **Mission Statement:** To help develop your mission statement, or general purpose in life, ask yourself, "What are my five biggest wishes in life?" These wishes give you a hint to your purpose because they point toward an ideal purpose in life. Feel free to think big, because mission statements tend toward being idealistic.

B. **Long-Range Goals to Support Mission Statement:** Now write down what long-range goals would support your mission statement. Suppose your mission statement related to "creating a better life for people who are disadvantaged." Your long-range goals might include establishing a foundation that would fund your efforts. You would also need to be successful enough in your career to get the foundation started.

C. **Intermediate-Range Goals to Support Long-Range Goals:** Write down the intermediate-range goals needed to support the long-range goals. You will probably need to complete your education, obtain broad experience, and identify a lucrative form of self-employment.

D. **Weekly Goals to Support Intermediate-Range Goals:** Write down what you have to do this week to help you complete your education, such as researching and writing a paper for a particular course, registering for courses for next term, and inquiring about career opportunities in your field.

E. **Today's Goals to Support Weekly Goals (My To-Do List):** Here's where your lofty purpose in life gets translated into reality. What do you have to do today to get that paper written? Do you need to get your car battery replaced so you can get to the library so you can write your paper, so you can graduate, so you can become rich, so you can ultimately help all those people who are disadvantaged? Get going.

messages like, "You have almost solved this tough problem for the customer. Don't blow it now." Intimidating comments like these hinder Self 2 from getting the job done. Self 2 encompasses all the inner resources—both actual and potential—of the individual.

Self 1 must be suppressed so Self 2 can accomplish its task and learn effectively without being lectured. The process required to move Self 1 aside is to focus your attention on a critical variable related to performance rather than on the performance you are attempting to achieve. An example would be for a customer service representative to focus on the amount of tension in a caller's voice. [39] Or, you might focus on the facial expressions of your manager as you attempt to sell him or her on an idea for improving productivity.

## Work Smarter, Not Harder

People caught up in trying to accomplish a job often wind up working hard, but not in an imaginative way that leads to good results. Much time and energy are therefore wasted. A working-smart approach also requires that you spend a few minutes carefully planning how to implement your task. An example of working smarter, not harder is to invest a few minutes of critical thinking before conducting a telemarketing campaign for home replacement windows. Develop a list of homeowners of houses of at least 15 years old. People with relatively new homes are poor prospects for replacing their windows.

A new perspective on working smarter, not harder is to keep perfecting your skills through **deliberate practice**—strong effort to improve target performance over time. Practice alone does not lead to nearly as much improvement as thinking through what you have done to look for areas for improvement. [40] Feedback from others is also helpful. Assume that a loan officer at a bank signs off on loans to small business owners. She engages in deliberate practice by following the history of these loans to evaluate which business owners proved to be good risks, and those that proved to be poor risks. She frequently asks herself, "What did I miss here? What did I do right here?" In this way, the loan officer is working smarter by honing her risk-evaluation skills.

## Value Orderliness and Cleanliness

An orderly desk, work area, briefcase, hard drive, or storage drive does not inevitably indicate an orderly mind. Yet it does help most people become more productive because they can better focus their mind. Being surrounded by a collection of small, unfinished tasks interferes with your ability to focus on major tasks. Also, less time is wasted and less energy is expended if you do not have to hunt for information that you thought you had on hand. The central message of the best-seller, *Getting Things Done* by David Allen is that to achieve maximum efficiency and relaxation is to clear clutter both outside and inside your mind. [41] If you are orderly, you clear clutter.

According to time-management consultant Barbara Hemphill, the average person spends 150 hours per year searching for misplaced information. Hemphill says, "Your ability to accomplish any task or goal is directly related to your ability to find the right information at the right time." [42] Knowing where information is and what information you have available is a way of being in control of your job. When your job gets out of control, you are probably working at less than peak efficiency. Valuing cleanliness improves productivity

---

■ **Deliberate practice**

strong effort to improve target performance over time

in several ways. According to the Japanese system, cleanliness is the bedrock of quality. Also, after you have thoroughly cleaned your work area, you will usually attain a fresh outlook.

As with any suggestions about human behavior, individual differences exist with respect to the impact of clutter on productivity. Internet guru, Esther Dyson, has a work area so cluttered she resembles a caricature of a person needing help from a personal productivity consultant. It has also been argued that focusing too much on tidiness might detract from creative thinking, and that many messy people, such as Albert Einstein, believe that a messy work area facilitates their creative thinking. To quote the great man, "If a cluttered desk is a sign of a cluttered mind, of what then, is an empty desk?" [43]

## Value Good Attendance and Punctuality

Good attendance and punctuality are expected of both experienced and inexperienced employees. You cannot be productive unless you are physically present in your work area. The same principle applies whether you work on company premises or at home. One exception is that some people can work through solutions to job problems while engaged in recreation. Keep in mind, too, that being late for or absent from meetings sends the silent message that you do not regard the meeting as being important.

The relationship of lateness to absenteeism and work performance has been researched. Based on 30 studies and over 9,000 workers, it was found that employees who were late also tended to have high absenteeism records. In addition, employees who were late tended to have poorer work performance than workers who were prompt, but the relationship was not strong. [44] Despite this weak association, being late must still be regarded as a productivity drain.

## Attain a Balance in Life and Avoid Being a Workaholic

A productive attitude to maintain is that overwork can lead to negative stress and burnout. Proper physical rest and relaxation can contribute to mental alertness and an improved ability to cope with frustration. Many people do not achieve enough rest and relaxation, as inferred from the fact that more than one half of American workers fail to take all their vacation days. [45] The environmentally induced attention deficit disorder and extreme jobs described earlier represent a life out of balance. A strategy for preventing overwork is to strive for a balance in which you derive satisfaction from various spheres of life. Major spheres in addition to work include family life, romance, sports, the arts and music, faith, and intellectual growth.

A strongly recommended technique for attaining balance between work and other spheres of life is to learn how to say no diplomatically to your boss and family members. [46] For example, your boss might ask you to take on a project when you are already overloaded. It would be necessary to *occasionally* explain that you are so overloaded that you could not do a good job with the new assignment. And, you might have to *occasionally* turn down your family's or friend's request to take a weekend vacation when you face heavy work demands.

Neglecting the normal need for rest and relaxation can lead to **workaholism**, an addiction to work in which not working is an uncomfortable experience. Some types of workaholics are perfectionists who are never satisfied with their work and

**Workaholism**

an addiction to work in which not working is an uncomfortable experience

therefore find it difficult to leave work behind, and have no real hobbies outside of the office. In addition, the perfectionist-type workaholic may become heavily focused on control of people and information, leading to rigid behavior and strained interpersonal relationships. Many workaholics take laptops to bed, and leave their cell phones on during the night to catch any potential calls from distant time zones. However, some people who work long and hard are classified as achievement-oriented workaholics who thrive on hard work and are usually highly productive. [47] For example, a person with strong family values might nevertheless work 65 hours per week for one year while establishing a new business. In contrast, giving up on the income and status you are striving for to avoid working long hours may not be a good idea.

## Increase Your Energy

According to Tony Schwartz, the founder of the Energy Project in New York City, increasing your energy is the best way to get more done faster and better. Becoming more energetic leads to more productivity gains than merely working longer hours. Schwartz believes that energy has four wellsprings—the body, emotions, mind, and spirit. Rituals can be established to build energy in the four areas, highlighted as follows:

1. *Body.* Increasing bodily energy closely follows some of the guidelines for stress management described earlier. Proper nutrition, moderate physical exercise, adequate rest, and taking brief breaks from work all enhance a person's energy level.

2. *Emotions.* Positive emotions bring us much more energy than do negative ones. Being in the fight-or-flight mode too frequently lowers emotional energy. Deep abdominal breathing can help ward off negative emotion. A powerful ritual that helps generate positive emotion is to express appreciation to others, following the suggestions for giving recognition presented in Chapter 13. Overcoming the idea that you are a victim can also bring about positive energy.

3. *Mind.* To enhance mental energy, it is particularly important to minimize distractions that lead to constant multitasking. Switching to another task increases the amount of time required to complete the primary tasks by up to 25 percent, a phenomenon know as *switching time*. Dan Cluna, a vice president at Wachovia, designed two rituals to enhance his mental energy by focusing his attention: (1) he leaves his desk to go to a conference room, away from phones and e-mail, when he has a task that requires concentration; (2) during meetings he lets his phone calls go to voice mail so he can focus completely on the person in front of him.

We recognize, however, that you still have to live in a modern world. If you are preparing a report and your boss sends you an urgent IM, or your sick parent or child calls you on your cell phone, it is natural to be distracted away from your primary task. The sensible strategy is to minimize distractions not eliminate them completely.

4. *Spirit.* Participating in activities that give you a sense of meaning and purpose, such as coaching and mentoring others, boosts the energy of the spirit. Being attentive to your deeper needs, such as being concerned about human or animal welfare, can boost your effectiveness and satisfaction on the job. [48]

You may have observed that this energy program for business executives is quite similar to what you have been studying in relation to developing interpersonal skills.

## ENHANCING PERSONAL PRODUCTIVITY THROUGH WORK HABITS AND SKILLS

■ Learning Objective 6

Overcoming procrastination and developing the right attitudes contribute to personal productivity. Effective work habits and skills are also essential for high productivity. Six key work habits and skills are described next. They represent a mixture of traditional productivity boosters and those geared toward information technology.

### Prepare a To-Do List and Set Priorities

At the heart of every time-management system is list making, whether the list is placed on an index card, in a leather-bound planner, or in a personal digital assistant such as the BlackBerry. As already described, the to-do list is the basic tool for achieving your daily goals, which in turn helps you achieve bigger goals and your mission. Almost every successful person in any field composes a list of important and less important tasks that need to be done. Before you compose a useful list, you need to set aside a few minutes of quiet time every day to sort out the tasks at hand. This is the most basic aspect of planning.

As is well known, it is helpful to set priorities for items on the to-do list. A typical system is to use A to signify critical or essential items, B to signify important items, and C for the least important ones. Although an item might be regarded as a C (for example, emptying the wood shavings from the electronic pencil sharpener), it still makes a contribution to your management of time and sense of well-being. Accomplishing anything reduces some stress. Also, many people obtain satisfaction from crossing off an item on their list, however trivial. If you are at all conscientious, small, unaccomplished items will come back to interfere with your concentration.

To-do lists contribute enormously to productivity, yet a to-do list may have to be revamped to meet the changing demands of the day. Marissa Mayer, vice president of Search Products and User Experience at Google, explains that she keeps a task list in a text file. She uses the list as high-priority things to focus on. "But at Google things can change pretty fast. This morning I had my list of what I thought I was going to do today, but now I'm doing entirely different things," says Mayer. [49] As a result, she quickly prepares a new to-do list.

Time-management consultant Harold Taylor warns that preparing to-do lists should not become an end in itself, with so much time devoted to list making that accomplishing some of the tasks get neglected. [50] Another danger is filling the to-do list with items you would have to accomplish anyway, such as "check e-mail." The to-do list can become so long that it becomes an overwhelming task.

## BACK TO THE OPENING CASE

Is Behnke's life crazy? Absolutely. Would she have it any other way? Absolutely not. She says, "When I see an opportunity, I have to go after it." Apparently this small business owner places high priority on both work and personal life. Behnke outsources her housekeeping and she schedules her occasional out-of-town trips for the seven consecutive days every month that her husband is at home. [51]

### Streamline Your Work and Emphasize Important Tasks

As companies continue to operate with fewer workers than in the past despite prosperity, more unproductive work must be eliminated. Getting rid of unproductive work is part of *business process improvement* in which work processes are radically redesigned and simplified. Every employee is expected to get rid of work that does not contribute to productivity or help customers. In general, to streamline your work, look for duplication of effort and waste. An example of duplication of effort would be to routinely send people e-mail and voice mail messages covering the same topic. An example of waste would be to call a meeting for disseminating information that could easily be communicated by e-mail.

Emphasizing important tasks means that you make sure to take care of A items on your to-do list. It also implies that you seek to accomplish a few work activities that, if done well, would make a big difference in your job performance. Although important tasks may take less time to accomplish than many routine tasks, they can represent the difference between success and failure. Five minutes of telephone conversation with a major customer might do more good for your company than three hours of arranging obsolete inventory in the warehouse.

### Concentrate on One Important Task at a Time Instead of Multitasking

While working on important tasks, concentrate on what you are doing. Effective executives and professionals have a well-developed capacity to concentrate on the problem or person facing them, however surrounded they are with other obligations. Intense concentration leads to crisper judgment and analysis and also minimizes major errors. Another useful by-product of concentration is that it helps reduce absentmindedness. If you really concentrate on what you are doing, the chances diminish that you will forget what you intended to do.

As you are concentrating on an important task, such as performing analytical work or writing a report, avoid multitasking, or performing more than one activity simultaneously. Common forms of multitasking include surfing the Internet or reading e-mail while engaged in a phone conversation with a coworker or customer. Both experimental evidence and opinion has accumulated that multitasking while performing important tasks leads to problems in concentration, along with significant errors—for most people. The information about mental energy described earlier applies here. Multitasking on routine tasks has less negative consequences, and can sometimes be a legitimate time saver.

David E. Meyer, the director of the Brain, Cognition and Action Laboratory at the University of Michigan, notes that when people attempt to perform two or more related tasks at the same time or alternating rapidly—instead of doing them sequentially—two negative consequences occur. Errors increase substantially, and the amount of time to perform the task may double. [52] Also, according to new research about the brain, few people can concentrate on more than four tasks at once. [53]

Personal finance advisor and television personality Suze Orman is a strong advocate of avoiding multitasking when doing serious work. She prides herself on her ability to focus on one thing at a time and adhere to her agenda. She says, "The people who multitask, I think, do everything to mediocrity at best. While they are getting a lot done, they are getting it done in such an inefficient way that they usually have to do it over again." [54]

Place the potential dangers of multitasking on a personal level. Would you want a cardiac surgeon to operate on a loved one while she was receiving personal calls on her cell phone? Would you want your commercial airline pilot to be sending text messages to "friends" on a social network while he was flying through a storm?

## Stay in Control of Paperwork and Electronic Work

Although it is fashionable to complain about paperwork in responsible jobs, the effective career person does not neglect paperwork. (Paperwork includes electronic work such as electronic mail and voice mail.) Paperwork involves taking care of administrative details such as correspondence, invoices, human resource reports, expense reports, and inventory forms. A considerable amount of electronic work results in paperwork because many e-mail messages and attachments wind up being printed. Unless paperwork and electronic work are attended to, a person's job may get out of control. A small amount of time should be invested in paperwork every day. Nonprime time (when you are at less than your peak of efficiency but not overfatigued) is the best time to take care of paperwork.

An effective technique is to respond quickly to high-priority e-mail messages, and permanently delete those you will most likely not need to refer to again. Print and file only those e-mail messages of high importance to avoid being overwhelmed with piles of old messages.

Communicating by e-mail or telephone with coworkers in distant time zones creates special challenges in terms of staying in control of electronic work. Assume that Pedro working in Washington, DC, has clients in London who want to have telephone conferences at 9 A.M. their time. Pedro has to be on the phone at 3 A.M. his time, so it is best to make all his 3 A.M. calls one morning per week rather than having a life out of control because he has to be on the phone many days at 3 A.M.

## Work Productively from Your Home Office or Virtual Office

■ **Virtual office**

a place of work without a fixed physical location, where the output is communicated electronically

A growing segment of the workforce works either full- or part-time from home or from a **virtual office**. Estimates vary considerably, but it appears that about 4 percent of corporate employees work primarily from the home. Such an office is a place of work without a fixed physical location from which the worker or workers communicate their output electronically. A virtual office might be in a car, train, airplane, or hotel room; on a park bench; or wherever the worker happens to be at the time. Many people adapt well to working at home and from virtual offices because they are self-starters and self-disciplined. Many other workers lack the self-discipline and effective work habits necessary to be productive outside of a traditional office. The following is a list of representative suggestions for being productive while working independently. [55]

■ Act as if you work in a traditional office. Set specific working hours, get dressed, go outside the house for a few minutes, then return and get to work. Also, close your office at home or virtual office at some regular time. Otherwise, you are open for business all the time. If you work at home, establish a clear workspace and let your family and friends know when you cannot be disturbed.

■ Stay in touch with teammates to enhance your team player skills and not lose out on important information that could lower your effectiveness (such as missing an appointment at the traditional office). Stay in touch with other workers also, such as visiting an office supply store or attending networking meetings. In this way you will feel less isolated from the workforce—assuming feeling isolated is a problem for you.

■ Minimize conducting your personal life at the same time as working (for example, working while watching television, talking to neighbors, or shopping over the Internet).

■ Schedule regular times for meals and snacks; otherwise, you will lose many minutes and gain many pounds taking food and beverage breaks.

The practice of working at home or from virtual offices is increasing rapidly, so these suggestions merit careful consideration. Several of the productivity ideas also fit the conventional office.

## Enhance Your Internet Search Skills

An important job skill is searching the Internet for a variety of information. It follows that if you develop your Internet search skills, you will be more productive by obtaining the results you need within a reasonable time. First, it is helpful to rely on several search engines to seek needed information. Several meta-search engines claim to be so comprehensive that no other engine is required. Such claims are exaggerated, because the same search word entered into several different comprehensive engines will reveal a different list of sources.

## Skill-Building Exercise 4-4

**Productivity Boosting Through Work Habits**

The chapter has already given you ideas about using work habits to increase productivity. Here is a chance to make some personal applications of your own. Gather into small teams or work individually to identify 10 ways in which good work habits, as well as using the Internet, can increase personal productivity either on the job or at home. To supplement your own thinking, you might search the Internet for ideas on how the Internet is supposed to boost productivity.

Second, give careful thought to the search word or phrase you use. The more specific you are, the better. Assume that you want to find software to enhance your productivity, and that you enter the word *software* into a search engine. You will probably receive a message indicating that 115 million entries have been located in response to your personal inquiry. You are better advised to use the search phrase *software for increasing personal productivity*.

Third, for many searches, framing the query as a phrase by enclosing it in quotation marks refines the number of hits (or sites) returned. Place quotation marks before and after the search word, such as "software for improving work habits." Fourth, if you don't find what you want in your initial search, reframe your question in another way or change the terms. How about *"software for time management"* or *"computer programs for increasing personal efficiency"*? Skill-Building Exercise 4-4 will help you make better use of the Internet to enhance your personal productivity.

## OVERCOMING TIME WASTERS

■ **Learning Objective 7**

Another basic thrust to improve personal productivity is to minimize wasting time. The average worker wastes 1.7 hours of a typical 8.5-hour workday, according to an informal survey by Salary.com. [56] Many of the techniques already described in this chapter help save time, such as eliminating nonessential work. Whether or not an activity is a time waster depends on the purpose of the activity. Suppose you play computer solitaire for 10 minutes to reduce stress and then return to work refreshed. In contrast, another worker who spends 10 minutes playing solitaire just for fun is wasting time.

Figure 4-7 presents a list of common time wasters. Being aware of time wasters will help sensitize you to the importance of minimizing them. Even if

1. Use a time log for two weeks to track time wasters. (See Skill-Building Exercise 4-5.)

2. Minimize daydreaming on the job by forcing yourself to concentrate.

3. Avoid the computer as a diversion from work, such as sending jokes back and forth to work members, playing video games, and checking out recreational Web sites during working hours.

4. Cluster together tasks such as returning phone calls or responding to e-mail messages. For example, in most jobs it is possible to be polite and productive by reserving two or three 15-minute periods per day for taking care of e-mail correspondence.

5. Socialize on the job just enough to build your network. Chatting with coworkers is a major productivity drain.

6. Be prepared for meetings by, for example, having a clear agenda and sorting through the documents you will be referring to. Make sure electronic equipment is in working order before attempting to use it during the meeting.

7. Keep track of important names, places, and things to avoid wasting time searching for them.

8. Set a time limit for tasks after you have done them once or twice.

9. Prepare a computer template for letters and computer documents that you send frequently. (The template is essentially a form letter, especially with respect to the salutation and return address.)

10. When you arrive at work, be ready to get started working immediately. Greet people quickly, avoid checking your personal e-mail, and shut off your cell phone.

11. Take care of as much e-mail correspondence as you can after you have finished your other work, unless a key part of your job is dealing with e-mail. It consumes substantial time.

12. Avoid perfectionism, which leads you to keep redoing a project. Let go and move on to another project.

13. Make use of bits of time—for instance, five minutes between appointments. Invest those five minutes in sending a work-related e-mail message or revising your to-do list.

14. Minimize procrastination, the number one time waster for most people.

15. Avoid spreading yourself too thin by doing too many things at once, such as having one project too many to handle. When you are overloaded, time can be wasted because of too many errors.

16. Manage interruptions by letting coworkers know when you are available for consultation, and when you need to work independently—except for emergencies. Respond to instant messages only if your job requires responding immediately. Batch your instant messages just as you would other e-mails.

**Figure  4-7**

**Ways to Prevent and Overcome Time Wasting.**

**Source:** Suggestions 4, 5, and 6 are based on Stephen R. Covey with Hyrum Smith, "What If You Could Chop an Hour from Your Day for Things That Matter Most?" *USA Weekend*, January 22–24, 1999, pp. 4–5; Suggestion 10 is from Anita Bruzzese, "Tips to Avoid Wasting Time," Gannet News Service, August 9, 2004. Support for suggestion 13 is found in Vince Thompson, "Make the Most of Your White Space," jobs@UpLadder. com, October 3, 2007. Data about the productivity drain of interruptions are analyzed in Quintus R. Jett and Jennifer M. George, "Work Interrupted: A Closer Look at the Role of Interruptions in Organizational Life," *Academy of Management Review*, July 2003, pp. 494–507.

you saved just 10 minutes per workday, the productivity gain over a year could be enormous.

To analyze whether you might be wasting time, do Skill-Building Exercise 4-5. Self-Assessment Quiz 4-2 gives you an opportunity to think through your tendencies toward a subtle type of time wasting.

## Skill-Building Exercise 4-5

### Maintaining a Time Log

An effective starting point to avoid wasting time is to identify how you spend the 168 hours you have each week (24 hours × 7 days). For two weeks, catalog all the time you spend, down to as much detail as you can tolerate. Include the large obvious items, as well as the small items that are easy to forget. Keep track of any activity that requires at least five minutes. Major items would include working, attending class, studying, reading, watching television, sleeping, eating, going places, time with loved ones and friends (hanging out). Small items would include visiting the coffee shop or vending machine, purchasing gum, and clipping your nails. If you multitask, such as walking and listening to music, do not double-count the time.

When your time logs have been completed, search for complete wastes of time, or activities that could be shortened. You might find, for example, that you spend about 45 minutes per day in the pursuit and consumption of coffee. If you reduced that time to 30 minutes you would have an additional 15 minutes per day that you could invest in your career. However, if coffee time includes forming alliances with people or maintaining relationships, maybe the 45-minute-per-day investment is worthwhile.

## Self-Assessment Quiz    4-2

### Tendencies toward Perfectionism

**Directions:** Many perfectionists hold some of the behaviors and attitudes described below. To help understand your tendencies toward perfectionism, rate how strongly you agree with each of the statements below on a scale of 0 to 4 by circling the appropriate number. 0 means disagree, 4 means agree.

| | | | | | | |
|---|---|---|---|---|---|---|
| 1. | Many people have told me that I am a perfectionist. | 0 | 1 | 2 | 3 | 4 |
| 2. | I often correct the speech of others. | 0 | 1 | 2 | 3 | 4 |
| 3. | It takes me a long time to write an e-mail because I keep checking and rechecking my writing. | 0 | 1 | 2 | 3 | 4 |
| 4. | I often criticize the color combinations my friends are wearing. | 0 | 1 | 2 | 3 | 4 |
| 5. | When I purchase food at a supermarket, I usually look at the expiration date so I can purchase the freshest. | 0 | 1 | 2 | 3 | 4 |
| 6. | I can't stand when people use the term *remote* instead of *remote control*, or *cell* instead of *cell phone*. | 0 | 1 | 2 | 3 | 4 |

*(continued)*

## Self-Assessment Quiz    4-2    *(Continued)*

| | | | | | |
|---|---|---|---|---|---|
| 7. If a company representative asked me, "What is your *social?*" I would reply with something like, "Do you mean my *social security number?*" | 0 | 1 | 2 | 3 | 4 |
| 8. I hate to see dust on furniture. | 0 | 1 | 2 | 3 | 4 |
| 9. I like the Martha Stewart idea of having every decoration in the home just right. | 0 | 1 | 2 | 3 | 4 |
| 10. I never put a map back in the glove compartment until it is folded just right. | 0 | 1 | 2 | 3 | 4 |
| 11. Once an eraser on a pencil of mine becomes hard and useless, I throw away the pencil. | 0 | 1 | 2 | 3 | 4 |
| 12. I adjust all my watches and clocks so they show exactly the same time. | 0 | 1 | 2 | 3 | 4 |
| 13. It bothers me that clocks on personal computers are often wrong by a few minutes. | 0 | 1 | 2 | 3 | 4 |
| 14. I clean the keyboard on my computer at least every other day. | 0 | 1 | 2 | 3 | 4 |
| 15. I organize my e-mail messages and computer documents into many different, clearly labeled files. | 0 | 1 | 2 | 3 | 4 |
| 16. You won't find old coffee cups or soft drink containers on my desk. | 0 | 1 | 2 | 3 | 4 |
| 17. I rarely start a new project or assignment until I have completed my present project or assignment. | 0 | 1 | 2 | 3 | 4 |
| 18. It is very difficult for me to concentrate when my work area is disorganized. | 0 | 1 | 2 | 3 | 4 |
| 19. Cobwebs in chandeliers and other lighting fixtures bother me. | 0 | 1 | 2 | 3 | 4 |
| 20. It takes me a long time to make a purchase such as a digital camera because I keep studying the features on various models. | 0 | 1 | 2 | 3 | 4 |
| 21. When I balance my checkbook, it usually comes out right within a few dollars. | 0 | 1 | 2 | 3 | 4 |
| 22. I carry enough small coins and dollar bills with me so when I shop I can pay the exact amount without requiring change back. | 0 | 1 | 2 | 3 | 4 |
| 23. I throw out any underwear or T-shirts that have even the smallest holes or tears. | 0 | 1 | 2 | 3 | 4 |
| 24. I become upset with myself if I make a mistake. | 0 | 1 | 2 | 3 | 4 |
| 25. When a fingernail of mine is broken or chipped, I fix it as soon as possible. | 0 | 1 | 2 | 3 | 4 |
| 26. I am carefully groomed whenever I leave my home. | 0 | 1 | 2 | 3 | 4 |

27. When I notice packaged goods or cans on the floor in a supermarket, I will often place them back on the shelf.    0    1    2    3    4

28. I think that carrying around antibacterial cleaner for the hands is an excellent idea.    0    1    2    3    4

29. If I am with a friend, and he or she has a loose hair on the shoulder, I will remove it without asking.    0    1    2    3    4

30. I am a perfectionist.    0    1    2    3    4

Total Score: _____

## Scoring and Interpretation

Add the numbers you circled to obtain your total score.

**91 or over:**    You have strong perfectionist tendencies to the point that it could interfere with your taking quick action when necessary. Also, you may annoy many people with your perfectionism.

**61–90:**    You have a moderate degree of perfectionism that could lead you to produce high-quality work and be a dependable person.

**31–60:**    You have a mild degree of perfectionism. You might be a perfectionist in some situations quite important to you, but not in others.

**0–30:**    You are not a perfectionist. You might be too casual about getting things done right, meeting deadlines, and being aware of details.

# SELF-ASSESSMENT QUIZZES IN OVERVIEW

Self-Assessment Quiz 4-1 measures tendencies toward procrastination. Thinking about the extent of your procrastination, and overcoming excessive amounts, can help you develop career thrust. You might be able to get by procrastinating small tasks, but delaying the completion of large, complex tasks like preparing a budget or developing a report about customer service will eventually result in low performance. Self-Assessment Quiz 4-2 measures perfectionism, which in large doses can lead to procrastination and not getting things done. However, like fat in the diet, a healthy dose of perfectionism is an asset because it can lead to high levels of performance. Oprah Winfrey and Donald Trump are both perfectionists without being obsessed over details.

# Concept Review and Reinforcement

## Key Terms

Corporate athletes, 98
Stress, 99
Stressor, 99
Fight-or-flight response, 99
Hindrance stressors, 101
Challenge stressors, 101
Burnout, 102

Perceived control, 103
Type A behavior, 103
Negative affectivity, 103
Role overload, 104
Extreme job, 105
Role ambiguity, 105
Carpal tunnel syndrome, 106

Support network, 109
Personal productivity, 110
Procrastination, 111
Deliberate practice, 116
Workaholism, 117
Virtual office, 122

## Summary of Key Concepts

A major challenge facing any worker who wants to stay healthy and have good interpersonal relationships is to manage stress effectively. Individual differences play a big role in determining whether an event will lead to stress. The physiological changes that take place within the body in response to stress are responsible for most of the stress symptoms. The fight-or-flight response is the battle against the stressor.

The activation of hormones, such as cortisol, when the body has to cope with a stressor produces short-term physiological reactions, including an increase in heart rate and blood pressure. When stress levels rarely subside, the physiological changes create damage. People under continual negative stress age quickly. However, the right amount of stress (challenge stressors) prepares us for meeting difficult challenges and improves performance. An optimum level of stress exists for most people and most tasks. In general, performance tends to be best under moderate amounts of stress.

One of the major problems of prolonged stress is that it may lead to burnout, a condition of emotional, mental, and physical exhaustion in response to long-term stressors. Burnout also creates cynicism and a distancing from tasks and people. Workers who perceive the cause of burnout to be external are more likely to become less committed to the firm and more cynical. Burnout also damages the physical health of workers.

Four personality factors predisposing people toward stress are low perceived control, low self-efficacy, Type A behavior and hostility, and negative affectivity. The heart attack triggers associated with Type A behavior are hostility, anger, cynicism, and suspiciousness, with hostility having the biggest impact. Four frequently encountered job stressors are role overload, role conflict and ambiguity, adverse environmental conditions including carpal tunnel syndrome and long commutes, environmentally induced attention deficit disorder, and job insecurity.

Managing stress refers to controlling stress by making it become a constructive force in your life. Coping with, or managing, stress includes hundreds of activities, with substantial individual differences in which technique is effective. Eight representative stress-management methods are to eliminate or modify the stressor, get appropriate physical exercise, rest sufficiently, maintain a healthy diet, build a support network, practice visualization and meditation, and practice everyday methods of stress reduction.

Achieving high personal productivity on the job is more in demand than ever. A starting point in improving productivity is to minimize procrastination, an enormous problem for many people that can be approached as follows: Commit to what you want in life; calculate the cost of procrastination; follow the worst in, first out (WIFO) principle; break the task into manageable chunks; make a commitment to other people; remove some clutter from your mind; satisfy your stimulation quota in constructive ways; and eliminate rewards for procrastinating.

Developing good work habits and time-management practices is often a matter of developing the right attitudes toward your work and toward time, as follows: (1) begin with a mission and goals; (2) play the inner game of work, (3) work smarter, not harder including the use of deliberate practice

(4) value orderliness and cleanliness; (5) value good attendance and punctuality; (6) attain a balance in life and avoid being a workaholic, and increase your energy (body, emotions, mind, and spirit).

Effective work habits and skills are essential for high productivity, including the following: (1) Prepare a to-do list and set priorities; (2) streamline your work and emphasize important tasks; (3) concentrate on one important task at a time instead of multitasking; (4) stay in control of paperwork and electronic work; (5) work productively from your home office or virtual office; and (6) enhance your Internet search skills.

Another basic thrust to improved personal productivity is to minimize time wasting. Whether or not an activity is a time waster depends on its purpose. Being aware of time wasters such as those presented in Figure 4-6 will sensitize you to the importance of minimizing them.

## Check your Understanding

1. Why might it be true that people who love their work live much longer than people who retire early because they dislike working?

2. Why might having your stress under control improve your interpersonal relationships?

3. What would be the advantages and disadvantages of an *extreme job* for you?

4. Interview a person in a high-pressure job in any field. Find out whether the person experiences significant stress and what method he or she uses to cope with it.

5. Provide an example from your own or somebody else's life of how having a major goal in life can help a person be better organized.

6. Executives at Toyota, among many other Japanese companies, emphasize that clean work areas in the factory enhance productivity. What might explain this relationship between cleanliness and productivity?

7. Describe any way in which you have used IT to make you more productive.

8. Use information in this chapter to explain how a person might be well organized yet still not get very far in his or her career.

9. For many young corporate professionals, a date often consists of the two people getting together in his or her place to spend three hours doing office work on their laptop computers, followed by a take-out meal. What is your evaluation of this approach to boosting personal productivity?

10. Ask an experienced high-level worker to identify his or her most effective method of time management. How effective do you think this technique would be for you?

## The Web Corner

*http://www.theinnergame.com*
(The inner game of work, sports, and team building.)

*http://www.stress.org*
(Institute for Stress Management.)

*http://stress.about.com*
(Considerable information about stress plus several self-quizzes.)

*http://ub-counseling.buffalo.edu/stressprocrast.shtml*
(Overcoming procrastination for students.)

### Internet Skill Builder: Getting Personal Help from Your Employer

Use your favorite search engines to learn about Employee Assistance Programs (EAPs). After visiting several sites, answer these questions: (1) What type of help can an employee expect to receive from an EAP? (2) How does an EAP help with stress management? (3) Does the EAP counselor typically tell the company the nature of the problem facing the employee who sought assistance? (4) What benefits do companies expect from offering an EAP to employees? (5) What would I tell the company if I needed help with problems that are causing me severe stress?

### Internet Skill Builder: What Are You Doing with Your Time?

Go to *http://www.getmoredone.com/tabulator.html* to find the Pace Productivity Tabulator. This interactive module enables you to enter the time you spend on 11 major activities (such as employment, eating, sleeping, and television watching) and compare your profile to others. You are also able to enter your ideal profile to see where you would like to be. You just follow the straightforward instructions. After arriving at your personal pie chart, ask yourself, "What have I learned that will enhance my personal productivity?"

# Developing Your Human Relations Skills

## Interpersonal Relations Case 4-1

### Rachel Runs the Treadmill

At 6:30 Tuesday morning, 38-year-old Rachel Mendez hops out of her bed while her husband Ben Mendez is still sleeping. Rachel's first stop is to wake up her nine-year-old daughter, and encourage her to start getting ready to meet the school bus on time. By 8 A.M. Rachel is in her car and on her way to her job as a business development specialist for a human resource outsourcing company. Her primary responsibility is to entice small- and medium-size companies to turn over most of their human resource functions to her firm.

Just as Rachel begins to manage her e-mail and plan her agenda for the day, she places her right hand about three inches to the right of her heart. Rachel can feel the tightness next to her heart, and in her left arm. She thinks to herself, "This feels like I'm going to have a heart attack, but it doesn't make sense for a woman my age to be a heart attack victim. But I'm happy that I have an appointment at the cardiology center on Thursday."

At the North Side Cardiology Center, Rachel is first interviewed by nurse practitioner Janet Trudeau before her interview with Dr. Harry Ching, the cardiologist. Trudeau first took a brief medical history, followed by an interview. Parts of the interview with Trudeau went as follows:

Trudeau: So tell me in more detail why you came to visit our cardiology center.

Mendez: I have these annoying chest pains next to my heart and in my left arm. The pains usually start when I am extremely aggravated and frustrated. I have the pains about once a day.

Trudeau: Do you ever faint or become light-headed during the pains?

Mendez: No, my problem is just the pains. I keep doing whatever I'm doing when the pain hits.

Trudeau: Tell me about the situations you find so aggravating and frustrating.

Mendez: I'm really stressing out. I have a ton of aggravations and worries. To begin, my nine-year-old daughter Samantha has seizures. She is under treatment but the problem remains, and it's worrisome. I worry every day that Samantha will have a seizure and strike her head or get involved in an accident.

My work is also quite worrisome. I work mostly on commission selling human resource services. Our business has grown rapidly in the last few years, but we have kind of dried up the territory. I have to travel more to find new clients. My earnings are taking a turn downward despite the extra travel.

Trudeau: Are you the sole breadwinner in the family?

Mendez: No, my husband Alex is an assistant manager at a Ruby Tuesday restaurant, and he makes a modest living. But talking about aggravation, my husband is a decent guy but he gives me chest pains. I think he cares much more about professional sports, especially the NFL and the NHL, than he does about Samantha and me. If he's watching a game, I can forget about talking about something serious.

And then, of course, Alex works the hours of a restaurant manager, which means that he's often working when I am not working, like on Saturdays and Sundays.

Trudeau: Any other major aggravations in your life?

Mendez: Yes, commuting on busy highways. I can feel my chest pains starting when I think of sitting still for 15 minutes during rush-hour traffic.

Trudeau: Thank you, Rachel. I will be studying this information before your interview with Dr. Ching. Have a seat in the waiting room. He will be with you in about 10 minutes.

Later that day, Mendez had an extensive cardiology exam, including an electrocardiogram. Dr. Ching informed her that despite the muscle tension she was experiencing, her heart was in excellent condition.

### Case Questions

1. What sources of stress does Rachel Mendez appear to be facing?
2. What do you recommend Mendez do about the stressors she is facing?
3. Given that Mendez does not have a heart problem, should she be concerned about the stressors in her life? Explain your answer.

## Interpersonal Relations Case 4-2

### *The Extreme Job Firefighter*

Jim Blaesi brings a strange mix to the world of work—he's an entrepreneur and a civil servant, a risk taker with a good pension and benefits package. But Blaesi, 32, a full-time Rochester, New York firefighter who owns an automotive repair shop on Hudson Avenue in the inner city, just sees himself as a guy who gets to do what he loves—even if it requires 80 to 100 hours a week.

"I kissed my wife goodbye yesterday and said 'I'll see you Friday,'" Blaesi said Tuesday. "But, you know, my accountant told me, 'The majority of people in life don't get to chase one of their dreams. You get to chase both of yours.'"

The son, grandson, and nephew of firefighters who developed an interest in mechanics at a young age, Blaesi opened Blaesi Automotive in 2000 when he was actively seeking a job as a city firefighter. He was hired in 2002, eight years after his submitted his first application.

It's not unusual for firefighters to own small businesses or hold second jobs because half their shifts are at night and the weekly rotation creates three and four-day "weekends" that often fall on weekdays. "It's a combination of a schedule that allows you to concentrate hours with a career that attracts high energy people," said Fire Capt. Dan McBride.

Blaesi, who has two full-time employees, works at his shop on his days off or when he's on the night shift. When he works days, he puts in a few hours of shop time in the later afternoon before taking his paperwork home for the night.

He works at a firehouse located hear the shop, so he often goes days at a time without seeing his suburban home. He and his wife Gina don't have children yet, and she has a full-time job as a tax specialist at Paychex, a national payroll and human resource services firm. "I love her to death because we're just getting to know each other," Blaesi said of his wife of four years.

Blaesi said he started working as a mechanic's apprentice for a friend's car dealership when he was 14. In high school he worked for oil-change and tune-up franchises and advanced to auto dealerships and a truck-rental company.

He started exploring the option of owning his own shop in the late 1990s and discovered a two-lift garage for sale on Hudson Avenue. Located in a part of the city known for high rates of crime and poverty, Blaesi remembers how his friends told him he was crazy to buy the shop. But at a price of $120,000 for more than 9,000 square feet, Blaesi saw an opportunity that other locations didn't offer. "It would cost you two, two and one-half million dollars in a suburb," he said. In the years since he opened the shop,

Blaesi has paid off the original loan and invested about $400,000 to expand the job to seven lifts.

Blaesi said he's making a profit with a strong client base that includes the fleets of several government agencies. Because he and his wife have good-paying jobs, he's been able to invest all the profit from his shop back into the business. Upgrades have also included a striking red-and-silver façade that stands out in an area with many vacant storefronts and rundown buildings. Blaesi designed the exterior himself, using the look of firehouses as an influence.

Blaesi, who said he may soon hire two more employees, is content to move slowly for now. He might soon buy more property in the neighborhood to build a parking lot large enough to open a towing service. He's also thinking of other real estate ventures. And of course, plans are in the works with his wife to grow a family.

"I'm always looking for the next adventure," he said.

## Case Questions

1. What advice can you offer Jim Blaesi about achieving balance in his life?
2. In what way does it appear that Blaesi might be making good use of contacts?
3. What is your evaluation of Blaesi's personal productivity?
4. Why might Blaesi's work be considered an *extreme job*?
5. What advice might you offer Blaesi's wife?

*Source:* Adapted from Patrick Flanigan, "Risk Taker Builds Business with Patience, Planning," *Rochester Democrat and Chronicle*, November 8, 2007, pp. 8D, 9D

# REFERENCES

1. Chris Penttila, "Time Out," *Entrepreneur*, April 2007, p. 71.
2. Cait Murphy, "The CEO Workout," *Fortune*, July 10, 2006, pp. 43–44.
3. Norman B. Anderson, "Toward Reducing Work Stress," *Monitor on Psychology*, February 2008, p. 9.
4. Jeffrey R. Edwards, "A Cybernetic Theory of Stress, Coping, and Well-Being in Organizations," *Academy of Management Review*, April 1992, p. 248.
5. Lea Winerman, "Reducing Stress Helps both Brain and Body," *Monitor on Psychology*, October 2006, p. 18.
6. Research reported in Christine Gorman, "6 Lessons for Handling Stress," *Time*, January 29, 2007, p. 82.
7. *British Medical Journal* study reported in "Trop de Stress au Travail Double le Risque de Mourir d'une Crise de Coeur," *Journal de Montréal*, 18 octobre, 2002, p. 7. [Too much work stress doubles the risk of dying from a heart attack.]
8. Jeffery A. Lapine, Nathan P. Podsakoff, and Marcie A. Lepine, "A Meta-Analytic Test of the Challenge-Stressor–Hindrance-Stressor Framework: An Explanation for Inconsistent Relationships among Stressors and Performance," *Academy of Management Journal*, October 2005, pp. 764–775.
9. Gillian E. Hardy, David Woods, and Toby D. Wall, "The Impact of Psychological Distress on Absence from Work," *Journal of Applied Psychology*, April 2003, pp. 306–314.
10. Quoted in "An Ounce of Prevention Beats Burnout," *HRfocus*, June 1999, p. 1.
11. Christina Maslach, *The Truth about Burnout* (San Francisco: Jossey-Bass, 1997). See also Dirk van Dierendonck, Wilmar B. Schaufeli, and Bram P. Buunk, "The Evaluation of an Individual Burnout Intervention Program: The Role of Equity and Social Support," *Journal of Applied Psychology*, June 1998, pp. 392–407.
12. Research reported in Deborah Smith Bailey, "Burnout Harms Workers' Physical Health through Many Pathways," *Monitor on Psychology*, June 2006, p. 11.
13. M. Afalur Rahim, "Relationships of Stress, Locus of Control, and Social Support to Psychiatric Symptoms and Propensity to Leave a Job: A Field Study with Managers," *Journal of Business and Psychology*, Winter 1997, p. 159.
14. Steve M. Jex and Paul D. Bliese, "Efficacy Beliefs as a Moderator of the Impact of Work-Related Stressors: A Multilevel Study," *Journal of Applied Psychology*, June 1999, pp. 349–361; Steve M. Jex, Paul O. Bliese, Sheri Buzell, and Jessica Primeau, "The Impact of Self-Efficacy on Stressor-Strain Relations: Coping Style as an Explanatory Mechanism," *Journal of Applied Psychology*, June 2001, pp. 401–409.
15. John Schaubroeck and Deryl E. Merrit, "Divergent Effects of Job Control on Coping with Work Stressors: The Key Role of Self-Efficacy," *Academy of Management Journal*, June 1997, p. 750.
16. Jeffrey R. Edwards and A. J. Baglioni, Jr., "Relationships between Type A Behavior Pattern and Mental and Physical Symptoms: A Comparison of Global and Component Measures," *Journal of Applied Psychology*, April 1991, p. 276; related research reported in Etienne Benson, "Hostility Is among Best Predictors of Heart Disease in Men," *Monitor on Psychology*, January 2003, p. 15.
17. Research reviewed in Nadja Geipert, "Don't Be Mad: More Research Links Hostility to Coronary Risk," *Monitor on Psychology*, January 2007, pp. 50–51.
18. Peter Y. Chen and Paul E. Spector, "Negative Affectivity as the Underlying Cause of Correlations between Stressors and Strains," *Journal of Applied Psychology*, June 1991, p. 398.
19. Families and Work Institute survey reported in Adam Geller, "Survey: Third of Americans Overworked," Associated Press, March 16, 2005.
20. Sylvia Ann Hewlett and Carolyn Buck Luce, "Extreme Jobs: The Dangerous Allure of the 70-Hour Work Week," *Harvard Business Review*, December 2006, pp. 49–59.
21. William Atkinson, "Causes of Workplace Stress," *HR Magazine*, December 2000, p. 107; Michele Conlin, "Is Your Office Killing You?" *Business Week*, June 5, 2000, pp. 114–128; "Sick Building Syndrome," http://www.doctorfungus.org, January 22, 2007, p. 1.
22. The data on vision and carpal tunnel syndrome are from the Computer Vision Syndrome Center reported in Anita Bruzzese, "Computer Users Often Strain Eyes," Gannett News Service, September 13, 2004; Christine A. Sprigg et al., "Work Characteristics, Musculoskeletal Disorders, and the Mediating Role of Psychological Strain: A Study of Call Center Employees," *Journal of Applied Psychology*, September 2007, pp. 1456–1466.
23. Study reported in Deborah Smith Bailey, "Longer Train Commutes Are More Stressful, Study Finds," *Monitor on Psychology*, September 2006, p. 12.
24. Larry Copeland, "Drivers Rising Earlier to Beat the Traffic," *USA Today* syndicated story, September 16, 2007.
25. Edward Hallowell, *CrazyBusy: Overstretched, Overbooked, and About to Snap—Strategies for Coping in a World Gone ADD* (New York: Ballantine Books, 2006); "Zen and the Art of Thinking Straight," *Business Week*, April 3, 2006, p. 116.
26. Richard S. DeFrank and John M. Ivancevich, "Stress on the Job: An Executive Update," *Academy of Management Executive*, August 1998, pp. 56–57.

27. Jan de Jonge and Christian Dormann, "Stressors, Resources, and Strain at Work: A Longitudinal Test of the Triple-Match Principle," *Journal of Applied Psychology*, November 2006, pp. 1359–1374.

28. Richard Corliss, "The Power of Yoga," *Time*, April 23, 2001, pp. 54–62; Stacy Forster, "Companies Say Yoga Isn't a Stretch," *The Wall Street Journal*, October 14, 2003, p. D4.

29. Lisa Belkin, "Some Respect, Please, for the Afternoon Nap," *The New York Times* (http://www.nytimes.com), February 25, 2007, p. 1.

30. Lea Winerman, "Sleep Deprivation Threatens Public Health, Says Research Award Winner," July/August 2004, p. 61.

31. Katherine Ellison, "Mastering Your Own Mind," *Psychology Today*, October 2006, p. 75.

32. Quoted in "How I Work: A.G. Lafley," *Fortune*, March 20, 2006, p. 74.

33. Gorman, "6 Lessons for Handling Stress," p. 80.

34. "A Put-It-Off Personality," *Psychology Today*, January/February 2007, p. 42; Data reported in Jared Sandberg, "Fans of Procrastination Say It Boosts Control, Self-Esteem," *The Wall Street Journal*, February 9, 2005, p. B1.

35. Maia Szalavitz, "Stand & Deliver," *Psychology Today*, July/August 2003, p. 50.

36. Cited in "A Put-It-Off Personality," p. 42.

37. Shale Paul, as cited in "Tips to Keep Procrastination Under Control," Gannett News Service syndicated story, November 9, 1998.

38. Dru Scott, *How to Put More Time in Your Life* (New York: New American Library, 1980), p. 1.

39. Cited in "The Voices in Your Head," *Entrepreneur*, July 2000, pp. 105–107.

40. Christopher Percy Collier, "The Expert on Experts," *Fast Company*, November 2006, p. 116.

41. David Allen, *Getting Things Done* (New York: Penguin, 2001, 2007).

42. Curtis Sittenfeld, "She's a Paper Tiger," *Fast Company*, August 2002, p. 34.

43. Quoted in Adrian Wooldridge, "Why Clean Up Your Desk? Delight in Disorder Instead," *The Wall Street Journal*, January 2, 2007, p. D7. Book review of Eric Abrahamson and David Freedman, *A Perfect Mess* (New York: Little, Brown & Co., 2007).

44. Meni Koslowky and Abraham Sagie, "Correlates of Employee Lateness: Some Theoretical Considerations," *Journal of Applied Psychology*, February 1997, pp. 79–88.

45. Survey cited in Michelle Conlin, "Do Us a Favor, Take a Vacation," *Business Week*, May 21, 2007.

46. Anne Fisher, "The Rebalancing Act," *Fortune*, October 6, 2003, p. 110; Andrea Kay, "Avoid 'Traps' to Gain the Free Time You Need," Gannet News Service, January 10, 2005.

47. Brenda Goodman, "A Field Guide To the Workaholic," *Psychology Today*, May/June 2006, p. 41; Mildred L. Culp, "Working Productively with Workaholics While Minimizing Legal Risks," Passage Media syndicated story, 1997.

48. Tony Schwartz, "Manage Your Energy, Not Your Time," *Harvard Business Review*, October 2007, pp. 63–74.

49. "Secrets of Greatness: Marissa Mayer," *Fortune*, March 20, 2006, p. 68.

50. Cited in Jared Sandberg, "To-Do Lists Can Take More Time Than Doing, but That Isn't the Point," *The Wall Street Journal*, September 8, 2004, p. B1.

51. Penttila, "Time Out," p. 73.

52. The scientific information about multitasking is reviewed in Claudia Wallis, "The Multitasking Generation," *Time*, March 27, 2006, pp. 48–55. See also Joshua S. Rubinstein, David E Meyer, and Jeffrey E. Evans, "Executive Control of Cognitive Processes in Task Switching," *Journal of Experimental Psychology—Human Perception and Performance*, January 2000, Vol. 26, No. 4, pp. 763–769.

53. Research from the University of Oregon reported in "The Problem with Extreme Multitasking," *The Wall Street Journal*, February 12, 2008, p. B4.

54. Quoted in Claudia Wallis and Sonja Steptoe, "The Case for Doing One Thing at a Time," *Time*, January 16, 2006, p. 76.

55. Amy Dunkin, "Saying 'Adios' to the Office," *Business Week*, October 12, 1998, p. 153; Sue Shellenbarger, "When Working at Home Doesn't Work: How Companies Comfort Telecommuters," *The Wall Street Journal*, August 24, 2006, p. D1; E. Jeffrey Hill, Brent C. Miller, Sara P. Weiner, and Joe Colihan, "Influences of the Virtual Office on Aspects of Work/Life Balance," *Personnel Psychology*, Autumn 1998, pp. 667–683.

56. Survey cited in "Average Worker Slacks for 1.7 Hours a Day," http://www.miamiherald.com, August 27, 2007.

# 5   Managing Conflict

## Learning Objectives

After studying the information and doing the exercises in this chapter, you should be able to:

1 Identify reasons why conflict between people takes place so often.

2 Pinpoint several helpful and harmful consequences of conflict.

3 Choose an effective method of resolving conflict.

4 Improve your assertion skills.

5 Improve your negotiating skill.

6 Develop anger management skills.

## Outline

1 **Why Does So Much Conflict Exist?** 138
Competition for Limited Resources
Personality Clashes
Aggressive Personalities Including Bullies
Culturally Diverse Teams and Factional Groups
Competing Work and Family Demands
Microinequities as a Source of Conflict
Sexual Harassment: A Special Type of Conflict

2 **The Good and Bad Sides of Conflict** 143

3 **What Are Some Techniques for Resolving Conflicts?** 145
Being Assertive
Confrontation and Problem Solving Leading to Win–Win
Disarm the Opposition
Cognitive Restructuring
Appeal to a Third Party
The Grievance Procedure
Company Programs for Lessening Work–Family Conflict
Negotiation and Bargaining Tactics

4 **What Are Some Suggestions for Managing Anger?** 158
Managing Your Own Anger
Managing Anger in Other People
Choosing a Tactic for Resolving a Conflict or Managing Anger

When Susan Siverson quit her Wall Street human resource job at a banking concern to stay home with her twin toddlers, she had no intention of returning for years. If asked then, she says, "I would have said, 'You'd have to drag me back kicking and screaming.'" But a campaign by Lehman Brothers to woo at-home mothers like Siverson—inviting her to an executive luncheon for ex-Wall Streeters, contacting her repeatedly, and offering flexible work—changed her attitude. She thought, "Maybe this is a tenable option for me," she says. She became a part-time consultant for the firm just recently. [1]

The situation just described illustrates a reality about the workplace and personal life. Conflict takes place frequently, and being able to manage it well contributes to your feeling of well-being. In this situation, the company helped the human resource professional resolve her conflict by offering her flexible work as a part-timer. **Conflict** is a condition that exists when two sets of demands, goals, or motives are incompatible. For example, if a person wants a career in retailing yet also wants to work a predictable eight-hour day with weekends off, that person faces a conflict. He or she cannot achieve both goals. A conflict can also be considered a dispute, feud, or controversy.

Our approach to studying conflict includes explaining why so much conflict exists, constructive approaches to resolving conflict, and the management of anger.

■ **Conflict**

condition that exists when two sets of demands, goals, or motives are incompatible

■ **Learning Objective 1**

# Why Does So Much Conflict Exist?

Many reasons exist for the widespread presence of conflict in all aspects of life. All these reasons are related to the basic nature of conflict—the fact that not every person can have what he or she wants at the same time. As with other topics in this book, understanding conflict helps you develop a better understanding of why people act as they do. Here we describe seven key sources of conflict.

## COMPETITION FOR LIMITED RESOURCES

A fundamental reason you might experience conflict with another person is that not everybody can get all the money, material, supplies, or human help they want. Conflict also ensues when employees are asked to compete for prizes, such as bonuses based on individual effort or company-paid vacation trips. Because the number of awards is so limited, the competition becomes intense enough to be regarded as conflict. Conflict stemming from limited resources has become prevalent as so many companies attempt to reduce expenses. Many units of the organization have to compete for the limited money available to hire new people or purchase new technology.

## PERSONALITY CLASHES

Various value and personality differences among people contribute to workplace conflict. Many disagreements on the job stem from the fact that some people simply dislike each other. A **personality clash** is thus an antagonistic relationship between two people based on differences in personal attributes, preferences, interests, values, and styles. People involved in a personality clash often have difficulty specifying why they dislike each other. The end result, however, is that they cannot maintain an amiable work relationship. A strange fact about personality clashes is that people who get along well may begin to clash after working together for a number of years. Many business partnerships fold because the two partners eventually clash.

■ **Personality clash**
antagonistic relationship between two people based on differences in personal attributes, preferences, interests, values, and styles

## AGGRESSIVE PERSONALITIES INCLUDING BULLIES

Coworkers naturally disagree about topics, issues, and ideas. Yet some people convert disagreement into an attack that puts down other people and damages their self-esteem. As a result, conflict surfaces. **Aggressive personalities** are people who verbally and sometimes physically attack others frequently. Verbal aggression takes the form of insults, teasing, ridicule, and profanity. The aggression may also be expressed as attacks on the victim's character, competence, background, and physical appearance. When people are verbally abused, they are put on the defensive making them feel uncomfortable. [2]

■ **Aggressive personalities**
people who verbally and sometimes physically attack others frequently

Aggressive personalities are also referred to as *bullies*. Among their typical behaviors are interrupting others, ranting in a loud voice, and making threats. A typical attitude of a bullying boss is "My way or the highway," sending the message that the employee's suggestions are unwelcome. One bullying manager would frequently ask people, "Are you going to be stupid the rest of your life?" Bullied workers complain of a range of psychological and physical ailments such as the following: anxiety, sleeplessness, headache, irritable bowel syndrome, skin problems, panic attacks, and low self-esteem. Human relations specialist Gary Namie of The Work Doctor—a firm that works with companies to help reduce hostility—says that bullying can have negative effects on employees and the organization. Bullying reduces morale and productivity by increasing absenteeism and sick leave. "If you have been pummeled and denigrated long enough, you will not be a peak performer," he said. [3]

Aggressiveness can also take the extreme form of the shooting or knifing of a former boss or colleague by a mentally unstable worker recently dismissed from the company. Violence has become so widespread that homicide is the second-highest cause of workplace deaths, with about 550 workplace homicides each year in the United States. [4] Most of these deaths result from a robbery or commercial crime. Many of these killings, however, are perpetrated by a disgruntled worker or former employee harboring an unresolved conflict. As companies have continued to reduce their workforce despite being profitable, these incidents have increased in frequency.

## CULTURALLY DIVERSE TEAMS AND FACTIONAL GROUPS

Conflict often surfaces as people work in teams whose members vary in many ways. Ethnicity, religion, and gender are three of the major factors that lead to clashes in viewpoints. Differing educational backgrounds and work specialties can also lead to conflict. Workers often shut out information that doesn't fit comfortably with their own beliefs, particularly if they do not like the person providing the information. When these conflicts are properly resolved, diversity lends strength to the organization because the various viewpoints make an important contribution to solving a problem. Groups that are reminded of the importance of effective communication and taught methods of conflict resolution that usually can overcome the conflict stemming from mixed groups. [5]

Another form of diversity occurs when groups contain different factions, such as those representing two different companies that merged. Often the factional group consists of two subgroups, each with several representatives, such as a cost-cutting task force consisting of three representatives each from marketing, operations, and finance. The potential for conflict within factional groups increases when the subgroups differ substantially in demographic characteristics such as age, gender, and educational levels. Professors Jiatao Li of Hong Kong University of Science and Technology and Donald C. Hambrick of the Pennsylvania State University studied factional groups at 71 Sino-foreign ventures in China. Five hundred and thirty-five managers completed surveys in either English or Chinese. Among the findings were that when there were large demographic differences between members of the joint venture teams, stereotyping, distrust, and discord mounted. These negative emotions led to conflict and a decrease in performance. [6]

## COMPETING WORK AND FAMILY DEMANDS

Balancing the demands of work and family life is a major challenge facing workers at all levels. Yet achieving this balance and resolving these conflicts is essential for being successful in career and personal life. The challenge of achieving balance is particularly intense for employees who are part of a two-wage-earner family. **Work–family conflict** occurs when the individual has to perform multiple roles: worker, spouse or partner, and often parent. From the standpoint of the individual, this type of conflict can be regarded as work interfering with family life. From the standpoint of the employer, the same conflict might be regarded as family life interfering with work.

Attempting to meet work and family demands is a frequent source of conflict because the demands are often incompatible. Imagine having to attend your child's championship soccer game and then being ordered at the last minute to attend a late-afternoon meeting. A survey revealed the following evidence of work–family conflict and the potential of such conflict:

- About 45 percent of students say their top consideration in selecting a first employer is the opportunity to achieve a balance between work and life outside of work.

- Approximately 80 percent of workers consider their effort to balance work and personal life as their first priority.

■ **Work–family conflict**

conflict that occurs when an individual has to perform multiple roles: worker, spouse or partner, and often parent

- More than one-third of employed Americans are working 10 or more hours a day, and 39 percent work on weekends.

- One-third of employees say that they are forced to choose between advancing in their jobs or devoting attention to their family or personal lives. [7]

The conflict over work versus family demands intensifies when the person is serious about both work and family responsibilities. The average professional working for an organization works approximately 55 hours per week, including five hours on weekends. Adhering to such a schedule almost inevitably results in some incompatible demands from work versus those from family members and friends. Conflict arises because the person wants to work sufficient hours to succeed on the job yet still have enough time for personal life.

The chapter opener described how one employer uses flexible work to help key workers deal with work–family conflict. Later in the chapter we present more information about what employers are doing to help resolve such conflict.

## MICROINEQUITIES AS A SOURCE OF CONFLICT

Growing attention is being paid to snubbing, or ignoring others, as a source of conflict. A **microinequity** is a small, semiconscious message we send with a powerful impact on the receiver. A microinequity might also be considered a subtle slight. Conflict occurs because a person's feelings are hurt, and he or she feels trivialized. Two examples of workplace microinequities follow:

- ■ **Microinequity**
  small, semiconscious message sent with a powerful impact on the receiver

- You check your messages on a cell phone, Blackberry, or computer screen while a coworker is talking to you. [You are devaluing the other person's time, and trivializing his or her importance.]

- A manager dismisses the first idea offered in a meeting by responding, "Okay, so who would like to get the ball rolling?" [The person who offered the idea feels like his or her suggestion is not even worth consideration and, therefore, has hurt feelings]

Many companies, including IBM and Wells Fargo, offer training seminars to help managers avoid microinequities, including those already mentioned as well as mispronouncing the name of subordinates and looking at a watch while someone else is talking. [8]

## SEXUAL HARASSMENT: A SPECIAL TYPE OF CONFLICT

Many employees face conflict because they are sexually harassed by a supervisor, coworker, or customers. **Sexual harassment** is an unwanted sexually oriented behavior in the workplace that results in discomfort or interference with the job. It can include an action as violent as rape or as subdued as telling a sexually toned joke. Sexual harassment creates conflict because the harassed person has to make a choice between two incompatible motives. One motive is to get ahead, keep the job, or have an unthreatening work environment. But to satisfy this motive, the person is forced to sacrifice the motive of holding on

- ■ **Sexual harassment**
  unwanted sexually oriented behavior in the workplace that results in discomfort or interference with the job

to his or her moral values or preferences. For example, a person might say, "I want a raise; but to do this, must I submit to being fondled by my boss?" Here we focus on the types and frequency of sexual harassment and guidelines for dealing with the problem.

## Types and Frequency of Harassment

Two types of sexual harassment are legally recognized. Both are violations of the Civil Rights Acts of 1964 and 1991 and are, therefore, a violation of your rights. In quid pro quo sexual harassment, the individual suffers loss (or threatened loss) of a job benefit as a result of his or her response to a request for sexual favors. The demands of a harasser can be blatant or implied. An implied form of quid pro quo harassment might take this form: A manager casually comments to one of his or her employees, "I've noticed that workers who become very close to me outside of the office get recommended for bigger raises."

The other form of sexual harassment is hostile-environment harassment. Another person in the workplace creates an intimidating, hostile, or offensive working environment. No tangible loss or psychological injury has to be suffered under this form of sexual harassment.

A major problem in controlling sexual harassment in the workplace is that most workers understand the meaning and nature of quid pro quo harassment but are confused about what constitutes the hostile-environment type. For example, some people might interpret the following behaviors to be harassing, whereas others would regard them as friendly initiatives: (1) calling a coworker "sweetie" and (2) saying to a subordinate, "I love your suit. You look fabulous."

An employee who is continually subjected to sexually suggestive comments, lewd jokes, or requests for dates is a victim of hostile-environment harassment. When the offensive behavior stems from customers or vendors, it is still harassment. Although the company cannot readily control the actions of customers or vendors, the company may still be liable for such harassment. According to several legal decisions, it is a company's job to take action to remedy harassment problems involving employees.

Surveys as well as the opinions of human resource professionals suggest that somewhere between 50 and 60 percent of women are sexually harassed at least once in their career. Aside from being an illegal and immoral act, sexual harassment has negative effects on the well-being of its victims. The harassed person may experience job stress, lowered morale, severe conflict, and lowered productivity. A study with both business and university workers found that even at low levels of frequency, harassment exerts a significant impact on women's psychological well-being and productivity. High levels of harassment, however, had even more negative effects. [9]

A related study of the long-term effects of sexual harassment indicated that the negative effects remained two years after the incident. For example, 24 months after an incident of sexual harassment, many women still experienced stress, a decrease in job satisfaction, and lowered productivity. [10]

Although much of the research on the consequences of sexual harassment has focused on the individual, one study indicates that harassment can negatively affect the team also. Professors of organizational psychology Jana L. Raver of Queen's University and Michele J. Gelfand of the University of Maryland studied sexual harassment in 35 teams within a food-service organization. It was found that the presence of sexual harassment in the form of insulting verbal and nonverbal behavior led to conflict about tasks (work to be performed) and people. The same type of harassment also led to lower group cohesion (team spirit) and lower financial performance. Another finding was that sexual harassment was more prevalent in the larger teams, suggesting that some workers feel they might be able to get away with misbehavior in a crowd. [11]

## Guidelines for Preventing and Dealing with Sexual Harassment

A starting point in dealing with sexual harassment is to develop an awareness of the type of behaviors that are considered sexual harassment. Often the difference is subtle. Suppose, for example, you placed copies of two nudes painted by Renoir, the French painter, on a coworker's desk. Your coworker might call that harassment. Yet if you took that same coworker to a museum to see the originals of the same nude paintings, your behavior would usually not be classified as harassment. This example illustrates that the setting of the words or behavior influences whether they are harassing. College courses in understanding and dealing with pornography have grown in popularity, and these courses often show adult (sexually explicit) films as part of the curriculum. [12] If an accounting professor in a college of business showed the same films to accounting students, he or she would most likely be charged with sexual harassment.

Education about the meaning of sexual harassment is, therefore, a basic part of any company program to prevent sexual harassment. The situation and your tone of voice, as well as other nonverbal behavior, contribute to perceptions of harassment. For example, the statement "You look wonderful" might be perceived as good natured versus harassing, depending on the sender's voice tone and facial expression.

The easiest way to deal with sexual harassment is to speak up before it becomes serious. The first time it happens, respond with statements such as, "I won't tolerate that kind of talk." "I dislike sexually oriented jokes." "Keep your hands off me." Write the harasser a stern letter shortly after the first incident. Confronting the harasser in writing dramatizes your seriousness of purpose in not wanting to be sexually harassed. If the problem persists, say something to the effect, "You're practicing sexual harassment. If you don't stop, I'm going to exercise my right to report you to management." Don't leave any room for doubt that the behavior or words you heard were unwelcome.

# The Good and Bad Sides of Conflict
■ Learning Objective 2

Conflict over significant issues is a source of stress. We usually do not suffer stress over minor conflicts such as having to choose between wearing one sweater or another. Like stress in general, we need an optimum amount of conflict to keep us mentally and physically energetic. Handled properly, moderate doses of conflict can be beneficial. Some of the benefits that might arise from conflict can be summarized around the following key points. Figure 5-1 outlines the positive, as well as the negative consequences of conflict.

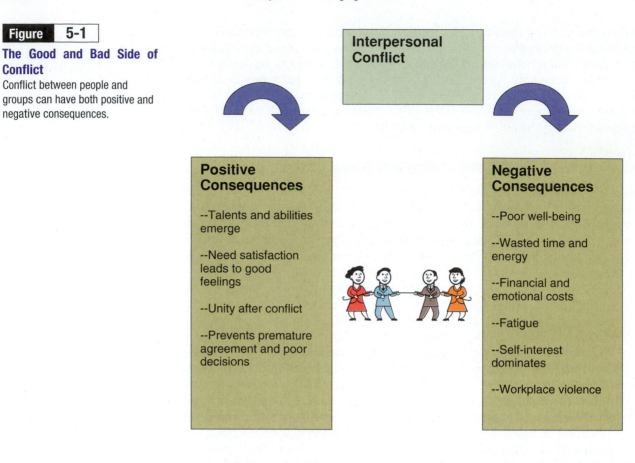

| Figure | 5-1 |
|--------|-----|

**The Good and Bad Side of Conflict**

Conflict between people and groups can have both positive and negative consequences.

**1. Talents and abilities may emerge in response to conflict.** When faced with a conflict, people often become more creative than they are in a tranquil situation. Assume that your employer told you that it would no longer pay for your advanced education unless you used the courses to improve your job performance. You would probably find ways to accomplish such an end.

**2. Conflict can help you feel better because it satisfies a number of psychological needs.** By nature, many people like a good fight. As a socially acceptable substitute for attacking others, you might be content to argue over a dispute on the job or at home.

**3. As an aftermath of conflict, the parties in conflict may become united.** Two warring supervisors may become more cooperative toward each other in the aftermath of confrontation. A possible explanation is that the shared experience of being in conflict with each other *sometimes* brings the parties closer.

**4. Conflict helps prevent people in the organization from agreeing too readily with each other, thus making some very poor decisions.** Groupthink is the situation that occurs when group members strive so hard to get along that they fail to critically evaluate each other's ideas.

Despite the positive picture of conflict just painted, it can also have detrimental consequences to the individual, the organization, and society. These harmful consequences of conflict make it important for people to learn how to resolve conflict:

1. **Prolonged conflict can be detrimental to some people's emotional and physical well-being.** As a type of stress, prolonged conflict can lead to such problems as heart disease and chronic intestinal disorders. President Lyndon B. Johnson suffered his first heart attack after an intense argument with a young newspaper reporter.

2. **People in conflict with each other often waste time and energy that could be put to useful purposes.** Instead of fighting all evening with your roommate, the two of you might fix up your place. Instead of writing angry e-mail messages back and forth, two department heads might better invest that time in thinking up ideas to save the company money.

3. **The aftermath of extreme conflict may have high financial and emotional costs.** Sabotage—such as ruining machinery—might be the financial consequence. At the same time, management may develop a permanent distrust of many people in the workforce, although only a few of them are saboteurs.

4. **Too much conflict is fatiguing, even if it does not cause symptoms of emotional illness.** People who work in high-conflict jobs often feel spent when they return home from work. When the battle-worn individual has limited energy left over for family responsibilities, the result is more conflict. (For instance, "What do you mean you are too tired to visit friends?" or "If your job is killing your interest in having friends, find another job.")

5. **People in conflict will often be much more concerned with their own interests than with the good of the family, organization, or society.** An employee in the shipping department who is in conflict with his supervisor might neglect to ship an order. And a gang in conflict with another might leave a park or beach strewn with broken glass.

6. **Workplace violence erupts, including the killing of managers, previous managers, coworkers, customers, as well as spouses and partners.** Intense conflict can release anger, leading to aggressive behavior and violence. Disgruntled employees, such as those recently fired, may attempt revenge by assassinating work associates. [13] People involved in an unresolved domestic dispute sometimes storm into the partner's workplace to physically attack him or her. Unresolved conflict and frustration from financial, marital, or other domestic problems increase the odds of a person "going ballistic" at work.

# What Are Some Techniques for Resolving Conflicts?

■ Learning Objective 3

Because of the inevitability of conflict, a successful and happy person must learn effective ways of resolving conflict. An important general consideration is to face conflict rather than letting conflict slide or smoothing over it. Ignoring or smoothing over conflict does little to resolve the real causes of conflict and seldom leads to an effective long-term solution. [14] Here we concentrate on methods of conflict resolution that you can use on your own. Most of them emphasize a collaborative or win–win philosophy. Several of the negotiating and bargaining tactics described may be close to the competitive orientation.

Human Relations Self-Assessment Quiz 5-1 gives you the opportunity to think through your style of managing conflict.

■ Learning Objective 4

## BEING ASSERTIVE

Several of the techniques for resolving conflict described here require assertiveness. Learning to express your feelings to make your demands known is also an important aspect of becoming an effective individual in general. Expressing your feelings helps you establish good relationships with people. If you aren't sharing your feelings and attitudes with other people, you will never get close to them. Here we examine the nature of assertiveness and then describe several techniques for building assertiveness.

## Human Relations Self-Assessment Quiz   5-1

### Collaborative versus Competitive Styles of Conflict Management

Answer on a 1-to-5 scale how well you agree with each of the following statements: disagree strongly, disagree, neutral, agree, agree strongly.

|  | Disagree Strongly | Disagree | Neutral | Agree | Agree Strongly |
|---|---|---|---|---|---|
| 1. I like to see the other side squirm when I resolve a dispute. | 5 | 4 | 3 | 2 | 1 |
| 2. Winning is everything when it comes to settling conflict. | 5 | 4 | 3 | 2 | 1 |
| 3. After I have successfully negotiated a price, I like to see the seller smile. | 1 | 2 | 3 | 4 | 5 |
| 4. I have a "smash-mouth" attitude toward resolving conflict. | 5 | 4 | 3 | 2 | 1 |
| 5. In most conflict situations one side is clearly right, and the other side is clearly wrong. | 1 | 2 | 3 | 4 | 5 |
| 6. I think there are effective alternatives to strikes for settling union versus management disputes. | 1 | 2 | 3 | 4 | 5 |
| 7. The winner should take all. | 5 | 4 | 3 | 2 | 1 |
| 8. Conflict on the job is like a prize fight: The idea is to knock out the opponent. | 5 | 4 | 3 | 2 | 1 |
| 9. I like the idea of tournaments in which first-round losers receive another opportunity to play. | 1 | 2 | 3 | 4 | 5 |
| 10. Nice guys and gals usually finish first. | 1 | 2 | 3 | 4 | 5 |

### Scoring and Interpretation:

Add the point value of your scores to obtain your total. Scores of 40 and higher suggest that you prefer a *collaborative*, or *win–win*, approach to resolving conflict. You tend to be concerned about finding long-term solutions to conflict that will provide benefits to both sides. Scores of 39 and lower suggest that you prefer a *competitive* approach to resolving conflict. You want to maximize gain for yourself, with little concern about the welfare of the other side.

## Assertive, Nonassertive, and Aggressive Behavior

As implied previously, **assertive** people state clearly what they want or how they feel in a given situation without being abusive, abrasive, or obnoxious. People who are assertive are open, honest, and "up-front" because they believe that all people have an equal right to express themselves honestly. Assertive behavior can be understood more fully by comparing it to that shown by two other types of people. **Nonassertive** people let things happen to them without letting their feelings be known. **Aggressive** people are obnoxious and overbearing. They push for what they want with almost no regard for the feelings of others.

Another representative assertive behavior is to ask for clarification rather than contradicting a person with whom you disagree. The assertive person asks for clarification when another person says something irritating, rather than hurling insults or telling the other person he or she is wrong. For example, assume someone says to you, "Your proposal is useless." Aggressively telling the person, "You have no right to make that judgment," shuts out any possible useful dialogue. You will probably learn more if you ask for clarification, such as "What is wrong with my proposal?"

Gestures as well as words can communicate whether the person is being assertive, nonassertive, or aggressive. Figure 5-2 illustrates these differences.

■ **Assertive**
characteristic of people who state clearly what they want or how they feel in a given situation without being abusive, abrasive, or obnoxious; open, honest, and "up-front" people who believe that all people have an equal right to express themselves honestly

■ **Nonassertive**
characteristic of people who let things happen to them without letting their feelings be known

■ **Aggressive**
characteristic of people who are obnoxious and overbearing; they push for what they want with almost no regard for the feelings of others

## Becoming More Assertive and Less Shy

Shyness, or not being assertive, is widespread, and about 50 percent of the U.S. population is shyer than they want to be. The personality trait of shyness has positive aspects, such as leading a person to think more deeply and become involved in ideas and things. (Where would the world be today if Bill Gates weren't shy as a youth?) However, shyness can also create discomfort and lower self-esteem. [15] There are a number of everyday actions a person can take to overcome being nonassertive or shy. Even if the actions described here do not elevate your assertiveness, they will not backfire and cause you discomfort. After reading the following five techniques, you might be able to think of others that will work for you. [16]

| Assertive | Nonassertive | Aggressive |
|---|---|---|
| Well-balanced | Covering mouth with hand | Pounding fists |
| Straight posture | Excessive head nodding | Stiff and rigid posture |
| Hand gestures, emphasizing key words | Tinkering with clothing or jewelry | Finger waving or pointing |
| | Constant shifting of weight | Shaking head as if other person isn't to be believed |
| | Scratching or rubbing head or other parts of the body | |
| | Wooden body posture | Hand on hips |
| Moderately loud voice | Voice too soft with frequent pauses | Voice louder than needed, fast speech |

**Figure   5-2**

**Assertive, Nonassertive, and Aggressive Gestures**

**1. Set a goal.** Clearly establish in your mind how you want to behave differently. Do you want to speak out more in meetings? Be able to express dissatisfaction to coworkers? You can overcome shyness only by behaving differently; feeling differently is not enough.

**2. Appear warm and friendly.** Shy people often communicate to others through their body language that they are not interested in reaching out to others. To overcome this impression, smile, lean forward, uncross your arms and legs, and unfold your hands.

**3. Conduct anonymous conversations.** Try starting a conversation with strangers in a safe setting, such as a sporting event, the waiting room of a medical office, or a waiting line at the post office or supermarket. Begin the conversation with the common experience you are sharing at the time. Among them might be

"How many people do you estimate are in the audience?"

"How long does it usually take before you get to see the doctor?"

"Where did you get that shopping bag? I've never seen one so sturdy before."

**4. Greet strangers.** For the next week or so, greet many of the people you pass. Smile and make a neutral comment such as "How ya doing?" or "Great day, isn't it." Because most people are unaccustomed to being greeted by a stranger, you may get a few quizzical looks. Many other people may smile and return your greeting. A few of these greetings may turn into conversations. A few conversations may even turn into friendships. Even if the return on your investment in greetings is only a few pleasant responses, it will boost your confidence.

**5. Practice being decisive.** An assertive person is usually decisive, so it is important to practice being decisive. Some nonassertive people are even indecisive when asked to make a choice from a restaurant menu. They communicate their indecisiveness by asking their friend, "What are you going to have?" or asking the server, "Could you please suggest something for me?" or "What's good?" Practice quickly sizing up the alternatives in any situation and reaching a decision. This will help you be assertive and also project an image of assertiveness.

## CONFRONTATION AND PROBLEM SOLVING LEADING TO WIN–WIN

■ **Confrontation and problem solving**

the most highly recommended way of resolving conflict; method of identifying the true source of conflict and resolving it systematically

The most highly recommended way of resolving conflict is **confrontation and problem solving.** It is a method of identifying the true source of conflict and resolving it systematically. The confrontation in this approach is gentle and tactful rather than combative and abusive. It is best to wait until your anger cools down before confronting the other person to avoid being unreasonable. Reasonableness is important because the person who takes the initiative in resolving the conflict wants to maintain a harmonious working relationship with the other party. Also, both parties should benefit from the resolution of the conflict.

Assume that Jason, the person working at the desk next to you, whistles loudly while he works. You find the whistling to be distracting and annoying; you think Jason is a noise polluter. If you don't bring the problem to Jason's attention, it will probably grow in proportion with time. Yet you are hesitant to enter into an argument about something a person might regard as a civil liberty (the right to whistle in a public place). An effective alternative is for you to approach Jason directly in this manner:

*You:* Jason, there is something bothering me that I would like to discuss with you.

*Jason:* Go ahead, I don't mind listening to other people's problems.

*You:* My problem concerns something you are doing that makes it difficult for me to concentrate on my work. When you whistle, it distracts me and grates on my nerves. It may be my problem, but the whistling does bother me.

*Jason:* I guess I could stop whistling when you're working next to me. It's probably simply a nervous habit. Maybe I can find a less disruptive habit, such as rolling my tongue inside my mouth.

An important advantage of confrontation and problem solving is that you deal directly with a sensitive problem without jeopardizing the chances of forming a constructive working relationship in the future. One reason that the method works so effectively is that the focus is on the problem at hand and not on the individual's personality.

The intent of confrontation and problem solving is to arrive at a collaborative solution to the conflict. The collaborative style reflects a desire to fully satisfy the desires of both parties. It is based on an underlying philosophy of **win–win,** the belief that after conflict has been resolved, both sides should gain something of value. The user of win–win approaches is genuinely concerned about arriving at a settlement that meets the needs of both parties or at least that does not badly damage the welfare of the other side. When collaborative approaches to resolving conflict are used, the relationships among the parties are built on and improved.

Here is an example of a win–win approach to resolving conflict. A manager granted an employee a few hours off on an occasional Friday afternoon because she was willing to be on call for emergency work on an occasional weekend. Both parties were satisfied with the outcome, and both accomplished their goals.

The opposite approach to win–win conflict resolution is *win–lose* in which one side attempts to maximize gain at the expense of the other side. Win–lose is also referred to as a *zero-sum game* in which one side wins nothing, and the other side wins everything. Common sense tells us that win–lose is the best approach to resolving conflict—and that is one reason so much conflict goes unresolved in the form of physical attacks on people and bankruptcies. A person with a competitive orientation is likely to engage in power struggles in which one side wins and the other loses. "My way or the highway" is a win–lose strategy. An extreme example of a win–lose strategy would be to bad-mouth a rival so he or she gets fired.

■ **Win–win**
belief that after conflict has been resolved both sides should gain something of value

"Many people avoid confronting day-to-day issues because they're not certain how to open the door to conversation in a productive manner that will preserve the relationship."
—Deb Koen, vice president of Career Development Services, Rochester, New York

If faced with an adversary who has a win–lose orientation, a plausible defense is to keep on pointing out the benefits of finding a solution that fits both sides. A sales representative for a company that makes steel buildings (often used for warehousing) was about to be laid off because of poor business. He proposed to his boss, "Please give me one more chance. Give me just enough salary to pay my rent and feed our newborn child. All the rest of my income will come from commissions on the sales I make." The owner conceded, and the sales rep did earn his way, so a win–lose situation emerged into a win–win.

## DISARM THE OPPOSITION

■ **Disarm the opposition**
method of conflict resolution in which you disarm the criticizer by agreeing with his or her criticism

When in conflict, your criticizer may be armed with valid negative criticism of you. The criticizer is figuratively clobbering you with knowledge of what you did wrong. If you deny that you have made a mistake, the criticism intensifies. A simple technique has been developed to help you deal with this type of manipulative criticism. **Disarm the opposition** is a method of conflict resolution in which you disarm the criticizer by agreeing with his or her criticism of you. The technique assumes that you have done something wrong. Disarm the opposition generally works more effectively than counterattacking a person with whom you are in conflict. Another reason this technique is effective is that it implies you are apologizing for a mistake or error you have made. An apology often gets the other person on your side, or at least softens the animosity.

Agreeing with criticism made of you by a manager or team leader is effective because, by so doing, you are in a position to ask that manager's help in improving your performance. Most managers and team leaders recognize that it is their responsibility to help employees to overcome problems, not merely to criticize them. Imagine that you have been chronically late in submitting reports during the past six months. It is time for a performance review and you know you will be reprimanded for your tardiness. You also hope that your boss will not downgrade all other aspects of your performance because of your tardy reports. Here is how disarming the situation would work in this situation:

*Your boss:* Have a seat. It's time for your performance review, and we have a lot to talk about. I'm concerned about some things.

*You:* So am I. It appears that I'm having a difficult time getting my reports in on time. I wonder if I'm being a perfectionist. Do you have any suggestions?

*Your boss:* I like your attitude. I think you can improve on getting your reports in on time. Maybe you are trying to make your reports perfect before you turn them in. Try not to figure out everything to four decimal places. We need thoroughness around here, but we don't want to overdo it.

## COGNITIVE RESTRUCTURING

■ **Cognitive restructuring**
technique of mentally converting negative aspects into positive ones by looking for the positive elements in a situation

An indirect way of resolving conflict between people is to lessen the conflicting elements in a situation by viewing them more positively. According to the technique of **cognitive restructuring,** you mentally convert negative aspects into positive ones by looking for the positive elements in a situation. The original purpose of cognitive restructuring was to help people overcome automatic, negative thinking about themselves or situations. An example would be recognize that a challenging situation, such as making a presentation in front of a group, is not as bad as it first seems. The idea is to overcome unhealthy thoughts. How you frame or choose your thoughts can determine the outcome of a conflict situation. Your thoughts can influence your actions. If you search for the beneficial elements in a situation, there will be less area for dispute. Although this technique might sound like a *mind game* to you, it can work effectively.

Imagine that a coworker of yours, Jennifer, has been asking you repeated questions about how to carry out a work procedure. You are about ready to tell Jennifer, "Go bother somebody else, I'm not paid to be a trainer." Instead, you look for the positive elements in the situation. You say to yourself, "Jennifer has been asking me a lot of questions. This does take time, but answering these questions is valuable experience. If I want to become a manager, I will have to help group members with problems."

After having completed this cognitive restructuring, you can then deal with the conflict more positively. You might say to Jennifer, "I welcome the opportunity to help you, but we need to find a mutually convenient time. In that way, I can better concentrate on my own work."

## APPEAL TO A THIRD PARTY

Now and then you may be placed in a conflict situation in which the other party either holds most of the power or simply won't budge. Perhaps you have tried techniques such as confrontation and problem solving or disarming the opposition, yet you cannot resolve your conflict. In these situations you may have to enlist the help of a third party with power—more power than you or your adversary has. Among such third parties is your common boss, union stewards, or human resource managers. Filing a lawsuit against your adversary is another application of the third-party technique, such as filing an age discrimination charge.

In some situations, simply implying that you will bring in a third party to help resolve the conflict situation is sufficient for you to gain advantage. One woman felt she was repeatedly passed over for promotion because of her sex. She hinted that if she were not given fairer consideration, she would speak to the Equal Employment Opportunity Commission (EEOC). She was given a small promotion shortly thereafter. Many conflicts about sexual harassment, as well as ethnic and racial harassment, are resolved through third-party appeal.

## THE GRIEVANCE PROCEDURE

The formal process of filing a complaint and resolving a dispute within an organization is the **grievance procedure.** It can also be regarded as a formal method of resolving conflict, in which a series of third parties are brought into the picture. The third-party appeal described previously skips the step-by-step approach of a formal grievance procedure. In a unionized firm, the steps in the grievance procedure are specified in the written contract between management and labor. The grievance procedure is a key part of a labor agreement because one of the union's

■ **Grievance procedure**
formal process of filing a complaint and resolving a dispute within an organization

goals is to obtain fair treatment for union members. An example of a grievance about favoritism would be, "I get the worst assignments because I'm not one of the boss's fishing buddies." An example of a grievance about discrimination would be, "I didn't get the transfer to the receptionist job because I'm 55 years old."

The steps in the grievance procedure may vary from one to six, depending on the labor agreement or company procedures. A summary of the typical steps in a grievance procedure is presented next and outlined in Figure 5-3. If the company does not have a labor union, a specialist from the human resources department might serve as a third party.

**Step 1.**   **Initiation of the formal grievance.** Suppose that an employee feels that he or she has been treated unfairly or that his or her rights have been

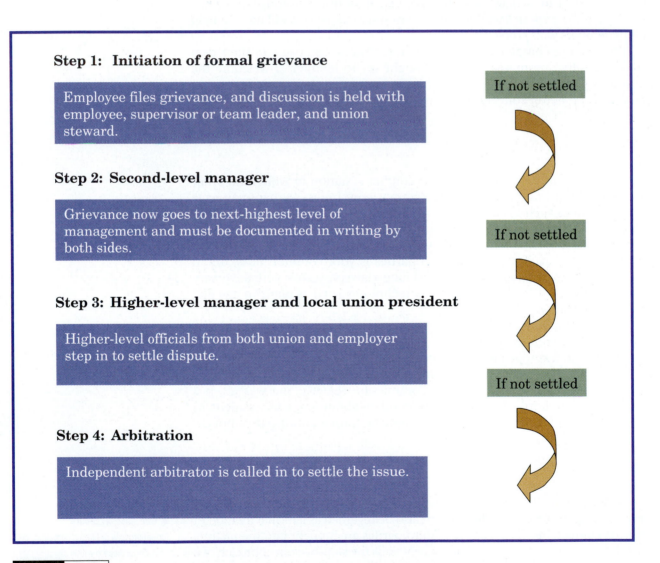

**Step 1: Initiation of formal grievance**

Employee files grievance, and discussion is held with employee, supervisor or team leader, and union steward.

If not settled

**Step 2: Second-level manager**

Grievance now goes to next-highest level of management and must be documented in writing by both sides.

If not settled

**Step 3: Higher-level manager and local union president**

Higher-level officials from both union and employer step in to settle dispute.

If not settled

**Step 4: Arbitration**

Independent arbitrator is called in to settle the issue.

**Figure**   **5-3**

**The Grievance Procedure**

violated in some way. The employee then files a grievance with the supervisor (or team leader). Most grievances end at step 1 by conversation among the employee, union steward, and the supervisor. At this stage, it makes sense to use some of the techniques for resolving conflict already described.

**Step 2.** **Second level of management.** If the steward, supervisor or team leader, and employee cannot reach a satisfactory solution to the conflict, it goes to the next-highest level in the organization. At this point, the grievance must be documented in writing by both sides. Which people are involved at this level depends on the size of the firm. In a small firm, a high-ranking manager might be involved in step 2.

**Step 3.** **A higher-level manager and the local union president.** If the grievance is not resolved at step 2, higher-level officials from both the union and the employer become involved in settling the dispute. A general principle is that at each higher step in the grievance process, comparable levels of management from both company and union face each other, or a higher-level representative from the human resources department might be involved.

**Step 4.** **Arbitration.** If the grievance cannot be settled at lower steps, an independent arbitrator may be called in to settle the issue. Only about 1 percent of grievances go all the way to arbitration. Arbitration is often used as an alternative to a strike. The arbitrator has the authority to settle the dispute and must be a person acceptable to both sides.

In a small organization, step 2 is sometimes omitted. After the grievance is discussed with the union steward, and it is not resolved, the grievance is taken to chief executive or business owner, and then to arbitration if necessary. [17]

*Mediation* is often confused with arbitration. A mediator is a third party who enters a controversy but holds no power of decision. The mediator helps the two sides find a resolution to their conflict. Relatively few labor agreements allow for mediation, yet mediation might be used to settle a strike. A mediator works like a marriage counselor by helping both sides come to agreement by themselves.

A grievance procedure used in many firms without a union is the **jury of peers,** whereby unresolved grievances are submitted to a panel of coworkers. The panel chosen is similar to a jury in a criminal case. Panel members weigh evidence and, after group discussion, vote for or against the grievant. The jury-of-peers method works well when the jury members are knowledgeable about organizational justice.

■ **Jury of peers**
grievance procedure used in many firms without a union whereby unresolved grievances are submitted to a panel of coworkers

The grievance processes described are formal and legalistic. Nevertheless, to represent your interests well, it is helpful to use the informal conflict resolution techniques described earlier, such as confrontation and problem solving. Grievances are less likely to lead to labor strikes in the current business environment partly because labor unions in manufacturing (not in the public service sector) are less powerful than in the past. As more and more manufacturing jobs are being outsourced to lower-wage regions, including other countries, employees fear job loss. Worldwide competition has taken a lot of bargaining power away from workers and unions in the manufacturing sector. [18] Also, an increasing number of manufacturing jobs are being automated, making workers feel more vulnerable.

## COMPANY PROGRAMS FOR LESSENING WORK–FAMILY CONFLICT

Employers have taken major steps in recent years to help employees balance the competing demands of work and family. One reason for giving assistance in this area is that balancing work and family demands helps both the worker and the company. Reducing work–family conflict is likely to reduce Workers' Compensation claims, medical expenses, absenteeism, and turnover. A study conducted with faculty members at 23 universities suggested that the positive effects of work–family programs are most likely to be forthcoming when the programs are administered in a just manner. Justice would include figuring out who needs the most help and avoiding favoritism. Furthermore, workers receiving assistance with work–family conflict should have a say as to what types of programs would be the most beneficial. [19]

A sampling of these work/family programs and practices follow. The accompanying Human Relations in Practice provides another example of how a company might help employees reduce work–family conflict.

1. **Flexible work schedules.**  Many employers allow employees to work flexible hours, provided that they work the full 40-hour schedule and are present at certain core times. A related program is the compressed workweek, whereby the person works 40 hours in four days or less. Some employees prefer the compressed workweek because it gives them longer weekends with their families. Yet compressed workweeks can also be family unfriendly and create major conflicts. An example is that for some workers, having to work three 12-hour days in one week creates family problems.

2. **Dependent-care programs.**  Assistance in dealing with two categories of dependents, children and elderly parents, lies at the core of programs and policies to help employees balance the demands of work and family. At one end of child-care assistance is a fully equipped nursery school on company premises. At the other end is simply a referral service that helps working parents find adequate child care. Many companies offer financial assistance for child care, including pretax expense accounts that allow employees to deduct dependent-care expenses.

■ **Job sharing**

work arrangement in which two people who work part time share one job

3. **Job sharing.**  Another way to reduce work–family conflict is to give workers half a job, a variation of part-time work. **Job sharing** is a work arrangement in which two people who work part time share one job. The sharers divide up the work according to their needs, including the family situation. Each may work selected days of the workweek. Or, one person might work mornings and the other afternoons. If you want to job share, workplace consultant Shari Rosen Ascher suggests approaching the arrangement from the employer benefit perspective. Among these benefits would be more coverage of a single job, twice the knowledge and expertise, increased productivity, and enhanced employee satisfaction and retention. [20]

4. **Employee sabbaticals.**  An extreme measure some companies offer to help selected employees reduce work–family conflict is to offer them paid sabbaticals—time off to recharge and reconnect with the family. A representative arrangement would be six weeks of leave after four years of employment. Sabbaticals are also thought to reduce turnover and retain wisdom that would be lost if a valuable worker burned out and quit. Among the companies offering

these sabbaticals (usually after five years of service) are Intel Corp., McDonald's Corp., and women's clothing designer Eileen Fisher, Inc. [21]

**5. Compassionate attitudes toward individual needs.** An informal policy that facilitates balancing work and family demands is for the manager to decide what can be done to resolve individual conflicts. Yet the manager cannot make arrangements with employees who would violate company policy. Being sensitive to individual situations could involve such arrangements as allowing a person time off to deal with a personal crisis. After the crisis is resolved, the employee makes up the lost time in small chunks of extra work time. In this way the manager helps the worker achieve success both on and off the job.

## NEGOTIATION AND BARGAINING TACTICS

■ **Learning Objective 5**

■ **Negotiating and bargaining** situation of conferring with another person to resolve a problem

Conflicts can be considered situations calling for **negotiating and bargaining,** conferring with another person to resolve a problem. When you are trying to negotiate a fair price for an automobile, you are also trying to resolve a conflict. At first the demands of both parties seem incompatible. After haggling for a while, you will probably reach a price that is satisfactory to both sides. Negotiation has many applications in the workplace, including buying, selling, arriving at a starting salary or raise, and deciding on a relocation allowance. Negotiation may also take place with coworkers when you need their assistance. For example, you might need to strike a bargain with a coworker to handle some of your responsibilities if you are faced with a temporary overload.

A sampling of negotiating tactics to help you resolve conflict is presented next. As with other techniques of resolving conflict already presented, choose those that best fit your style and the situation. Many people feel awkward at the prospects of negotiating with a stranger, yet speaker and attorney Marc Deiner says that by learning and practicing new skills most people can become better negotiators. [22]

### Create a Positive Negotiating Climate

Negotiation proceeds much more swiftly if a positive tone surrounds the session, so it is helpful to initiate a positive outlook about the negotiation meeting. A good opening line in a negotiating session is, "Thanks for fitting this meeting into your hectic schedule." Nonverbal communication such as smiling and making friendly gestures helps create a positive climate. A calm voice helps build the trust necessary for creating a positive climate.

In negotiating with coworkers for assistance, a positive climate can often be achieved by phrasing demands as a request for help. Most people will be more accommodating if you say to them, "I have a problem that I wonder if you could help me with." The problem might be that you need the person's time and mental energy. By giving that person a choice of offering you help, you have established a much more positive climate than by demanding assistance. [23]

### Allow Room for Compromise, but Be Reasonable

The basic strategy of negotiation is to begin with a demand that allows room for compromise and concession. Anyone who has ever negotiated the price of

## Human Relations in Practice

### Best Buy Helps Employees Resolve Work–Family Conflicts

Cali Ressler, manager of the work–life balance program for Best Buy, helped a troubled division of the retail group in Minneapolis deal with sinking employee morale. Ressler encouraged the manager to try flexible scheduling, trusting his team to work as it suited them. "He said, 'Well, trust doesn't cost me anything,'" she recalls. The innovation was that the whole team did it together. Although the sample size was fewer than 300 employees, the early results were promising. Turnover in the first three months of employment fell from 14 to 0 percent, job satisfaction rose 10 percent, and their team-performance scores rose 13 percent.

When Jody Thompson, Best Buy's "organizational change" guru, heard about Ressler's work, she pushed the company's management to make total flexibility available to everyone. No one is forced into it; teams sign up when they're ready. Best Buy expects that ROWE (results-oriented work environment) one day will apply to the whole company. Under ROWE, headquarters employees can work when and where they like, as long as they get the job done. At the moment, it is working on a version for the 100,000 retail employees in its stores, a much more difficult task because most of those employees are hourly, and their work is regulated by federal law.

Source: Jyoti Thottam, "Reworking Work," *Time*, July 25, 2005, pp. 51, 52.

an automobile, house, or used furniture recognizes this vital strategy. If you are a buyer, begin with a low bid. (You say, "I'll give you $60 for that painting" when you are prepared to pay $90.) If you are the seller, begin with a high demand. (You say, "You can have this painting for $130" when you are ready to sell it for as low as $100.) As negotiations proceed, the two of you will probably arrive at a mutually satisfactory price. This negotiating strategy can also be used for such purposes as obtaining a higher starting salary or purchasing excess inventory.

Common sense propels many negotiators to allow *too much* room for compromise. They begin negotiations by asking way beyond what they expect to receive or offering far less than they expect to give. As a result of these implausible demands, the other side may become hostile, antagonistic, or walk away from the negotiations. Beginning with a plausible demand or offer is also important because it contributes to a positive negotiating climate.

### Focus on Interests, Not Positions

Rather than clinging to specific negotiating points, keep your overall interests in mind and try to satisfy them. A negotiating point might be a certain amount of money or a concession that you must have. Remember that the true object of negotiation is to satisfy the underlying interests of both sides. Among the interests you and the other side might be trying to protect include money, lifestyle, power, or the status quo. For example, instead of negotiating for a particular starting salary, your true interests might be to afford a certain lifestyle. If the company pays all your medical and dental coverage, you can get by with a lower salary. Or your cost of living might be much lower in one city than in another. Therefore, you can accept a lower starting salary in the city with a lower cost of living.

## Make a Last and Final Offer

In many circumstances, presenting a final offer will break a deadlock. You might frame your message something like this. "All I can possibly pay for your guitar is $250. You have my number. Call me when it is available at that price." Sometimes the strategy will be countered by a last and final offer from the other side: "Thanks for your interest. My absolute minimum price for this guitar is $300. Call us if that should seem OK to you." One of you will probably give in and accept the other person's last and final offer.

## Role-Play to Predict What the Other Side Will Do

An advanced negotiating technique is to prepare in advance by forecasting what the other side will demand or offer. Two marketing professors from New Zealand, J. Scott Armstrong and Kesten Green, have discovered that when people role-play conflicts their ability to predict outcomes jumps remarkably. The researchers presented 290 participants with descriptions of six actual conflicts and asked them to choose the most likely eventual decisions. The conflicts involved labor–management, commercial, and civil disputes. Five of these conflicts were chosen for role playing. Without the use of role playing, the participants did not much better than chance, with a 27 percent success ratio. Next, the researchers asked 21 international game theorists (specialist in predicting outcomes of events) to forecast the conflict outcomes. The game theorists were correct only 28 percent of the time. (Chance here would be one-fifth, or 20 percent.)

Next, 352 students were instructed to role-play the conflicts in the five situations. The average correct decision was 61 percent versus 27 percent for the comparable group. The authors note that in more than 40 years of studying forecasting, they have never seen a technique that led to such improvement in predictive accuracy. [24]

The implication for making you a better negotiator is to role-play with a friend in advance of the negotiating session you will be facing. The role-play should help you predict what the other side and you will do so you will be better prepared. For example, if your role-play suggests that the company would be willing to give you a 15 percent bonus for incredible performance, ask for a 15 percent bonus.

## Allow for Face-Saving

We have saved one of the most important negotiating and conflict resolution strategies for last. Negotiating does not mean that you should try to squash the other side. You should try to create circumstances that will enable you to continue working with that person if it is necessary. People prefer to avoid looking weak, foolish, or incompetent during negotiation or when the process is completed. If you do not give your opponent an opportunity to save face, you will probably create a long-term enemy.

Face-saving could work in this way. A small-business owner winds up purchasing a network system for about twice what he originally budgeted. After the sale is completed, the sales rep says, "I know you bought a more professional networking rig than you originally intended. Yet I know you made the right decision. You will be able to do boost productivity enough with the networked PCs to pay back the cost of the networking system in two years."

# What Are Some Suggestions for Managing Anger?

■ **Learning Objective 6**

Limited ability to manage anger damages the careers and personal lives of many people. The ability to manage your anger, and the anger of others, is an important human relations skill now considered to be part of emotional intelligence. A person who cannot manage anger well cannot take good advantage of his or her intellectual intelligence. As an extreme example, a genius who swears at the manager regularly will probably lose his or her job despite being so talented. Concerns about employees becoming violent have prompted many companies to offer employees training in anger management. Also, employees who become verbally abuse on the job are often sent to such training. [25] Anger-management training is likely to encompass most of the suggestions presented next. Our concern here is with several tactics for managing your own anger and that of others effectively.

## MANAGING YOUR OWN ANGER

A starting point in dealing with your anger is to recognize that at its best, anger can be an energizing force. Instead of letting it be destructive, channel your anger into exceptional performance. If you are angry because you did not get the raise you thought you deserved, get even by performing so well that there will be no question you deserve a raise next time. Develop the habit of expressing your anger before it reaches a high intensity. Tell your coworker that you do not appreciate his or her listening to an iPod while you are having dinner together the first time the act of rudeness occurs. If you wait too long, you may wind up grabbing the iPod and slamming it to the floor.

As you are about to express anger, *slow down*. (The old technique of counting to 10 is still effective.) Slowing down gives you the opportunity to express your anger in a way that does not damage your relationship with the other person. Following your first impulse, you might say to the other person, "You're a stupid fool." If you slow down, this might translate into "You need training on this task."

Closely related to slowing down is a technique taught in anger-management programs: Think about the consequences of what you do when you are worked up. Say to yourself as soon as you feel angry, "Oops, I'm in the anger mode now.

I had better calm down before I say something or do something that I will regret later." To gauge how effectively you are expressing your anger, ask for feedback. Ask a friend, coworker, or manager, "Am I coming on too strong when I express my negative opinion?" [26]

## MANAGING ANGER IN OTHER PEOPLE

A variation of confrontation and problem solving has developed specifically to resolve conflict with angry people: confront, contain, and connect. *Confront* in this context means that you jump right in and get agitated workers talking to prevent future blowups. The confrontation, however, is not aimed at arguing with the angry person. If the other person yells, you talk more softly. *Contain* refers to moving an angry worker out of sight and out of earshot. At the same time you remain impartial. The supervisor is advised not to choose sides or appear to be a friend.

You *connect* by asking open-ended questions such as "What would you like us to do about your concern?" to get at the real reasons behind an outburst. Using this approach, one worker revealed he was upset because a female coworker got to leave early to pick up her daughter at daycare. The man also needed to leave early one day a week for personal reasons but felt awkward making the request. So instead of being assertive (explicit and direct) about his demands, he flared up.

An important feature of the confront–contain–connect technique is that it provides angry workers a place where they can vent their frustrations and report the outbursts of others. Mediator Nina Meierding says, "Workers need a safe outlet to talk through anger and not feel they will be minimized or put their job in jeopardy." [27]

## CHOOSING A TACTIC FOR RESOLVING A CONFLICT OR MANAGING ANGER

How does a person know which of the tactics or strategies presented in this chapter will work best for a given problem? The best answer is to consider both your personality and the situation. With respect to your personality, or personal style, pick a tactic for resolving conflict that you would feel comfortable using. One person might say, "I would like the tactic of make a last and final offer because I like to control situations." Another person might say, "I prefer confrontation because I'm an open and up-front type of person." Still another person might say, "I'll avoid disarming the opposition for now. I don't yet have enough finesse to carry out this technique."

In fitting the strategy to the situation, it is important to assess the gravity of the topic for negotiation or the conflict between people. A woman might say to herself, "My boss has committed such a blatant act of sexual harassment that I had best take this up with a higher authority immediately." Sizing up your opponent can also help you choose the best strategy. If she or he appears reasonably flexible, you might try to compromise. Or if your adversary is especially upset, give that person a chance to simmer down before trying to solve the problem.

# Concept Review and Reinforcement

## Key Terms

Conflict, 138
Personality clash, 139
Aggressive personalities, 139
Work–family conflict, 140
Microinequity, 141
Sexual harassment, 141

Assertive, 147
Nonassertive, 147
Aggressive, 147
Confrontation and problem
  solving, 148
Win–win, 149

Disarm the opposition, 150
Cognitive restructuring, 150
Grievance procedure, 151
Jury of peers, 153
Job sharing, 154
Negotiating and bargaining, 155

## Summary and Review

Conflict occurs when two sets of demands, goals, or motives are incompatible. Such differences often lead to a hostile or antagonistic relationship between people. A conflict can also be considered a dispute, feud, or controversy. Among the reasons for widespread conflict are

- competition for limited resources
- personality clashes
- aggressive personalities, including bullies
- culturally diverse teams and factional groups
- competing work and family demands
- microinequities (semiconscious slights)
- sexual harassment

Sexual harassment is one of two types: quid pro quo (a demand for sexual favors in exchange for job benefits) and creating a hostile environment. It is important for workers to understand what actions and words constitute sexual harassment and how to deal with the problem.

The benefits of conflict include the emergence of talents and abilities, constructive innovation and change, and increased unity after the conflict is settled. Among the detrimental consequences of conflict are physical and mental health problems, wasted resources, the promotion of self-interest, and workplace violence.

Techniques for resolving conflicts with others include the following:

- Being assertive. To become more assertive, set a goal, appear warm and friendly, conduct anonymous conversations, greet strangers, and practice being decisive.
- Confrontation and problem solving leading to win–win. Get to the root of the problem and resolve it systematically. The intention of confrontation and problem solving is to arrive at a collaborative solution to the conflict. The opposite of win–win is win–lose, where each side attempts to maximize gain at the expense of the other.
- Disarm the opposition. Agree with the criticizer and enlist his or her help.
- Cognitive restructuring. Mentally convert negative aspects into positive ones by looking for the positive elements in a situation.
- Appeal to a third party (such as a government agency).
- Use the grievance procedure (a formal organizational procedure for dispute resolution), used extensively in unionized companies.
- Use company programs to help reduce work–family conflict including flexible work schedules, dependent-care programs, job sharing, employee sabbbitacals, and compassionate attitudes toward individual needs. Such programs increase productivity.

- Use negotiation and bargaining tactics, including creating a positive negotiating climate; allowing room for compromise but being reasonable; focusing on interests, not positions; making a last and final offer; role-playing to predict what the other side will do; and allowing for face-saving.

Limited ability to manage anger damages the careers and personal lives of many people. The ability to manage anger is part of emotional intelligence. In managing your own anger, remember that anger can be an energizing force.

- Express your anger before it reaches a high intensity.

- As you are about to express your anger, slow down.
- Ask for feedback on how you deal with anger.
- In dealing with the anger of others, use the confront, contain (move the angry worker out of sight), and connect (ask open-ended questions to get at the real reason behind the outburst) method.

In choosing a tactic for resolving conflict, consider both your personality or style and the nature of the situation facing you. The situation includes such factors as the gravity of the conflict and the type of person you are facing.

## Check Your Understanding

1. Many former students of human relations or organizational behavior contend that the most useful information they learned in the course pertained to conflict resolution. Why might their contention be true?
2. Give an example from your own life of how competition for limited resources can breed conflict.
3. Some conflicts go on for decades without being resolved, such as disputes between countries that last for up to 100 years. Why is it so difficult to resolve such conflicts?
4. Imagine that after two weeks on a new job that you want, your boss begins to treat you in a bullying, intimidating manner. What would you say to that boss?
5. Many male managers who confer with a female worker in their offices leave the door open to avoid any charges of sexual harassment. Are these managers using good judgment, or are they being overly cautious?

6. Why is it that during a game, same-sex professional athletes touch (even on the buttocks), hug, and kiss each other yet such behavior is frowned on or forbidden in other workplaces, such as the office or factory?
7. Identify several occupations in which conflict resolution skills are particularly important.
8. How might a person use cognitive restructuring to help deal with the conflict of having received a below-average raise yet expecting an above-average raise?
9. What is your explanation of the research showing that role-playing a negotiation scenario helps people make more accurate predictions about the outcome of conflicts?
10. Ask a successful person how much conflict he or she experiences in balancing the demands of work and personal life. Be prepared to report your findings in class.

## Web Corner

*Cognitive restructuring:*

http://www.mindtools.com/stress/rt/Cognitive Restructuring.htm

*Assertiveness training:*

http://www.psychologyinfo. com/treatment/asssertiveness.html

*Shyness:*

www.shyness.com (self-quizzes about shyness, plus the opportunity to participate in research about shyness)

*Internet Skill Builder:*

WWW.NEGOTIATORS.COM/60SECONDS.HTM presents a teaser of a program that suggests you can learn to negotiate within one minute, based on slides presented. As you read the presentation, identify the concepts and skills that you think would be the most beneficial to you. What else would you have to do in addition to absorbing the presentation on this Web site to enhance your negotiating skills? Compare the techniques in the 60-second presentation to those described in the text. What similarities do you see?

# Developing Your Human Relations Skills

*Human Relations Application Exercises*

## Applying Human Relations Exercise 5-1

### Win–Win Conflict Management

The class is organized into groups of six, with each group being divided into conflict resolution teams of three each. The members of the team would like to find a win–win solution to the issue separating each side. The team members are free to invent their own pressing issue or choose among the following:

■ Management wants to control costs by not giving cost-of-living adjustments in the upcoming year. The employee group believes that a cost-of-living adjustment is absolutely necessary.

■ The marketing team claims it could sell 250,000 units of a toaster large enough to toast bagels if the toasters could be produced at $15 per unit. The manufacturing group says it would not be feasible to get the manufacturing costs below $20 per unit.

■ Starbucks Coffee would like to build in a new location, adjacent to a historic district in one of the oldest cities in North America. The members of the town planning board would like the tax revenue and the jobs that the Starbucks store would bring, but they still say they do not want a Starbucks store adjacent to the historic district.

After the teams have developed win–win solutions to the conflicts, the creative solutions can be shared with teammates. Explain why each of your solutions should be classified as win–win. Describe the benefits each side received from the resolution of conflict and why you classified the outcome as a benfit.

## Applying Human Relations Exercise 5-2

### Learning to Manage Anger

The next few times you are really angry with somebody or something, use one or more of the following good mental health statements. Each statement is designed to remind you that you are in charge, not your anger. To begin, visualize something that has made you angry recently. Practice making the following statements in relation to that angry episode.

■ I'm in charge here, not my emotional outbursts.
■ I'll breathe deeply a few times and then deal with this.

■ I feel _____ when you _____.
■ I can handle this.
■ I'm going to take time out to cool down before I deal with this.
■ Yes, I'm angry and I'll just watch what I say or do.

Now describe the effect making these statements had on your anger.

**Source:** Based on Lynne Namka, "A Primer on Anger: Getting a Handle on Your Mads," available at http://members.aol.com/AngriesOut/grown2.htm, p. 4, retrieved April 21, 1998.

## Applying Human Relations Exercise 5-3

### Conflict Resolution

Imagine that Heather in the case presented, next decides that her job is taking too big a toll on her personal life. However, she still values her job and does not want to quit. She decides to discuss her problem with her team leader, Tyler. From Tyler's standpoint, a professional person must stand ready to meet unusual job demands and cannot expect an entirely predictable work schedule. One person plays the role of Heather and another the role of Tyler as they attempt to resolve this incident of work–family conflict.

Observers will look for (a) how well the conflict appears to have been resolved and (b) which techniques of conflict resolution Heather and Tyler used. Other feedback observations will also be welcome.

## Human Relations Case Study 5-1

### Caught in a Squeeze

Heather Lopez is a product development specialist at a telecommunications company. For the past seven months she has worked as a member of a product development team composed of people from five different departments within the company. Heather's previously worked full time in the marketing department. Her primary responsibilities were to research the market potential of an idea for a new product. The product development team is now working on a product that will integrate a company's printers and copiers.

Heather's previous position in the marketing department was a satisfactory fit for her lifestyle. Heather thought that she was able to take care of her family responsibilities and her job without sacrificing one for the other. As Heather explains, "I worked about 45 predictable hours in my other job. My hours were essentially 8:30 A.M. to 4:30 P.M. with a little work at night and on Saturdays. But I could do the work at night and on Saturdays at home.

"Brad, my husband, and I had a smooth-working arrangement for sharing the responsibility for getting our son, Christopher, off to school and picking him up from the after-school child-care center. Brad is a devoted accountant, so he understands the importance of giving high priority to a career yet still being a good family person."

In her new position as a member of the product development team, Heather is encountering some unanticipated demands. Three weeks ago, at 3 P.M. on a Tuesday, Tyler Watson, Heather's team leader, announced an emergency meeting to discuss a budget problem with the new product. The meeting would start at 4 and probably end at about 6:30. "Don't worry folks," said the team leader, "if it looks like we are going past 6:30, we will order in some Chinese food."

With a look of panic on her face, Heather responded to Tyler, "I can't make the meeting. Christopher will be expecting me at about 5 at the child-care center. My husband is out of town, and the center closes at 6 sharp. So count me out of today's meeting."

Tyler said, "I said that this is an emergency meeting and that we need input from all the members. You need to organize your personal life better to be a contributing member to this team. But do what you have to do, at least this once."

Heather chose to leave the office at 4:30 so she could pick up Christopher. The next day, Tyler did not comment on her absence. However, he gave her a copy of the minutes and asked for her input. The budget problem surfaced again one week later. Top-level management asked the group to reduce the cost of the new product and its initial marketing costs by 15 percent.

Tyler said to the team on a Friday morning, "We have until Monday morning to arrive at a reduced cost structure on our product development. I am dividing up the project into segments. If we meet as a team Saturday morning at 8, we should get the job done by 6 at night. Get a good night's rest so we can start fresh tomorrow morning. Breakfast and lunch will be on the company."

Heather could feel stress overwhelming her body, as she thought to herself, "Christopher is play-ing in the finals of his Little League soccer match tomorrow morning at 10. Brad has made dinner reservations for 6, so we can make it to the *The Lion King* at 8 P.M. Should I tell Tyler he is being unreasonable? Should I quit? Should I tell Christopher and Brad that our special occasions together are less important than a Saturday business meeting?"

## Questions

1. What type of conflicts is Heather facing?
2. What should Heather do to resolve her conflicts with respect to family and work responsibilities?
3. What should the company do to help deal with the type of conflict Heather is facing? Or should the company not consider Heather's dilemma to be their problem?

## Human Relations Case Study 5-2

### Wal-Mart Plays Tough in Quebec

In electronics, only "Le Gros Albert" (Fat Albert) and a few other leftover DVDs remain. Over in household goods, liquidation tags dangle beside thin skillets as the Wal-Mart in Jonquiere, Quebec (Canada), prepares to close. The company shut the doors here May 6, 2005, after workers voted to make this the first unionized Wal-Mart in North America.

The closure left 190 bitter employees out of work and the town uneasy over the future of unions. Supporters of organized labor also say it serves as a warning for workers at other Wal-Mart stores who might contemplate defying founder Sam Walton's sharp distaste for unions. The world's largest retail chain has fiercely and successfully resisted unionization attempts at its 3,600 stores in the United States.

In Canada, the battle has been pitched, pitting the country's still-healthy union movement against what is now its largest retailer. Wal-Mart Stores Inc. now takes 52 percent of the retail market share in Canada and is opening about 30 stores a year. Jonquiere was the first store to be unionized.

Andrew Pelletier, head of corporate affairs for Wal-Mart Canada Corp., said that, although the union may have succeeded in organizing a store in Jonquiere, Wal-Mart workers have on five other occasions voted against unionization. "I think that says we are a good employer," Pelletier said.

Jonquiere, 120 miles north of Quebec City, is a French-speaking mill town of 60,000. Its bland neighborhoods of square clapboard homes attest to its origins a century ago as a center for the pulp-and-paper industry. The Wal-Mart here is one of three in the area, and it was welcomed when it opened more than three years ago. The town's manufacturing legs are getting old: The two paper mills closed lines in their plants in 2004, costing 1,200 jobs. "Economically, it's not a good time for us," said the mayor of the Saguenay area, Jean Tremblay. The new Wal-Mart was swamped with applications, and those who were hired thought themselves lucky.

"I never had a job as good as this before," said Lynn Morissette, 44, who tracks inventory in the store. "I worked in the daytime. I thought I had a good wage, and I was a shareholder, too, so I could save up some money. I was going to retire here." But others were not so thrilled about Wal-Mart's pay—starting at about $6.20 (U.S.) an hour, its floating shifts for part-timers, or the rules that limited some full-time employees to 28 hours of work a week. In an area built on union jobs, with higher wage scales, it wasn't long before some employees tried to organize.

Those involved in the organizing effort claim they were harassed by the company. "We were targeted fairly quickly by Wal-Mart," said Pierre Martineau, a 60-year-old maintenance man who helped organize the union. He said he was humiliated and ridiculed by managers at a storewide meeting and followed around by supervisors who made implied threats.

Those who did not want a union, say organizers, harassed them to join. "People signed the cards just to get some peace" from the union organizers, said Noella Langlois, 53, who works in the clothing department. "They thought they would vote against it in a secret vote." In fact, there was a vote last April that rejected the union. But under Quebec labor laws, the organizers could try again. When they collected signed union cards from 51 percent of the employees, the law declared the Jonquiere Wal-Mart a union shop.

Pelletier, the Wal-Mart spokesperson, says the Quebec laws are unfair, and only a secret ballot would show the true feelings of the workers. "Signing a union card, when there's someone on your doorstep at night saying, 'Sign this card,' should not be the last word," he said. "A democratic, secret vote is the only way to avoid intimidation by either the union or an employer."

But it became moot in February, when Wal-Mart announced it would close the store. Company officials said it was losing money, and the demands of the union would have made it even less tenable. "You can't take a store that is a struggling store anyway and add a bunch of people and a bunch of work rules," said Wal-Mart chief executive H. Lee Scott, Jr.

Some here in Jonquiere don't believe the company's claim that the store was losing money. They say the chain sacrificed the store to make a point to its employees across Canada and the United States, where union organizers are involved in dozens of organizing drives and court battles. "They closed it to be a threat to other unions," said Tremblay, the mayor. "We know that for Wal-Mart, Jonquiere is nothing. They wanted to close it to make a lesson to other Wal-Marts."

The announcement deepened animosities among the employees. Those who liked their jobs and said they were happy at Wal-Mart are bitter at the union for its tactics, which they blame for the store closure.

Sylvie Lavoie, 40, said she is unsure how, as a single mother, she will support herself and her 10-year-old daughter after the store closes. But the backup cashier, who earns $7.55 an hour, said she does not regret joining the union drive. "We can't regret trying to make our lives better," she said at the union hall. "I don't know what I'll do, but I know my daughter will be proud of me."

### Questions

1. Which technique of conflict resolution might have made it possible for Wal-Mart to stay open in Jonquiere?
2. How might the Wal-Mart workers who opposed the union and those that favored the union have approached their differences?
3. What has this case got to do with human relations skills?

**Source:** Excerpted from Doug Struck, "Wal-Mart Leaves Bitter Chill: Quebec Store Closes after Vote to Unionize," *Washington Post Foreign Service*, April 14, 2005, p. E01.

# REFERENCES

1. Sue Shellenbarger, "Employers Step Up Efforts to Lure Stay-at-Home Mothers Back to Work," *The Wall Street Journal*, February 9, 2006, p. D1.

2. Dominic A. Infante, *Arguing Constructively* (Prospects Heights, IL: Waveland Press, 1992); Siobhan Leftwich, "Hey, You Can't Say That! How to Cope with Verbally Abusive People," *Black Enterprise*, January 2006, p. 95.

3. Julie Ellis, "Knock Down Workplace Bullying; Improve Office Morale," *Managing Workplace Conflict* (The Dartnell Corporation sample issue, 2002), p. 6.

4. "Safety and Health Topics: Workplace Violence," U.S. Department of Labor, Occupational Safety and Health Administration, available at www.osha.gov, retrieved April 2, 2006.

5. Angela Pirisi, "Teamwork: The Downside of Diversity," *Psychology Today*, November/December 1999, p. 18.

6. Jiatao Li and Donald C. Hambrick, "Factional Groups: A New Vantage on Demographic Faultlines, Conflict, and Disintegration in Work Teams," *Academy of Management Journal*, October 2005, pp. 794–813.

7. "When Work and Private Lives Collide," *Workforce*, February 1999, p. 27.

8. The examples, but not the interpretations, are from Julie Fawe, "Why Your Boss May Start Sweating the Small Stuff," *Time*, March 20, 2006, p. 80. See also, Joann S. Lublin, "How to Stop the Snubs that Demoralize You and Your Colleagues," *The Wall Street Journal*, December 7, 2004, p. B1.

9. Kimberly T. Schneider, Suzanne Swan, and Louise F. Fitzgerald, "Job-Related and Psychological Effects of Sexual Harassment in the Workplace: Empirical Evidence in Two Organizations," *Journal of Applied Psychology*, June 1997, p. 406.

10. Theresa M. Glomb, Liberty J. Munson, and Charles L. Hulin, "Structural Equation Models of Sexual Harassment: Longitudinal Explorations and Cross-Sectional Generalizations," *Journal of Applied Psychology*, February 1999, pp. 14–28.

11. Jana L. Raver and Michele J. Gelfand, "Beyond the Individual Victim: Linking Sexual Harassment, Team Processes, and Team Performance," *Academy of Management Journal*, June 2005, pp. 387–400.

12. Lisa Takeuchi Cullen, "Sex in the Syllabus," *Time*, April 3, 2006, pp. 80–81.

13. Data reported in Anne Fisher, "How to Prevent Violence at Work," *Fortune*, February 21, 2005.

14. "Right and Wrong Ways to Manage Conflict," *Manager's Edge*, October 2001, p. 5

15. Bernardo J. Carducci, *Shyness: A Bold Approach* (New York: HarperCollins, 1999).

16. Philip Zimbardo, *Shyness: What It Is, What to Do about It* (Reading, MA: Addison-Wesley, 1977), pp. 220–226; Mel Silberman with Freda Hansburg, *PeopleSmart* (San Francisco: Berrett-Koehler, 2000), pp. 75–76.

17. Stephen P. Robbins and David A. DeCenzo, *Supervision Today!* 4th ed. (Upper Saddle River, NJ: Pearson Prentice Hall, 2004), p. 438.

18. David Welch, "Twilight of the UAW," *Business Week*, April 10, 2006, p. 62.

19. Timothy A. Judge and Jason A. Colquitt, "Organizational Justice and Stress: The Mediating Role of Work–Family Conflict," *Journal of Applied Psychology*, June 2004, pp. 395–404.

20. Cited in Marcia A. Reed-Woodward, "Share and Share Alike: A New Option for Work/Life Balance." *Black Enterprise*, April 2006, p. 63.

21. Michael Arndt, "Nice Work If You Can Get It," *Business Week*, January 9, 2006, pp. 56–57.

22. Marc Deiner, "Speak Up: Hate to Negotiate? That's Still No Excuse to Avoid Learning the Skill," *Entrepreneur*, September 2004, p. 79.

23. Joseph D'O'Brian, "Negotiating with Peers: Consensus, Not Power," *Supervisory Management*, January 1992, p. 4.

24. J. Scott Armstrong, "Forecasting in Conflicts: How to Predict What Your Opponents Will Do," *Knowledge@ Wharton*, February 13, 2002, p.1.

25. Linda Wasmer Andrews, "When It's Time for Anger Management," *HR Magazine*, June 2005, pp. 131–135.

26. Fred Pryor, "Is Anger Really Healthy?" *The Pryor Management Newsletter*, February 1996, p. 3.

27. The quote and technique are both from Kathleen Doheny, "It's a Mad, Mad Corporate World," *Working Woman*, April 2000, pp. 71–72.

# Developing Teamwork Skills

## Learning Objectives

After reading and studying this chapter and doing the exercises, you should be able to:

1 Identify several types of teams in organizations.

2 Understand the advantages and disadvantages of teams.

3 Identify various team member roles.

4 Apply interpersonal-related tactics for effective team play.

5 Apply task-related tactics for effective team play.

## Outline

1 **Types of Teams   171**
Self-Managing Work Teams
Cross-Functional Teams
Virtual Teams
Crews

2 **The Advantages and Disadvantages of Teams and Teamwork   176**
Advantages of Group Work and Teamwork
Disadvantages of Group Work and Teamwork

3 **Team Member Roles   180**

4 **Guidelines for the Interpersonal Aspects of Team Play   184**
Trust Team Members
Display a High Level of Cooperation and Collaboration
Recognize the Interests and Achievements of Others
Give and Receive Helpful Criticism
Share the Glory
Take Care Not to Rain on Another Person's Parade

5 **Guidelines for the Task Aspects of Team Play   189**
Provide Technical Expertise (or Knowledge of the Task)
Assume Responsibility for Problems
See the Big Picture
Believe in Consensus
Focus on Deadlines
Help Team Members Do Their Jobs Better
Be a Good Organizational Citizen

It seemed like a typical company holiday party. The brandy and eggnog flowed freely, although it didn't seem to loosen up any of the attendees. "Smile and make pleasant talk while you serve, please," instructed the fellow who had cast himself as Santa. There were plenty of gag gifts: a luxury flat overlooking the Kremlin for Victoria, who was moving to Moscow; growth-enhancing supplements for Domas, who hovers at 6-foot-4. And of course, the requisite taste-less humor. All standard fare for an office party—except that there was no office. Thomas Basil, director of support at MySQL, a $40 million software maker, staged the event online, playing Santa while dispensing virtual drinks and gifts to staffers scattered in such outposts as Russia, England, and Germany.

*To accommodate the different geographics, Basil started the festivities on a December day at 10 A.M. in Baltimore, where he lives. (His clocks are actually set seven hours ahead to Helsinki time, the time zone of many of his team members.) "When a company is as spread out as this one," Basil explains, "you have to think of virtual ways to imitate the dynamics of what goes one in a more familiar employment situation." [1]*

*The activities of the executive just described are directed toward nurturing a bond among workers who, as participants on a virtual team, rarely, if ever, meet. The reason Basil bothers attempting to create bonds among team members is that bonds enhance team-work, and the modern organization depends on teamwork throughout the company. Many firms rely more on teamwork than on individuals acting alone to accomplish work. To be successful in the modern organization, it is therefore necessary to be an effective team player. You have to work smoothly with other members of the team to accomplish your goals. Teamwork is more important as people work their way up through the organization. Executives, such as CEOs, preach teamwork but tend to dominate meetings and make more decisions by themselves. [2]*

■ **Team**

a small number of people with complementary skills who are committed to a common purpose, set of performance goals, and approach for which they hold themselves mutually accountable

The challenges a team member faces come to light when the true nature of a team is recognized. A **team** is a special type of group. Team members have complementary skills and are committed to a common purpose, a set of performance goals, and an approach to the task. In other words, the members of a team work together smoothly, and all pull in the same direction. A workplace team should be more like an effective athletic team than a group of individuals out for individual glory. [3]

This chapter gives you the information, insights, and preliminary practice necessary to develop effective teamwork skills. Self-Assessment Quiz 6-1 will help you assess your current mental readiness to be a contributing team member.

## Self-Assessment Quiz  6-1

### Team Player Attitudes

**Directions:** Describe how well you agree with each of the following statements, using the following scale: disagree strongly (DS); disagree (D); neutral (N); agree (A); agree strongly (AS). Circle the number in the appropriate column.

|  | DS | D | N | A | AS |
|---|---|---|---|---|---|
| 1. I am at my best when working alone. | 5 | 4 | 3 | 2 | 1 |
| 2. I have belonged to clubs and teams ever since I was a child. | 1 | 2 | 3 | 4 | 5 |
| 3. It takes far too long to get work accomplished with a group. | 5 | 4 | 3 | 2 | 1 |
| 4. I like the friendship of working in a group. | 1 | 2 | 3 | 4 | 5 |
| 5. I would prefer to run a one-person business than to be a member of a large firm. | 5 | 4 | 3 | 2 | 1 |
| 6. It's difficult to trust others in the group on key assignments. | 5 | 4 | 3 | 2 | 1 |
| 7. Encouraging others comes to me naturally. | 1 | 2 | 3 | 4 | 5 |
| 8. I like the give-and-take of ideas that is possible in a group. | 1 | 2 | 3 | 4 | 5 |
| 9. It is fun for me to share responsibility with other group members. | 1 | 2 | 3 | 4 | 5 |
| 10. Much more can be accomplished by a team than by the same number of people working alone. | 1 | 2 | 3 | 4 | 5 |

Total score: _____

### Scoring and Interpretation:

Add the numbers you circled to obtain your total score.

**41–50**   You have strong positive attitudes toward being a team member and working cooperatively with other members.

**30–40**   You have moderately favorable attitudes toward being a team member and working cooperatively with other members.

**10–29**   You much prefer working by yourself to being a team member. To work effectively in a company that emphasizes teamwork, you may need to develop more positive attitudes toward working jointly with others.

# Types of Teams

■ **Learning Objective 1**

All teams in the workplace have the common element of people working together cooperatively and members possessing a mix of skills. Nevertheless, many specific types of work teams can be identified. Successful people will usually have the opportunity to be a member of several different types of teams.

Four representative work teams are self-managing work teams, cross-functional teams, virtual teams and crews. Projects, task forces, and committees are similar in design to cross-functional teams, so they do not receive separate mention here. No matter what label the team carries, its broad purpose is to contribute to a *collaborative workplace* in which people help each other achieve constructive goals. The idea is for workers to collaborate (a high level of cooperation) rather than compete with or prevent others from getting their work done.

As teams have become more common in the workplace, effort has been directed toward specifying the skills and knowledge a person needs to function effectively on a team, particularly a self-managing work team.

## SELF-MANAGING WORK TEAMS

■ **Self-managing work team**
a small group of employees responsible for managing and performing technical tasks to deliver a product or service to an external or internal customer

The best-known work team is a group of workers who take much of the responsibility for managing their own work. The same type of team is referred to as a self-managing work team, a self-directing work team, a production work team, or a team. A **self-managing work team** is a small group of employees responsible for managing and performing technical tasks to deliver a product or service to an external or internal customer. [4] The majority of large- and medium-size firms make some use of self-managing work teams. Work teams are used in a variety of activities including the production of motorcycles, telephone directories, or a major component for a large computer.

Members of a self-managing work team typically work together on an ongoing, day-by-day basis, thus differentiating it from a task force or a committee. The work team is often given total responsibility for or "ownership" of an entire product or service, such as producing a telephone directory. At other times, the team is given responsibility for a major chunk of a job, such as building an airplane engine (but not the entire airplane).

A major hurdle in forming self-managing teams is to help employees overcome the attitude reflected in the statement "I'm not paid to think." Work teams rely less on supervisors and more on the workers assuming more responsibilities for managing their own activities. For example, work team members may be required to discipline other team members who have attendance, performance, or behavioral problems. [5]

As with all teams, mutual trust among members contributes to team effectiveness. A study conducted with business students, however, showed that if the members trust each other too much they may not monitor (check up on) each other's work enough. As a result, group performance will suffer. This problem of too much trust surfaces primarily when the team members have individual assignments that do not bring them into frequent contact with each other. [6] An example of an individual, or autonomous, project would be preparing a statistical report that would later be given to the group.

## CROSS-FUNCTIONAL TEAMS

■ **Cross-functional team**
a work group composed of workers from different specialties, and about the same organizational level, who come together to accomplish a task

It is common practice for teams to be composed of workers from different specialties. A **cross-functional team** is a work group composed of workers from different specialties, who come together to accomplish a task. The purpose of the cross-functional team is to get workers from different specialties to blend their talents toward accomplishing a task that requires such a mix.

## Self-Assessment Quiz  6-2

### Team Skills

A variety of skills is required to be an effective member of various types of teams. Several different business firms use the skill inventory here to help guide team members toward the competencies they need to become high-performing team members.

**Directions:** Review each team skill listed and rate your skill level for each one using the following classification:

**S** = strong (capable and comfortable with effectively implementing the skill)
**M** = moderate (demonstrated skill in the past)
**B** = basic (minimum ability in this area)
**N** = not applicable (not relevant to the type of work I do)

| Communication skills | Skill level (S, M, B, or N) |
|---|---|
| Speak effectively | _____ |
| Foster open communications | _____ |
| Listen to others | _____ |
| Deliver presentations | _____ |
| Prepare written communication | _____ |
| *Self-management skills* | |
| Act with integrity | _____ |
| Demonstrate adaptability | _____ |
| Engage in personal development | _____ |
| Strive for results | _____ |
| Display a commitment to work | _____ |
| *Thought process skills* | |
| Innovate solutions to problems | _____ |
| Use sound judgment | _____ |
| Analyze issues | _____ |
| Think "outside the box" | _____ |
| *Organizational skills* | |
| Know the business | _____ |
| Use technical/functional expertise | _____ |
| Use financial/quantitative data | _____ |
| *Strategic (broad business perspective) skills* | |
| Recognize "big picture" impact | _____ |
| Promote corporate citizenship | _____ |
| Focus on customer needs | _____ |
| Commit to quality | _____ |
| Manage profitability | _____ |

### Interpretation:

There is no scoring key for this questionnaire. Its purpose is to raise your awareness of the types of skills that are required to be a successful team member in business.

A typical application of a cross-functional team would be to develop a new product such as a video cell phone. Among the specialties needed on such a team would be computer science, engineering, manufacturing, industrial design, marketing, and finance. (The finance person would help guide the team toward producing a video cell phone that could be sold at a profit.) When members from different specialties work together, they can take into account each other's perspectives when making their contribution. For example, if the manufacturing representative knows that a video cell phone must sell for about one-half the price of a plasma screen TV, then he or she will have to build the device inexpensively. A major advantage of cross-functional teams for product development is that they enhance communication across groups, thereby saving time. In addition to product development, cross-functional teams are used for such purposes as improving quality, reducing costs, and running a company (in the form of a top management team).

To perform well on a cross-functional team, a person would have to think in terms of the good of the larger organization, rather than in terms of his or her own specialty. For example, a manufacturing technician might say, "If I proposed using expensive components for the video phone, would the product cost too much for its intended market?"

## VIRTUAL TEAMS

Some teams conduct most of their work by sending electronic messages to each other rather than conducting face-to-face meetings. A **virtual team** is a small group of people who conduct almost all of their collaborative work by electronic communication rather than face-to-face meetings. E-mail, including IM (instant messaging), is the usual medium for sharing information and conducting meetings. *Groupware* is another widely used approach to conducting an electronic meeting. Using groupware, several people can edit a document at the same time, or in sequence. Desktop videoconferencing is another technological advance that facilitates the virtual team.

Most high-tech companies make some use of virtual teams and electronic meetings. Strategic alliances in which geographically dispersed companies work with each other are a natural for virtual teams. It is less expensive for the field technician in Iceland to hold an electronic meeting with her counterparts in South Africa, Mexico, and California than it is to bring them all together in one physical location. Virtual teams are sometimes the answer to the challenge of hiring workers with essential skills who do not want to relocate. With team members geographically dispersed, precise communications are all the more important for virtual teams. The virtual team members usually need a formal document outlining the objectives, job responsibilities, and team goals. Another communication problem takes place when the virtual team is composed of both in-house workers and those in remote locations. The office-bound members become jealous of the seemingly cushy setup enjoyed by the telecommuters. One solution to this problem is for every member of the team to be given a chance to prove he or she can work off-site. [7]

Establishing trust is a major challenge in a virtual team because the team members have to rely on people they never see to carry out their fair share of the workload, and to exchange reliable information. Trust is also needed in terms of what information should be shared outside of the team. For example, if the team is behind schedule on a project, can each member be trusted not to inform outsiders about the problem? For example, one virtual team had an external communication norm that prohibited team members from conveying negative information to anyone outside the team. [8]

Despite the efficiency of virtual teams, there are times when face-to-face (or at least telephone) interaction is necessary to deal with complex and emotional issues. Negotiating a new contract between management and a labor union, for example, is not well suited to an electronic meeting.

## CREWS

We are all familiar with common use of the term *crew* in relation to such groups as those who operate airplanes, boats, and firefighting equipment. The technical meaning of the term means virtually the same thing. A **crew** is a group of specialists each of whom have specific roles, perform brief events that are closely synchronized with each other, and repeat these events under different environmental conditions. A crew is identified by the technology it handles, such as an aircraft crew, or a deep-sea salvage operation. The crew members rarely rotate specialties, such as the flight attendant taking over for the chief pilot. (Special training and licensing would be required.) The following are several criteria of a group qualifying as a crew [9]:

- Clear roles and responsibilities
- Work flow well established before anyone joins the team
- Careful coordination required with other members to perform the task
- Group needs to be in a specific environment to complete its task
- Different people can join the group without interfering with its operation or mission

Because of the specialized roles they play and the essential tasks they perform, much is expected of crews. The future of crews is promising. For example,

> "Virtual teams need to know that their coworkers are "real people." It's the personal information they learn from one another that will foster the social ties that allow collaboration to occur naturally."
> —Tammy Burch, CEO of Virtual Concepts International in Milford, Michigan

■ **Crew**
a group of specialists each of whom have specific rules, perform brief events that are closely synchronized with each other, and repeat these events under different environmental conditions

---

### BACK TO THE OPENING CASE

The software company executive believed strongly that a feeling of teamwork is not easy to accomplish among workers who are geographically dispersed. So instead of going to the expense and difficulty of have a physical holiday party, he held a virtual party. Although a virtual holiday party may not be a substitute for the real thing, it reflected a sincere effort on the executive's part to help enhance team spirit. Because almost all of the workers attended the holiday party from their homes, the company did not have to worry about employees driving home from the party under the influence of alcohol.

computer-virus-fighting crews would be a welcome addition to business and society. Mutual trust is especially important in a crew because good cooperation could save one's life, such as in a firefighting crew. Experience with sailing crews strongly suggests that team members should be technically excellent and have good personal chemistry with each other. [10] Under life-threatening circumstances, such as navigating a storm, it is best to have strong bonds with each other.

■ Learning Objective 2

# The Advantages and Disadvantages of Teams and Teamwork

■ **Synergy**
a situation in which the group's total output exceeds the sum of each individual's contribution

Groups have always been the building blocks of organizations. Yet groups and teams have recently grown in importance as the basic unit for organizing work. In an attempt to cope with numerous changes in the outside world, many organizations have granted teams increased independence and flexibility. Furthermore, teams are often required to work more closely with customers and suppliers.

The increased acceptance of teams suggests that group work offers many advantages. Nevertheless, it is useful to specify several of these advantages and examine the potential problems of groups. Being aware of these potential pitfalls can often help a person avoid them. These same advantages and disadvantages also apply to group decision making.

## ADVANTAGES OF GROUP WORK AND TEAMWORK

Group work and group decision making offer several advantages over individual effort. If several knowledgeable people are brought into the decision-making process, a number of worthwhile possibilities may be uncovered [10] It is also possible to gain **synergy**, whereby the group's total output exceeds the sum of each individual's contribution. For example, it would be a rare person working alone who could build a racing car.

Group decision making is also helpful in gaining acceptance and commitment. The argument is that people who contribute to making a decision will feel some ownership about implementing the decision. Team members often evaluate each other's thinking, so the team is likely to avoid major errors. An advertising specialist was developing an advertising campaign to attract seniors to live in a retirement community. The proposed ads had photographs of senior citizens engaged in playing shuffleboard, visiting the pharmacy, and sleeping in a hammock. Another team member on the project pointed out that many seniors perceive themselves to be energetic and youthful. Ads emphasizing advanced age might therefore backfire. A successful advertising campaign was then developed that featured seniors in more youthful activities such as jogging and dancing.

A major justification for relying on teams in the workplace is that under the right circumstances, they can enhance productivity and profitability. The right circumstances include an atmosphere that promotes teamwork and financial bonuses for high-performing teams. A classic example is American steelmaker Nucor Corp. The company is committed to the spirit of teamwork, and bonuses for teams of steelworkers average 170 percent to 180 percent. Since Nucor implemented its team incentive plan in 1966, the company has been profitable each quarter through 2007 despite foreign competition. [11]

Working in teams and groups also enhances the job satisfaction of members. Being a member of a work group makes it possible to satisfy more needs than working alone. Among these needs are affiliation, security, self-esteem, and self-fulfillment. (Chapter 13 provides more details about psychological needs.)

## DISADVANTAGES OF GROUP WORK AND TEAMWORK

Group activity has some potential disadvantages for both individuals and the organization. Teams and other groups often waste time because they talk too much and act too little. Committees appear to suffer from more inaction than teams. Abigail Johnson, president of Fidelity Employer Services Co. (Fesco), says that committees are not effective decision makers. "They have tended to be slow and overly risk averse. Even worse, I believe, they can drain an organization of talent, because the group can only be as good as the average." [12] A major problem is that members face pressures to conform to group standards of performance and conduct, as just implied. Some teams might shun a person who is much more productive than his or her coworkers. Shirking of individual responsibility is another problem frequently noted in groups. Unless work is assigned carefully to each team member, an under-motivated person can often squeeze by without contributing his or her fair share to a group effort.

**Social loafing** is the psychological term for shirking individual responsibility in a group setting. The social loafer risks being ostracized (shunned) by the group but may be willing to pay the price rather than work hard. Loafing of this type is sometimes found in groups such as committees and project teams. Have you ever encountered a social loafer on a group project at school?

■ **Social loafing**
the psychological term for shirking individual responsibility in a group setting

At their worst, teams and other groups foster conflict on the job. People within the work group often bicker about such matters as doing a fair share of the undesirable tasks within the department. Cohesive work groups can also become xenophobic (fearful of outsiders). As a consequence, they may grow to dislike other groups and enter into conflict with them. A customer service group might put considerable effort into showing up a sales group because the latter makes promises to customers that the customer service group cannot keep. For example, a sales representative might promise that a customer can get a loaner if his or her equipment needs repair, although customer service has no such policy.

A well-publicized disadvantage of group decision making is **groupthink**, a deterioration of mental efficiency, reality testing, and moral judgment in the interest of group solidarity. Simply put, groupthink is an extreme form of consensus. The group atmosphere values getting along more than getting things done. The group thinks as a unit, believes it is

■ **Groupthink**
a deterioration of mental efficiency, reality testing, and moral judgment in the interest of group solidarity

impervious to outside criticism, and begins to have illusions about its own invincibility. As a consequence, the group loses its powers of critical analysis. [13] Groupthink appears to have contributed to several of the major financial scandals of the previous decade. Members of top management got together to vote themselves huge bonuses just before filing

- The team has clear-cut goals linked to organizational goals so that group members feel connected to the entire organization. Group members are empowered so they learn to think for themselves rather than expecting a supervisor to solve all the difficult problems. At the same time, the group believes it has the authority to solve a variety of problems without first obtaining approval from management.

- Group members are assigned work they perceive to be challenging, exciting, and rewarding. As a consequence, the work is self-rewarding.

- Members depend on one another to accomplish tasks, and work toward a common goal.

- Members learn to think "outside the box" (are creative).

- Members receive extensive training in technical knowledge, problem-solving skills, and interpersonal skills.

- Members inspect their own work for quality.

- Members receive part of their pay related to team or group incentives rather than strictly based on individual performance.

- Group size is generally about 6 people, rather than 10 or more.

- Team members have good intelligence and personality factors such as conscientiousness, openness to experience, collectivism (as opposed to individualism), and pride that contribute to good performance.

- There is honest and open communication among group members and with other groups in the organization.

- Members have the philosophy of working as a team—25 brains, not just 50 hands.

- Members are familiar with their jobs, coworkers, and the work environment. This experience adds to their expertise. The beneficial effects of experience may diminish after awhile because the team needs fresh ideas and approaches.

- The team has emotional intelligence in the sense that it builds relationships both inside and outside the team. Included in emotional intelligence are norms that establish mutual trust among members, a feeling of group identity, and group efficacy.

**Figure   6-1**

**Key Characteristics of Effective Teams and Work Groups.**
**Source:** Gerben S. Van Der Vegt et al., "Patterns of Interdependence in Work Teams: A Two-Level Investigation of the Relations with Job and Team Satisfaction," *Personnel Psychology*, Spring 2001, pp. 51–69; Shawn L. Berman, Vanessa Urch Druskat, and Steven B. Wolff, "Building the Emotional Intelligence of Groups," *Harvard Business Review*, March 2001, pp. 80–90; Claus W. Langred, "Too Much of a Good Thing? Negative Effects of High Trust and Individual Autonomy in Self-Managing Work Teams," *Academy of Management Journal*, June 2004, pp. 385–389; Suzanne T. Bell, "Deep Level Composition Variables as Predictors of Team Performance: A Meta-Analysis," *Journal of Applied Psychology*, May 2007, pp. 595–615.

bankruptcy for their company. Several of the executives, including a few from Enron Corporation, were later sent to prison for their outrageous decisions.

Related to groupthink is the idea that groups often breed conformity in thinking and behavior. In an effort to be accepted by members of the group, some members will attempt to think and act like other members in terms of speech, thinking, and even dress. This tendency is pronounced among teenagers, and takes place on the job as well. You might want to examine a photo of Google, Microsoft, or Apple employees and observe how much conformity in dress you find. Self-Assessment Quiz 6-3 gives you an opportunity to think about your tendencies toward conformity.

Two conditions are important for overcoming the potential disadvantages of teams and groups. First, the members must strive to act like a team, [14] following some of the suggestions given in the upcoming pages. Second, the task given to the group should require collective effort instead of being a task that could better be performed by individuals. For example, an international business specialist would probably learn to conjugate verbs in a foreign language better by working alone than on a team. What is your opinion on this issue? Figure 6-1 presents more information about key factors associated with effective work teams and groups. The more of these factors that are present, the more likely it is that a given team or group will be productive.

## Self-Assessment Quiz 6-3

### The Conformity Quiz

**Directions:** Circle the extent to which each of the following statements describes your behavior or attitude: agree strongly (AS); agree (A); neutral (N); disagree (D); disagree strongly (DS). You may have to respond in terms of any team or group experience you have had if you are not currently a member of a work team, a class project team, or a sports team. Consider having someone who is familiar with your behavior and attitudes help you respond accurately.

|  | AS | A | N | D | DS |
|---|---|---|---|---|---|
| 1. I rarely question the decision reached by the team. | 5 | 4 | 3 | 2 | 1 |
| 2. Whatever the group wants is fine with me. | 5 | 4 | 3 | 2 | 1 |
| 3. My clothing distinguishes me from the other members of the team. | 1 | 2 | 3 | 4 | 5 |
| 4. I consider myself to be one of the gang. | 5 | 4 | 3 | 2 | 1 |
| 5. I rarely express disagreement during a group discussion. | 5 | 4 | 3 | 2 | 1 |
| 6. I routinely have lunch with other members of the team. | 5 | 4 | 3 | 2 | 1 |
| 7. My teammates sometimes complain that I think too independently. | 1 | 2 | 3 | 4 | 5 |
| 8. My preference is to piggyback on the ideas of others rather than contribute the ideas of my own. | 5 | 4 | 3 | 2 | 1 |
| 9. When I notice that the other members of the team make the same error in speech, I will copy them rather than sound different. | 5 | 4 | 3 | 2 | 1 |

*(continued)*

## Self-Assessment Quiz   6-3   (Continued)

| | | | | | |
|---|---|---|---|---|---|
| 10. I am often the first person to get up at the scheduled ending of the meeting. | 1 | 2 | 3 | 4 | 5 |
| 11. I do almost all of my creative thinking for the team task when I'm with the team. | 5 | 4 | 3 | 2 | 1 |
| 12. I'm particularly careful not to criticize an idea submitted by the team leader. | 5 | 4 | 3 | 2 | 1 |
| 13. The number of hours I work per week corresponds closely to the number worked by my teammates. | 5 | 4 | 3 | 2 | 1 |
| 14. When I think it is necessary, I bring information to the group conflicting with the path we are following. | 1 | 2 | 3 | 4 | 5 |
| 15. I would rather keep my mouth closed than point out weaknesses in a teammate's ideas. | 5 | 4 | 3 | 2 | 1 |
| 16. I've been called a maverick on more than one occasion by teammates. | 1 | 2 | 3 | 4 | 5 |
| 17. I encourage team members to express doubts about proposed solutions to problems. | 1 | 2 | 3 | 4 | 5 |
| 18. I invite criticism of my ideas. | 1 | 2 | 3 | 4 | 5 |
| 19. When the team laughs at a comment, I laugh too even if I don't think the comment was funny. | 5 | 4 | 3 | 2 | 1 |
| 20. Most of my social life centers around activities with my teammates. | 5 | 4 | 3 | 2 | 1 |

### Interpretation:

Calculate your score by adding the numbers you have circled, and use the following guide:

**80–100**     You are a high-conforming individual who readily goes along with the team without preserving your individuality. In an effort to be liked, you might be overcompromising your thinking.

**40–79**     You have probably achieved the right balance between following group norms (standards of conduct) and expressing your individuality. With actions and attitudes like this, you are on your way to becoming a good team player, yet also in a position to attain individual recognition.

**20–29**     You are highly individualistic, perhaps to the point of not working smoothly in a team setting. Be careful that you are not going out of your way to be a nonconformist, thereby interfering with your ability to be an effective team player.

### Skill Development:

Examine your responses to the 20 questions because the response might give you a clue to needed development, often just by making a subtle change within your control. Here are two examples: If you answered agree strongly or agree to Question 8, you might work toward contributing ideas of your own. If you answered disagree or disagree strongly to Question 14, you might work toward helping the team think more critically about the path it is following.

■ **Learning Objective 3**

# Team Member Roles

A major challenge in learning to become an effective team member is to choose the right roles to occupy. A role is a tendency to behave, contribute, and relate to others in a particular way. If you carry out positive roles, you will be perceived as a contributor to team effort. If you neglect carrying out these roles, you will be perceived as a poor contributor. Self-Assessment Quiz 6-4

## Self-Assessment Quiz  6-4

**Team Player Roles**

**Directions:** For each of the following statements about team activity, check *mostly agree* or *mostly disagree.* If you have not experienced such a situation, imagine how you would act or think if placed in that situation. In responding to the statements, assume that you are taking the questionnaire with the intent of learning something about yourself.

| | Mostly Agree | Mostly Disagree |
|---|---|---|
| 1. It is rare that I ever miss a team meeting. | _____ | _____ |
| 2. I regularly compliment team members when they do something exceptional. | _____ | _____ |
| 3. Whenever I can, I avoid being the note taker at a team meeting. | _____ | _____ |
| 4. From time to time, other team members come to me for advice on technical matters. | _____ | _____ |
| 5. I like to hide some information from other team members so I can be in control. | _____ | _____ |
| 6. I welcome new team members coming to me for advice and learning the ropes. | _____ | _____ |
| 7. My priorities come first, which leaves me with very little time to help other team members. | _____ | _____ |
| 8. During a team meeting, it is not unusual for several other people at a time to look toward me for my opinion. | _____ | _____ |
| 9. If I think the team is moving in an unethical direction, I will say so explicitly. | _____ | _____ |
| 10. Rarely will I criticize the progress of the team even if I think such criticism is deserved. | _____ | _____ |
| 11. It is typical for me to summarize the progress in a team meeting, even if not asked. | _____ | _____ |
| 12. To conserve time, I attempt to minimize contact with my teammates outside our meetings. | _____ | _____ |
| 13. I intensely dislike going along with a consensus decision if the decision runs contrary to my thoughts on the issue. | _____ | _____ |
| 14. I rarely remind teammates of our mission statement as we go about our work. | _____ | _____ |
| 15. Once I have made up my mind on an issue facing the team, I am unlikely to be persuaded in another direction. | _____ | _____ |
| 16. I am willing to accept negative feedback from team members. | _____ | _____ |
| 17. Just to get a new member of the team involved, I will ask his or her opinion. | _____ | _____ |
| 18. Even if the team has decided on a course of action, I am not hesitant to bring in new information that supports another position. | _____ | _____ |
| 19. Quite often I talk negatively about one team member to another. | _____ | _____ |
| 20. My teammates are almost a family to me because I am truly concerned about their welfare. | _____ | _____ |

*(continued)*

## Self-Assessment Quiz  6-4  *(Continued)*

21. When it seems appropriate, I joke and kid with teammates.   _____   _____
22. My contribution to team tasks is as important to me as my   _____   _____
    individual work.
23. From time to time I have pointed out to the team how we can   _____   _____
    all improve in reaching our goals.
24. I will fight to the last when the team does not support my   _____   _____
    viewpoint and wants to move toward consensus.
25. I will confront the team if I believe that the members are   _____   _____
    thinking too much alike.

Total score: _____

### Scoring and Interpretation:

Give yourself one point (+1) for each statement you gave in agreement with the keyed answer. The keyed answer indicates carrying out a positive, as opposed to a negative, role.

| Question number | Positive role answer | | Question number | Positive role answer |
|---|---|---|---|---|
| 1. | Mostly agree | | 14. | Mostly disagree |
| 2. | Mostly agree | | 15. | Mostly disagree |
| 3. | Mostly disagree | | 16. | Mostly agree |
| 4. | Mostly agree | | 17. | Mostly agree |
| 5. | Mostly disagree | | 18. | Mostly agree |
| 6. | Mostly agree | | 19. | Mostly disagree |
| 7. | Mostly disagree | | 20. | Mostly agree |
| 8. | Mostly agree | | 21. | Mostly agree |
| 9. | Mostly agree | | 22. | Mostly agree |
| 10. | Mostly disagree | | 23. | Mostly agree |
| 11. | Mostly agree | | 24. | Mostly disagree |
| 12. | Mostly disagree | | 25. | Mostly agree |
| 13. | Mostly disagree | | | |

**20–25**   You carry out a well-above-average number of positive team roles. Behavior of this type contributes substantially to being an effective team player. Study the information in this chapter to build upon your already laudable sensitivity to occupying various positive roles within the team.

**10–19**   You carry out an average number of positive team roles. Study carefully the roles described in this chapter to search for ways to carry out a greater number of positive roles.

**0–9**   You carry out a substantially above average number of negative team roles. If becoming an effective team player is important to you, you will have to diligently search for ways to play positive team roles. Study the information in this chapter carefully.

will help you evaluate your present inclinations toward occupying effective roles as a team member. In this section we describe a number of the most frequently observed positive roles played by team members. [15] We also mention a group of negative roles. The description is followed by an activity in which the roles can be practiced.

According to the role theory developed by R. Meredith Belbin and his group of researchers, there are nine frequent roles occupied by team members. All of these roles are influenced to some extent by an individual's personality.

1. **Creative problem solver.** The creative problem solver is creative, imaginative, and unorthodox. Such a person solves difficult problems. A potential weakness of this role is that the person tends to ignore fine details and becomes too immersed in the problem to communicate effectively.

2. **Resource investigator.** The resource investigator is extraverted and enthusiastic, and communicates freely with other team members. He or she will explore opportunities and develop valuable contacts. A potential weakness of this role is that the person can be overly optimistic and may lose interest after the initial enthusiasm wanes.

3. **Coordinator.** The coordinator is mature, confident, and a natural team leader. He or she clarifies goals, promotes decision making, and delegates effectively. A downside to occupying this role is that the person might be seen as manipulative and controlling. Some coordinators delegate too much by asking others to do some of the work they (the coordinators) should be doing.

4. **Shaper.** The shaper is challenging, dynamic, and thrives under pressure. He or she will use determination and courage to overcome obstacles. A potential weakness of the shaper is that he or she can be easily provoked and may ignore the feelings of others.

5. **Monitor-evaluator.** The monitor-evaluator is even tempered, engages in strategic (big picture and long-term) thinking, and makes accurate judgments. He or she sees all the options and judges accurately. A potential weakness of this role occupant is that he or she might lack drive and the ability to inspire others.

6. **Team worker.** The team worker is cooperative, focuses on relationships, and is sensitive and diplomatic. He or she is a good listener who builds relationships, dislikes confrontation, and averts friction. A potential weakness is that the team worker can be indecisive in a crunch situation or crisis.

7. **Implementer.** The implementer is disciplined, reliable, conservative, and efficient. He or she will act quickly on ideas, and convert them into practical actions. A potential weakness is that the implementer can be inflexible and slow to see new opportunities.

8. **Completer-finisher.** The completer-finisher is conscientious and eager to get the job done. He or she has a good eye for detail, and is effective at searching out errors. He or she can be counted on for finishing a project and

delivering on time. A potential weakness is that the completer-finisher can be a worrier and reluctant to delegate.

9. **Specialist.** The specialist is a single-minded self-starter. He or she is dedicated and provides knowledge and skill in rare supply. A potential weakness of the specialist is that he or she can be stuck in a niche with little interest in other knowledge and may dwell on technicalities.

The weaknesses in the first nine roles point to problems the team leader or manager can expect to emerge, and therefore an allowance should be made. Belbin refers to these potential problems as *allowable weaknesses* because an allowance should be made for them. To illustrate, if a team worker has a tendency to be indecisive in a crisis, the team should not have high expectations of the team worker when faced with a crisis. Team workers will be the most satisfied if the crisis is predicted and decisions involving them are made before the pressure mounts. [16]

Another perspective on team roles is that team members will sometimes engage in *self-oriented* roles. Members will sometimes focus on their own needs rather than those of the group. The individual might be overly aggressive because of a personal need such as wanting a bigger budget for his or her project. The individual might hunger for recognition or power. Similarly, the person might attempt to dominate the meeting, block others from contributing, or serve as a distraction. One of the ploys used by distracters recently is to engage in cell phone conversations during a meeting, blaming it on "those people who keep calling me."

The many roles just presented overlap somewhat. For example, the implementer might engage in specialist activities. Do not be concerned about the overlap. Instead, pick and choose from the many roles as the situation dictates—whether or not overlap exists. Skill-Building Exercise 6-1 gives you an opportunity to observe these roles in action. The behavior associated with the roles just described is more important than remembering the labels. For example, remembering to be creative and imaginative is more important than remembering the specific label "creative problem solver."

■ **Learning Objective 4**

# Guidelines for the Interpersonal Aspects of Team Play

The purpose of this and the following section is to help you enhance your effectiveness as a team player by describing the skills, actions, and attitudes required to be an effective team player. You can regard these behaviors (the collective term for skills, actions, and attitudes) as goals for personal improvement. Identify the actions and attitudes for which you need the most improvement, and proceed accordingly with self-development.

One convenient method for classifying team activities in pursuit of goals is to categorize them as people related or task related. Remember, however, that the categorization of people- versus task-related activities is not entirely accurate. For example, if you are challenging your teammates

# Skill-Building Exercise 6-1

## Team Member Roles

A team of approximately six people is formed to conduct a 20-minute meeting on a significant topic of their choosing. The possible scenarios follow:

**Scenario A: Management Team.** A group of managers are pondering whether to lay off one-third of the workforce to increase profits. The company has had a tradition of caring for employees and regarding them as the company's most precious asset. However, the CEO has said privately that times have changed in our competitive world, and the company must do whatever possible to enhance profits. The group wants to think through the advisability of laying off one-third of the workforce, as well as explore other alternatives.

**Scenario B: Group of Sports Fans.** A group of fans have volunteered to find a new team name to replace "Redskins" for the local basketball team. One person among the group of volunteers believes that the name "Redskins" should be retained because it is a compliment, rather than an insult to Native Americans. The other members of the group believe that a name change is in order, but they lack any good ideas for replacing a mascot team name that has endured for over 50 years.

**Scenario C: Community Group.** A community group is attempting to launch an initiative to help battered adults and children. Opinions differ strongly as to what initiative would be truly helpful to battered adults and children. Among the alternatives are establishing a shelter for battered people, giving workshops on preventing violence, and providing self-defense training. Each group member with an idea strongly believes that he or she has come up with a workable possibility for helping with the problem of battered people.

While the team members are conducting their heated discussion, other class members make notes on which team members carry out which roles. Students should watch for the different roles as developed by Belbin and his associates, as well as the self-oriented roles. For example, students in the first row might look for examples of the creative problem solver.

Use the role worksheet that follows to help make your observations. Summarize the comment that is indicative of the role. An example would be noting in the shaper category: "Linda said naming the team the 'Washington Rainbows' seems like too much of an attempt to be politically correct."

Creative Problem Solver _____

Resource Investigator _____

Coordinator _____

Shaper _____

Monitor-Evaluator _____

*(Continued)*

## Skill-Building Exercise 6-1  *(Continued)*

Team Worker _____

Implementer _____

Completer-Finisher _____

Specialist _____

Self-Oriented Roles _____

Understanding team member roles will contribute to working effectively as a member of a team. However, a contributor to the foundation of effective team play is recognizing individual differences and having good communication skills. The same two factors are fundamental for effectiveness in any setting involving interaction between and among people. Here is an example of how recognizing individual differences and having effective communication skills can help in a team setting: Max and Beth are teammates, and Max notices that Beth is shy and somewhat sullen. (He observes individual differences.) Max gives Beth a playful fist in the air, and says, "Come on Beth, we need your contribution in the 10 o'clock meeting. You have one of the sharpest minds on the team, and you're hiding it from us." With such warm encouragement, Beth then has the courage to contribute more to the morning meeting.

**Figure 6-2**

**Interpersonal Aspects of Team Play**

1. Trust team members.
2. Display a high level of cooperation and collaboration.
3. Recognize the interests and achievements of others.
4. Give and receive helpful criticism.
5. Share the glory.
6. Take care not to rain on another person's parade.

with a difficult goal, are you focusing more on the people (offering them a motivational challenge) or the task (achieving the goal)? We begin first with people-related actions and attitudes (see also Figure 6-2), followed in the next section by task-related actions and attitudes.

## TRUST TEAM MEMBERS

The cornerstone attitude of an outstanding team player is to trust team members, including the leader. Working on a team is akin to a small business partnership. If you do not believe that the other team members have your best interests at heart, it will be difficult for you to share opinions and ideas. You will fear that others will make negative statements behind your back.

Trusting team members also includes believing that their ideas are technically sound and rational until proven otherwise. Another manifestation of trust is taking risks with others. You can take a risk by trying out one of their unproved ideas. You can also take a risk by submitting an unproved idea and not worrying about being ridiculed.

## DISPLAY A HIGH LEVEL OF COOPERATION AND COLLABORATION

Cooperation and collaboration are synonymous with teamwork. If you display a willingness to help others by working cooperatively with them, you will be regarded as a team player. If you do not cooperate with other team members, the team structure breaks down. Collaboration at a team level refers to working jointly with others to solve mutual problems. Although working with another person on a given problem may take longer than working through a problem alone, the long-term payoff is important. You have established a climate favorable to working on joint problems where collective action is necessary.

Achieving a cooperative team spirit is often a question of making the first move. Instead of grumbling about poor teamwork, take the initiative and launch a cooperative spirit in your group. Target the most individualistic, least cooperative member of the group. Ask the person for his or her input on an idea you are formulating. Thank the person, then state that you would be privileged to return the favor.

Another way of attaining good cooperation is to minimize confrontations. If you disagree with the opinion of another team member, patiently explain the reasons for your differences and look for a workable way to integrate both your ideas. A teammate might suggest, for example, that the team stay until midnight to get a project completed today. You have plans for the evening and are angered by the suggestion. Instead of lashing out at your teammate, you might say, "I agree we need to put in extra time and effort to get the job done. But why can't we spread out this extra effort over a few days? In this way those of us who cannot work until midnight this evening can still contribute."

Skill-Building Exercise 6-2 is a widely used technique for demonstrating the importance of cooperation and collaboration.

## RECOGNIZE THE INTERESTS AND ACHIEVEMENTS OF OTHERS

A fundamental tactic for establishing yourself as a solid team player is to actively recognize the interests and achievements of others. Let others know you care about their interests. After you make a suggestion during a team meeting, ask: "Would my suggestion create any problems for anybody else?" or "How do my ideas fit into what you have planned?"

Recognizing the achievements of others is more straightforward than recognizing interests. Be prepared to compliment any tangible achievement. Give realistic compliments by making the compliment commensurate with the achievement. To do otherwise is to compromise your sincerity. For example, do not call someone a genius just because he or she showed you how to compute an exchange rate from one currency to another. Instead, you might say, "Thank you. I am very impressed by your knowledge of exchange rates."

## Skill-Building Exercise 6-2

### The Scavenger Hunt

The purpose of this teamwork exercise is to demonstrate the importance of cooperation and collaboration in accomplishing a task under pressure. The class is divided into teams of about five students. How much time you can devote to the task depends upon your particular class schedule. The instructor will supply each team with a list of items to find within a prescribed period of time—usually about 35 minutes. Given the time constraints, the group will usually have to conduct the hunt on campus. What follows is a representative list of items to find in an on-campus scavenger hunt:

- A floppy disk
- A tie
- A brick
- A cap from a beer bottle
- A pocket knife
- A flash drive

When the groups return within 30 minutes, you hold a public discussion about what you learned about teamwork and what insights you acquired.

A technique has been developed to enable the entire team to recognize the interests and achievements of others. Playing the anonymous praise game, each team member lists what he or she admires about a specific coworker. The team leader collects the responses and sends each team member the comments made about him or her. Using this technique, team members see a compilation of praise based on how coworkers perceive them. The anonymous praise game helps overcome the hesitancy some people have to praise another person face-to-face. [17]

## GIVE AND RECEIVE HELPFUL CRITICISM

The outstanding team player offers constructive criticism when needed, but does so diplomatically. To do otherwise is to let down the team. A high-performance team demands sincere and tactful criticism among members. No matter how diplomatic you are, keep your ratio of criticism to praise small. Keep two time-tested principles in mind. First, attempt to criticize the person's work, not the person. It is better to say "The conclusion is missing from your analysis" than "You left out the conclusion." (The latter statement hurts because it sounds like your teammate did something wrong.)

Another key guideline for criticism is to ask a question rather than to make a declarative statement. By answering a question, the person being criticized is involved in improving his or her work. In the example at hand, it would be effective to ask, "Do you think your report would have a greater impact if it contained a conclusion?" In this way, the person being criticized contributes a judgment about the conclusion. The person has a chance to say, "Yes, I will prepare a conclusion."

Criticism works both ways, so the effective team player is willing to accept helpful criticism, such as "You are speaking too fast for several of our team members for whom English is their second language." Becky Blalock, the vice president and chief information officer (CIO) of the electric utility, the Southern Company, regards being open to feedback as one of the core principles of teamwork. [18]

## SHARE THE GLORY

An effective team player shares praise and other rewards for accomplishment even if he or she is the most deserving. Shared praise is usually merited to some extent because teammates have probably made at least some contribution to the achievement that received praise. For example, if a team member comes up with a powerful suggestion for cutting costs, it is likely that somebody else in the group sparked his or her thinking. Effective examples of sharing glory are easy to find. Think back to watching athletes and other entertainers who win a title or an award. Many of them are gracious enough to share the glory. Shortly after he retired, hockey legend Wayne Gretzky told a television reporter, "I never would have accomplished what I did if I hadn't played with such a great group of guys."

## TAKE CARE NOT TO RAIN ON ANOTHER PERSON'S PARADE

As teamwork specialist Pamela Lovell observes, we all have achievements and accomplishments that are sources of pride. Belittling the achievements of others for no legitimate reason brings about tension and anger. Suppress your feelings of petty jealousy. [19] An example would be saying to someone who is proudly describing an accomplishment, "Don't take too much credit. It looks to me like you were at the right place at the right time." If you support teammates by acknowledging their accomplishments, you are more likely to receive their support when needed.

# Guidelines for the Task Aspects of Team Play

■ Learning Objective 5

The task aspects of team play also make a key contribution to becoming an effective team player. Here we describe six major task-related tactics, as outlined in Figure 6-3. As mentioned earlier, a task aspect usually has interpersonal consequences.

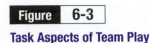

**Task Aspects of Team Play**

1. Provide technical expertise (or knowledge of the task).
2. Assume responsibility for problems.
3. See the big picture.
4. Believe in consensus.
5. Focus on deadlines.
6. Help team members do their jobs better.
7. Be a good organizational citizen.

## PROVIDE TECHNICAL EXPERTISE (OR KNOWLEDGE OF THE TASK)

Most people are selected for a work team primarily because of their technical expertise. *Technical* refers to the intimate details of any task, not just tasks in engineering, physical science, and information technology. The sales promotion specialist on a product development team has technical expertise about sales promotion, whether or not sales promotion requires knowledge of engineering or computers.

As team consultant Glenn Parker observes, to use your technical expertise to outstanding advantage you must have the willingness to share that expertise. [20] Some experts perceive their esoteric knowledge as a source of power. As a consequence, they are hesitant to let others share their knowledge for fear of relinquishing power. It is also necessary for the technical expert to be able to communicate with team members in other disciplines who lack the same technical background. The technical person who cannot explain the potential value of his or her contribution may fail to receive much attention.

## ASSUME RESPONSIBILITY FOR PROBLEMS

The outstanding team player assumes responsibilities for problems. If a problem is not yet assigned to anybody, he or she says, "I'll do it." One team member might note that true progress on the team's effort is blocked until the team benchmarks (compares itself) with other successful teams. The effective team player might say, "You are right, we need to benchmark. If it's okay with everybody else, I'll get started on the benchmarking project tomorrow. It will be my responsibility." Taking responsibility must be combined with dependability. The person who takes responsibility for a task must produce, time after time.

## SEE THE BIG PICTURE

Effective team players need to think conceptually, or see the big picture. A trap in team effort is that discussion can get bogged down in small details and the team might lose sight of what it is trying to accomplish. The team player (including the team leader) who can help the group focus on its broader purpose plays a vital role. The following case history illustrates what it means to see the big picture.

*A group of retail sales associates and customer service representatives were sent to a one-day seminar about customer-service training. The group was sent to training because customer-service ratings at their store were below the level store executives thought acceptable. During the lunch breaks, the conversation quickly turned to the fact that the coffee was not as hot as desired, the snacks were mediocre, the restrooms were too far from the meeting room, and the presenter had a phony smile and told goofy jokes. Next came a few complaints about a couple of the PowerPoint slides having too much detail.*

*Alyssa, an experienced sales associate, stepped in with a comment. She noted, "I think all of you have valid complaints, but your points are minor. We are here to learn how to improve customer service. If we want our store to survive, and for us to earn bigger bonuses, we have to learn what we can to help us do our jobs better. Whether or not you like our trainer's smile or jokes, he is trying to be helpful." The group returned after lunch with a more determined effort to focus on the purpose of the seminar—picking up ideas to improve customer service.*

## BELIEVE IN CONSENSUS

A major task-related attitude for outstanding team play is to believe that consensus has merit. **Consensus** is general acceptance of a decision by the group. Every member may not be thrilled about the decision, yet they are unopposed and are willing to support the decision. Believing that consensus is valuable enables you to participate fully in team decisions without thinking that you have sacrificed your beliefs or the right to think independently. To believe in consensus is to believe that the democratic process has relevance for organizations and that ideal solutions are not always possible.

■ **Consensus**
general acceptance by the group of a decision

## FOCUS ON DEADLINES

A notable source of individual differences among work group members is how much importance they attach to deadlines. Some work group members may regard deadlines as a moral contract, to be missed only in case of emergency. Others may view deadlines as an arbitrary date imposed by someone external to the group. Other work group members may perceive deadlines as moderately important. Differences in perception about the importance of deadlines influence the group's ability to meet deadlines. [21]

## Skill-Building Exercise 6-3

### Habitat for Homeless People

Organize the class into teams of about six people. Each team takes on the assignment of formulating plans for building temporary shelters for homeless people. The task will take about one hour and can be done inside or outside the class. The dwellings you plan to build, for example, might be two-room cottages with electricity and indoor plumbing.

During the time allotted to the task, formulate plans for going ahead with Habitat for Homeless People. Consider dividing up work by assigning certain roles to each team member. Sketch out tentative answers to the following questions:

1. How will you obtain funding for your venture?
2. Which homeless people will you help?
3. Where will your shelters be located?
4. Who will do the actual construction?

After your plan is completed, evaluate the quality of the teamwork that took place within the group. Specify which teamwork skills were evident and which ones did not surface. Search the chapter for techniques you might use to improve teamwork. The skills used to accomplish the habitat task could relate to the team skills the interpersonal aspects of team play, the task aspects of team play, or some team skill not mentioned in this chapter. Here is a sampling of the many different skills that might be relevant in this exercise:

- Speaks effectively
- Listens to others
- Innovates solutions to problems
- Thinks outside the box
- Displays a high level of cooperation and collaboration
- Provides knowledge of the task
- Sees the big picture
- Focuses on deadlines

Keeping the group focused on the deadline is a valuable task behavior because meeting deadlines is vital to team success. Discussing the importance of the deadlines is helpful because of the varying attitudes about deadlines likely to be found among group members.

## HELP TEAM MEMBERS DO THEIR JOBS BETTER

Your stature as a team player will increase if you take the initiative to help coworkers make needed work improvements. Helping other team members

## Self-Assessment Quizzes in Overview

Self-Assessment Quiz 6-1 gave you an opportunity to think through the extent to which you really enjoy, or are interested, in teamwork. Being part of a close-knit team is important for many types of work, but there is always room for some people who prefer to work alone doing analytical or creative work. For example, at Microsoft Corp. the office layout gives space to people who want to work alone and not be distracted by other people. Self-Assessment Quiz 6-2 follows up your interests and attitudes about teamwork with an opportunity to review your skills. Interest and skills are not the same. A given individual who likes the idea of skydiving might lack the eye—hand coordination to pull the cord under pressure, and therefore would be a disaster as a skydiver.

If you have the attitudes for teamwork, another subtle factor about teamwork can influence your effectiveness. As measured in Self-Assessment Quiz 6-3, your level of conformity can influence your effectiveness. Too much or too little conformity can detract from your effectiveness. Self-Assessment Quiz 6-4 takes you even further into the intricacies of teamwork by measuring your tendency to play positive team roles. With few exceptions, a person needs to focus on positive team roles to be a successful team member.

with their work assignments is a high-level form of cooperation. Make the suggestions in a constructive spirit rather than displaying an air of superiority. Identify a problem that a coworker is having, and then suggest alternatives he or she might be interested in exploring. Avoid saying to team members that they "should" do something, because many people become defensive when told what they should do. The term *should* is usually perceived as a moral judgment given to one person by another, such as being told that you should save money, should learn a second language, or should improve your math skills.

## BE A GOOD ORGANIZATIONAL CITIZEN

A comprehensive way of carrying out the task aspects of team play (as well as relationship aspects) is to help out beyond the requirements of your job description. As discussed in Chapter 3, such extra-role activity is referred to as "organizational citizenship behavior"—working for the good of the organization even without the promise of a specific reward. As a result of many workers being good organizational citizens, the organization functions more effectively in such ways as improved product quantity and quality. [22] Good citizenship on the job encompasses many specific behaviors, including helping a coworker with a job task and refraining from complaints or petty grievances. A good organizational citizen would carry out such specific acts as picking up litter in the company parking lot. He or she would also bring a reference to the office that could help a coworker solve a job problem. Most of the other team player tactics described here are related to organizational citizenship behavior.

Two experiments, one with business students and one with managers, suggested that organizational citizenship behavior is even more important when people depend on each other to accomplish a task. [23] An example is filling an order with components from different departments. Given that most tasks on a team are interdependent, organizational citizenship behavior is quite important for effective teamwork.

# Concept Review and Reinforcement

## Key Terms

Team, 170
Self-managing work team, 172
Cross-functional team, 172

Virtual team, 174
Crew, 175
Synergy, 176

Social loafing, 177
Groupthink, 177
Consensus, 191

## Summary of Key Concepts

To be successful in the modern organization it is necessary to be an effective team player. Team members have complementary skills and are committed to a common purpose. All teams have some elements in common, but four key types of teams are self-managing work teams, cross-functional teams, virtual teams, and crews. (A virtual team does most of its work electronically instead of in face-to-face meetings.)

Groups and teams offer such advantages as gaining synergy, avoiding major errors, and gaining increased acceptance of and commitment to decisions. Working in groups can also enhance job satisfaction. Groups and teams also have disadvantages, such as more talk than action, conformity in thinking and action, social loafing, and the creation of conflict. A serious potential problem is groupthink, whereby bad decisions are made as a by-product of strong consensus. Key characteristics of effective work groups are outlined in Figure 6-1.

An important part of being an effective team player is to choose effective roles. The roles studied here are: creative problem solver, resource investigator, coordinator, shaper, monitor-evaluator, team worker, implementer, completer-finisher, and specialist. Self-oriented roles are less effective and detract from group productivity. Understanding roles does not supplant the need for recognizing individual differences and communicating well.

Guidelines for effectively contributing to the interpersonal aspects of team play include (1) trusting team members, (2) displaying a high level of cooperation and collaboration, (3) recognizing the interests and achievements of others, (4) giving and receiving helpful criticism, (5) sharing the glory, and (6) taking care not to rain on another person's parade.

Guidelines for effectively contributing to the task aspects of team play include (1) providing technical expertise, (2) assuming responsibility for problems, (3) seeing the big picture, (4) believing in consensus, (5) focusing on deadlines, and (6) helping team members do their jobs better.

## Check Your Understanding

1. Part of being a good team player is helping other members. How can members of a workplace team help each other?
2. How do team members know when they have achieved synergy?
3. What should the other team members do when they uncover a social loafer?
4. What is the potential downside of heavily emphasizing the *specialist* role?

5. How can the *monitor-evaluator* role backfire for a person?
6. Assume that you are a team member. What percent of your pay would you be willing to have based on a group reward? Explain your reasoning.
7. Many retail companies, banks, and medical offices require customer-contact employees to wear the same uniform. In what ways might these uniforms enhance teamwork?
8. A number of companies have sent employees to a team-building exercise in which they prepare a gourmet meal. Why would preparing a gourmet meal help build teamwork?
9. The "little picture" in studying this chapter is learning details about teamwork skills. What is the "big picture"?
10. How can a person achieve individual recognition yet still be a team player?

## The Web Corner

http://www.adventureassoc.com/workshops/teamwork.html
(Development of teamwork skills, including the use of the MBTI.)

http://www.quintcareers.com/team_player_quiz.html
(Take the quiz, "Are You a Team Player? A Quintessential Careers Quiz.")

### Internet Skill Builder: Becoming a Better Team Player
The purpose of this exercise duplicates the major purpose of the chapter—finding practical suggestions for improving your teamwork skills. Visit several Web sites that deal with enhancing teamwork skills from the standpoint of the individual, not the manager. An example of such a Web site is http://www.confidencecenter.com. Write down at least three concrete suggestions you find, and compare these suggestions to those made in this chapter. If the opportunity arises, practice one of these skills in the next 10 days and observe the results.

# Developing Your Human Relations Skills

### Mark Wants to Look Good

Certified public accountant (CPA) Mark was looking for a way to document his contribution to a team whose work directly supported the mission of his firm. Mark's firm was experiencing a business plateau. As more large business firms gobbled up smaller companies, the demand for accounting services decreased. (Fewer companies were available to hire accountants.) In addition, more companies were doing their work internally and using software to replace some of the contributions of outside accountants.

Mark served on a client-development team that uncovered several productive ways of expanding the firm's practice. Among these initiatives was to advertise and hold tax seminars free to the public. The team received ample credit from the senior partners for helping the accounting practice grow. However, Mark believed that he deserved more credit than several of the other team members. Nevertheless, he did not want to appear tacky by stating this observation to the senior partners. Instead, he wrote an e-mail message describing his contribution without asking for credit. His e-mail stated:

Hello Senior Partners,

Thanks for the opportunity to serve on the client-development team. I'm pleased that the team accomplished its mission. My major assignment was to conduct tax seminars for the public. I am so pleased that the team accomplished its mission. I found that to be a professionally rewarding experience. Should the opportunity arise to help the firm again by conducting seminars, please consider me a candidate.

Sincerely,

Mark Davenport

Mark thought to himself, "This e-mail should work. I'll be seen as a fine team player and a great individual contributor at the same time."

#### Case Questions

1. What is your evaluation of Mark as a team player?
2. If Mark had asked your advice about sending this e-mail, what would you have told him?
3. If you were a senior partner in Mark's firm, how would you reply to his memo?

### Ruth Waves a Red Flag

Carlos is the team leader of a cost-reduction team within a well-established baked-goods company that produces bakery products under its own label, as well as private labels for grocery-store chains such as Giant and Winn-Dixie. Top-level management formed the team to arrive at suggestions for reducing costs throughout the organization. A transcript of one of the meetings is presented next.

Carlos: We've been gathering information for a month now. It's about time we heard some specific suggestions.

Jack: At the top of my list is cutting pension benefits. Our pension payments are higher than the minimum required by law. Our medical benefits are way above average. If we cut back on pension benefits, no current employees would be adversely affected.

Melissa: I like your analysis, Jack. No sense risking laying off employees just to keep retirees happy.

Jordan: We should make absolutely certain there are no legal complications here. Then we can sharpen our cost-cutting knives and dig right in.

Gunther: I'd support cutting pension benefits. It would probably reduce expenses more dramatically than the ways I have uncovered.

Carlos: There seems to be consensus so far that we should considered making recommendations about cutting pension benefits. Ruth, what do you think?

Ruth: I think it is much too early to reach consensus on such a sensitive issue. Cutting pension benefits would create panic among our retirees. Our older employees would be screaming as well. We'll have an avalanche of negative publicity in the media.

Jordan: Hold on, Ruth. I said the team should first check out this idea with the legal department.

Ruth: Just because cutting pension benefits could squeeze by legally doesn't mean that it's a good idea. We haven't examined the negative ramifications of cutting pension benefits. Let's study this issue further before word leaks out that we're taking away the golden egg.

Carlos: Maybe Ruth has a point. Let's investigate this issue further before making a recommendation.

## Case Questions

1. What role, or roles, is Ruth occupying on the cost-reduction team?
2. How effective does she appear to be in her role?
3. What role, or roles, is Jack occupying on the cost-reduction team?
4. How effective does he appear to be in his role?
5. How effective is Carlos in his role as a team leader?

# REFERENCES

1. Josh Hyatt, "The Soul of a New Team," *Fortune*, June 12, 2006. pp. 134, 135.
2. Conference Board report cited in "CEO Leadership Skips Teamwork, Article Says," *Rochester Democrat and Chronicle*, February 17, 2002, p. 1E.
3. Jon R. Katzenbach and Douglas K. Smith, "The Discipline of Teams," Harvard Business Review, March–April 1993, p. 112.
4. Deal E. Yeatts and Coyd Hyten, *High Performing Self-Managed Work Teams: A Comparison of Theory and Practice* (Thousands Oaks, CA: Sage, 1998), p. xiii.
5. Rudy M. Yandrick, "A Team Effort," *HR Magazine*, June 2001, p. 138.
6. Claus W. Langfred, "Too Much Trust a Good Thing? Negative Effects of High Trust and Individual Autonomy in Self-Managing Teams," *Academy of Management Journal*, June 2004, pp. 385–399.
7. "Shepherding Communications When the Flock Is Scattered," *Flexible Workplace Management*, sample issue, 2001.
8. Arvind Malhotra, Ann Majchrzak, and Benson Rosen, "Leading Virtual Teams," *Academy of Management Perspectives*, February 2007, p. 62.
9. Shelia Simsarian Webber and Richard J. Klimoski, "Crews: A Distinct Type of Work Team," *Journal of Business and Psychology*, Spring 2004, pp. 261–279.
10. Carol Hymowitz, "A High-Seas Race Can Tell Tales about Executive Roles," *The Wall Street Journal*, August 9, 2005, p. B1.
11. Matt Bolch, "Rewarding the Team," *HR Magazine*, February 2007, pp. 91–93.
12. "When Committees Spell Trouble: Don't Let Individuals Hide Within a Group," *WorkingSMART*, August 1998, p. 1; Ross Kerber, "For Abigail Johnson, a Leadership Test," *The Boston Globe* (http://www.boston.com), August 21, 2007, p. 1.
13. Irving L. Janus, *Victims of Groupthink: A Psychological Study of Foreign Policy Decisions and Fiascos* (Boston: Houghton Mifflin, 1972); Glen Whyte, "Groupthink Reconsidered," *Academy of Management Review*, January 1989, pp. 40–56.
14. Martha A. Peak, "Treating Trauma in Teamland," *Management Review*, September 1997, p. 1.
15. "R. Meredith Belbin," in *Business: The Ultimate Resource* (Cambridge, MA: Perseus, 2002), pp. 966–967; Belbin, *Management Teams* (London: Elsevier Butterworth-Heinemann, 2003); Belbin® Team-Roles, http://www.belbin.com/belbin-team roles.htm.
16. From a review of Meredith Belbin, *Management Teams*, by Colin Thomson, appearing in http://www.accountingweb.co.uk, accessed April 14, 2004.
17. "Fly in Formation: Easy Ways to Build Team Spirit," *WorkingSMART*, March 2000, p. 6.
18. "Score a Perfect '10' on Teamwork," *Manager's Edge*, May 2006, p. 1.
19. Pamela Lovell, "Healthy Teams Display Strong Vital Signs," *Teamwork*, sample issue, the Dartnell Corporation, 1997.
20. Glenn M. Parker, *Cross-Functional Teams: Working with Allies, Enemies, & Other Strangers* (San Francisco: Jossey-Bass, 1994), p. 170.
21. Mary J. Waller et al., "The Effect of Individual Perceptions of Deadlines on Team Performance," *Academy of Management Review*, October 2001, p. 597.
22. Mark G. Ehrhant and Stefanie E. Naumann, "Organizational Citizenship Behavior in Work Groups: A Group Norms Approach," *Journal of Applied Psychology*, December 2004, pp. 960–974.
23. Daniel G. Bachrach, Benjamin C. Powell, Elliot Bendoly, and R. Glenn Richey, "Organizational Citizenship Behavior and Performance Evaluations: Exploring the Impact of Task Interdependence," *Journal of Applied Psychology*, January 2006, pp. 193–201.

# 7

# Diversity and Cross-Cultural Competence

## Learning Objectives

After studying the information and doing the exercises in this chapter, you should be able to:

1 Explain some of the major ways in which cultures differ from one another.

2 Pinpoint barriers to cross-cultural relations.

3 Describe techniques for improving cross-cultural relations.

4 Be sensitive to potential cultural bloopers.

5 Be prepared to overcome cross-cultural communication barriers.

6 Recognize and understand gender differences in leadership style.

7 Be aware of some of the legal aspects of working in a culturally diverse environment.

## Outline

1 **What Are the Major Dimensions of Differences in Cultural Values?** 202
Multicultural Identities and the Cultural Mosaic
Applying Knowledge of Cultural Differences in Values

2 **What Are Some Barriers to Good Cross-Cultural Relations?** 206
Perceptual Expectations
Ethnocentrism
Stereotypes in Intergroup Relations
Different Norms and Codes of Conduct
Microinequities

3 **What Are Some Approaches to Improving Cross-Cultural Relations?** 209
Develop Cultural Sensitivity and Cultural Intelligence
Focus on Individuals Rather Than Groups
Respect All Workers and Cultures
Value Cultural Differences
Minimize Cultural Bloopers
Participate in Cultural Training
Participate in Diversity

4 **How Do You Overcome Cross-Cultural Communication Barriers?** 219

5 **Why Are Gender Differences in Leadership Style Regarded as Cultural Differences?** 221

6 **What Are Some of the Legal Aspects of Working in a Culturally Diverse Environment?** 222
Federal Laws Prohibiting Job Discrimination
Affirmative Action

S oon after he arrived at the Wegmans Food Market Stores in Dulles, Virginia, executive chef Llewellyn Correia discovered that many of the 120 employees he supervised had not been attending the company's mandatory safety and sanitation classes. The reason he said: "The courses were in English, and many of my employees don't speak English."

Correia said some of his Asian cooks needed training in U.S. food handling standards, which are more rigorous than the ones in their home countries and more likely to be enforced by government inspectors. "It's very hard to break old habits," he said. The lack of training also was raising safety issues. "We had lots of issues like slips and falls," he said.

Today, the Dulles Wegmans offers a Web-based version of its safety and sanitation courses in Mandarin and Spanish in addition to English—only one nod the supermarket says it is making to a multilingual workplace in which more than 200 of its 650 employees do not speak English as their primary language. Wegmans has hired language instructors for its Dulles and Fairfax, Virginia, stores to teach employees a bit more English and their managers un poco Español [a little Spanish].

Having a diverse workforce can boost sales and build loyalty among non-English–speaking customers who can ask a question—Are the Pepsi's 12-packs still on sale?—in their native languages. [1]

The supermarket experience described illustrates how people from different cultures can learn to work together, sometimes by using a basic technique such as offering training in several languages to facilitate learning. Being able to work well with people from other cultures, both outside and inside your own country, is important for career success. Being able to relate to a culturally diverse customer base is also necessary for success. Not only is the workforce becoming more diverse but also business has become increasingly international. Small and medium-size firms, as well as corporate giants, are increasingly dependent on trade with other countries. Furthermore, as an increasing number of jobs are sent overseas, more U.S. workers will have contact with personnel in foreign countries.

This chapter presents ideas and techniques you can use to sharpen your ability to work effectively with people from diverse backgrounds. The buzzword for this activity is to be *inclusive* in your relationships with people. We also include a discussion of antidiscrimination legislation that protects the rights of workers.

# What Are the Major Dimensions of Differences in Cultural Values?

■ **Learning Objective 1**

Everything we do in work and personal life is influenced by a combination of heredity and culture, or nature and nurture. You might be thirsty at this moment because a genetically produced mechanism in your brain tells you it is time to ingest fluid. However, if you choose to drink a Diet Pepsi or papaya juice with a coworker, you are engaging in culturally learned behavior. **Culture** is a learned and shared system of knowledge, beliefs, values, attitudes, and norms. As such, culture includes an enormous amount of behavior. Here we describe seven dimensions (or facets) of cultural values that help us understand how cultures differ from each other. [2] In other words, various cultures value different types of behavior.

Recognize that these dimensions are stereotypes, representing a typical value for a person in a given culture. You might find, for example, that most Chinese people are oriented more toward the group than seeking individual recognition. However, you might meet some Chinese people who are egotistical and self-centered.

■ **Culture**
a learned and shared system of knowledge, beliefs, values, attitudes, and norms

1. **Individualism versus collectivism.** At one end of the continuum is individualism, a mental set in which people see themselves first as individuals and believe that their own interests take priority. Members of a society who value individualism are more concerned with their careers than with the good of the firm. Members of a society who value collectivism, in contrast, are typically more concerned with the organization or the work group than with themselves. An example of individualistic behavior would be to want to win an employee-of-the month award; an example of collectivisitic behavior would be to want to win an award for the team. Highly individualistic cultures include the Unites States, Canada, and the Netherlands. Japan and Mexico are among the countries that strongly value collectivism. However, with the increasing emphasis on teamwork in American culture, more U.S. workers are becoming collectivistic.

2. **Acceptance of power and authority.** People from some cultures accept the idea that members of an organization have different levels of power and authority. In a culture that believes in concentration of power and authority, the boss makes many decisions simply because he or she is the boss. Group members readily comply because they have a positive orientation toward authority, including high respect for elders. In a culture with less acceptance of power and authority, employees do not recognize a power hierarchy. They accept directions only when they think the boss is right or when they feel threatened. Cultures that readily accept power and authority include France, China, and India. Countries that have much less acceptance of power and authority are the United States and, particularly, the Scandinavian countries (e.g., Sweden).

3. **Materialism versus concern for others.** In this context, materialism refers to an emphasis on assertiveness and the acquisition of money and material objects. It also means a deemphasis on caring for others. At the other end of the continuum is concern for others, an emphasis on personal relations, and a concern for the welfare of others. Materialistic countries include Japan and Italy. The United States is considered to be moderately materialistic, as evidenced by the high participation rates in charities. Scandinavian countries all emphasize caring as a national value.

4. **Formality versus informality.** A country that values formality attaches considerable importance to tradition, ceremony, social rules, and rank. At the other extreme, informality refers to a casual attitude toward these same aspects of culture. Workers in Latin American countries highly value formality, such as lavish public receptions and processions. Americans, Canadians, and

Scandinavians are much more informal. Casual observation suggests that most of the industrialized world is becoming more informal through such practices as an emphasis on using the first name only during business introductions.

**5. Urgent time orientation versus casual time orientation.** Individuals and nations attach different importance to time. People with an urgent time orientation perceive time as a scarce resource and tend to be impatient. People with a casual time orientation view time as an unlimited and unending resource and tend to be patient. Americans are noted for their urgent time orientation. They frequently impose deadlines and are eager to get started doing business. Asians and Middle Easterners, in contrast, are patient negotiators. Many corporate workers and entrepreneurs engaged in international business recognize the importance of building relationships slowly overseas.

**6. Work orientation versus leisure orientation.** A major cultural difference is the number of hours per week and weeks per year people expect to invest in work versus leisure or other nonwork activities. American corporate professionals typically work about 55 hours per week, take 45-minute lunch breaks, and take two weeks of vacation. Japanese workers share similar values with respect to time invested in work. In contrast, many European countries have steadily reduced the workweek in recent years while lengthening vacations.

**7. High-context versus low-context cultures.** Cultures differ in how much importance they attach to the surrounding circumstances, or context, of an event. People from a high-context culture place more emphasis on *how* something is said rather than *what* is said. (They emphasize nonverbal communication.) For example, a person from a high-context culture is not likely to take you seriously if you smile when you say that you do not like his or her service.

High-context cultures make more extensive use of body language as part of their emphasis on nonverbal communication. Some cultures, such as the Hispanic and African American cultures, are high context. In contrast, northern European cultures are low context and make less use of body language. The Anglo American culture is considered to be medium-low context. People in low-context cultures seldom take time in business dealings to build relationships and establish trust.

## MULTICULTURAL IDENTITIES AND THE CULTURAL MOSAIC

■ **Multicultural identities**
individuals who incorporate the values of two or more cultures because they identify with both their primary culture and another culture or cultures

Another complexity about understanding cultural differences is that many people have **multicultural identities** because they identify with both their primary culture and another culture or cultures. As a consequence, these people may incorporate the values of two cultures. Young people develop a global identity that gives them a feeling of belonging to a worldwide culture. The feeling of belongingness enables them to communicate with people from diverse places when they travel, when others travel to where they live, and when they communicate globally using e-mail and the telephone. Television and movies also help us develop a global identity.

Further, according to this theory, people retain a local identity along with their global identity. Young people in India provide an apt example.

The country has a rapidly growing high-tech sector led mostly by young people. Yet most of these well-educated young people still cling to local traditions, such as a marriage arranged by the parents and the expectation that they will care for their parents in old age. [3]

Another complexity of culture is that a person's country is but one cultural influence. For example, people from the upper-socioeconomic group within one country or ethnic group might value education and the use of grammatically correct speech more than people from a lower-socioeconomic group.

The fact of multicultural identities and different values among people from the same country and ethnic groups has recently been labeled the cultural mosaic by management professors Georgia T. Chao from Michigan State University and Henry Moon of Emory University. The **cultural mosaic** refers to an individual's unique mixture of multiple cultural identities that yields a complex picture of the cultural influences on that person. Rather than choosing a particular "tile" such as race, gender, or country of origin, people develop an identity based on a mix of smaller tiles. [4] Every reader of this book is probably an example of a cultural mosaic. One of thousands of possible examples is that one person could derive a cultural identity from being a (1) U.S. citizen, (2) African American, (3) Baptist, (4) male, (5) musician, (6) football player, (7) accountant, and (8) southerner.

■ **Cultural mosaic**
an individual's unique mixture of multiple cultural identities that yields a complex picture of the cultural influences on that person

The religious value part of the cultural mosaic often affects when people are willing to work or not work. One potential cultural clash is that the rights of an individual to freely practice and observe religious beliefs sometimes collide with company goals. Differences in religious practices must be recognized because the number of religions in the workplace has increased substantially.

Religious diversity can create problems as more companies move to 24/7 (around-the-clock, seven-days-per-week) schedules. Employers, therefore, need more flexibility from employees, yet religious beliefs often limit times at which employees are willing to work. The message for improved understanding is that employers must recognize workers' religious beliefs. At the same time, workers must understand the importance of a company meeting the demands of the marketplace, such as having 24-hour customer service support. Workers, for example, can trade off working on each others' religious holidays.

## APPLYING KNOWLEDGE OF CULTURAL DIFFERENCES IN VALUES

How might you use this information about cultural differences to improve interpersonal relationships on the job? A starting point would be to recognize that a person's national values might influence his or her behavior. Assume that you wanted to establish a good working relationship with a person from a high-context culture. Make sure your facial expression fits the content of your words. For example, do not smile when, as a supervisor, you say, "No, you cannot take off tomorrow afternoon to have your French Poodle groomed." You would also want to emphasize body language when communicating with that individual. A related point is that people from high-context cultures are more likely to touch and kiss strangers. As Fernando, who was raised in the Dominican Republic and is studying in the United States, said, "In my country I hug people I meet for the first time. When I do it here, they think I'm very rude."

# What Are Some Barriers to Good Cross-Cultural Relations?

■ **Learning Objective 2**

Many logical reasons exist as to why people often encounter difficulties in developing good relations and communicating with people from different cultures. The fact that cultures differ in key dimensions creates some friction in cross-cultural relations. A go-getter from Brooklyn, New York, might say to himself, "Why do I have to spend three days here in Hong Kong wining and dining customers just so I can sell them an enterprise software system?"

Here we look at several of the underlying factors that create problems in developing smooth cross-cultural relations. Not being aware of the type of barriers presented next blocks effective cross-cultural relations because such lack of awareness often leads to misunderstandings. The techniques presented in the following section of the chapter are designed to overcome some these barriers. To get you started thinking about your readiness to work in a culturally diverse environment, as well as to minimize cross-cultural barriers, take Human Relations Self-Assessment Quiz 7-1.

## PERCEPTUAL EXPECTATIONS

Achieving good cross-cultural relations is hampered somewhat by people's predisposition to discriminate. They do so as a perceptual shortcut, much like stereotyping. A bank customer, for example, might be communicating with a 24-year-old man about a mortgage application. Dissatisfied with his concerns about her creditworthiness, the customer might say, "Let me speak to a mortgage officer." In reality, the man *is* a mortgage officer, but the woman expects an older person to be occupying such a position. The message in this anecdote about perceptual expectations is important. We have to overcome this form of discrimination to enhance cross-cultural relations.

Positive expectations or stereotypes can also create some barriers to cross-cultural relations. Two company representatives were entertaining Sophie, a work associate from Jamaica. They assumed that because Sophie was black and Jamaican, she enjoyed dancing, so they invited her to a dance club. Sophie was a little taken back and said, "What makes you think I like to dance? Not every Jamaican lady has natural rhythm." Similarly, on the job, we sometimes think that everybody from a certain national group has the characteristics of that group. For example, not all Chinese workers are methodical or precise or have good eye–hand coordination and exceptional math skills.

## ETHNOCENTRISM

■ **Ethnocentrism**
the assumption that the ways of one's culture are the *best* ways of doing things

A key barrier to good cross-cultural relations is **ethnocentrism,** the assumption that the ways of one's culture are the *best* ways of doing things. Another part of ethnocentrism is to believe that our own way of living is essentially the only way. Most cultures consider themselves to be the center of the world, such as the French believing that any cultivated person must appreciate French painters and French wine. One consequence of ethnocentrism is that people from one culture prefer people from other cultures similar to themselves.

# Human Relations Self-Assessment Quiz 7–1

## Cross-Cultural Skills and Attitudes

Following are various skills and attitudes that various employers and cross-cultural experts think are important for relating effectively to coworkers in a culturally diverse environment.

| | Applies to Me Now | Not There Yet |
|---|---|---|
| 1. I have spent some time in another country. | _____ | _____ |
| 2. At least one of my friends is deaf or blind or uses a wheelchair. | _____ | _____ |
| 3. Currency from other countries is as real as the currency from my own country. | _____ | _____ |
| 4. I can read in a language other than my own. | _____ | _____ |
| 5. I can speak in a language other than my own. | _____ | _____ |
| 6. I can write in a language other than my own. | _____ | _____ |
| 7. I can understand people speaking in a language other than my own. | _____ | _____ |
| 8. I use my second language regularly. | _____ | _____ |
| 9. My friends include people of races different from my own. | _____ | _____ |
| 10. My friends include people of different ages. | _____ | _____ |
| 11. I feel (or would feel) comfortable having a friend with a sexual orientation different from mine. | _____ | _____ |
| 12. My attitude is that although another culture may be very different from mine, that culture is equally good. | _____ | _____ |
| 13. I would be willing to (or already do) hang art from different countries in my home. | _____ | _____ |
| 14. I would accept (or have already accepted) a work assignment of more than several months in another country. | _____ | _____ |
| 15. I have a passport. | _____ | _____ |

## Interpretation:

If you checked Applies to Me Now to 10 or more of the preceding items, you most likely function well in a multicultural work environment. If you answered Not There Yet to 10 or more of the preceding items, you need to develop more cross-cultural awareness and skills to work effectively in a multicultural work environment. You will notice that being bilingual gives you at least five points on this quiz.

**Source:** Several ideas for statements on this quiz are derived from Ruthann Dirks and Janet Buzzard, "What CEOs Expect of Employees Hired for International Work," *Business Education Forum,* April 1997, pp. 3–7; Gunnar Beeth, "Multicultural Managers Wanted," *Management Review,* May 1997, pp. 17–21.

English people, therefore, would have more positive attitudes toward Australians than they would toward Mexicans. Despite this generalization, some countries that appear to have similar cultures are intense rivals. Many Japanese and Korean people dislike each other, as do the French and Belgians. In what way do you feel your country's way of doing something is the best?

## STEREOTYPES IN INTERGROUP RELATIONS

We described perceptual expectations as a form of stereotype that could interfere with effective cross-cultural relations. Stereotypes, in general, create some problems. As a result of stereotypes, people overestimate the probability that a given member of a group will have an attribute of his or her category. People tend to select information that fits the stereotype and reject inconsistent information. As a consequence, we readily draw conclusions about people from another cultural group without carefully listening and observing. As an Indian American business graduate reports

> I took a job with a systems consulting company. The job was supposed to involve a lot of contact with users. But because I look and sound Indian, the managers just assumed that I'm heavy into information technology. Writing code all day gives me a headache. I try to explain my preferences, but all I get is a puzzled look from my manager. [The problem here is that being placed in the wrong job can lead to dissatisfaction and costly turnover.]

## DIFFERENT NORMS AND CODES OF CONDUCT

Various cultural groups have norms of their own, such as in some countries men walking ahead of the women. Also, what is permissible conduct in one group may be frowned on and even punished in another group. In the United States it is permissible for people to publish nasty (even X-rated) cartoons about political leaders without fear of reprisal by the government. In some countries such behavior will lead to long-term imprisonment. In some countries copying the products and ideas of others is an accepted business strategy, but it is considered illegal piracy in another country.

At times, we may make the mistake that others are similar to us and from become confused when they act differently from our expectations. We may unknowingly insult others from a different culture, or they many unknowingly insult us. If you are from a culture that highly values time, such as the Americans and the English (James Bond is always on time), you may be angry when your new Brazilian acquaintance arrives 30 minutes late for a party. Because most Brazilians do not adhere to rigid time schedules for social events, you have just experienced a clash of different cultural norms.

## MICROINEQUITIES

Many barriers to effective cross-cultural relations surface because a person is unaware that he or she is slighting another individual, according to Mary Row, a researcher on gender and racial differences. These slights are referred to as microinequities, as you may have studied in relation to interpersonal conflict. Understanding microinequities can lead to changes in one-on-one relationships that may profoundly irritate others. [5] For example, a manager was introducing a new office assistant to the group, mentioning the name of each member one by one. However, the manager omitted mentioning the name of the one Philippine American group member.

As part of a training program in understanding microinequities, the people who are slighted are taught to confront the issue rather than let resentment build. The Philippine American worker might say tactfully to the manager, "Diane, the new assistant, was introduced to everybody but me. And I am the only Philippine in the department. Was this a coincidence?"

# What Are Some Approaches to Improving Cross-Cultural Relations?

 **Learning Objective 3**

By now you are probably already aware of how to improve cross-cultural relations by avoiding some of the mistakes already mentioned or implied, such as relying too heavily on group stereotypes. In this section, we take a systematic look at approaches you can use on your own along with training programs designed to improve cross-cultural relations. [6] The methods and techniques for such improvement are outlined in Figure 7-1.

## DEVELOP CULTURAL SENSITIVITY AND CULTURAL INTELLIGENCE

In order to relate well to someone from a foreign country, a person must be alert to possible cultural differences. When working in another country, one must be willing to acquire knowledge about local customs and learn how to speak the

**Methods and techniques**

**Figure    7-1**

**Improving Cross-Cultural Relations**

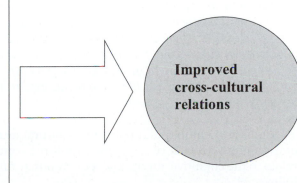

1. Develop cultural sensitivity and cultural intelligence.
2. Focus on the individual rather than groups.
3. Respect all workers and cultures.
4. Value cultural differences.
5. Minimize cultural bloopers.
6. Participate in cultural training.
7. Participate in diversity training.

Improved cross-cultural relations

native language, at least passably. When working with people from different cultures, even from one's own country, the person must be patient, adaptable, flexible, and willing to listen and learn.

These characteristics mentioned are part of **cultural sensitivity,** an awareness of and a willingness to investigate the reasons why people of another culture act as they do. [7] A person with cultural sensitivity will recognize certain nuances in customs that will help build better relationships with people from cultural backgrounds other than his or her own. A culturally sensitive person will also recognize that humor does not easily translate from one culture to another, and that some types of humor might be offensive in another culture. Assume, for example, you are having lunch with a group of Japanese workers on a trip to Japan. You begin your joke with, "This old guy walks into a bar. . . . " The Japanese workers might take offense because older people are highly respected in Japan.

One approach to enhancing cultural sensitivity is to keep in mind the types of cultural differences mentioned throughout this chapter, even down to such details as holding a fork in your left hand when dining in England and India. Another approach is to raise your antenna and observe carefully what others are doing. Suppose you are on a business trip to a different region of your country and are invited to have dinner at the plant general manager's house. You notice that she takes off her street shoes on entering the house. You do likewise to establish better rapport, even if your host says, "Oh, please don't bother." It is obvious from your host's behavior that she observes a "shoe code" in her house.

An advanced aspect of cultural sensitivity is to be able to fit in comfortably with people of another culture by observing the subtle cues they give about how a person should act in their presence. **Cultural intelligence (CQ)** is an outsider's ability to interpret someone's unfamiliar and ambiguous behavior the same way that person's compatriots would. [8] (CQ refers to a cultural quotient.) With high cultural intelligence a person would be able to figure out what behavior would be true of all people and all groups, such as rapid shaking of a clenched fist to communicate anger. Also, the person with high cultural intelligence could figure out what is peculiar to this group, and those aspects of behavior that are neither universal nor peculiar to the group. These ideas are so abstract, that an example will help clarify.

> *An American expatriate manager served on a design team that included two German engineers. As other team members floated their ideas, the engineers condemned them as incomplete or underdeveloped. The manager concluded that the Germans in general are rude and aggressive.*
>
> *With average cultural intelligence the American would have realized he was mistakenly equating the merit of an idea with the merit of the person presenting it. The Germans, however, were able to make a sharp distinction between the two. A manager with more advanced cultural intelligence might have tried to figure out how much of the two German's behavior was typically German and how much was explained by the fact that they were engineers.*

Similar to emotional intelligence, cultural intelligence encompasses several different aspects of behavior. The three sources of cultural intelligence relate to the cognitive, emotional/motivational, and the physical, explained as follows: [9]

■ **Cultural sensitivity**

an awareness of and a willingness to investigate the reasons why people of another culture act as they do

> "We have somehow been tabbed with the term Ugly Americans. It's a bad rap. I don't think we are Ugly Americans, but we are often Unprepared Americans."
> —Roger Axtell, author of eight books on business etiquette.

■ **Cultural intelligence (CQ)**

an outsider's ability to interpret someone's unfamiliar and ambiguous behavior the same way that person's compatriots would

1. **Cognitive (the head).** The cognitive part of CQ refers to what a person knows and how he or she can acquire new knowledge. Here you acquire facts about people from another culture such as their passion for football (soccer in North America), their business practices, and their promptness in paying bills. Another aspect of this source of cultural intelligence is figuring out how you can learn more about the other culture.

2. **Emotional/motivational (the heart).** The emotional/motivational aspect of CQ refers to energizing one's actions and building personal confidence. You need both confidence and motivation to adapt to another culture. A man on a business trip to the Ivory Coast in Africa might say to himself, "When I greet a work associate in a restaurant, can I really pull off kissing him on both cheeks. What if he thinks I'm weird?" With strong motivation, the same person might say, "I'll give it a try. I kind of greet my grandfather the same way back in the United States."

3. **The body (physical).** The body aspect of CQ is the action component. The body is the element for translating intentions into actions and desires. Kissing the same-sex African work associates on both cheeks is the *physical* aspect previously mentioned. We often have an idea of what we should do, but implementation is not so easy. You might know, for example, that when entering an Asian person's home you should take off your shoes, yet you might not actually remove them—thereby offending your Asian work (or personal life) associate.

To practice high cultural intelligence, the mind, heart, and body would have to work together. You would have to figure out how you have to act with people from another culture; you would need motivation and confidence to change; and you would have to translate your knowledge and motivation into action. So when you are on a business trip to Tokyo, go ahead and bow when you are introduced to the plant manager.

## FOCUS ON INDIVIDUALS RATHER THAN GROUPS

Understanding broad cultural differences is a good starting point in building relationships with people from other cultures. Nevertheless, it is even more important to get to know the individual rather than relying exclusively on an understanding of his or her cultural group. Instead of generalizing about the other person's characteristics and values (such as assuming that your Mexican American coworker chooses to be late for meetings), get to know his or her personal style. You might find that this particular Mexican American values promptness and becomes anxious when others are late for a meeting. A consultant in the area of cross-cultural relations suggests that the best way to know individuals is to build personal relationships with people and not to generalize. [10]

## RESPECT ALL WORKERS AND CULTURES

An effective strategy for achieving cross-cultural understanding is to simply respect all others in the workplace, including their cultures. An important component of respect is to believe that although another person's culture is different from yours, it is equally good. Respect comes from valuing differences, such as one person speaking standard English and the other favoring American Sign Language. Respecting other people's customs can translate into specific attitudes, such as respecting one coworker for wearing a yarmulke on Friday or another for wearing an African costume to celebrate Kwanzaa. Another way of being respectful would be to listen carefully to the opinion of a senior worker who says the company should never have converted to voice mail in place of assistants answering the phone (even though you disagree). An aspect of respecting all workers is the importance of respecting the rights of majorities, including white males.

Another way of showing respect for all workers and cultures is to develop supportive peer relations in the workplace with people from different cultural groups. A supportive relationship includes a feeling of closeness and trust, the sharing of thoughts and feelings, and the feeling that one is able to seek assistance from another. Such respect in the form of support doubles in importance because the creativity advantage of a diverse group is more likely to surface when there is a supportive relationship among coworkers who differ demographically. A study with New York state employees found that peer support tends to decline when the proportion of racially different others increases. [11] A tentative interpretation of these findings is that workers find it easier to support somebody culturally different when they can focus their supportive efforts on only a few coworkers.

A major consequence of lack of respect is that it can lead to job discrimination intentionally or unintentionally. In 2006, the trendy retailer Abercrombie & Fitch settled sex discrimination and racial lawsuits. The company agreed to modify its well-known collegiate, All-American, mostly white, image by adding more African Americans, Hispanics, and Asians to its marketing materials. Abercrombie paid $40 million in fines, and agreed to hire 25 diversity recruiters and a vice president for diversity so that its hiring and promotion of minorities and women was in proportion to its applicant pool. The settlement also called for the company to increase diversity not only in hiring and promotions but also in advertisements and in catalogs.

When Abercrombie & Fitch was sued in June 2003, several Hispanic, African American, and Asian plaintiffs said that when they applied for jobs, they were steered toward backroom operations rather than sales positions. [12] If these charges were true, it would reflect lack of respect for the affected groups.

## VALUE CULTURAL DIFFERENCES

■ **Multicultural worker**
one who can work effectively with people of different cultures

Recognizing cultural differences is an excellent starting point in becoming a **multicultural worker,** one who can work effectively with people of different cultures. More importantly, however, is to *value* cultural differences. The distinction goes well beyond semantics. If you place a high value on cultural differences, you will perceive people from other cultures to be different but equally good. Gunnar Beeth, an executive placement specialist in Europe, notes that you cannot motivate anyone, especially someone of another culture, until that person first accepts you. A multilingual sales representative has the ability to explain the advantages of a product in other languages. In contrast, a multicultural sales rep can motivate foreigners to make the purchase. The difference is substantial. [13]

A challenge in showing respect for other cultures is not to act revolted or shocked when a member of another culture eats something that lies outside your area of what is acceptable as food. Some westerners are shocked and repelled to find that some easterners eat insects, cats, dogs, sheep's eyeballs, chicken soup containing the feet, and rattlesnakes. Some easterners are shocked and repelled to find that westerners eat a sacred animal such as cow and are surprised about popcorn. [14]

Other cross-cultural differences in customs also represent a challenge when trying to respect another culture. An American might find it difficult to respect the Pakistani practice of having young children work in factories. In contrast, the Pakistani might find it difficult to respect the American practice of putting old relatives in nursing homes and hospices. Sometimes it takes careful reflection on one's own culture to be able to respect another culture.

A current trend in valuing cultural differences, as well as showing respect, is to be mindful of the rights of gay, lesbian, bisexual, and transgender (GLBT) employees. A leading example is Eastman Kodak Company that has earned an award from the Human Rights Campaign, a gay rights organization. Kodak executives believe that providing equitable treatment toward gay employees makes its products more appealing to the 15 million domestic gay consumers who tend to be brand-loyal. [15]

## MINIMIZE CULTURAL BLOOPERS

■ Learning Objective 4

An effective way of being culturally sensitive is to minimize actions that are likely to offend people from another culture based on their values and customs. Cultural bloopers are most likely to take place when you are visiting another country. The same bloopers, however, can also be committed with people from a different culture within your own country. To avoid these bloopers, you must carefully observe persons from another culture. Studying another culture through reading is also helpful. Even small behaviors, such as while in France asking for ketchup to accompany an omelet, can strain a business relationship.

E-commerce and other forms of Internet communication have created new opportunities for creating cultural bloopers. The Web site developers and the workers responsible for adding content must have good cross-cultural literacy, including an awareness of how the information might be misinterpreted. Here is a sampling of potential problems:

■ Numerical date formats can be readily misinterpreted. To an American, 4/9/08 would be interpreted as April 9, 2008 (or 1908!). However, many Europeans would interpret the same numerical expression as September 4, 2008.

■ Colors on Web sites must be chosen carefully. For example, in some cultures purple is the color of royalty, whereas in Brazil purple is associated with death.

■ Be careful of metaphors that may not make sense to a person for whom your language is a second language. Examples include "We've encountered an ethical meltdown" and "Our biggest competitor is over the hill."

International business specialist Rick Borelli recommends that being able to communicate your message directly in your customer's mother tongue provides a competitive advantage. [16] Consumers are four times more likely to purchase from a Web site written in their native language. The translator, of course, must have good knowledge of the subtleties of the language to avoid a blooper. An English-to-French translator used the verb *baiser* instead of *baisser* to describe a program of lowering prices. *Baisser* is the French verb "to lower," whereas *baiser* is the verb "to kiss." Worse, in everyday language, *baiser* is a verb that refers to having an intimate physical relationship!

Keep two key facts in mind when attempting to avoid cultural mistakes. One is that members of any cultural group show individual differences. What one member of the group might regard as an insensitive act another might welcome. Recognize also that one or two cultural mistakes will not peg you permanently as a boor. Figure 7-2 will help you minimize certain cultural bloopers.

## PARTICIPATE IN CULTURAL TRAINING

■ **Cultural training**

set of learning experiences designed to help employees understand the customs, traditions, and beliefs of another culture

For many years companies and government agencies have prepared their workers for overseas assignments. The method most frequently chosen is **cultural training,** a set of learning experiences designed to help employees understand the customs, traditions, and beliefs of another culture. In today's diverse business environment and international marketplace, learning about individuals raised in different cultural backgrounds has become more important. Many industries, therefore, train employees in cross-cultural relations. Cultural training is considered essential for international workers involved with people from other cultures because negotiating styles differ across cultures. For example, the Japanese prefer an exchange of information to confrontation. Russians, in contrast, enjoy combat in negotiations. [18] (Again, we are dealing with cultural stereotypes.)

Much of the information presented in this chapter, such as understanding cultural values and bloopers, is often incorporated into cultural training. Here we describe some of the learning skills emphasized in cultural training as well as one of its frequent components, language training.

### Learning Skill Dimensions of Cross-Cultural Training Program

Cultural training includes a wide variety of information and skill development, and cultural training programs vary considerably in terms of what knowledge and skills they teach. Two professors of organizational behavior, Yoshitaka Yamazaki of the International University of Japan and D. Christopher Kayes of the George Washington University, have synthesized what goes into cultural training. They identified 73 skills that are useful for expatriates (those people who live in a foreign land) in adapting to another culture. As part of their analysis, the researchers organized the 73 skills into five learning skill dimensions. [19] Figure 7-3 highlights and summarizes some of the competencies and knowledge or skill associated with the five dimensions. You will observe that much of cultural training relates to the development of human relations skills, including cultural sensitivity and cultural intelligence.

**Western Europe**

| Great Britain | • Asking personal questions. The British protect their privacy. |
| --- | --- |
| | • Thinking that a business person from England is unenthusiastic when he or she says, "Not bad at all." English people understate positive emotion. |
| | • Gossiping about royalty. |
| France | • Expecting to complete work during the French two-hour lunch. |
| | • Attempting to conduct significant business during August—*les vacances* (vacation time). |
| | • Greeting a French person for the first time and not using a title such as "sir" or "madam" (or *monsieur, madame,* or *mademoiselle*). |
| Italy | • Eating too much pasta, as it is not the main course. |
| | • Handing out business cards freely. Italians use them infrequently. |
| Spain | • Expecting punctuality. Your appointments will usually arrive 20 to 30 minutes late. |
| | • Make the American sign for "OK" with your thumb and forefinger. In Spain (and many other countries) this is vulgar. |
| Scandinavia (Denmark, Sweden, Norway) | • Being overly rank conscious in these countries. Scandinavians pay relatively little attention to a person's place in the hierarchy. |
| | • Introducing conflict among Swedish work associates. Swedes go out of their way to avoid conflict. |
| Greece | • Waving good-bye by using the American hand shake. Greeks regard this practice to be an insult. |

**Asia**

| All Asian countries | • Pressuring an Asian job applicant or employee to brag about his or her accomplishments. Asians feel self-conscious when boasting about individual accomplishments and prefer to let the record speak for itself. In addition, they prefer to talk about group rather than individual accomplishments. |
| --- | --- |
| Japan | • Shaking hands or hugging Japanese (as well as other Asians) in public. Japanese consider the practices to be offensive. |
| | • Looking directly in the eye of a business acquaintance for more than a few seconds. |
| | • Not interpreting "We'll consider it" as a *no* when spoken by a Japanese businessperson. Japanese negotiators mean *no* when they say, "We'll consider it." |
| | • Not giving small gifts to Japanese when conducting business. Japanese are offended by not receiving these gifts. |
| | • Giving your business card to a Japanese businessperson more than once. Japanese prefer to give and receive business cards only once. |
| China | • Using black borders on stationary and business cards because black is associated with death. |
| | • Giving small gifts to Chinese when conducting business. Chinese are offended by these gifts. |
| | • Making cold calls on Chinese business executives. An appropriate introduction is required for a first-time meeting with a Chinese official. |
| Korea | • Saying *no*. Koreans feel it is important to have visitors leave with good feelings. |
| India | • Telling Indians you prefer not to eat with your hands. If the Indians are not using cutlery when eating, they expect you to do likewise. |

**Mexico and Latin America**

| Mexico | • Flying into a Mexican city in the morning and expecting to close a deal by lunch. Mexicans build business relationships slowly. |
| --- | --- |
| Brazil | • Attempting to impress Brazilians by speaking a few words of Spanish. Portuguese is the official language of Brazil. |
| Most Latin American countries | • Wearing elegant and expensive jewelry during a business meeting. Most Latin Americans think people should appear more conservative during a business meeting. |

**Note:** A cultural mistake for Americans to avoid when conducting business in most countries outside the United States and Canada is to insist on getting down to business quickly. Other stereotyped American traits to avoid are aggressiveness, impatience, and frequent interruptions to get your point across. North Americans in small towns also like to build a relationship before getting down to business. Another general mistake for Americans is to use a familiar, laid-back style in locales where "business casual" is unacceptable and first names are reserved for family and friends.[17]

**Figure 7-2**

**Cultural Mistakes to Avoid with Selected Cultural Groups**

## Foreign Language Training

Learning a foreign language is often part of cultural training yet can also be a separate activity. Knowledge of a second language is important because it builds better connections with people from other cultures than does relying on a translator. Many workers aside from international business specialists also choose to develop skills in a target language. Speaking another language can help build rapport with customers and employees who speak that language. Almost all language training has elements similar to taking a course in another language or self-study. Companies invest heavily in helping employees learn a target language because it facilitates conducting business in other countries. Medical specialists, police workers, and firefighters also find second-language skills to be

| Learning Skill Dimension | Cross-Cultural Competency Cluster | Knowledge or Skill Required |
|---|---|---|
| Interpersonal | Building relationships | Ability to gain access to and maintain relationships with members of host culture |
| | Valuing people of different cultures | Empathy for differences; sensitivity to diversity |
| Information | Listening and observation | Knows cultural history and reasons for cultural actions and customs |
| | Coping with ambiguity | Recognizes and interprets implicit behavior, especially nonverbal cues |
| Analytical | Translating complex information | Knowledge of local language, symbols, or other forms of verbal language and written language |
| Action | Taking action and initiative | Understands intended and potentially unintended consequences of actions |
| | Managing others | Ability to manage details of a job including maintaining cohesion in a group |
| Adaptive | Adaptability and flexibility | Views change from multiple perspectives |
| | Managing stress | Understands own and other's mood, emotions, and personality |

**Figure 7-3**

**Competencies for Successful Cross-Cultural Adaptation of Expatriates**
**Source:** Abridged from Yoshitaka Yamazaki and D. Christopher Kayes, "An Experiential Approach to Cross-Cultural Learning: A Review and Integration of Competencies for Successful Expatriate Adaptation," *Academy of Management Learning and Education*, December 2004, p. 372.

quite helpful. Clients under stress, such as an injured person, are likely to revert to their native tongue.

Many multinational companies have downplayed the importance of American workers being fluent in a second language because English has become the standard language of commerce. [20] Despite the merits of this observation, speaking and writing well in the language of your target can help establish rapport. Furthermore, from the standpoint of career management it is worth noting that more and more highly placed managers in large companies are bilingual. Another value of foreign-language training is to better communicate with subordinates, coworkers, and customers. For example, it is estimated that in the United States, nearly two-thirds of U.S. construction workers do not speak English as their primary language. Construction supervisors who speak Spanish can prevent many accidents. [21]

As with any other skill training, these investments can only pay off if the trainee is willing to work hard developing the new skill outside the training session. It is unlikely that almost anyone can develop conversational skills in another language by listening to foreign language cassette tapes or taking classes for 30 days. The quick training program, however, helps you develop a base for further learning. Allowing even 10 days to pass without practicing your target language will result in a sharp decline in your ability to use that language.

## PARTICIPATE IN DIVERSITY TRAINING

The general purpose of cultural training is to help workers understand people from other cultures. Understanding can lead to dealing more effectively with them as work associates or customers. **Diversity training** has a slightly different purpose. It attempts to bring about workplace harmony by teaching people how to get along with diverse work associates. Quite often the program is aimed at minimizing open expressions of racism and sexism. Diversity training takes a number of forms. Nevertheless, all center on increasing awareness of and empathy for people who are different in some noticeable way from oneself.

■ **Diversity training**
program that attempts to bring about workplace harmony by teaching people how to get along with diverse work associates; often aimed at minimizing open expressions of racism and sexism

A starting point in diversity training is to emphasize that everybody is different is some way and that all these differences should be appreciated. The subtle point here is that cultural diversity does not refer exclusively to differences in race, ethnicity, age, and sex. As the United States Office of Civil Rights explains, "Diversity is a term used broadly to refer to many demographic variables, including but not limited to race, religion, color, gender, national origin, disability, sexual orientation, age, education, geographic origin, and skill characteristics." [22]

Diversity training emphasizes *inclusion,* or including everybody when appreciating diversity. The accompanying Human Relations in Practice illustrates both the scope of diversity, and how much importance companies attach to having a diverse workforce. Figure 7-4 presents a broad sampling of the ways in which workplace associates can differ from one another. All these differences are tucked under the welcoming *diversity umbrella.* Studying this list can help you anticipate the type of differences to understand and appreciate in a diverse workplace. The differences include cultural as well as individual factors. Individual factors are also important because people can be discriminated against for personal characteristics as well as group characteristics. Many people who

## Human Relations In Practice

### The Corporate Diversity Policy of Alliant Energy

A core corporate value of Alliant Energy is to be a responsible corporate citizen, caring for the environment and the communities where we do business and **encouraging diversity** in our employee and supplier ranks.

Diversity includes, but is not limited to, race, gender, age, physical and mental abilities, lifestyles, culture, education, ideas and background.

At Alliant Energy we recognize, respect, and appreciate the valuable and different perspectives that each of us bring to the work environment, our company and our customers.

Our goal is to break down barriers and create an environment that maximizes the contributions of all employees.

Source: "Corporate Diversity Policy," available at www.alliantenergy.com. (Madison, Wisconsin) Retrieved April 24, 2006.

- Race
- Sex or gender
- Religion
- Age (young, middle aged, and old)
- Generation differences, including attitudes (e.g., baby boomers versus the Net generation)
- Ethnicity (country of origin)
- Education
- Abilities
- Mental disabilities (including attention deficit disorder)
- Physical status (including hearing status, visual status, able-bodied, wheelchair user)
- Values and motivation
- Sexual orientation (heterosexual, homosexual, bisexual, transsexual)
- Marital status (married, single, cohabitating, widow, widower)
- Family status (children, no children, two-parent family, single parent, grandparent, opposite-sex parents, same-sex parents)
- Personality traits
- Functional background (area of specialization, such as marketing, manufacturing)
- Technology interest (high tech, low tech, technophobe)
- Weight status (average, obese, underweight, anorexic)
- Hair status (full head of hair, bald, wild hair, tame hair, long hair, short hair)
- Style of clothing and appearance (dress up, dress down, professional appearance, casual appearance, tattoos, body piercing including multiple earrings, nose rings, lip rings)
- Tobacco status (smoker versus nonsmoker, chewer versus nonchewer)
- Your creative suggestion

**Figure    7-4**

**The Diversity Umbrella**

are disfigured believe they are held back from obtaining a higher-level job because of their disfigurement, such as a facial birthmark.

Another important part of diversity training is to develop empathy for diverse viewpoints. To help training participants develop empathy, representatives of various groups explain their feelings related to workplace issues. In one segment of such a program, a minority group member was seated in the middle of a circle. The other participants sat at the periphery of the circle. First, the coworkers listened to a Vietnamese woman explain how she felt excluded from the in-group composed of whites and African Americans in her department. "I feel like you simply tolerate me. You do not make me feel that I am somebody important. You make me feel that because I am Vietnamese I don't count." The next person to sit in the middle of the circle was Muslim. He complained about people wishing him Merry Christmas. "I would much prefer that my coworkers would stop to think that I do not celebrate Christian holidays. I respect your religion, but it is not my religion."

A criticism of many diversity training programs is that too many angry feelings are expressed and that negative stereotypes are reinforced, leading to strained relationships. Another criticism is that the program might be considered patronizing because the majority of participants are already respectful of people different from themselves and know how to work harmoniously with a wide variety of people.

Support for the importance of diversity training comes from a five-year study of the impact of diversity on business results conducted by Thomas A. Kochan, a professor of both management and engineering systems, at the Massachusetts Institute of Technology. He concludes that a culturally diverse workforce enhances business performance only when proper training is provided to employees. An organizational culture that supports diversity, meaning that the values and atmosphere of the firm welcome inclusion, is also required. [23] Also, a study by the Urban League found that at eight companies where diversity is a fact of life, productivity growth during the four-year period studied, exceeded that of the economy as a whole by 18 percent. "Getting serious about workforce diversity isn't just the right thing to do," notes League President Marc Morial, "It's the smart thing to do." [24]

An example of a company in the service industry that emphasizes diversity is the MGM Mirage. One of its many initiatives is the Management Associate Program, a six-month training program to prepare recent minority college graduates for careers in management. The program includes mentors, classroom instruction, job shadowing (following around a mentor) and hands-on experience. [25]

# How Do You Overcome Cross-Cultural Communication Barriers?

■ **Learning Objective 5**

A key part of developing good cross-cultural relations is to overcome or prevent communication barriers stemming from cultural differences. Personal life, too, is often more culturally diverse today than previously, leading to culturally based communication problems. The information about avoiding cultural bloopers presented in this chapter might also be interpreted as a way to prevent communication barriers. Here we describe eight additional strategies and tactics to help overcome cross-cultural communication barriers.

**1. Be alert to cultural differences in customs and behavior.** To minimize cross-cultural communication barriers, recognize that many subtle job-related differences in customs and behavior may exist. For example, Asians typically feel uncomfortable when asked to brag about themselves in the presence of others. From their perspective, calling attention to yourself at the expense of another person is rude and unprofessional.

**2. Use straightforward language and speak slowly and clearly.** When working with people who do not speak your language fluently, speak in an easy-to-understand manner. Be patient for many reasons including the fact that your accent in your native tongue may not be the same as the person from whom your target learned your language. (For example, English as learned in India is quite different from English as learned in Ohio.) Minimize the use of idioms and analogies specific to your language. For example, in North America the term "over the hill" means outdated or past one's prime. A person from another culture may not understand this phrase yet be hesitant to ask for clarification. Speaking slowly is also important because even people who read and write a second language at an expert level may have difficulty catching the nuances of conversation. Facing the person from another culture directly also improves communication because your facial expressions and lips contribute to comprehension.

**3. When the situation is appropriate, speak in the language of the people from another culture.** Americans who can speak another language are at a competitive advantage when dealing with businesspeople who speak that language. The language skill, however, must be more advanced than speaking a few words and phrases. A new twist in speaking another language has surged recently: As more deaf people have been integrated into the workforce, knowing American Sign Language can be a real advantage to a worker when some of his or her coworkers or customers are deaf.

**4. Observe cultural differences in etiquette.** Violating rules of etiquette without explanation can erect immediate communication barriers. A major rule of etiquette is that in some countries older people in high-status positions expect to be treated with respect. Formality is important, unless invited to do otherwise. When visiting a company in Asia, for example, it is best to be deferent (appeal to the authority of) to company dignitaries. Visualize yourself as a company representative of a high-tech American firm that manufactures equipment for legally downloading music over the Internet. You visit Sony Corporation in Japan to speak about a joint venture. On meeting the marketing vice president, bow slightly and say something to the effect; "Mr. _____, it is my honor to discuss doing business with Sony." Do not commit the etiquette mistake of saying something to the effect, "Hi Charlie, how's the wife and kids?" (An American actually said this at a Japanese company shortly before being escorted out the door.)

**5. Be sensitive to differences in nonverbal communication.** Stay alert to the possibility that a person from another culture may misinterpret your nonverbal signal. To use positive reinforcement, some managers will give a sideways hug to an employee or will touch an employee's arm. People from some cultures resent touching from workmates and will be offended. Koreans in particular dislike being touched or touching others in a work setting. (Refer back to the discussion of cultural bloopers.)

**6. Do not be diverted by style, accent, grammar, or personal appearance.** Although all these superficial factors are related to business success, they are difficult to interpret when judging a person from another culture. It is, therefore, better to judge the merits of the statement or behavior. [26] A brilliant individual from another culture may still be learning your language and thus make basic mistakes in speaking your language. He or she might also not have developed a sensitivity to dress style in your culture.

**7. Listen for understanding, not agreement.** When working with diverse teammates, the differences in viewpoints can lead to conflict. To help overcome such conflict, follow the *LUNA rule:* Listen for Understanding, Not Agreement. In this way you gear yourself to consider the viewpoints of others as a first resort. For example; some older workers may express some intense loyalty to the organization, whereas their younger teammates may speak in more critical terms. By everyone listening to understand, they can begin to appreciate each others' paradigms and accept differences of opinion. [27] Listening is a powerful tool for overcoming cross-cultural communication barriers.

**8. Be attentive to individual differences in appearance.** A major cross-cultural insult is to confuse the identity of people because they are members of the same race or ethnic group. Psychological research suggests that people have difficulty seeing individual differences among people of another race because they code race first, such as thinking, "He has the nose of an African American." However, people can learn to search for more distinguishing features, such as a dimple or eye color. [28]

# Why Are Gender Differences in Leadership Style Regarded as Cultural Differences?

■ **Learning Objective 6**

Differences in the way men and women lead can be interpreted as cultural differences because gender is one of the factors contributing to the cultural mosaic. A number of factors may contribute to a person's cultural identity, with maleness or femaleness being one contributor. Several researchers and writers argue that women have certain acquired traits and behaviors that suit them for a people-oriented leadership style. [29] Consequently, women leaders frequently exhibit a cooperative, empowering style that includes nurturing team members. According to this same perspective, men are inclined toward a command-and-control, somewhat militaristic leadership style. Women find participative management more natural than do men because they feel more comfortable interacting with people. Furthermore, it is argued that women's natural sensitivity to people gives them an edge over men to encouraging group members to participate in decision making.

The gender differences in leadership style that do exist could be attributable in part to differences in communication style between men and women. Men are more concerned about transmitting information and gaining status while they communicate, whereas women are more concerned about building social connections.

Assume that these differences in the preferred leadership style between men and women were generally true. Women managers, therefore, would be better suited for organizations that have shifted to participation and empowerment. It may be true that more women than men gravitate naturally toward the consultative, consensus, and democratic leadership styles, and men toward the autocratic. Nevertheless, there are many male leaders who find the participative style to be a good fit, and many women who are autocratic.

Even if gender differences in leadership style exist, this type of cultural difference requires a minimum of adaptation by most people. Fewer and fewer people in the workforce find it unusual or difficult to work with members of the opposite sex, even if they have a preference for working with members of their own sex.

# What Are Some of the Legal Aspects of Working in a Culturally Diverse Environment?

■ Learning Objective 7

In this chapter we have emphasized the interpersonal aspects of building good relationships with work associates who are demographically and culturally diverse. The legal side of diversity focuses on such matters as protecting workers from being discriminated against, such as not being denied a job you are qualified for because of race, gender, age, or physical disability. However, legislation does not require workers to develop constructive relationships with each other or to develop cultural intelligence. Here we look briefly at relevant employment legislation, as well as affirmative action.

## FEDERAL LAWS PROHIBITING JOB DISCRIMINATION

Workers are protected by a series of federal laws that prohibit job discrimination. In addition, states, provinces (Canada), and municipalities have their own laws governing fair treatment of employees. Furthermore, many employment lawyers bring forth law suits for discrimination not specifically mentioned in federal laws. For example, a job candidate might claim that he was denied a position for which he was qualified because he was obese. A state or local judge could then decide whether the claim was justified. The general purpose of job discrimination laws is to protect individuals who have been disadvantaged in the past because of demographic (not cultural) characteristics. Employment legislations began with prohibiting employment discrimination based on race, color, religion, sex, or national origin. Figure 7-5 summarizes Federal Equal Employment Opportunity (EEO) Laws. These laws apply to all private employers, state and local governments, and educational institutions that employ 15 or more individuals.

An effective way of understanding how these laws might affect the individual is to specify the discriminatory practices prohibited by these laws. Under Title VII, the ADA, and the ADEA, it is illegal to discriminate in any aspect of employment, including hiring and firing; compensation, assignment, or classification of employees; transfer, promotion, layoff, or recall; job advertisements; recruitment; testing; use of company facilities; training and apprenticeship programs; fringe benefits; pay, retirement plans, and disability leave; or other terms and conditions of employment. Discriminatory practices under these laws also include the following:

1. Harassment on the basis of race, color, religion, sex, national origin, disability, or age;

2. Retaliation against an individual for filing a charge of discrimination, participating in an investigation, or opposing discriminatory practices;

3. Employment decisions based on stereotypes or assumptions about the abilities, traits, or performance of individuals of a certain sex, race, age, religion, or ethnic group, or individuals with disabilities; and

4. Denying employment opportunities to a person because of marriage to, or association with, an individual of a particular race, religion, national origin, or an individual with a disability. Title VII also prohibits discrimination because of participation in schools or places of worship associated with a particular racial, ethnic, or religious group.

Although all of these forms of discrimination may appear clear-cut, a good deal of interpretation is required to decide whether a given employee is the subject of discrimination. For example, assume that a woman files a charge of sexual harassment. Later, she is bypassed for promotion. She claims she is now

- Title VII of the Civil Rights Act of 1964 (Title VII) prohibits employment discrimination based on race, color, religion, sex, or national origin.
- The Equal Pay Act of 1963 (EPA) protects men and women who perform substantially equal work in the same establishment from sex-based wage discrimination.
- The Age Discrimination in Employment Act of 1967 (ADEA) protects individuals who are 40 years of age or older.
- Title I and Title V of the Americans with Disabilities Act of 1990 (ADA) prohibits employment discrimination against qualified individuals with disabilities in the private sector, and in state and local governments.
- Sections 501 and 505 of the Rehabilitation Act of 1973 prohibits discrimination against qualified individuals with disabilities who work in the federal government.
- The Civil Rights Act of 1991, among other things, provides monetary damages in cases of intentional employment discrimination.

The U.S. EEOC enforces all of these laws. EEOC also provides oversight and coordination of all federal equal employment opportunity regulations, practices, and policies.

**Source:** Available at www.eeoc.gov/facts/ganda.html.

**Figure 7-5**

**Federal Laws Prohibiting Job Discrimination**

the victim of discrimination, yet the company claims that she did not have the appropriate interpersonal skills to be promoted to a supervisory position.

Among the remedies awarded to individuals judged to be discriminated against are back pay, promotion, reinstatement, and the employer paying attorney's fees, and court costs. Compensatory and punitive damages are also possible.

## AFFIRMATIVE ACTION

■ **Affirmative action**

programs that comply with antidiscrimination laws and attempt to correct past discriminatory practices

A key aspect of implementing the spirit and letter of antidiscrimination law in the United States has been affirmative action programs. **Affirmative action** consists of complying with antidiscrimination laws and correcting past discriminatory practices. Under an affirmative action program, employers actively recruit, employ, train, and promote minorities and women who have been discriminated against by an employer in the past. As a result, women and minority group members are underrepresented in certain positions. Part of an affirmative action plan might be to actively recruit Hispanic business graduates to place them in a company management training program.

Affirmative action has been the subject of continuing debate. Proponents of affirmative action believe that it provides the opportunity many people need to prove their capability and earn just rewards. Opponents of affirmative action believe that it provides preferential treatment for certain groups and winds up discriminating against workers who are qualified but do not fit an affirmative action category. The National Leadership Network of Black Conservatives is an example of a group strongly opposed to affirmative action. The National Leadership Network supports the position that affirmative action is wrong because it is "a system rooted in the belief that blacks and certain other minorities cannot hope to win if they have to compete on a level playing field." [30] What is your opinion about the merits of affirmative action?

# Concept Review and Reinforcement

## Key Terms

Culture, 203
Multicultural identities, 204
Cultural mosaic, 205
Ethnocentrism, 206

Cultural sensitivity, 210
Cultural intelligence(CQ), 210
Multicultural worker, 212
Cultural training, 214

Diversity training, 217
Affirmative action, 224

## Summary and Review

Being able to work well with people from other cultures, both outside and inside your own country, is important for career success. Seven dimensions of cultural values that help us understand how cultures differ from one another are as follows:

- individualism versus collectivism
- acceptance of power and authority
- materialism versus concern for others
- formality versus informality
- urgent time orientation versus casual time orientation
- work orientation versus leisure orientation
- high-context versus low-context cultures (with an emphasis on body language)

Many people have multicultural identities because they identify with their own culture as well as other cultures. Similarly, according to the cultural mosaic, people have a rich mixture of cultural identities. The religious value part of the cultural mosaic often affects when people are willing to work or not work. It is important to be alert to possible cultural differences.

Certain underlying factors create problems in developing smooth cross-cultural relations, including communication problems.

- Perceptual expectations are much like stereotypes that lead to misunderstandings.
- Ethnocentrism, or thinking that one's culture is best, leads to misunderstandings.

- Misunderstandings also come about from stereotypes in intergroup relations.
- Different cultural norms and codes of conduct can lead to confusion.
- Microinequities also create problems.

Six specific methods and techniques for improving cross-cultural relations are as follows:

- Develop cultural sensitivity (being aware of differences) and cultural intelligence (cognitive, emotional, and body components).
- Focus on individuals rather than groups.
- Respect all workers and cultures.
- Value cultural differences (this also involves showing respect).
- Minimize cultural bloopers (embarrassing mistakes).
- Participate in cultural training, including language training. (The skill dimensions of cross-cultural training are interpersonal, information, analytic, action, and adaptive.)
- Participate in diversity training, or learning to get along with diverse work associates.

Cross-cultural communication barriers can often be overcome by the following:

- being alert to cultural differences in customs and behavior
- using straightforward language and speaking slowly and clearly

■ speaking in the language of the other group
■ observing cultural differences in etiquette
■ being sensitive to differences in nonverbal communication
■ not being diverted by style, accent, grammar, or personal appearance
■ listening for understanding, not agreement
■ being attentive to individual differences in appearance.

Gender differences in leadership style have been observed that could be interpreted as cultural differences between men and women. Women tend toward a cooperative, empowering style that includes nurturing team members. It is argued that men lean toward a command-and-control autocratic style.

The legal side of diversity focuses on such matters as protecting workers from discrimination, but is not part of developing cross-cultural competence. Workers are protected by a series of federal, state, and municipal laws that govern fair treatment of employees. It is illegal to discriminate in any aspect of employment including hiring and firing, compensation, and recruitment. Affirmative action programs consist of complying with antidiscrimination laws and correcting past discriminatory practices.

## Check your Understanding

1. What does it really mean to say that every member of the workforce is different in some way?
2. In what way might having a high acceptance for power and authority make it difficult for a person to work well on a team that has very little supervision?
3. Identify three positive stereotypes about cultural groups that are related to job behavior. (An example would be the observation that Mexican laborers are known for their hard work and dependability.)
4. When you meet someone from another culture, what can you do to demonstrate that you respect that person's culture?
5. Provide an example of cultural insensitivity of any kind that you have seen, read about, or could imagine.
6. Imagine that you are trying hard to "Do as Romans do when in Rome" in a foreign country. You are attending a business dinner and your host invites you to eat a meal that is composed of an animal you consider to be a household pet. How would you handle this situation?

7. All the cultural bloopers presented in Figure 7-2 dealt with errors people make in regard to people who are not American. Give an example of a cultural blooper that a person from another country might make in the United States.
8. In an era of welcoming cultural diversity, does a company have the right to exclude employees with visible body piercings from any type of positions?
9. Suppose a company wants to promote cross-cultural understanding. Should the executives then discourage students from one racial or ethnic group from forming a club or sitting together in the company cafeteria? Explain your position.
10. Many people speak loudly to deaf people, blind people, and those who speak a different language. Based on the information presented in this chapter, what mistakes are these people making?
11. Why are gender differences in leadership style referred to as cultural differences?

## Web Corner

*Cultural training:*
www.berlitz.com; www.culturalsavvy.com (Click on/ "Tips & Info.")

*Cultural diversity:*
www.DiversityInc.com

### Internet Skill Builder: Developing Your Multicultural Skills

A useful way of developing skills in a second language and learning more about another culture is to create a cover page (the page that appears when you open a Web site) written in your target language. In this way, each time you go the Internet on your own computer, your cover page will contain fresh information in the language you want to develop.

Assume that your target language is French. Enter a phrase such as "French language newspaper" or "French current events" in the search probe. Once you find a suitable choice, insert that newspaper as your cover page. The search engine might have brought you to www.france2.fr or www.cyberpresse.ca. These Web sites keep you abreast of French and French Canadian international news, sports, and cultural events—written in French. Now every time you access the Internet, you can spend a few minutes becoming multicultural. You can save lot of travel costs and time using the Internet to help you become multicultural.

# Developing Your Human Relations Skills

*Human Relations Application Exercises*

## Applying Human Relations Exercise 7–1

### Avoiding Cultural Mistakes

Refer back to Figure 7-2, Cultural Mistakes to Avoid with Selected Cultural Groups. Review the list of cultural groups mentioned. After you have chosen one or two cultural groups, imagine how and where you might have an opportunity to relate to someone from one of these culture groups. During the next 30 days, look for an opportunity to relate to a person from another culture in the way described in these suggestions. You may have to be creative to find a target with whom you can practice your cross-cultural skills. Before approaching your target, answer these questions:

1. What would be my usual approach to dealing with a person from that culture? (An example here would be as follows: "Usually when I visit the neighborhood convenience store operated by a Korean family, I attempt to place the money for purchases directly in the hands of the cashier.)

2. What will I do differently after studying the suggestions in Figure 7-2? (Because touching a Korean's hand might be uncomfortable for him or her, I will lay the money on the counter and let the cashier pick it up.)

Observe the reaction of the other person for feedback on your cross-cultural effectiveness. Then assess whether your approach to improving cross-cultural relations had any effect on your target.

## Applying Human Relations Exercise 7–2

### Developing Empathy for Differences

Class members come up to the front of the room one by one and give a brief presentation (perhaps even three minutes) of any way in which they have been perceived as different and how they felt about this perception. The difference can be of any kind, relating to characteristics such as ethnicity, race, major field of study, physical appearance, height, weight, hair color, or body piercing. (Here is an example repeatedly heard from very tall people: "I am so tired of the same old stupid comment, 'How is the weather up there.' It also annoys me that so many people ask me to change a light bulb in a highly placed fixture. Even worse, because I'm tall, people think I would want to help them move furniture." An example heard frequently from information technology students is as follows: "When I'm out socially, people are forever asking me about some software problem they are facing. They think I know all about every software package ever written. Even worse, they think I have no life outside of computers. Why should I want to talk about computer problems when I'm partying?"

After each member of the class has presented (perhaps even the instructor), class members discuss what they learned from the exercise. Points to look for include the following:

- What pattern do you see in the ways people perceive themselves to be different?
- What is the most frequent difference reported by class members?
- What kind of perceptions by others seem to hurt the most?

It is also important to discuss how this exercise can improve relationships on the job. What would be at least one take-away from the exercise?

## Human Relations Case Study 7–1

### *Are Americans Abroad Really That Bad?*

Trying to combat anti, U.S. sentiment abroad, a campaign is underway to give the "ugly American" a makeover and improve the business manners of business travelers overseas. Employees and executives of some big corporations who are bound for other countries will receive a "World Citizens Guide" brochure with 16 tips to improve the image of the United States, such as trying to speak a little of foreign languages and refraining from too much talk about wealth, power, status, or American pride. The program began in May 2006 and expanded in the fall of that year to include a one-day seminar.

"We are broadly seen throughout the world as an arrogant people, totally self-absorbed and loud," said Keith Reinhard, chair emeritus of DDB Worldwide Inc. who is leading the effort through a group called Business for Diplomatic Action Inc., a nonprofit organization that tries to get U.S. companies to work to improve the reputation of the United States in the world.

AMR Corp.'s American Airlines, Lowe's Cos. and Novell Inc. have signed up for the program, the group says. Exxon Mobil Corp., Microsoft Corp., and Weyerhaeuser Co. have officials on the Board of Business for Diplomatic Action, and are expected to join the campaign, which is being funded by the National Business Travelers Association, a group of corporate travel managers. More than 40 large companies have been approached so far, according to NBTA, and about half expressed interest in participating.

Some companies cringe at the suggestion that their employees and executives are in need of "Miss Manners"–style lessons, and Reinhard's group runs into doubters who say personal interactions will do little to greatly shift the perception of U.S. citizens around the world. A State Department effort to enlist Madison Avenue to boost American's image globally fell flat shortly after September 11, 2001.

Business for Diplomatic Action has held discussions with the State Department about distributing its World Citizens Guide to every U.S. passport holder and putting it on the State Department's Web site. No decision has been reached.

The group's advice includes tried-and-true international travel suggestions, such as reminders that in Japan it is considered rude to look directly in the eye for more than a few seconds, and in Greece the hand-waving gesture commonly used in America for goodbye is considered an insult.

But it also covers stereotypical American traits such as boastfulness, loudness, and speed. The guide urges travelers to eat slower, speak slower, move slower, and dress up when abroad because casual dress can be a sign of disrespect. Tone down talk of religion, politics, and national pride, as well as your voice. "Listen as much as you talk," the guide says, and "save the lectures for your kids."

"Anger, impatience, and rudeness are universal turnoffs," the guide says, imploring employees to "Help your country while you travel for your country."

Reinhard, a prominent advertising executive who created slogans such as "You deserve a break today" and "Two all-beef patties. . .," said he started looking for ways to polish the image of the United States when he heard President Bush express dismay shortly after September 11 that "people did not like us" in other parts of the world.

Many of the suggestions offered in the World Citizens Guide stem from the results of a survey taken by an affiliate of DDB in 130 countries. The questions asked about how America was viewed and what Americans could do to make a better impression overseas. Business executives around the world were also interviewed for their opinion on the same topic.

## Questions

1. How effective do you think the World Citizens Guide will be in fostering cross-cultural understanding?

2. How effective do you think the World Citizens Guide (and related seminars) will be in developing better relations between American businesspeople and their customers and affiliates overseas?

3. One criticism of this initiative by the Business for Diplomatic Action is that major U.S. foreign-policy decisions and events such as the Iraq war far outweigh manners when it comes to shaping the perception of Americans overseas. What do you think of this criticism?

**Source:** Adapted from Scott McCartney, "Teaching Americans How to Behave Abroad: Fearing Anti-U.S. Backlash, Big Companies Team Up to Offer Advice to Executives," *The Wall Street Journal*, April 11, 2006, pp. D1, D4.

## Human Relations Case Study 7–2

### The Multicultural Dealership

Manuel Ortiz is the owner and operator of Futura Motors, a large automobile and small-truck dealership in Brooklyn, New York. The dealership represents several Japanese and Korean vehicle manufacturers. For more than a decade, Ortiz and his management team have invested time, effort, and money into building culturally diverse sales and service staffs to better serve the many ethnic, cultural, and racial groups that make up the dealership's customer base. Ortiz brags that in total his sales staff speaks 13 different languages. "In this way we can communicate in the native tongue of almost any customer or sales prospect who shows up on the floor," says Ortiz. (A *sales prospect* is anyone who visits Futura without the full intention of purchasing a vehicle from the dealership, including the people who are "just looking.") The culturally diverse sales and service staffs apparently have contributed to the growth and profitability of Futura, although such an assertion would be difficult to prove. For example, Ortiz has not been able to compare the dollar volume of Futura to a comparable size foreign dealership in Brooklyn that has a more homogeneous workforce.

Penny Shakelford, the office manager at Futura, has recently brought a potential problem to Ortiz's attention that has caused him some concern about how well he and his staff are managing diversity. According to Shakelford, the multicultural sales staff appears to be well accepted by most customers and prospects, yet some problems are surfacing. Based on direct concerns expressed by both customers and prospects, Shakelford believes that they are being patronized on the basis of their demographic group. She explains:

"My impression is that some customers think we are bending over backwards to make them feel at home. If a person who walks on the floor appears to be an African American, immediately an African American sales rep walks up to him or her. The same goes for several other visible ethnic or racial groups. Two different Asiatic Indians wrote down on customer service survey cards that they thought it was too obvious that an Indian rushed out on the floor as soon as they appeared.

"A Mexican American woman said she thought it was a little bit much that three minutes after she and her husband walked into the dealership, a young sales rep introduced himself in Spanish. The customer said she was in Brooklyn, not Mexico City, and wanted to be treated like an American."

Ortiz said that it appears that the vast majority of customers and prospects find no problem with our attempt to make a direct appeal to their racial or ethnic group but that maybe some adjustment needs to be made.

"We need to give this problem some thought. We don't want to insult anybody, but neither do we want to lose our competitive edge of having a multicultural workforce."

## Questions

1. What is your opinion of the merits of a vehicle dealership attempting to match the demographic group of a customer with a sales rep of the same demographic group?
2. What do you recommend Ortiz and his management team do about the several complaints the Futura dealership has received.
3. To help you analyze this case, get the input from a few people in your network about how they would feel about having a person from their demographic group approach them when they visited a dealership. (Perhaps a few classmates representing different ethnic groups can provide useful input.)

# REFERENCES

1. Bill Brubaker, "Diverse Work Force Creates Challenges for Wegmans," *Washington Post* syndicated story, December 28, 2005.

2. Geert Hofstede, *Culture's Consequences: International Differences in Work-Related Values* (Beverly Hills, CA: Sage, 1980); updated and expanded in "A Conversation with Geert Hofstede," *Organizational Dynamics,* Spring 1993, pp. 53–61; Harry Triandis, The Many Dimensions of Culture," *Academy of Management Executive,* February 2004, pp. 88–93.

3. Jeffrey Jensen Arnett, "The Psychology of Globalization," *American Psychologist,* October 2002, pp. 777–778.

4. Georgia T. Chao and Henry Moon, "The Cultural Mosaic: A Methodology for Understanding the Complexity of Culture," *Journal of Applied Psychology,* November 2005, pp. 1128–1140.

5. Gary M. Stern, "Small Slights Bring Big Problems," *Workforce,* August 2002, p. 17.

6. Based on the contribution of Terri Geerinck in Andrew J. DuBrin and Terri Geerinck, *Human Relations for Career and Personal Success,* 2nd Canadian ed. (Toronto: Prentice Hall, 2001), p. 201. Geerinck also contributed the idea of a separate chapter on cross-cultural competency.

7. Arvind V. Phatak, *International Dimensions of Management* (Boston: Kent, 1983), p. 167.

8. P. Christopher Earley and Elain Mosakowski, "Cultural Intelligence," *Harvard Business Review,* October 2004, p. 140. The example is from the same source, same page.

9. Earley and Mosakowski, "Toward Cultural Intelligence: Turning Cultural Differences into Workplace Advantage," *Academy of Management Executive,* August 2004, pp. 154–155.

10. Todd Raphael, "Savvy Companies Build Bonds with Hispanic Employees," *Workforce,* September 2001, p. 19.

11. Samuel B. Bacharach, Peter A. Bamberger, and Dana Vashdi, "Diversity and Homophilly at Work: Supportive Relations among White and African-American Peers," *Academy of Management Journal,* August 2005, pp. 619–644.

12. Steven Greenhouse, "Abercrombie & Fitch Bias Case Is Settled," *The New York Times,* available at nytimes.com, retrieved November 17, 2004.

13. Gunnar Beeth, "Multicultural Managers Wanted," *Management Review,* May 1997, p. 17.

14. A few of these tasty morsels are from Lillian H. Chaney and Jeannette S. Martin, *Interpersonal Business Communication,* 3rd ed. (Upper Saddle River, NJ: Pearson Prentice Hall, 2004), p. 190.

15. Todd Henneman, "Acceptance of Gays, Lesbians, Is a Big Part of Kodak's Diversity Picture," *Workforce Management,* December 2004, p. 68.

16. Rick Borelli, "A Worldwide Language Trap," *Management Review,* October 1997, pp. 52–54.

17. The comment about informality is credited to Jacqueline Whitmore as cited in Michael Peltier, "Etiquette Lessons," *Time,* January 31, 2005, p. A4.

18. Marc Diener, "Culture Shock," *Entrepreneur,* July 2003, p. 77.

19. Yoshitaka Yamazaki and D. Christopher Kayes, "An Experiential Approach to Cross-Cultural Learning: A Review and Integration of Competencies for Successful Expatriate Adaptation," *Academy of Management Learning & Education,* December 2004, pp. 362–379.

20. Gretchen Weber, "English Rules," *Workforce Management,* May 2004, p. 48.

21. Donna M. Owens, "Multilingual Workforces," *HR Magazine,* September 2005, p. 127.

22. Definition from the U.S. Department of the Interior, Office of Civil Rights, as quoted in Janet Perez, "Diversity Inside-Out," *Hispanic Business,* April 2006, p. 64.

23. Research reported in Fay Hansen, "Diversity's Business Case Doesn't Add Up," *Workforce,* April 2003, pp. 28–32.

24. Facts and quote from Anne Fisher, "How You Can Do Better on Diversity," *Fortune,* November 15, 2004, p. 60.

25. Janet Perez, "A Fresh Deck: Publicly Traded MGM Begins Dealing Diversity," *Hispanic Business,* January/February 2006, p. 62.

26. David P. Tulin, "Enhance Your Multi-Cultural Communication Skills," *Managing Diversity,* 1, 1992, p. 5.

27. "Use Team's Diversity to Best Advantage, *ExecutiveSTRATEGIES,* April 2000, p. 2.

28. Siri Carpenter, "Why Do 'They All Look Alike'?" *Monitor on Psychology,* December 2000, p. 44.

29. One example of this research is Robert J. Kabacoff, "Gender Differences in Organizational Leadership," Management Research Group, Portland, Maine, as reported in "Do Men and Women Lead Differently?" *Leadership Strategies,* Premier Issue, copyright 2001, Briefings Publishing Group.

30. The National Leadership Network of Black Conservatives, Affirmative Action Information Center, available at *www.nationalcenter.org/AA.html*; Retrieved April 23, 2006, Jeff Jacoby, "On Flattering Minorities, *townhall.com,* May 19, 2004.

# 8

# Problem Solving and Creativity

# Learning Objectives

# Outline

**After studying the information and doing the exercises in this chapter, you should be able to:**

1 Understand how personal characteristics influence the ability to solve problems and make decisions.

2 Apply the problem-solving and decision-making steps to complex problems.

3 Summarize the characteristics of creative people.

4 Describe various ways of improving your creativity.

1 **What Are Some Personal Characteristics That Influence Your Problem-Solving Ability?** 236
Cognitive Intelligence, Education, and Experience
Emotional Intelligence
Flexibility versus Rigidity
Intuition
Concentration
Decisiveness and Perfectionism
Risk Taking and Thrill Seeking
Values of the Decision Maker
Gender Differences in Decision Making

2 **What Are the Problem-Solving and Decision-Making Steps?** 240
Awareness of the Problem
Identify Causes of the Problem
Find Creative Alternatives
Weigh Alternatives and Make the Choice
Implement the Choice
Evaluate the Choice
Brain Teasers for Improving Your Problem-Solving Ability

3 **What Do I Need to Know About Creativity in Decision Making?** 245
Measuring Your Creative Potential
Characteristics of Creative Workers
The Conditions Necessary for Creativity

4 **How Do I Improve My Creativity?** 252
Concentrate Intensely on the Task at Hand
Overcome Traditional Mental Sets
Discipline Yourself to Think Laterally
Conduct Brainstorming Sessions
Establish Idea Quotes for Yourself
Play the Roles of Explorer, Artist, Judge, and Laywer

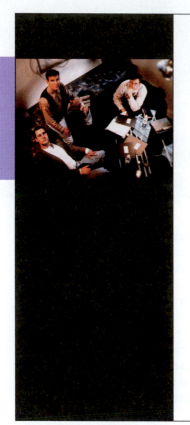

Peter Labaziewicz, an Eastman Kodak Co. scientist, was riding on the train to work one day in Japan when he reached back across the decades for an idea that could push the digital era to new frontiers. He started thinking about the old "turret" film cameras—beastly looking models containing multiple lenses on a "plate" that rotates in front of a shutter. His concept: building similar flexibility in choice of lenses into a digital camera. "Wouldn't it be interesting?" Labaziewicz says he wondered.

*It's not only interesting but also possible, and very, very successful, as Labaziewicz and his colleagues have found out. His musings helped trigger the creation of the Kodak imaging into an important new phase. The V750 is the first camera with two lenses and image sensors—one for wide-angle picture taking, the other for regular zoom. It's considered the first attempt by an industry mainstay to design digital products with attributes that are unique in their own right, free of the constraints of the film era.*

*Since its introduction in early January 2006, the V750 has become a miniphenomenon, capturing the imagination of snap shooters and celebrities alike. It has drawn thousands of e-mails and numerous requests for product placements and donations. Kodak gave out diamond-encrusted models of the V750 to nominees for best actress at the 2006 Academy Awards. The attention is largely because of its sleek, unusual, space-age look and the allure of the camera offering something different. [1]*

■ **Problem**
gap between what exists and what you want to exist

■ **Decision making**
choosing one alternative from the various alternative solutions that can be pursued

The new turret digital camera may not rival the light bulb or the computer as creative brilliance. Yet it does illustrate a few basic facts about problem solving, decision making, and creativity. The inventor of the new camera found a **problem,** a gap between what exists and what you want to exist. His employer was looking to push the digital era to new frontiers. Part of being a creative problem solver is to rely on a storehouse of information, such as knowledge about old turret film cameras. **Decision making** refers to choosing one alternative from the various alternative solutions that can be pursued. The developers of the new camera undoubtedly were sifting through hundreds of new product ideas to find a breakthrough camera.

The general purpose of this chapter is to help you become a more effective and creative problem solver when working individually or in groups. Whether you are solving problems by yourself or as part of a group, the principles apply equally well.

# What Are Some Personal Characteristics That Influence Your Problem-Solving Ability

■ **Learning Objective 1**

Many personal characteristics and traits influence the type of problem solver and decision maker you are or are capable of becoming. Fortunately, some

Figure 8-1

Influences on Problem-Solving Skill

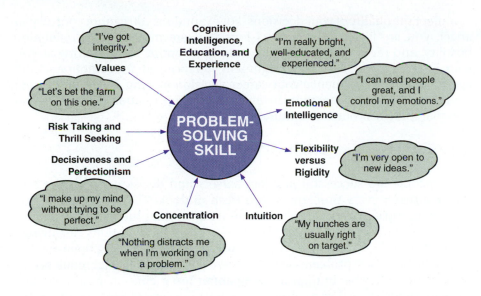

personal characteristics that influence your decision-making ability can be improved through conscious effort. For instance, if you make bad decisions because you do not concentrate on the details of the problem, you can gradually learn to concentrate better. Most of the personal characteristics described next can be strengthened through the appropriate education, training, and self-discipline. Figure 8-1 outlines these characteristics.

## COGNITIVE INTELLIGENCE, EDUCATION, AND EXPERIENCE

In general, if you are intelligent, well educated, and well experienced, you will make better decisions than people without these attributes. (The term *cognitive intelligence* refers to the intellectual, or traditional, type of intelligence that is necessary for such tasks as solving math problems and conjugating verbs.) Cognitive intelligence helps because, by definition, intelligence denotes the ability to solve problems. Education improves the problem-solving and decision-making process because it gives you a background of principles and facts on which to rely.

Experience facilitates decision making because good decisions tend to be made by people who have already faced similar situations in the past. All things being equal, would you prefer to take your computer problem to an experienced or an inexperienced specialist?

## EMOTIONAL INTELLIGENCE

Being able to deal effectively with your feelings and emotions and those of others can help you make better decisions. This type of intelligence has to do with the ability to connect with people and understand their emotions. A worker with high emotional intelligence would be able to engage in such behaviors as sizing up people, pleasing others, and influencing them. [2]

Emotional intelligence is important for decision making because how effective you are in managing your feelings and reading those of other people can affect the quality of your decisions. For example, if you cannot control your anger, you are likely to make decisions that are motivated by retaliation, hostility, and revenge. An example would be shouting and swearing at your team leader because of a work assignment you received. Your emotional intelligence could also influence your career decision making. If you understand your own feelings, you are more likely to enter an occupation or accept a position that matches your true attitude.

## FLEXIBILITY VERSUS RIGIDITY

Some people are successful problem solvers and decision makers because they approach every problem with a fresh outlook. They are able to avoid developing rigid viewpoints. Flexible thinking enables the problem solver to think of original—and therefore creative—alternative solutions to solving a problem. Another perspective on the same issue is that being open-minded helps a person solve problems well. In recent years several major retailers have become more flexible in their thinking about inner cities as profitable locations for their stores. For example, the Kmart division of Sears Holdings Inc. has been successful with many of its new inner-city stores. The link between flexibility and creativity will be described in more detail in the discussion of the characteristics of creative people.

## INTUITION

■ **Intuition**

an experience-based way of knowing or reasoning in which weighing and balancing of evidence are done automatically

Effective decision makers do not rely on careful analysis alone. Instead, they also use their **intuition,** an experience-based way of knowing or reasoning in which weighing and balancing of evidence are done automatically. Recent research about intuition suggests that it is composed of the interplay between knowing (intuition-as-expertise) and sensing (intuition-as-feeling). The best use of intuition, therefore, involves both bring past facts in mind to deal with the situation and a sudden emotional hunch at the same time. [3] An experienced real estate developer might look at an old building and within 10 minutes decide it would be a good investment to rehabilitate the structure. Based on hundreds of property evaluations, the developer knows that rehabilitating an old building can be profitable. At the same time the developer visualizes what the old building would look like when rehabilitated.

Relying on intuition is like relying on your instincts when faced with a decision. Intuition takes place when the brain gathers information stored in memory and packages it as a new insight or solution. Intuitions, therefore, can be regarded as stored information that is reorganized or repackaged. Developing good intuition may take a long time because so much information has to be stored. Cognitive psychologist Gary Klein, the founder of Klein Associates, explains it this way:

> We sometimes think that experts are weighted down by information, by facts, by memories—that they make decisions slowly because they must search through so much data. But in fact, we've got it backward. The accumulation of experience does not weight people down—it lightens them up. It makes them fast. [4]

Intuition has become perhaps the hottest topic in decision making, including being the subject of a bestseller (*Blink* by Malcolm Gladwell). [5]

Nevertheless, intuition has its drawbacks. Our hunches based on the combination of experience and emotion can sometimes lead us astray when a more analytical approach would have led to a better decision. For example, a charming and articulate job candidate might be chosen mostly on the basis of intuition. A background check based on rational analysis might have revealed that the candidate is a procrastinator and a criminal. One way to improve intuition is to get feedback on the decisions we make, so we can sharpen future decisions. [6] For example, a credit analyst in a bank profits from feedback about the future payment records of the loans he or she approved.

## CONCENTRATION

Mental concentration is an important contributor to making good decisions. Many people who solve problems poorly do so because they are too distracted to immerse themselves in the problem at hand. In contrast, effective problem solvers often achieve the **flow experience**—total absorption in their work. When flow occurs, things seem to go just right. The person feels alive and fully attentive to what he or she is doing. As a by-product of the flow experience, a good solution to a problem may surface. If you fail to concentrate hard enough, you may overlook an important detail that could affect the outcome of the decision. For example, a person about to purchase an automobile might be excited about the high gas mileage but forget to check the vehicle's ability to withstand a crash.

■ **Flow experience**
total absorption in work; when flow occurs, things seem to go just right

## DECISIVENESS AND PERFECTIONISM

Some people are ill suited to solving problems and making decisions because they are fearful of committing themselves to any given course of action. "Gee, I'm not sure, what do you think?" is their typical response to a decision forced on them. If you are indecisive, this characteristic will have to be modified if you are to become successful in your field. A manager has to decide which person to hire. And a photographer has to decide which setting is best for the subject. As the old saying goes, at some point "you have to fish or cut bait." The combination of being indecisive and a perfectionist can lead to procrastination. Also, being a procrastinator can make one indecisive. Perfectionism contributes to delayed decision making because the person keeps working on a project before deciding to submit it to somebody else.

## RISK TAKING AND THRILL SEEKING

The need for taking risks and seeking thrills is yet another personality characteristic that influences problem-solving skill. For some types of problems, the high risk taker and thrill seeker is at an advantage. Firefighters have to take risks to save people from burning buildings and remove people trapped in collapsed buildings. An information technology specialist might have to engage in a risky maneuver to salvage data from a crashed hard drive. Risk taking and thrill seeking can also lead to poor problem solving and decision making, such as a merchandiser buying a huge inventory of a highly original fashion. The experienced decision maker needs to know when to take high risks and seek thrills and when to be more conservative.

## VALUES OF THE DECISION MAKER

Values influence decision making at every step. The right values for the situation will improve problem solving and decision making, whereas the wrong values will lead to poor decisions. Ultimately, all decisions are based on values. A manager who places a high value on the well-being of employees tries to avoid alternatives that create hardships for workers. Another value that significantly influences problem solving and decision making is the pursuit of excellence. A worker who embraces the pursuit of excellence (and is, therefore, conscientious) will search for the high-quality alternative solution.

## GENDER DIFFERENCES IN DECISION MAKING

Gender is a possible source of differences in the types of decisions people make, even if gender does not influence the quality of decisions. According to some research men and women in managerial positions have different decision making styles. Rita Mano-Negrin of the human services department of the University of Haifa in Israel observes that women collaborate, listen, and strive to build teamwork. Men are more likely to direct, blame others, and frequently say "I." A personality assessment by Hagberg Consulting concluded that women give most weight to two factors in making a decision: how it will affect the team and whether it will affect short-term goals. In contrast, men focus on the competitive environment and long-term results. [7] Furthermore, according to cultural stereotypes, women typically rely more on intuition when making decisions, and men tend to rely more on analytical reasoning.

# What Are the Problem-Solving and Decision-Making Steps?

■ Learning Objective 2

Whatever complex problem you face, it is best to use the standard problem-solving and decision-making steps as a guide. These steps are similar to the systematic approach used in the scientific method. Figure 8-2 summarizes the steps involved in problem solving and decision making. It assumes that problem solving should take place in an orderly flow of steps. Paying attention to this model is important because deviating too far will often result in decision failure. Paul C. Nutt studied 356 decisions in medium to large organizations in the United States and Canada. He found that one-half of these decisions failed, meaning that the decision was not fully used after two years. The typical reason for failure is that the decision makers did not take a systematic approach, such as searching for many alternative solutions. The managers involved also committed the human relations error of not involving enough people in the decisions. [8]

Although the problem-solving and decision-making steps appear logical, we emphasize again that people are frequently not entirely rational when making decisions. Emotions and personality traits can cloud decision making. In fact, psychologist Daniel Kahneman won a Nobel Prize in economics for his research on how people often behave irrationally in ordinary situations, such as holding on to losing mutual funds or buying insurance for inexpensive appliances. [9]

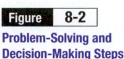

**Figure  8-2**

**Problem-Solving and Decision-Making Steps**

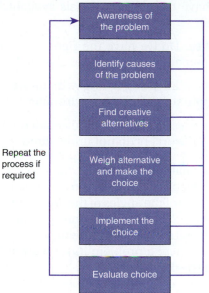

## AWARENESS OF THE PROBLEM

Problem solving and decision making begin when somebody is aware that a problem exists. In most decision-making situations, problems are given to another person. At other times, people create their own problems to solve, or they find problems. Scotch Tape had its origins more than 75 years ago because somebody noticed a problem. The story goes like this:

> Richard Drew, a young engineer working for the Minnesota Mining and Manufacturing Co. (3M today), a small sandpaper manufacturer, noticed that car painters were having trouble masking one section while painting another in a different color. In 1925, Drew invented a masking tape using crepe paper with lines of pressure-sensitive glue running along the edges. Trouble was, the tape kept falling off. An automotive painter told a 3M representative to go back to his "Scotch" (negative stereotype that Scotch people are cheap) bosses and tell them to put adhesive all over the tape, not just on the edges. They did, the tape worked and the name stuck. Five years later Drew overcame numerous production hurdles and developed the clear, cellophane tape today that has become a worldwide staple. [10]

After you are aware that a problem exists or have identified it, recognize that it may represent an important opportunity. For example, if you are bothered enough by a problem facing your company, you might volunteer to be the person in charge of overcoming the problem.

## IDENTIFY CAUSES OF THE PROBLEM

The causes of problems should be diagnosed and clarified before any action is taken because they are not always what they seem to be on the surface. Some may be more complicated than suspected or may even be the wrong problem you need to solve in a particular situation. Five key elements to ask questions about (along with some sample questions) are as follows:

- **People.** What do the people involved contribute to the problem? Are they competent? Do they have an attitude problem?

- **Materials.** Do we have the right materials available? Is the quality of the materials adequate?

- **Machines and facilities.** Do we have the right machines and facilities to do the job? Have the machines and facilities changed?

- **Physical environment.** Is anything wrong with the environment (such as toxic fumes making people sick)? Has the environment changed?

- **Methods.** Are the processes and procedures adequate? Have new methods been introduced that workers do not understand?

The approach to analyzing causes is often place in a cause-and-effect diagram, as shown in Figure 8-3. The approach is sometimes referred to as a *fishbone diagram* because of the angles of the lines leading to the various causes. Notice that all the causes contribute to the problem at the right. Even when you have identified the general source of a problem, you may still need to dig further as to what, when, and where a problem *did not* occur. Suppose a friend talks about a fear of public speaking. By asking a few "but not" questions, you might be able to identify a major cause of the problem. Let's try out the method:

*Your friend:*   I'm horribly afraid of public speaking. I hate going up in front of class.

*You:*   But have you ever not been afraid of speaking to a group of people?

*Your friend:*   Yes, I can remember once feeling OK speaking at a victory dinner for my high school soccer team. We came in first place in the region.

*You:*   What did you talk about?

*Your friend:*   I told a cute story about how my mother and father put a soccer ball in my crib. I hugged it every day like it was a teddy bear.

*You:*   So why weren't you afraid of giving that talk?

*Your friend:*   I knew what I was talking about. I didn't have to rehearse.

**Figure    8-3**

**Basic Cause-and-Effect Diagram**

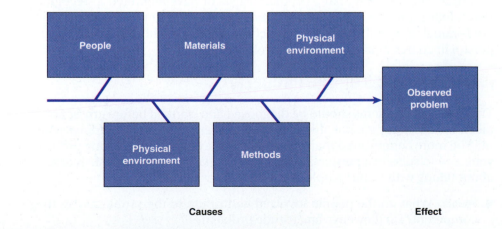

*You:*            What else was different about the talk?

*Your friend:*    It wasn't like talking to strangers. I was just there with my buddies and our coaches.

*You:*            What you are really telling me is that public speaking is OK when you are well prepared and you are in a comfortable surrounding?

*Your friend:*    Thanks for helping me understand my problem.

## FIND CREATIVE ALTERNATIVES

Creativity and imagination enter into problem solving and decision making. Successful decision makers have the ability to think of different alternatives. The person who pushes to find one more alternative to a problem is often the person who finds a breakthrough solution. The more alternatives you generate, the more likely you will find a useful solution to your problem. In the words of business strategy expert and consultant Gary Hamel, "Innovation is a numbers game. It takes 1,000 wacky ideas to find 100 things worth putting any money at all on, to find 10 ideas worth really investing in, to wind up with one really great idea." [11]

## WEIGH ALTERNATIVES AND MAKE THE CHOICE

This stage refers simply to examining the pros and cons of the various alternatives in the previous stages and then making a choice. In a major decision, each alternative would have to be given serious consideration. In practice, weighing alternatives often means jotting down the key good and bad points of each possible choice. The essence of decision making is selecting the right course of action to follow. You have to choose an alternative, even if it is not to go ahead with a new plan of action. For instance, after conducting a job campaign, you could decide *not* to change jobs. Instead of coming to a decision, some people overanalyze a problem. Do you suffer from "analysis paralysis," or do you make up your mind after a reasonable amount of thought?

In choosing an alternative, it is helpful to remember that most problems really have multiple solutions. You, therefore, do not have to be overly concerned with finding the only correct answer to your problem. For instance, there might be several effective ways of reducing the costs of running a department.

## IMPLEMENT THE CHOICE

After you decide which course of action to take, you have to put the choice into effect. Some decisions are more difficult to implement than others. Decisions made by top management, for example, are sometimes so difficult to implement that they have to be reversed. An executive at a major on-line retailer announced a new policy that all customer problems would have to be resolved by e-mail and that the toll-free number for customer assistance would be disbanded. Hundreds of customers complained about the new policy by e-mail, and many customer accounts became inactive. The executive reconsidered the decision in terms of its effect on customer service and goodwill and reinstated the toll-free telephone call option. The general point is that to implement many decisions, the human element must be taken into consideration.

## EVALUATE THE CHOICE

The decision-making sequence is not complete until the decision has been evaluated. Evaluation may take a considerable period of time because the results of your decision are not always immediately apparent. Suppose you receive two job offers. It might take several months to a year to determine whether you are satisfied with the job you accepted. It would be necessary to look at the factors you think are most important in a job. Among them might be "Is there opportunity for advancement?" "Are the people here friendly?" "Is the work interesting?"

Evaluating your choice would be further complicated by the difficulty of determining how you might have fared in the job you didn't accept. Now and then, you might obtain some information to suggest what that alternative held in store for you, as did a woman who turned down a job offer with a new and promising company. She questioned that decision until she read one morning a year later that the company had gone into bankruptcy.

What happens when your evaluation of a decision is negative? You go back to the drawing board, as the line and arrow on the left-hand side of Figure 8-1 indicates. Because your first decision was not a good one, you are faced with another problem situation. A helpful decision-making aid is to visualize what you would do if the alternative you chose proved to be dreadful—the **worst-case scenario.** Suppose, for example, you choose a job that proves to be unsuited to your talents. Would you resign as soon as your mistake became apparent, or would you sweat it out for a year to show some employment stability? Or would you retain the job while starting to look for a more suitable job? Developing a worst-case scenario helps prevent you from becoming overwhelmed by a bad decision. Closely related to the worst-case scenario is establishing an **exit strategy** that determines in advance how you will get out of a bad decision, such as having joined a failing family business.

## BRAIN TEASERS FOR IMPROVING YOUR PROBLEM-SOLVING ABILITY

A widely accepted belief is that solving difficult problems and puzzles enhances your problem-solving ability. Among these brain teasers could be crossword puzzles, some types of video games, and various types of word puzzles. Just to give you a brief mental workout, here we present an example of a frame game (Figure 8-4) and Sudoko (Figure 8-5). Performing activities such as these regularly might sharpen your mental acuity for problem solving on the job and in school. The answers to the Sudoku and the Frame Games are presented following the References in this chapter.

■ **Worst-case scenario**

helpful decision-making aid is that involves visualizing what you would do if the alternative chosen proved to be dreadful

■ **Exit strategy**

determining in advance how to get out of a bad decision, such as having joined a failing family business

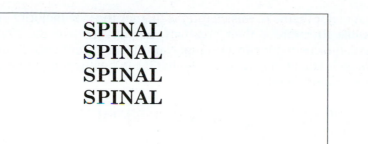

**Figure 8-4**
**Frame Games**
**Source:** The frame games are from Terry Stickels, "Frame Games," *USA Weekend*, March 10–12, 2006, p. 26.

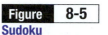

**Figure 8-5**
**Sudoku**
Fill in the Sudoko grid so that every row, every column, and every $3 \times 3$ box contains the digits 1 through 9.

# What Do I Need to Know About Creativity in Decision Making?

Creativity is helpful at any stage of problem solving but is essential for being aware of problems, analyzing their causes, and searching for alternative solutions. Simply put, **creativity** is the ability to develop good ideas that can be put into action. Finding a creative idea usually involves a flash of insight as to how to solve a problem, such as that experienced by the person who thought of Scotch tape.

When many people see or hear the word *creativity,* they think of a rarefied talent. A more helpful perspective is to recognize that not all creativity requires wild imagination. The emphasis here is on creativity applied to business and personal life rather than on creativity in science, technology, and the arts. Creativity is important for companies of all sizes, not only for large firms.

■ **Creativity**
the ability to develop good ideas that can be put into action

■ Learning Objective 3

A major theme of this chapter is that for the vast majority of people, it is possible to improve their creativity. As explained in the *Encyclopedia of Creativity,* creativity can be taught and learned, enhanced, and mastered. Enough is known about creativity that it can be integrated into every level in the educational system [12].

## MEASURING YOUR CREATIVE POTENTIAL

One way to understand creativity is to try out exercises used to measure creative potential. Begin with Human Relations Self-Assessment Quiz 8-1 that measures creativity based on verbal ability.

## CHARACTERISTICS OF CREATIVE WORKERS

Creative workers tend to have different intellectual and personality characteristics from their less creative counterparts. In general, creative people are more mentally flexible than others, which allows them to overcome the traditional ways of looking at problems. This flexibility often shows up in practical jokes and other forms of playfulness, such as making up a rap song about the company's product line. The characteristics of creative workers can be grouped into three broad areas: knowledge, intellectual abilities, personality. [13]

### Knowledge

Creative thinking requires a broad background of information, including facts and observations. Knowledge supplies the building blocks for generating and combining ideas. This is particularly true because, according to some experts, creativity always comes down to combining things in a new and different way. The introductory case about the scientist who linked knowledge of old turret cameras with knowledge about digital cameras illustrates how combining facts can be helpful. Taking Human Relations Self-Assessment Quiz 8-2, will help you appreciate how possessing knowledge contributes to thinking creatively.

### Intellectual Abilities

■ **Insight**

an ability to know what information is relevant, to find connections between the old and the new, to combine facts that are unrelated, and to see the "big picture"

In general, creative workers tend to be bright rather than brilliant. Extraordinarily high intelligence is not required to be creative, but creative people are good at generating alternative solutions to problems in a short period of time. According to Yale University professor of psychology and education, Robert Sternberg, the key to creative intelligence is **insight,** an ability to know what information is relevant, to find connections between the old and the new, to combine facts that are unrelated, and to see the "big picture." [14] Creative people also maintain a youthful curiosity throughout their lives, and the curiosity is not centered on only their own field of expertise. Instead, their range of interests encompasses many areas of knowledge, and they generate enthusiasm toward almost any puzzling problem.

Creative people are able to think divergently. They can expand the number of alternatives to a problem, thus moving away from a single solution. Yet the creative thinker also knows when it is time to think convergently, narrowing

## Human Relations Self-Assessment Quiz  8-1

### Creative Personality Test

Answer each of the following statements as Mostly True or Mostly False. We are looking for general trends, so do not be concerned that under certain circumstances your answer might be different in response to a particular statement.

| | Mostly True | Mostly False |
|---|---|---|
| 1. I think novels are a waste of time, so I am more likely to read a nonfiction book. | _____ | _____ |
| 2. You have to admit, some crooks are ingenious. | _____ | _____ |
| 3. I pretty much wear the same style and colors of clothing regularly. | _____ | _____ |
| 4. To me most issues have a clear-cut right side or wrong side. | _____ | _____ |
| 5. I enjoy it when my boss hands me vague instructions. | _____ | _____ |
| 6. When I'm surfing the Internet, I sometimes investigate topics, about which I know very little. | _____ | _____ |
| 7. Business before leisure activities is a hard-and-fast rule in my life. | _____ | _____ |
| 8. Taking a different route to work is fun, even if it takes longer. | _____ | _____ |
| 9. From time to time I have made friends with people of a different sex, race, religion, or ethnic background from myself. | _____ | _____ |
| 10. Rules and regulations should be respected, but deviating from them once in a while is acceptable. | _____ | _____ |
| 11. People who know me say that I have an excellent sense of humor. | _____ | _____ |
| 12. I have been known to play practical jokes or pranks on people. | _____ | _____ |
| 13. Writers should avoid using unusual words and word combinations. | _____ | _____ |
| 14. Detective work would have some appeal to me. | _____ | _____ |
| 15. I am much more likely to tell a rehearsed joke than make a witty comment. | _____ | _____ |
| 16. Almost all national advertising on television bores me. | _____ | _____ |
| 17. Why write letters or send e-mail greetings to friends when there are so many clever greeting cards already available in the stores or on-line? | _____ | _____ |
| 18. For most important problems in life, there is one best solution available. | _____ | _____ |
| 19. Pleasing myself means more to me than pleasing others. | _____ | _____ |
| 20. I'm enjoying taking this test. | _____ | _____ |

### Scoring and Interpretation:

Give yourself a plus 1 for each answer scored in the creative direction as follows:

| | | |
|---|---|---|
| 1. Mostly False | 5. Mostly True | 9. Mostly True |
| 2. Mostly True | 6. Mostly True | 10. Mostly True |
| 3. Mostly False | 7. Mostly False | 11. Mostly True |
| 4. Mostly False | 8. Mostly True | 12. Mostly True |

*(continued)*

## Human Relations Self-Assessment Quiz **8-1** *(Continued)*

**13.** Mostly False    **16.** Mostly False    **19.** Mostly True

**14.** Mostly True     **17.** Mostly False    **20.** Mostly True

**15.** Mostly False    **18.** Mostly False

A score of 15 or more suggests that your personality and attitudes are similar to those of a creative person. A score of between 9 and 14 suggests an average similarity with the personality and attitudes of a creative person. A score of 8 or less suggests that your personality is dissimilar to that of a creative person. You are probably more of a conformist and not highly open-minded in your thinking at this point in your life. To become more creative, you may need to develop more flexibility in your thinking and a higher degree of open-mindedness.

## Human Relations Self-Assessment Quiz **8-2**

### Rhyme and Reason

A noted creativity expert says that exercises in rhyming release creative energy; they stir imagination into action. While doing the following exercises, remember that rhyme is frequently a matter of sound and does not have to involve similar or identical spelling. This exercise deals with light and frivolous emotions. After each "definition," write two rhyming words to which it refers.

**Examples**

| | | |
|---|---|---|
| **1.** Large hog | Big | pig |
| **2.** Television | Boob | tube |
| **3.** A computer command tool for the home | House | mouse |

Now try these:

**1.** Happy father
**2.** False pain
**3.** Formed like a simian
**4.** Highest-ranking police worker
**5.** Voyage by a large boat
**6.** Corpulent feline
**7.** Melancholy fellow
**8.** Clever beginning
**9.** Heavy and unbroken slumber
**10.** Crazy custom

11. Lengthy melody
12. Weak man      _____      _____
13. Instruction at the seashore      _____      _____
14. Criticism lacking in effectiveness      _____      _____
15. A person who murders for pleasurable excitement      _____      _____
16. Musical stringed instrument with full, rich sounds      _____      _____
17. Courageous person who is owned as property by another      _____      _____
18. Mature complaint      _____      _____
19. Strange hair growing on the lower part of a man's face      _____      _____
20. Drooping marine crustacean      _____      _____
21. A computer whiz with a ridiculous sense of humor      _____      _____
22. You make one up now for the most important question of all      _____      _____

## Answers and Interpretation:

The more of these rhymes you were able to come up with, the higher your creative potential. You would also need an advanced vocabulary to score very high (for instance, what is a *simian* or a *crustacean*?). Ten or more correct rhymes would tend to show outstanding creative potential, at least in the verbal area. Here are the answers:

| | | |
|---|---|---|
| 1. Glad dad | 9. Deep sleep | 16. Mellow cello |
| 2. Fake ache | 10. Mad fad | 17. Brave slave |
| 3. Ape shape | 11. Long song | 18. Ripe gripe |
| 4. Top cop | 12. Frail male | 19. Weird beard |
| 5. Ship trip | 13. Beach teach | 20. Limp shrimp |
| 6. Fat cat | 14. Weak critique | 21. Absurd nerd |
| 7. Sad lad | 15. Thriller killer | 22. Two bonus points |
| 8. Smart start | | |

If you can think of a sensible substitute for any of these answers, give yourself a bonus point. For example, for number 21, how about a freak geek?

**Source:** The current test is an updated version of Eugene Raudsepp with George P. Hough, Jr., *Creative Growth Games* (New York: Harcourt Brace Jovanovich, 1977). Reprinted with permission.

the number of useful solutions. For example, the divergent thinker might think of 27 different names for a Web site to sell high-fashion buttons. Yet at some point, he or she will have to converge toward choosing the best name, such as ***www.chicbutton.com.***

Creativity can stem from both *fluid intelligence* and *crystallized intelligence*. Fluid intelligence depends on raw processing ability, or how quickly you learn information and solve problems. Like raw athletic ability, fluid intelligence begins to decline by age 30, particularly because our nerve conduction slows. Crystallized intelligence is accumulated knowledge that increases with age and experience.

## Personality

The emotional and other nonintellectual aspects of a person heavily influence creative problem solving. Creative people tend to have a positive self-image without being blindly self-confident. Because they are self-confident, creative people are able to cope with criticism of their ideas. Creative people have the ability to tolerate the isolation necessary for developing ideas. Talking to others is a good source of ideas. Yet at some point, the creative problem solver has to work alone and concentrate.

Creative people are frequently nonconformists and do not need strong approval from the group. Many creative problem solvers are thrill seekers who find developing imaginative solutions to problems to be a source of thrills. Creative people are also persistent, which is especially important for seeing that a new idea is implemented. Selling a creative idea to the right people requires considerable follow-up. Creative people enjoy dealing with uncertainty and chaos. A creative person, for example, would enjoy the challenge of taking over a customer service department that was way behind schedule and ineffective. Less creative people become frustrated quickly when their jobs are unclear and disorder exists.

Self-reflection and a concentration on feelings are characteristic of many creative people. The quiet thinking is helpful in finding useful ideas, as in thinking of how to solve a difficult problem while walking alone or taking a shower. Creative people are also open and responsive to feelings and emotions in the world around them.

## THE CONDITIONS NECESSARY FOR CREATIVITY

Creativity is not simply a random occurrence. Well-known creativity researcher and professor of business administration at Harvard Business School Teresa M. Amabile has summarized 22 years of her research about creativity in the workplace. Her findings are also supported by others. [15] Creativity takes place when three components come together: expertise, creative thinking skills, and the right type of motivation. *Expertise* refers to the necessary knowledge to put facts together. The more ideas floating around in your head, the more likely you are to combine them in some useful way, as already described.

*Creative thinking* refers to how flexibly and imaginatively individuals approach problems. If you know how to keep digging for alternatives and to avoid getting stuck in the status quo, your chances of being creative multiply. Along these same lines, you are much more likely to be creative if you are intentionally seeking ideas, such always being on the lookout for money-saving ideas. Persevering, or sticking with a problem to a conclusion, is essential for finding creative solutions. A few rest breaks to gain a fresh perspective may be helpful, but the creative person keeps coming back until a solution emerges.

The right type of *motivation* is the third essential ingredient for creative thought. A fascination with or passion for the task is much more important then searching for external rewards. People will be the most creative when they are motivated primarily by the satisfaction and challenge of the work itself. A Dutch psychologist attempted to analyze what separated chess masters from chess grand masters. He subjected groups of each to a variety of mental ability tests but found no difference between the two groups. The only difference was found in motivation: grand masters simply loved chess more and had more passion and commitment for the game. [16]

Passion for the task and high intrinsic motivation contribute to a total absorption in the work and intense concentration, resulting in the flow experience. A creative businessperson, such as an entrepreneur developing a plan for worldwide distribution of a product, will often achieve the experience of flow. One analysis of creativity suggests that hard work and the love of the task can be at least as important as raw talent in ensuring creative success. [17] In addition to the internal conditions that foster creativity, five factors outside the person are key:

**1. An environmental need must stimulate the setting of a goal.** This is another way of saying, "Necessity is the mother of invention." For example, several years ago independent hardware stores were faced with the challenge of large chains, such as Home Depot and Lowe's, driving them out of business. Many of these independent stores survived by forming buying alliances with each other so that they could purchase inventory in larger quantities—and, therefore, lower prices. The independents also emphasize doing home repairs, such as fixing ripped screens and broken windows.

**2. Another condition that fosters creativity is enough conflict and tension to put people on edge.** Robert Sutton advises managers to prod happy people into fighting among themselves to stimulate creativity. The fights should be about ideas, not personality conflicts and name calling. For example, a group member should be given time to defend his or her work, and then the ideas should be sharply criticized by the other group members. [18] Cirque du Soleil, the world-famous circus, capitalizes on the importance of conflict for creativity. Cirque officials generally ensure there is a mix of nationalities and viewpoints when they assemble a creative team. Daniel Lamarre, the troupe's president, says that easy consensus is the enemy of groundbreaking ideas. The ideas, in this context, usually refer to fascinating acts. [19]

**3. Another external factor for creativity is encouragement, including a permissive atmosphere that welcomes new ideas.** A manager or team leader who encourages imagination and original thinking and does not punish people for making honest mistakes is likely to receive creative ideas from people. 3M is highly regarded as a company with many innovations in addition to Scotch tape and Post-it® notes. The company encourages creativity in many ways, such as granting people time off from regular responsibilities simply to think about new ideas. W. L Gore is often cited among the world's most innovative companies. You may be familiar with their waterproof fabrics and guitar strings. The cornerstone of Gore's innovative culture has been a permissive atmosphere. In the words of human resources associate, Jackie Brinton, "We believe in the power of the individual who is given the freedom to do great things and in the beauty of small teams, even though we're now operating on a global, coordinated scale." [20]

**4. Humor is a key environmental condition for enhancing creativity.** Humor has always been linked to creativity. Humor gets the creative juices flowing, and effective humor requires creativity. Thomas Edison started every workday with a joke-telling session. Mike Vance, chair of the Creative Thinking Association of America, says, "Humor is unmasking the hypocritical. What makes us laugh often is seeing how things are screwed up—then sometimes seeing how we can fix them. Whenever I go into a company and don't hear much laughter, I know it's not a creative place." [21]

**5.   A final key environmental condition to be considered here is how much time pressure the problem solver should face to trigger creativity.**   Conventional wisdom says that people produce the best when pressure is highest, for example, thinking of ways to keep a business running after a disaster, such as a fire, flood, or terrorist attack. Yet studies show that the more workers feel pressed for time, the less likely they are to produce creative output, such as solving a tricky problem or envisioning a new product, or to have other such "aha" experiences that result in innovation. Time pressures may diminish creativity because they limit a worker's freedom to think through different options and directions. A subtle finding, however, is that time pressures may help creativity if the worker is focused on a single task he or she considers important. [22] So if you are under heavy time pressure to arrive at a creative solution, focus on one task.

Despite the theme of permissiveness in several of the conditions for enhancing creativity, constraints also have their place. Individuals or teams with budget constraints and time constraints sometimes find that these constraints help them rise to the occasion. Marissa Ann Mayer, the vice president for search products and user experience at Google contends that constraints can actually speed product development. Google often gets a sense of just how good a new concept is if they simply prototype it (try it out) for a single day or week. Another constraint would be limiting team size to two or three people. [23]

■ Learning Objective 4

# How Do I Improve My Creativity?

Because of the importance of creative problem solving, many techniques have been developed to improve creativity. Here we look at both specific techniques and general strategies for becoming more creative. The goal of these experiences is to think like a creative problem solver. Such a person lets his or her imagination wander. He or she ventures beyond the constraints that limit most people. The result of thinking more creatively is to bring something new into existence. *Something new* can be a totally new creation or a combination of existing things and ideas. To focus again on the subject, when we refer to creativity in business we are not necessarily thinking of revolutionary ideas that create a new industry. The new design of containers for prescription medicine is a representative example. Old prescription bottles are difficult to open and read, whereas the new prescription bottles are color-coded to specific medicines and easy to read and open. [24]

## CONCENTRATE INTENSELY ON THE TASK AT HAND

The ability to concentrate was mentioned earlier as a characteristic that contributes to effective problem solving in general. The ability to eliminate distractions also contributes mightily to generating new ideas. At times we think we are thinking intently about our problem yet in reality we may be thinking about something that interferes with creativity. Among the office distractions that interfere with concentration are phone calls, a computer beep informing you of an incoming message, a person in the next cubicle talking loudly on the phone, and a friendly hello from a work associate walking past your cubicle. All the methods that follow for creativity enhancement require concentration.

## OVERCOME TRADITIONAL MENTAL SETS

An important consequence of becoming more intellectually flexible is that you can overcome a **traditional mental set,** a fixed way of thinking about objects and activities. Overcoming traditional mental sets is important because the major block to creativity is perceiving things in a traditional way. All creative examples presented so far in this chapter involved this process, and here is another one. You may be familiar with the Nalgene sports bottle for carrying water and other fluids. Aside from its decorative colors, a key feature is its durability. The bottle had its origins in chemical laboratories—the traditional use for a durable plastic bottle. However, by the 1970s, managers at Nalgene noticed that scientists were using the durable bottles to hold water for camping and hiking. The company soon started a division to market its "laboratory" bottles to Boy Scouts and other hikers. [25] Today, the company is challenged to keep up with the demand for the Nalgene bottle.

■ **Traditional mental set**
fixed way of thinking about objects and activities

An effective way of overcoming a traditional mental set (or thinking outside the box) is to challenge the status quo. If you want to develop an idea that will impress your boss or turn around an industry, you must use your imagination. Question the old standby that things have always been done in a particular way.

## DISCIPLINE YOURSELF TO THINK LATERALLY

A major challenge in developing creative thinking skills is to learn how to think laterally in addition to vertically. **Vertical thinking** is an analytical, logical process that results in few answers. The vertical thinker is looking for the one best solution to a problem, much like solving an equation in algebra. In contrast, **lateral thinking** spreads out to find many different alternative solutions to a problem. In short, critical thinking is vertical, and creative thinking is lateral. A vertical thinker might say, "I must find a part-time job to supplement my income. My income is not matching my expenses." The lateral thinker might say, "I need more money. Let me think of the various ways of earning more money. I can find a second job, get promoted where I am working, cut my expenses, run a small business out of my home. . . ."

■ **Vertical thinking**
analytical, logical process that results in few answers; the vertical thinker looks for the one best solution to a problem, much like solving an equation in algebra

■ **Lateral thinking**
process of spreading out to find many different alternative solutions to a problem

To learn to think laterally, you have to develop the mental set that every problem has multiple alternative solutions. Do not leave the problem until you have sketched out multiple alternatives. Use a pencil or pen and paper or a computer screen, but do not walk away from your problem until you have thought of multiple alternatives. The accompanying Human Relations in Practice box insert provides an industrial example of lateral thinking.

## Human Relations in Practice

### Robot Maker Thinks Laterally to Find New Use for Product

The KR 500, designed to lift car parts, is sold by Kuka Robotics, Europe's largest manufacturer of automated industrial machines. In 2000, several Kuka engineers wondered aloud whether the KR 500 could also lift people. "We could attach a chair to the end of it," one said. "It could make a fun ride." At any other industrial manufacturer, such an idea might have been laughed at and forgotten. But at Kuka, which has long built robots not only to perform but also to delight, it breathed new life into the company.

Only five years ago, Kuka was a century-old supplier of manufacturing equipment whose profits were disappearing because of its overreliancce on automakers. By taking on its engineers challenge to break down the barrier between man and machine, Kuka has found lucrative customers in a range of new industries and made its robots the stars of internationally renowned movies (for example, *Die Another Day*) and theme parks. Says Donald Vincent, executive vice president of Robotic Industries Association, "Kuka has stretched the envelope in growing new markets."

### Questions

1. Why is the new use for an industrial robot an example of lateral thinking?
2. Why are Kuka's ideas for new uses for their products more about business creativity than scientific creativity?

Source: Siri Schubert, "Taking Robots for a Ride," *Business 2.0*, August 2005, p. 46.

## CONDUCT BRAINSTORMING SESSIONS

■ **Brainstorming**

technique by which group members think of multiple solutions to a problem

The best-known method of improving creativity is **brainstorming**, a technique by which group members think of multiple solutions to a problem. Using brainstorming, a group of six people might sit around a table generating new ideas for a product. During the idea-generating part of brainstorming, potential solutions are not criticized or evaluated in any way. In this way, spontaneity is encouraged. Brainstorming continues as a standard procedure for producing creative ideas in all types of organizations. IDEO, the famous design firm that now teaches other companies how to be innovative, uses brainstorming to design products and improve consumer services for clients. Among its successes are the stand-up toothpaste tube for Procter & Gamble Co.'s Crest and the Oral-B toothbrush for children. [26] Rules for brainstorming are presented in Figure 8-6. Brainstorming has many variations, including an electronic approach and brainwriting.

An important strategy for enhancing the outcome of brainstorming is to have intellectually and culturally diverse group members. Some group leaders purposely choose people of different problem-solving styles (such as sensation

1. Use groups of about five to seven people.
2. Encourage the spontaneous expression of ideas. All suggestions are welcome, even if they are outlandish or outreageous. The least workable ideas can be edited out when the idea-generation phase is completed.
3. Quantity and variety are very important. The greater the number of ideas, the greater the likelihood of a breakthrough idea.
4. Encourage combination and improvement of ideas. This process is referred to as *piggybacking* or *hitchhiking*.
5. One person serves as the secretary and records the ideas, perhaps posting them on a whiteboard or a computer with a projection device.
6. Do not overstructure by following any of the preceding rules too rigidly. Brainstorming is a spontaneous process.

**Figure    8-6**

**Rules and Guidelines for Brainstorming**

types and intuitive types) to encourage more diverse thinking. The sensation type might have more "brainstorms" based on facts, whereas the intuitive type might have more brainstorms based on hunches. Cultural diversity is likely to improve brainstorming because people with different cultural experiences often bring different viewpoints to bear on the problem. A basic example is that when developing new food products, members with different ethnic backgrounds are chosen for a brainstorming group. You will recall that Cirque du Soleil relies on heterogeneous groups to produce new ideas.

## Electronic Brainstorming

In electronic brainstorming, group members simultaneously enter their suggestions into a computer. The ideas are distributed to the screens of other group members. Although the group members do not talk to each other, they are still able to build on each other's ideas and combine ideas. Electronic brainstorming helps overcome certain problems encountered in traditional brainstorming. Shyness, domination by one or two members, and participants who loaf tend to be less troublesome than in face-to-face situations.

## Brainwriting

In many situations, brainstorming by yourself produces as many or more useful ideas than does brainstorming in groups. **Brainwriting** is arriving at creative ideas by jotting them down yourself. The creativity-improvement techniques discussed so far will help you develop the mental flexibility necessary for brainstorming. After you have loosened up your mental processes, you will be ready to tackle your most vexing problems. Self-discipline is very important for brainwriting because some people have a tendency to postpone something as challenging as thinking alone. A variation of brainwriting is for group members to pass along their ideas from working alone to another member who reads them and adds his or her own ideas.

   In the various types of brainstorming just discussed, collecting wild ideas is only the start of the process. After ideas are collected, the group or each member carefully evaluates and analyzes the various alternatives. (You also need to refine your ideas from brainwriting.) It is usually important to also

■ **Brainwriting**
arriving at creative ideas by jotting them down

specify the implementation details. For example, how do you actually convert an industrial robot into an amusement park ride?

### Borrow Creative Ideas

Copying the successful ideas of others is a legitimate form of creativity. Be careful, however, to give appropriate credit. Knowing when and which ideas to borrow from other people can help you behave as if you were an imaginative person. Creative ideas can be borrowed through such methods as the following:

- speaking to friends, relatives, classmates, and coworkers

- reading newspapers, newsmagazines, trade magazines, textbooks, nonfiction books, and novels and surfing the Internet

- watching television and listening to radio programs

- subscribing to computerized information services (expensive but worth it to many ambitious people)

■ **Benchmarking**
business firms borrowing ideas from each other regularly as part of quality improvement and improving productivity; representatives from one company visiting another to observe firsthand the practices of the other company

Business firms borrow ideas from each other regularly as part of quality improvement and improving productivity. The process is referred to as **benchmarking** because another firm's product, service, or process is used as a standard of excellence. Benchmarking involves representatives from one company visiting another to observe firsthand the practices of another company. The company visited is usually not a direct competitor. It is considered unethical to visit a competitor company for the purpose of appropriating ideas.

## ESTABLISH IDEA QUOTAS FOR YOURSELF

To enhance creativity, many companies assign idea quotas to workers. For example, workers might be instructed to bring one good idea for earning or saving money to every meeting. Establishing idea quotas is similar to brainwriting with a goal in mind. An easy way of getting started is to establish a monthly minimum quota of one creative idea to improve your personal life and one to improve your job or school performance. Although this exercise might only take about five minutes of thinking each month, it could have a tremendous impact on your life.

A strategy for producing ideas is similar to the techniques for borrowing ideas previously described. To force-feed your creative thinking, follow the suggestion of science fiction writer Ray Bradbury: Read something daily that stimulates your imagination. "If you stuff yourself full," says Bradbury, "you will automatically explode every morning like Old Faithful." [27]

## PLAY THE ROLES OF EXPLORER, ARTIST, JUDGE, AND LAWYER

A method for improving creativity has been proposed that incorporates many of the suggestions already made. The method calls for you to adopt four roles in your thinking. [28]

**1. Be an explorer.** Speak to people in different fields and get ideas that you can use. For example, if you are a telecommunications specialist, speak to salespeople and manufacturing specialists.

**2. Be an artist by stretching your imagination.** Strive to spend about 5 percent of your day asking "what if" questions. For example, a sales manager at a fresh-fish distributor might ask, "What if some new research suggests that eating fish causes intestinal cancer in humans?" Also, remember to challenge the commonly perceived rules in your field. A bank manager challenged why customers needed their canceled checks returned each month. This questioning led to some banks not returning canceled checks unless the customer paid an additional fee for the service. (As a compromise, most banks send customers photocopies of about 10 checks on one page.)

**3. Know when to be a judge.** After developing some wild ideas, at some point you have to evaluate them. Do not be so critical that you discourage your own imaginative thinking. However, be critical enough to prevent attempting to implement weak ideas.

**4. Achieve results by playing the role of a lawyer.** Negotiate and find ways to implement your ideas within your field or place of work. The explorer, artist, and judge stages of creative thought might take only a short time to develop a creative idea. Yet you may spend months or even years getting your brainstorm implemented. For example, it took a long time for the developer of the electronic pager to finally get the product manufactured and distributed on a large scale.

# Concept Review and Reinforcement

## Key Terms

Problem, 236
Decision making, 236
Intuition, 238
Flow experience, 239
Worst-case scenario, 244

Exit strategy, 244
Creativity, 244
Insight, 246
Traditional mental set, 253
Vertical thinking, 253

Lateral thinking, 253
Brainstorming, 254
Brainwriting, 255
Benchmarking, 256

## Summary and Review

Problem solving occurs when you try to remove an obstacle that is blocking a path you want to take or when you try to close the gap between what exists and what you want to exist. Decision making takes place after you encounter a problem and you select one alternative from the various courses of action that can be pursued. Many traits and characteristics influence the type of problem solver you are now or are capable of becoming. Among them are:

- cognitive intelligence, education, and experience
- emotional intelligence
- flexibility versus rigidity
- intuition
- concentration
- decisiveness and perfectionism
- risk taking and thrill seeking
- values of the decision maker

Gender differences may exist in decision making, including the fact that women are more concerned about how a decision will affect the team and short-term results, whereas men focus more on the competitive environment and long-term results.

The decision-making process outlined in this chapter uses both the scientific method and intuition for making decisions in response to problems. Decision making follows an orderly flow of events:

1. You are aware of a problem or create one of your own.
2. You identify causes of the problem.
3. You find creative alternatives.
4. You weigh the alternatives and make a choice.
5. You implement the choice.
6. You evaluate whether you have made a sound choice. If your choice was unsound, you are faced with a new problem, and the cycle repeats itself.

Creativity is the ability to look for good ideas that can be put into action. Creative workers tend to have different intellectual and personality characteristics than their less creative counterparts. In general, creative people are more mentally flexible than others, which allows them to overcome the traditional way of looking at problems.

- **Knowledge.** Creative thinking requires a broad background of information, including facts and observations.
- **Intellectual abilities.** Creative workers tend to be bright rather than brilliant. The key to creative intelligence is insight. Creativity can stem from both fluid (raw) intelligence and crystallized (accumulated) intelligence.
- **Personality.** The emotional and other nonintellectual aspects of a person heavily influence creative problem solving. For example, creative people are frequently nonconformists and thrill seekers.

Creativity takes place when three components come together:

- expertise
- creative thinking skills (being flexible and imaginative)
- right type of motivation (passion for the task and intrinsic motivation)

Four factors outside the person play a key role in fostering creativity: an environmental need, enough conflict and tension to put people on edge, encouragement from management, and the presence of humor. Unless a person is working on a highly focused task, time pressures are likely to diminish creativity. Constraints, such as time and budgets, can often enhance creativity.

Methods of improving your creativity include the following:

- Concentrate intensely on the task at hand.
- Overcome traditional mental sets.
- Discipline yourself to think laterally.
- Conduct brainstorming sessions, including electronic brainstorming and brainwriting.
- Borrow creative ideas.
- Establish idea quotas for yourself.
- Play the roles of explorer, artist, judge, and lawyer.

## Check your Understanding

1. What would be some of the symptoms or signs of a "rigid thinker"?
2. Furnish an example from your own life in which you became aware of a problem. What led to this awareness?
3. Why does concentration improve problem solving?
4. Why is intuition often referred to as a "sixth sense"?
5. Why does knowledge lead to creativity?
6. How can a person still be creative in his or her work without having much talent?
7. Provide an example of how a supervisor or teacher of yours encouraged you to be creative. How effective was this encouragement?
8. Give an example of one work problem and one personal problem for which brainstorming might be useful.
9. Why is being passionate about the task at hand almost essential for being creative?
10. Ask an experienced manager or professional how important creative thinking has been in his or her career. Be prepared to report back to class with your findings.

## Web Corner

*Problem solving techniques:*
WWW.MNDTOOLS.COM

*Development of Creative Thinking:* WWW.CRE8NG.
COM

### Internet Skill Builder

Many Web sites offer creativity training. One such site is www.before-after.com, which mentions many reasons for improving creativity, including "Bring greater creativity to our sales process," "Infuse our meeting with creative energy," and "I'm just looking for creative inspiration." We especially recommend going to the two-minute Creative IQ test. How do the results of this test compare to the creativity test you took in this chapter? If before-after.com is no longer in operation, insert "creativity training" in your search engine to find a comparable site.

# Developing Your Human Relations Skills

*Human Relations Application Exercises*

## Applying Human Relations Exercise 8-1

### Using the Problem-Solving Process

Imagine that you have received $2 million in cash with the income taxes already paid. The only stipulation is that you will have to use the money to establish some sort of enterprise, either a business or a charitable foundation. Solve this problem using the following worksheet. Describe what thoughts you have or what actions you will take for each step of problem solving and decision making.

I. *Identify causes of the problem.* Have you found your own problem, or was it given to you?
II. *Diagnose the problem.* What is the true decision that you are facing? What is your underlying problem?
III. *Find creative alternatives.* Think of the many alternatives facing you. Let your imagination flow and be creative.
IV. *Weigh alternatives and make the choice.* Weigh the pros and cons of each of your sensible alternatives.

| Alternatives | Advantages | Disadvantages |
|---|---|---|
| 1. | | |
| 2. | | |
| 3. | | |
| 4. | | |
| 5. | | |

V. Based on your analysis in step IV, choose the best alternative.
VI. *Implement the choice.* Outline your action plan for converting your chosen alternative into action.
VII. *Evaluate the choice.* Do the best you can here by speculating how you will know if the decision you reached was a good one.

## Applying Human Relations Exercise 8-2

### Choose an Effective Domain Name

Using conventional brainstorming or one of its variations, huddle in small groups. Your task is to develop original domain names for several products or services. An effective domain name is typically one that is easy to remember and will capture potential customers in an uncomplicated Web search. One reason this exercise is difficult is that "cybersquatters" grab unclaimed names they think business owners might want, and then sell these names later. For example, a cybersquatter (or domain name exploiter) might develop or buy the domain name www.dogfood.com, hoping that an e-tailer of dog food will want this name in the future. The owner of dogfood.com would charge a company such as Pet Smart every time a surfer looking to purchase dog food over the Internet, entered www.dogfood.com and was then linked to Pet Smart.

After your team has brainstormed a few possible domain names, search the Internet to see if your domain name is already in used. Simply enter www plus the name you have chosen into your browser. Or visit the site of a company such as DomainCollection.com Inc. After you have developed your list of domain names not already in use, present your findings to the rest of the class.

- Funeral homes
- Replacement parts for antique or classic autos
- A used-car chain
- Personal loans for people with very poor credit ratings
- Clothing for cross-dressers
- A dating (introduction) service
- You choose one of your own

## Questions

1. Suppose the domain names you come up with are also developed by other groups in the class. What might this tell you about the creative process?

**Source:** Several of the facts for this skill-building exercise (but not the exercise) stem from Kelly K. Spors, "Pick a Domain Name," *The Wall Street Journal*, May 9, 2005, p. R8.

2. What do you think of the ethics of cybersquatters holding the rights to obvious domain names such as www.usedautoparts or www.asthma treatment.com?

3. Why not become a cybersquatter and attempt to sell your domain names, sharing the profits with the group?

## Human Relations Case Study 8-1

### L.L. Bean Changes Its Mind

A few years ago, outdoor-clothing retailer L.L. Bean Inc. began building a call center near Waterville, Maine. Then, in November, mobile-phone carrier T-Mobile USA Inc. said it would build its own call center next door. Within a week, Bean chief executive Christopher McCormick halted construction—literally stopping bulldozers in their tracks. A few weeks later, Bean said it would abandon the Waterville site; it ultimately chose to open the new call center in Bangor, about 55 miles away.

McCormick wasn't concerned about appearing wishy-washy. He simply wanted to make the best decision for the closely held Freeport, Maine, retailer. A 23-year veteran who was named CEO in 2001, 50-year-old McCormick is the first chief executive from outside the founding family.

Bean, which does much of its business through catalog telephone sales, opened a call center in an old Waterville shopping center in 1997. But the storefront was cramped and offered limited parking, so Bean executives in early 2004 began scouting for another site. By summer, they had settled on the FirstPark business center in nearby Oakland. Bean purchased the land, drew up the plans for a 50,000-square-foot office that could accommodate up to 800 workers and began grading the site.

Then T-Mobile disclosed plans for a 77,000 square-foot center in FirstPark, housing 700 or more employees. McCormick says he worried immediately whether Waterville, a city of 16,000 had enough workers to supply both companies. He was especially concerned because much of Bean's workforce is seasonal, peaking near the Christmas holidays. He feared that experienced call-center workers would prefer relatively stable year-round employment with T-Mobile, leaving Bean out in the cold.

Within days, he called a meeting of his top lieutenants and told them he wanted to stop work at FirstPark. "You want to do what?" he recalls one asking. "There were certainly some shocked looks." It didn't help that the reappraisal came at Bean's busiest time of the year, when executives were already stretched thin to accommodate holiday sales. Moreover, McCormick wanted the new call center ready by the fall of 2005, then only about nine months away.

McCormick says he has never before reversed such a significant decision. Beyond the land cost, Bean had already sunk more than $500,000 into plans and preliminary construction. But he also wanted to send a signal to other executives. "I want my people to consider all the options. I want objective decision making," he says. "I don't want them to be a champion of one point of view."

Bean began searching for a new call-center site, employing the same real estate broker that had steered T-Mobile to FirstPark. By spring, Bean executives settled on a vacant office building in Bangor, where the city offered the company a break on the rent. When it came time to formally abandon the Waterville deal and commit to Bangor, McCormick says the Bean executive team agreed unanimously.

In disagreement with state officials, McCormick says he couldn't take the chance on moving forward with the Waterville call center. "It was too risky to build this huge building" without more confidence about the potential labor supply. McCormick briefly considered locating the call center outside Maine. He says Bean could have saved money, but he rejected the move because Bean's connection to the state is crucial to the company's branding.

### Questions

1. To what extent did McCormick use the problem-solving and decision-making steps described in the chapter?
2. How will CEO McCormick know if he made a good decision?
3. What is your opinion of the ethics of McCormick backing off on the deal to construct a call center in Waterville?

**Source:** Adapted from Scott Thurm, "Seldom-Used Executive Power: Reconsidering," *The Wall Street Journal*, February 6, 2006, p. B3.

---

## Human Relations Case Study 8-2

### *Hanging on to a Vulnerable Account*

Henry Sanderson is an outsourcing manager at Mercury Products, an office equipment manufacturer. He manages 17 customer sites and 35 employees who work at the sites. Sanderson described a recent problem his group faced. Business was good in that the customers were pleased with the management of their office equipment but had concerns over their monthly costs, which ranged from $37,000 to $43,000. It seemed like a great deal of money to them.

About two years before the five-year account was going to be up for renewal, Alice Reuben, an on-site technician telephoned Sanderson and said there had been a couple of sales reps from one of their competitors in to visit with a customer. Furthermore, the customer had agreed to allow them to make a formal presentation the following week.

Sanderson realized that this account could be taken by a worthy outsourcing competitor, so he listed this major account as vulnerable in his customer database. The consequences of losing an account were tremendous because of lost revenues and layoffs of the on-site employees.

Sanderson decided to conduct a brainstorming session to deal with possible loss of the account. After this the brainstorming began, Betty Yang acted as the scribe to capture every thought on a flip chart. The big question the team sought answers to was, "What can we do better with the customer?" The ideas thrown out included the following: (A few of the ideas were accompanied by action plans.)

■ We need to do better training of end users. A lot of the service calls were needed because the end users did not know how to perform certain functions on our copiers. Although all end users had been trained three years earlier when the equipment was installed, this growing business had added a lot of new employees who didn't know how to use the equipment. Fewer calls to service meant techs would spend less time at this site. This would have a positive effect on their overall performance and budget.

- Improve overall customer service.
- Seek an early renewal to the contract.
- Find a way to lock out the competition. One of the sales strategies for the new contract was to remove the labor component. This would bring the cost down by $3,800 per month.
- Take the misery out of billing.
- Create a roles and responsibilities document. The document will help organize our individual efforts so we can present a unified organization to the customer.
- Give more value to the customer. The sales team, led by Shawn Elliot will determine the appropriate new equipment for the account and determine the pricing with the standard net profit margin. The monthly charge to the customer will probably be higher because of the buyout and the fact that installing networked equipment costs more. However, it will be the task of sales and technical to present a value-added solution that also saves the customer money in terms of time-in-motion, while increasing their productivity.
- Respond more quickly to service problems. Stephanie Johnson reported that the group's average response time to service calls has been 2.4 hours. This is at the very high end of acceptability as the industry average is more than 7 hours.
- Find some quick ways to delight the customer. Mercury's invoice would be put on "auto-pay,"

meaning it did not need any corporate-level approval and the company could be paid immediately.

- Go for seven-year contracts instead of the traditional five-year contract.

Sanderson scheduled another day for solution presentations in one week. The sales group was asked to present their results. Based on a seven-year contract, we would accomplish all of our goals:

➡ The on-site labor component would remain at 100 percent.
➡ The cost to the customer would be reduced by $1,719 per month.
➡ The biggest possible savings for the customer would be $8,000 per month.

The customer would save approximately four cents for each print. The sales group concluded that the customer was printing about 200,000 prints to desktop printers per month, at a cost of about five cents per print; $10,000 for printing documents. The cost of printing with our products would only be one cent, or $2,000 per month, representing a new savings of $8,000 per month. Additional savings would come through the removal of the desktop printers and the supplies and service that accompanied them. A new contract was signed four days after this presentation.

### Questions

1. In what way did the Mercury group make effective use of brainstorming?
2. In what way did the Mercury group deviate from traditional brainstorming?
3. What advice can you offer Sanderson when he conducts his next brainstorming session?

**Source:** Case researched by Henry Soric, Liverpool, New York, March 2006.

# REFERENCES

1. Ben Rand, "Kodak Seeks Digital's Future via Past: V570's Dual Lenses Harken to 'Turret' Cameras," Rochester, New York, *Democrat and Chronicle*, March 12, 2006, pp. 1E, 4E.
2. Daniel Goleman, *Working with Emotional Intelligence* (New York: Bantam, 1998).
3. Eugene Sadler-Smith and Erella Shefy, "The Intuitive Executive: Understanding and Applying 'Gut Feel' in Decision-Making," *Academy of Management Executive*, November 2004, p. 76.
4. Quoted in Bill Breen, "What's Your Intuition?" *Fast Company*, September 2000, p. 300.
5. Malcolm Gladwell, *Blink: The Power of Thinking without Thinking* (New York: Little, Brown, 2005).
6. Lea Winerman, "What We Know without Knowing," *Monitor on Psychology*, March 2005, p. 52.
7. Research cited in Janet Guyon, "The Art of the Decision," *Fortune*, November 14, 2005, p. 144.
8. Paul C. Nutt, "Surprising but True: Half the Decision in Organizations Fail," *Academy of Management Executive*, November 1999, pp. 75–90; Nutt, *Why Decisions Fail* (San Francisco: Berrett-Koehler, 2002).
9. Peter Coy, "Laurels for an Odd Couple: A Psychologist and a Traditionalist Share This Year's Nobel," *BusinessWeek*, October 21, 2002, p. 50.
10. Carol Polsky, "This Invention Is So Useful, It Has Stuck around for 75 Years," *Newsday* syndicated story, May 13, 2000.
11. Quoted in Ann Pomeroy, "Cooking Up Innovation," *HR Magazine*, November 2004, pp. 49–50.
12. Mark A. Runco and Steven R. Pritzker, eds., *Encyclopedia of Creativity*, vol. 1 (San Diego: Academic Press, 1999), p. xv.
13. Richard W. Woodman, John E. Sawyer, and Ricky W. Griffin, "Toward a Theory of Organizational Creativity," *Academy of Management Review*, April 1993, pp. 293–321; Greg R. Oldham and Anne Cummings, "Employee Creativity: Personal and Contextual Factors at Work," *Academy of Management Journal*, June 1996, pp. 607–634; Robert J. Sternberg, "Creativity as a Decision," *American Psychologist*, May 2002, p. 376; Zak Stambor, "Self-Reflection May Lead Independently to Creativity, Depression," *Monitor on Psychology*, June 2005, p. 13.
14. Robert J. Sternberg, ed., *Handbook of Creativity* (New York: Cambridge University Press, 1999).
15. Teresa M. Amabile, "How to Kill Creativity," *Harvard Business Review*, September–October 1998, pp. 78–79.
16. Research cited in "What Happens in the Brain of an Einstein in the Throes of Creation?" *USA Weekend*, January 1–3, 1999, p. 11.
17. Teresa M. Amabile, "Beyond Talent: John Irving and the Passionate Craft of Creativity," *American Psychologist*, April 2001, p. 335.
18. Robert I. Sutton, "The Weird Rules of Creativity," *Harvard Business Review*, September 2001, p. 101.
19. Linda Tischler, "Join the Circus," *Fast Company*, July 2005, p. 56.
20. Patrick J. Kiger, "Small Groups: Big Ideas," *Workforce Management*, February 27, 2006, p. 2
21. Cited in Robert McGarvey, "Turn It On," *Entrepreneur*, November 1996, pp. 156–157.
22. Research cited in Bridget Murray, "A Ticking Clock Means a Creativity Drop," *Monitor on Psychology*, November 2002, p. 24; Interview with Teresa M. Amabile in Bill Breen, "The 6 Myths of Creativity," *Fast Company*, December 2004, pp. 77–78.
23. Marissa Ann Mayer, "Creativity Loves Constraints," *Business Week*, February 13, 2006, p. 102.
24. Bruce Nussbaum, "Get Creative! How to Build Innovative Companies," *Business Week*, August 1, 2005, pp. 66, 67.
25. "Sports Bottles Oh So Cool," *Rochester (NY) Democrat and Chronicle*, August 23, 2003, p. 14D.
26. Bruce Nussbaum, "The Power of Design," *Business Week*, May 17, 2004, p. 88.
27. "Leadership Tips," *Executive Leadership*, December 2005, p. 8.
28. "Be a Creative Problem Solver," *Executive Strategies*, June 6, 1989, pp. 1–2.

*Answers to brain teasers are as follows:*

The answers to the Frame Games are (1) Spinal column and (2) Too much to do and too little time. The Sudoko solution is presented in the grid.

| 9 | 6 | 3 | 1 | 7 | 4 | 2 | 5 | 8 |
|---|---|---|---|---|---|---|---|---|
| 1 | 7 | 8 | 3 | 2 | 5 | 6 | 4 | 9 |
| 2 | 5 | 4 | 6 | 8 | 9 | 7 | 3 | 1 |
| 8 | 2 | 1 | 4 | 3 | 7 | 5 | 9 | 6 |
| 4 | 9 | 6 | 8 | 5 | 2 | 3 | 1 | 7 |
| 7 | 3 | 5 | 9 | 6 | 1 | 8 | 2 | 4 |
| 5 | 8 | 9 | 7 | 1 | 3 | 4 | 6 | 2 |
| 3 | 1 | 7 | 2 | 4 | 6 | 9 | 8 | 5 |
| 6 | 4 | 2 | 5 | 9 | 8 | 1 | 7 | 3 |

# 9

# Getting Ahead in Your Career

## Learning Objectives

After studying the information and doing the exercises in this chapter, you should be able to:

1 Identify job-finding methods and use the Internet to assist you in your job search.

2 Prepare an effective cover letter and job résumé, and prepare for the job interview.

3 Select several strategies and tactics for getting ahead in your career by taking control of your own behavior.

4 Select several strategies and tactics for advancing your career by exerting control over your environment.

5 Understand networking techniques and be ready to implement them.

## Outline

1 What Are the Basics of Conducting a Job Search?  270
Target Your Job Search
Job-Finding through Networking and the Internet

2 What Are Some Effective Career Advancement Strategies and Tactics?  277
Taking Control of Yourself
Exerting Control over the Outside World

3 Developing Your Networking Skills  287

M indy Gikas was interviewing a senior Level manager on the phone when suddenly the job candidate paused. He said he was reading an e-mail, recalls Ms. Gikas, a managing director for Ogilvy Public Relations Worldwide, a unit of WPP Group of London. "It showed me that his conversation with me wasn't very important," she explains. He wasn't invited to interview in person. [1]

You might be saying to yourself, "How could any senior level manager be so stupid when conducting a job search? Doesn't he have any common sense? Doesn't he know any telephone etiquette?" In reality, when it comes to job finding and career management many people can use a refresher about the basics. In this chapter we review a few basic ideas about conducting a job campaign as part of the major theme of getting ahead in your career. We have divided the vast information about career advancement into three sections. The first section deals with approaches to managing or taking control of your own behavior to advance or retain a good position. The second section deals with approaches to exerting control over your environment to improve your chances for success. The third section deals with networking, the most widely accepted career advancement strategy. To begin relating career development to yourself, do Human Relations Self-Assessment Quiz 9-1.

# What Are the Basics of Conducting a Job Search?

■ Learning Objective 1

The purpose of this section is to provide a review of a few key ideas you need to conduct a successful job search, including sources of job leads, preparation of a cover letter and job résumé, and performing well in a job interview. Although job search knowledge is readily available, this concise information can be used as a refresher and a reminder to be systematic in finding a new position. We also present a few fine points to help give you an edge over those who do the minimum necessary to find a new position.

## TARGET YOUR JOB SEARCH

A job search begins with a reasonably flexible description of the type of job or jobs for which you are looking. Flexibility is called for because, with so many different jobs available, it is difficult to be too specific. Also, flexibility with respect to the type of employer is important. For example, many job seekers overlook the possibilities of working for the U.S. government. The federal government hires graduates in dozens of fields, and the starting pay is competitive with similar private-sector jobs. [2] Your chances of finding suitable employment are directly proportional to the number of positions that will satisfy your job objectives. One person with a degree in information technology might be

# Human Relations Self-Assessment Quiz    9-1

## The Career Development Inventory

Career development activities inevitably include answering some penetrating questions about yourself, such as the 12 questions that follow. You may need several hours to do a competent job answering these questions. After individuals have answered these questions by themselves, it may be profitable to hold a class discussion about the relevance of the specific questions. A strongly recommended procedure is for you to date your completed inventory and put it away for safekeeping. Examine your answers in several years to see (1) how well you are doing in advancing your career and (2) how much you have changed.

Keep the following information in mind in answering this inventory: People are generous in their self-evaluations when they answer career development inventories. So you might want to discuss some of your answers with somebody else who knows you well.

1. How would you describe yourself as a person?
2. What are you best at doing? Worst?
3. What are your two biggest strengths or assets?
4. What skills and knowledge will you need to acquire to reach your goals?
5. What are your two biggest accomplishments?
6. Write your obituary as you would like it to appear.
7. What would be the ideal job for you?
8. What career advice can you give yourself?
9. Describe the two peak work-related experiences in your life.
10. What are your five most important values (the things in life most important to you)?
11. What goals in life are you trying to achieve?
12. What do you see as your niche (spot where you best fit) in the modern world?

interested exclusively in working in the information systems division of a major corporation. Another person with the same background is willing to work in the information technology field for a large company, a small company, a high-tech start-up, a government agency, or an educational institution. The second person has a better chance than the first of finding a job in a geographic location he or she wants.

Closely tied in with the type of work you are seeking is the type of organization in which you would prefer to work. You are much more likely to be successful in your new job and your career when you find a good **person–organization fit,** the compatibility of the individual and the organization. In other words, what type of organization culture (or atmosphere) would fit you best? Based on many studies, the evidence is strong that your job satisfaction will be higher, and you are likely to stay longer with an employer, when there is a good person–organization fit. In addition to fitting in well with the organization, it is also important to fit your job, group, and supervisor. [3]

■ **Person–organization fit**
the compatibility of the individual and the organization

Unless you have had exposure to different types of organizations, you may have only tentative answers to this question. Questioning people who work at different places can provide you with some useful clues. A vital source of input about a prospective employer is present and past employees. Further, plant tours open to the public can provide valuable tips about what it is like to work in a particular firm.

Visits to stores, restaurants, and government agencies will provide informal information about the general nature of working conditions in those places. Using the Internet to find facts about a company has become standard practice. The Internet search includes the firm's Web site as well as news stories about the company. Also, the time spent talking to your prospective supervisor and coworkers is time well spent.

## JOB-FINDING THROUGH NETWORKING AND THE INTERNET

Two cornerstone principles of conducting a job campaign are to use several different methods and keep trying. These two principles should be applied because most approaches to job finding are inefficient yet effective. *Inefficient* refers to the fact that a person might have to make many contacts to find only one job. Yet the system is *effective* because it does lead to a desired outcome—finding a suitable position. He we look at two of dozens of possible methods for conducting a job search, social networking and the Internet.

### Networking (Contacts and Referrals)

**Networking**
the process of establishing a group of contacts who can help you in your career; establishing contacts to find a better position, become a customer, become a valuable supplier, solve difficult problems, or find a mentor; people in a network also offer emotional support

The most effective method of finding a job is through personal contacts. **Networking** is the process of establishing a group of contacts who can help you in your career. Networking is particularly helpful because it taps you into the "insider system" or "internal job market." The internal job market is the large array of jobs that haven't been advertised and are usually filled by word of mouth or through friends and acquaintances of employees. Traditional wisdom states that the vast majority of job openings are found in the internal job market. However, according to recruiting specialists, the insider system is no longer so dominant. Recruiter Gerry Crispin estimates that job seekers can track down as many as 80 to 90 percent of existing job openings by sifting through the career section of an employer's Web site in addition to searching other Internet sites and print media. [4]

The best way to reach the jobs in the internal market is by getting someone to recommend you for one. When looking for a job, it is, therefore, important to tell every potential contact of your job search. The more influential the person, the better. Be specific about the type of job you are seeking. When workers are in short supply, some companies give cash bonuses and prizes to employees for referring job candidates to them. To use networking effectively, it may be necessary to create contacts aside from those you already have. Networking is time consuming yet is usually well worth the effort. Potential sources of contacts for your network include the following: friends, family members, faculty and staff, athletic team members, professional associations, and career and job fairs.

A growing development in job-search networking is to join an on-line networking site, such as *LinkedIn.com* or *Friendster.com*. The major purpose of these sites is for members to help each other find jobs. Some sites emphasize professional contacts, whereas others focus on developing friendships. A growing number of employers recruit directly through these sites. The usefulness of on-line networking increases when you meet face-to-face a few of the most promising contacts.

An important caution about networking: Too many people are consuming too much of other people's time to help them with their job searches. Keep your request for assistance brief and pointed. Ask to reciprocate in any way you can. For example, you might prepare a chart or conduct research for a manager who gave you a job lead.

## The Internet and Résumé Database Services

Using the Internet, for little or no cost, the job seeker can post a résumé or scroll through hundreds of job opportunities. Web sites such as Career Mosaic and E-Span are résumé database services because they give employers access to résumés submitted by job hunters. It is also helpful to look for job Web sites for a specific field, such as information technology, finance, or sales. Also, as implied previously, the employment section of company Web sites can be as effective as general job boards in finding job leads.

Job hunting on the Internet can lead to a false sense of security. Using the Internet, a résumé is cast over a wide net, and hundreds of job postings can be explored. As a consequence, the job seeker may think that he or she can sit back and wait for a job offer to come through the e-mail. In reality, the Internet is only one source of leads that should be used in conjunction with other job-finding methods. Thousands of other job seekers can access the same job openings, and many of the positions listed have already been filled.

A major challenge of job hunting through the Internet is finding a way to speak to a company representative about your application. Telephoning the human resources department of a large company usually leads to a voice mail system with a lengthy menu and rarely a return call. A plausible approach to making a personal contact is to call the main number of your target company and tap the operator button. Ask for the department where you hope to work, and you may be able to establish a personal contact—provided that you do not encounter another lengthy menu. Marc Cenderella, the president of an electronic newsletter and job board for high-level positions, offers this advice: "Hitting 'send' is not the end. You still need to get on the phone, take people to lunch, and work your way to the top of the résumé pile the old-fashioned way." [5]

Despite the cautions mentioned, many job seekers do find jobs through job boards and company Web sites. Keep in mind that the Internet is only one approach to conducting a job search.

## The T-Form Cover Letter

■ **Learning Objective 2**

We all know that a cover letter must accompany a résumé sent on-line or through the postal mail. A novel format for a cover letter to consider is one that systematically outlines how the applicant's qualifications match up against the job requirements posted in the position announcement. The T-form (or column) approach gives the reader a tabular outline of how the applicant's background fits the position description. The T-form cover letter, presented in Figure 9-1, is also recommended because it has an attention-getting format. [6]

Dear Sales Manager:

In response to your recent advertisement in the Atlanta Gazette and on the Monster Board for telemarketing sales professionals, please consider the following:

| REQUIREMENTS | MY QUALIFICATIONS |
|---|---|
| Prior sales experience a must | Two years of full-time and part-time selling including retail and magazine subscription renewals |
| Great communicator | Two different managers praised my communication skills; received an A in two communication skills courses |
| Self-motivated | Worked well without supervision; considered to be a self-starter |
| Reliable | Not one sick day in two years; never late with a class assignment |

Your opportunity excites me, and I would be proud to represent your company. My résumé is enclosed for your consideration.
Sincerely,

**Figure   9-1**

**The T-Form Cover Letter**

## Preparing an Effective Job Résumé

The major purpose of a résumé is to present a targeted message that will help you obtain a job interview, not a job. A résumé is needed both as an outside candidate and often when seeking a transfer within a large firm. Effective résumés are straightforward, factual presentations of a person's experiences, education, skills, and accomplishments. A challenge in preparing an effective résumé is to suit many different preferences. To add to the confusion, some people spell *résumé* with the acute accents (*résumé* is a French word) and some without.

Résumé length illustrates how employers hold different opinions about the best résumé format. For people of limited job experience, a one-page résumé is usually sufficient. For candidates with more experience, two pages may suffice. A *curriculum vitae* (CV) is used to provide a more comprehensive work and education history of the sender and can easily run to more than six pages. [7] A CV is used primarily by professors and scientists and would include such detailed information as publications, patents, and committee experience.

Information about résumé construction is readily available. For example, Microsoft Word includes job résumé templates under File | New | Other Documents. You will find there templates for contemporary, elegant, and professional résumés plus a résumé wizard that helps you construct an individualized résumé. Done properly, a résumé can lead to an interview with a prospective employer. Done poorly, it will block you from further consideration. *Poor* refers to such features as misspellings, misuse of words, disorganization, lack of accurate contact information, too many abbreviations and acronyms, and too much unaccounted for blocks of time. Job candidates who are found to have misrepresented facts (such as pretending to have graduated from a particular school) on a résumé are immediately disqualified.

Whichever style of résumé you choose, it should include a section about your job-related skills and accomplishments. A *skill* is an activity, such as preparing a PowerPoint presentation, compiling a research report on consumer preferences, or translating documents from Spanish to English. Most employers hire for skills, so being specific about your skills in a résumé is essential. (Skill description is also quite important during a job interview.) Skills can be based on academic pursuits, paid work, volunteer work, and sometimes sports such as a team captain mentioning "activity scheduling" as a skill. Remember though, a skill is something you can do now and does not refer to a course you once took, unless you have practiced the skill learned in the course.

The skills mentioned on your résumé might be incorporated into the summary section. Jeevan DeVore, vice president of operations for **Career-Perfect.com** writes that a résumé should have a brief but compelling summary to catch the potential employer's within the first 10 seconds. After that, enough depth and detail can be presented to hold the reader's interest. [8]

## The Successful Job Interview

A successful job campaign results in one or more employment interviews. Screening interviews are often conducted by telephone, particularly for customer service positions requiring telephone skills. An effective way of preparing for a telephone interview is to prepare a 30-second presentation of yourself including your name, your schooling, job experience, and the type of job you want. Keep working at your presentation until you reduce it to 30 seconds of clear, useful information.

More extensive interviews are usually conducted in person. Being interviewed by one person at a time is still standard practice. Many firms, however, also conduct group interviews in which the job candidates speak to several prospective work associates at the same time. Often the group interview is conducted in a casual environment, such as a restaurant or company cafeteria. The candidate may not be aware that meeting with the group is actually an interview and that he or she is being judged.

Another important development in employee interviewing is the **behavioral interview,** in which a candidate is asked how he or she handled a particular problem in the past. Such an interview is essentially a job sample because the interviewee is asked how a problem was dealt with in the past. An example of a behavioral interview questions is as follows: "Tell me how you dealt with an angry customer. What was the problem, and what was the outcome?" Behavioral interviews are used frequently because they seem more related to job behavior than personal characteristics, general interview impressions, or test scores. Of course, this assertion neglects the important fact that a person with strong potential may never have handled the type of job situation presented yet could do so in the future.

Becoming a skillful interviewee requires practice. You can acquire this practice as you go through the job-finding process. In addition, you can rehearse simulated job interviews with friends and other students. Practice answering the questions posed in Figure 9-2. You might also think of several questions you would not like to be asked and develop answers for them. Think through how you have handled difficult job situations, such as dealing with a tight deadline or resolving conflict with a customer, so you can describe these situations during an interview.

■ **Behavioral interview**
a candidate is asked how he or she handled a particular problem in the past

Videotaping the practice interviews is especially helpful because it provides feedback on how you presented yourself. In watching the replay, pay particular attention to your spoken and nonverbal communication skills. Then make adjustments as needed. Many colleges of business and career schools require students to be videotaped before they go out on job interviews.

A general guide for performing well in the job interview is to present a positive but accurate self-picture. Your chances of performing well in a job increase if you are suited for the job. An effective job-getting tactic is to explain to a prospective employer what you think you can do to help the company. Look for opportunities to make **skill–benefit statements**—brief explanations of how your skills can benefit the company. If you were applying for a billing specialist position in a company that you knew was having trouble billing customers correctly, you might make this skill–benefit statement: "Here is how I would apply my skill and experience in setting up billing systems to help develop a billing system with as few glitches as possible." Or, you might state that your previous employer had a billing problem and then explain how you helped solve the problem.

A final note here about job finding is to avoid widely practiced tactics that disqualify candidates. Executive coach and corporate trainer Jim Pawiak spoke to a panel of HR specialists and hiring managers on how not to get a job. His findings encompass much wisdom:

> Being rude to the receptionist or administrative assistant, "cute" e-mail account names (e.g., babygirl44@, and bookworm@); busy signals (use voice mail rather than an answering machine); taking a call waiting interruption while talking with an employer; smelling like tobacco smoke, wearing perfume or aftershave lotion when interviewing; the dead-fish handshake; not making eye contact; not asking questions; not knowing anything–asking anything about the company; not saying "Thank you" at the end of the interview. [9] (Also, complaints are surfacing of job candidates who receive cell-phone calls while being interviewed.)

■ **Skill–benefit statements**
brief explanations of how an individual's skills can benefit the company

---

The following questions are of the same basic type and content encountered in most employment interviews. Practice answering them in front of a friend, camcorder, or mirror.

1. Why did you apply for this job?
2. What are your short-term and long-term goals?
3. What are your strengths? Areas for improvement?
4. Why should we hire you?
5. What do you know about our firm?
6. Describe how well you work under pressure.
7. Here's a sample job problem. How would you handle it?

**Note:** Questions 6 and 7 are often asked as part of a behavioral interview.

**Figure   9-2**

**Seven Questions Frequently Asked of Job Candidates**

# What Are Some Effective Career Advancement Strategies and Tactics?

■ Learning Objective 3

As you look to advance your career, it is helpful to divide your approach into developing your personal qualities and developing qualities that focus more on your interaction with the environment.

## TAKING CONTROL OF YOURSELF

The unifying theme to the strategies, tactics, and attitudes described in this section is that you must attempt to control your own behavior. You can advance your career by harnessing the forces under your control. Such a perspective is important because individuals have the primary responsibility for managing their own careers. The late management guru Peter Drucker placed responsibility for career and life development on the individual. He said, "The stepladder is gone, and there's not even an implied structure of an industry's rope ladder. It's more like vines, and you bring your own machete." [10] (Professor Drucker liked to exaggerate a little.)

Some companies have career development programs, but the individual is still responsible for achieving his or her goals. The following section concentrates on getting ahead by trying to control your external environment in some small way. Do not be concerned about overlap between the general categories of controlling yourself and controlling the environment. Instead, be concerned about the meaning and application of the strategies and tactics.

### Develop Expertise, Passion, and Pride

A starting point in getting ahead is to develop a useful job skill. This tactic is obvious if you are working as a specialist, such as an insurance underwriter. Being skilled at the task performed by the group is also a requirement for being promoted to a supervisory position. After being promoted to a supervisor or another managerial job, expertise is still important for further advancement. It helps a manager's reputation to be skilled in such things as memo writing, computer applications, preparing a budget, and interviewing job candidates.

Athough expertise is highly recommended, the workplace also demands that a person perform a variety of tasks as is required in working on a team. A finance specialist assigned to a product development team would also be expected to know something about marketing, such as how to analyze a marketing survey. A recommended approach is to have depth in your primary field but also have breadth by having several lesser areas of expertise. A widespread example is that no matter what your specialty field, you are also expected to have information technology skills.

Passion goes hand in hand with expertise; it contributes to problem solving and is a major requirement for being an effective leader. It is difficult to sustain expertise if you are not passionate about your specialty field. A work-passionate person, for example, would regularly read printed and electronic information about his or her specialty. In support of job passion, career coach and author Cynthia Shapiro advises that "Companies are running scared. They're looking for the kind of passion that creates a competitive edge. Employers rarely get rid of cheerleaders. Even in a drastic layoff, their jobs are safe." [11]

Developing expertise and being passionate about your work leads naturally to being proud of what you produce. People who take pride in their work are likely to achieve higher quality and a good reputation. From the standpoint of management, proud workers are major contributors because their pride motivates them to excel.

## Develop a Code of Professional Ethics

Another solid foundation for developing a career is to establish a personal ethical code. An ethical code determines what behavior is right or wrong, good or bad, based on values. The values stem from cultural upbringing, religious teachings, peer influences, and professional or industry standards. A code of professional ethics helps a worker deal with such issues as accepting bribes, backstabbing coworkers, and sexually harassing a work associate.

## Perform Well Including Going beyond Your Job Description

Good job performance is the bedrock of a person's career. In rare instances, a person is promoted on the basis of favoritism alone. In all other situations, an employee must have received a favorable performance appraisal (evaluation) to be promoted. Before an employee is promoted, the prospective new boss asks, "How well did this person perform for you?" To be an outstanding performer, it is also necessary to go outside your job description by occasionally taking on tasks not expected of you. Going beyond your job description is part of being a good organizational citizen. Another way of looking at the same issue is that people tend to get promoted not because they perform their jobs well but because they take the initiative to do more than expected.

Performing well on all your assignments is also important because it contributes to the **success syndrome,** a pattern in which the worker performs one assignment well and then has the confidence to take on an even more difficult assignment. Each new assignment contributes to more self-confidence and more success. As you succeed in new and more challenging assignments, your reputation grows within the firm.

## Develop a Proactive Personality

If you are an active agent in taking control of the forces around you, you stand a better chance of capitalizing on opportunities. Also, you will seek out opportunities such as seeing problems that need fixing. A **proactive personality** is a person relatively unconstrained by forces in the situation and who brings about environmental change. People who are highly proactive identify opportunities and act on them, showing initiative, and keep trying until they bring

---

> "Nothing is more important than your reputation. You can't build a reputation on what you say you are going to do—you have to build it on what you do. I learned early on in this business that I was going to live or die by my reputation."
>
> —Jerome Henderson, team leader at HomeBanc Mortgage Corp, Raleigh, North Carolina, and defensive back for nine years in the NFL

■ **Success syndrome**
pattern in which the worker performs one assignment well and then has the confidence to take on an even more difficult assignment

■ **Proactive personality**
characteristic of a person who is relatively unconstrained by forces in a situation and who brings about environmental change; highly proactive people identify opportunities and act on them, showing initiative, and keep trying until they bring about meaningful change

about meaningful change. Jeffery A. Thompson, a professor of organizational behavior at Brigham University found that one reason proactive personalities perform better is that they develop the social networks they need to help them achieve their goals. For example, the person with a proactive personality would know who to contact for help with a specific business or technical problem. [12]

A health and safety specialist with a proactive personality might identify a health hazard others had missed. She would identify the nature of the problem and urge management for funding to control the problem, making use of her network. Ultimately, her efforts in preventing major health problems would be recognized. Having a proactive personality makes it easier for a person to be a good corporate citizen because such behavior is "built into your DNA."

Managers prefer workers with a proactive personality because these workers become proactive employees, or those who take the initiative to take care of problems. Today's employee is supposed to be enterprising. Instead of relying solely on the manager to figure out what work needs to be accomplished, he or she looks for projects to undertake. The proactive employee, however, may clash with an old-fashioned manager who believes that an employee's job is strictly to follow orders. A study conducted with close to 500 men and women workers in diverse occupations examined the relationship between career success and a proactive personality. Proactive personality, as measured by a test, was related to salary, promotions, and career satisfaction. [13] It may not be easy to develop a proactive personality, but a person can get started by taking more initiative to fix problems and attempt to be more self-starting.

## Create Good First Impressions and a Favorable Appearance

Every time you interact with a new person inside or outside your company, you create a first impression. Fair or not, these first impressions have a big impact on your career. If your first impression is favorable, you will often be invited back by an internal or external customer. Your first impression also creates a halo that may influence perceptions about the quality of your work in the future. If your first impression is negative, you will have to work extra hard to be perceived as competent later on.

Looking successful contributes to a positive first impression. Your clothing, your desk and office, and your speech should project the image of a successful, but not necessarily flamboyant, person. Your standard of dress should be appropriate to your particular career stage and work environment. At the extreme, highly placed business executives often dress as if they were walking advertisements for the beauty and fashion industry.

Appropriate dress for an inventory specialist is not the same as that for an outside salesperson dealing with industrial customers. Yet in the past few years, more formal business attire, such as suits for men and women, is making a comeback. Many salespeople and managers today maintain a flexible clothing style by such means as keeping a jacket and extra jewelry in the car or office. When an unanticipated meeting with a customer or some other special occasion arises, a quick modification of clothing style is possible. Appearing physically fit is also part of the success image.

Projecting a sense of control is another key factor contributing to a positive first impression. Show that you are in control of yourself and the environment and that you can handle job pressures. Avoid letting your body language betray you—fidgeting or rubbing your face sends negative nonverbal messages. Make your gestures project self-assurance and purpose. A verbal method of appearing in control is to make a positive assertion such as, "This is a demanding assignment and I welcome the challenge."

The factors mentioned so far contribute to a favorable appearance, which can be an asset in a career. Physical attractiveness continues to play a major role in many employment decisions—especially for workers who are in contact with customers and clients. Patrick Hicks, an attorney in a Las Vegas employment law firm, notes" "Everything else being equal, certain businesses—retail is the best example—would prefer people who are physically attractive." [14]

Body art in the form of tattoos and piercing often figures into physical appearance. More companies today accept such decorations as a fact of modern culture. Tatooing is one of the faster-growing retail businesses in the United States. Ford Motor Co. permits employees from the most senior executives on down to have tattoos and piercings—except those that could endanger factory workers. Despite this general acceptance of body art, excessive decoration in visible places could be a career deterrent. [15] Visualize a man with a pierced tongue and snake tattooed on his neck applying for a sales representative position at Hewlett Packard!

## Document Your Accomplishments

Keeping an accurate record of your job accomplishments can be valuable when you are being considered for promotion, transfer, or assignment to a team or project. Documenting your accomplishments can also be used to verify new learning. In addition, a record of accomplishments is useful when your performance is being evaluated. You can show your manager what you have done for the company lately. Many professional-level workers maintain a portfolio of their accomplishments, such as samples of work accomplished. The portfolio is much like that used by photographers, artists, and models when applying for a job. Here are two examples of documented accomplishments from different types of jobs:

1. A bank teller suggested that at least one person in the bank should be fluent in American Sign Language to facilitate serving deaf customers. After implementing the idea, the bank attracted many more deaf customers.

2. A maintenance supervisor decreased fuel costs in the office by 27 percent in one year by installing ceiling fans.

After documenting your accomplishments, it pays to advertise. Let key people know in a tasteful way of your tangible accomplishments. You might request an opportunity to make a presentation to your boss to review the status of one of your successful projects. Or you could use e-mail for the same purpose if it would be presumptuous for you to request a special meeting to discuss your accomplishments.

## Keep Growing through Continuous Learning and Self-Development

Many employers expect employees to keep learning, either through company sponsored programs or on their own. It is particularly important to engage in new learning in areas of interest to the company, such as developing proficiency in a second language if the company has customers and employees in other countries. Continuous learning can take many forms, including formal schooling, attending training programs and seminars, and self-study. To engage in continuous learning, it is essential to remain open to new viewpoints on your established beliefs. A belief (or stereotype) that has been true for a long time may no longer hold true. A person might think, for example, that almost all workers older than 60 are simply putting in time until they reach the traditional retirement age of 65. In reality, many workers plan to continue to work well into their 70s and 80s.

## Observe Proper Etiquette

Proper etiquette is important for career advancement because such behavior is considered part of acting professionally. **Business etiquette** is a special code of behavior required in work situations. Both *etiquette* and *manners* refer to behaving in an acceptable and refined way. In the digital era, etiquette is just as important as ever because of the new challenges that high-tech devices bring. For example, is it good etiquette to read the information on a coworker's computer screen when visiting his or her cubicle? The globalization of business also creates challenges, such as figuring out when visiting another country whether handshakes are acceptable.

Deciphering what constitutes proper etiquette and business manners requires investigation. One approach is to use successful people as models of behavior and sources of information. Another approach is to consult a current book about business etiquette. The basic rules of etiquette are to make the other person feel comfortable in your presence, be considerate, and strive not to embarrass anyone. Also, be cordial to all, remembering that everyone deserves our respect. Specific guidelines for practicing etiquette stem from these basic rules. Figure 9-3 presents examples of good business etiquette and manners.

> ■ **Business etiquette**
> special code of behavior required in work situations

## Develop the Brand Called You

Well-known business consultant Tom Peters urges career-minded people to develop their credentials and their reputations to the extent that they stand out so much that they become a brand name. Although the analogy of each person becoming a recognizable brand name such as Nike is far-fetched, the idea of becoming a trusted person with value is sound. As Peters sees it, you don't belong to any company for life, and your chief affiliation isn't any particular function or department (such as accounting). You are not defined by your job title or your job description. "Starting today you are a brand." [16]

You begin developing brand You by identifying the qualities or characteristics that distinguish you from coworkers. What have you done recently to make you stand out? What benefit do you offer? Do you deliver high-quality work on time? Are you a creative problem solver? Next, you would make yourself visible so you can cash in your uniqueness (your brand). Almost all the ideas in this chapter will help you develop brand You!

Following are 13 specific suggestions about business etiquette and manners that should be considered in the context of a specific job situation. For example, "make appointments with high-ranking people" is not so relevant in a small, informal company when the company places less emphasis on formality.

1. *Be polite to people in person.* Say "good morning" and "good evening" to work associates at all job levels. Smile frequently. Offer to bring coffee or another beverage for a coworker if you are going outside to get some for yourself. When somebody shakes your hand, stand up instead of remaining in your chair.

2. *Write polite letters and e-mail messages.* An important occasion for practicing good etiquette is the writing of business and personal letters and e-mail messages. Include the person's job title in the inside address and spell the person's name correctly. Use supportive rather than harsh statements. (For example, say "It would be helpful if you could" rather than "You must.") When writing a hard-copy letter, avoid right margin justification (block writing) because it is much harsher than indented lines. Thank-you notes for gifts should be handwritten rather than sent by e-mail, but at least an e-mail note is better than not offering thanks.

3. *Practice good table manners.* Avoid smacking your lips or sucking your fingers. If someone else is paying the bill, do not order the most expensive item on the menu (such as a $195 bottle of Dom Pérignon champagne). Offer to cut bread for the other person and do not look at the check if the other person is paying. A pet peeve of many executives is having to dine with people who eat with their mouths open.

4. *Names should be remembered.* It is good manners and good etiquette to remember the names of work associates, even if you see them only occasionally. If you forget the name of a person, it is better to admit this rather than guessing and coming up with the wrong name. Just say, "I apologize, but I have forgotten your name. Tell me once more, and I will not forget your name again."

5. *Males and females should receive equal treatment.* Amenities extended to females by males in a social setting are minimized in business settings. During a meeting, a male is not expected to hold a chair or a door for a woman, nor does he jump to walk on the outside when the two of them are walking down the street. Many women resent being treated differently from males with respect to minor social customs. In general, common courtesies should be extended by both sexes to one another. A handshake and a smile are a better greeting than a kiss on the cheek of the opposite-sex person. Yet if a client or customer initiates the light kiss, it is acceptable to follow suit.

6. *Shouting is out.* Emotional control is an important way of impressing superiors. Following the same principle, shouting in most work situations is said to detract from you image.

7. *The host or hostess pays the bill.* An area of considerable confusion about etiquette surrounds business lunches and who should pay the check—the man or the woman. The rule of etiquette is that the person who extends the invitation pays the bill.

8. *Introduce the higher-ranking person to the lower-ranking person.* Your boss's name will be mentioned before a coworker's, you introduce the older person to the younger person, and a client is introduced first to coworkers. ("Ms. CEO I would like you to meet our new custodial assistant.")

9. *Address superiors and visitors in their preferred way.* As the modern business world has become more informal, a natural tendency has developed to address people at all levels by their first names. It is safer to first address people by a title and their last names and then wait for them to correct you if they desire. You will probably find that more than 90 percent of people want to be addressed by their first name. However, important exceptions exist. J.C. Penney only recently shifted to a culture where senior managers are addressed by their first name, and many Asian executives prefer to be referred to by a title such as Mr, Mrs., Ms., or Dr.

10. *Make appointments with high-ranking people rather than dropping in.* Although the business world has become increasingly informal, it is taboo in most firms for lower-ranking employees to casually drop in to the office of an executive. Use e-mail instead to contact higher-ranking managers directly.

11. *When another person is opening a door to exit a room or building, do not jump in ahead of him or her.* Many people have developed the curious habit of quickly jumping in past another person (moving in the opposite direction) who is exiting. Not only is this practice rude, but it can also lead to an uncomfortable collision.

12. *Be sensitive to cross-cultural differences in etiquette.* When dealing with people from different cultures, regularly investigate possible major differences in etiquette. For example, using the index finger to point is considered rude in most Asian and Eastern countries. The American sign for okay (thumb and index finger forming a circle) is considered a vulgarity in most other countries. Another example is that Finns are very private people, so don't ask questions about their private life unless they bring up the topic first. Instead, talk about the safe topic of sports. Don't blow your nose in public in Belgium where it is considered an offensive gesture. (It's not too cool elsewhere, either.)

13. *Minimize social kissing in an American workplace, but welcome it in Europe.* Kissing in business is generally regarded as rude except among close acquaintances, yet is more frequent in Europe. However, European kissing amounts to pecks on both cheeks, or top of the head, and never on the lips.

**Caution:** Although all the points could have some bearing on the image you project, violation of any one of them would not necessarily have a negative impact on your career. It is the overall image you project that counts the most. Therefore, the general principle of being considerate of work associates is much more important than any one act of etiquette or manners.

**Source:** Jim Rucker and Jean Anna Sellers, "Changes in Business Etiquette," *Business Education Forum*, February 1998, p. 45; "Business Etiquette: Teaching Students the Unwritten Rules," *Keying In*, January 1996, pp. 1–2; "Meeting and Greeting," *Keying In*, January 1996, p. 3; compilation from other sources in Andrea Sachs, "Corporate Ps and Qs," *Time*, November 1, 1999, p. 23; Sachs, "Learn How to Behave," *Time*, August 2005, p. A5; Letitia Baldrige, *The Executive Advantage* (Washington, DC: Georgetown Publishing House, 1999).

| Figure | 9-3 |
|--------|-----|

**Business Etiquette and Manners**

# EXERTING CONTROL OVER THE OUTSIDE WORLD

■ Learning Objective 4

In this section we emphasize approaches that require you to exert some control over the outside environment. If you do not control it, at least you can try to juggle it to your advantage. For example, the "Find a Mentor" section suggests that you search out a friendly and supportive person in your field who can help you advance in your career.

## Develop a Flexible Career Path

Planning your career inevitably involves some form of goal setting. If your goals are laid out systematically to lead to your ultimate career goal, you have established a **career path,** a sequence of positions necessary to achieve a goal. Here we describe two types of career paths. One type emphasizes climbing up the ladder in a traditional organization. The other emphasizes the horizontal movements that fit better the new model of career advancement.

■ **Career path**
sequence of positions necessary to achieve a goal

*The Traditional Career Path.* A traditional career path is based on the assumption that a person will occupy a series of positions, each at a higher level of responsibility than the previous one. A person thus climbs the organizational ladder or hierarchy. If a career path is laid out in one firm, it must be related to the present and future demands of that firm. If you aspire toward a high-level manufacturing position, you would need to know the future of manufacturing in that company. Many U.S. firms, for example, continue to conduct more of their manufacturing in China. If you were really determined, you might study the appropriate language and ready yourself for a global position.

Before establishing the goals on the career path, it is helpful to clarify your values. These are probably the same values that enabled you to choose a career in the first place. Questions to think about are "Can you name the three things most important to your job satisfaction? What do you really look for in a job? Do you want to be part of a team? To think creatively? Are you passionate about helping people and improving the world? Do you want to carefully follow directions, or do you want to decide which tasks are important?" [17]

While sketching out a career path, you should list your personal goals. They should mesh with your work plans to help avoid major conflicts in your life. Some lifestyles, for example, are incompatible with some career paths. You might find it difficult to develop a stable home life (spouse, children, friends, community activities, garden) if you aspired toward holding field positions in international marketing.

Your career path is a living document and may need to be modified as your circumstances change. Keep in mind changes in your company and industry. If becoming a branch manager is an important step in your career path, check to see if your company or industry still has branch managers. The changing preferences of your family can also influence your career path. A family who wanted to stay put may now be willing to relocate, which could open up new possibilities on your career path.

Contingency ("what if?") plans should also be incorporated into a well-designed career path. For instance, "If I don't become an agency supervisor by age 35, I will seek employment in the private sector." Or, "If I am not promoted within two years, I will enroll in a business school program."

Career paths can be laid out graphically, as shown in Figure 9-4. One benefit of a career path laid out in chart form is that it gives a clear perception of climbing steps toward your target position. As each position is attained, the corresponding step can be shaded in color or crosshatched.

Most goals in a career path include a time element, which is crucial to sound career management. Your long-range goal might be clearly established in your mind (such as owner and operator of a health spa). At the same time you must establish short-range goals (get any kind of job in health spa) and intermediate-range goals (manager of a health spa by age 30). Goals set too far in the future that are not supported with more immediate goals may lose their motivational value. The career path in Figure 9-4 features a steady progression of promotions yet a reasonable number of years in each position. Such planning is realistic because promotions often take a long time to achieve.

**Figure** **9-4**

**A Vertical Career Path**

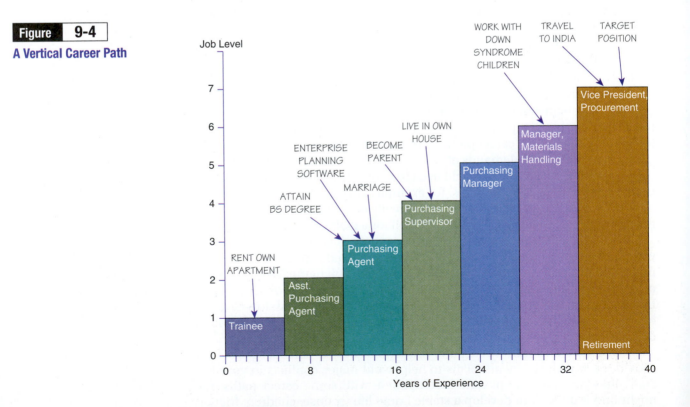

*The Horizontal Career Path.* Many organizations today have no fixed career paths. Instead of plotting a series of moves over a long time period, many individuals can only make predictions about the type of work they would like to be doing rather than target specific positions. A significant feature of the horizontal career path is that people are more likely to advance by moving sideways than moving up. Or, at least, people who get ahead will spend a considerable part of their career working in different positions at or near the same level. In addition, they may occasionally move to a lower-level position to gain valuable experience. With a horizontal career path, the major reward is no longer promotion but the opportunity to gain more experience and increase job skills. Figure 9-5 presents a horizontal career path.

A horizontal career path, as well as a traditional (or vertical) career path, does not necessarily mean the person stays with the same firm. For example, a worker might spend three years in one company as an electronics technician, three years in another as an e-commerce coordinator, and then three years as a customer service specialist in a third company. All three positions would be approximately at the same level. The third company then promotes the individual to a much-deserved position as the marketing team leader.

## Achieve Broad Experience

Most people who land high-ranking positions usually have broad experience. Therefore, a widely accepted strategy for advancing in responsibility is to strengthen your credentials by broadening your experience. Workers who follow the alternative model of career advancement, as illustrated by the horizontal career path, are automatically achieving broad experience. It is best to achieve breadth early in your career because it is easier to transfer when an individual's compensation is not too high. Broadening can come about by performing a variety of jobs or sometimes by performing essentially the same job in different organizations. You can also achieve breadth by working on committees and special assignments.

Breadth can also be attained through self-nomination. Have the courage and assertiveness to ask for a promotion or a transfer. Your manager or team leader may not know that you are actually seeking more responsibility. An

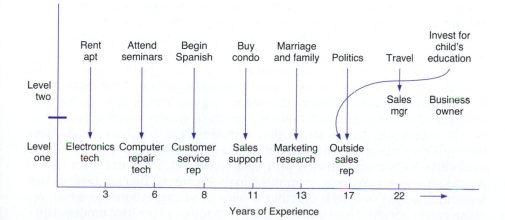

**Figure 9-5**

**A Horizontal Career Path**

effective method of convincing him or her is to volunteer for specific job openings or for challenging assignments. A boss may need convincing because many more people will be seeking advancement than are actually willing to handle more responsibility.

A major benefit of broad experience is that you achieve more career portability, allowing you to move to another employer should the need exist. The employability derives from being a more flexible person with a broader perspective. A person, for example, who has worked in both the underwriting (setting rates for risks) and the claims aspects of insurance would be well regarded by insurance companies.

## Find a Mentor

■ **Mentor**

a more experienced person who guides, teaches, and coaches another individual

The vast majority of successful career people have had one or more mentors during their careers. A **mentor** is a more experienced person who guides, teaches, and coaches another individual. In years past, mentors were almost always higher-ranking people. Today mentors can be peers and even lower-ranking individuals. A lower-ranking individual, for example, can educate you on how other parts of the organization work—something you may need to know to advance. Sometimes you are able to develop a mentor from the contacts you make on the Internet. After the person becomes your mentor, much of the mentoring can take place through e-mail and messaging. (Busier mentors may prefer e-mail because they can respond at their leisure.) E-mentoring will sometimes increase the pool of potential mentors and allow relationships to develop without social bias, such as people being suspicious of the nature of a mentoring relationship between a middle-age man and a young woman. [18]

Mentorship is an important development process in many occupations: master–apprentice, physician–intern, teacher–student, and executive–junior executive. An emotional tie exists between the less experienced person (the protégé) and the mentor. The mentor serves as a positive model and a trusted friend. In return, the person being mentored expresses appreciation, gives positive feedback to the mentor, and shares victories. It is also important to offer a concrete service in return for the mentor's advice. Possibilities include offering to collect information, prepare computer graphics, or run a few errands.

Finding a mentor involves the same process as networking (described later in this chapter). One possibility to mention for now is that you can ask people you already know if they could think of a possible mentor for you. With e-mentoring, geographic distance does not create a substantial barrier. With any prospective mentor, it is best to begin gradually by asking for some advice and then see how the relationship develops. The accompanying Human Relations in Practice box insert provides an example of e-mentoring.

The advantages of being mentored are widely accepted by managers and human relations specialists, so it is encouraging to know that data based research supports the contention that mentoring can benefit a protégé's career. A team of five researchers synthesized a group of studies covering more than 10,000 individuals. It was found that compensation and promotions were slightly higher for mentored than nonmentored individuals. Also, the mentored individuals were more satisfied with their career, felt more optimistic about promotions, and were more committed to their careers. Two key reasons that mentoring helps protégés is that they receive good suggestions from mentors about career advancement and they use the mentors as positive models. [19]

## Human Relations in Practice

### KPMG Offers Employees On-line Mentoring

KPMG LLP, a New York–based tax and audit firm with about 18,200 employees in the United States, has attained success using an on-line mentoring database. Although informal mentoring was taking place (partners mentored junior staff to help them move through the ranks), the company enacted a more formal voluntary nationwide mentoring program in 2004. "For a variety of reasons, wanted to expand on informal mentoring," says Barbara Wankoff, KPMG's director of workplace solutions which is part of HR. "We set out to encourage people and establish mentoring relationships."

The KPMG program is on the company's HR Web site and is "customized to match our competencies," says Wankoff. The system uses key words such as "boardroom skills" or "negotiation" to help find suitable mentors for employees who seek mentoring. And before accepting an assignment, a mentor agrees to terms that include confidentiality.

KPMG officials describe the on-line program as "user friendly" and easy to navigate, with information that is prominently displayed and readily accessible. "We feel the message is being put out there," says Wankoff. Employees know we support this and it's available to them if they want it. We also recognize not everyone is ready and willing to commit to mentoring, but we hope to see it grow and increase greatly." So far, there's been a positive response—about 6,000 mentoring relationships have been formed.

Source: Donna M. Owens, "Virtual Mentoring," *HR Magazine*, March 2006, p. 106.

## Balance Your Life

Balancing your life among the competing demands of work, social life, and personal interests can help you advance your career. Having balance gives you additional energy and vitality that will help you in your career. Without balance, a career person runs the risk of burnout and feeling that work is not worthwhile. Stephen Covey writes, "Always being the last to leave the office does not make you an indispensable employee. In fact, those who work long hours for extended periods are prone to burnout. The trick is to have your priorities clear, honor your commitments, and keep a balance in life." [20]

# Developing Your Networking Skills

■ Learning Objective 5

Developing a network of contacts is important for finding a job. As a career advancement tactic, networking has several purposes. The contacts you establish can help you find a better position, offer you a new position, become a customer, become a valuable supplier, help you solve difficult problems, or find a mentor. People in your network can also offer you emotional support during periods of adversity.

A recommended approach to networking is to keep a list of at least 25 people whom you contact at least once a month. The contact can be as extensive as a luncheon meeting or as brief as an e-mail message. The starting point in networking is to obtain an ample supply of business cards. You then give a card to any person you meet who might be able to help you now or in the future. While first developing your network, be inclusive. Later, as your network develops, you can strive to include a greater number of influential and successful people. People in your network can include relatives; people you meet while traveling, vacationing, or attending trade shows; and classmates.

Community activities and religious organizations can also be a source of contacts. Golf is still considered the number one sport for networking because of the high-level contacts the sport generates. A substantial amount of social networking also takes place on the Internet. The range of potential people in your network is much greater over the Internet than if networking is done locally and in person. The people in these groups can become valuable business contacts. On-line networking includes newsgroups, mailing lists, chat rooms, and e-mail. Corporate Web sites usually have a listing of contact people for a company, and it is possible that some of these people will become part of your network. Figure 9-6 offers some additional networking suggestions, and Exercise 9-1 provides a worksheet for networking.

Networking is obviously beneficial in a field such as direct selling whereby you contact people you know to purchase your goods or services. For example, if you sell products such as financial services, Avon, or Tupperware, you are expected to capitalize on personal contacts. Almost any successful businessperson you meet uses networking, at least to some extent. A representative example is Anna Garcia, the owner of Anko Metal Services in Denver, Colorado. She attributes some of her success to networking with women. Garcia said, "Latina women used to get together in a religious setting. Now, it's in the business atmosphere." A specific event is a Latina business-development event, held throughout the United States. The gathering focuses on networking, and courting potential clients is expected behavior. [21]

We caution again to be selective about your networking. Overreliance on networking, such as contacting people who probably have no interest in hearing from you, can be annoying to the recipient. Kenneth Norton, the director of product management at Yahoo! has coined the term *snam* (a mutant of *spam*) in reference to unwanted e-mail generated by such social networking sites as Friendster, LinkedIn, and Tribe. [22]

The following networking suggestions are gathered from a number of career counselors and business writers. Select and choose from among the list those ideas that appear fit your personality and circumstances.

- Expand and diversify your network. Everyone you come in contact with is a potential resource to help you in your career. Even someone whose sole purpose is to cheer you on during downturns can be a valuable ally. Keep filling your network with new contacts because older contacts may fade away. Retired people who have had a successful careers can be a valuable source of contacts. Also, retired people typically enjoy assisting people at earlier stages in their careers.
- Add value as well as asking for assistance. Consider how you can help the other person and listen as much as you talk.
- When networking by e-mail, include your telephone number and address. The other person may want to contact you by means other than an e-mail. Also, be persistent because e-mail messages may get deleted by accident or simply disappear because of technical problems.
- When approaching someone to be part of your network, explain how you received his or her name or refresh the person's mind as to how you met previously.
- If you attend a formal networking event (such as a professional meeting), "work the room." Engage in professional conversations with as many people as feasible.
- Create good relationships with your peers and fellow students. Some of them will occupy influential positions in the future. Stay in touch with your more promising classmates. In other words, "Look at the paws on those pups."
- Strive to develop a personal relationship with at least two people at higher levels in your place of work. Keep these people informed of what you are doing and ask for their advice.
- Be memorable for positive reasons. Making a lasting positive impression is a promising way of keeping a network alive.
- When you have a change of status, such as accepting a new position, let this be an opportunity to notify network members. Let everyone know should you change your e-mail address or telephone number.

**Source:** Anita Bruzzese, "Restrain Yourself and Think When Networking by E-Mail," *Gannett News Service*, June 30, 2003; "Networking Isn't for Spectators: Meeting People, Discovering Trends, and Arriving Early Can Pay Dividends," Knight Ridder, February 24, 2003; Deb Koehn, "Networking Vital in Ever-Evolving Workplaces," *Rochester (NY) Democrat and Chronicle*, July 14, 2002, p. 4E; Deb Koehn, "Know Etiquette of Networking," *Rochester (NY) Democrat and Chronicle*, October 27, 2002, p. 4E; "'85 Broads' Shares Networking Tips," *Executive Leadership*, February 2002, p. 3; Anne Fisher, "How Do I Network When I Don't Even Know Anyone?" *Fortune*, July 22, 2002, p. 226.

**Figure  9-6**

**Networking Suggestions**

# Concept Review and Reinforcement

## Key Terms

Person–organization fit, 271
Networking, 272
Behavioral interview, 275

Skill–benefit statements, 276
Success syndrome, 278
Proactive personality, 278

Business etiquette, 281
Career path, 283
Mentor, 286

## Summary and Review

The job search begins with a reasonably flexible statement of the type of job you are seeking (your job objective). Knowing what type of organization you would prefer to work for will help focus your job search. Use different methods of job searching and keep trying.

- The most effective method of finding a job is through personal contacts, or networking. Getting someone on the inside to recommend you for a job is the best way to reach the internal job market.
- Job hunting on the Internet can be done through job boards and company Web sites. Despite using the Internet, it is important to speak to a person to conclude your job search.

A novel format for a cover letter is the T-form approach that systematically outlines how the applicant's qualifications match up against the job requirements.

The major purpose of a résumé is to help you obtain a job interview. There is no one best way to prepare a résumé. Effective résumés are straightforward, factual presentations of a person's experiences, skills, and accomplishments. Avoid making untrue statements on your résumé. A résumé should include a section about your job-related skills and accomplishments.

Rehearse being interviewed and then present yourself favorably but accurately in the interview. Behavioral interviews are growing in importance.

- To perform well in an interview, present a positive but accurate self-picture.
- Look for opportunities to make a skill–benefit statement about how your skills can help the company.

One set of strategies and tactics for getting ahead can be classified as taking control of your own behavior. Included are these approaches:

- Develop expertise, passion, and pride.
- Develop a code of professional ethics.
- Perform well including going beyond your job description.
- Develop a proactive personality.
- Create good first impressions and a favorable appearance.
- Document your accomplishments.
- Keep growing through continuous learning and self-development.
- Observe proper etiquette.
- Develop the brand called You.

Another set of strategies and tactics for career advancement centers around taking control of your environment, or at least adapting it to your advantage. Included are following:

- Develop a flexible career path (including the traditional and lateral types).
- Achieve broad experience.
- Find a mentor.
- Balance your life.

Developing networking skills is a major career advancement tactic that can help you find a new position, become a customer, become a valuable supplier, solve difficult problems, find a mentor, and receive emotional support. Keep a list of at least 25 people whom you contact monthly and add value as well as asking for assistance.

## Check your Understanding

1. During times when there is a shortage of skilled workers, why is it still important to study how to conduct a job campaign?
2. During a period in which there is a dire shortage of jobs available, which job-hunting tactics do you think would be the most relevant?
3. What can you do today to help you develop a contact that could someday lead to a job?
4. Visit the employment section of the Web site of three large companies of interest to you. Identify several jobs you perceive to match your qualifications or for which you have a reasonable chance of being regarded as a bona fide candidate.
5. Make up a behavioral interview question that you might be asked, and develop a good answer.

6. With the upcoming labor shortage, the future for graduates in almost all business-related specialties looks bright for at least the next 10 years. So why be concerned with strategies for career advancement?
7. Identify several jobs for which observing good business etiquette would be particularly important.
8. What similarities do you see between a person with a *proactive personality* and one who displays good *organizational citizenship behavior*?
9. Identify several tactics you would be willing to use to attract a mentor in a large company.
10. How might a person go about networking for career advancement in an airport or on an airplane?

## Web Corner

*Image building through image consultants:*
www.aic.org

*Career advice including job search and salaries:*
www.vault.com.

*Career advancement suggestions from The Wall Street Journal:*
www.CareerJournal.com.

*Find a mentor:*
www.AdvanceMentoring.com

*Internet Skill Builder:*
So many job boards exist on the Internet that conducting a Web-based job search can be baffling. A direct approach is to visit Yahoo! Hot Jobs (on the front page of www.Yahoo.com) and enter three

specific job titles of interest to you. You will be directed to loads of job opportunities closely matching the job titles you entered. It may be helpful to enter variations of the same job title, such as both "office manager" and "administrative assistant." Your assignment is to identify five jobs for which you appear to be qualified. Even if you have no interest in conducting a job search, it is informative to be aware of job opportunities in your field. Seek answers to the following questions:

1. Do I appear to have the qualifications for the type of job I am seeking?
2. Is there a particular geographic area where the job or jobs I want are available?
3. How good are opportunities in my chosen field?

# Developing Your Human Relations Skills

## Applying Human Relations Exercise 9-1

### Building Your Network

Networking can be regarded as the process of building a team that works with you to achieve success. You can start the following exercise now, but it will probably take your entire career to implement completely. To start networking or make your present networking more systematic, take the following steps:

**Step 1:** Jot down your top three goals or objectives for the following three months, such as obtaining a new job or promotion, starting a small business, or doing a field research study.

1. _____

2. _____

3. _____

**Step 2:** List family members, friends, or acquaintances who could assist you in meeting your goals or objectives. Prepare a contact card or database entry for each person on your list, including as many details as you can about the person and the person's family, friends, employers, and contacts.

**Step 3:** Identify what assistance you will request of your contact or contacts. Be realistic in light of your prior investment in the relationship. Remember, you have to be a friend to have a friend.

**Step 4:** Identify how you will meet your contact or contacts during the next month. Could it be for lunch or at an athletic field, nightclub, sports club, recreational facility on campus, cafeteria, and so forth? Learn more about your contacts during your face-to-face meetings. In some cases you may have to use the telephone or e-mail to substitute for an in-person meeting. Look for ways to mutually benefit from the relationship. At the beginning of each week, verify that you have made a small investment in building these relationships.

**Step 5:** Ask for the help you need. A network must benefit you. Thank the contact for any help given. Jot down on your planner a reminder to make a follow-up call, letter, or e-mail message to your contacts. In this way, you will have less work to do before you make another request for help.

**Step 6:** For each person in your network, think of a favor, however small, that you can return to him or her. Without reciprocity, a network fades rapidly.

**Source:** Adapted and expanded from Cheryl Kitter, "Taking the Work Out of Networking," Success Workshop, supplement to The Pryor Report, March 1998, pp. 1–2.

## Applying Human Relations Exercise 9-2

### Career Pathing

1. Each class member will develop a tentative career path, perhaps as an outside assignment. About six volunteers will then share their paths with the rest of the class. Feedback of any type will be welcomed. Class members studying the career paths of others should keep in mind such issues as the following:
   a. How logical does it appear?
   b. Is this something the person really wants, or is it simply an exercise in putting down on paper what the ambitious person is supposed to want?
   c. How well do the individual's work plans mesh with personal plans?
2. Each class member will interview an experienced working person outside of class about his or her career path. Most of the people interviewed will have already completed a portion of their path. Therefore, they will have less flexibility (and perhaps less idealism) than people just getting started in their careers. The conclusions reached about these interviews will make a fruitful class discussion. Among the issues raised might be the following:
   a. How familiar were these people with the idea of a career path?
   b. How willing were they to talk about themselves?
   c. Were many actual "paths" discovered, or did a series of jobs simply come about by luck or "fate?"

## Human Relations Case Study 9-1

### Stacy Sings the Blues

Stacy, age 27, was proud to be an architectural technician student. She liked the idea of combining her interest in art with being part of something important. As she reasoned, "I will be helping architects erect skyscrapers, small office buildings, and houses that will last for a century. I will help provide beautiful environments in which fellow human beings will work and live."

To help fund her schooling and pay her living expenses while at career school, Stacy tended bar at the Big Boar Inn, a trendy bar frequented mostly by young people. Stacy had worked on and off as a bartender before attending career school. For several years after high school, she traveled around the world finding work at bars and resorts wherever she could. During her travels, Stacy made notes of the designs of buildings and prepared many sketches of her own ideas about building designs. She knew that she wanted someday to work in the field of architecture.

Several months before graduation, Stacy's father and several friends asked her when she would be starting her job hunt. Stacy explained that she was too busy finishing her studies at school and working at the Big Boar to get seriously involved in a job hunt. "After graduation in May, I'll take a couple of months to unwind and then begin searching for a job. Besides, most architectural firms don't get serious about hiring recent graduates until after Labor Day." Stacy's dad thought she was being a little laid back in her job-hunting approach but did not think he was in a position to tell her what to do.

After graduation, Stacy continued to work at the Big Boar about 25 hours per week. She spent a lot of time at the beach and developed a deep skin tan. One day she ran into her mentor, Professor Bill Byron, at the supermarket. Byron asked Stacy how her job search was going.

Stacy replied, "I will be getting to working on my résumé soon. With the job market for architectural technicians being soft right now, I didn't see any need to rush. Would it be OK to drop by your office to get some advice on my résumé?"

Stacy met with Mr. Byron a week later. He gave Stacy a few suggestions about résumé construction and also noted that her portfolio of architectural renderings needed more work before she could present the portfolio to prospective employers. Stacy then decided to sharpen her portfolio before beginning her job search.

At the urging of a friend, Stacy bought a few out-of-town newspapers to search the classified sections. She chose Washington, DC, Atlanta, and Miami because of their warm climates. Stacy spotted a total of three openings for architectural technicians and sent a résumé and cover letter to the addresses indicated in the ads.

Two months passed, and Stacy had not heard back from any of the firms to which she sent letters. Stacy's next approach was to give a copy of her résumé to a friend who sold furniture to an architectural firm in New Jersey. The friend said he would give the résumé to a personal contact he had at the firm.

During a work break at the Big Boar, a server asked Stacy how her job hunt was proceeding. Stacy replied, "Right now, I'm just sitting back and waiting to hear. There's not much else I can do."

## Questions

1. What is your evaluation of the effectiveness of Stacy's job campaign?
2. What recommendations can you make to Stacy to help her find a position as an architectural technician?
3. You be the career counselor. Does Stacy really want to leave her job as a bartender at the Big Boar Inn and become an architectural technician?

## Human Relations Case Study 9-2

### San Deep Wants the Fast Track

At age 25, San Deep already had impressive leadership experience. She was the head of her Girl Scout troop at age 11, the president of the Asian Student Association in high school, and the captain of her soccer team in both high school and college. She also organized a food drive for homeless people in her hometown for three consecutive summers. Deep believed that these experiences, in addition to her formal education, were preparing her to be a corporate leader. At college, Deep majored in information systems and business administration.

Deep's first position in industry was a business analyst at a medium-size consulting firm that helped clients implement large-scale systems, such as enterprise software. She explained to her team leader at the outset that she wanted to be placed on a management track rather than a technical track because she aspired to becoming a corporate executive. Deep's team leader explained, "San, I know you are in a hurry to get ahead. Lots of capable people are looking to climb the ladder. But you first have to build your career by proving that you are an outstanding analyst."

Deep thought, "It looks like the company may need a little convincing that I'm leadership material, so I'm going to dig in and perform like a star." And Deep did dig in, much to the pleasure of her clients, her team leader, and her coworkers. Her first few performance evaluations were outstanding, yet the company was still not ready to promote San to a team leader position. Deep's team leader explained, "Bob [the team leader's manager] and I both agree that you are doing an outstanding job, but promotions are hard to come by in our company these days. The company is shrinking more than expanding, so talks about promotion are a little futile right now."

Deep decided that it would take a long time to be promoted to team leader or manager in her present company, so she began to quietly look for a new position in her field. Her job hunt proceeded more swiftly than she anticipated. Through a sports club contact, Deep was granted a job interview with a partner in a larger consulting firm offering similar services. After a series of four interviews, Deep was hired as a senior business analyst performing work on a system similar to the one she had been working with for two years. During her interviews, Deep emphasized her goals of occupying a leadership position as soon as the company believed that she was ready for such a role. Her first client assignment would be helping a team of consultants install a state income tax call center.

After a one-month-long orientation and training program, Deep was performing billable work at her new employer. At the outset, she reminded her new manager and team leader again that she preferred the managerial route to remaining in a technical position. After six months of hard work, Deep looked forward to her first formal performance evaluation. Deep's team leader informed her that her performance was better than average but short of outstanding. Deep asked for an explanation of why her performance was not considered outstanding. She informed her team leader and manager, "I need an outstanding rating to help me achieve my goals of becoming a leader in our company."

The manager replied, "Our performance evaluations are based on your contribution to the company. We care much less about writing performance evaluations to help a senior business analyst reach her career goals. Besides, San, you've made your point enough about wanting to be a leader in our firm. Let your performance speak for itself."

That evening, Deep met with her fiancé, Ryan, to discuss her dilemma. "The problem, Ryan, is that they don't get it. I'm leadership material, and they don't see it yet. I'm performing well and letting my intentions be known, but my strategy isn't working. The company is missing out on a golden opportunity by not putting me on a fast leadership track. I have to convince them of their error in judgment."

Ryan, a human resources specialist, replied, "I'm listening to you, and I want to give you good advice. Let me be objective here despite the fact that I love you. What have you done lately to prove to the company that you are leadership material?"

### Questions

1. Who has the problem here, San or the consulting firm in question?
2. What advice can you offer San to help her increase her chances of being promoted to a formal leadership position in the company?
3. What is your evaluation of the validity of the advice Ryan offered San?

# REFERENCES

1. Sarah E. Needleman, "Be Prepared When Opportunity Calls," *The Wall Street Journal*, February 7, 2006, p. B4.

2. Mary Ellen Slayter, "Job Hunters Take Note: Your Best Fit May Be Federal," available at *washingtonpost.com*, retrieved December 25, 2005.

3. Amy L. Kristof-Brown, Ryan D. Zimmerman, and Erin C. Johnson, "Consequences of Individuals' Fit at Work: A Meta-Analysis of Person–Job, Person–Organization, Person–Group, and Person–Supervisor Fit," *Personnel Psychology*, Summer 2005, p. 310.

4. Cited in Kris Maher, "The Jungle: Focus on Recruitment, Pay and Getting Ahead," *The Wall Street Journal*, June 17, 2003, p. B8.

5. Quoted in Anne Fisher, "How to Run an Online Job Hunt," *Fortune*, June 28, 2004, p. 43.

6. Based on form used by Garrett Associates, Alexandria, Virginia.

7. Amy Lindgren, "CV or Résumé? Depends on Purpose, Reader," *Atlanta Journal Constitution*, January 29, 2006, p. R4.

8. Laura Egodigwe, "Extreme Makeover," *Black Enterprise*, September 2004, p. 106.

9. Jim Pawlak, "Interviewing 101: How Not to Get a New Job," *The Detroit News*, available at detnews.com, retrieved September 30, 2005.

10. Peter F. Drucker, *Classic Drucker: Essential Wisdom of Peter Drucker from the Pages of Harvard Business Review* (Boston: Harvard Business School Press, 2006).

11. Quoted in Anne Fisher, "Disaster-Proofing Your Career," *Fortune*, October 3, 2005, p. 174.

12. Jeffery A. Thompson, "Proactive Personality and Job Performance: A Social Capital Perspective," *Journal of Applied Psychology*, September 2005, pp. 1011–1017.

13. Scott E. Seibert, J. Michael Crant, and Maria L. Kraimer, "Proactive Personality and Career Success," *Journal of Applied Psychology*, June 1999, pp. 416–427.

14. Quoted in Michael Barrier, "Should Looks Count: Are You Discriminating against Employees Because of Their Appearance?" *HR Magazine*, September 2004, p. 66.

15. Mielikki Org, "The Tatooed Executive: Body Art Gains Acceptance in Once-Staid Office Settings; Corporate Counsel's Yin-Yang," *The Wall Street Journal*, August 28, 2003, pp. D1, D 15; Karen Dybis, "While No Longer Taboo, Body Art Still Can Be a Sticky Issue at Work," *Detroit News*, available at detnews.com, June 21, 2005.

16. Tom Peters, "The Brand Called You: You Can't Move Up If You Don't Stand Out," *Fast Company*, August–September 1997, pp. 83–94. The quote is from p. 86.

17. Deb Koen, "Identifying Values Clarifies Career Goals," *Rochester (NY) Democrat and Chronicle*, June 4, 2000, p. D4.

18. Betti A. Hamilton and Terri A. Scandura, "E-Mentoring: Implications for Organizational Learning and Development in a Wired World," *Organizational Dynamics*, 32, no. 4, 2003, p. 388; Donna M. Owens, "Virtual Mentoring," *HR Magazine*, March 2006, pp. 105–107.

19. Tammy D. Allen et al., "Career Benefits Associated with Mentoring for Protégés: A Meta-Analysis," *Journal of Applied Psychology*, February 2004, pp. 127–136.

20. Stephen Covey, "How to Succeed in Today's Workplace," *USA Weekend*, August 29–31, 1997, pp. 4–5.

21. Will Shanley, "Latina Exec's Success Story Inspires," *Denver Post*, available at *denverpost.com*, March 21, 2005.

22. Scott Kirsner, "Networking Overload," *Fast Company*, April 2004, p. 38.

# 10

# Job Search and Career Management Skills

## Learning Objectives

After reading and studying this chapter and doing the exercises, you should be able to:

1 Acquire new insights into conducting a job search, including writing an impressive cover letter, preparing a résumé, and being interviewed.

2 Describe the difference between a vertical and a horizontal career path.

3 Identify a handful of career-enhancing strategies and tactics you intend to use.

## Outline

1 **Conducting a Job Search** 301
Job-Hunting Tactics
The Job Résumé and Cover Letter
Performing Well in a Job Interview

2 **The Vertical and Horizontal Career Paths** 315
The Vertical (Traditional) Career Path
The Horizontal Career Path

3 **Career Advancement Strategies and Tactics** 319
Capitalize on Your Strengths and Build Your Personal Brand
Be Passionate about and Proud of Your Work
Develop a Code of Professional Ethics
Develop a Proactive Personality
Keep Growing through Continuous Learning and Self-Development
Document Your Accomplishments
Project a Professional Image
Perceive Yourself as a Provider of Services
Develop Depth and Breadth
Rely on a Network of Successful People
Work with a Mentor
Find a Good Person–Organization Fit
Take Sensible Risks
Emphasize Relationships to Combat Being Outsourced

Ellis Rowe, Group President, Mars Drinks Group and Mars Developing Pet Care, at age 54, was interviewed by *Black Enterprise*, about his career. A portion of the interview follows:

*BE:*  *You've been in a manufacturing role, moved into information systems, then finance. You were responsible for all pet care and snack foods factories in North America, held a corporate staff officer role in finance, were general manager of the confectionary business, and held a corporate HR role. You attribute your varied career in almost 30 years at Mars Inc., where you've had more than 20 staff and line jobs crossing many function areas, to your internal network. [Staff jobs are support positions, whereas line jobs deal with the primary purpose of the business, such as manufacturing.]*

*ER:*  *An internal network allows you to connect with individuals who can influence your career as well as guide you through opportunities that you might not otherwise be aware of. Internal networking is building a wall brick by brick. You can start on the foundation level, and if you're with the business for a while, you just keep adding bricks until one day you have a wall.*

*BE:*  *How can executives build internal networks?*

*ER:*  *They need to identify where they want their careers to go and the people who can help them get there. If you want something, you have to move toward it. To do that, you have to find a way to add value, whether it's exchanging information or identifying what you can do to help that person—be it a colleague or someone senior to you. We work in teams in our business, and if you help your team and individuals on the team succeed, they can support you in building your career.*

*You become a senior person in business not because of time but because you've built relationships with individuals of influence who recognize that value you can add. In your career, there'll be opportunities that you'll want to be considered for. The best way is to not have to interview for those jobs but to be considered by people who want you on their team. [1]*

As the experience of the business executive just described suggests, being systematic about advancing your career can pay big dividends. In this case, the person effectively capitalized on internal networks. This final chapter of the book focuses on career success, including a description of strategies and tactics that will help you gain advantage.

Our approach to achieving career success is divided into three major segments: conducting a job campaign, understanding two major types of career paths, and using career advancement strategies and tactics. However, the information presented in this chapter is more specifically about managing your career.

# Conducting a Job Search

■ **Learning Objective 1**

The vast majority of workers have to conduct a job search at various times in their careers. Job searches are conducted to find employment in a firm the job seeker is not already working for, or sometimes to find a new position within one's own firm. When job openings are on short supply, job search skills are especially important. Even during the most prosperous of times, when jobs are in ample supply, learning more about conducting a job search is useful. It can help you land an excellent position. Included in the job search are job-hunting tactics and preparing a résumé and cover letter.

## JOB-HUNTING TACTICS

Most people already have usable knowledge about how to find a job. Some of the ideas discussed next will therefore be familiar; some will be unfamiliar. We recommend using this list of tactics as a checklist to ensure that you have not neglected something important. Also, it is important to search for employment systematically. It is easy to overlook the obvious when job hunting because your emotions may cloud your sense of logic.

### Identify Your Job Objectives

An effective job search begins with a clear perception of what kind of position (or positions) you want. If you express indecision about the type of work you seek, the prospective employer will typically ask in a critical tone, "What kind of work are you looking for?" Your chances of finding suitable employment increase when several different types of positions will satisfy your job objectives. Assume that one person who majored in business administration is only willing to accept a position as an office manager in a corporation. Another person with the same major is seeking a position as (1) an office manager; (2) a management trainee in a corporation; (3) an assistant manager in a retail store, restaurant, or hotel; (4) a sales representative; (5) an assistant purchasing agent; or (6) a management analyst. The second person has a much better chance of finding a suitable position.

### Be Aware of Qualifications Sought by Employers

What you are looking for in an employer must be matched against what an employer is looking for in an employee. If you are aware of what employers are seeking, you can emphasize those aspects of yourself when applying for a position. For example, applicants for almost any type of position should emphasize their IT skills. Job interviewers and hiring managers do not all agree on the qualifications they seek in employees. Nevertheless, a number of traits, characteristics, skills, and accomplishments are important to many employers. Self-Assessment Quiz 10-1 summarizes these qualifications in a way that you can apply to yourself as you think about your job hunt.

### Identify Your Skills and Potential Contribution

The job market has been skill based for some time. Employers typically seek out job candidates with tangible skills (including interpersonal skills) that can

## Self-Assessment Quiz   10-1

### Qualifications Sought by Employers

**Directions:** The following is a list of qualifications widely sought by prospective employers. After reading each qualification, rate yourself on a 1 to 5 scale by circling the appropriate number: 1 = very low, 2 = low, 3 = average, 4 = high, 5 = very high.

| | | | | | |
|---|---|---|---|---|---|
| 1. Appropriate education for the position under consideration and satisfactory grades | 1 | 2 | 3 | 4 | 5 |
| 2. Relevant work experience | 1 | 2 | 3 | 4 | 5 |
| 3. Communication and other interpersonal skills | 1 | 2 | 3 | 4 | 5 |
| 4. Motivation and energy | 1 | 2 | 3 | 4 | 5 |
| 5. Problem-solving ability (intelligence) and creativity | 1 | 2 | 3 | 4 | 5 |
| 6. Judgment and common sense | 1 | 2 | 3 | 4 | 5 |
| 7. Adaptability to change | 1 | 2 | 3 | 4 | 5 |
| 8. Emotional maturity (acting professionally and responsibly) | 1 | 2 | 3 | 4 | 5 |
| 9. Teamwork (ability and interest in working in a team effort) | 1 | 2 | 3 | 4 | 5 |
| 10. Positive attitude (enthusiasm about work and initiative) | 1 | 2 | 3 | 4 | 5 |
| 11. Emotional intelligence (ability to deal with own feelings and those of others) | 1 | 2 | 3 | 4 | 5 |
| 12. Customer service orientation (wanting to meet customer needs) | 1 | 2 | 3 | 4 | 5 |
| 13. Information technology skills | 1 | 2 | 3 | 4 | 5 |
| 14. Willingness to continue to study and learn about the job, company, and industry | 1 | 2 | 3 | 4 | 5 |
| 15. Likableness and sense of humor | 1 | 2 | 3 | 4 | 5 |
| 16. Dependability, responsibility, and conscientiousness (including good work habits and time management) | 1 | 2 | 3 | 4 | 5 |
| 17. Willingness and ability to work well with coworkers and customers from different cultures | 1 | 2 | 3 | 4 | 5 |
| 18. Behaves ethically toward customers and company employees and obeys laws and regulations | 1 | 2 | 3 | 4 | 5 |

### Interpretation

Consider engaging in some serious self-development, training, and education for items on which you rated yourself low or very low. If you accurately rated yourself as 4 or 5 on all the dimensions, you are an exceptional job candidate.

be put to immediate use in accomplishing work. Job-relevant skills you might identify include IT skills, written communication skills, oral communication skills, math skills, and listening skills. The cornerstone of a job search should be a thorough list of assets and accomplishments, because they point to useful skills and abilities you can use to help the employer.

A successful candidate for a customer service position at a telecommunications company told the interviewer, "I know I can help your customers with their software and hardware problems. I worked at the technical support center at college, and my friends and family members are forever coming to me with their computer problems. I even get long-distance calls for help. Give me a chance to help your customers." (Notice that the candidate implied that he or she had good listening skills.)

## Develop a Comprehensive Marketing Strategy

A vital job-finding strategy is to use multiple approaches to reach the right prospective employer. This is particularly true when the position you seek is in short supply. Among the many approaches employers use to recruit candidates are employee referrals, newspaper ads, job boards, employer Web sites, social networking Web sites, college and professional school recruitment, job fairs, temporary help firms, walk-ins, unsolicited résumés and phone calls, and government employment services.

## Use Networking to Reach Company Insiders

The majority of successful job campaigns stem from personal contacts. Employers rely heavily on referrals from employees to fill positions, even though many good positions are also announced publicly, such as through Web sites and classified ads. In regard to job hunting, networking is contacting friends and acquaintances and building systematically on these relationships to create a still wider set of contacts that might lead to employment. Formal mechanisms to develop network contacts have been introduced in recent years, such as bar parties in metropolitan areas devoted just to making job contacts.

Figure 10-1 presents a list of potential network contacts. In addition, a skill-building exercise about networking as a method of career advancement, including a job search, is presented toward the end of this chapter.

The networking technique is so well known today that it suffers from overuse. It is therefore important to use a tactful, low-key approach with a contact. For example, instead of asking a person in your network to furnish you a job lead, ask that person how someone with qualifications similar to yours might find a job. In addition, guard against taking up a

- Coworkers and previous employers
- Friends and neighbors
- Faculty and staff
- Graduates of any schools you have attended
- Former employers
- Present employers (assuming you hold a temporary position)
- Professional workers such as bankers, brokers, and clergy
- Political leaders at the local level
- Members of your club or athletic team
- Community groups, churches, temples, and mosques
- Trade and professional associations
- Student professional associations
- Career fairs
- People met in airports and on airplanes
- People met in aerobic classes and health clubs
- People you get to know through Internet social networks

**Figure 10-1**

**Potential Sources of Network Contacts**

large portion of a busy person's workday, for instance, by insisting on a luncheon meeting.

Another way of reaching company insiders is to write dozens of e-mail messages or hard-copy letters to potential employers. A surprisingly large number of people find jobs by contacting employers directly. Most large company Web sites have a section allocated to inviting job inquiries as part of the employee recruitment program. Prepare a prospective employer list, including the names of executives to contact in each firm. The people who receive your letters and e-mail messages become part of your network. A variation of this approach is to develop a 30-second telephone presentation of your background. After you have researched firms that may have opportunities for you, call them and make your pitch. However, voice-mail systems usually make it difficult to speak directly to your target person.

### Use Multiple Online Approaches

The Internet is a standard avenue for job hunting, even for middle-management and executive positions. Sources of job leads on the Internet include general job boards, specialty job boards, company Web sites, and social networking Web sites.

With a job board (or job search site), the job seeker can post a résumé or scroll through hundreds of job opportunities. A number of job board Web sites are résumé database services because they give employers access to résumés submitted by job hunters. Many position announcements on the Internet require the job seeker to send a résumé by attached file. A few position announcements still request that the résumé be sent by fax or paper mail. Figure 10-2 lists some of the leading job boards, and dozens of others can be found quickly with an Internet job search. Job boards post positions by both field and geographic region. Specialty job boards, such as those listed in Figure 10-2, are preferred by some job seekers and employers because these boards are less flooded with positions and applicants. An Internet search will quickly reveal any specialty job site in your field.

Many managers prefer the employment section of their Web site over commercial job boards. Some of the more advanced company job sites, such as GE, present possible career paths for people who enter the company in the position sought.

**Figure 10-2**

**General and Specialty Job Boards**

1. *Leading General Job-Search Web Sites*
   www.CareerBuilder.com
   www.Monster.com
   www.HotJobs.Yahoo.com
   www.Job.com
   www.Indeed.com

2. *Examples of Specialized Job-Search Web Sites*
   www.Dice.com (technology positions)
   www.SalesAnimals.com (sales positions)
   www.Healthcaresource.com (health-care positions)
   www.cruisejobfinder.com (cruise and hospitality positions)

A growing number of employers believe that the best way to find good job candidates is to advertise on Web sites where these candidates are likely to be spending considerable time, such as MySpace or Linkedin. Job boards also have a presence on social networking sites, as do recruiting firms. HotJobs has an application form on the social networking site Facebook. The potential applicant can send an e-mail or instant message to a particular posting. Another example of using social networking sites to find applicants is that recruiting companies have set up shop on Second Life. Job possibilities on this site on found on the job board, SLJobFinder.com. [2] Hundreds of people every day land jobs they first learned about through a job board or company Web site, so this approach offers some promise. A caution is that job hunting on the Internet can lead to a false sense of security. Using the Internet, a résumé is cast over a wide net, and hundreds of job postings can be explored. As a consequence, the job seeker may think that he or she can sit back and wait for a job offer to come through e-mail. In reality, the Internet is just one source of leads that should be used in conjunction with other job-finding methods, especially personal contacts that might lead to an interview. Employers still extensively use print ads in newspapers to recruit employees. Remember also that thousands of other job seekers can access the same job opening, and many of the positions listed have already been filled.

Skill-Building Exercise 10-1 will give you an opportunity to learn firsthand about job hunting on the Internet.

## Skill-Building Exercise 10-1

### Job Hunting on the Internet

Job hunting on the Internet can be a rewarding or frustrating experience, depending on your skill in navigating job search Web sites and the availability of positions for a person with your qualifications. Use several job boards to locate a position opening for the following three persons:

**Position 1:** You.
Find a position listed on the Internet that would appear to be an excellent fit for you at this time in your career.

**Position 2:** Sales Representative, Fluent in English and Chinese.
Attempt to find an opening for an industrial sales representative or retail sales position that requires the applicant to be fluent in English and Chinese.

**Position 3:** Sports Administrator.
Attempt to find an opening for a sports administrator, typically a person who does administrative work for a professional sports team. Set a time limit for your surfing, perhaps 60 minutes. If you are working in a team, each team member can search for one position. Share with each other your approaches and job boards that appear to achieve the best results.

Establishing your own Web site or blog, with résumé included, will some-times attract an employer who conducts an Internet search for potential candidates. For example, Ryan Loken, a Wal-Mart Stores, Inc., recruitment manager, says he spends a couple hours per week scanning blogs for new talent or additional information about candidates already interviewed. [3] A blog is most likely to attract a recruiter's attention if it relates to work in your contemplated field, such as explaining how you helped your employer save energy.

### Smile at Network Members and Interviewers and Be Enthusiastic

Assuming that you have the right qualifications, the simple act of smiling can be an effective job-hunting technique. One reason that smiling is effective at any stage of the job search is that it helps build a relationship, however brief. If you use a Webcam or video as part of your job search, smile on camera. Closely related to smiling is to display enthusiasm and excitement when speaking to people who can help you land a position. Conducted properly, a job search should be exciting and invigorating, and you should express these emotions to your contacts. [4] The excitement and invigoration stem from each small step you take leading to your goal of finding suitable employment.

### Smooth Out Rough Spots in Your Background

About 95 percent of employers routinely conduct background investigations of prospective employees. A background investigation by a firm hired for the purpose could include speaking to neighbors and coworkers about your reputation. In addition, the investigator may delve into your driving record, check for criminal charges or convictions, survey your credit record, and find out whether you have had disputes with the government about taxes. The information just mentioned is used to supplement reference checks because so many employers are hesitant to say anything negative about past employees. The information uncovered through the background check is often compared to the information presented on your résumé. A discrepancy between the two sends up an immediate red flag.

A job seeker's credit history has gained importance as part of a background investigation. Rightfully or wrongfully, many otherwise qualified candidates are rejected because of a poor credit history. Whether or not the law is usually followed, U.S. law requires companies to get permission from applicants to run credit checks. Applicants should also be given the opportunity to respond. [5] Concerns about hiring someone with a poor credit record include (a) worries that finances will interfere with his or her concentration, (b) the person is unreliable in general, or (c) that being in dire need of money, he or she might steal from the company. Under ideal circumstances an employer would give the applicant a chance to explain a poor credit history. For example, many reliable people have poor credit records because their medical bills went into collection while they waited for an insurance company to pay, or were victims of identity theft. [6]

Any job seeker who has severe negative factors in his or her background cannot readily change the past. Yet the job seeker can receive copies of a credit bureau report to make sure it is fair and accurate. If inaccuracies exist, or certain credit problems have been resolved, the credit report might be changed in the applicant's favor. Or, bring up the negative credit rating during an interview to present your side of the story. Perhaps you had cosigned a loan for a friend who fell behind on his or her payments. It might also be possible to obtain a more favorable reference from an employer by making a polite request. A third step can be to request a copy of the consumer report, which is a report of your reputation based on interviews with coworkers, neighbors, and others. A person might be able to negotiate a deletion of damaging information that is incorrect or exaggerated. [7]

Another way to learn about what public information exists about you is to place your own name into a couple of search engines. Sometimes another person with the same name as yours—particularly if many people have the same name as you—might have been involved in criminal activity, so be prepared to defend yourself! "Googling" candidates has become standard practice to uncover both positive and negative information about job applicants. Going one step further, many employers search social Web sites like MySpace to see if the candidate has engaged in outrageous behavior such as swimming in a public fountain while under the influence of alcohol—and then bragged about the episode on the social Web site.

Concerns about having negative information about one self somewhere on the Internet have prompted several entrepreneurs to help job seekers, as well as others, help buy negative or embarrassing postings on other people's Web sites. Reputation Defender, Inc., is one such firm. [8]

## THE JOB RÉSUMÉ AND COVER LETTER

A résumé is usually an essential part of the job hunt. Yet you can sometimes join a family business for a friend's enterprise without submitting a résumé. In some instances you will be asked to complete a job application form instead of, or in addition to, a résumé. Résumés are also important for job hunting within your own firm. You may need one to be considered for a transfer with a large firm, or to be assigned to a team or project.

### Résumé Purpose

Regard your résumé as a marketing tool for selling your skills and potential to handle new responsibilities. The most specific purpose of a résumé is to help you obtain an interview that can lead to a job. Your résumé, whether electronic, paper, or video, must therefore attract enough attention for an employer to invite you for an interview. A poorly prepared résumé often leads to an immediate rejection of the candidate. Recognize that you are competing against many carefully prepared résumés, some of which have been prepared with assistance from others. If the demand for your skills is high enough, it is conceivable that you will be hired without an interview.

### Résumé Length and Format

Opinions vary about the desirable length for a résumé. For a recent graduate with limited work experience, a one-page résumé may be acceptable. One page might seem too short for more experienced workers. Employers today demand considerable detail in résumés, particularly about the candidate's skills, accomplishments, and teamwork and leadership experience. Nevertheless, a three-page or longer résumé may irritate an impatient reader. Two pages are therefore recommended for early stages in your career. Professors and scientists often use a CV (curriculum vitae) instead of a résumé. The CV goes into considerable detail about their research activities and publications, and might take about seven pages. To add to the confusion of terms, Europeans and Canadians are more likely to use the term *curriculum* vitae rather than *résumé*.

A general-purpose résumé is presented in Figures 10-3 and 10-4. Recognize that hiring managers and human resource professionals have

---

Scott Wayland<br>
170 Glenview Drive<br>
Dallas, Texas 75243<br>
Phone/Fax (312) 555-3986<br>
swayland@gmail.com<br>
http://www.scottwayland.com

**Qualification Summary**
Experience in selling industrial machinery. Education in business administration, combined with apprenticeship in tool and die making. In one year sold $500,000 worth of excess machine inventory. Received letter of commendation from CEO.

**Job Objective**
Industrial sales, handling large, complex machinery. Willing to work largely on commission basis. Want to use my skill and contacts to help employer gain market share.

**Job Experience**
2009–present
Industrial account representative, Bainbridge Corporation, Dallas, Texas. Sell line of tool and die equipment to companies in Southwest. Responsibilities include servicing established accounts and canvassing new ones.

2007–2009
Inside sales representative, Bainbridge Corporation. Answered customer inquiries through e-mail, Web site, and telephone. Filled orders for replacement parts. Trained for outside sales position. Served as sales team representative on company productivity-improvement team.

2003–2007
Tool and die maker apprentice, Texas Metals, Inc., Dallas. Assisted senior tool and die makers during four-year training program. Worked on milling machines, jigs, punch presses, computer-assisted manufacturing, computer-assisted design (CAD/CAM).

**Formal Education**
2003–2009
Madagascar College, Dallas. Associate Degree in Business Administration; graduated with 3.16 grade point average. Courses in marketing, sales techniques, consumer behavior, accounting, and statistics. President of Commuter's Club.

1999–2003
Big Horn High, Dallas. Honors student; academic major with vocational elective. Played varsity football and basketball. Earned part of living by selling magazine subscriptions.

**Job-Related Skills**
Professional sales representative. Able to size up customer manufacturing problem and make recommendations for appropriate machinery. Precise in preparing call reports and expense accounts. Good skill in gathering input from the field for market research purposes.

**Personal Interests and Hobbies**
Information technology enthusiast (developed and installed own Web site), scuba diving, recreational golf player, read trade and business magazines. Auto enthusiast, including restoring a 1976 Corvette.

**References**
On file with placement office at Madagascar College.

**Figure  10-3**

**A General Purpose Résumé**

**Jennifer A. Koster**

700 Anderson St., Apt. B ∞ Fairfax, VA 22033 ∞ (703) 555-2121 ∞ Email: jakerwin@yahoo.com

| | |
|---|---|
| **Objective** | Sales management trainee position, leading eventually to becoming a sales manager |
| **Education** | **B.A. Business Administration, Marketing Major, Advertising Minor, December 2010**<br>George Mason University, Fairfax, VA<br>GPA: In-major, 3.4/4.0   Overall, 2.7/4.0<br>Earned 40% of educational expenses |

**Accomplishments and skills**

**Marketing / Sales / Promotion**
- Grossed $16,000 in three months with summer landscaping business
- Raised $75,000 in advertising space for environmental club folder project
- Raised $50,000 for sorority sponsored car show
- Cold canvassed community for potential clients
- Created informational brochure for apartment leasing company
- Developed advertising campaign for class project

**Mangement / Training / Organizational Ability**
- Managed daily activities of own landscaping business including renting/purchasing equipment and supplies, hiring assistants, budgeting, payroll
- Arranged client contracts for landscaping business
- Coordinated sales presentation strategy for sorority car show and trained others in sales techniques
- Trained new fast-service restaurant employees
- Aided in refurbishing and renovating a restaurant
- Performed restaurant duties ranging from server to night manager

**Communications / Language / Creative Projects**
- Created multimedia presentation using slides, music, and narration to brief incoming George Mason students during orientation
- Developed sales presentations and assisted with advertising campaigns including radio spots, newspaper ads, billboards, posters, brochures
- Designed and distributed flyers for landscaping business
- Conversational Spanish skills; write reasonably well in Spanish

| | |
|---|---|
| **Work Experience** | **Self-Employed,** (Partnership) Whole Earth Landscaping, Reston, VA, Summer 2008<br>**Waiter,** Rainbow's of Washington, Washington, DC, Summers 2007, 2008, 2009 |
| **Activities** | **Theater Arts,** George Mason, several roles in dramas and musicals. Regularly participate in clothing and fund drives for homeless people in Washington, DC |

**Figure 10-4**

**A Job Résumé for a Recent Business Graduate**

widely different perceptions of what constitutes an effective résumé. Both résumés include job duties performed as well as a chronological history, and could therefore be referred to as *chronological* résumés. A résumé that focuses on work performed rather than a job chronology is referred to as a *functional* résumé. This type of résumé can be helpful in directing attention toward skills and away from employment gaps. [9] Check at least two résumé guides before preparing a final version of your résumé. Microsoft Word includes several templates for job résumés. A study conducted with 64 business professionals provides some useful information about which résumé characteristics are perceived positively enough to invite a job candidate for an interview. The business professionals reviewed résumés for new business graduates. The following résumé characteristics were more likely to lead to first choices for an interview: One page in contrast to two pages, a specific objective statement in comparison to a general objective statement, relevant coursework better than no coursework listed, GPAs of 3.0 in contrast to no GPA listed, GPAs of 3.50 in contrast to GPAs of 2.75, and accomplishment statements in contrast to no accomplishment statement. [10] In support of these findings, a résumé that does not list the candidate's skills and accomplishments is considered insufficient today.

In writing your résumé, keep in mind that certain key words attract the attention of managers and specialists who scan job résumés manually or with software. Among these key words are *languages, wireless, WiFi, global outsourcing, hands-on, flexible, results-driven, communication skills, e-commerce, cultural diversity,* and *sustainable environment.* The attention-grabbing words and terms are often referred to as *Google-optimized key words* because they show up frequently in an Internet search. You can find the key words that apply to your field by studying relevant ads. Key words are particularly important for online submission of your credentials because software is used by human resource departments of large companies to reduce a large stack of candidates into a manageable list of finalists. [11]

When submitting your résumé and cover letter electronically, make it easy for the employer to access, such as using an attached Word file. Many employers will refuse to open a link to your Web site or a PowerPoint presentation. Furthermore, concerns about computer viruses have prompted some employers to refuse to open any attached file. So you might send an attached word processing file, plus insert your résumé on the e-mail message. Make sure the formatting is not lost when cutting and pasting your document into e-mail. Send your cover letter and résumé to yourself to check for lost formatting.

Although an up-to-date job search may require online submission, recognize that you may be subject to identify theft. In one scam, the job seeker is sent an e-mail claiming to be from a recruiter representing a company seeking personal details for a pre-employment background check. Your identifying information is then used for identity theft. Sometimes you are asked for bank account information so your prospective new employer can make direct deposits to your account. [12]

Also, you may receive phony job offers requiring you to engage in such tasks as sending packages to an overseas country. The packages are usually stolen merchandise, and you never receive payment for your work. Another frequent scam is paying you a commission to transfer money overseas. You are sent a phony check, and then asked to send your own check overseas for perhaps 80 percent of the value of the check.

### Video Résumés and Creative Formats

A rapidly growing approach to résumé construction is the online video résumé. Turning the camcorder or Webcam on yourself, you present much of the basic information that would be found on a written résumé. The video approach is good for capturing your appearance, personality, and oral communication skills. Some job seekers place their video on their Web site or on YouTube, or simply as an attachment.

Unless you are highly skilled at video presentation, it is best to get professional help in constructing your video résumé. Careful editing might be needed to eliminate vocalized pauses and inadvertent distracting expressions.

Another potential problem with the video résumé is that it focuses too much attention on soft skills for a candidate who wants to emphasize hard skills. Because some employers do not wish to spend the time watching a video, it is a good human relations tactic is also include a more conventional résumé. If an employer uses a video on its job site, the climate is probably right for you to submit a video résumé.

Another alternative to developing a distinctive résumé is to create an unusual format in factors such as color, size, and layout, including presenting the résumé in the form of a marketing brochure. If aesthetically pleasing, the offbeat résumé could suggest that you are creative and courageous. Allan Zander, a vice president of SolaCom Technologies in Quebec, receives up to 300 résumés when he has a position open, with fewer than 5 percent having creative designs. Among the more appealing ones, Zander says, are those that display corporate logos representing an applicant's current and past employers. (A school logo might also be eye appealing.) Another design element Zander admires is the pull-out quote—a short amount of text displayed in large type. [13] An example would be, "Have quickly developed a reputation as a finisher."

Whatever type of résumé you choose, and whatever mode of transmission, honesty is important. Many managers believe that a person who lies on a résumé might also behave unethically once on the job. ResumeDoctor.com, a résumé-preparation business, discovered that of 1,000 résumés checked for truthfulness, 43 percent contain significant inaccuracies. A background screening company found that 14 percent of U.S. job applicants lie about education on their résumés. [14]

## The Cover Letter

A résumé should be accompanied by a cover letter explaining who you are and why you are applying for a particular position. The cover letter customizes your approach to a particular employer, whereas the résumé is a more general approach. Sometimes it is helpful to prepare an attention-getting cover letter in which you make an assertive statement about how you intend to help the employer deal with an important problem. A person applying for a credit manager position might state, "Let me help you improve your cash flow by using the latest methods for getting customers to pay on time, or even early."

Career advisor Jim Pawlak suggests that the cover letter should take no longer than one minute to read, and should focus on the skills and background you'll bring to the job. Follow this with a brief bulleted list of your accomplishments. A useful alternative to the bulleted list is a two-column table that compares the requirements stated by the employer with your qualifications. [15] An example follows:

| Your Requirements | My Qualifications |
|---|---|
| Sales experience | Four years of part-time selling including working a newspaper subscription and renewal kiosk at a shopping mall. |
| Ability to resolve conflict | Worked three seasons as lifeguard, and frequently had to stop rule violators and people in fights. Worked as Little League baseball coach, and resolved many conflicts between parents and myself, or between parents and the umpires. |

If possible, mention a company insider in your network, and then close the cover letter with appreciation for any consideration your qualifications might be given. Figure 10-5 presents a traditional, yet quite brief, cover letter. Use this approach if you are concerned about being too bold in your cover letter, or if you are applying to a highly traditional business firm.

## PERFORMING WELL IN A JOB INTERVIEW

After a prospective employer has reacted favorably to your cover letter and résumé, the next step is a telephone screening interview or a more comprehensive job interview. The purpose of the telephone screening interview is generally to obtain some indication of the candidate's oral communication skill. Such an interview is most likely when one applies for a customer contact position or one that requires knowledge of a second language. Having passed the screening interview, the candidate is invited for an in-person job interview.

Some job candidates overlook the fact that the phone interview is a serious contact with their employer, and do not differentiate between a social interview and a professional one. Outrageously wrong behaviors during the screening interview include having a television set turned on, letting a dog bark, using call waiting, and conducting the interview while washing dishes. When asked by a phone interviewer, why he could hear water splashing, one candidate replied, "I'm taking a bath, that's the way I relax." It is preferable to use a landline, nonportable phone for a screen interview because you will be less likely to be distracted if you are stationary.

**Figure 10-5**

**A Traditional Cover Letter**

27 Running Brook Road
Baton Rouge, Louisiana 70801
(507) 825-6742
swooden@aol.com

Ms. Melissa Flowers
Director of Human Resources
Medical Supplies Corporation
7385 South Clinton Avenue
New Orleans, Louisiana 70130

Dear Ms. Flowers:

Please accept my application for the position of purchasing assistant, posted on your company Web Site and also in the *Times Picayune*, March 27.
My company, Wentworth Industries, is currently sending its manufacturing operations to Malaysia, and my position will be terminated April 30. I am strongly interested in being considered a candidate for the position of purchasing assistant. As shown in my job resume, I have the following key qualifications:

&infin;    Two years of experience in a purchasing department, including one year as an office assistant and one year as a purchasing assistant

&infin;    An appropriate academic background with a major in business administration

&infin;    Courses in purchasing and inventory management, and computer applications

Thank you for considering my application.
Cordially,
Sara Wooden

Another type of screening interview is to respond to computerized questions, including a sample job problem. Your answers are printed for the interviewer to review. Candidates who get through the computer-assisted interview get to be interviewed by a company representative.

Typically one person at a time interviews the job candidate, yet team interviews are becoming more commonplace. In this format, members of the team or department with whom you would be working take turns asking you questions. One justification for team interviews is to observe how the candidate fits in with the team. Another variation on the traditional interview is that you meet for a brief interview with a series of interviewers. The process is referred to as *speed interview*, because of its similarity to speed dating in which the relationship-seeker meets briefly with a series of prospective dates or mates at a planned event. Busy employers like speed interviews because they can quickly screen several candidates for the same position. [16]

A general guide for performing well in the job interview is to present a positive but accurate picture of you. Your chances of performing well in a job increase if you are suited for the job. Tricking a prospective employer into hiring you when you are not qualified is therefore self-defeating in terms of your career. What follows is a list of some key points to keep in mind when being interviewed for a job you want:

1. **Be prepared, look relaxed, and make the interviewer feel comfortable.** Coming to the interview fully prepared to discuss yourself and your background and knowing key facts about the prospective employer will help you look relaxed. Use the company Web sites to gather background information about the prospective employer. Check out stories found on the Web about the employer. Many middle-age job hunters take Botox treatments to appear relaxed (rather than frowning) during the job interview, and after being hired as well.

2. **Avoid talking too much during the interview.** It is natural to think that during a job interview, you will be expected to talk. However, talking too much, including the presentation of your thoughts in a rambling, disorganized manner, will be perceived quite negatively by experienced interviewers. Being perceived as a compulsive talker will often lead to immediate rejection. Display effective communication skills by presenting your ideas in depth, yet concisely. A facilities administrator ruined her chances of employment at an accounting firm in this manner: When asked to describe her strengths, she delivered a long-winded reply focused on how she cleaned every cabinet in her home. "She probably went on for three to four minutes," recalls the human resources director. "I doubted she could get the job done in an eight-hour day." Rehearsing answers to typical interview questions beforehand, such as those presented in Figure 10-6, can help you present your ideas more concisely. Also, if the interviewer looks bored, you may be rambling. [17]

3. **Establish a link between you and the prospective employer.** A good way to build rapport between you and the prospective employer is to mention some plausible link you have with that firm. To illustrate, if being interviewed for a position at a Sears store, one might say, "It's fun to visit the office part of Sears. Our family has been shopping here for years. In fact, I bought a DVD player here last month. It works great."

| Figure | 10-6 |
| --- | --- |

**Questions Frequently Asked of Job Candidates**

**Source:** Questions 1 and 9 are from "Questions Job Interviewers Are Asking Most," http://www.csmonitor.com/2003/0317/pl5s01-wmno.html, April 20, 2003.

An effective way of preparing for job interviews is to rehearse answers to the types of questions you will most likely be asked by the interviewer. The following questions are a sampling of the types found in most employment interviews. Rehearse answers to them prior to going out on job interviews. One good rehearsal method is to role-play the employment interview with a friend who asks these typical questions or to videotape yourself.

1. What would be your ideal job?
2. What are your career goals?
3. What are your salary requirements?
4. What new job skills would you like to acquire in the next few years?
5. Give me an example of how you displayed good teamwork.
6. Describe how you have shown leadership on the job or off the job.
7. What are your strengths (or good points)?
8. What are your weaknesses (or areas for needed improvement)?
9. What would a former boss say about you?
10. How well do you work under pressure?
11. What positions with other companies are you applying for?
12. What makes you think you will be successful in business?
13. What do you know about our company?
14. Here is a sample job problem. How would you handle it?
15. How would you use the Internet to perform better in this job?
16. What questions do you have for me?

> "Share your achievements and qualifications with confidence, but not arrogance."
>
> —Marie Artim, assistant vice president for recruiting, Enterprise Rent-A-Car, quoted in *Business Week*, September 24, 2007, p. 54

4. **Ask perceptive questions.** The best questions are sincere ones that reflect an interest in the content of the job (intrinsic motivators) and job performance, rather than benefits and social activities. A good question to ask is, "What would you consider to be outstanding performance in this job?" If the issue of compensation is not introduced by the interviewer, ask about such matters after first discussing the job and your qualifications.

5. **Be prepared to discuss your strengths and developmental opportunities.** Most interviewers will ask you to discuss your strengths and developmental opportunities. (These and other frequently asked questions are presented in Figure 10-6.) Knowledge of strengths hints at how good your potential job performance will be. If you deny having areas for improvement, you will appear uninsightful or defensive. Some candidates describe developmental opportunities that could be interpreted as strengths. A case in point: "I have been criticized for expecting too much from myself and others." Do you think this approach is unethical?

6. **Be prepared to respond to behavioral interview questions.** A behavioral interview asks questions directly about the candidate's behavior in relation to an important job activity. The job candidate is expected to give samples of important job behaviors. The behavioral interview is therefore more applicable to candidates with substantial work experience. Two behavioral inquiries are "Tell me about a time in which your ability to work well on a team contributed to the success of a project" and "Give me an example of a creative suggestion you made that was actually implemented. In what way did it help the company?" Instruction 6 and Question 14 in

Figure 10-6 are also behavioral interview questions. To prepare for such questions, think of some examples of how you handled a few difficult job challenges. The idea is to document specific actions you took or behaviors you engaged in that contributed to a favorable outcome.

7. **Show how you can help the employer.** A prospective employer wants to know whether you will be able to perform the job well. Direct much of your conversation toward how you intend to help the company solve problems and get important work accomplished. Whatever the question, think about what details of your skills and experiences will be useful to the employer. Joe Hodowanes, a career strategy advisor, recommends that before your interview, think of an answer to "What value do I bring to a company and why should they hire me?" As you think of your key selling points, write them down. [18]

8. **Use body language that projects confidence and decisiveness.** A job interviewer will often carefully observe the candidate's body language. Monitor your body language to appear confident and decisive. A case in point: An executive coach helped a manager hone his nonverbal communication skills. The manager was concerned because he came close to getting three job offers but did not get hired. The coach showed the manager how his relaxed posture and habit of picking up anything in reach made him appear indecisive. Therefore, the manager practiced sitting upright and keeping his hands at his sides. Soon thereafter the manager was hired into a position he wanted. [19] Being carefully groomed, looking crisp and fresh, and having clean, unbroken nails also help project self-confidence.

9. **Practice good etiquette during the interview, including during a meal.** Under the pressures of applying for a job, it is easy to let etiquette slip. To display poor etiquette and manners, however, could lead to a candidate being rejected from consideration. Most of the suggestions made about etiquette apply to the job interview, but be particularly sensitive to allowing company officials to talk without interrupting them, and practicing good table manners. Even interviewers who are rude themselves, such as taking phone calls while interviewing you, expect *you* not to do the same.

10. **Send a follow-up letter.** As part of displaying good manners, mail a courteous follow-up letter or send an e-mail message several days after the interview, particularly if you want the job. A follow-up letter is a tip-off that you are truly interested in the position. You should state your attitudes toward the position, the team, and the company and summarize any conclusions reached about your discussion.

Now do Skill-Building Exercise 10-2 to practice the job interview.

# The Vertical and Horizontal Career Paths

■ Learning Objective 2

Career planning can begin at any point, including a kindergarten child saying, "I want to be an astronaut." Many other people think about developing their career after they have worked in a full-time professional position for several

## Skill-Building Exercise 10-2

### The Job Interview

"As described in Figure 10-6, a good way to prepare for a job interview is to rehearse answers to frequently asked questions. In this role-play, one student will be the interviewer and one will be the interviewee (job applicant). The job in question is that of property manager for a large apartment complex in Phoenix, Arizona. Assume that the applicant really wants the job. The interviewer, having taken a course in human resource management, will ask many of the questions in Figure 10-3.

In addition, the interviewer will ask at least one behavioral question, perhaps about teamwork. The interviewer might also have other questions, such as, "Why do you want to live in Phoenix?"

Before proceeding with the role-play, both people should review the information in this chapter about the job interview.

■ **Career path**
a sequence of positions necessary to achieve a goal

years. Planning and developing your career involves some form of goal setting. If your goals are laid out systematically to lead to your ultimate career goal, you have established a **career path**, a sequence of positions necessary to achieve a goal. Here we look at the more traditional career path with an emphasis on moving upward, along with the more contemporary path that emphasizes acquiring new skills and knowledge.

## THE VERTICAL (TRADITIONAL) CAREER PATH

The vertical, or traditional, career path is based on the idea that a person continues to grow in responsibility with the aim of reaching a target position, such as becoming a top-level manager. The vertical career path is synonymous with "climbing the corporate ladder." The same path is based somewhat on the unwritten contract that a good performer will have the opportunity to work for one firm for a long time and receive many promotions in the process. However, a vertical career path can be spread out over several employers.

A career path should be related to the present and future demands of one firm or the industry. If you aspire toward a high-level manufacturing position, it would be vital to know the future of manufacturing in that firm and in the industry. Many U.S. firms, for example, outsource much of their manufacturing to China and Mexico. If you were really determined, you might study the appropriate language and ready yourself for a foreign position.

While laying out a career path, it is also helpful to list your personal goals. They should mesh with your work plans to avoid major conflicts in your life. Some lifestyles, for example, are incompatible with some career paths. It would be difficult to develop a stable home life (spouse, children, friends, community activities, sports team, and garden) if a person aspired toward holding field positions in international marketing. Contingency ("what if") plans should also be incorporated into a well-designed career path. For instance, "If I am not promoted within two years, I will pursue an advanced degree."

Mary Gonzalez, an ambitious 20-year-old, formulated the career path shown in Figure 10-7 prior to receiving an associate degree in business management. After she presented her tentative career path to her classmates, several exclaimed that Mary was aiming too high. Mary's career goals are high, but she has established contingency plans.

A career path laid out in chart form gives a person a clear perception of climbing steps toward his or her target position. As each position is attained, the corresponding step can be shaded in color or cross-hatched. The steps, or goals, include a time element, which is helpful for sound career management even in work environments that are less predictable than they used to be. Your long-range goal might be clearly established in your mind (such as to become regional manager of a hotel chain). At the same time, you must establish short-range (get any kind of job in a hotel) and intermediate-range (be manager of a hotel by age 27) goals. Goals set too far in the future that are not supported with more immediate goals may lose their motivational value.

Skill-Building Exercise 10-3 gives you the opportunity to practice building a career path—an activity that could have an enormous impact on your professional and personal life.

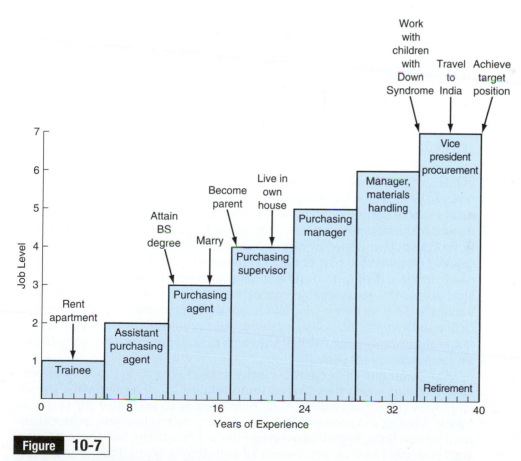

**Figure 10-7**

**A Vertical (or Traditional) Career Path**

## Skill-Building Exercise 10-3

### Developing a Career Path

1. Each class member will develop a tentative career path, perhaps as an outside assignment. About six volunteers will then share their paths with the rest of the class. Feedback of any type will be welcomed. Class members studying the career paths of others should keep in mind such issues as the following:
   a. How logical does it appear?
   b. Is this something the person really wants, or is it simply an exercise in putting down on paper what the ambitious person is supposed to want?
   c. How well do the individual's work plans mesh with personal plans?

2. Each class member will interview an experienced working person outside of class about his or her career path. Most of the people interviewed will have already completed a portion of their path. They will therefore have less flexibility (and perhaps less idealism) than people who are just getting started in their careers. The conclusions reached about these interviews will make a fruitful class discussion. Among the issues raised might be the following:
   a. How familiar were these people with the idea of a career path?
   b. How willing were they to talk about themselves?
   c. Were many actual "paths" discovered, or did a series of jobs simply come about by luck or "fate"?

## THE HORIZONTAL CAREER PATH

In many organizations, the hope of staying for a long time and receiving a long series of promotions has vanished. Instead of climbing the ladder, the person makes a series of horizontal moves, as illustrated in Figure 10-8. A significant feature of the horizontal career path is that people are more likely to advance by moving sideways than by moving up. Or, at least people who get ahead will spend a considerable part of their career working in different positions at or nearly at the same level. In addition, they may occasionally move to a lower-level position to gain valuable experience. With a horizontal career path, the major reward is no longer promotion, but the opportunity to gain more experience and increase job skills. Organizations that reward people for good work, rather than simply because they have high rank, is another force encouraging the horizontal career path. [20]

The horizontal career path is closely linked to the contemporary employment contract that offers shared responsibility for career growth. The old employment contract was lifetime employment in exchange for corporate loyalty. Instead, today employees get a chance to develop new technical and professional skills. Rather than being offered job security, they become more employable because of the diversity of skills they acquire. The company provides the environment for learning, and the employees are responsible for developing their skills. Another justification for the horizontal career path is

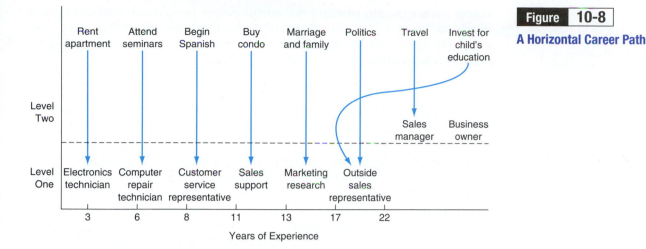

**Figure** 10-8

**A Horizontal Career Path**

that many employees want the option of decelerated rather than accelerated career progress—they want to take their time in developing their career.

Furthermore, they would rather have a work–life balance rather than aim for promotions that could mean long work weeks and work overload, including considerable business travel and time away from home. [21]

Despite this trend, many employers are reverting to the traditional promises of an opportunity to climb the organizational ladder. Furthermore, it is not unusual for workers to aspire toward holding higher level, higher-paying positions, or a corner office or corner cubicle.

A horizontal career path, as well as a traditional (or vertical) career path, does not necessarily mean the person stays with the same firm. For example, a worker might spend three years in one company as an electronics technician, three years in another as a sales representative, and then three years as a customer service specialist in a third company. All three positions would be approximately at the same level. The third company then promotes the individual to a much-deserved position as the marketing team leader. Figure 10-8 illustrates a horizontal career path for Larry Chang, a career school graduate who did attempt to make long-range predictions about his career. Notice that all the positions through Year 17 are at the first level, and the positions for Year 22 and beyond are at the second level. Chang's career contingency plans are as follows:

*(1) If I cannot obtain experience as a market research analyst, customer service rep, or sales rep, I will continue to develop as an electronics technician. (2) If I cannot find employment as a sales manager, I will attempt to become supervisor of electronic technicians. (3) If I do not raise sufficient funds for starting my own business, I will continue in a corporate job until retirement.*

# Career Advancement Strategies and Tactics

■ Learning Objective 3

The many ways of improving interpersonal relationships described in this book can help advance and enhance a person's career. People who enhance their relationships with others are laying a foundation for career advancement. The following section discusses 14 other key strategies and tactics for career advancement, whether the advancement be vertical, horizontal, or a combination of the two. The first 8 of the methods described deal more with controlling your own characteristics and behaviors, whereas the remaining 6 deal more with interacting with the environment.

## CAPITALIZE ON YOUR STRENGTHS AND BUILD YOUR PERSONAL BRAND

A long-established principle of getting ahead in your career, as well as managing others, is to capitalize on strengths rather than focus solely on overcoming areas for improvement. A recent bestselling book, Go *Put Your Strengths to Work* by Marcus Buckingham, elaborates on this idea. [22] Visualize Sam, who has excellent interpersonal skills, but is mediocre in quantitative skills. Sam will go far as a manager or sales representative if he continues to hone his interpersonal skills. Yet as hard as he tries to strengthen his quantitative skills, he probably would become only a mediocre accountant, research analyst, or actuary.

One key point made by Buckingham is that you should forget the myth that fixing one's weaknesses is the path to success. Another key point is that you should identify your strengths in realms in which you have delivered near-perfect performance. One flaw in Buckingham's thinking is that some weaknesses need to be patched reasonably well before you can capitalize on your strengths over time. For example, you might be masterful at composing pop-up ads that people click on and then make a purchase. However, if you cannot overcome your urge to steal from the company and sexually harass coworkers, you won't last long in your position.

Understanding your basket of strengths forms the basis for developing your **personal brand** (or, the *brand called you*). Your personal brand makes you unique, thereby distinguishing you from the competition. Perhaps your brand will not reach the recognition of Nike or Rolex, but it will help develop your reputation. Your personal brand also helps you attract employers and perhaps potential clients. Your identity as shown on the Internet including social networking sites such as Facebook is also part of your personal brand. Here is an example of a brand identity developed for a 25-year old college graduate, Rob Borden:

> *The branding consultants learned that Borden had opened a landscaping business in college, captained an NCAA-championship lacrosse team and was deeply interested in land development and conservation. They drafted a marketing plan around five qualities: a passion for commercial real estate, strong business experience, leadership abilities, and a sparkling wit when not nervous. In job interviews, Borden hammered away at those key points and, after meeting with about eight companies land a job that he loves in commercial real estate.* [23]

Your personal brand will be more effective if it is authentic in the sense of accurately reflecting who you are. You might add a little drama to your strengths, but the strengths should still be true. For example, if Lisa regularly volunteers time to feed homeless people, she might describe herself as having "enduring humanitarian values." Yet it would be a stretch for her to say that she "is committed to ending world hunger." As business advisors Jack and Suzy

■ **Personal brand**

the qualities based on your basket of strengths that make you unique, thereby distinguishing you from the competition

Welch suggest, "The most powerful thing you can do to get a head is, well, be real. As in not phony. As in authentic." [24]

## BE PASSIONATE ABOUT AND PROUD OF YOUR WORK

Successful people in all fields are passionate about their work. Without passion, you rely too heavily on external rewards to sustain effort. Passion contributes to both your career growth and company productivity. Effective leaders and business owners are usually passionate about their work, and group members expect their leader to be passionate. [25] For example, a joyous small-business owner is so excited about a product or service that it makes a difference. Bob Werts, the owner of Waxman Candles, says, "I love coming in the morning and pouring wax." [26] Being passionate is also important because it is linked to developing expertise and high job performance. Taking pride in your work stems naturally from passion. If you invest the emotional energy into having passion, you are likely to be proud of your work.

The surest path to career success is to identify your area of expertise and then build a career around it. The more passionate and proud you are about your area of expertise, the better. Becoming wealthy and achieving recognition are by-products of making effective use of your talents. Expertise combined with passion helps you attain high job performance. Consistently good job performance is the foundation on which you build your career. Job competence is still the major success ingredient in all but the most political organizations (those where favoritism outweighs merit).

## DEVELOP A CODE OF PROFESSIONAL ETHICS

Another solid foundation for developing a career is to establish a personal ethical code. An ethical code determines what behavior is right or wrong, good or bad, based on values. The values stem from cultural upbringing, religious teachings, peer influences, and professional or industry standards. As implied in Chapter 9, a code of professional ethics helps a worker deal with such issues as accepting bribes, backstabbing coworkers, and sexually harassing a work associate.

## DEVELOP A PROACTIVE PERSONALITY

If you are an active agent in taking control of the forces around you, you stand a better chance of capitalizing on opportunities. Also, you will seek out opportunities such as seeing problems that need fixing. A **proactive personality** is a person who is relatively unconstrained by situational forces and who brings about environmental change. The proactive personality has high perceived control over situations. Self-Assessment Quiz 10-2 offers you an opportunity to learn about your tendencies toward having a proactive personality.

People who are highly proactive identify opportunities and act on them, show initiative, and keep trying until they bring about meaningful change. A health and safety specialist with a proactive personality might identify a health hazard others had missed. She would identify the nature of the problem

■ **Proactive personality**
a person who is relatively unconstrained by situational forces and who brings about environmental change

## Self-Assessment Quiz 10-2

### Proactive Personality Scale

Indicate on a 1-to-7 scale how much you agree with the following statements: 1 = *strongly disagree*, 2 = *disagree*, 3 = *disagree somewhat*, 4 = *neutral*, 5 = *agree somewhat*, 6 = *agree*, 7 = *strongly agree*.

*No.  Statement about Proactive Behavior*                                        *Answer (1– 7)*
1. I am constantly on the lookout for new ways to improve my life.
2. Wherever I have been, I have been a powerful force for constructive change.
3. Nothing is more exciting than seeing my ideas turn into reality.
4. If I see something I don't like, I fix it.
5. No matter what the odds, if I believe in something, I will make it happen.
6. I love being a champion for my ideas, even against the opposition of others.
7. I excel at identifying opportunities.
8. I am always looking for better ways to do things.
9. If I believe in an idea, no obstacles will prevent me from making it happen.
10. I can spot a good opportunity long before others can.

                                            Total Score _____

### Interpretation

**60–70**    You have a strong proactive personality, which should help advance your career providing you are not too impatient for progress.

**41–59**    You appear to be about average with respect to being a proactive personality. You may need to take the initiative about identifying and solving problems in order to capitalize on your career potential.

**10–40**    You might have a tendency to wait to take action until circumstances are forced on you. Also, you might be highly laid back. You may need to take the initiative more about problem solving in order to advance in your career.

**Source:** The quiz is adapted from T. S. Batemen and J. M. Crant, *Journal of Organizational Behavior*, Vol. 14, 1993, pp. 103–118. Copyright 1993 by John Wiley & Sons Limited. Reprinted with permission.

and urge management to supply funding to control the problem. Ultimately, her efforts in preventing major health problems would be recognized. The proactive employee can also be regarded as displaying organizational citizenship behavior because he or she is a good citizen who will step outside the job description to be helpful. For example, he or she might take the initiative to help a coworker without being asked, or report a leaking faucet to the maintenance department.

   Two studies conducted with close to 700 male and female workers in diverse occupations examined the relationship between career success and a proactive personality. Proactive personality, as measured by a test, was related to salary, promotions, taking the initiative in one's career, and career satisfaction. [27]

Another reason that being proactive facilitates career success is that employees are expected to be self-managing more so than in the past. The proactive employee will identify and resolve many problems without being directed to do so by the manager. A more recent study indicated that a proactive personality influenced job search success among 180 graduating college students. The students took the test of proactive personality presented here. Search success was measured in terms of being offered follow-up interviews and receiving offers. [28] It may not be easy to develop a proactive personality, but a person can get started by taking more initiative to fix problems and attempt to be self-starting. Asking for permission to assume responsibility for a project that needs doing is also helpful. Many newcomers to an organization have enhanced their reputation by asking for permission to organize the current year's office party.

## KEEP GROWING THROUGH CONTINUOUS LEARNING AND SELF-DEVELOPMENT

Given that continuous learning is part of the new employment contract, engaging in regular learning can take many forms, including formal schooling, attending training programs and seminars, and self-study. An everyday method of continuous learning is to ask intelligent questions about processes or procedures that will help you understand the business. For example, a manager might say that she checks out the competition every week by going to the Internet. You might ask, "Specifically, how do you get the information? Where do you look? The process sounds fascinating."

It is particularly important to engage in new learning in areas of interest to the company, such as developing proficiency in a second language if the company has customers and employees in other countries. Many companies support continuous learning because they perceive themselves to be *learning organizations*. It may therefore be easy for you to implement the tactic of growth through continuous learning.

## DOCUMENT YOUR ACCOMPLISHMENTS

An accurate record of what you have accomplished in your career can be valuable when being considered for reassignment, promotion, or a position outside your company. The same log of accomplishments is useful for résumé preparation and to bring to a performance review. Sending e-mail updates to your manager about your noteworthy accomplishments is effective if not done to the point of being an annoyance. It is preferable to point to tangible, quantifiable accomplishments than to another person's subjective impression of your performance. Let's assume that a retail store manager, Kelly, reduced inventory shrinkage by 30 percent in one year. It would be better to state that fact than to record a statement from her manager saying, "Kelly shows outstanding ability to reduce inventory shrinkage."

Career coach Peggy Klaus recommends that you weave your accomplishments into an interesting story to tell other people. [29] The story approach has more appeal than a straightforward list of your accomplishments. Here is a fragment of a story that a man who worked for a food supplier to restaurants, schools, and hospitals used to document his accomplishments:

> *Our area was hit with a vicious lightning storm last March 12. Our computer and telephone systems went haywire because of power outages. We had to be in touch with our customers. I rounded up 10 people in the company who had cell phones with them. Using all the battery power we had left in our phones, we were able to contact all our customers. My manager said my cell phone rescue effort saved the day.*

Documenting your accomplishments in a business field is similar to a person in the arts such as a photographer, interior designer, or architect developing a portfolio of work. When the person applies for a job or assignment, he or she carries along the portfolio of representative work.

Documentation enables you to promote yourself in a dignified, tactful way. When discussing work with key people in the company, let them know of your good deeds without taking too much credit for team accomplishments. If you distinguish yourself in the community, for example, by fund-raising for a shelter for homeless people, let your manager know of your activities. The rationale is that most companies want their workers to be responsible community members.

## PROJECT A PROFESSIONAL IMAGE

Your clothing, desk and work area, speech, and general knowledge should project the image of a professional, responsible person if you seek career advancement. A positive scent also contributes to a person's professional image, with light perfume, toilet water, or cologne *often* contributing to a positive image. Good grammar and sentence structure can give you the edge because so many people use highly informal patterns of speech. Being a knowledgeable person is important because today's professional businessperson is supposed to be aware of the external environment. Also, as noted by a human relations specialist, projecting a professional image hastens the development of trust and rapport in business relationships. [30]

A subtle part of projecting a professional image is to have a positive attitude. Assume that things are not going well in the office, such as the CEO announcing that no year-end bonuses will be forthcoming this year. Instead of joining the complainers, you might say to your coworkers, "A bonus would be wonderful, but I am happy to know that by not giving bonuses there will be no layoffs." Joining in the negativity makes you appear unprofessional. Yet offering constructive criticisms can be quite professional.

A challenge in projecting a professional image is to figure out what constitutes a professional image in your particular environment. Less restrictive dress codes have made it more confusing to select clothing that will create a favorable appearance. For the last several years, business formal attire for both men and women has been making a strong comeback. Yet, the IT field in Silicon Valley is still extremely informal. A programmer who wore a tank top and running shoes and brought a parrot to the office might be considered to project a professional image. Yet a marketing specialist for a health insurance provider behaving in the same way in Boston would be perceived as unprofessional.

Hairstyle is a superficial part of appearance that the career-minded person must ponder, whether or not standards for coiffeur border on being discriminatory. Some employers prefer that men in customer contact positions do not wear shoulder-length hair. The short-hair stereotype is also pronounced for women. Research suggests that both sexes perceive women with short, high-lighted hairstyles as smart and confident, but not sexy, finds Marianne LaFrance, a psychologist at Yale University. "More hair equals more femininity, but also less intelligence," she says. [31]

A general guideline is to dress somewhat like the successful people in your firm or the customer's firm. It might pay to contact a company you plan to visit in advance and inquire about the dress standards for key people in the company. Skill-Building Exercise 10-4 is designed to sensitize you to what constitutes a professional image in a specific environment.

## PERCEIVE YOURSELF AS A PROVIDER OF SERVICES

A useful perspective for upgrading your professional self-image and enhancing your feelings of job security is to perceive yourself as something other than a traditional employee. According to career specialist John A. Thomson, each person should see him- or herself as a personal service business entity. Basically you are a business, offering the company (also your client from this perspective) a valuable service. You keep offering the service so long as the company keeps you on the payroll and you enjoy the work. Note the similarity to a high-level professional such as a dentist or IT consultant. You are offering a service that many people need. Part of the same perception is that you own your skills, and that these are the service your business (you) offers to others. [32]

## Skill-Building Exercise 10-4

### The Professional Image Investigation

Find out what constitutes a *professional image* in a specific job environment, either where you work or at another employer. Ask a handful of people, "What makes for a professional image here?" Speak to or correspond by e-mail with a top-level manager, as well as a few workers without managerial responsibility. Another approach to this assignment is to make some observations directly in a retail establishment like Safeway, Albertson's, Target, or Nordstrom. How do the people in supervisory positions appear to dress, behave, and talk? Maybe you can conduct a one-minute interview with a service worker or two.

Share your observations with classmates, and see what conclusions can be drawn. For example, how does the type of company influence what constitutes a professional image? Are there different standards for men and women?

Another way of perceiving yourself as different from a traditional employee is to think of yourself as a professional-level temporary employee. Sometimes you will have a long stay with one employer, acting like a permanent temporary employee. At other times, you will move on to another company where your skills are more in need.

## DEVELOP DEPTH AND BREADTH

A continuing concern about career management is whether to acquire substantial depth in a specialty or to obtain broader experience. Is it better to be a specialist or a generalist? Typically it pays to have good depth in one area of expertise, yet also to acquire broad experience. A distribution specialist who helped set up shipping systems in an automobile supply company, an office supply company, and a hospital supply company would have excellent credentials. Yet some career specialists would argue that knowing one industry well has its merits.

If your goal is to become an executive, broadening your experience is a career enhancer. A person who held positions in sales and manufacturing would have broad experience. Breadth could also come about by experience in different industries, such as retailing and mining, or by holding positions in different companies. Being assigned to different teams, projects, and committees is another natural broadening experience. Conducting a job search within your company can often lead to a broadening experience, such as working with marketing people after having worked primarily with accountants. Another approach to broadening is to self-study different aspects of the business.

## RELY ON A NETWORK OF SUCCESSFUL PEOPLE

Networking has already been described as a major assist to finding a job. Members of your network can also help you by assisting with difficult job problems, providing emotional support, buying your products or services, and offering you good prices on their products or services. On the negative side, being excluded from informal networks in your company can block your career advancement. The starting point in face-to-face networking is to obtain an ample supply of business cards. You then give a card to any person you meet who might be able to help you now or in the future. As the recognition of the importance of networking for career advancement and career finding continues to grow, new suggestions emerge. One such suggestion is to hold brunch or dinner parties at your home, and invite an interesting cross section of guests. [33] Professional and trade groups, such an association of bankers or sales professionals, are ideal for networking and are found in virtually every city.

While first developing your network, be inclusive by inviting any plausible person into your network. Later, as your network develops, you can strive to include a greater number of influential and successful people. One reason that playing golf persists as a networking technique is that so many influential and successful people play golf.

Social networking Web sites such as MySpace, Facebook, and even YouTube can often be used to find members for your professional network despite their social emphasis. A couple of years ago there were already 40,000 MySpace groups devoted to companies or coworkers, and 8,000 work-related networks at Facebook. A strictly professional site such as Linkedin is directly targeted toward making professional contacts. Millions of professionals turn to Linkedin to swap job details and contact information, often for recruiting purposes. To use these social networking sites for professional purposes, you will need to create an online profile including your résumé. An example of successful online networking is that a graphic designer named Angela Glenn developed a contact through a blog that led to the formation of a new advertising agency. [34]

Posting your own blog and visiting the blogs of other people can also be a source of valuable contacts. Be prepared to go through hundreds, if not thousands, of message exchanges before making one good contact. Converting some of these virtual contacts into in-person meetings will enhance the effectiveness of social networking on the Internet.

Skill-Building Exercise 10-5 provides suggestions for systematically building your network.

## WORK WITH A MENTOR

Mentoring was presented as a way of helping people grow and develop. Here I reemphasize that having a mentor can facilitate career advancement. Ideally, a person should develop a small network of mentors who give advice and counsel on different topics such as job advancement opportunities and how to solve a difficult problem. Many people who receive exceptional promotions within their own firms, or receive excellent job offers from other companies, are chosen by their mentors. At the root of mentoring is the ability to attract and build a relationship with a person who is more experienced and talented than you.

A mentor can help the career beginner overcome hurdles such as being disappointed about the first job, such as not being listened to or receiving enough feedback. Another disappointment might occur when a recent grad anticipates that all workers will be fired up and eager to help the company. Yet on the job, the grad might encounter workers who are bored with their work. The newcomer might ask a mentor in a senior position, "Did you go through this? Is this normal? When does it all change, if at all?" [35]

## FIND A GOOD PERSON–ORGANIZATION FIT

Assuming that you have the luxury of selecting among different prospective employers, it is best to work for a company where your personality and style fit the organization culture. As implied at several places in the text, an **organization culture** is a system of shared values and beliefs that influence worker behavior. You have to study the culture through observation and questioning to understand its nature. A good starting point is to ask, "In order to succeed, what is really expected of workers?" You might find out, for example, that pleasing customers and being honest is the path to success.

A **person–organization** fit is the compatibility of the individual and the organization. Job interviews represent a good opportunity for evaluating a

■ **Organization culture**
a system of shared values and beliefs that influence worker behavior

■ **Person–organization fit**
the compatibility of the individual and the organization

# Skill-Building Exercise 10-5

## Building Your Network

From a career standpoint, networking involves developing a list of personal contacts who can help you achieve goals, and whom you offer something of value in exchange.

Networking is a career-long process, but the time to begin is now. Quite often the people who have been in your network the longest become your most valuable contacts. To begin networking, or systematizing the networking you are now doing, implement the following steps:

**Step 1:** Write down the type of assistance you are seeking for the next several months. Perhaps you need leads for a job, advice about getting ahead in your industry, or help with a difficult computer problem.

**Step 2:** List all the people who might be able to provide you the assistance you need. Among them might be fellow students, former employers, neighbors, and faculty members. Prepare a contact card, or database entry, for each person on your list as if they were sales prospects. Include relevant details such as name, position, major, e-mail address, phone numbers, postal address, and favorite pastimes. (Setting up a table with a word processor would work quite well for list and entries, or use a spreadsheet.)

**Step 3:** Identify an action step for making contact with the potential network members. Quite often the initial contact will be by e-mail. Gently mention that you would enjoy a telephone conversation or face-to-face meeting if it fit the contact's interest and schedule. You might also be able to think of creative ways to make the initial contact in person, such as attending professional meetings, or talking to a neighbor while he or she is washing a car or doing yard work.

**Step 4:** Identify how you might be able to help each person in your contact list, or how you can reciprocate. For example, if a marketing person gives you an idea for a job lead, you can become part of his or her company's *guerilla marketing team* (you say nice things about the company product to friends and in public, or use the product in public). Sometimes the best approach is to ask the person who becomes part of your network, what you can do to reciprocate.

**Step 5:** Maintain a log of all the contacts you make, and what took place, such as an agreed-upon face-to-face meeting, or specific assistance received. Indicate how you responded to the assistance, such as, "I visited my contact's company Web site, went to the career section, and included her name as a person who is familiar with my work." Write down carefully your plans for reciprocity. Make a check list for whether you remembered to thank the person for any courtesy he or she extended to you.

**Step 6:** Update your log weekly, even if the activity requires only a few minutes of your attention. A network of helpers is a dynamic list, with people entering and exiting your network frequently. Each week ask yourself, "Whom can I add to my network this week?"

person–organization fit for both the applicant and the employer. [36] During a visit to the company to learn whether a culture tends to be formal or informal, you might observe the formality of the people and the emphasis on procedures such as a lengthy document to obtain a travel reimbursement.

The compatibility in question often centers on the extent to which a person's major work-related values and personality traits fit major elements of the organization culture. Following this idea, a person who is adventuresome and risk taking would achieve the highest performance and satisfaction in an organization in which adventuresome behavior and risk-taking are valued. Conversely, a methodical and conservative individual should join a slow-moving bureaucracy. How much an organization emphasizes individual effort versus teamwork is another important area for person–organization fit. Workers who enjoy teamwork would fit better in a teamwork-oriented culture.

Person–organization fit can also include superficial aspects of behavior such as physical appearance and dress. For example, a person who dresses like a Wall Street investment banker might not feel comfortable working in a high-tech firm in California where jeans and sandals are standard work attire. As a consequence of not feeling comfortable in your work environment, you might not perform at your best.

The consequences of a person fitting both the organization and the job have been systematically researched based on 25 studies. One of the conclusions reached was that commitment to the organization (a willingness to stay) was strongly associated with the person–organization fit. The study cautioned that it is not always easy for the job applicant to diagnose the fit in such areas as the conformance between the ethics of the individual and the company. When the topic arises, the hiring manager might be less than candid in explaining the company's true ethics. [37]

An interesting twist on person–organization fit is that it is more strongly linked to job satisfaction when the worker does not perceive a good fit between his or her needs and the characteristics of the work environment. This conclusion came from a study of 300 participants in a 12-week internship program. [38] An example of such a mismatch between needs and the work environment would be to want a job heavy on interaction with people, yet the job holder spent most of the workday isolated in a cubicle. So if your job is a little disappointing, fitting in with the company takes away some of the sting.

## BACK TO THE OPENING CASE

Ellis Rowe has not only used internal networking to obtain new positions, he also uses internal networking to solicit ideas that will help him perform better. One of Rowe's contacts is four levels below him, yet because they have connected before, the person feels comfortable calling Rowe and saying, "Do you have five minutes?" Once or twice a month the contact submits an idea to Rowe, and the latter listens carefully for ideas that could help the business.

## TAKE SENSIBLE RISKS

People who make it big in their careers usually take sensible risks on their journey to success. Sensible risk taking means about the same thing as *moving outside your comfort zone*, because you stretch your capabilities but do not plunge recklessly into a new venture. Among these risks would be to work for a fledgling company that offers big promises but a modest starting salary, or to take an overseas assignment with no promise of a good position when you return. Purchasing stock in start-up companies is sometimes a sensible risk, if you do not absolutely need the funds for living expenses. Fran Briggs, a motivational speaker and author says, "If you plan to advance in your career, experience fulfilling relationships, earn more money, and achieve your goals sooner, you must plan on taking the respective risks." [39]

## EMPHASIZE RELATIONSHIPS TO COMBAT BEING OUTSOURCED

A major concern of many workers is that their job will be *outsourced* or *offshored* to a lower paid worker in a country where a competent worker will perform the same job at lower pay. As companies throughout the world struggle to stay competitive in a global economy, more and more jobs are outsourced. Call center and IT positions are the most frequently outsourced but so is a variety of design work, some legal research, and medical diagnostic work. The positions least likely to be outsourced are those requiring the physical presence of the worker and cannot easily be done remotely. Examples include nursing, real estate selling, teaching, funeral technician, massage therapist, and hairstylist. Managing people requires a physical presence, but not if your workers' positions have been outsourced. [40]

Another way to decrease the chance of your job being outsourced is to make relationship building a key part of your job, whether or not you are performing mostly technical work. An obvious part of relationship building is to be physically present in the workplace, so working from home might make you more susceptible to your job being outsourced. [41] A real estate agent with hundreds of personal contacts cannot be replaced by a Web site. And an information systems specialist who performs hands-on work with internal clients cannot be replaced by an IT specialist working 7,000 miles away in another country.

In short, good interpersonal relationships will not only advance your career but also help you preserve your position through the turmoil of technological change.

## SELF-ASSESSMENT QUIZZES IN OVERVIEW

Self-Assessment Quiz 10-1 measures qualifications sought by employers. As you move through your career, it is helpful to reflect on whether you are strengthening your standing on many of these qualifications. For example, you might ask yourself if you are making progress in developing judgment and common sense, and teamwork skills. Self-Assessment Quiz 10-2 measures a more subtle qualification or characteristic—being a proactive personality. Initiative taking, providing you do not go well beyond the limits of your authority, is a quality welcome in most organizations.

# Concept Review and Reinforcement

## Key Terms

career path, 316
personal brand, 320

proactive personality, 321
organization culture, 327

person–organization fit, 327

## Summary of Key Concepts

Recommended job-hunting tactics include the following:

1. Identify your job objectives.
2. Be aware of qualifications sought by employers.
3. Identify your skills and potential contribution.
4. Develop a comprehensive marketing strategy.
5. Use networking to reach company insiders.
6. Use multiple online approaches.
7. Smile at network members and interviewers and be enthusiastic.
8. Smooth out the rough spots in your background.

Job hunting almost always requires a résumé. A length of one page is recommended for a less experienced person, and two pages for a more experienced person. Résumés should emphasize skills and accomplishments. Be aware of the problems of identity theft and scams associated with online résumés. Video résumés can be important, as well as creative formats. A résumé should almost always be accompanied by a cover letter explaining how you can help the organization and why you are applying for this particular job. Comparing job requirements to your qualifications can be helpful. Screening interviews, including computer-assisted ones, precede a full job interview. A general guide for performing well in an interview is to present a positive but accurate picture of yourself. More specific suggestions include the following:

1. Be prepared, look relaxed, and make the interviewer feel comfortable.
2. Avoid talking too much during the interview.
3. Establish a link between you and the prospective employer.
4. Ask perceptive questions.
5. Be prepared to discuss your strengths and developmental opportunities.
6. Be prepared to respond to behavioral interview questions (examples of job behaviors).
7. Show how you can help the employer.
8. Use body language that projects confidence and decisiveness.
9. Practice good etiquette during the interview, including during a meal.
10. Send a follow-up letter.

The vertical, or traditional, career path is based on the idea that a person continues to grow in responsibility with the aim of reaching a target position, such as becoming a top-level manager. A vertical path is based on the traditional employment contract. A vertical career path should be related to the present and future demands of one firm or the industry. The horizontal career path is less predictable, and emphasizes lateral moves with an opportunity to gain more experience and increase job skills. A horizontal path is closely linked to the new employment contract that offers shared responsibility for career growth. Receiving rewards for good work rather than for rank fits the horizontal career path. Career paths should have contingency plans.

Improving interpersonal relationships assists career advancement. In addition, the following strategies and tactics are relevant:

1. Captitalize on your strengths and build your personal brand.
2. Be passionate about and proud of your work.
3. Develop a code of professional ethics.
4. Develop a proactive personality.
5. Keep growing through continuous learning and self-development.
6. Document your accomplishments.
7. Project a professional image.
8. Perceive yourself as a provider of services.
9. Develop depth and breadth.
10. Rely on a network of successful people.
11. Work with a mentor.
12. Find a good person–organization fit.
13. Take sensible risks.
14. Emphasize relationships to combat being outsourced.

## Check your Understanding

1. Identify four situations in a career in which conducting a job campaign would be necessary or desirable.
2. During a labor shortage (when there are more positions open than qualified applicants), why is it still important to have good job search skills?
3. What is your evaluation of the effectiveness of a job hunter using the Internet as his or her only method of finding a job?
4. In what ways might video résumés both help and hinder a company attain the goal of having a diverse workforce?
5. Why is a vertical career path still the dream of so many workers?
6. Give an example from your own life in which you behaved as if you were a proactive personality.
7. In what way do political tactics assist career advancement?
8. How might a person use a Webcam to help build and sustain a network?
9. Assume that you are attempting to create a personal brand. What key features about yourself do you would feature in your personal brand?
10. What is the most useful idea you picked up from this chapter about either conducting a job campaign or managing your career? Explain your reasoning.

## The Web Corner

*http://www.JobHuntersBible.com*
(Career guru Dick Bolles guides career changers and suggests actions to take after they have exhausted Internet job sites.)

*http://www.Vault.com*
(Wealth of information about career advancement, job finding, and occupational profiles.)

*http://www.mentoringgroup.com*
(Suggestions for having a good mentoring relationship.)

### Internet Skill Builder: Finding a Job Efficiently

So many job boards exist on the Internet that conducting a Web-based job search can be baffling. A direct approach is to visit Yahoo! Hot Jobs (on the front page of http://www.Yahoo.com) and enter three specific job titles of interest to you. You will be directed to loads of job opportunities closely matching the job titles you entered. It may be helpful to enter variations of the same job title, such as both "office manager" and "administrative assistant." Your assignment is to identify five jobs for which you appear to be qualified. Even if you have no interest in conducting a job search, it is informative to be aware of job opportunities in your field. Seek answers to the following questions:

1. Do I appear to have the qualifications for the type of job I am seeking?
2. Is there a particular geographic area where the job or jobs I want are available?
3. How good are opportunities in my chosen field?

# Developing Your Human Relations Skills

## Interpersonal Relations Case 10.1

### Why Isn't My Résumé Getting Results?

Billy Joe Wentworth was working in the family business as a manufacturing technician while he attended career school. Although he got along well with his family members, Billy Joe wanted to find employment elsewhere so he could build a career on his own. Billy Joe's job objective was a position in industrial sales. He compiled a long list of prospective employers from personal contacts, classified ads in newspapers, and job openings on the Internet. Billy Joe clipped a business card with a brief handwritten note to each résumé. The note usually said something to the effect, "Job sounds great. Let's schedule an interview at your convenience."

After mailing out 200 résumés, Billy Joe still did not have an interview. He asked his uncle and mentor, the owner of the family business, "Why isn't my résumé getting results?" The résumé is shown in Exhibit 10-1.

### Case Questions

1. What suggestions can you make to Billy Joe for improving his résumé? Or does it require improvement?
2. What is your evaluation of Billy Joe's approach to creating a cover letter?

---

**BILLY JOE WENTWORTH**
275 Birdwhistle Lane
Cleveland, Ohio 44131
(216) 555-7512 (Please call after 7 P.M. weekday nights)
Billyjoe@wentworth.com

#### Objective
Long-range goal is Vice President of sales of major corporation. For now, industrial sales representative paid by salary and commission.

#### Job Experience
- Five years experience in Wentworth industries as manufacturing technician, tool crib attendant, shipper, and floor sweeper. Voted as "employee of the month" twice.
- Two years' experience in newspaper delivery business. Distributed newspapers door-to-door, responsible for accounts receivable and development of new business in my territory.

#### Education
- Justin Peabody Career College, business administration major with manufacturing technology minor. Expect degree in June 2010. 2.65 GPA. Took courses in sales management and selling. Received a B+ in professional selling course.
- Cleveland Heights High School, business and technology major, 1994–1998. Graduated 45th in class of 125. 82% average.

#### Skills and Talents
Good knowledge of manufacturing equipment; friends say I'm a born leader; have been offered supervisory position in Wentworth Industries; real go-getter.

#### References
Okay to contact present employer except for my immediate supervisor, Jill Baxter, with whom I have a personality clash.

---

**Exhibit 10-1**

**Résumé of Billy Joe Wentworth**

## Interpersonal Skills Role-Play 10-1

### Helping Billy Joe with His Résumé

One student plays the role of a friend whom Billy Joe consults about his job résumé. Billy Joe is quite proud of the résumé, and is looking for encouragement and support. The friend consulted, however, attempts to be objective and professional whenever he or she offers assistance. Run the role-play for about eight minutes. Outsiders can judge if Billy Joe is on the road to being helped.

## Interpersonal Relations Case 10-2

### The Brand Called Brandy

As Brandy Barclay navigated the challenging highways toward her job interview in Los Angeles, she rehearsed in her mind the importance of communicating that she is a unique brand. "I have to get across the idea that I am special, even if my brand is not as well established as Godiva Chocolates or Dr. Pepper. This administrative assistant position at the hotel and resort company will be a good way to launch my career and brand."

An excerpt of her job interview with the hiring manager Gloria Gomez follows:

Gomez:  Welcome, Brandy, I am pleased that you made it through the online job application and the telephone screening interview. Tell me again why you would like to join our hotel company as an administrative assistant.

Barclay:  Oh, I really don't want to join you as an administrative assistant. I would prefer a vice president job, but I have to start somewhere. [Smiling] Seriously, I like the hotel field. It fits my brand called "Brandy." I am a great support person,

and a great people person. I'm so unique because I'm great with details and great with people.

Gomez:  Tell me specifically, what key strengths would you bring to this job?

Barclay:  As found in my brand called "Brandy," I am high info tech and high touch. I'm a whiz at Microsoft Office Suite, and I'm sweet with people. Kind of catchy, don't you think? Come to think of it, have you seen my business card? It contains loads of details about my skills and strengths on the back. The card is laminated so it will last, and it contains my photo, and even is like a hologram with a 3-D look.

Gomez:  Yes, Brandy, I do have your card. You gave one to the receptionist, and she gave it to me. And why do you keep referring to yourself as a brand? Is this just a gimmick to get you noticed?

Barclay:  Being a brand is the modern way to tell you that Brandy Barclay is one of a kind. I've got a skill set that is hard to beat.

Besides, I want to build a reputation fast that will propel me to the top as an executive in the hotel field.

Gomez: On your trip to the top, what do you plan to do for us as an administrative assistant?

Barclay: I will live up to the brand called Brandy by getting the job done big time. Just ask me to do something, and it will be done. Don't forget, I will be building my brand image while in this beginning assignment.

Gomez: Now let's talk about details like the job assignment, salary, and benefits.

Barclay: Fine with me. We have to deal with the mundane at some point.

## Case Questions

1. How effectively is Brandy Barclay presenting herself as a brand?
2. What suggestions can you offer Barclay for presenting herself as a brand more effectively?
3. What suggestions can you offer Barclay for conducting herself better during her next job interview?

# REFERENCES

1. Laura Egodigwe, "Power Play: Using the Network," *Black Enterprise*, May 2007, p. 63.

2. Emily Steel, "Job-Search Sites Face a Nimble Threat," *The Wall Street Journal*, October 9, 2007, p. B10; John Zappe, "Recruiting Firms Setting Up Shop in Second Life," *Workforce Management*, March 26, 2007, p. 4.

3. Cited in Sarah E. Needleman, "How Blogging Can Help You Get a New Job," *The Wall Street Journal*, April 10, 2007, p. B1.

4. "Kat & Dale Talk Jobs," King Features Syndicate, April 14, 2002.

5. "Checking Credit of Job Candidates Drives Concerns about Civil Rights," *Christian Science Monitor*, January 19, 2007.

6. Chris Pentila, "Risky Business," *Entrepreneur*, September 2003, pp. 78–79.

7. Edward A. Robinson, "Beware—Job Seekers Have No Secrets," *Fortune*, December 29, 1997, p. 285.

8. M. P. McQueen, "Why You Should Spy on Yourself," *The Wall Street Journal*, April 21–22, 2007, p. B1.

9. Joann S. Lublin, "Silence Is Golden Rule for Résumés of People Who Have Broken It," *The Wall Street Journal*, October 2, 2007, p. B1.

10. Peg Thomas et al., "Resume Characteristics as Predictors as an Invitation to Interview," *Journal of Business and Psychology*, Spring 1999, pp. 339–356.

11. Douglas MacMillan, "The Art of the Online Résumé," *Business Week*, May 7, 2007, p. 86.

12. Dana Mattioli, "Who's Reading Online Résumés? Identity Crooks," *The Wall Street Journal*, October 17, 2006, p. B9.

13. Sarah E. Needleman, "Special Résumé Looks Can Do Quite a Job at Getting You Noticed," *The Wall Street Journal*, August 21, 2007, p. B6.

14. Data presented in Lisa Takeuchi Cullen, "Getting Wise to Lies," *Time*, May 1, 2006, p. 59.

15. Jim Pawlak, "Keep Job Application Cover Letter Short," http://detnews.com, April 15, 2005.

16. Sarah E. Needleman, "Speed Interviewing Grows as Skills Shortage Looms," *The Wall Street Journal*, November 6, 2007, p. B15.

17. Joann S. Lublin, "Talking Too Much On a Job Interview May Kill Your Chance," *The Wall Street Journal*, October 30, 2007, p. B1.

18. Quoted in Eileen Alt Powell, "Research, Practice Can Lead to a Stronger Job Interview," *MiamiHerald.com* (http://www.miamiherald.com), p. 1.

19. Anne Field, "Coach, Help Me Out with This Interview," *BusinessWeek*, October 22, 2001, p. 134E2.

20. Diane Brady, "Yes, Winning Is Still the Only Thing," *Business Week*, August 21/28, p. 52.

21. Alison Maitland, "Flexible Careers May Be Key to Worker Retention," *Financial Times* syndicated story, October 21, 2007; George Anders, "What Is Success, Anyway?" *The Wall Street Journal*, September 18, 2006, p. R10.

22. Marcus Buckingham, *Go Put Your Strengths to Work* (New York: Free Press, 2007).

23. Jeninne Lee-St. John, "It's a Brand-You World," *Time*, November 6, 2006, pp. 60–61.

24. Jack and Suzy Welch, "Get Real, Get Ahead," *Business Week*, May 14, 2007, p. 100.

25. Richard Boyatzis, Annie McKee, and Daniel Goleman, "Reawakening Your Passion for Work," *Harvard Business Review*, April 2002, pp. 86–94.

26. Jeff Bailey, "Devoted Work Wins Customers Willing to Pay," *The Wall Street Journal*, October 14, 2003.

27. Scott E. Seibert, Maria L. Kraimer, and J. Michael Crant, "What Do Proactive People Do? A Longitudinal Model Linking Proactive Personality and Career Success," *Personnel Psychology*, Winter 2001, pp. 845–874; Scott E. Seibert, J. Michael Crant, and Maria L. Kraimer, "Proactive Personality and Career Success," *Journal of Applied Psychology*, June 1999, pp. 416–427.

28. Douglas J. Brown et al., "Proactive Personality and the Successful Job Search: A Field Investigation with College Graduates," *Journal of Applied Psychology*, May 2006, pp. 717–726.

29. Cited in Cheryl Dahle, "Showing Your Worth Without Showing Off," http://www.nytimes.com, September 19, 2004; http://www.bragbetter.com.

30. Philip L. Hunsaker, "Projecting the Appropriate Image," *Supervisory Management*, May 1989, p. 26.

31. Quoted in Louise Dobson, "Skirting the Line: In the Office, Wardrobe Mistakes Can Be Disastrous," *Psychology Today*, July/August 2006, p. 13.

32. Quoted in "Taking Charge in a Temp World," *Fortune*, October 21, 1998, pp. 247–248.

33. Anne Fisher, "How to Network—and Enjoy It," *Fortune*, April 4, 2005, p. 38.

34. Jessica E. Vascellaro, "Social Networking Goes Professional," *The Wall Street Journal*, August 28, 2007, p. D1, D2; Ed Frauenheim, "Social Revolution: Social Networking Technology Is Colliding with the Workplace—Whether Employers Like It or Not," *Workforce Management*, October 22, 2007, p. 1.

35. Erin White, "The First Job Blues: How to Adjust, When to Move On," *The Wall Street Journal*, July 25, 2006, p. B7.

36. Daniel L. Cable and Timothy A. Judge, "Interviewers' Perceptions of Person–Organization Fit and Organizational Selection Decisions," *Journal of Applied Psychology*, August 1997, pp. 546–561.

37. Amy L. Kristof-Brown, Ryan D. Zimmerman, and Erin C. Johnson, "Consequences of Individuals' Fit at Work: A Meta–Analysis of Person–Job, Person-Organization,

Person–Group, and Person–Supervisor Fit," *Personnel Psychology*, Summer 2005, pp. 281–342.

38. Christian J. Resick, Boris B. Baltes, and Cynthia Walker Shantz, "Person–Organization Fit and Work-Related Attitudes and Decisions: Interactive Effects with Job Fit and Conscientiousness," *Journal of Applied Psychology*, September 2007, pp. 1446–1455.

39. Quoted in Robyn D. Clarke, "Rewards of Risk Taking: How to Move Out of Your Comfort Zone," *Black Enterprise*, March 2006, p. 105.

40. David Wessel, "The Future of Jobs: New Ones Arise, Wage Gap Widens," *The Wall Street Journal*, April 2, 2004; Peter Svensson, "Hands-On Jobs May Be the Safest," Associated Press, July 9, 2004.

41. Jack and Suzy Welch, "The Importance of Being There," *Business Week*, April 16, 2007, p. 92.

# 11 Building Self-Esteem and Self-Confidence

## Learning Objectives

After reading and studying this chapter and doing the exercises, you should be able to:

1 Describe the nature, development, and consequences of self-esteem.

2 Explain how to enhance self-esteem.

3 Describe the importance of self-confidence and self-efficacy.

4 Pinpoint methods of enhancing and developing your self-confidence.

## Outline

1 **The Meaning of Self-Esteem and its Development and Consequences 343**
How Self-Esteem Develops
The Consequences of Self-Esteem

2 **Enhancing Self-Esteem 348**
Attain Legitimate Accomplishments
Be Aware of Personal Strengths
Rebut the Inner Critic
Practice Self-Nurturing
Minimize Settings and Interactions That Detract from Your Feelings of Competence
Get Help from Others
Model the Behavior of People with High Self-Esteem
Create a High Self-Esteem Living Space

3 **The Importance of Self-Confidence and Self-Efficacy 354**

4 **Techniques For Developing and Enhancing Your Self-Confidence 355**
Develop a Solid Knowledge Base
Use Positive Self-Talk
Avoid Negative Self-Talk
Use Positive Visual Imagery
Set High Expectations for Yourself (the Galeta Effect)
Develop the Explanatory Style of Optimists
Strive for Peak Performance
Bounce Back from Setbacks and Embarrassments

S usan Chapman, age 37, is the Global Head of Operations, Citigroup Reality Services. She oversees 14,000 properties representing 90 million square feet of space in 96 countries. Chapman talks about herself and her career in an interview with *Black Enterprise* magazine.

*BE: What obstacles have you faced in your career?*
*SE: There were times when I wasn't given opportunities because of my gender or the color of my skin. Part of me wanted to stay and stick it out because that's what we do, we don't quit. But then the other part of me realized that I needed to make a change. When I did, the whole world opened up to me.*

*BE: What strategies have you employed?*
*SC: Having people around me who are willing to tell you the truth is key. Oftentimes it's very hard to get feedback from those who are culturally different from you. But it's critically important to develop relationships so that others feel comfortable telling you where you need to improve.*

*BE: How do you handle constructive feedback?*
*SC: I seek it. Early in my career, I didn't really seek out feedback. One day a mentor told me, "You need to get a lot more quality feedback because something's going on that you don't know about."*

*BE: What was the problem?*
*SC: There were a couple of problems in terms of not getting promoted and in being in an environment where people weren't engaging me the way I needed in order for me to be successful in my job. I hadn't built the relationships the way I needed to. I have to go out of my way to build the relationships.*

*BE: What traits or skills do you think are most important in overcoming obstacles?*
*SC: Be ambitious about setting goals, and do a self-check regularly. Ask yourself: Who am I? What am I doing? Why am I doing this? And is it working for me? You also have to be very giving, which allows a channel of things to come back to you when you really need it. When you're trying to overcome an obstacle and you need some help, it's hard to ask for help if you've never given it." [1]*

One of many possible interpretations of this executive's answers to the interview questions is that she scores high in self-esteem and self-confidence. She thinks highly enough about herself to believe that she can advance to great heights in her career. At the same time she has the self-confidence to ask for and handle feedback that can set her in the right direction. Many other people you will meet in this book score high in self-esteem and self-confidence—otherwise they would never have been so successful. In this chapter we focus on two of the biggest building blocks for more effective human relations: the nature and development of self-esteem and self-confidence. The development of both self-esteem and self-confidence includes refining certain skills.

# The Meaning of Self-Esteem and its Development and Consequences

■ Learning Objective 1

Understanding the self from various perspectives is important because who you are and what you think of you influences many different facets of your life both on and off the job. A particularly important role is played by **self-esteem**, the overall evaluation people make about themselves, whether positive or negative. [2] A useful distinction is that our self-concept is what we *think* about ourselves, whereas self-esteem is what we *feel* about ourselves. [3] People with positive self-esteem have a deep-down, inside-the-self feeling of their own worth. Consequently, they develop a positive self-concept. Before reading further, you are invited to measure your current level of self-esteem by doing Human Relations Self-Assessment Quiz 11-1. We look next at the development of self-esteem and many of its consequences.

■ **Self-esteem**
the overall evaluation people make about themselves, whether positive or negative

## HOW SELF-ESTEEM DEVELOPS

Part of understanding the nature of self-esteem is to know how it develops. Self-esteem develops and evolves throughout our lives based on interactions with people, events, and things. [4] As an adolescent or adult, your self-esteem might be boosted by a key accomplishment. A 44-year-old woman who was studying to become a licensed practical nurse (LPN) said that her self-esteem increased when she received an A in a pharmacology course. Self-esteem can also go down in adulthood by means of a negative event such as being laid off and not being able to find new employment.

Early life experiences have a major impact on self-esteem. People who were encouraged to feel good about themselves and their accomplishments by family members, friends, and teachers are more likely to enjoy high self-esteem. Early life experiences play a key role in the development of both healthy self-esteem and low self-esteem, according to research synthesized at The Counseling and Mental Health Center of the University of Texas. [5] Childhood experiences that lead to health self-esteem include

- Being praised
- Being listened to
- Being spoken to respectfully
- Getting attention and hugs
- Experiencing success in sports or school

In contrast, childhood experiences that lead to low self-esteem include

- Being harshly criticized
- Being yelled at or beaten
- Being ignored, ridiculed, or teased

## Human Relations Self-Assessment Quiz   11-1

### The Self-Esteem Checklist

Indicate whether each of the following statements is Mostly True or Mostly False as it applies to you.

| | Mostly True | Mostly False |
|---|---|---|
| 1. I am excited about starting each day. | _____ | _____ |
| 2. Most of any progress I have made in my work or school can be attributed to luck. | _____ | _____ |
| 3. I often ask myself, "Why can't I be more successful?" | _____ | _____ |
| 4. When my manager or team leader gives me a challenging assignment, I usually dive in with confidence. | _____ | _____ |
| 5. I believe that I am working up to my potential. | _____ | _____ |
| 6. I am able to set limits to what I will do for others without feeling anxious. | _____ | _____ |
| 7. I regularly make excuses for my mistakes. | _____ | _____ |
| 8. Negative feedback crushes me. | _____ | _____ |
| 9. I care very much how much money other people make, especially when they are working in my field. | _____ | _____ |
| 10. I feel like a failure when I do not achieve my goals. | _____ | _____ |
| 11. Hard work gives me an emotional lift. | _____ | _____ |
| 12. When others compliment me, I doubt their sincerity. | _____ | _____ |
| 13. Complimenting others makes me feel uncomfortable. | _____ | _____ |
| 14. I find it comfortable to say, "I'm sorry." | _____ | _____ |
| 15. It is difficult for me to face up to my mistakes. | _____ | _____ |
| 16. My coworkers think I am not worthy of promotion. | _____ | _____ |
| 17. People who want to become my friends usually do not have much to offer. | _____ | _____ |
| 18. If my manager praised me, I would have a difficult time believing it was deserved. | _____ | _____ |
| 19. I'm just an ordinary person. | _____ | _____ |
| 20. Having to face change really disturbs me. | _____ | _____ |
| 21. When I make a mistake, I have no fear owning up to it in public. | _____ | _____ |
| 22. When I look in the mirror, I typically see someone who is attractive and confident. | _____ | _____ |
| 23. When I think about the greater purpose in my life, I feel like I am drifting. | _____ | _____ |
| 24. When I make a mistake, I tend to feel ashamed and embarrassed. | _____ | _____ |
| 25. When I make a commitment to myself I usually stick to it with conviction and await the rewards that I believe will come from it. | _____ | _____ |

## Scoring and Interpretation:

The answers in the high self-esteem direction are as follows:

| | | | |
|---|---|---|---|
| **1.** Mostly True | **8.** Mostly False | **15.** Mostly False | **22.** Mostly True |
| **2.** Mostly False | **9.** Mostly False | **16.** Mostly False | **23.** Mostly False |
| **3.** Mostly False | **10.** Mostly False | **17.** Mostly False | **24.** Mostly False |
| **4.** Mostly True | **11.** Mostly True | **18.** Mostly False | **25.** Mostly True |
| **5.** Mostly True | **12.** Mostly False | **19.** Mostly False | |
| **6.** Mostly True | **13.** Mostly False | **20.** Mostly False | |
| **7.** Mostly False | **14.** Mostly True | **21.** Mostly True | |

**20–25**    You have very high self-esteem. Yet if your score is 25, it could be that you are denying any self-doubts.

**14–19**    Your self-esteem is in the average range. It would probably be worthwhile for you to implement strategies to boost your self-esteem (described in this chapter) so that you can develop a greater feeling of well-being.

**0–13**    Your self-esteem needs bolstering. Talk over your feelings about yourself with a trusted friend or with a mental health professional. At the same time, attempt to implement several of the tactics for boosting self-esteem described in this chapter.

**Questions: 1.** How does your score on this quiz match your evaluation of your self-esteem?

   **2.** What would it be like being married to somebody who scored 0 on this quiz?

**Source:** Statements 21–25 are based on information in the National Association for Self-Esteem, "Self-Esteem Self-Guided Tour—Rate Your Self-Esteem," http://www.self-esteem-nase.org/jssurvey.shtml, May 6, 2005, pp. 1–4.

- Being expected to be "perfect" all the time

- Experience failures in sports or school

- Often being given messages that failed experiences (losing a game, getting a poor grade, and so forth) were failures of their whole self

A widespread explanation of self-esteem development is that compliments, praise, and hugs alone build self-esteem. Yet many developmental psychologists seriously question this perspective. Instead, they believe that self-esteem results from accomplishing worthwhile activities and then feeling proud of these accomplishments. Receiving encouragement, however, can help the person accomplish activities that build self-esteem.

Leading psychologist Martin Seligman argues that self-esteem is caused by a variety of successes and failures. To develop self-esteem, people need to improve their skills for dealing with the world. [6] Self-esteem therefore comes about by genuine accomplishments, followed by praise and recognition. Heaping undeserved praise and recognition on people may lead to a temporary high, but it does not produce genuine self-esteem. The child develops self-esteem not from being told he or she can score a goal in soccer, but from scoring that goal.

In attempting to build the self-esteem of children and students, many parents and teachers give children too many undeserved compliments. Researchers suggest that inappropriate compliments are turning too many adults into narcissistic praise-junkies. As a result, many young adults feel insecure if they do not receive compliments regularly. [7]

As mentioned earlier, experiences in adult life can influence the development of self-esteem. David De Cremer of the Tilburg University (Netherlands) and his associates conducted two studies with Dutch college students about how the behavior of leaders, and fair procedures, influence self-esteem. The focus of any given leader's behavior was whether he or she motivated the workers–students to reward *themselves* for a job well done, such as a self-compliment. Procedural fairness was measured in terms of whether the study participants were given a voice in making decisions. Self-esteem was measured by a questionnaire somewhat similar to Self-Assessment 11-1 in this chapter. The study questionnaire reflected the perceived value that individuals have of themselves as organizational members.

The study found that self-esteem was related to procedural fairness and leadership that encourages self-rewards. When leadership that encouraged rewards was high, procedural fairness was more strongly related to self-esteem. The interpretation given of the findings is that a leader or supervisor can facilitate self-esteem when he or she encourages self-rewards and uses fair procedures. Furthermore, fair procedures have a stronger impact on self-esteem when the leader encourages self-rewards. [8] A takeaway from this study would that rewarding yourself for a job well done, even in adult life, can boost your self-esteem a little.

## THE CONSEQUENCES OF SELF-ESTEEM

No single factor is as important to career success as self-esteem, as observed by psychologist Eugene Raudsepp. People with positive self-esteem understand their own competence and worth, and a positive perception of their ability to cope with problems and adversity. [9]

One of the major consequences of high self-esteem is good mental health. People with high self-esteem feel good about themselves and have a positive outlook on life. One of the links between good mental health and self-esteem is that high self-esteem helps prevent many situations from being stressful. Few negative comments from others are likely to bother you when your self-esteem is high. A person with low self-esteem might crumble if somebody insulted his or her appearance. A person with high self-esteem might shrug off the insult as simply being the other person's point of view. If faced with an everyday setback, such as losing keys, the high self-esteem person might think, "I have so much going for me, why fall apart over this incident?"

Positive self-esteem also conributes to good mental health because it helps us ward off being troubled by feelings of jealousy and acting aggressively toward others because of our jealousy. Particularly with adolescents, lower self-worth leads to jealousy about friends liking other people better. [10]

Although people with high self-esteem can readily shrug off undeserved insults, they still profit well from negative feedback. Because they are secure, they can profit from the developmental opportunities suggested by negative feedback. Workers with high self-esteem develop and maintain favorable work attitudes and perform at a high level. These positive consequences take place because such attitudes and behavior are consistent with the personal belief that they are competent individuals. Mary Kay Ash, the legendary founder of a beauty-products company, put it this way: "It never occurred to me I couldn't do it. I always knew that if I worked hard enough, I could." Furthermore, research has shown that high-self-esteem individuals value reaching work goals more than do low-self-esteem individuals. [11]

The combined effect of workers having high self-esteem helps a company prosper. Long-term research by Nathaniel Branden, as well as more recent studies, suggests that self-esteem is a critical source of competitive advantage in an information society. Companies gain the edge when, in addition to having an educated workforce, employees have high self-esteem, as shown by such behaviors as the following:

- Being creative and innovative

- Taking personal responsibility for problems

- A feeling of independence (yet still wanting to work cooperatively with others)

- Trusting one's own capabilities

- Taking the initiative to solve problems [12]

Behaviors such as these help workers cope with the challenge of a rapidly changing workplace where products and ideas become obsolete quickly. Workers with high self-esteem are more likely to be able to cope with new challenges regularly because they are confident they can master their environment.

High self-esteem can sometimes have negative consequences, particularly because individuals with high self-esteem work hard to preserve their high status relative to others. When people with high self-esteem are placed in a situation where undermining others helps them maintain their status, they will engage in behaviors that diminish others. In one study it was shown that high self-esteem individuals who are also a little neurotic (somewhat emotionally unstable) will often engage the following undermining behaviors: Criticizing group members in front of others, intentionally ignoring others, talking down to other group members, going back on their word, giving others the silent treatment, belittling others, and not listening to people. [13]

Another potential danger exists in having highly inflated self-esteem. A controversial study conducted in England found that people with high self-esteem might have an unrealistic sense of themselves. "They expect to do well at things, discount failure, and feel beyond reproach." Furthermore, people with exaggerated self-esteem are sometimes intolerant of people who are different from them. [14]

A potential negative consequence of low self-esteem is envying too many people. If you perceive that many individuals have much more of what you want, and are more worthwhile than you, you will suffer from enormous envy. To decrease pangs of envy, it is best to develop realistic standards of comparison between you and other people in the world. If high school basketball player Joshua measures his self-esteem in terms of how well he stacks up with basketball superstar and supermillionaire LeBron James, young Joshua will

> "Research shows people who feel good about themselves take better care of themselves."
> —Christy Greenleaf, assistant professor in the Department of Kinesiology, Health Promotion and Recreation at the University of North Texas. Quoted in Jorge Cruise, "Self-Image Matters," *USA Weekend*, March 17–19, 2006, p. 4.

take a lot of blows to his self-esteem. However, if Joshua compares himself to other players on his team and in his league, his self-esteem will be higher because he has chosen a more realistic reference group.

According to economist Robert H. Frank of Cornell University, our own reference group has the biggest impact on self-esteem. He writes: "When you see Bill Gates' mansion, you don't actually aspire to have one like it. It's who is local, who is near you physically and who is most like you—your family members, coworkers and old high school classmates—with whom you compare yourself. If someone in your reference group has a little more, you get a little anxious." [15]

Low self-esteem can have negative consequences for romantic relationships because people with self-doubts consistently underestimate their partners' feelings for them. People with low self-respect distance themselves from the relationship—often devaluing their partner—to prepare themselves for what they think will be an inevitable breakup. John G. Holmes, a psychologist at the University of Waterloo in Ontario, Canada, says, "If people think negatively about themselves, they think their partner must think negatively about them—and they're wrong." [16]

The consequences of self-esteem are related to its source. People who evaluate their self-worth on how others perceive them and not on their value as human beings often suffer negative mental and physical consequences. In a series of studies, developmental psychologist Jennifer Crocker found that college students who based their self-worth on external sources reported more stress, anger, academic problems, and interpersonal conflicts. In addition, these students had higher levels of drug and alcohol use and symptoms of eating disorders. (External sources of self-worth include appearance, approval from others, and grades in school.) Students who based their self-esteem (or self-worth) on internal sources generally received higher grades and were less likely to consume alcohol and drugs or develop eating disorders. [17] (An internal source would be thinking of yourself as a kind and charitable person.)

# Enhancing Self-Esteem

■ **Learning Objective 2**

Improving self-esteem is a lifelong process because self-esteem is related to the success of your activities and interactions with people. Following are approaches to enhancing self-esteem that are related to how self-esteem develops (see also Figure 11-1). Each of these approaches has a skill component, such as learning to avoid situations that make you feel incompetent.

## ATTAIN LEGITIMATE ACCOMPLISHMENTS

To emphasize again, accomplishing worthwhile activities is a major contributor to self-esteem (as well as self-confidence) in both children and adults. Social science research suggests this sequence of events: Person establishes a goal; person pursues the goal; person achieves the goal; person develops

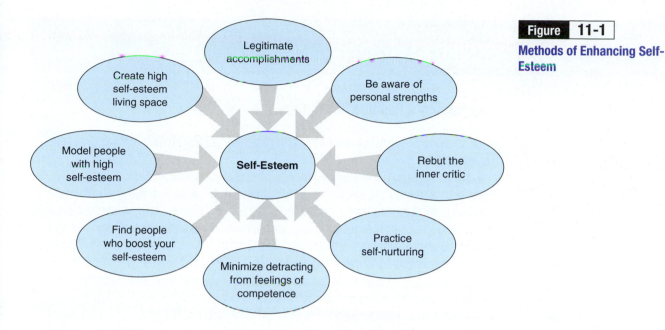

Figure   11-1

**Methods of Enhancing Self-Esteem**

esteem-like feelings. [18] The opposite point of view is this sequence: Person develops esteem-like feelings; person establishes a goal; person pursues the goal; person achieves the goal. Similarly, giving people large trophies for mundane accomplishments is unlikely to raise self-esteem. More likely, the person will see through the transparent attempt to build his or her self-esteem and develop negative feelings about the self. What about you? Would your self-esteem receive a bigger boost by (1) receiving an A in a course in which 10 percent of the class received an A or by (2) receiving an A in a class in which everybody received the same grade?

## BE AWARE OF PERSONAL STRENGTHS

Another method of improving your self-esteem is to develop an appreciation of your strengths and accomplishments. Research a while back with over 60 executives has shown that their self-concepts become more positive after one month of practicing this exercise for a few minutes every day. [19] A good starting point is to list your strengths and accomplishments on a word processing document or paper. This list is likely to be more impressive than you expected.

You can sometimes develop an appreciation of your strengths by participating in a group exercise designed for such purposes. A group of about seven people meet to form a support group. All group members first spend about 10 minutes answering the question, "What are my three strongest points, attributes, or skills?" After each group member records his or her three strengths, the person discusses them with the other group members.

Each group member then comments on the list. Other group members sometimes add to your list of strengths or reinforce what you have to say. Sometimes you may find disagreement. One member told the group, "I'm handsome, intelligent, reliable, athletic, self-confident, and very moral. I also

## Skill-Building Exercise 11-1

### Reinforcing a Positive Self-Image

To do this exercise, you will need a piece of paper and a pencil or pen or a word processor, and a timer or clock.

Set a timer for 10 minutes or note the time on your watch, cell phone, or a clock. Write your name across the top of the document. Then write everything positive and good you can think of about yourself. Include special attributes, talents, and achievements. You can use single words or sentences. You can write the same things over and over if you want to emphasize them. Your ideas do not have to be well organized. Write down whatever comes to mind. You are the only one who will see this document. Avoid using any negative words. Use only positive ones.

When the 10 minutes are up, read the document over to yourself. You may feel sad when you read it over because it is a new, different, and positive way of thinking about yourself. Your document will contradict some of the negative thoughts you have had about yourself. Those feelings will diminish as you reread this document. Read the document over again several times. Print the document if written by computer, and put it in a convenient place, such as in your pocket, purse, wallet, or your bedside table. Read it over at least once a day to keep reminding yourself of how great you are! Find a private space and read it aloud. If you have a good friend or family member who is supportive, read it to that person. Maybe your confidant can think of a positive attribute that you have missed.

Source: Adapted from "Building Self-esteem: A Self-Help Guide," http://mentalhealth.samhsa.gov/, accessed September 7, 2007.

have a good sense of humor." Another group member retorted, "And I might add that you're unbearably conceited."

Skill-Building Exercises 11-1 and 11-2 provide additional ways of developing self-esteem, both of which focus on appreciation of strengths.

## REBUT THE INNER CRITIC

Another early step in attaining better self-esteem is to rebut your inner critic—the voice inside you that sends negative messages about your capabilities. Rebutting critical statements about you might also be considered another way of appreciating your strengths. Two examples of rebutting your inner critic follow [20]:

*Your unfairly harsh inner critic says:* "People said they liked my presentation, but it was nowhere as good as it should have been. I can't believe no one noticed all the places I messed up. I'm such an imposter."

## Skill-Building Exercise 11-2

### The Self-Esteem Building Club

You and your classmates are invited to participate in one of the most humane and productive human-relations skill-building exercises, membership in the "self-esteem building club." Your assignment is, for three consecutive weeks, to help build the self-esteem of one person. Before embarking upon the exercise, review the information about self-esteem development in this chapter. One of the most effective tactics would be to find somebody who has a legitimate accomplishment, and give that person a reward or thank you. Record carefully what the person did, what you did, and any behavioral reactions of the person whose self-esteem you attempted to build. An example follows, written by a 46-year old student of human relations:

Thursday night two weeks ago I went to the athletic club to play racquetball. Different than usual, I had a date after the club. I wanted to look good, so I decided to wear my high school class ring. The ring doesn't have much resale value, but I was emotionally attached to it, having worn it for special occasions for 28 years. I stuffed the ring along with my watch and wallet in my athletic bag.

When I was through with racquetball, I showered and got dressed. My ring was missing from my bag, but my wallet and watch were still there. I kind of freaked out because I hate to lose a prized possession. I shook the bag out three times, but no luck. Very discouraged, I left my name, telephone number, and e-mail address at the front desk just in case somebody turned in the ring. I kept thinking that I must have lost the ring when I stopped at the desk to check in.

The next morning before going to class, I got a phone call from a front-desk clerk at the club. The clerk told me that Karl, from the housekeeping staff, heard a strange noise while he was vacuuming near the front desk. He shut off the vacuum cleaner immediately, and pulled out my ring. To me, Karl was a hero. I made a special trip to the club that night to meet with Karl. I shook his hand, and gave him a $10 bill as a reward. I also explained to Karl what a difference he had made in my mood. I told him that honest, hardworking people like him who take pride in their work make this world a better place. It made my day when Karl smiled and told me it was a pleasure to be helpful.

Your instructor might organize a sharing of self-esteem building episodes in the class. If the sharing does take place, look for patterns in terms of what seemed to work in terms of self-esteem building. Also, listen for any patterns in failed attempts at self-esteem building.

*Your reassuring rebuttal:* "Wow, they really liked it. Maybe it wasn't perfect, but I worked hard on that presentation and did a good job. I'm proud of myself. This was a great success."

*Your harsh inner critic makes leaps of illogic:* "He is frowning. He didn't say anything, but I know it means that he doesn't like me!"

*Your rebuttal that challenges the illogic:* "Okay, he's frowning, but I don't know why. It could have nothing to do with me. Maybe I should ask."

These are but two examples of the type of put-downs we often hear from our inner critic. To boost your self-esteem in spite of such criticism, you need to develop the skill of rebuttal by rebutting your inner critic frequently.

## PRACTICE SELF-NURTURING

Although you may be successful at pointing to your strengths and rebutting the inner voice that puts you down, it is also helpful to treat yourself as a worth-while person. Start to challenge negative experiences and messages from the past by nurturing and caring for yourself in ways that show how valuable, competent, deserving, and lovable you really are. Self-nurturing is often referred to "as treating yourself well" or "spoiling yourself." Here are two suggestions for self-nurturing, both of which involve a modest amount of skill development.

- **Administer self-rewards for a job well done.** When you have carried out an activity especially well in relation to your typical performance, reward yourself in a small, constructive way. You might dine at a favorite restaurant, take an afternoon off to go for a nature walk, or spend an hour at a Web site you usually do not have the time to visit.

- **Take good care of yourself mentally and physically.** Make sure you get enough sleep and rest, eat nutritious foods, avoid high-bacteria environments such as a public keyboard unless you use a bacteria spray, and participate in moderate physical exercise. Even taking an extra shower or bath can give you a physical and mental boost. The suggestions just mentioned are also part of stress management.

Real estate agent Laura provides a helpful example of how self-nurturing can help bolster self-esteem. While watching her son play soccer at four in the afternoon, she was asked by another soccer parent, "How's business?" Laura replied, "I haven't made a deal in two weeks, but I know times will get better. So for now, I'm enjoying myself watching Todd [her son] play his little heart out. Afterwards we are going for pizza, and a few video games. My soul will be energized again."

## MINIMIZE SETTINGS AND INTERACTIONS THAT DETRACT FROM YOUR FEELINGS OF COMPETENCE

Most of us have situations in our work and personal lives that make us feel less than our best. If you can minimize exposure to those situations, you will have fewer feelings of incompetence. The problem with feeling incompetent is that it lowers your self-esteem. An office supervisor said she detested company picnics, most of all because she was forced into playing softball. At her own admission, she had less aptitude for athletics than any able-bodied person she knew. In addition, she felt uncomfortable with the small-talk characteristic of picnics. To minimize discomfort, the woman attended only those picnics she thought were absolutely necessary. Instead of playing on the softball team, she volunteered to be the equipment manager.

A problem with avoiding all situations in which you feel lowly competent is that it might prevent you from acquiring needed skills. Also, it boosts your self-confidence and self-esteem to become comfortable in a previously uncomfortable situation.

## GET HELP FROM OTHERS

Self-esteem is strongly shaped by how others perceive us, so getting help from others is a major step a person can take to improve his or her self-esteem. However, getting help from others can also be difficult. People with low self-esteem often do not ask for help because they may not think they are worthy of receiving help. Yet help from others is effective in overcoming the negative messages received from others in the past.

Asking for support from friends can include such basic steps as these: (1) Ask friends to tell you what they like about you or think that you do well. (2) Ask someone who cares about you to listen to you complain about something without offering a solution to your problem. (3) Ask for a hug. (4) Ask someone who loves you to remind you that he or she does.

Getting help from teachers and other helpers can include these steps: (1) Ask professors or tutors for help with work you find challenging. (2) If you lack self-confidence in certain areas, take classes or attempt new activities to increase your self of competence. An increasing number of retired people today are taking classes in such subjects as computer utilization and digital photography to help catch up with younger people whose skills have challenged their self-esteem. [21]

Another way of getting help from others is to talk and socialize frequently with people who can boost your self-esteem. Psychologist Barbara Ilardie says that the people who can raise your self-esteem are usually those with high self-esteem themselves. They are the people who give honest feedback because they respect others and themselves. Such high self-esteem individuals should not be confused with yes-people who agree with others just to be liked. The point is that you typically receive more from strong people than weak ones. Weak people will flatter you but will not give you the honest feedback you need to build self-esteem. [22]

For many people with low self-esteem, casual help with others will not increase self-esteem. In these situations, discussing low self-esteem with a mental health specialist might be the most effective measure.

## MODEL THE BEHAVIOR OF PEOPLE WITH HIGH SELF-ESTEEM

Observe the way people who you believe to have high self-esteem stand, walk, speak, and act. Even if you are not feeling so secure inside, you will project a high self-esteem image if you act assured. Eugene Raudsepp recommends, "Stand tall, speak clearly and with confidence, shake hands firmly, look people in the eye and smile frequently. Your self-esteem will increase as you notice encouraging reactions from others." [23] (Notice here that self-esteem is considered to be about the same idea as self-confidence.)

Choose your models of high self-esteem from people you know personally, as well as celebrities you might watch on television news and interview shows. Observing actors on the large or small screen is a little less useful because they are guaranteed to be playing a role. Identifying a teacher or professor as a self-esteem model is widely practiced, as is observing successful family members and friends.

### CREATE A HIGH SELF-ESTEEM LIVING SPACE

A panel of mental health specialists recommends that to enhance your self-esteem you should make your living space one that honors the person you are. [24] Whether you live in a single room, a small apartment, or a large house, make that space comfortable and attractive for you. If you have a clean, inviting living space, others are likely to treat you with more respect, which will contribute to your self-esteem. If you share your living space with others, dedicate some space just for you—a place where you can keep your things and know that they will not be disturbed and that you can decorate any way you choose.

Your living space is part of your self-image, so you want to ask yourself if your living space projects the right self-image. Also, if you arrange your living space to fit your preferences, you will feel better about yourself.

# The Importance of Self-Confidence and Self-Efficacy

■ **Learning Objective 3**

■ **Self-efficacy**
the confidence in your ability to carry out a specific task

Although self-confidence can be considered part of self-esteem (or almost its equivalent), it is important enough to study separately. **Self-efficacy** is confidence in your ability to carry out a specific task, in contrast to generalized self-confidence. Various studies have shown that people with a high sense of self-efficacy tend to have good job performance, so being self-confident is important for your career. They also set relatively high goals for themselves. [25] Self-confidence has also long been recognized as a trait of effective leaders. A straightforward implication of self-efficacy is that people who think they can perform well on a task do better than those who think they will do poorly.

Research by college professors and psychological consultants George P. Hollenbeck and Douglas T. Hall suggests that our feelings of self-confidence stem from five sources of information. [26] The first source is the *actual experience,* or *things we have done.* Having done something before and succeeded is the most powerful way to build self-confidence. If you successfully inserted a replacement battery into your watch without destroying the watch, you will be confident to make another replacement.

The second source of self-confidence is the *experiences of others,* or *modeling.* You can gain some self-confidence if you have carefully observed others perform a task, such as resolving conflict with a customer. You might say to yourself, "I've seen Tracy calm down the customer by listening and showing sympathy, and I'm confident I can do the same thing." The third source of self-confidence is *social comparison,* or *comparing yourself to others.* If you see other people with capabilities similar to your own perform a task well, you will gain in confidence. A person might say to him- or herself, "If that person can learn how to work with enterprise software, I can do it also. I'm just as smart."

The fourth source of self-confidence is *social persuasion, the process of convincing another person.* If a credible person convinces you that you can accomplish a particular task, you will often receive a large enough boost in self-confidence to give the task a try. If the encouragement is coupled with guidance on how to perform the task, your self-confidence gain will be higher. So the boss or teacher who says, "I know you can do it, and I'm here to help you," knows how to build self-confidence.

The fifth source of information for making a self-confidence judgment is *emotional arousal,* or *how we feel about events around us and manage our emotions.* We rely somewhat on our inner feelings to know if we are self-confident enough to perform the task. Imagine a person standing on top of a high mountain ready to ski down. However, he is she is trembling and nauseated from fear. Contrast this beginner to another person who simply feels mildly excited and challenged. Skier number one has a self-confidence problem, whereas skier number two has enough confidence to start the descent. (Have your emotional sensations ever influenced your self-confidence?)

The more of these five sources of self-confidence are positive for you, the more likely your self-confidence will be positive. A subtle point about self-confidence is that being too low in self-confidence is a problem yet being too high is also a problem. The overly self-confident person may not listen carefully to the suggestions of others, and may be blind to criticism.

Human Relations Self-Assessment Exercise 11-2 provides some insight into your level of self-confidence.

# Techniques For Developing and Enhancing Your Self-Confidence

■ **Learning Objective 4**

Self-confidence is generally achieved by succeeding in a variety of situations. A confident civil engineering technician may not be generally self-confident unless he or she also achieves success in activities such as forming good personal relationships, navigating complex software, writing a letter, learning a second language, or displaying athletic skills.

Although this general approach to self-confidence building makes sense, it does not work for everyone. Some people who seem to succeed at everything still have lingering self-doubt. Low self-confidence is so deeply ingrained in this type of personality that success in later life is not sufficient to change things. Following are seven specific strategies and tactics for building and elevating self-confidence, as outlined in Figure 11-2. They will generally work unless the person has deep-rooted feelings of inferiority. The tactics and strategies are arranged approximately in the order in which they should be tried to achieve best results.

## DEVELOP A SOLID KNOWLEDGE BASE

A bedrock strategy for projecting self-confidence is to develop a base of knowledge that enables you to provide sensible alternative solutions to problems.

## Human Relations Self-Assessment Quiz 11-2

### How Self-Confident Are You?

Indicate the extent to which you agree with each of the following statements. Use a 1–5 scale: (1) disagree strongly (DS); (2) disagree (D); (3) neutral (N); (4) agree (A); (5) agree strongly (AS).

|  | DS | D | N | A | AS |
|---|---|---|---|---|---|
| 1. I frequently say to people, "I'm not sure." | 5 | 4 | 3 | 2 | 1 |
| 2. I perform well in most situations in life. | 1 | 2 | 3 | 4 | 5 |
| 3. I willingly offer advice to others. | 1 | 2 | 3 | 4 | 5 |
| 4. Before making even a minor decision, I usually consult with several people. | 5 | 4 | 3 | 2 | 1 |
| 5. I am generally willing to attempt new activities for which I have very little related skill or experience. | 1 | 2 | 3 | 4 | 5 |
| 6. Speaking in front of the class or other group is a frightening experience for me. | 5 | 4 | 3 | 2 | 1 |
| 7. I experience stress when people challenge me or put me on the spot. | 5 | 4 | 3 | 2 | 1 |
| 8. I feel comfortable attending a social event by myself. | 1 | 2 | 3 | 4 | 5 |
| 9. I'm much more of a winner than a loser. | 1 | 2 | 3 | 4 | 5 |
| 10. I am cautious about making any substantial change in my life. | 5 | 4 | 3 | 2 | 1 |

Total score: _____

### Scoring and Interpretation:

Calculate your total score by adding the numbers circled. A tentative interpretation of the scoring is as follows:

**45–50** Very high self-confidence with perhaps a tendency toward arrogance.

**38–44** A high, desirable level of self-confidence.

**30–37** Moderate, or average, self-confidence.

**10–29** Self-confidence needs strengthening.

**Questions:** 1. How does your score on this test fit with you evaluation of your self-confidence?

2. What would it be like working for a manager who scored 10 on this quiz?

Intuition is very important, but working from a base of facts helps you project a confident image. Formal education is an obvious and important source of information for your knowledge base. Day-by-day absorption of information directly and indirectly related to your career is equally important. A major purpose of formal education is to get you in the right frame of mind to continue your quest for knowledge. In your quest for developing a solid knowledge base to project self-confidence, be sensitive to abusing this technique. If you

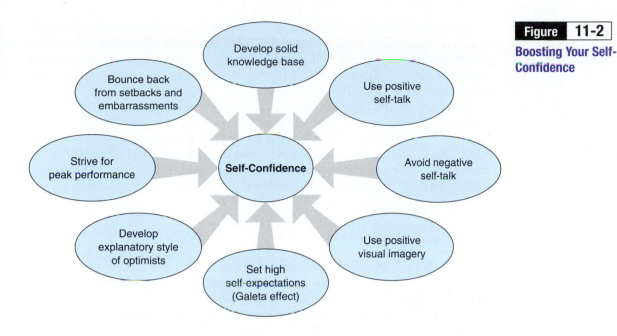

**Figure   11-2**

**Boosting Your Self-Confidence**

bombard people with quotes, facts, and figures, you are likely to be perceived as an annoying know-it-all.

## USE POSITIVE SELF-TALK

A basic method of building self-confidence is to engage in **positive self-talk**, saying positive things about yourself. The first step in using positive self-talk is to objectively state the incident that is casting doubt about self-worth. [27] The key word here is *objectively*. Terry, who is fearful of poorly executing a report-writing assignment, might say, "I've been asked to write a report for the company, and I'm not a good writer."

The next step is to objectively interpret what the incident *does not* mean. Terry might say, "Not being a skilled writer doesn't mean that I can't figure out a way to write a good report or that I'm an ineffective employee."

Next, the person should objectively state what the incident *does* mean. In doing this, the person should avoid put-down labels such as "incompetent," "stupid," "dumb," "jerk," or "airhead." All these terms are forms of negative self-talk. Terry should state what the incident does mean: "I have a problem with one small aspect of this job."

The fourth step is to objectively account for the cause of the incident. Terry would say, "I'm really worried about writing a good report because I have very little experience in writing along these lines."

The fifth step is to identify some positive ways to prevent the incident from happening again. Terry might say, "I'll get out my textbook on business communications and review the chapter on report writing" or "I'll enroll in a course or seminar on business report writing."

The final step is to use positive self-talk. Terry imagines his boss saying, "This report is really good. I'm proud of my decision to select you to prepare this important report."

■ **Positive self-talk**

saying positive things about yourself

Positive self-talk builds self-confidence and self-esteem because it programs the mind with positive messages. Making frequent positive statements or affirmations about the self creates a more confident person. An example would be, "I know I can learn this new equipment rapidly enough to increase my productivity within five days."

Business coach Gary Lockwood emphasizes that positive self-talk is also useful for getting people past difficult times. "It's all in your head," he said. "Remember, you are in charge of your feelings. You are in control of your attitude." Instead of berating yourself after making a mistake, learn from the experience and move on. Say to yourself, "Everyone makes mistakes," "Tomorrow is another day," or "What can I learn from this?" [28]

## AVOID NEGATIVE SELF-TALK

As implied, you should minimize negative statements about yourself to bolster self-confidence. A lack of self-confidence is reflected in statements such as "I may be stupid, but …," "Nobody asked my opinion," "I know I'm usually wrong, but …," "I know I don't have as much education as some people, but …" Self-effacing statements like these serve to reinforce low self-confidence.

It is also important not to attribute to yourself negative, irreversible traits, such as "idiotic," "ugly," "dull," "loser," and "hopeless." Instead, look on your weak points as areas for possible self-improvement. Negative self-labeling can do long-term damage to your self-confidence. If a person stops that practice today, his or her self-confidence may begin to increase.

## USE POSITIVE VISUAL IMAGERY

**■ Positive visual imagery**
picturing a positive outcome in
your mind

Assume you have a situation in mind in which you would like to appear confident and in control. An example would be a meeting with a major customer who has told you by e-mail that he is considering switching suppliers. Your intuitive reaction is that if you cannot handle his concerns without fumbling or appearing desperate, you will lose the account. An important technique is this situation is **positive visual imagery,** or picturing a positive outcome in your mind. To apply this technique in this situation, imagine yourself engaging in a convincing argument about why your customer should retain your company as the primary supplier. Imagine yourself talking in positive terms about the good service your company offers and how you can rectify any problems.

Visualize yourself listening patiently to your customer's concerns and then talking confidently about how your company can handle these concerns. As you rehearse this moment of truth, create a mental picture of you and the customer shaking hands over the fact that the account is still yours.

Positive visual imagery helps you appear self-confident because your mental rehearsal of the situation has helped you prepare for battle. If imagery works for you once, you will be even more effective in subsequent uses of the technique.

## SET HIGH EXPECTATIONS FOR YOURSELF (THE GALETA EFFECT)

If you set high expectations for yourself and you succeed, you are likely to experience a temporary or permanent boost in self-confidence. The **Galeta effect** is a type of self-fulfilling prophecy in which high expectations lead to high performance. Similar to positive self-talk, if you believe in yourself, you are more likely to succeed. You expect to win, so you do. The Galeta effect does not work all the time, but it does work some of the time for many people.

Workplace behavior researchers D. Brian McNatt and Timothy A. Judge studied the Galeta effect with 72 auditors within three offices of a major accounting firm over a three-month period. The auditors were given letters of encouragement to strengthen their feelings of self-efficacy. Information in the letters was based on facts about the auditors, such as information derived from their résumés and company records. The results of the experiment showed that creating a Galeta effect bolstered self-efficacy, motivation, and performance. However, the performance improvement was temporary, suggesting that self-expectations need to be boosted regularly. [29]

■ **Galeta effect**
a type of self-fulfilling prophecy in which high expectations lead to high perfomance

## DEVELOP THE EXPLANATORY STYLE OF OPTIMISTS

According to the research and observations of consultant and trainer Price Pritchett, optimism is linked to self-confidence. Explaining events in an optimistic way can help preserve self-confidence and self-esteem. When experiencing trouble, optimists tend to explain the problems to themselves as temporary. Bad events are expected to be short-lived, and optimists look to the future when times will be better. Another aspect of optimists' explanatory style protects their self-confidence. Rather then condemn themselves for failures, they look for how other factors or circumstances have contributed to the problem. Optimists, then, do not take all the blame for a problem, but look to external factors to help explain what went wrong.

Interpreting difficulties in this way gives the optimists a sense of control. Instead of looking at the unfortunate situation as hopeless, they have faith in their ability to deal with the problem. [30] Suppose an optimist purchases a computer workstation that comes packed in a box with many parts along with directions. A problem arises: some of the screws and dowels do not fit, and the directions are unclear. A pessimist might suffer a drop in self-confidence and self-esteem, saying to himself or herself, "What a fool I am. I can't even assemble a piece of office furniture." In contrast, the optimist might say, "I'm doing something wrong here, and I will get a buddy to help show me my mistake. But the manufacturer can also be blamed. The instructions are terrible, and all the parts may not fit together." In this way the optimist does not take such a big hit to self-confidence and self-esteem.

## STRIVE FOR PEAK PERFORMANCE

■ **Peak performance**
exceptional accomplishment in a given task

A key strategy for projecting self-confidence is to display **peak performance**, or exceptional accomplishment in a given task. The experience is transient but exceptionally meaningful. Peak performance refers to much more than attempting to do your best. Experiencing peak performance in various tasks over a long time period would move a person toward self-actualization. [31] To achieve peak performance, you must be totally focused on what you are doing. When you are in the state of peak performance, you are mentally calm and physically at ease. Intense concentration is required to achieve this state. You are so focused on the task at hand that you are not distracted by extraneous events or thoughts. To use an athletic analogy, you are *in the zone* while you are performing the task. In fact, many sport psychologists and other sports trainers work with athletes to help them attain peak performance.

The mental state achieved during peak performance is akin to a person's sense of deep concentration when immersed in a sport or hobby. On days when tennis players perform way above their usual game, they typically comment, "The ball looked so large today, I could read the label as I hit it." On the job, focus and concentration allow the person to sense and respond to relevant information coming both from within the mind and from outside stimuli. When you are at your peak, you impress others by responding intelligently to their input. While turning in peak performance, you are experiencing a mental state referred to as *flow*.

Although you are concentrating on an object or sometimes on another person during peak performance, you still have an awareness of the self. You develop a strong sense of the self, similar to self-confidence and self-efficacy, while you are concentrating on the task. Peak performance is related to self-confidence in another important way. Achieving peak performance in many situations helps you develop self-confidence.

Skill-Building Exercise 11-3 gives you and opportunity to work on enhancing your self-confidence.

## BOUNCE BACK FROM SETBACKS AND EMBARRASSMENTS

Resilience is a major contributor to personal effectiveness. Overcoming setbacks also builds self-confidence, as implied from the description of the explanatory style of optimists. An effective self-confidence builder is to convince yourself that you can conquer adversity such as setbacks and embarrassments, thus being resilient. The vast majority of successful leaders have dealt successfully with at least one significant setback in their careers, such as being fired or demoted. In contrast, crumbling after a setback or series of setbacks will usually lower self-confidence. Two major suggestions for bouncing back from setbacks and embarrassments are presented next.

### Get Past the Emotional Turmoil

Adversity has enormous emotional consequences. The emotional impact of severe job adversity can rival the loss of a personal relationship. The stress from adversity leads to a cycle of adversity followed by stress, followed by

# Human Relations Self-Assessment Quiz 11-3

## Building Your Self-Confidence and Self-Efficacy

Most people can use a boost to their self-confidence. Even if you are a highly confident individual, perhaps there is room for building your feelings of self-efficacy in a particular area, such as a proud and successful business owner learning a new skill such as editing digital photos or speaking a foreign language. For this skill-building exercise, enhance your self-confidence or self-efficacy in the next two weeks by trying out one of the many suggestions for self-confidence building described in the text.

As part of planning the implementation of this exercise, think about any area in which your self-confidence could use a boost. A candid human relations student, who was also a confident cheerleader, said, "Face it. I'm terrible at PowerPoint presentations. I put up so many details on my slides that the audience is trying to read my slides instead of looking at me. I have to admit that my PowerPoint presentation consists mostly of my reading my slides to the audience. I'm much better at cheerleading." So this student studied information in her human relations text about making better graphic presentations. She revamped her approach to using her slides as headlines and talking points. She tried out one presentation in class, and one at her church. She received so many compliments about her presentations that she now has much higher self-efficacy with respect to PowerPoint presentations.

Your instructor might organize a sharing of self-confidence building episodes in the class. If the sharing does take place, look for patterns in what seemed to work for self-confidence or self-efficacy building. Also, listen for any patterns in failed attempts at self-confidence building.

more adversity. A starting point in dealing with the emotional aspects of adversity is to *accept the reality of your problem.* Admit that your problems are real and that you are hurting inside. A second step is *not to take the set-back personally.* Remember that setbacks are inevitable so long as you are taking some risks in your career. Not personalizing setbacks helps reduce some of the emotional sting. If possible, *do not panic.* Recognize that you are in difficult circumstances under which many others panic. Convince yourself to remain calm enough to deal with the severe problem or crisis. Also, *get help from your support network.* Getting emotional support from family members and friends helps overcome the emotional turmoil associated with adversity.

## Find a Creative Solution to Your Problem

An inescapable part of planning a comeback is to solve your problem. You often need to search for creative solutions. Suppose a person faced the adversity of not having enough money for educational expenses. The person might search through standard alternatives such as applying for financial aid, looking for more lucrative part-time work, and borrowing from family members. Several students have solved their problem more creatively by asking strangers to lend them money as intermediate-term investments. An option the investors have is to receive a payback based on the future earnings of the students.

## Self-Assessment Quizzes in Overview

The two self-assessment quizzes presented in this chapter support each other well. Self-Assessment Quiz 11-1 is a self-esteem checklist. People who score high on The Self-Esteem Checklist should theoretically score high on Self-Assessment Quiz 11-2, How Self-Confident Are You? The reason is that self-esteem and self-confidence are closely related and may be part of the same concept. An exception is that some people might like themselves even though they are not particularly self-confident in many situations. Perhaps their attitude is, "So who cares if I am not self-confident? I like me anyway."

# Concept Review and Reinforcement

## Key Terms

Self-esteem, 343

Self-efficacy, 354

Positive self-talk, 357

Positive visual imagery, 358

Galeta effect, 359

Peak performance, 360

## Summary of Key Concepts

Self-esteem refers to the overall evaluation people make about themselves. People with high self-esteem develop a positive self-concept. Self-esteem develops from a variety of early-life experiences. People who were encouraged to feel good about themselves and their accomplishments by key people in their lives are more likely to enjoy high self-esteem. Of major significance, self-esteem also results from accomplishing worthwhile activities, and then feeling proud of these accomplishments. Praise and recognition for accomplishments also help develop self-esteem.

Self-esteem is important for career success. Good mental health is another major consequence of high self-esteem. One of the links between good mental health and self-esteem is that high self-esteem helps prevent many situations from being stressful. Workers with high self-esteem develop and maintain favorable work attitudes and perform at a high level. A company with high self-esteem workers has a competitive advantage.

High self-esteem can sometimes have negative consequences, such as undermining others to preserve one's own status. A potential negative consequence of low self-esteem is envying too many people. Our own reference group has the biggest impact on self-esteem. Low self-esteem can have negative consequences for romantic relationships because people with self-doubts consistently underestimate their partners' feelings for them. A series of studies showed that students who based their self-esteem on internal sources generally received higher grades and were less likely to consume alcohol and drugs or develop eating disorders.

Self-esteem can be enhanced in many ways: (a) attain legitimate accomplishments; (b) be aware of your personal strengths; (c) rebut the inner critic; (d) practice self-nurturing; (e) minimize settings and interactions that detract from your feelings of competence; (f) get help from others, including talking and socializing frequently with people who boost your self-esteem; (g) model the behavior of people with high self-esteem; and (h) create a high self-esteem living space.

Various studies have shown that people with a high sense of self-efficacy tend to have good job performance, so self-confidence is important for your career. Our feelings of self-confidence stem from five sources of information: actual experiences, or things that we have done; experiences of others, or modeling; social comparison, or comparing yourself to others; social persuasion, the process of convincing another person; and emotional arousal, or how we feel about events around us and manage our emotions.

A general principle of boosting your self-confidence is to experience success (goal accomplishment) in a variety of situations. The specific strategies for building self-confidence described here are (a) develop a solid knowledge base, (b) use positive self-talk, (c) avoid negative self-talk, (d) use positive visual imagery, (e) set high expectations for yourself (the Galeta effect), (f) develop the explanatory style of optimists, (g) strive for peak performance, and (h) bounce back from setbacks and embarrassments.

## Check your Understanding

1. Why does holding an important job contribute to a person's self-esteem?

2. A study by economists indicated that workers with higher levels of self-esteem tended to be more productive. What would be an explanation for this finding?

3. Having workers with high self-esteem is supposed to give a company a competitive edge. If you were responsible for hiring a few new workers, how would you evaluate a given applicant's level of self-esteem?

4. Exercises to boost self-esteem and self-confidence often emphasize focusing on your positive qualities. Why might it also be important to be aware of your weak points to develop self-esteem?

5. A study mentioned in this chapter showed that people with high self-esteem are sometimes intolerant of people quite different from themselves. How would you explain these findings?

6. When you meet another person, on what basis do you conclude that he or she is self-confident?

7. What positive self-talk can you use after you have failed on a major assignment?

8. In what way does your program of studies contribute to building your self-esteem and self-confidence?

9. Many pharmaceutical firms actively recruit cheerleaders as sales representatives to call on doctors to recommend their brand of prescription drugs. The firms in question say that cheerleaders make good sales reps because they are so self-confident. What is your opinion on this controversial issue?

10. Interview a person whom you perceive to have a successful career. Ask that person to describe how he or she developed high self-esteem. Be prepared to discuss your findings in class.

## The Web Corner

*http://www.more-self-esteem.com*
(Measuring and building your self-esteem.)

*http://www.self-confidence.co.uk*
(Developing your self-confidence.)

*http://www.mindtools.com/selfconf.html*
(The difference between self-confidence and low self-confidence.)

### Internet Skills Builder: Learning More About Your Self-Esteem

The Self-Esteem Checklist in this chapter gave you one opportunity to assess you self-esteem. To gain additional insights into your self-esteem, visit http://www.more-selfesteem.com. Go to "Quizzes" under Free Resources, and take the self-esteem test. How does your score on this quiz compare to your score on The Self-Esteem Checklist? If your level of self-esteem as measured by the two quizzes is quite different (such as high vs. low), explain why this discrepancy might occur.

# Developing Your
# Human Relations Skills

### The Confetti Man

Nick Jablonski works for a manufacturer of property maintenance and recreational vehicles such as lawn mowers, snowblowers, and all-terrain vehicles. The company prospers even during downturns in the economy. This is true because when economic conditions are worrisome, many people invest more money in taking care of their property and enjoying themselves close to home instead of traveling. Nick holds the job title "celebrations assistant" as part of his work duties. The more traditional part of his job is to organize company events like picnics, sales meetings, and shareholder meetings.

When asked to explain the celebrations assistant part of his job in more detail, Nick replied with a smile, "My job is to help workers throughout the company celebrate accomplishments that help the company reach its goals. I'll give you a couple of examples. Suppose I learn that a production technician has exceeded quota on inserting dashboards on riding mowers. I will visit the factory floor and help the technician celebrate. Sometimes I will attach a smiley face to his or her work area. I might shake his or her hand or pat the person on the back. Yet to be dramatic, I will shower the person with confetti.

"Just last week I was told by her supervisor that one of our customer service reps was working on the phone with a woman suffering from arthritis. The customer was having a difficult time starting one of our lawn mowers. The rep stayed on the phone 20 minutes with the lady until she could pull the start cord correctly. The customer was so pleased that she wrote a letter to the CEO praising the helpfulness of the rep.

"My response was to visit the customer service rep's area and have a little celebration. Not only did I throw two bags of confetti, I blew a fog horn. I could tell the rep became a little embarrassed because she blushed. Yet I knew that I really boosted her self-esteem."

When Nick was asked why his work as a celebrations assistant boosted worker self-esteem, he answered as follows: "My job is to make our employees feel good about themselves. My smiley faces, my encouraging message, and especially my confetti throwing make people feel great. If people feel great about themselves and their accomplishments, their self-esteem heads north. It's that simple."

### Case Questions

1. To what extent do you think that the celebrations assistant is really boosting the self-esteem of workers?

2. Assume that Nick is successful in boosting worker self-esteem. How might this help the company?

3. Advise the CEO of the company in question as to whether having a celebrations assistant on the payroll is a good investment of company money.

**Source:** Several facts in this case are based on Jeffrey Zaslow, "The Most-Praised Generation Goes to Work," *The Wall Street Journal*, April 20, 2007, pp. W1, W7.

## Interpersonal Relations Case 11-2

### *Building Up Kristina*

Kristina Wright entered the front door of the half of a house she was sharing with Wendy Lopez. Her housemate said, "I don't see a smile on your face. How did the job hunt go today?"

"Not too well," replied Wright. "I had two interviews, but I doubt I'll be called back. After all, there are dozens of applicants looking for administrative assistant positions with better qualifications than mine. In this economy you really have to know the right people to land a job."

"Will you please stop it, Kristina? You're as good or better than the competition. You have your degree, and you have experience as an administrative intern. Besides that, you look great."

"That's easy for you to say, Wendy. You have a good job, and people like you. I'm just average, average, average. Even Lucky [Kristina's cocker spaniel] has an average name. And thousands of girls are named Kristina."

"With an attitude like that," replied Wendy, "you won't get hired. Be proud of who you are. You're somebody special."

"Thanks for the ego boost, my ever faithful friend. But I almost don't have the courage to go back out there tomorrow and face any more interviews."

### Case Questions

1. What seems to be Kristina's problem based on the brief information you have been given?
2. What recommendations can you make to Kristina to boost her self-confidence enough to get through any upcoming job interviews she might have?
3. How helpful might be the words of encouragement and advice that Wendy has given Kristina so far?

# REFERENCES

1. Excerpted from Laura Egodigwe, "Working it Out! How a Young Executive Overcomes Obstacles on the Job," *Black Enterprise*, January 2007, p. 55.
2. Michelle K. Duffy et al., "The Moderating Roles of Self-Esteem and Neuroticism in the Relationships Between Group and Individual Undermining Behavior," *Journal of Applied Psychology*, September 2006, p. 1067.
3. April O'Connell, Vincent O'Connell, and Lois-Ann Kuntz, *Choice and Change: The Psychology of Personal Growth and Interpersonal Relationships*, 7th edition (Upper Saddle River, NJ: Pearson/Prentice Hall, 2005), p. 3.
4. "Better Self-Esteem," http://www.utexas.edu/student/cmhc/booklets/selfesteem/selfest.html, 1999, p. 2.
5. Ibid.
6. Randall Edwards, "Is Self-Esteem Really All That Important?" *The APA Monitor*, May 1995, p. 43.
7. Research reported in Jeffrey Zaslow, "The Most-Praised Generation Goes to Work," *The Wall Street Journal*, April 20, 2007, p. W7.
8. David De Cremer et al., "Rewarding Leadership and Fair Procedures as Determinants of Self-Esteem," *Journal of Applied Psychology*, January 2005, pp. 3–12.
9. Eugene Raudsepp, "Strong Self-Esteem Can Help You Advance," *CareerJournal.com* (*The Wall Street Journal*, http://online.wsj.com/careers), August 10, 2004.
10. Research reported in Melissa Dittman, "Study Links Jealousy with Aggression, Low Self-Esteem," *Psychology Today*, February 2005, p. 13.
11. Jon L. Pierce, Donald G. Gardner, Larry L. Cummings, and Randall B. Dunman, "Organization-Based Self-Esteem: Construct Definition, Measurement, and Validation," *Academy of Management Journal*, September 1989, p. 623.
12. Nathaniel Branden, *Self-Esteem at Work: How Confident People Make Powerful Companies* (San Francisco: Jossey-Bass, 1998); Timothy A. Judge and Joyce E. Bono, "Relationship of Core Self-Evaluations Traits—Self-Esteem, Generalized Self-Efficacy, Locus of Control, and Emotional Stability—with Job Satisfaction and Job Performance: A Meta-Analysis," *Journal of Applied Psychology*, February 2001, pp. 80–92.
13. Duffey et al., "The Moderating Role of Self-Esteem and Neuroticism," p. 1069.
14. Research reported in David Dent, "Bursting the Self-Esteem Bubble," *Psychology Today*, March/April 2002, p. 16.
15. Quoted in Carlin Flora, "The Measuring Game: Why You Think You'll Never Stack Up," *Psychology Today*, September/October 2005, p. 44.
16. Cited in Julia M. Klein, "The Illusion of Rejection," *Psychology Today*, January/February 2005, p. 30.
17. Research reported in Melissa Dittmann, "Self-Esteem That's Based on External Sources Has Mental Health Consequences, Study Says," *Monitor on Psychology*, December 2002, p. 16.
18. Research mentioned in book review by E. R. Snyder in *Contemporary Psychology*, July 1998, p. 482.
19. Daniel L. Aroz, "The Manager's Self-Concept," *Human Resources Forum*, July 1989, p. 4.
20. "Better Self-Esteem," pp. 3–4.
21. Ibid, pp. 4–5.
22. Cited in "Self-Esteem: You'll Need It to Succeed," *Executive Strategies*, September 1993, p. 12.
23. Raudsepp, "Strong Self-Esteem Can Help You Advance."
24. "Building Self-Esteem: A Self-Help Guide," http://mentalhealth.samhsa.gov/, p. 2, accessed September 7, 2007.
25. Marilyn E. Gist and Terence R. Mitchell, "Self-Efficacy: A Theoretical Analysis of Its Determinants and Malleability," *Academy of Management Review*, April 1992, pp. 183–211.
26. George P. Hollenbeck and Douglas T. Hall, "Self-Confidence and Leader Performance," *Organizational Dynamics*, Issue 3, 2004, pp. 261–264.
27. Jay T. Knippen and Thad B. Green, "Building Self-Confidence," *Supervisory Management*, August 1989, pp. 22–27.
28. Quoted in "Entrepreneurs Need Attitude: Power of Being Positive Can Help You to Succeed in Spite of Setbacks," Knight Ridder, September 16, 2002.
29. D. Brian McNatt and Timothy A. Judge, "Boundary Conditions of the Galeta Effect: A Field Experiment and Constructive Replication," *Academy of Management Journal*, August 2004, 550–565.
30. Price Pritchett, *HardOptimism: Developing Deep Strengths for Managing Uncertainty, Opportunity, Adversity, and Change* (Dallas, TX: Pritchett, 2004), p. 16.
31. Frances Thornton, Gayle Privette, and Charles M. Bundrick, "Peak Performance of Business Leaders: An Experience Parallel to Self-Actualization Theory," *Journal of Business and Psychology*, Winter 1999, pp. 253–264.

# 12

# Becoming an Effective Leader

## Learning Objectives

**After reading and studying this chapter and doing the exercises, you should be able to**

1 Identify key leadership traits for personal development.

2 Develop several attitudes and behaviors that will help you appear charismatic.

3 Develop your team leadership skills.

4 Understand how you can develop your leadership potential.

## Outline

1 **Key Leadership Traits to Develop    371**
Self-Confidence
Assertiveness
Trustworthiness and Morality
Emotional Stability
Sense of Humor
Self-Awareness and Self-Objectivity
Cognitive Skills and Clarity
Emotional Intelligence
Passion and Enthusiasm

2 **Suggestions for Developing Charisma    380**

3 **Developing Team Leadership Skills    383**
Build a Mission Statement
Show Your Team Members That They Are Trusted
Establish a Sense of Urgency and High Performance Standards
Hold Question-and-Answer Sessions with the Team
Encourage Team Members to RecognizeEach Other's Accomplishments
Encourage Honest Criticism
Use Team Symbols
Use Peer Evaluations
Help Team Members See the Big Picture
Minimize Formation of In-Groups and Out-Groups

4 **Developing Your Leadership Potential    391**

Mary DiSalvo is the director of operations of a printing company that specializes in printing shrink-wrapped labels for food and consumer products including bottled water, orange juice, and packaged meat. Company CEO Bruce Denton observed that over a six-year period, DiSalvo's group had the highest produxctivity and lowest employee turnover at the company. Denton had a hunch that DiSalvo's passion for people and her love of printing had something to do with her outstanding record. However, he wanted more insight into what made for superb leadership at his company. So with Mary's permission, an outside human relations specialist interviewed several people about their experiences working in the company, and what they thought of Mary's leadership.

*Cheryl, a shipping supervisor, described DiSalvo's leadership in these terms: "Mary is so gung ho about labels and production efficiency that her excitement rubs off on you. She makes us feel that we are on a crusade to produce the best labels in the business. At the same time, she really cares about everybody who works at the company. I remember when she personally went to help out a production worker whose house was severely damaged by a tree falling on it."*

*Jeff, a quality technician, expressed these ideas to the human relations interviewer: "I don't have too much direct contact with Mary because she is two levels up the ladder from me. But I feel her impact almost every day. Mary is committed to quality, and her e-mails to the company about quality make me feel that my work is very important. Mary is the hardest worker in the plant, so she sets a good example for us. She also has a great warm smile and a cheerful attitude that makes you want to do your best."* [1]

■ **Leadership**

the ability to inspire support and confidence among the people who are needed to achieve common goals

As in the story just presented, effective leaders have a combination of admirable qualities, including expertise, a passion to succeed, high energy, and the ability to inspire others. In working toward improving your leadership ability, the following definition is a goal to strive for. **Leadership** is the ability to inspire support and confidence among the people who are needed to achieve company goals. A company president might have to inspire thousands of people, while a team leader is concerned with inspiring about six people. Both of these leaders nonetheless play an important role.

Leadership has also been defined in many other ways. Bill Bradley, former U.S. senator and professional basketball player, uses a definition of leadership that points to what a leader actually accomplishes. Bradley perceives leadership as getting people to think, believe, see, and do what they might not have without your presence. [2] In other words, the leader makes a difference.

Becoming a leader does not necessarily mean that the company has to put you in charge of others (or assign you a formal leadership position). You can also rise to leadership when people come to respect your opinion and personal characteristics and are thus influenced by you. Leadership is thought by many to exist at all levels with people anywhere in the organization being able to influence others if they have the right skills or know the right work procedures. [3] Your greatest opportunity for exerting leadership will come about from a combination of holding a formal position and exerting personal influence. An individual with appealing personal characteristics and expertise who is placed in a position of authority will find it relatively easy to exert leadership.

The purpose of this chapter is twofold. One is to make you aware of the basic concepts you need to become a leader. The other purpose is to point you toward developing skills necessary for leadership effectiveness.

# Key Leadership Traits to Develop

An important part of being an effective leader is to have the *right stuff.* This section and the following one about charisma describe personal attributes that help a person lead others in many situations. Recognize, however, that radically different situations require a different set of leadership characteristics. For example, a leader might have to be more assertive with group members performing distasteful work than with those whose work is enjoyable.

■ **Learning Objective 1**

Each of the nine leadership traits described next, and shown in Figure 12-1, can be developed. For such development to take place, you need to be aware of the importance of the personal characteristic, and then monitor your own behavior to make progress. To assist you with such development, the description of each trait is accompanied by a suggestion for improvement.

## SELF-CONFIDENCE

In virtually every leadership setting, it is important for the leader to be realistically self-confident. A leader who is self-assured without being bombastic or overbearing instills confidence in group members. Self-confidence was among the first leadership traits researchers identified. Current research with leaders in many situations has continued to underscore the importance of this trait. A series of research studies have shown that increased self-confidence can bring about improvement in performance, including helping a group attain its goals. [4] In addition to being self-confident, the leader must project that self-confidence to the group. [5] Self-confidence is not only a personality trait. It also refers to the behavior a person exhibits in a number of situations. It is similar to being cool under pressure. We can conclude that a person is a self-confident leader when he or she retains composure during a crisis, such as when the company suffers flood damage during a busy season.

You can appear more self-confident to the group by using definitive wording, maintaining good posture, and making appropriate gestures such as pointing an index finger outward. Developing self-confidence is a lifelong process of performing well in a variety of situations. You need a series of easy victories to establish self-confidence. Further development of your self-confidence requires performing well in challenging circumstances. Taking risks, such as volunteering to work on an unfamiliar project, contributes to self-confidence when the risk proves to be worthwhile.

## ASSERTIVENESS

A widely recognized leadership trait is **assertiveness**, being forthright in expressing demands, opinions, feelings, and attitudes. If you are self-confident, it is easier to be assertive with people. An assertive team leader might say, "I know that the ice storm put us out of business for 4 days, but we can make up the time by working smart and pulling together. Within 30 days, we will have met or sur-

■ **Assertiveness**
being forthright in expressing demands, opinions, feelings, and attitudes

**Figure    12-1**

**Nine Key Leadership Traits**
People who possess the traits listed in this figure are usually well suited to being an effective leader. However, many other traits and behaviors are also important contributors to effective leadership.

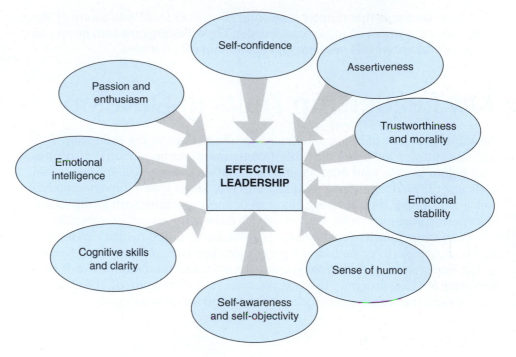

passed our goals for the quarter." This statement reflects self-confidence in her leadership capabilities and assertiveness in expressing exactly what she thinks.

Assertiveness helps leaders perform many tasks and achieve goals. Among them are confronting group members about their mistakes, demanding higher performance, and setting high expectations. An assertive leader will also make legitimate demands on higher management, such as asking for equipment needed by the group.

To be assertive differs significantly from being aggressive or passive (or nonassertive). Aggressive people express their demands in an overly pushy, obnoxious, and abrasive manner. Passive people suppress their own ideas, attitudes, feelings, and thoughts as if they were likely to be perceived as controversial. Nonassertive people are also too accommodating. A series of three studies with a variety of workers indicated that leaders with moderate assertiveness were considered more effective than leaders low (passive) or high (aggressive) in this trait. [6]

Developing assertiveness is much like attempting to become less shy. You must force yourself to take the opportunity to express your feelings and demands. For example, if something a teammate does annoys you, make the statement, "I enjoy working with you in general, but what you are doing now annoys me." You can also practice expressing positive emotion, such as telling a coworker, "I'm happy that you and I are working on this project together, because I like your approach to work."

Expressing demands is easier for most people to practice than expressing feelings. People who do start expressing their demands are often surprised at the result. For example, if you are contemplating the purchase of an item that is beyond your budget, try this statement: "I like this product very uch. Yet all I have to spend is $75 below your asking price. Can we do business?" For a reading on your own level of assertiveness, do Self-Assessment Quiz 12-1.

# Self-Assessment Quiz 12-1

## The Assertiveness Scale

**Directions:** Check whether each of the following statements is *mostly true* or *mostly false* as it applies to you. If in doubt about your reaction to a particular statement, think of how you would generally respond.

| | Mostly True | Mostly False |
|---|---|---|
| 1. It is extremely difficult for me to turn down a sales representative if he or she is a nice person. | _____ | _____ |
| 2. I express criticism freely. | _____ | _____ |
| 3. If another person were being very unfair, I would bring it to his or her attention. | _____ | _____ |
| 4. Work is no place to let your feelings show. | _____ | _____ |
| 5. There's no use in asking for favors; people get what they deserve. | _____ | _____ |
| 6. Business is not the place for tact; say what you think. | _____ | _____ |
| 7. If a person looked as if he or she were in a hurry, I would let that person in front of me in a supermarket line. | _____ | _____ |
| 8. A weakness of mine is that I'm too nice a person. | _____ | _____ |
| 9. I usually give other people what they want rather than do what I think is best, just to avoid an argument. | _____ | _____ |
| 10. If the mood strikes me, I will laugh out loud in public. | _____ | _____ |
| 11. People would describe me as too outspoken. | _____ | _____ |
| 12. I am quite willing to return merchandise that I find has even a minor blemish. | _____ | _____ |
| 13. I dread having to express anger toward a coworker. | _____ | _____ |
| 14. People often say that I'm too reserved and emotionally controlled. | _____ | _____ |
| 15. Nice guys and gals finish last in business. | _____ | _____ |
| 16. I fight for my rights down to the last detail. | _____ | _____ |
| 17. I have no misgivings about returning an overcoat to the store if it doesn't fit me right. | _____ | _____ |
| 18. After I have an argument with a person, I try to avoid him or her. | _____ | _____ |
| 19. I insist on my spouse (or roommate or partner) doing his or her fair share of undesirable chores. | _____ | _____ |
| 20. It is difficult for me to look directly at another person when the two of us are in disagreement. | _____ | _____ |
| 21. I have cried among friends more than once. | _____ | _____ |
| 22. If someone near me at a movie kept up a conversation with another person, I would ask him or her to stop. | _____ | _____ |

*(continued)*

## Self-Assessment Quiz **12-1** (*Continued*)

23. I am able to turn down social engagements with people I do not particularly care for.   _____   _____

24. It is in poor taste to express what you really feel about another individual.   _____   _____

25. I sometimes show my anger by swearing at or belittling another person.   _____   _____

26. I am reluctant to speak up at a meeting.   _____   _____

27. I find it relatively easy to ask friends for small favors such as giving me a ride to work while my car is being repaired.   _____   _____

28. If another person were talking very loudly in a restaurant and it bothered me, I would inform that person.   _____   _____

29. I often finish other people's sentences for them.   _____   _____

30. It is relatively easy for me to express love and affection toward another person.   _____   _____

Total score   _____   _____

### Scoring and Interpretation:

The answers for determining your assertiveness are as follows:

| | | | |
|---|---|---|---|
| 1. Mostly false | 9. Mostly false | 17. Mostly true | 25. Mostly true |
| 2. Mostly true | 10. Mostly true | 18. Mostly false | 26. Mostly false |
| 3. Mostly true | 11. Mostly true | 19. Mostly true | 27. Mostly true |
| 4. Mostly false | 12. Mostly true | 20. Mostly false | 28. Mostly true |
| 5. Mostly false | 13. Mostly false | 21. Mostly true | 29. Mostly true |
| 6. Mostly true | 14. Mostly false | 22. Mostly true | 30. Mostly true |
| 7. Mostly false | 15. Mostly true | 23. Mostly true | |
| 8. Mostly false | 16. Mostly true | 24. Mostly false | |

Score yourself a +1 for each of your answers that agrees with the scoring key. If your score is 15 or less, it is probable that you are currently nonassertive. A score of 16 through 24 suggests that you are assertive. A score of 25 or higher suggests that you are aggressive. Retake this quiz about 30 days from now to give yourself some indication of the stability of your answers. You might also discuss your answers with a close friend to determine whether that person has a similar perception of your assertiveness.

## TRUSTWORTHINESS AND MORALITY

Group members consistently believe that leaders must display honesty, integrity, and credibility—and therefore must be trustworthy. Right Manage-ment Consultants conducted a survey of 570 employees in which they found that the white-collar workers value honesty and integrity in a manager more than any other trait. When asked, "What is the most important trait or attribute that the leader of your company should possess?" 24 percent of the survey participants cited honesty and 16 percent named integrity/morals, or ethics. [7] Leaders themselves believe that honesty makes a difference in their effectiveness.

Being honest with team members helps build trust, which in turn leads to good cooperation and team spirit. In recent years, trust in business leaders has been damaged by financial scandals in well-known companies. Executives in those companies enriched themselves by selling company stock just before the time they correctly forecast that the stock price would tumble. At the same time, the executives encouraged employees to not sell their stock, or to purchase more. Also, records were falsified to enhance the value of stock purchases by executives.

To trust group members, the leader has to be willing to give up some control over them, such as letting group members make more decisions and not challenging their expense accounts. The following anecdote, told by Fred Smith, the founder of FedEx, illustrates what trust can mean in an organization:

> *A blizzard shut down a radio relay located on top of a mountain, cutting phone service to several FedEx offices. The phone company said it would take five days to repair the problem. On his own, a FedEx telecommunications expert named Hal chartered a helicopter to get to the site. The pilot was unable to land, but he got close enough to the ground for Hal to jump safely. Hal slogged through the deep snow and fixed the problem.*

According to Smith, Hal went to such great lengths to keep the organization going because there was mutual trust between employer and employee. Hal knew he would not be reprimanded for going to such expense to fix the telephone problem. [8]

Being moral is closely linked to trustworthiness because a moral leader is more likely to be trusted. A leader with high morality would perceive that he or she had an ethical responsibility to group members, as well as outsiders. [9] The moral leader would therefore not give preferential treatment to workers with whom he had an friendship outside of work. At the same time, the moral leader would not try to fool customers or make up false excuses for not paying bills on time to suppliers.

Chapter 14, about ethical behavior, provides details about honesty on the job. Being honest is an effective way of getting others to trust you. A starting point in developing a strong sense of honesty and morality is to follow a variation of the Golden Rule: Be as honest with others as you want them to be with you.

## EMOTIONAL STABILITY

Anyone who has ever worked for an unstable supervisor will attest to the importance of emotional stability as a leadership trait. (As described in Chapter 3, emotional stability is equivalent to scoring low on neuroticism in the Five-Factor Model.) Emotional stability is important for a leader because group members expect and need consistency in the way they are treated.

Kenneth Chenault, the chief executive officer of American Express—and the first African American man to be the top executive of a Fortune 500 company—is known for his even temperament. Although an assertive and tough executive, he is calm and in control. A survey of Chenault's former and present colleagues found that his personality is free of the rough edges that usually accompany fierce ambition. Nobody questioned could recall Chenault losing his temper or even raising his voice. Chenault's emotional stability was also demonstrated by how well he led AmEx cope with the difficult times following the terrorist attacks of 9/11. Part of his recovery plan was to shift the company from primarily an offline business to one that was mostly online. Chenault emphasizes that having the right values (such as caring for people) gives stability to a person's career. [10]

Emotional stability is difficult to develop, but people can learn to control many of their emotional outbursts. People who cannot control their emotions, yet still want to become leaders, should seek assistance from a mental health professional.

## SENSE OF HUMOR

A sense of humor is on the borderline between being a trait and a behavior. However you classify it, the effective use of humor is considered an important part of a leader's role. Humor serves such functions in the workplace as relieving tension and boredom and defusing hostility. Because humor helps the leader dissolve tension and defuse conflict, it helps him or her exert power over the group. A study conducted in a large financial institution indicated that leaders who made frequent use of humor had higher-performing units. (Another interpretation is that it's easier to laugh when the group is performing well!) Among the forms of humor used by the managers were "[using] humor to take the edge off during stressful periods" and "[making] us laugh at ourselves when we are too serious." [11]

Self-effacing humor is the choice of comedians and organizational leaders alike. When you are self-effacing, nobody else is insulted or slighted, yet a point can be made. A marketing executive at Gateway (now part of Acer Computer) said a few years ago to a subcontractor, "I want you people to design photo software so uncomplicated that even managers at my level could learn how to use it."

Creativity is required for humor. Just as creativity can be enhanced with practice, so can a sense of humor. To gather some experience in making humorous comments in the workplace, do Skill-Building Exercise 12-1.

## SELF-AWARENESS AND SELF-OBJECTIVITY

Effective leaders are aware of their strengths and limitations. This awareness enables them to capitalize upon their strengths and overcome their weaknesses. A leader, for example, might realize that he or she is naturally distrustful of others. Awareness of this problem cautions the leader to not distrust people without good evidence. Another leader might realize that he or she is adept at counseling team members. This leader might then emphasize that activity in an effort to improve performance. Self-objectivity refers to being detached or nonsubjective about your perceived strengths and limitations.

Another way in which self-awareness and self-objectivity contribute to leadership effectiveness is that these traits help a person become an authentic leader. Such a leader demonstrates passion for his or her pupose, practices values consistently, and leads with the heart as well as the head. Instead of being

## Skill-Building Exercise 12-1

### The Witty Leader

Students gather in problem-solving groups of about five to invent humorous comments a leader might make in the following scenarios. After the problem-solving groups have formulated their witty comments, the comments can be shared and compared. Groups also have the option of deciding that a particular scenario is too grim for humor.

**Scenario 1:** A store manager wants to communicate to employees how bad business has been lately. Sales have declined about 20 percent for three consecutive weeks.

**Scenario 2:** A leader has to communicate to the group that salaries have been frozen for another year because of limited business. The leader knows that group members have been eagerly awaiting news about the salary increase.

**Scenario 3:** Owing to an unprecedented surge in orders, all salaried personnel will be required to work about 65 hours per week for the next 10 weeks. Furthermore, the office and factory must be staffed on Saturdays and Sundays.

**Scenario 4:** A consulting firm that specializes in helping companies downsize their workforce has seen the demand for its services decline substantially in recent months. The company must therefore downsize itself. The company founder has to announce the layoff decision to the company.

Observers might rate the attempts at humor on a 1 (low) to 10 (high) scale. Observe also if any of the role players made you laugh.

---

a phony, or acting out of character, the person is genuine. Authenticity helps the leader be perceived as trustworthy. [12] "Being yourself" thus contributes to leadership effectiveness assuming that you have personal qualities, such as those presented in this chapter, that facilitate leadership. Mary DiSalvo, the leader described in the chapter opener, appears to be an authentic leader.

You can enhance your self-awareness and self-objectivity by regularly asking for feedback from others. You then compare the feedback to your self-perception of your standing on the same factor. You might, for example, think that you communicate in colorful, interesting terms. In speaking to others about your communication style, you might discover that others agree. You can then conclude that your self-awareness about your communication skills is accurate.

Another technique for improving self-awareness and self-objectivity is to take several self-examination exercises such as those found in this text. Even if they do not describe you exactly, they stimulate you to reflect on your characteristics and behaviors.

## COGNITIVE SKILLS AND CLARITY

Mental ability, as well as personality, is important for leadership success. To inspire people, bring about constructive changes, and solve problems

■ **Cognitive factors**
the collective terms for problem-solving and intellectual skills

creatively, leaders need to be mentally sharp. Problem-solving and intellectual skills are referred to collectively as **cognitive factors.** The term *cognition* refers to the mental process or faculty by which knowledge is gathered.

A major reason that cognitive skills have increased in importance for leadership is that they enable the leader to acquire knowledge. The processing of knowledge is now considered to be the *core competence* (key ability) of organizations. The leader's role is to both originate useful ideas and collect them from smart people throughout the organization. [13] Two cognitive skills were discussed in Chapter 3: mental ability and the personal factor of openness to experience. Another cognitive skill of major importance is *knowledge of the business,* or technical skill. An effective leader has to be technically or professionally competent in some discipline, particularly when leading a group of specialists. It is difficult for the leader to establish rapport with group members when he or she does not know what they are doing. A related damper on leadership effectiveness is when the group does not respect the leader's technical skill.

High intelligence is particularly important for leaders, when they have the opportunity to make decisions by themselves and provide direction (such as giving technical instructions) to group members. [14] Problem-solving ability is less important when the leader delegates most of his or her responsibilities to others (or empowers them). High intelligence is important for three major aspects of the leader's job. One aspect is dealing with tasks such as developing ideas for cost cutting. A second aspect is working with and through other people, or the human relations focus. The third is judging oneself and adapting one's behavior accordingly as in self-awareness and self-objectivity. [15]

Closely related to cognitive skills is the leader's ability to be clear about what needs to be accomplished to build a better future, even if the future is next week. Based on his study of some of the world's most successful business leaders, Marcus Buckingham concludes that the leader should define the future in vivid terms so people can see where they are headed. The leader also has to be clear about such matters as who the group is trying to serve. [16] For example, when Deborah Wahl Meyer was appointed as chief marketing officer for Chrysler, he reasoned that her main challenge would be crafting a clear identity for the Chrysler brand. She noted that the Jeep and Dodge nameplates "have a lot of strength and equity in the market." [17] Meyer had in mind serving the consumer group of those who purchase vehicles. A beauty salon operator could provide clarity to her hairstylists with a statement such as, "Our real purpose here is to boost our customers' self-esteem. Every customer who leaves our salon should feel a little better about himself or herself."

Increasing one's mental ability, or raw intelligence, may not be easy to accomplish. Yet people can develop their cognitive skills by continuous study and by working on challenging problems. The mere act of keeping up with developments in your field can keep you mentally sharp. For a leader to provide clarity, the leader would have to think through clearly what it is that he or she is really attempting to accomplish.

# EMOTIONAL INTELLIGENCE

Emotional intelligence, as described in Chapter 3, refers to the ability to recognize your emotions and those of people around you. Emotional intelligence also refers to being able to work effectively with the emotions of others to resolve problems, including listening and empathizing. As such, emotional intelligence is a blend of psychological skills that enable the leader to relate effectively to people. Research conducted by Daniel Goleman in many different firms suggests that superb leaders all have one trait in common: superb emotional intelligence. [19] A specific example is that an effective manager or leader can often recognize the motives behind an employee's actions.

> "Leadership is first figuring out what's right, and then explaining it to people, as opposed to having people explain to you what's right, and then just saying what they want to hear."
> —Rudy Giuliani, former former mayor of New York City, and president of a consulting firm. [18]

*Visualize yourself as a team leader. Vanessa, one of the team members, says to you, "I'm worried about Rick. I think he needs help. He looks like he has a drinking problem." If you have good emotional intelligence, you might think to yourself, "I wonder why Vanessa is telling me this. Is she simply being helpful? Or is she out to backstab Rick?" Therefore, you would seek some tangible evidence about Rick's alleged problem before acting. You would also seek to spend more time with Vanessa so you can better understand her motives.*

*With much less emotional intelligence, you would immediately get in touch with Rick, accuse him of having a drinking problem, and tell him to get help or get fired.*

Emotional intelligence is also reflected in a leader who incorporates the human touch into business activities, such as building personal relationships with employees and customers. Several years ago Robert A. Eckert was recruited from Kraft Foods to become chair and CEO of toy maker Mattel. At the time Mattel was in deep financial trouble, and key managers were leaving the company. Eckert moved quickly to bring the famous toy manufacturer back to health. The first steps he took were to share meals with employees in the company cafeteria at every opportunity. During these lunches he engaged in candid dialogue with employees chosen at random. He reassured employees that their personal growth and development were integral to his plans for rebuilding Mattel. Eckert notes, "In this case the emotional intelligence I'd developed over the years was even more important to my success than my traditional, analytical management skills were." [20]

Leaders with emotional intelligence are in tune with the thoughts and emotions of their own and those of other people. The emotionally intelligent leader recognizes that emotions are contagious, such as optimists making other workers optimistic, and pessimists making other workers pessimistic. At the same time, these leaders know that their own emotions are powerful drivers of their group member's moods, and ultimately performance. [21]

Emotional intelligence can be developed through working on some of its components, as described in Chapter 3. It is also important to develop the habit of looking to understand the feelings and emotions of people around you. Ask yourself, "How do I feel about what's going on here?" When you have a hunch about people's motives, look for feedback in the future to see if you were right. For example, a little investigation might indicate that Vanessa and Rick are indeed rivals and have a personality clash.

## PASSION AND ENTHUSIASM

A prominent characteristic of effective leaders is the passion and enthusiasm they have for their work, much like the same quality in creative people. The passion reflects itself in such ways as an intense liking for the business, the customers, and employees. Passion is also reflected in a relentless drive to get work accomplished and an obsession for achieving company goals. Passion for their work is especially evident in entrepreneurial leaders and small business owners who are preoccupied with growing their businesses. Many leaders use the term *love* to describe their passion for their work, business, and employees.

To display passion and enthusiasm for your work, you must first find work that creates an inner spark. The work that you choose should be equally or more exciting than your favorite pastime. If not everything about your job excites you, search for its most satisfying or intrinsically motivating elements. For example, the Mattel executive described previously is so excited about the interpersonal aspects of his work that his passion inspires employees.

■ **Learning Objective 2**

# Suggestions for Developing Charisma

■ **Charisma**

a special quality of leaders whose purposes, powers, and extraordinary determination differentiate them from others. (However, people besides leaders can be charismatic.)

The study of leadership in recent years has emphasized the importance of inspirational leaders who guide others toward great heights of achievement. Such leaders are said to possess **charisma,** a special quality of leaders whose purposes, powers, and extraordinary determination differentiate them from others. [22] Being charismatic can make a leader's job easier, because leaders have to energize group members. [23]

An important fact about charisma is that it reflects a subjective perception on the part of the person being influenced. Many people regard a leader such as Steve Jobs of Apple Corp. as being powerful and inspirational. Yet he is also disliked by many people who consider him to be arrogant, prone to throwing tamper tantrums, and a control freak.

The term *charisma* is most frequently used in association with nationally and internationally known leaders. Yet first-level supervisors, team leaders, and minor sports coaches can also be charismatic. Possessing a naturally dynamic personality is a major contributor to charisma, but a person can engage in many tangible actions that also contribute to charisma. What follows are a number of suggestions for behaving charismatically, all based on characteristics and behaviors often found among charismatic leaders. If you are not currently a leader, remember that being perceived as charismatic will help you become one.

1. **Communicate a vision.** A charismatic leader offers an exciting image of where the organization is headed and how to get there. A vision is more than a forecast because it describes an ideal version of the future of an entire organization or an organizational unit such as a department. Richard Branson, the colorful British entrepreneur, has inspired hundreds of employees with his vision of the Virgin brand being a leader in dozens

of fields. Among his accomplishments to reach this vision are the Virgin Atlantic airline, Virgin Megastores, and Virgin Cinema. The supervisor of paralegal services might communicate a vision such as, "Our paralegal group will become known as the most professional and helpful paralegal group in Arizona." A visionary leader should also have the courage to communicate the vision to others, and to help implement the vision. [24] For the paralegal supervisor, part of implementing the vision might be teaching new technology skills to the paralegals.

Skill-Building Exercise 12-2 will give you a chance to develop visioning skills (a buzzword in business).

2. **Make frequent use of metaphors and analogies.** To inspire people, the charismatic leader uses colorful language and exciting metaphors and analogies. Develop metaphors to inspire people around you. A metaphor commonly used after a group has

## Skill-Building Exercise 12-2

### Creating a Vision

The class organizes into small problem-solving groups. Each group constructs a vision for a unit of an organization or for a total organization of its choosing. Students can choose a well-known business firm, government agency, or an organization with which they are familiar. The vision should be approximately 25 words long and depict a glorious future. A vision is not simply a straightforward goal, such as, "In 2010 our firm will gross $10 million in sales." Remember, the vision statement drawn should inspire people throughout the organization.

If class time permits, volunteers can share their visions with other class members who will provide feedback on the clarity and inspirational qualities of the visions presented.

### Back to the Opening Case

Several of Mary DiSalvo's leadership qualities were mentioned in the opening case. She also is a leader with vision. She says, "As food-product safety becomes more of an issue in our world, the importance of secure labeling and packaging will multiply, and our company will be at the forefront."

suffered a setback is, "Like the phoenix, we will rise from the ashes of defeat." To pick up the spirits of her maintenance group, a maintenance supervisor told the group, "We're a lot like the heating and cooling system in a house. A lot of people don't give us much thought, but without us their lives would be very uncomfortable."

3. **Inspire trust and confidence.** Make your deeds consistent with your promises. As mentioned earlier in this chapter, being trustworthy is a key leadership trait. Get people to believe in your competence by making your accomplishments known in a polite, tactful way. The *socialized charismatic* is likely to inspire trust and confidence because such a leader is ethical and wants to accomplish activities that help others rather than pursuing personal ends such as glory and power. [25]

4. **Be highly energetic and goal oriented.** Impress others with your energy and resourcefulness. To increase your energy supply, exercise frequently, eat well, and get ample rest. Closely related to being goal oriented is being optimistic about what you and the group can accomplish. People also associate optimism with energy. Being grumpy is often associated with being low on energy. You can add to an image of energy by raising and lowering your voice frequently, and avoiding a slow pace.

5. **Be emotionally expressive and warm.** A key characteristic of charismatic leaders is the ability to express feelings openly. Assertiveness is therefore an important component of charisma. In dealing with team members, refer to your feelings at the time, such as, "I'm excited because I know we are going to hit our year-end target by mid-October." Nonverbal emotional expressiveness, such as warm gestures and occasional touching (nonsexual) of group members, also exhibits charisma. Remember, however, that many people resent being touched when at work. Frequent smiling is another way of being emotionally expressive. Also, a warm smile seems to indicate a confident, caring person, which contributes to a perception of charisma.

6. **Make ample use of true stories.** An excellent way of building rapport is to tell stories that deliver a message. People like to hear stories about how a department or company went through hard times when it started, such as how Dell Computer began in a dormitory room at the University of Texas. Telling positive stories has become a widely accepted technique for building relationships with employees. Storytelling adds a touch of warmth to the teller and helps build connections among people who become familiar with the same story.

7. **Be candid and direct.** Practice being direct in saying what you want, rather than being indirect and evasive. If you want someone to help you, don't ask, "Are you busy?" Instead, ask, "Can you help me with a problem I'm having right now?"

8. **Make everybody you meet feel that he or she is important.** For example, at a company social gathering, shake the hand of every person you meet. Also, thank people frequently both orally and by written notes.

9. **Multiply the effectiveness of your handshake.** Shake firmly without creating pain, and make enough eye contact to notice the color of the other

person's eyes. When you take that much trouble, you project care and concern. [26]

10. **Stand up straight and use other nonverbal signals of self-confidence.** Practice good posture. Minimize fidgeting, scratching, foot tapping, and speaking in a monotone. Walk at a rapid pace without appearing to be panicked. Dress fashionably without going to the extreme that people notice your clothes more than they notice you.

11. **Be willing to take personal risks.** Charismatic leaders are typically risk takers, and risk taking adds to their charisma. Risks you might take would include extending additional credit to a start-up business, suggesting a bright but costly idea, and recommending that a former felon be given a chance in your firm.

12. **Be self-promotional.** Charismatic leaders are not shy. Instead, they toot their own horns and allow others to know how important they are. Without appearing self-absorbed, you, too, might let others know of your tangible accomplishments. Explain to others the key role that you played on your team or how you achieved a few tough goals.

Despite the importance of developing charisma, being excessively and flamboyantly charismatic can backfire because others may perceive you as self-serving. Therefore, the idea is to sprinkle your charisma with humility, such as admitting when you make a mistake. Also, in recent years top-level management at some companies have replaced highly charismatic, rock-star-like leaders with those who concentrate more on running the business instead of gathering publicity for themselves.

# Developing Team Leadership Skills

■ Learning Objective 3

As organizations rely heavily on teams, some of the best opportunities for practicing leadership occur as a team leader. A team leader typically reports to a higher-level manager. The team leader is not a boss in the old-fashioned sense, but a facilitator or coach who shares decision making with team members. (A facilitator is a person who helps make things happen without taking control.) A team leader practices **participative leadership,** or sharing authority with the group. Being a participative leader does not mean that the leader just stays out of the way and provides no guidance or encouragement to team members. Recent research conducted with Norwegian companies supports the belief that danger lurks in the hands of leaders who turn over all responsibility to the group. Employees who received almost no direction from their boss suffered from role ambiguity—confusion about what needs to be done. As a result, these employees suffered from stress, and often found themselves in conflict with each other, including bullying. [27] (The conflict and bullying may have stemmed from workers in dispute over who should do what.)

■ **Participative leadership**
sharing authority with the group

Self-Assessment Quiz 12-2 gives you an opportunity to gauge your attitudes toward being a participative leader. We next discuss ten techniques that would contribute to your effectiveness as a team leader, as outlined in Figure 12-2.

## Self-Assessment Quiz   **12-2**

### What Style of Leader Are You or Would You Be?

**Directions:** Check whether each of the following questions is *mostly true* or *mostly false*, keeping in mind what you have done, or think you would do, in the scenarios and attitudes described.

| | Mostly True | Mostly False |
|---|---|---|
| 1. I am more likely to take care of a high-impact assignment myself than turn it over to a group member. | _____ | _____ |
| 2. I would prefer the analytical aspects of a manager's job rather than working directly with group members. | _____ | _____ |
| 3. An important part of my approach to managing a group is to keep the members informed almost daily of any information that could affect their work. | _____ | _____ |
| 4. It's a good idea to give two people in the group the same problem, and then choose what appears to be the best solution. | _____ | _____ |
| 5. It makes good sense for the leader or manager to stay somewhat aloof from the group, so he or she can make a tough decision when necessary. | _____ | _____ |
| 6. I look for opportunities to obtain group input before making a decision, even on straightforward issues. | _____ | _____ |
| 7. I would reverse a decision if several of the group members presented evidence that I was wrong. | _____ | _____ |
| 8. Differences of opinion in the work group are healthy. | _____ | _____ |
| 9. I think that activities to build team spirit, like the team fixing up a low-income family's house on a Saturday, are an excellent investment of time. | _____ | _____ |
| 10. If my group were hiring a new member, I would like the person to be interviewed by the entire group. | _____ | _____ |
| 11. An effective team leader today uses e-mail for about 98 percent of communication with team members. | _____ | _____ |
| 12. Some of the best ideas are likely to come from the group members rather than the manager. | _____ | _____ |
| 13. If our group were going to have a banquet, I would get input from each member on what type of food should be served. | _____ | _____ |
| 14. I have never seen a statue of a committee in a museum or park, so why bother making decisions by a committee if you want to be recognized? | _____ | _____ |
| 15. I dislike it intensely when a group member challenges my position on an issue. | _____ | _____ |
| 16. I typically explain to group members what method they should use to accomplish an assigned task. | _____ | _____ |

17. If I were out of the office for a week, most of the important work in the department would get accomplished anyway.          _____          _____

18. Delegation of important tasks is something that would be (or is) very difficult for me.          _____          _____

19. When a group member comes to me with a problem, I tend to jump right in with a proposed solution.          _____          _____

20. When a group member comes to me with a problem, I typically ask that person something like, "What alternative solutions have you thought of so far?"          _____          _____

Total score          _____          _____

## Scoring and Interpretation:

The answers for determining what style of leader you are (or would be) are as follows:

| | | | |
|---|---|---|---|
| 1. Mostly false | 6. Mostly true | 11. Mostly false | 16. Mostly false |
| 2. Mostly false | 7. Mostly true | 12. Mostly true | 17. Mostly true |
| 3. Mostly true | 8. Mostly true | 13. Mostly true | 18. Mostly false |
| 4. Mostly false | 9. Mostly true | 14. Mostly false | 19. Mostly false |
| 5. Mostly false | 10. Mostly true | 15. Mostly false | 20. Mostly true |

If your score is 15 or higher, you are most likely (or would be) a participative or team-style leader. If your score is 5 or lower, you are most likely (or would be) an authoritarian-style leader.

## Skill Development:

The quiz you just completed is also an opportunity for skill development. Review the 20 questions and look for implied suggestions for engaging in participative leadership. For example, Question 20 suggests that you encourage group members to work through their own solutions to problems. If your goal is to become an authoritarian (one who makes decisions primarily on his or her own), the questions can also serve as useful guidelines. For example, Question 19 suggests than an authoritarian leader looks first to solve problems for group members.

## BUILD A MISSION STATEMENT

A starting point in developing teamwork is to specify the team's mission. The mission should contain a specific goal and purpose, and it should be optimistic and uplifting. Here is an example from a service team at a Cadillac dealership:

> *To plan and implement a level of automobile service and repair of the highest quality, at a competitive price, that will delight customers and retain their loyalty.*

The leader can help develop the mission statement when the team is first formed or at any other time. Developing a mission statement for a long-standing team breathes new life into its activities. Being committed to a mission improves teamwork, as does the process of formulating a mission statement. Skill-Building Exercise 12-3 gives you practice in developing a mission statement for a team.

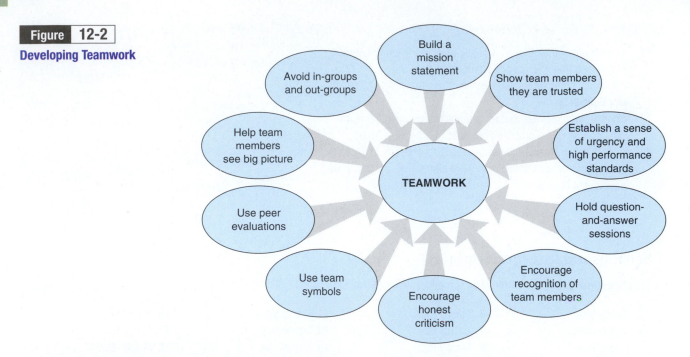

**Figure** **12-2**
**Developing Teamwork**

---

# Skill-Building Exercise 12-3

## Developing a Team Mission Statement

The class organizes into teams of about six people and appoints a team leader. Each team plays the role of a specific team within a company, government agency, or hospital. An example would be the customer service team at a utility company. The task is to develop a mission statement approximating the type described in the text. The team leader might also take notes for the group.

Remember that a mission statement contains a goal and a purpose, and it is uplifting and optimistic. Allow about 15 minutes for preparing the mission statements. The groups then compare mission statements. One representative from each group presents the mission statements to the rest of the class.

## SHOW YOUR TEAM MEMBERS THAT THEY ARE TRUSTED

An effective leader is perceived as honest and trustworthy, and he or she trusts team members. The leader should recognize and reward ethical behavior, particularly when there is a temptation to be dishonest—such as not reporting a quality defect to a customer or cheating on tax returns. Raise expectations of honesty by telling group members you are confident they will act in ways that bring credit to the organization. [28]

A practical way of demonstrating trust in group members is to avoid closely monitoring their work and second-guessing their decisions about minor matters such as the best type of border for a report. A **micromanager** is one who closely monitors most aspects of group members' activities, sometimes to the point of being a control freak. As a result, the group members do not feel that the leader or manager trusts them to make even the smallest decisions. One manager checked travel Web sites himself for the best deal after a team member booked plans for a business trip. As a result, team members felt that they were not trusted to care about the financial welfare of the company.

■ **Micromanager**
one who closely monitors most aspects of group members' activities, sometimes to the point of being a control freak

## ESTABLISH A SENSE OF URGENCY AND HIGH PERFORMANCE STANDARDS

To build teamwork, members need to believe that the team has urgent, constructive purposes. A demanding performance challenge helps create and sustain the team. Team members also want to know exactly what is expected of them. The more urgent and relevant the rationale, the more likely it is that the team will perform well. [29] Based on this information, as a team leader you might project a sense of urgency and encourage setting high goals.

## HOLD QUESTION-AND-ANSWER SESSIONS WITH THE TEAM

An effective way of demonstrating participative or team leadership is to hold question-and-answer sessions with team members. Both leader and members ask and answer questions, such as, "How can we make an even bigger contribution to the company?" The Quality Department at Delta Dental Plan of California used question-and-answer sessions with success. The process not only boosted morale and made managers more accessible to employees, but also yielded more than 1,000 employee suggestions in the first year. The department head said, "This program totally revolutionized the company. Now employees from other divisions are eager to work in our department." [30]

## ENCOURAGE TEAM MEMBERS TO RECOGNIZE EACH OTHER'S ACCOMPLISHMENTS

Members of a high-spirited team look for ways to encourage and praise each other, including the traditional "high five" signifying an important contribution to the team. Encouragement and praise from the team leader is important, but team members also play an important role in giving positive reinforcement to each other. Team spirit develops as members receive frequent positive feedback from each other. [31] Skill-Building Exercise 12-4 gives you the opportunity to practice the skill of recognizing team accomplishments.

## ENCOURAGE HONEST CRITICISM

A superficial type of camaraderie develops when team members avoid honestly criticizing each other for the sake of group harmony. Avoiding criticism

## Skill-Building Exercise 12-4

### Recognizing Team Accomplishments

The class organizes into teams of about six, ideally into teams or groups that already worked with each other during the course. If you have not worked with each other, you will have to rely on any impressions you have made of the other members of the team during the course. Team members will be equipped with about six 3 x 5 index cards. However, any other small-size piece of paper will work. Each member of the team thinks carefully about what other members of the team have accomplished during the course, including contribution to team problem solving, class participation, or perhaps some accomplishment outside of class.

Assume you have six members on the team. Prepare a card for each member by jotting down whatever accomplishments you have observed of the other team members. Each person therefore prepares five cards that will be handed to the person whose name is on the card and then given to that person. Each team member will receive five "accomplishment cards," one from the other five members. Each member studies his or her accomplishment cards, consisting of statements of accomplishments and perhaps a couple of words of praise. Here are two examples:

"I like the way you showed up on time for our study group, and were prepared for action. Nice job, Ben."

"A few times you came up with great ideas in our problem-solving groups. Shauna, you are a really nice team player."

After all cards have been read carefully, discuss your feelings about their cards and their potential contribution to teamwork. Include observations such as the following:

- How much closer to the group do you feel now?
- How much have your efforts in being a team player paid off?
- How useful a technique would this technique of accomplishment recognition be for a workplace team?
- What potential disadvantages do you see to the technique?

can result in groupthink. As a team leader, you should therefore explain that being a good team player includes offering honest feedback on mistakes and flawed ideas. The team benefits from mutual criticism. A stronger team spirit will develop because team members realize they are helping each other through honest feedback. An example of honest criticism took place in the shipping department of a manufacturer of small kitchen appliances:

*One member of a customer service team had designed a satisfaction survey to mail to customers. The purpose of the survey was to investigate whether the packing materials were of satisfactory quality. Another member said, "Are you sure you want to do this? Would we just annoy our customers by asking about packing ingredients? Why waste more paper? We've never had a complaint about packing materials."*

The person whose idea was challenged was miffed at first, but then expressed appreciation. She said, "I guess I went a little overboard on trying to measure customer satisfaction. Maybe we should save our survey dollars for a more important issue."

## USE TEAM SYMBOLS

Teamwork on the athletic field is enhanced by team symbols such as uniforms and nicknames. The term *Lady Vols*, for example, deserves some credit for contributing to the mystique of the University of Tennessee women's basketball team. Symbols can also be an effective team builder in business. Trademarks, logos, mottoes, and other indicators of products both advertise the company and signify a joint effort. Company jackets, caps, T-shirts, mugs, ballpoint pens, and business cards can be modified to symbolize a work unit. As a team leader, you might therefore invest part of your team's budget in an appropriate symbol. Use the opportunity to practice participative leadership. Conduct a group problem-solving session to develop a team logo to place on a T-shirt or cap.

## USE PEER EVALUATIONS

In the traditional performance-evaluation system, the manager evaluates group members at regular intervals. With peer-evaluation systems, the team members contribute to the evaluation by submitting evaluations of each other. The evaluations might consist of filling out rating forms about each other's performance. Sometimes brief essays are written about each other and then synthesized by the team leader.

Peer evaluations contribute to teamwork because team members realize that helping each other becomes as important as helping the boss. Similarly, team members recognize that pleasing each other counts as much as pleasing the boss. A potential disadvantage of peer evaluations, however, is that the group members will agree to give each other outstanding evaluations, or to get even with coworkers they do not like.

As a team leader, you might not have the authority to initiate a peer-evaluation system without first checking with your manager. Making a recommendation for peer input into evaluations might demonstrate that you are committed to participative leadership.

## HELP TEAM MEMBERS SEE THE BIG PICTURE

The team is likely to work together more smoothly when members have a clear understanding of how their work contributes to the company. Communicating the mission as described earlier is a good starting point. Showing the team its specific contribution to the overall organization is equally important. As the team leader, you might create a flowchart that tracks an order from the time it is taken to when it is delivered. Show the team its role at each step. The team members may be aware how they contribute to the team, but not how the team contributes to the success of the organization. [32] The team leader of a shipping department at a distribution center explains to his team regularly, "Let's keep this clearly in mind. A big factor in determining whether a customer stays with us is whether the goods arrive on time and in good shape."

## MINIMIZE FORMATION OF IN-GROUPS AND OUT-GROUPS

■ **Leader-member exchange model**
a theory explaining that group leaders establish unique working relationships with group members, thereby creating in-groups and out-groups

An established leadership theory, the **leader–member exchange model**, provides useful information for the aspiring team leader. According to this theory, leaders establish unique working relationships with group members. By so doing, they create in-groups and out-groups. The in-groups become part of a smoothly functioning team headed by the leader. Out-group members are less likely to experience good teamwork. [33] Figure 12-3 depicts the major concept of the leader–member exchange model.

The in-group may come about because the leader prefers certain group members and therefore is motivated to form good working relationships with them. Conversely, the leader may neglect to form good relationships with people with whom he or she has limited rapport. First impressions count heavily when the leader decides on who is "in" and who is "out." Team leaders should therefore guard against the formation of out-groups just because they are not fond of a few team members, or because a given team member gives a poor first impression.

The leader–member exchange model does not mean that the team leader should avoid forming unique relationships with team members. What should be avoided is forming an out-group. A study investigated the relationships a group of female sales managers established with both men and women members of their sales groups. Treating members differently based on their needs contributed to leadership effectiveness, such as producing good results. [34] An example of a unique relationship would be to give more recognition to a sales representative who craved recognition.

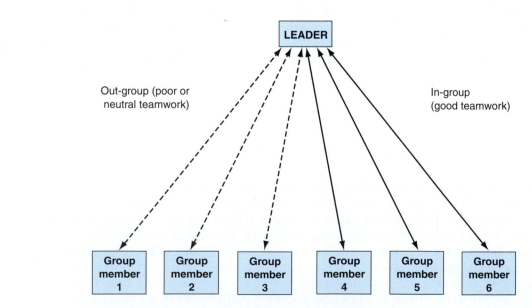

**Figure 12-3**

**The Leader–Member Exchange Model**

# Developing Your Leadership Potential

■ **Learning Objective 3**

Much of this book deals directly and indirectly with information that could improve your leadership effectiveness. Improving your communications effectiveness would be one way to enhance your ability to lead people. Formal education and leadership development programs also contribute to enhancing leadership potential. (Many such programs include some of the activities found in this chapter.) Here we describe six strategies for developing your leadership potential, in addition to studying and participating in formal programs.

Our approach to developing leadership potential is based on the assumption that leaders are both born and made. [35] You need some basic cognitive and personality characteristics to have the potential to be a leader, yet you need to develop these characteristics through experience and practice. A person who has good problem-solving ability and is charismatic, still needs to assume leadership responsibility and engage in certain actions to become an

## Skill-Building Exercise 12-5

### My Personal Leadership Journal

A potentially important assist in your development as a leader is to maintain a journal or diary of your leadership experiences. Make a journal entry within 24 hours after you have carried out a leadership action of any kind, or failed to do so when the opportunity arose. You will therefore have entries dealing with leadership opportunities both capitalized upon and missed. An example would be as follows: "A few of my neighbors were complaining about trash flying around the neighborhood on trash pick-up days, particularly when the wind was strong. I took the initiative to send e-mails and flyers to neighborhood residents discussing what could be done about the problem. I suggested that people pack their recycling boxes more tightly. I also suggested ever-so-politely that people should pick up their own flying trash. Soon the problem just about disappeared."

Also include in your journal such entries as feedback you receive on your leadership ability, leadership traits that you appear to be developing, and leadership ideas you learn about. Also, keep a list of leadership articles and books you intend to read. You might also want to record observations about significant acts of leadership or leadership blunders that you have observed in others, either firsthand or through the media.

Review your journal monthly, and make note of any progress you think you have made in developing your leadership skills. Also consider preparing a graph of your progress in developing leadership skills. The vertical axis can represent skill level on a 1–100 scale, and the horizontal axis might be divided into time intervals, such as calendar quarters.

## Self-Assessment Quizzes in Overview

Self-Assessment Quiz 12-1, The Assertiveness Scale, gave you an opportunity to measure your degree of assertiveness, a key personality trait that is important for leadership as well as many other interpersonal activities such as resolving conflict, volunteering for assignments, getting noticed by your manager, and finding companionship. Self-Assessment Quiz 12-2, What Style of Leader Are You or Would You Be?, takes you more specifically into the basics of leadership. For many situations it will be helpful to emphasize participative or team leadership because organizations have become more democratic. For example, imagine yourself as the supervisor of a credit and collection group. It would probably be to your advantage to ask the credit specialists in your group what they think would be a few good ways to collect more payments on time. Yet in crises, it may be more helpful to be more directive and tell people what to do without emphasizing group participation. For example, if you were the supervisor of credit and collections, the company might ask you to bring in some money fast to help fend off bankruptcy.

effective leader. Among these dozens of activities would be recognizing the accomplishments of others. Skill-Building Exercise 12-5, about maintaining a personal leadership journal, provides a start in practicing and refining leadership skills.

First-level supervisory jobs are an invaluable starting point for developing your leadership potential. It takes considerable skill to manage a rapid-service (fast-food) restaurant or direct a public playground during the summer. First-level supervisors frequently face situations in which group members are poorly trained, poorly paid, and not well motivated to achieve company objectives. Motivating and inspiring entry-level workers is one of the major challenges facing organizations. One of the lessons from the U.S. Marines is that if you want to fire up the frontline, you must use discipline to develop pride. The point is that entry-level workers often take pride in being able to abide by tough rules. [36]

1. **Acquire broad experience.** Because leadership varies somewhat with the situation, a sound approach to improving leadership effectiveness is to attempt to gain supervisory experience in different settings. A person who wants to become an executive is well advised to gain supervisory experience in at least two different organizational functions, such as marketing and operations.

2. **Model effective leaders.** Another strategy for leadership development is to observe capable leaders in action and then model some of their approaches. You may not want to copy a particular leader entirely, but you can incorporate a few of the behavior patterns into your own leadership style. For instance, most inexperienced leaders have difficulty confronting others. Observe how a skilled confronter handles the situation, and try that person's approach the next time you have unfavorable news to communicate to another person.

3. **Self-develop leadership traits and behaviors.** Study the leadership traits and behaviors described earlier in this chapter. As a starting point,

identify several attributes you think you could strengthen within your-self, given some determination and perhaps combined with the right training program. For example, you might decide that with some effort you could improve your sense of humor. You might also believe that you could remember to encourage honest criticism within the team. It is also helpful to obtain feedback from valid sources (such as a trusted manager) about which traits and behaviors you particularly need to develop.

4. **Become an integrated human being.** A philosophical approach to leadership suggests that the model leader is first and foremost a fully functioning person. According to William D. Hitt, mastering the art of leadership comes with self-mastery. Leadership development is the process of self-development. As a result, the process of becoming a leader is similar to the process of becoming an integrated human being. For example, you need to develop values that guide your behavior before you can adequately guide the behavior of others.

   The model (or ideal) leader, according to Hitt, must possess six char-acter traits: identity (know thyself), independence, authenticity, responsi-bility, courage, and integrity. [37] A more recent analysis of leadership development suggests that self-understanding is a major vehicle for improvement. After attaining self-insight, you can move forward with leadership development. [38] Suppose you discover that you feel intimi-dated by people who are older and more experienced than you. Armed with this self-insight you can gradually overcome the problem and feel more comfortable leading workers who are older and more experienced than you. All of the traits Hitt mentions have everyday meanings, but they can also have personal meanings. Part of becoming an integrated person is to answer such questions as, "What do I mean when I say I have integrity?"

   Another approach to becoming an integrated human being, and therefore a more effective leader, is to figure out how you perceive the world. For example, if you perceive yourself as inferior to most people, you will forever be in competition with others to impress them. You will even compete rather than work collaboratively with team members. [39]

5. **Practice a little leadership.** An effective way to develop your leadership skills is to look for opportunities to exert a small amount of helpful leadership in contrast to waiting for opportunities to accomplish extraordinary deeds. The "little leadership" might involve such behaviors as mentoring a strug-gling team member, coaching somebody about how to use a new high-tech dSevice, or making a suggestion about improving a product. In the words of Michael E. McGill and John W. Slocum, Jr., "For those who want to stand atop the dugout, dance with the elephants, fly with the buffaloes, soar with eagles, or perform other mystical and heroic acts of large leader-ship, our little leadership may seem all too managerial, too modest, and too mundane." [40]

6. **Help your leader lead.** According to Michael Useem, leaders need your assis-tance so they can do a good job. "If people are afraid to help their leaders lead, their leaders will fail." [41] A group member is often closer to the

market and closer to how the product is used. Therefore, he or she can provide useful information to the person in the formal leadership position. When you help the people above you avoid a mistake or capitalize upon an opportunity, you help the entire company. At the same time, you are developing your ability to take the initiative and lead.

# Concept Review and Reinforcement

## Key Terms

Leadership, 370
Assertiveness, 371
Cognitive factors, 378

Charisma, 380
Participative leadership, 383

Micromanager, 387
Leader–member exchange
   model, 390

## Summary of Key Concepts

Effective leadership depends on having the right personal characteristics and taking the appropriate actions. Leadership is the ability to inspire support and confidence among the people who are needed to achieve company goals. People can exercise leadership whether or not they occupy a formal leadership position.

Certain traits contribute heavily to leadership effectiveness. Among them are self-confidence, assertiveness, trustworthiness and morality, emotional stability, sense of humor, self-awareness and self-objectivity, cognitive skills and clarity, emotional intelligence, and passion and enthusiasm.

Possessing a naturally dynamic personality is a major contributor to charisma, but a person can engage in many tangible actions that contribute to charisma. Suggestions for behaving charismatically include the following:

1. Communicate a vision.
2. Make frequent use of metaphors and analogies.
3. Inspire trust and confidence.
4. Be highly energetic and goal oriented.
5. Be emotionally expressive and warm.
6. Make ample use of true stories.
7. Be candid and direct.
8. Make everyone you meet feel that he or she is important.
9. Multiply the effectiveness of your handshake.
10. Stand up straight and use other nonverbal signals of self-confidence.
11. Be willing to take personal risks.
12. Be self-promotional.

A team leader acts as a facilitator or coach who shares decision making with team members, thus practicing participative leadership. The following are some techniques for effective team leadership:

1. Build a mission statement.
2. Show your team members that they are trusted.
3. Establish a sense of urgency and high performance standards.
4. Hold question-and-answer sessions with the team.
5. Encourage team members to recognize each other's accomplishments.
6. Encourage honest criticism.
7. Use team symbols.
8. Use peer evaluations.
9. Help team members see the big picture.
10. Minimize formation of in-groups and out-groups.

In addition to participating in formal leadership-development programs, six strategies for developing leadership potential are to (1) acquire broad experience, (2) model effective leaders, (3) self-develop leadership traits and behaviors, (4) become an integrated human being (a fully functioning person), (5) practice a little leadership, and (6) help your leader lead.

## Check Your Understanding

1. Informal observation suggests that people who were voted "most likely to succeed" in high school are frequently found in leadership positions later in life. What explanation can you offer for these predictions about success so often being true?

2. What is your reaction to Rudy Giuliani's statement that the leader should tell people what is right, rather than the people telling him or her what is right and then the leader telling them what they want to hear?

3. What does it mean to say that a person has the "right stuff" for being a leader?

4. How can a person demonstrate to others in the company that he or she is trustworthy enough to be considered for a leadership position?

5. Why does a leader need good emotional intelligence? Shouldn't a leader be a take-charge person focused on obtaining results like making money or winning ball games?

6. What does the term *self-objectivity* mean to you, and why is it important for leadership?

7. What can you do this week to increase your charisma?

8. What kind of *clarity* could your instructor provide for you in his or her role as the leader of this course?

9. In what ways do the concepts of charismatic leadership and participative leadership differ substantially from each other?

10. Assume that a student obtains a part-time job as an assistant store manager. What can this person do to capitalize on this position for leadership experience?

## The Web Corner

*http://www.ccl.org*
(Center for Creative Leadership.)

*http://www.core-edge.com*
(Attaining power and charisma.)

*http://www.SelfGrowth.com*
(Developing your charisma.)

*Internet Skill Builder: Developing Your Charisma*
You have already received in this chapter suggestions for developing your charisma. Visit http://www.core-edge.com to search for additional ideas for charisma development. Go to the section on *charismatology*, and read a couple of the case histories to uncover ideas you might try to enhance your charisma. After digging through core-edge.com, list two concrete ideas you might implement to enhance your charisma.

# Developing Your Human Relations Skills

## Jim Press Wants to Steer Chrysler in the Right Direction

His hiring from Toyota Motor Corp. rocked the auto industry, but James Press didn't join Chrysler LLC to be its savior. Instead, the 60-year-old veteran had a pretty simple view of his role as vice chairman and chief product strategist for Chrysler: "My role is to be the voice of the consumer and to represent the needs of the dealers in the marketplace," he said. "That's my passion."

Press's departure after 37 years with Toyota was one of the most dramatic personnel moves in the recent history of Detroit's Big Three automakers. As Toyota's top North American executive, Press enjoyed a stellar reputation as perhaps the savviest sales and marketing executive in the business. Next, he turned his talents to reviving the product lineup and invigorating sales at Chrysler, which had recently been acquired by the investment group Cerberus Capital Management.

In one of his first interviews since joining Chrysler, Press said he saw great opportunities and some challenges in the automaker's product portfolio. "There are some products that may go away, and there are probably some products that we need to add," he said. "We need a more strategic product portfolio going forward that is customer-driven."

Press's role in the new management team at Chrysler was to take a hard look at Chrysler's place in the brutally competitive U.S. market. He saw Chrysler as a company with strong heritage, capable people, and a chance for quick improvement.

He gave other executives a taste of his vision during a product review of the new Jeep Grand Cherokee. As members of the executive product committee looked on, Press meticulously critiqued the design of the SUV, all the way down to the placement of its cup holders. Afterward, chief executive Bob Nardelli said, "That's why we hired him."

Chrysler dealers welcomed Press into the fold, but were realistic about his ability to improve sales in the short term. "Jim is a great listener and knows the business," said Martin "Hoot" McInerney, a longtime Chrysler and Toyota dealer. "But all the Jim Presses in the world won't help if you don't have a good product."

The president of an automobile consulting firm said about Press, "The dealers loved him. He is very approachable, and very smart. He asks good questions and he's very engaged with the product."

Over time, Press said that he will push to empower engineers and designers to have freedom of expression and more influence on products, and give dealers a bigger say in Chrysler's overall direction. "I brought no Toyota secrets along with me," said Press. "But the company I came from definitely proves the strength of bottom-up management."

### Case Questions

1. What leadership qualities and traits does Press appear to demonstrate?
2. What does the cup holder incident tell you about Press's approach to leadership?
3. To what extent does Press appear to believe in participative leadership and empowerment?
4. How trustworthy can Press be if he would jump ship from Toyota to work for a rival?
5. What suggestions can you offer James Press to help him move Chrysler forward?

**Source:** Bill Vlasic, "Chrysler Executive Sees Vehicle Tuneup," *Detroit News* (*detnews.com*), October 2, 2007.

## Interpersonal Relations Case 12-2

### So Is This How You Learn Leadership?

Len Olsen, age 23, was proud to be selected as part of the leader's program at a national chain of family restaurants. Workers selected for the leadership program are considered to be in line for running individual restaurants and as potential candidates in the long run for leadership positions in corporate headquarters. Before entering the key phase of the leadership program, all candidates must first work a minimum of one year as a server or bartender at one of the company stores (restaurants).

Olsen worked one year as a server in a downtown Chicago restaurant, and then was assigned to another Chicago restaurant to begin his formal leadership training as an assistant manager. Olsen's assignments as an assistant manager included scheduling the wait staff, conducting preliminary screen interviews of job applicants, and resolving problems with customers. After three months on the job, Olsen was asked by a member of the corporate human resources staff how his leadership training program was going. Olsen replied, "I'm a little bit skeptical. I don't think I'm learning much about leadership."

When asked why he didn't think he was learning much about leadership, Olsen listed what he considered three recent examples of the type of responsibilities he faced regularly:

■ "At 11 yesterday morning, I received a phone call from Annie, one of the servers. She told me she wouldn't be to work that afternoon because her Labrador retriever had become quite ill and she had to take the Lab to the vet. I told Annie that we desperately needed her that afternoon because of a large luncheon party. Annie told me her dog was more important to her than the job."

■ "Two weeks ago, Gus, one of our salad chefs, showed up to work absolutely drunk. I told him that working while drunk was absolutely against company rules. He got a little belligerent, but I did get him to take a taxi home at company expense."

■ "Two days ago a customer in the restaurant spilled a cup of hot coffee on herself while answering a call on her cell phone. She told me that the coffee was too hot and that she was going to sue the restaurant. I explained to her tactfully that unless she was truly burned, she had no claim. I offered to have the restaurant pay for her dry cleaning, and then she calmed down."

Olsen then said to the human resources manager, "What has stuff like this got to do with leadership? I mean, I'm not creating great visions or inspiring hordes of people. In what way am I becoming a leader?"

### Case Questions

1. What is your opinion of the contribution of Olsen's representative experiences to his development as a leader?
2. What else can the restaurant chain do to help Olsen, and others in the leadership program, develop as leaders?

# REFERENCES

1. Case history collected in Rochester, New York, January 2008.
2. Bill Bill Bradley, "Whatever the Score—Bounce Back," *Parade Magazine*, October 18, 1998, p. 6.
3. Joseph A. Raelin, *Creating Leaderful Organizations: How to Bring Out Leadership in Everyone* (San Francisco: Berrett-Koehler, 2003).
4. George P. Hollenbeck and Douglas T. Hall, "Self-Confidence and Leader Performance," *Organizational Dynamics*, no. 3, 2004, pp. 254–269.
5. Shelley A. Kirkpatrick and Edwin A. Locke, "Leadership: Do Traits Matter?" *Academy of Management Executive*, May 1991, pp. 26–27.
6. Daniel R. Ames and Francis J. Flynn, "What Breaks a Leader: The Curvilinear Relation between Assertiveness and Leadership," *Journal of Personality and Social Psychology*, Volume 92, 2007, pp. 307–324.
7. Survey cited in "What Are the Most Important Traits for Bosses?" *Employee Recruitment & Retention*, Sample Issue, 2006.
8. Reported in "Developing Trust Pays Off," *Manager's Edge*, April 1999, p. 9.
9. Douglas R. May, Adrian Y. L. Chan, Timothy D. Hodges, and Bruce J. Avolio, "Developing the Moral Component of Authentic Leadership," *Organizational Dynamics*, no. 3, 2003, pp. 247–260.
10. Anthony Bianco, "The Rise of a Star," *BusinessWeek*, December 21, 1998, p. 63; "AmEx's Ken Chenault Talks about Leadership, Integrity, and the Credit Card Business," Knowledge@Wharton (http://knowledge.wharton.upenn), April 2005, p. 2.
11. Bruce J. Avolio, Jane M. Howell, and John J. Sosik, "A Funny Thing Happened on the Way to the Bottom Line: Humor as a Moderator of Leadership Style Effects," *Academy of Management Journal*, April 1999, pp. 219–227.
12. Bill George, Peter Sims, Andrew N. McLean, and Diana Mayer, "Discovering Your Authentic Leadership," *Harvard Business Review*, February 2007, p. 129.
13. Dale E. Zand, *The Leadership Triad: Knowledge, Trust, and Power* (New York: Oxford University Press, 1997), p. 8.
14. Studies on this topic are reviewed in Timothy A. Judge, Amy Colbert, and Remus Ilies, "Intelligence and Leadership: A Quantitative Review and Test of Theoretical Propositions," *Journal of Applied Psychology*, June 2004, p. 548.
15. John Menkes, *Executive Intelligence: What All Great Leaders Have* (New York: Collins, 2006).
16. Gina Chon, "Chrysler Challenge: Burnish Image," *The Wall Street Journal*, August 24, 2007, p. B3.
17. Bill Breen, "The Clear Leader," *Fast Company*, March 2005, pp. 65–67.
18. Quoted in Brian M. Carney, "Of Tax Cuts and Terror," *The Wall Street Journal*, June 30–July 1, 2007, p. A7.
19. Daniel Goleman, "What Makes a Leader?" *Harvard Business Review*, November–December 1998, p. 92; Goleman, "Never Stop Learning," *Harvard Business Review*, January 2004, pp. 28–28.
20. Robert A. Eckert, "Where Leadership Starts," *Harvard Business Review*, November 2001, pp. 53–61. The quote is from page 54.
21. Richard Boyatzis and Annie McKee, *Resonant Leadership* (Boston: Harvard Business School Press, 2005).
22. Jay A. Conger, *The Charismatic Leader: Behind the Mystique of Exceptional Leadership* (San Francisco: Jossey-Bass, 1989).
23. Jack and Suzy Welch, "It's Not about Empty Suits," *Business Week*, October 16, 2006, p. 132.
24. Luisa Beltran, "Standout Performer," *Hispanic Business*, April 2007, p. 26.
25. Michael E. Brown and Linda K. Treviño, "Socialized Charismatic Leadership, Values, Congruence, and Deviance in Work Groups," *Journal of Applied Psychology*, July 2006, p. 955.
26. Suggestions 7, 9, and 10 are from Roger Dawson, *Secrets of Power Persuasion* (Upper Saddle River, NJ: Prentice Hall, 1992), pp. 181–183.
27. A. Skogtad et al., "The Destructiveness of Laissez-Faire Leadership Behavior," *Journal of Occupational Health Psychology*, January 2007, pp. 80–92.
28. "Bring Out the Leader in Everyone," *Managing People at Work*, sample issue, 2000, p. 4.
29. Jon R. Katzenbach and Douglas K. Smith, "The Discipline of Teams," *Harvard Business Review*, March–April 1993, p. 118.
30. "Pump Up Your Leadership Style," *Manager's Edge*, March 2007, p. 3. Adapted from Patricia Fripp, "Leadership Lesson 2: 'I'm Glad You Asked,'" http://www.fripp.com.
31. "Bring Out the Leader in Everyone," p. 4.
32. "What It Takes to Be an Effective Team Leader," *Manager's Edge*, March 2000, p. 6.
33. Terri A. Scandura and Chester A. Schrieisheim, "Leader–Member Exchange and Supervisor Career Mentoring as Complementary Constructs in Leadership Research," *Academy of Management Journal*, December 1994, pp. 1588–1602; George Graen and J. F. Cashman, "A Role Making Model of Leadership in Formal Organizations: A Developmental Approach," in J. G. Hunt and L. L. Larson, eds., *Leadership Frontiers* (Kent, OH: Kent State University Press, 1975), pp. 143–165.
34. Francis J. Yammarino, Alan J. Dubinsky, Lucette B. Comer, and Marvin A. Jolson, "Women and Transformational and Contingent Reward Leadership: A Multiple-Levels-of-Analysis Perspective," *Academy of Management Journal*, February 1997, pp. 205–222.

35. This issue is treated at length in Bruce J. Avolio, *Leadership in Balance: Made/Born* (Mahwah, NJ: Earlbaum, 2005).

36. Jon R. Katzenbach and Jason A. Santamaria, "Firing Up the Front Line," *Harvard Business Review,* May–June 1999, pp. 116–117.

37. William D. Hitt, *The Model Leader: A Fully Functioning Person* (Columbus, OH: Battelle Press, 1993).

38. Manuel London, *Leadership Development: Paths to Self-Insight and Professional Growth* (Mahwah, NJ: Erlbaum, 2002).

39. Cheryl Dahle, "Natural Leader," *Fast Company,* December 2000, p. 270.

40. Michael E. McGill and John W. Slocum, Jr., "A *Little* Leadership Please?" *Organizational Dynamics,* Winter 1998, p. 48.

41. Bill Breen, "Trickle-Up Leadership," *Fast Company,* November 2001, pp. 70–72.

# Motivating Others

## Learning Objectives

After reading and studying this chapter and doing the exercises, you should be able to:

1 Motivate people by responding to their self-interests.

2 Make effective use of positive reinforcement to motivate people in many situations.

3 Make effective use of recognition to motivate others.

4 Apply expectancy theory as a comprehensive way of motivating others.

5 Diagnose situations to analyze the strength of motivation present.

## Outline

1 Motivation Skill Based on the Principle of "What's in it for me?"   406

2 Using Positive Reinforcement to Motivate Others   407

3 Using Recognition to Motivate Others   411

4 Using Expectancy Theory to Motivate Others   414
Capsule Overview of Expectancy Theory
Basic Components of Expectancy Theory
How Moods Influence Expectancy Theory
Diagnosing Motivation with Expectancy Theory
Guidelines for Applying Expectancy Theory

The Commercial Division of the Toro Company supplies mowing, utility, and turf cultivation products to domestic and international golf courses. For many years, Toro has engaged Maritz Travel to design and execute group travel incentive programs as part of their commitment to superior customer care, and recognition of their top sales performers. Over the past 10 years, Toro distributor teams have competed for the chance to win luxury trips to destinations ranging from Munich to Australia to Kauai.

*In addition to reaching sales goals, top performers demonstrated improved product knowledge and customer satisfaction scores. Still, in reviewing overall costs, senior management raised questions about the impact of the travel incentive programs, wondering if the dollars spent were cost-effective. Toro engaged a third-party researcher to evaluate the effects that the Maritz travel programs had on their business. The research compared the growth of the Commercial Division over 11 years, including both promotional and non-promotional years. (A promotion year is one in which the luxury trip incentives were available.)*

*The research clearly showed the positive impact of the group travel incentive programs: (1) Sales growth averaged 19% in promotion years versus 12% in non-promotion years. (2) Increased gross profits (after program costs) amounted to millions of dollars over the 10-year period. (3) Winning distributors tended to have high customer satisfaction scores. [1]*

■ **Motivation**

an internal state that leads to effort expended toward objectives; an activity performed by one person to get another to accomplish work

The case history about Toro demonstrates that by rewarding workers for good performance, they will often increase their performance. You may not be in a position to offer a trip to Australia to a coworker who does what you want, but the principle of being systematic about motivating others remains the same. **Motivation** has two meanings: (1) an internal state that leads to effort expended toward objectives, and (2) an activity performed by one person to get another to accomplish work. We often think of a manager or leader as the one attempting to motivate group members. Yet many people in the workplace have a need to motivate others. To accomplish their work, people must motivate individuals who report to them, coworkers, supervisors, or customers. Developing motivational skills will therefore help you accomplish more work than you would if you relied strictly on the good nature and team spirit of others.

This chapter describes how to develop motivational skills based on four related explanations of motivation. We progress from the simplest to the most complex explanation. As a starting point in thinking through how to motivate others, do Self-Assessment Quiz 13-1.

## Self-Assessment Quiz   13-1

### My Approach to Motivating Others

**Directions:** Describe how often you act or think in the way indicated by the following statements when you are attempting to motivate another person. Circle the appropriate number for each statement using the following scale: Very infrequently (VI); Infrequently (I); Sometimes (S); Frequently (F); Very frequently (VF).

| | VI | I | S | F | VF |
|---|---|---|---|---|---|
| 1. I ask the other person what he or she is hoping to achieve in the situation. | 1 | 2 | 3 | 4 | 5 |
| 2. I attempt to figure out whether the person has the ability to do what I need done. | 1 | 2 | 3 | 4 | 5 |
| 3. When another person is heel-dragging, it usually means he or she is lazy. | 5 | 4 | 3 | 2 | 1 |
| 4. I explain exactly what I want to the person I'm trying to motivate. | 1 | 2 | 3 | 4 | 5 |
| 5. I like to give the other person a reward up front so he or she will be motivated. | 5 | 4 | 3 | 2 | 1 |
| 6. I give lots of feedback when another person is performing a task for me. | 1 | 2 | 3 | 4 | 5 |
| 7. I like to belittle another person enough so that he or she will be intimidated into doing what I need done. | 5 | 4 | 3 | 2 | 1 |
| 8. I make sure that the other person feels treated fairly. | 1 | 2 | 3 | 4 | 5 |
| 9. I figure that if I smile nicely I can get the other person to work as hard as I need. | 5 | 4 | 3 | 2 | 1 |
| 10. I attempt to get what I need done by instilling fear in the other person. | 5 | 4 | 3 | 2 | 1 |
| 11. I specify exactly what needs to be accomplished. | 1 | 2 | 3 | 4 | 5 |
| 12. I generously praise people who help me get my work accomplished. | 1 | 2 | 3 | 4 | 5 |
| 13. A job well done is its own reward. I therefore keep praise to a minimum. | 5 | 4 | 3 | 2 | 1 |
| 14. I make sure I let people know how well they have done in meeting my expectations on a task. | 1 | 2 | 3 | 4 | 5 |
| 15. To be fair, I attempt to reward people similarly no matter how well they have performed. | 5 | 4 | 3 | 2 | 1 |
| 16. When somebody doing work for me performs well, I recognize his or her accomplishments promptly. | 1 | 2 | 3 | 4 | 5 |
| 17. Before giving somebody a reward, I attempt to find out what would appeal to that person. | 1 | 2 | 3 | 4 | 5 |
| 18. I make it a policy not to thank somebody for doing a job he or she is paid to do. | 5 | 4 | 3 | 2 | 1 |
| 19. If people do not know how to perform a task, motivation will suffer. | 1 | 2 | 3 | 4 | 5 |
| 20. If properly laid out, many jobs can be self-rewarding. | 1 | 2 | 3 | 4 | 5 |

**Total score**  _____

### Scoring and Interpretation:

Add the circled numbers to obtain your total score.

**90–100**   You have advanced knowledge and skill with respect to motivating others in a work environment. Continue to build on the solid base you have established.

**50–89**   You have average knowledge and skill with respect to motivating others. With additional study and experience, you will probably develop advanced motivational skills.

**20–49**   To effectively motivate others in a work environment, you will need to greatly expand your knowledge of motivation theory and techniques.

**Source:** The idea for this quiz, and a few items, are from David A. Whetton and Kim S. Cameron, *Developing Management Skills*, 5th ed. (Upper Saddle River, NJ: Prentice Hall, 2002), pp. 302–303.

■ **Learning Objective 1**

# Motivation Skill Based on the Principle of "What's in it for me?"

The most fundamental principle of human motivation is that people are motivated by self-interest. This principle is referred to as "What's in it for me?" or WIIFM (pronounced wiff'em). Reflect on your own experience. Before working hard to accomplish a task, you probably want to know how you will benefit. If your manager asks you to work extra hours to take care of an emergency, you will most likely oblige. Yet underneath you might be thinking, "If I work these extra hours, my boss will think highly of me. As a result, I will probably receive a good performance evaluation and maybe a better-than-average salary increase."

If your instructor asks you to prepare a lengthy research paper, you might be motivated to work to the best of your ability. But before getting down to the task, it is likely that questions have raced through your mind, such as, "Will this paper elevate my grade?" or, "Will I pick up information that will help me in my career?"

A perplexing issue is how the WIIFM principle explains why people are motivated to help others. Why would a company CEO donate gift baskets of food to homeless people? Why hire a virtually unemployable person for a non-productive job in the mailroom? People who perform acts of social good receive the reward of feeling better about themselves. In psychological terms, they satisfy their needs to nurture (take care of) others. More cynically, helping those less fortunate leads to recognition for being a Good Samaritan.

To use the WIIFM principle in motivating others, you have to be aware of the intensity of the person's desire. [2] A person can be highly motivated, mildly motivated, or only slightly motivated, depending on the intensity of his or her WIIFM principle. A company might offer outstanding performers the opportunity to work at home one day per week. Employees who are intensely motivated to work at home will work virtually up to capacity to achieve a rating of outstanding performer.

Applying the WIIFM principle irequires you to find out what needs, desires, or motives a person is attempting to satisfy. A need acts as an internal energy force. In simple language, responding to the needs of people is referred to as touching their hot buttons. You find out what these needs are by asking people what they want or by observing what interests them. For instance, the way a manager might motivate a recognition-hungry group member is to tell that person, "If you perform 10 percent above quota for six consecutive months, we will get you a plaque signifying your achievement to hang on the wall."

One of the reasons needs are so important in understanding motivation is that needs lead to behavior, or what people actually do. A person might be extraverted because of a need to affiliate with others, so that person might be motivated by the opportunity to work closely with others. Another person might be conscientious partly because of a need for achievement. This individual might be motivated by the opportunity to accomplish useful work. [3]

Employee needs have been classified in many ways, yet most of these lists overlap. According to a representative classification, 99 percent of employees are motivated by one or more of the following seven needs:

1. **The need for achievement.** Employees with strong achievement needs seek the satisfaction of completing projects successfully. They want to apply

their talents to attain success, and they find joy in accomplishment for its own sake.

2. **The need for power.** Employees with a strong power need derive satisfaction from influencing and controlling others, and they aspire to become executives. These employees like to lead and persuade and be in charge of resources such as budgets.

3. **The need for affiliation.** Employees with a strong need for affiliation derive satisfaction from interacting with others, being part of a work group, and forming friendships. The same employees are motivated to avoid working alone for long periods of time.

4. **The need for autonomy.** Employees with a strong need for autonomy seek freedom and independence, such as having almost complete responsibility for a project. The same employees are motivated to avoid working in a team effort for long periods of time. Many industrial sales representatives (those who sell to companies) have a strong need for autonomy.

5. **The need for esteem.** Employees with a strong need for esteem want to feel good about themselves, and they judge their worth largely based on how much recognition and praise they receive.

6. **The need for safety and security.** Employees with strong needs for safety and security seek job security, steady income, ample medical and dental insurance, and a hazard-free work environment.

7. **The need for equity.** Employees with a strong need for equity seek fair treatment. They often compare working hours, job responsibilities, salary, and privileges to those of coworkers, and they will become discouraged if coworkers are receiving better treatment. [4]

Recognizing such needs, as well as other needs and interests, helps you apply the WIIFM principle. Skill-Building Exercise 13-1 gives you the opportunity to do the preliminary work needed for applying the WIIFM principle.

# Using Positive Reinforcement to Motivate Others

■ **Learning Objective 2**

The most widely used formal method of motivating people in the workplace is **behavior modification**, an attempt to change behavior by manipulating rewards and punishments. Behavior modification is based on a fundamental principle of human behavior: the law of effect. According to the **law of effect,** behavior that leads to a positive consequence for the individual tends to be repeated, whereas behavior that leads to a negative consequence tends not to be repeated.

The focus of behavior modification on the job is to reward employees for behaving in ways that support what the organization is attempting to accomplish, such as improved productivity. Our approach to skill development in

■ **Behavior modification**
an attempt to change behavior by manipulating rewards and punishments

■ **Law of effect**
behavior that leads to a positive consequence for the individual tends to be repeated, whereas behavior that leads to a negative consequence tends not to be repeated

# Skill-Building Exercise 13-1

## Background Work for WIIFM

Divide the class into pairs of students. In each pair, one student plays the role of a team leader who is developing a plan to highly motivate the team member being interviewed. The other student plays the role of the team member being interviewed. The twist to this role-play, however, is that the team member reflects on his or her actual motivators.

The team leader might ask several or all of these questions while conducting an interview for approximately 15 minutes. In addition, when the team member reveals an important piece of information, the team leader will dig for more details. The team leader should use effective listening skills, Suggested interview questions are as follows:

1. Why are you working on this team?
2. What can the company do to make you really happy?
3. What would be a fair reward for performing up to your capacity? On a 1-to-10 scale, how badly do you want this reward?
4. What would be an outstanding reward for performing up to your capacity? On a 1-to-10 scale, how badly do you want this reward?
5. What would be a fantasy reward for performing up to your capacity? On a 1-to-10 scale, how badly do you want this reward?
6. What do you hope to get out of this job?

A brief class discussion might follow the completion of the interviews. A key issue to address in the discussion is the extent to which the interview would be helpful in motivating the team member.

■ **Positive reinforcement**
increasing the probability that behavior will be repeated by rewarding people for making the desired response

behavior modification is to emphasize positive reinforcement because this is the modification strategy most widely used in the workplace. **Positive reinforcement** means increasing the probability that behavior will be repeated by rewarding people for making the desired response. The phrase *increasing the probability* means that positive reinforcement improves learning and motivation, but is not 100 percent effective. The phrase *making the desired response* is also noteworthy. To use positive reinforcement properly, a reward must be contingent upon doing something right. Simply paying somebody a compliment or giving the person something of value is not positive reinforcement. Behavior modification involves linking consequences to what the person has or has not accomplished.

Positive reinforcement is easy to visualize with well-structured jobs such as data entry or producing parts. Yet positive reinforcement is also used to encourage desired behavior in highly paid, complex jobs. An accountant who developed a new method for the company getting paid faster might be rewarded with two extra days of vacation.

**Negative reinforcement** (or **avoidance motivation**) means rewarding people by taking away an uncomfortable consequence of their behavior. Negative reinforcement is a reward because a disliked consequence is avoided or withdrawn. You are subject to negative reinforcement when you are told, "Your insurance rate will go down if you receive no traffic violations for 12 months." The uncomfortable consequence removed is a high insurance premium. Removing the undesirable consequence is contingent upon your making the right response—driving within the law.

Be careful not to make the common mistake of confusing negative reinforcement with punishment. Negative reinforcement is the opposite of punishment. It involves rewarding someone by removing a punishment or uncomfortable situation.

To use positive reinforcement effectively, certain rules and procedures must be followed, as outlined in Figure 13-1. Although using rewards to motivate people seems straightforward, behavior modification requires a systematic approach. The rules are specified from the standpoint of the person trying to motivate another individual, such as a group member, coworker, supervisor, or customer.

## Rule 1: State Clearly What Behavior Will Lead to a Reward

The nature of good performance, or the goals, must be agreed upon by the manager and group member. Clarification might take this form: "We need to decrease by 40 percent the number of new credit card customers who have delinquent accounts of 60 days or more."

## Rule 2: Choose an Appropriate Reward

An appropriate reward is effective in motivating a given person and feasible from the standpoint of the individual or the company. If one reward does not motivate the person, try another. The importance of choosing the right reward underscores the fact that not all rewards are reinforcers. A reward is something of perceived value by the person giving the reward. However, if the reward does not lead to strengthening a desired response (such as wearing safety goggles), it is not a true reinforcer. [5]

Figure 13-2 lists the factors that employees indicated would satisfy them on the job. At the same time, these factors can be translated into potential rewards for employees. For example, if employees value bonuses, a high-performing employee might be given some assurance of receiving a bonus for above-average

**■ Negative reinforcement (avoidance motivation)**

rewarding people by taking away an uncomfortable consequence of their behavior

---

1. State clearly what behavior will lead to a reward.
2. Choose an appropriate reward.
3. Supply ample feedback.
4. Schedule rewards intermittently.
5. Make the reward follow the observed behavior closely in time.
6. Make the reward fit the behavior.
7. Make the reward visible.
8. Change the reward periodically.
9. Reward the group or team also.

**Figure 13-1**

**Rules and Procedures for Positive Reinforcement**

| Figure | **13-2** |
| --- | --- |

**What Workers Want from Their Jobs and Their Employers**

**Note:** Although only factors 1, 2, and 3 are in rank order, factors 4 through 8 are also considered important for job satisfaction.

**Source:** Table prepared from survey of 1,051 workers presented in "Listen up Employers: Employees Know What They Want This Labor Day," http://www.kronos.com, August 2, 2006, p. 1. The survey was conducted by Harris Interactive® and sponsored by Kronos® Incorporated.

1. Competitive salary
2. 100 percent of health care coverage paid by employers
3. Company-matched 401(k) investments
4. Bonus programs
5. Flexible schedules
6. Compressed workweek
7. Good relationship with the boss
8. Being treated with respect

"The real opportunity for growth comes in utilizing your strengths. Great managers catch people doing the right things."
—Curt Coffman of the Gallup Organization

■ **Intermittent rewards**
rewards given for good performance occasionally, but not always

employment. Because all of these factors are ranked as *important* job factors by employees, all of them are potentially appropriate rewards.

### Rule 3: Supply Ample Feedback

Positive reinforcement cannot work without frequent feedback to individuals. Feedback can take the form of simply telling people they have done something right or wrong. Brief e-mail messages or handwritten notes are other forms of feedback. Many effective motivators, including Jack Welch, the legendary former CEO of General Electric, made extensive use of handwritten thank-you notes. Negative feedback by e-mail should be written tactfully to avoid resentment.

### Rule 4: Schedule Rewards Intermittently

Rewards should not be given on every occasion of good performance. **Intermittent rewards** sustain desired behaviors longer and slow down the process of behaviors fading away when they are not rewarded. If each correct performance results in a reward, the behavior will stop shortly after a performance in which the reward is not received. Another problem is that a reward given continuously may lose its impact. Also, automatic rewards for doing the right thing become perceived as entitlements. As the reward becomes almost guaranteed, the employee feels entitled to it, and the reward loses its motivational effectiveness, much like a weekly paycheck. A practical value of intermittent reinforcement is that it saves time. Few managers or team leaders have enough time to dispense rewards for every correct action by group members.

### Rule 5: Make the Reward Follow the Observed Behavior Closely in Time

For maximum effectiveness, people should be rewarded soon after doing something right. A built-in, or intrinsic, feedback system, such as software working or not working, capitalizes on this principle. If you are administering rewards and punishments, strive to administer them the same day they are earned. Suppose a coworker feeds you exactly the information you need to make a PowerPoint presentation for the group. Send your coworker an e-mail or text message of appreciation that very day. Or, be old-fashioned and thank him or her in person.

### Rule 6: Make the Reward Fit the Behavior

People who are inexperienced in applying positive reinforcement often overdo the intensity of spoken rewards. When an employee does something of an ordinary nature correctly, simple praise such as "Good job" is preferable to

"Fantastic performance." A related idea is that the magnitude of the reward should vary with the magnitude of the accomplishment.

### Rule 7: Make the Reward Visible

Another important characteristic of an effective reward is the extent to which it is visible, or noticeable, to other employees. When other workers notice the reward, its impact multiplies because other people observe what kind of behavior is rewarded. [6] Assume that you are being informed about a coworker having received an exciting assignment because of high performance. You might strive to accomplish the same level of performance. Rewards should also be visible, or noticeable, to the employee. A reward of $10 per week added to a person's paycheck might be hardly noticeable, after payroll deductions. However, a bonus check for $300 might be very noticeable.

### Rule 8: Change the Reward Periodically

Rewards do not retain their effectiveness indefinitely. Employees and customers lose interest in striving for a reward they have received many times in the past. This is particularly true of a repetitive statement such as "Nice job" or "Congratulations." It is helpful for the person giving out the rewards to study the list of potential rewards and try different ones from time to time. A general approach relating to the previous rules is to look for creative ways to apply behavior modification. The creativity might be in the selection of the reward, or how the reward is administered. Several illustrative ideas include:

- *Applause:* Choose an especially effective employee, and at the end of the week or month have coworkers gather and clap for the person.

- *Giraffe award*: Give a certificate saying, "Thanks for sticking your neck out." The name of the reward and the certificate reward risk taking.

- *Safety jackpot*: Managers give five "lottery" cards to employees who follow safety practices. Workers scratch off the cards to learn how many points they have won. Points are then redeemed via a gift catalog or Web site. [7]

### Rule 9: Reward the Group or Team Also

Positive reinforcement applies to groups as well as individuals in the sense that individuals within the group can be rewarded collectively. An obvious rule is that the group should receive a reward commensurate with its accomplishment. However, several of the other eight rules also apply. An example of a team reward is to implement a "Team of the Month" program. [8]

Perform Skill-Building Exercise 13-2 to practice several of these rules for using positive reinforcement.

# Using Recognition to Motivate Others

■ Learning Objective 3

Motivating others by giving them recognition and praise can be considered a direct application of positive reinforcement. Nevertheless, recognition is such a potentially powerful motivator that it merits separate attention. Also, recog-

## Skill-Building Exercise 13-2

### Positive Reinforcement

In both of the following scenarios, one student plays the role of the person attempting to give positive reinforcement, and therefore motivate, the other individual. Another student plays the role of the person who is the recipient of these attempts at motivation.

**Scenario 1: Rewarding a Customer Service Representative.** The customer service manager carefully reviews customer service reports to discover that one service rep has resolved the most complaints for four consecutive weeks. Because this rep has been on the job only six months, the manager wants to make sure the rep feels amply rewarded and appreciated. The manager calls the rep into his office to discuss this outstanding performance and give an appropriate reward.

**Scenario 2: Rewarding Your Boss.** The group member has just received a wonderful assignment from the boss, offering the opportunity to spend a few days with key customers who are located out of town. This is the group member's first exciting extra assignment. As a consequence, the worker wants to encourage the boss to keep him or her in mind for future assignments of this nature. The boss was not expecting to be rewarded for making an assignment that fit the company's needs.

Others in the class observe the two scenarios so they can provide feedback on how well behavior modification principles were applied.

nition programs to reward and motivate employees are standard practice in business and nonprofit firms. Examples would be rewarding high-performing employees with a crystal vase (company logo inscribed) or designating them "employee of the month." Outstanding Mary Kay sales representatives ("beauty consultants") receive recognition and rewards in the form of pink cell phones, pink Buicks, and pink Cadillacs—in the United States, as well as in China and other countries. [9] The pink, however, is just a tinge of pink to give it a modern look. In keeping with the theme of this book, the emphasis is on individual, rather than organizational, use of recognition to motivate.

Recognition is a strong motivator because it is a normal human need to crave recognition. At the same time, recognition is effective because most workers feel they do not receive enough notice. Several studies conducted over a 50-year time span have indicated that employees welcome praise for a job well done as much as a regular paycheck. Furthermore, according to one estimate, 79 percent of employees who quit their job point to lack of appreciation as a key factor for leaving. This finding should not be interpreted to mean that praise is an adequate substitute for salary. Employees tend to regard compensation as an entitlement, whereas recognition is perceived as a gift. [10] Workers, including your coworkers, want to know that their output is useful to somebody. To appeal to the recognition need of others, identify a meritorious behavior and then recognize that behavior with an oral, written, or material reward. E-mail, instant messaging, and text messaging are useful vehicles for providing quick recognition when in-person appreciation is not feasible. Also, sometimes people like to print a copy of the recognition they receive. The rules for the use of positive reinforcement are directly applicable. An additional suggestion relates closely to making rewards visible: Time your praise for when it will do the most good. Praise delivered during a staff meeting, for example, can be a potent form of recognition. [11] The recognition award should help the employee feel appreciated for having made a contribution. The economic value of the award, such as engraved metal bowl, is much less important.

Some specific examples of using recognition to sustain desired behavior (a key aspect of motivation) follow:

- A coworker shows you how to more effectively perform an important task on the Internet. Three days later, you send her an e-mail message with a copy to the boss: "Hi, Jessica. Your suggestion about copying company logos was dynamite. I've used it five times with success since you showed me what to do." (You are reinforcing Jessica's helpful and cooperative behavior.)

- As the team leader, you receive a glowing letter from a customer about how Kent, one of your team members, solved his or her problem. You have the letter laminated and present it as a gift to Kent. (The behavior you are reinforcing is good customer service.)

- One member of your department, Jason, is a mechanical engineer. While at a department lunch taking place during National Engineers Week, you stand up and say, "I want to toast Jason in celebration of National Engineers Week. I certainly wouldn't want to be sitting in this office building today if a mechanical engineer hadn't assisted in its construction." (Here the only behavior you are reinforcing is the goodwill of Jason, so your motivational approach is general rather than specific.)

As you might have inferred from the examples presented, statements of recognition tend to be more effective when they are expressed in specific, rather than general, terms. "You're doing a great job" is an example of a general recognition statement. Here are a few more specific recognition statements:

"You really made a difference by . . ."

"You're right on the mark with . . ."

"We couldn't have done it without your . . ." [12]

An outstanding advantage of recognition, including praise, as a motivator is that it is no cost or low cost, yet powerful. Recognition thus provides an enormous return on investment in comparison to a cash bonus. A challenge in using recognition effectively is that not everyone responds well to the same form of recognition. A good example is that highly technical people tend not to like general praise such as "Great job" or "Awesome." Instead, they prefer a laid-back, factual statement of how their output made a contribution.

Furthermore, women are slightly more responsive to praise than are men, as revealed in a study of working adults. [13]

Giving recognition to others as a motivational tactic is more likely to be effective if a culture of recognition exists within the company. This is true because the person giving the recognition will feel that what he or she is doing fits what top management thinks is appropriate behavior. At the same time, the recipient of the recognition is likely to take it seriously.

■ Learning Objective 4

# Using Expectancy Theory to Motivate Others

So far, we have described motivating others through applying the principle of WIIFM and behavior modification, including recognition. We now shift to expectancy theory, a more comprehensive explanation of motivation that includes elements of the two other approaches. Expectancy theory is given special attention here for these reasons. First, expectancy theory can help you diagnose motivational problems. Second, it is comprehensive because it incorporates many different aspects of motivating others. Third, it gives the person attempting to motivate others many guidelines for triggering and sustaining constructive effort from group members.

## CAPSULE OVERVIEW OF EXPECTANCY THEORY

■ **Expectancy theory**
a motivation theory based on the premise that the effort people expend depends on the reward they expect to receive in return

The **expectancy theory** of motivation is based on the premise that how much effort people expend depends on the reward they expect to receive in return. (Notice the similarity to WIIFM?) Expectancy theory assumes that people are rational and logical, and the process resembles rational gambling. In any given situation, they want to maximize gain and minimize loss. The theory assumes that people choose among alternatives by selecting the one they think they have the best chance of attaining. Furthermore, they choose the alternative that appears to have the biggest personal payoff. How intensely they want that alternative is also an important consideration. Given a choice, people select an assignment they think they can handle and that will benefit them the most.

An example will help clarify the central thesis of expectancy theory. Hector, a 27-year-old credit analyst at a machine tool company, recognizes that he needs to increase his income by about $500 per month to cover his expenses. After carefully reviewing his options, Hector narrows his alternatives to the following three choices:

1. Work as a dining-room server one night a week and on most weekends, with a variable income of somewhere between $600 and $850 per month.

2. Work for an income tax preparation service about four months per year for 20 hours per week, yielding an annual income of about $7,000.

3. Work extra hard at his regular job, including taking a course in corporate finance, to improve his chances of receiving a promotion and a salary increase of $700 per month.

Hector rejects the first choice. Although he knows he can do the work, he anticipates several negative outcomes. He would much prefer to engage in extra work related to his field of expertise. The unpredictable income associated with being a dining-room server is also a concern. Hector sees merit in the second alternative because income tax preparation work relates to his accounting background. Furthermore, the outcome (amount of pay) is relatively certain. But Hector also has some concerns that working so many extra hours for four months a year could hurt his performance on his day job.

Hector decides to take a chance with the third alternative of going all out to position himself for promotion. He is confident he can elevate his performance, but he is much less certain that hard work will lead to promotion. Yet Hector attaches such high value to being promoted and upgrading his professional credentials that he is willing to gamble.

## BASIC COMPONENTS OF EXPECTANCY THEORY

All versions of expectancy theory have the following three major components: effort-to-performance expectancy, performance-to-outcome expectancy, and valence. [14] Figure 13-3 presents a glimpse of expectancy theory.

### Effort-to-Performance Expectancy

**Effort-to-performance expectancy** is the probability assigned by the individual that effort will lead to performing the task correctly. An important question rational people ask themselves before putting forth effort to accomplish a task is this: "If I put in all this work, will I really get the job done properly?" Each behavior is associated in the individual's mind with a certain expectancy, or subjective hunch of the probability of success.

Expectancies range from 0 to 1.0. The expectancy would be 0 if the person thought that there was no chance of performing the task correctly. An expectancy of 1.0 would signify absolute faith in being able to perform the task properly. Expectancies thus influence whether you will even strive to earn a reward. Self-confident people have higher expectancies than do those with low self-confidence. Being well trained will also increase your subjective hunch that you can perform the task.

The importance of having high expectancies for motivation meshes well with a thrust in work motivation that emphasizes the contribution of **self-efficacy**, the confidence in your ability to carry out a specific task. If you have high self-efficacy about the task, your motivation will be high. Low self-efficacy leads to low motivation. [15] Some people are poorly motivated to skydive because they doubt they will be able to pull the ripcord while free-falling at 120 mph.

■ **Effort-to-performance expectancy**
the probability assigned by the individual that effort will lead to performing the task correctly

■ **Self-efficacy**
the confidence in your ability to carry out a specific task

**Figure 13-3**

**Basic Version of Expectancy Theory**

Person will be motivated under these conditions {

A. Effort-to-performance expectancy is high: Person believes he or she can perform the task.
B. Performance-to-outcome expectancy is high: Person believes that performance will lead to certain outcomes.
C. Valence is high: Person highly values the outcomes.

### Performance-to-Outcome Expectancy

■ **Performance-to-outcome expectancy**

the probability assigned by the individual that performance will lead to outcomes or rewards

**Performance-to-outcome expectancy** is the probability assigned by the individual that performance will lead to certain outcomes or rewards. When people engage in a particular behavior, they do so with the intention of achieving a desired outcome or reward. Performance-to-outcome expectancies also range from 0 to 1.0. If you believe there is no chance of receiving the desired reward, the assigned probability is 0. If you believe the reward is certain to follow from performing correctly, the assigned probability is 1.0; for example: "I know for sure that if I show up for work every day this month, I will receive my paycheck."

### Valence

■ **Valence**

the value, worth, or attractiveness of an outcome

A **valence** is the value, worth, or attractiveness of an outcome. It signifies how intensely you want something (as described in WIIFM). In each work situation there are multiple outcomes, each with a valence of its own. Remember Hector, the credit analyst? The potential outcomes of working part time as an income tax preparer would include extra income, new experience, and interference with his day job.

In the version of expectancy theory presented here, valences range from −100 to +100. A valence of +100 means that you desire an outcome strongly. A valence of −100 means that you are strongly motivated to avoid an outcome, such as being fired. A valence of 0 means that you are indifferent toward an outcome, and it is therefore no use as a motivator. An outcome with a probable valence of 0 would be as follows: To gain the cooperation of coworkers, you promise them gold stars as a reward (or outcome).

Skill-Building Exercise 13-3 will help sensitize you to the importance of estimating valences when attempting to motivate others. A major problem faced by managers and others who attempt to motivate others is that they have limited knowledge about the valences of their motivators (or rewards).

## HOW MOODS INFLUENCE EXPECTANCY THEORY

Expectancy theory emphasizes the rational side of people, yet emotions still play a key role in determining the impact of expectancies, instrumentalities, and valences. Moods are relatively long-lasting emotional states that do not appear tied to a clear source of the emotion. For example, a person might be in a good mood despite experiencing a negative situation such as an automobile breaking down. Also, people may feel glum despite good news such as having won a prize.

Several studies have shown that moods shape people's perceptions of expectancies and valence in expectancy theory. A positive mood increases the perceived connection between effort and performance (E → P expectancy), between performance and desired outcome (P → O expectancy), and in the valence attached to those outcomes. When we are in a good mood, we are more likely to believe that we can accomplish a task, so we have more of a "can do" attitude. We are also more optimistic about the outcomes (rewards) of our effort,

## Skill-Building Exercise 13-3

### Estimating Valences for Applying Expectancy Theory

**Directions:** Listed here are rewards and punishments (outcomes) stemming from job scenarios. Also included is a space for rating the reward or punishment on a scale of +100 to −100. Work with about six teammates, with each person rating all the rewards and punishments. Compute the mean (average) rating for each reward and punishment.

| Potential Outcome | *Rating* (−100 to +100) |
|---|---|
| 1. A 20-percent salary increase | _____ |
| 2. Profit-sharing plan in successful company | _____ |
| 3. Stock ownership in company | _____ |
| 4. Fully paid three-day leave | _____ |
| 5. A $8,000 performance bonus | _____ |
| 6. A $400 gift certificate | _____ |
| 7. Outstanding performance review | _____ |
| 8. Above-average performance review | _____ |
| 9. One-step promotion | _____ |
| 10. Two-step promotion | _____ |
| 11. Flexible working hours | _____ |
| 12. Chance to work at home one day per week | _____ |
| 13. Chance to do more of preferred task | _____ |
| 14. Take over for supervisor when supervisor is away | _____ |
| 15. Fancy job title without change in pay | _____ |
| 16. Bigger cubicle | _____ |
| 17. Private office | _____ |
| 18. Company-paid cell phone | _____ |
| 19. Wall plaque indicating accomplishment | _____ |
| 20. Employee-of-the-month designation | _____ |
| 21. Warm smile and word of appreciation | _____ |
| 22. Compliment in front of others | _____ |
| 23. Threat of being suspended for a month | _____ |
| 24. One-month suspension without pay | _____ |
| 25. Demotion to undesirable job | _____ |
| 26. Being fired | _____ |
| 27. Being fired combined with promise of negative references | _____ |
| 28. Being placed on probation | _____ |
| 29. Being ridiculed in front of others | _____ |
| 30. A 30-percent pay reduction | _____ |

*(Continued)*

# Skill-Building Exercise 13-3 (*Continued*)

After completing the ratings, discuss the following topics:

1. Which outcomes received the most variable ratings?
2. Which outcomes received the most similar ratings?
3. Which are the three most desirable rewards?
4. Which are the three most undesirable punishments?

Another analytical approach would be to compute the class mean for all 30 outcomes. Each student could then compare his or her rating with the class average.

To apply this technique to the job, modify the preceding outcomes to fit the outcomes available in your work situation. Explain to team members that you are attempting to do a better job of rewarding and disciplining and that you need their input. The ratings made by team members will give strong clues to which rewards and punishments would be the most effective in motivating them.

and the outcomes look even better to us. [16] The opposite might also be true—when we are in a bad mood we feel less capable of task accomplishment, we are more pessimistic about getting the reward, and the reward appears less enticing.

■ Learning Objective 5

## DIAGNOSING MOTIVATION WITH EXPECTANCY THEORY

An important potential contribution of expectancy theory to interpersonal relations is that it helps a person diagnose whether motivation is present and the intensity of the motivation. In performing your diagnosis, seek answers to the following questions:

1. Does the person I am attempting to motivate have the skills and self-efficacy to do the job? If the person feels ill-equipped to perform, he or she will be discouraged and show very little motivation.

2. What assurance does the person have that if he or she performs the work, the promised reward will be forthcoming? Does the company have a decent reputation for following through on promises? What about me? Have I established my credibility as a person who follows through on promises? (If you or the company is not trusted, motivation could be reduced to zero.)

3. How badly does the person want the reward being offered in the situation? Am I offering a reward that will make it worthwhile for the person to do what I need done? If the sum of the valences of the outcomes in the situation is close to 0 (some positive, some negative), motivation will be absent.

4. Are there any zeroes in response to the first three questions? If there are, motivation will be absent, because the expectancy theory equation is Motivation = (effort-to-performance expectancies) × (performance-to-outcome

expectancies) × (the sum of the valences for all the outcomes). Remember what happens when you multiply by 0 in an equation.

5. Is the person in a reasonably good mood? Perhaps the person is poorly motivated today because of being in a bad mood.

## BACK TO THE OPENING CASE

Management at the Commercial Division of Toro correctly diagnosed the motivation of its sales force. Although these industrial sales representatives take considerable pride in their work, they still respond well to external incentives. The opportunity to win expense-paid vacations to exotic locales gave them a motivational boost strong enough to boost sales growth by 7 percent—a substantial amount of revenue for Toro.

## GUIDELINES FOR APPLYING EXPECTANCY THEORY

The information about expectancy theory presented so far provides ideas for motivating others. Here we discuss several additional specific guidelines to improve your skill in motivating others.

1. **Train and encourage people.** If you are a manager, you should give employees the necessary training and encouragement to be confident that they can perform the required tasks. Some employees who appear poorly motivated simply lack the right skills and self-efficacy.

2. **Make explicit the link between rewards and performance.** Employees should be reassured that if they perform the job up to standard, they will receive the promised reward. It is sometimes helpful for employees to speak to coworkers about whether they received promised rewards.

3. **Make sure the rewards are large enough.** Some rewards fail to motivate people because, although they are the right kind, they are not in the right amount. The promise of a large salary increase might be motivational, but a 1 percent increase will probably have little motivational thrust for most workers.

4. **Understand individual differences in valences.** To motivate others in the workplace effectively, you must discover individual differences in preferences for rewards. An attempt should be made to offer a worker rewards to which he or she attaches a high valence. For instance, one employee might value a high-adventure assignment; another might attach a high valence to a routine, tranquil assignment. Also keep individual differences in mind when attempting to motivate customers. One customer might attach a high valence to a volume discount, while another might favor follow-up service.

5. **Use the Pygmalion effect to increase effort-to-performance expectancies.** The **Pygmalion effect** refers to the phenomenon that people will rise (or fall) to the expectations another person has of them. Even if these expectations are not communicated explicitly, the other person will catch on to the nonverbal language. As the levels of expectation increase, so will performance. The high expectations thus become a self-fulfilling prophecy.

■ **Pygmalion effect**
the phenomenon that peoplewill rise (or fall) to theexpectations that anotherperson has of them

It is difficult to keep all the points made about expectancy theory in your head at the same time. Nevertheless, with practice and by referring to this book and your notes, you can apply many of the ideas. Skill-Building Exercise 13-4 will help you get started applying expectancy theory. Skill-Building Exercise 13-5 will help you apply the information in this chapter to self-motivation.

## Skill-Building Exercise 13-4

### Applying Expectancy Theory

One student plays the role of the manager of a telemarketing firm (selling over the telephone). Another student plays the role of Terry, a telemarketing specialist who has been with the company for three months. Terry is 40 percent below target in selling magazine renewals. The manager calls Terry into the office for a discussion of the problem.

Terry goes on at length to explain how confusing the job has become. Terry makes comments such as, "I don't even know if I have the right kind of voice for this job. People I reach on the phone think I'm just a kid." Terry also wonders what kind of money he can make in this job and whether it is a dead-end job. (The student who plays the role of Terry can improvise about more of these kinds of problems.)

The manager will apply expectancy theory to motivate Terry to achieve satisfactory performance. Other class members should jot down statements the manager makes that indicate the use of expectancy theory. Also, observe whether it appears that Terry is being helped.

## Skill-Building Exercise 13-5

### Working on My Own Motivators

The focus of this chapter has been the skill of motivating others. Yet, if you neglect motivating yourself, you (a) might not gain a formal position in which you can motivate others, and (b) you will not be able to motivate others by leading through example. Apply some of the concepts in this chapter to help work through this exercise.

*What Motivates Me?*
Think back on what situations, and factors within a situation, have prompted you to put forth your best effort and work the hardest—on the job, at community work, at school, in sports, or in other recreational activities such as being a band member. Which needs were you attempting to satisfy? Which tangible or intangible rewards were you pursuing? Here is a portion of a sample answer:

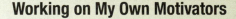

*(Continued)*

## Skill-Building Exercise 13-5 (*Continued*)

"I was lucky enough to be entered in Domino's national speed contest for making a store-usable pizza. I jumped into the situation like somebody obsessed. Here I was at 20 years old with a chance to win a national contest and be lifted up over the head of my buddies. I would have been King Pizza for a day. I didn't win, but I came close.

"Now I know that competition and recognition get my adrenalin flowing. I think that's why I will be successful in industrial sales. I need that big carrot dangling out in front of me."

*What Can I Do to Capitalize on My Motivators?*
It is helpful to know what motivates you, but it is even more helpful to follow up by placing yourself in situations in which you will be highly motivated. The Pizza King aspirant provides us a good example. Attempt to manage your career by placing yourself in highly motivational situations. For example, if the opportunity to work alone without supervision and the opportunity to schedule your own time motivates you, strive to work at home in the near future.

Now write down the type of situations that will most likely enable you to work at your motivated best.

## Self-Assessment Quiz in Overview

Self-Assessment Quiz 13-1 is different from the other quizzes presented in this text because it emphasizes cognitive knowledge about the subject (in this case motivation). Nevertheless, your attitudes toward people often become translated into knowledge about motivation. For example, if you are warm and supportive toward people, you would likely respond "very frequently" to Statement 8, "I make sure that the other person feels treated fairly." And, if you were essentially hostile toward people, you would respond "very frequently" to Statement 3, "When another person is heel-dragging, it usually means he or she is lazy."

# Concept Review and Reinforcement

## Key Terms

Motivation, 404
Behavior modification, 407
Law of effect, 407
Positive reinforcement, 408
Negative reinforcement
   (Avoidance motivation), 409

Intermittent rewards, 410
Expectancy theory, 414
Effort-to-performance
   expectancy, 415
Self-efficacy, 415

Performance-to-outcome
   expectancy, 416
Valence, 416
Pygmalion effect, 419

## Summary of Key Concepts

Motivation refers to an internal state that leads to effort expended toward objectives and to an activity performed by one person to get another person to work. Managers, as well as people working by themselves, often need to motivate others.

The most fundamental principle of human motivation is that people are motivated by self-interest, referred to as "What's in it for me?" (WIIFM). Even those who help others are simultaneously helping themselves by feeling good. In using the WIIFM principle, be aware of the intensity of a person's desire for a reward.

Behavior modification is an attempt to change behavior by manipulating rewards and punishments. Its key principle is the law of effect—behavior that leads to a positive effect tends to be repeated, while the opposite is also true. Negative reinforcement, or avoidance motivation, can be used to supplement positive reinforcement. Rules for the effective use of positive reinforcement include the following:

1. State clearly what behavior will lead to a reward.
2. Choose an appropriate reward.
3. Supply ample feedback.
4. Schedule rewards intermittently.
5. Make the reward follow the observed behavior closely in time.
6. Make the reward fit the behavior.
7. Make the reward visible.
8. Change the reward periodically.
9. Reward the group or team also.

A general approach to applying these rules is to look for creative ways to apply positive reinforcement.

Motivating others by giving them recognition and praise is a direct application of positive reinforcement. Recognition is a strong motivator because it is a normal human need to crave recognition, and most workers feel they do not get enough recognition. Choosing when to deliver recognition can be important. Statements of recognition tend to be more effective when they are specific. Recognition and praise are low-cost, powerful motivators. Recognition is more likely to be an effective motivator in a culture of recognition.

The expectancy theory of motivation assumes that people are decision makers who choose among alternatives by selecting the one that appears to have the biggest personal payoff at the time. Expectancy theory has three major components: expectancies about being able to perform, expectancies about performance leading to certain outcomes, and valence (the value attached to the reward). A positive mood state can enhance the components of expectancy theory.

Expectancy theory is useful in diagnosing whether motivation is present by examining the strength of the expectancies and the valences of the rewards. If any element is 0, motivation will not be present. Expectancy theory provides important ideas for motivating others, including the following:

1. Train and encourage people.
2. Make explicit the link between rewards and performance.

3. Make sure the rewards are large enough.
4. Understand individual differences in valences.
5. Use the Pygmalion effect to increase effort-to-performance expectancies.

## Check your Understanding

1. Explain whether the ability to motivate others is a soft skill or a hard skill.
2. A recent Google search identified 68,600,600 listings for the subject of "work motivation." With all this information available, why is motivating workers still such a hassle for so many managers?
3. For what purpose would someone need to motivate his or her supervisor?
4. If people really live by the WIIFM principle, how can a leader still achieve teamwork?
5. What evidence can you suggest that some people prefer exciting and interesting work over exceptional financial rewards?

6. Identify several factors in Figure 13-1 that you think would be particularly effective in motivating managers and professional-level workers. Explain your reasoning.
7. Answer Question 6 for entry-level service workers, such as supermarket cashiers.
8. How do individual differences show themselves in attempting to motivate others?
9. How might you use expectancy theory to improve your own level of work motivation?
10. How might cultural differences affect the valence ratings in Skill-Building Exercise 13-3?

## The Web Corner

*http://www.awards.com*
(One-stop supersite for rewards and recognition.)

*http://www.ZeroMillion.com*
(Go to Positive Reinforcement in the Workplace.)

*http://www.Entrepreneur.com*
(Go to "Think Positive," which deals with positive reinforcement in the workplace.)

*Internet Skill Builder: Motivating Other People*
Visit *http://www.nelson-motivation.com* to watch a five-minute video clip of one of Bob Nelson's talks. After watching the video, answer the following questions: (1) What have I learned that I could translate into a skill motivating other people as well as employees? (2) Which theory, or approach, to motivation does Nelson emphasize in his presentation?

## Interpersonal Relations Case 13-1

### *Motivating the Kitchen Staff at the Blue Gardenia*

Jimmy Gomez aspires to someday be the manager of a large hotel. To help work toward that goal, he is working part-time on a degree in hospitality administration. He attends classes at various times to fit his demanding full-time position as the kitchen staff supervisor at the Blue Gardenia, a well-established downtown hotel. Gomez supervises a staff of about 45 kitchen workers, including food preparers, butchers, bakers, and cooks. The highly paid chefs report to the restaurant manager, Sonya Rosato, who is also Gomez's manager.

The average wage is $9.50 per hour for the kitchen staff reporting to Gomez. Half of these workers work part-time and receive almost no benefits. Full-time staff members receive a few modest benefits, such as vacation, a $25,000 life insurance policy, and medical insurance. Blue Gardenia management believes strongly that the company pays competitive wages for kitchen staff and that paying them much more would eat into profits too much.

During a goal-setting conference with Rosato, Gomez agreed that an important area for improvement in his operation would be to reduce turnover and increase productivity among the kitchen staff. Rosato pointed out that although the turnover rate for Gomez's employees was about average for kitchen staff in the geographic area (75 percent per year), it was still too high. If the turnover rate could be trimmed down to about 45 percent, it would save the hotel thousands of dollars in hiring and training costs. Also, less food would be wasted because trainees make so many mistakes in food preparation. Skilled workers also drop fewer dishes and glasses.

Rosato and Gomez also agreed that lower turnover would mean more kitchen staff would have good job skills and therefore would be able to produce more. For example, a skilled salad maker can make twice as many salads as a beginner. Another concern Rosato expressed was that many of the kitchen staff seemed lazy.

During the week following the meeting with his boss, Gomez kept thinking about the problem. He decided tentatively that he was really dealing with a motivational issue. He reasoned that if the staff were better motivated, they would stay with the job longer and obviously should not appear lazy. As a starting point in attempting to better motivate the kitchen staff, Gomez conducted a few informal interviews with them during breaks and toward the end of the workday. He asked 12 of the kitchen workers what Blue Gardenia management could do to keep kitchen staff on the job longer and working harder. A few of the comments Gomez collected were as follows:

- "What do you expect for $9.50 an hour? Some kind of superman? I work as hard as a factory worker, but I don't get paid like a factory worker in a union plant."
- "This is like a dead-end job. If I could find a job with a better future, I'd be out of here in no time."
- "I like this job fine. But just like a few of the other guys here, I've got a problem. My wife and I are expecting a child. If I stay in this job, I won't be able to support my child. My wife wants to drop out of work for a year to care for the baby."
- "Not me, but I think some of the workers here think management doesn't care much about them. So if they can find another job that pays even 50¢ more per hour, they're gone."
- "I like this kind of work. I mean, we're really doing some good. People like nice entertainment, and eating good food is a form of entertainment. Also, we're keeping people healthy and helping them live longer. Our food is made with the best ingredients. Even the beef we prepare is lean and healthy."
- "My gripe is not with the work, but that we don't get enough respect. The chef gets the glory, but

we do a lot of the real work. I think I'm doing important work, but nobody tells me I am. Sometimes I think I'm treated like just another piece of kitchen equipment. A few of the other guys and gals feel the same way about how they're treated."

After the interviews were completed, Gomez thought to himself that he had a lot of information. Yet he wondered how he could translate all this information into an action plan that would reduce turnover and keep the kitchen staff working harder.

### Case Questions

1. How effective do you think it was for Jimmy Gomez to interview members of the kitchen staff to investigate possible motivational problems?
2. What does the information revealed by the kitchen staff tell you about their valences?
3. Which needs among the people interviewed are not being satisfied?
4. What recommendations can you make to Blue Gardenia management about decreasing the turnover and increasing the productivity of the kitchen staff?

## Interpersonal Relations Case 13-2

### On Time at Prime Time

Prime Time Furniture is a manufacturer and distributor of inexpensive, ready-to-assemble furniture for the home and small business, including home-based businesses. Among their products are bookcases, television stands, computer workstations, and kitchen tables. Some of the higher-end products are manufactured at the Wisconsin factory and distribution center. The vast majority of products, however, are imported from Malaysia and then placed in the distribution center until sold.

Demand for ready-to-assemble furniture has increased steadily as more people are looking for ways to reduce household expenses. To meet the increased demand, more companies have entered the field, making the business more competitive and therefore reducing prices.

Eton Westin, the distribution center manager, searches continuously for ways to make the center more efficient. During a two-hour productivity meeting with supervisors, Westin learned that employee lateness is costing Prime Time a lot of money. Ashley Novak explained the problem in these terms:

"We are short-handed as it is. When an employee is late, it makes it more difficult to ship on time. We have learned the hard way that when we do not ship on time, we lose some business. A big part of our business now comes from online sales through Amazon and other resellers. These outfits promise rapid delivery, and when we don't ship on time, we get heat from both the resellers and the end customers." (The resellers inform the end customer that Prime Time Furniture is the source of the furniture.)

Jimmy Gerber, the director of administration and human resources, said he had an idea for improving punctuality that has worked in other companies. The program is set up by a company specializing in performance improvement. Gerber then outlined the basics of the program.

"We run a punctuality race, with each department being represented by a horse, assigned a name by the department. The consulting company sets up the race with its own software, and we visit our race Web site any time we want. The setup looks like a video game. You can see graphically the relative positions of the horses as they run the 'punctuality race.'

"Every time a worker arrives on time, that fact is entered into the database, and the department's horse gets two points. Every time a worker is late, the department's horse is penalized two points. Coming back from breaks on time earns one point, and coming back late is a one-point penalty. Leaving work, or leaving early, also follows the same one-point value.

"At the end of each month, the points are totaled. The team with the winning horse can then convert the points into gifts from a catalog or gift certificates to a few selected restaurants."

Westin asked the group for their opinion on the horse race to improve punctuality. "I'm a little concerned," he said. "Isn't this too child-like? I mean, running a horse race for coming to work on time. Let's get real."

"In all respect, Eton," said Liz Lopez, the shipping supervisor. "Adults are motivated by games and small prizes. We are all children at heart, even Prime Time employees."

### Case Questions

1. What do you predict will be the outcome of the horse-race motivation program if implemented?
2. Which approach, or approaches, to motivating people does this horse-race program represent?
3. What other program for improving punctuality might you recommend?

# REFERENCES

1. "Travel Incentives Shown to Grow Sales," http://www.martizetravel.com/travel-toro.html, 2007, p. 1.

2. Gerald Kushel, *Reaching the Peak Performance Zone: How to Motivate Yourself and Others to Excel* (New York: AMACOM, 1994), p. 66.

3. Piers Steel and Cornelius J. König, "Integrating Theories of Motivation," *Academy of Management Review,* October 2006. pp. 895–896.

4. Research summarized in "One of These Seven Things Will Motivate Any Employee in the Company," *Motivational Manager,* sample issue, 1998 (Lawrence Ragan Communications, Inc.).

5. Fred Luthans and Alexander D. Stajkovic, "Reinforce for Performance: The Need to Go Beyond Pay and Even Rewards," *Academy of Management Executive,* May 1999, p. 52.

6. Steven Kerr, *Ultimate Rewards: What Really Motivates People to Achieve* (Boston: Harvard Business School Publishing, 1997).

7. "Simple Rewards Are Powerful Motivators," *HRfocus,* August 2001, p. 10.

8. "5 Ways to Create Team Motivation," *Manager's Edge,* November 2007, p. 4.

9. Martin Booe, "Sales Force at Mary Kay China Embraces the American Way," *Workforce Management,* April 2005, pp. 24–25.

10. Jennifer Laabs, "Satisfy Them with More Than Money," *Workforce,* November 1998, p. 43; Charlotte Garvey, "Meaningful Tokens of Appreciation," *HR Magazine,* August 2004, pp. 101–106; 10. Adrian Gostick and Chester Elton, *The Carrot Principle* (New York: The Free Press, 2007).

11. "Time Your Praise to Make It Last," *WorkingSMART,* June 2000, p. 2.

12. "Ten Sentences That Will Help You Retain Your Best Employees," *Employee Recruitment & Retention,* sample issue, 2004 (Lawrence Ragan Communications Inc.).

13. Andrew J. DuBrin, "Self-Perceived Technical Orientation and Attitudes Toward Being Flattered," *Psychological Reports*, vol. 96, 2005, pp. 852–854.

14. The original version of expectancy theory applied to work motivation is Victor Vroom, *Work and Motivation* (New York: Wiley, 1964). A scholarly update of the theory is presented in Steel and König, "Integrating Theories of Motivation," pp. 893–895.

15. Alexander D. Stajkovic and Fred Luthans, "Social Cognitive Theory and Self-Efficacy: Going Beyond Traditional Motivational and Behavioral Approaches," *Organizational Dynamics,* Spring 1998, p. 66.

16. Steve McShane, "Getting Emotional about Employee Motivation," *Currents* (published by McGraw-Hill), September 2004, p. 1; Amir Erez and Alice M. Isen, "The Influence of Positive Affect on the Components of Expectancy Motivation," *Journal of Applied Psychology,* December 2002, pp. 1055–1067.

# 14 Enhancing Ethical Behavior

## Learning Objectives

After reading and studying this chapter and doing the exercises, you should be able to:

1 Recognize the importance of ethical behavior for establishing good interpersonal relationships in organizations.

2 Describe why the character trait of virtuousness contributes to being ethical in the workplace.

3 Identify job situations that often present ethical dilemmas.

4 Use a systematic method for making ethical decisions and behaving ethically.

## Outline

1 **Why be Concerned about Business Ethics?**    430

2 **Why we Have so Many Ethical Problems**    433
Why Being Ethical Isn't Easy
A Survey of the Extent of Ethical Problems
Frequent Ethical Dilemmas
Choosing between Two Rights: Dealing with Defining Moments

3 **Guidelines for Behaving Ethically**    441
Developing Virtuousness
Following a Guide to Ethical Decision Making
Developing Strong Relationships with Work Associates
Using Corporate Ethics Programs
Being Environmentally Conscious
Following an Applicable Professional Code of Conduct
Be Ready to Exert Upward Leadership

F or Tina Byles Williams hiring ethical employees is doing the smart thing as much as doing the right thing. The pension funds and other institutions that pay her 10-year-old firm, FIS Group Inc., for investment advice and management naturally expect that none of her 16 employees will make off with their funds. They also expect no conflicts of interest or other improprieties—a matter brought into high relieve three years ago when a former employee's activities made Williams consider measures to prevent unethical employee behavior.

*Since the incident, the $6 million company has re-examined its process for hiring, evaluating, and retaining ethical employees. Williams, 45, how regards hiring ethical employees to be a core mission: "If part of what we're selling is trust, it's critical to hire people of integrity and high ethics."*

*Williams pays for background checks on job applicants, and notices how cheerfully employees complete reports on personal investments, which detect conflicts of interest. [As described later in the chapter, a conflict of interest occurs when you are not in position to be entirely objective about an issue.] Williams says, "I think people are fundamentally good. But you need to establish a framework of expectations and monitoring." [1]*

The scenario just described illustrates that ethical issues in the workplace are not just about big business and corporate executives. People performing all types of work need a good sense of ethics (and etiquette) to be successful. Also, you often need to have an ethical reputation to get the job you want. *Ethics* refers to what is good and bad, right and wrong, just and unjust, and what people should do. Ethics is the vehicle for turning values into action. If you value fair play, you will do such things as giving honest performance evaluations to members of your group.

We study ethics here because a person's ethical code has a significant impact on his or her interpersonal relationships. This chapter's approach will emphasize the importance of ethics, common ethical problems, and guidelines for behaving ethically. Self-Assessment Quiz 14-1 gives you the opportunity to examine your ethical beliefs and attitudes.

■ Learning Objective 1

# Why be Concerned about Business Ethics?

When asked why ethics is important, most people would respond with something to the effect that "Ethics is important because it's the right thing to do. You behave decently in the workplace because your family and religious values have taught you what is right and wrong." All this is true, but the justification for behaving ethically is more complex, as described next. [2]

A major justification for behaving ethically on the job is to recognize that people are motivated by both self-interest and moral commitments. Most

## Self-Assessment Quiz  14-1

### The Ethical Reasoning Inventory

**Directions:**  Describe how well you agree with each of the following statements, using the following scale: disagree strongly (DS); disagree (D); neutral (N); agree (A); agree strongly (AS). Circle the number in the appropriate column.

|  | DS | D | N | A | AS |
|---|---|---|---|---|---|
| 1. When applying for a job, I would cover up the fact that I had been fired from my most recent job. | 5 | 4 | 3 | 2 | 1 |
| 2. Cheating just a few dollars in one's favor on an expense account is okay if a person needs the money. | 5 | 4 | 3 | 2 | 1 |
| 3. Employees should report on each other for wrongdoing. | 1 | 2 | 3 | 4 | 5 |
| 4. It is acceptable to give approximate figures for expense account items when one does not have all the receipts. | 5 | 4 | 3 | 2 | 1 |
| 5. I see no problem with conducting a little personal business on company time. | 5 | 4 | 3 | 2 | 1 |
| 6. Just to make a sale, I would stretch the truth about a delivery date. | 5 | 4 | 3 | 2 | 1 |
| 7. I would fix up a purchasing agent with a date just to close a sale. | 5 | 4 | 3 | 2 | 1 |
| 8. I would flirt with my boss just to get a bigger salary increase. | 5 | 4 | 3 | 2 | 1 |
| 9. If I received $400 for doing some odd jobs, I would report it on my income tax return. | 1 | 2 | 3 | 4 | 5 |
| 10. I see no harm in taking home a few office supplies. | 5 | 4 | 3 | 2 | 1 |
| 11. It is acceptable to read the e-mail messages and faxes of coworkers, even when not invited to do so. | 5 | 4 | 3 | 2 | 1 |
| 12. It is unacceptable to call in sick to take a day off, even if only done once or twice a year. | 1 | 2 | 3 | 4 | 5 |
| 13. I would accept a permanent, full-time job even if I knew I wanted the job for only six months. | 5 | 4 | 3 | 2 | 1 |
| 14. I would first check company policy before accepting an expensive gift from a supplier. | 1 | 2 | 3 | 4 | 5 |
| 15. To be successful in business, a person usually has to ignore ethics. | 5 | 4 | 3 | 2 | 1 |
| 16. If I felt physically attracted toward a job candidate, I would hire that person over a more qualified candidate. | 5 | 4 | 3 | 2 | 1 |
| 17. On the job, I tell the truth all the time. | 1 | 2 | 3 | 4 | 5 |
| 18. If a student were very pressed for time, it would be acceptable to either have a friend write the paper or purchase one. | 5 | 4 | 3 | 2 | 1 |

*(continued)*

## Self-Assessment Quiz  **14-1**  (*Continued*)

| | | | | | |
|---|---|---|---|---|---|
| 19. I would be willing to put a hazardous chemical in a consumer product if the product made a good profit for the company. | 5 | 4 | 3 | 2 | 1 |
| 20. I would never accept credit for a coworker's ideas. | 1 | 2 | 3 | 4 | 5 |

Total score: _____

### Scoring and Interpretation:

Add the numbers you have circled to obtain your total score.

**90–100**   You are a strongly ethical person who may take a little ribbing from coworkers for being too straitlaced.

**61–90**   You show an average degree of ethical awareness, and therefore should become more sensitive to ethical issues.

**41–59**   Your ethics are underdeveloped, but you at least have some awareness of ethical issues. You need to raise your level of awareness of ethical issues.

**20–40**   Your ethical values are far below contemporary standards in business. Begin a serious study of business ethics.

people want to maximize gain for themselves (remember the expectancy theory of motivation?). At the same time, most people are motivated to do something morally right. As one of many examples, vast numbers of people donate money to charity, although keeping that amount of money for themselves would provide more personal gain.

Many business executives want employees to behave ethically because a good reputation can enhance business. A favorable corporate reputation may enable firms to charge premium prices and attract better job applicants. A favorable reputation also helps attract investors, such as mutual fund managers who purchase stock in companies. Certain mutual funds, for example, invest only in companies that are environmentally friendly. Managers want employees to behave ethically because unethical behavior—for example, employee theft, lost production time, and lawsuits—is costly.

Behaving ethically is also important because many unethical acts are illegal as well, which can lead to financial loss and imprisonment. According to one estimate, the cost of unethical and fraudulent acts committed by U.S. employees totals $400 billion per year. A company that knowingly allows workers to engage in unsafe practices might be fined and the executives may be held personally liable. Furthermore, unsafe practices can kill people. In recent history, two employees burned to death in a fire they could not escape in a chicken processing plant. Management had blocked the back doors to prevent employees from sneaking chicken parts out of the plant. Low ethics have also resulted in financial hardship for employees as company executives raid pension funds of other companies they purchase, sharply reducing or eliminating the retirement funds of many workers.

A subtle reason for behaving ethically is that high ethics increases the quality of work life. Ethics provides a set of guidelines that specify what makes for acceptable behavior. Being ethical will point you toward actions that make life more satisfying for work associates. A company code of ethics specifies what constitutes ethical versus unethical behavior. When employees follow this code, the quality of work life improves. Several sample clauses from ethical codes are as follows:

- Demonstrate courtesy, respect, honesty, and fairness.

- Do not use abusive language.

- Do not bring firearms or knives to work.

- Do not offer bribes.

- Maintain confidentiality of records.

- Do not harass (sexually, racially, ethnically, or physically) subordinates, superiors, coworkers, customers, or suppliers.

To the extent that all members of the organization abide by this ethical code, the quality of work life will improve. At the same time, interpersonal relations in organizations will be strengthened.

# Why we Have so Many Ethical Problems

■ **Learning Objective 2**

To become more skilled at behaving ethically, it is important to familiarize yourself with common ethical problems in organizations. Whether or not a given situation presents an ethical problem for a person depends to some extent on its **moral intensity**, or how deeply others might be affected. [3] A worker might face a strong ethical conflict about dumping mercury into a water supply but would be less concerned about dumping cleaning fluid. Yet both acts would be considered unethical and illegal. Here we first look at why being ethical is not as easy as it sounds. We then look at some data about the frequency of ethical problems and an analysis of predictable ethical temptations, and examine the subtle ethical dilemma of choosing between rights.

■ **Moral intensity**
in ethical decision making, how deeply others might be affected by the decision

## WHY BEING ETHICAL ISN'T EASY

As analyzed by Linda Klebe Treviño and Michael E. Brown, behaving ethically in business is more complex than it seems on the surface for a variety of reasons. [4] To begin with, ethical decisions are complex. For example, someone might argue that hiring children for factory jobs in overseas countries is unethical. Yet if these children lose their jobs, many would starve or turn to crime to survive. Second, people do not always recognize the moral issues involved in a decision. The home-maintenance worker who finds a butcher knife under the bed might not think that he has a role to play in perhaps preventing murder. Sometimes language hides the moral issue involved, such as when the term *file sharing* music replaces *stealing* music.

Another complexity in making ethical decisions is that people have different levels of moral development. At one end of the scale, some people behavior morally just to escape punishment. At the other end of the scale, some people are morally developed to the point that they are guided by principles of justice and want to help as many people as possible. The environment in which we work also influences whether we behave ethically. Suppose a restaurant owner encourages such practices as serving customers food that was accidentally dropped on the kitchen floor. An individual server is more likely to engage in such behavior to obey the demands of the owner—even though the server knows that dangerous bacteria may have attached to the food.

A fundamental reason that being unethical is not always easy is that some people have a predisposition to be unethical. The predisposition works almost like a personality trait, compelling certain people to be devious. A person with a **utilitarian predisposition** believes that the value of an act's outcomes should determine whether it is moral. [5] A server with this predisposition might be willing to serve food that dropped on the floor as long as no customer became sick or sued the restaurant. A small business owner with a utilitarian predisposition might be willing to sell fake luxury goods on the Internet as long as nobody complained and he or she was not caught. When asked about why he sold imitation watches, one vendor said, "What's the difference? My watches look like the real thing, and they tell time."

■ **Utilitarian predisposition**
a belief that the value of an act's outcomes should determine whether it is moral

## A SURVEY OF THE EXTENT OF ETHICAL PROBLEMS

The ethical misdeeds of executives have received substantial publicity in recent years. However, recent surveys show that ethical violations by rank-and-file employees are widespread, particularly with respect to lying. According to two separate surveys, more than one-third of U.S. workers admit to having fabricated about their need for sick days. More employees are stretching the reasons for taking time off. Job applicants reporting false or embellished academic credentials have hit a three-year high. [6]

Figure 14-1 presents data about unethical behavior noticed by employees. Notice that the type of bullying behavior described in Chapter 11 is perceived to be unethical. As found in other surveys, lying is another widespread ethical problem in the workplace. Although these findings might suggest that unethical behavior is on the increase, another explanation is possible. Workers today might be more observant of ethical problems and more willing to note them on a survey.

## FREQUENT ETHICAL DILEMMAS

Certain ethical mistakes, including illegal actions, recur in the workplace. Familiarizing oneself can be helpful in monitoring one's own behavior. The following subsections describe a number of common ethical problems faced by business executives as well as workers at lower job levels. [7] Figure 14-2 outlines these problems.

Despite a heightened emphasis on business ethics following scandals earlier this decade, a significant number of employees say they still witness questionable workplace behavior. Here is the percentage of employees who say they observed certain behaviors in the previous year, according to a survey of 3,015 workers by the Ethics Resource Center.

| | |
|---|---|
| Abusive or intimidating behavior toward employees | 21% |
| Lying to employees, customers, vendors, or public | 19% |
| Violations of safety regulations | 16% |
| Misreporting of actual time worked | 16% |
| Race, sex, or other discrimination | 12% |
| Theft | 11% |
| Sexual harassment | 9% |

**Figure 14-1**

**Questionable Workplace Behavior as Reported by Employees**

**Source:** Ethics Resource Center as reported in Erin White, "What Would You Do? Ethics Courses Get Context," *The Wall Street Journal*, June 12, 2006, p. B3.

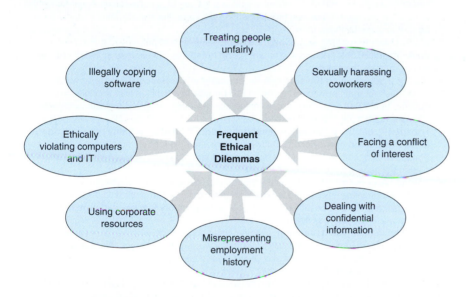

**Figure 14-2**

**Frequent Ethical Dilemmas**

Many ethical temptations face the individual on the job, forcing him or her to think through ethical issues practically every workday.

## Illegally Copying Software

A rampant ethical problem is whether or not to illegally copy computer software. According to the Business Software Alliance, approximately 35 percent of applications used in business are illegal. [8] Figure 14-3 offers details about and insight into this widespread ethical dilemma.

## Treating People Unfairly

Being fair to people means equity, reciprocity, and impartiality. Fairness revolves around the issue of giving people equal rewards for accomplishing equal amounts of work. The goal of human resource legislation is to make decisions about people based on their qualifications and performance—not on the basis of demographic factors such as gender, race, or age. A fair working environment is where performance is the only factor that counts (equity). Employer–employee expectations must be understood and met (reciprocity). Prejudice and bias must be eliminated (impartiality).

A flagrant unethical and **illegal** job behavior is unauthorized copying of software. When confronted with software pirating, people are quick to rationalize their actions. Here are the top ten defenses of software pirates. (None of them are likely to hold up if you are caught.)

1. **I'm allowed to make a backup disk in case something happens to the original, so it must be okay to use it on another machine.** A backup is strictly a backup to be used on the same computer. The original should be safely locked away, and the copy should be stored away only as a backup.
2. **I didn't copy it—a friend gave it to me.** Technically you are right. You would not be guilty of illegally copying software in this case, although your friend would. However, since illegally copied software is regarded as stolen property, you are just as guilty as you would be for stealing it in the first place.
3. **My boss (or department head, or instructor) told me to. It's that person's problem.** The defense "I was just following orders" is a weak one. Complying with your boss's demands to commit an illegal act does not get you off the hook. You could be fired for obeying an order to commit a crime.
4. **I bought the software; shouldn't I be able to do what I want with it?** Software is seldom ever sold to individuals. What is sold is a license to use the software, not full rights to do what you want. When you break open the package, the law assumes that you have agreed to abide by those terms.
5. **It's not like I'm robbing somebody.** Software is intellectual property just like a song, a book, an article, or a trademark. You are taking bread from the table of software engineers when you copy their work.
6. **It's OK if you're using the software for educational purposes.** If education were a justification for theft, driving instructors would be able to steal cars with impunity. There is a doctrine of **fair use** that allows some limited use of written materials in classrooms without permission from the copyright holder.
7. **I needed it, but the price was unreasonably high. If I had to actually pay for it, there is no way I could ever afford it.** Software prices are high for the same reason the price of houses is high: both require a lot of highly skilled labor to create. You cannot steal a DVD player just because you cannot afford one.
8. **I didn't know it was illegal.** Unauthorized duplication of software is a felony in many states and provinces. State and federal laws provide for civil and criminal penalties if you are convicted. It would be difficult to convince a judge or jury that you had no idea that unauthorized copying was illegal.
9. **It's only illegal if you get caught.** Criminal behavior is illegal whether or not you are caught. If you do get caught illegally copying software, you could face fines, imprisonment, and/or civil penalties. Some educational institutions take disciplinary action against software pirates, including suspension.
10. **Oh, come on, everyone is doing it.** This excuse has been used to justify everything from speeding to lynching. The popularity of a criminal act does not make it legal.

Treating people fairly—and therefore ethically—requires a deemphasis on political factors, or favoritism. Yet this ethical doctrine is not always easy to implement. It is human nature to want to give bigger rewards (such as fatter raises or bigger orders) to people we like.

A major contributor to treating people unfairly is cronyism, or giving jobs to people who have done personal favors for you. Often the unqualified friend is given a position when competent and qualified candidates are available. Cronyism is often practiced in government, where heads of government agencies are sometimes appointed mostly because they are a supporter and friend of the person in power. Earl E. Devaney, the Interior Department's inspector general, said at a hearing, "Simply stated, short of a crime, anything goes at the highest levels of the Department of the Interior." Among the ethical charges were cronyism and cover-ups of incompetence. [9] Cronyism is also sometimes found in business, with buddies, relatives, and lovers often being chosen over more qualified workers for a variety of positions.

> "Follow the Platinum Rule: Treat people the way they wish to be treated."
> —Eric Harvey and Scott Airitam, authors of Ethics 4 Everyone

## Sexually Harassing Coworkers

Sexual harassment is also an ethical issue because it is morally wrong and unfair. All acts of sexual harassment flunk an ethics test. Before sexually harassing another person, the potential harasser should ask, "Would I want a loved one to be treated this way?"

## Facing a Conflict of Interest

Part of being ethical is making business judgments only on the basis of the merits or facts in a situation. Imagine that you are a supervisor who is romantically involved with a worker within the group. When it comes time to assign raises, it will be difficult for you to be objective. A **conflict of interest** occurs when your judgment or objectivity is compromised. Conflicts of interest often take place in the sales end of business. If a company representative accepts a large gift from a sales representative, it may be difficult to make objective judgments about buying from the rep. Yet being taken to dinner by a vendor would not ordinarily cloud one's judgment. Another common example of a conflict of interest is making a hiring decision about a friend who badly needs a job, but is not well qualified for the position.

■ **Conflict of interest**
a situation that occurs when a person's judgment or objectivity is compromised

Conflicts of interest have been behind some of the major business scandals in recent times, such as Enron Corporation auditors giving the company a favorable rating. The accounting and consulting firm Arthur Andersen had earned $25 million in auditing fees and $27 million for consulting prior to the company's collapse. The conflict of interest was that if the Arthur Andersen auditors were too critical of Enron, the firm might not have received such lucrative consulting contracts. [10] Some financial research analysts give glowing public reports about the fiscal condition of a company when that company is a client of the analyst's own firm. The analyst's firm sells services for issuing new stock and assisting with corporate mergers and acquisitions.

## Dealing with Confidential Information

An ethical person can be trusted by others not to divulge confidential information unless the welfare of others is at stake. Suppose a coworker tells you in confidence that she is upset with the company and is therefore looking for another job. Behaving ethically, you do not pass along this information to your supervisor even though it would help your supervisor plan for a replacement. Now suppose the scenario changes slightly. Your coworker tells you she is looking for another job because she is upset. She tells you she is so upset that she plans to destroy company computer files on her last day. If your friend does find another job, you might warn the company about her contemplated activities.

The challenge of dealing with confidential information arises in many areas of business, many of which affect interpersonal relations. If you learned that a coworker was indicted for a crime, charged with sexual harassment, or facing bankruptcy, there would be a temptation to gossip about the person. A highly ethical person would not pass along information about the personal difficulties of another person.

### Misrepresenting Employment History

Many people are tempted to distort in a positive direction information about their employment history on their job résumé, on job application form, and during the interview. Distortion, or lying, of this type is considered unethical and can lead to immediate dismissal if discovered. A well-known case in point is George O'Leary, who was dismissed after five days on the job as head coach of the Notre Dame Football team. After his résumé distortions were uncovered, O'Leary resigned and admitted he falsified his academic and athletic credentials for decades. He had falsely claimed to have a master's degree in education and to have played college football for three years. [11] Shortly thereafter, O'Leary made good use of his network of professional contacts and was hired by the Minnesota Vikings professional football team in a coaching position. Despite being disgraced nationally, O'Leary's political skills provided him with a safety net. O'Leary later became the head football coach at the University of Central Florida, showing that people can recover from a single ethical lapse.

### Using Corporate Resources

A corporate resource is anything the company owns, including its name and reputation. If Jake Petro worked for Ford Motor Company, for example, it would be unethical for him to establish a body shop and put on his letterhead and Web site, "Jake Petro, Manufacturing Technician, Ford Motor Company." (The card and Web site would imply that the Ford Motor Co. supports this venture.) Other uses of corporate resources fall more into the gray area. It might be quite ethical to borrow a laptop computer for the weekend from your employer to conduct work at home. But it would be less ethical to borrow the laptop computer to prepare income taxes. In the latter case, you might be accused of using corporate resources for personal purposes. Loading personal software on company computers so you can access your bank account and so forth also can be considered an ethical violation.

### Ethically Violating Computers and IT

As computers dominate the workplace, many ethical issues have arisen in addition to pirating software. One ethical dilemma that surfaces frequently is the fairness of tracking the Web sites a person visits and those he or she buys from. Should this information be sold, like a mailing list? The scams that appear on e-mail everyday are another prime example of the unethical use of information technology. Another issue is the fairness of having an employee work at a keyboard for 60 hours in one week when such behavior frequently leads to repetitive motion disorder. Figure 14-4 lists some major ethical issues involved in computer use.

You may have observed that these common ethical problems are not always clear-cut. Aside from obvious matters such as prohibitions against stealing, lying, cheating, and intimidating, subjectivity enters into ethical decision making. Skill-Building Exercise 14-1 provides an opportunity to try out your ethical reasoning.

1. Do not use a computer to harm other people. Avoid all obscene, defamatory, threatening, or otherwise harassing messages. Take precautions against others developing repetitive motion disorders.
2. Do not interfere with other people's computer work. (This includes intentionally spreading computer viruses.)
3. Do not snoop around in other people's files.
4. Do not use a computer to steal.
5. Do not use a computer to bear false witness.
6. Do not use or copy software for which you have not paid (see Figure 14-1).
7. Do not use other people's resources without authorization.
8. Do not appropriate other people's intellectual output.
9. Do not use the employer's computer for the personal promotion of commercial goods or services, unless granted permission by the employer.
10. Do think about the social consequences of the program you write.
11. Do use a computer in ways that show consideration and respect.

**Figure  14-4**

**Eleven Commandments for Computer Ethics**
**Source:** Adapted and updated from Arlene H. Rinaldi and Florida Atlantic University, rinaldi@acc.fau.edu; "Code of Conduct for Computer and Network Use," *http://www.rit.edu/computerconduct*.

# Skill-Building Exercise 14-1

## The Ethics Game

Many companies teach ethics by asking small teams of employees to confront difficult scenarios such as those that follow. Discuss these ethical problems in teams. As you discuss the scenarios, identify the ethical issues involved.

**Scenario 1:** One of your assignments is to find a contractor to conduct building maintenance for your company headquarters. You invite bids for the job. High-Performance Cleaners, a firm staffed largely by teenagers from troubled families who have criminal records, bids on the job.

Many of these teenagers also have severe learning disabilities and cannot readily find employment. High-Performance Cleaners proves to be the second-highest bidder. You:

**A.**  advise High-Performance Cleaners that its bid is too high for consideration and that your company is not a social agency.
**B.**  award the bid to High-Performance Cleaners and justify your actions with a letter to top management by talking about social responsibility.
**C.**  falsify the other bids in your report to management, making High-Performance Cleaners the low bidder—and thus the contract winner.
**D.**  explain to High-Performance Cleaners that it lost the bid, but you will award the company a piece of the contract because of its sterling work with teenagers in need.

**Scenario 2:** You live in Texas and your company sends you on a three-day trip to New York City. Your business dealings in the Big Apple will keep you there Wednesday, Thursday, and Friday morning. You have several friends and relatives in New York, so you decide to stay there until Sunday afternoon. Besides, you want to engage in tourist activities such as taking a boat tour around Manhattan and visiting Radio City Music Hall.

*(Continued)*

## Skill-Building Exercise 14-1 (*Continued*)

When preparing your expense report for your trip, you request payment for all your business-related costs up through Friday afternoon, plus:

**A.**   your return trip on Sunday.

**B.**   the return trip and the room cost for Friday and Saturday nights.

**C.**   the return trip, one-half of your weekend food expenses, and two extra nights in the hotel.

**D.**   the return trip and your food costs for the weekend (which you justify because you ate at fast-food restaurants on Wednesday, Thursday, and Friday).

**Scenario 1:** You are the leader of a self-managing work team in a financial services company. The work of your team has expanded to the point where you are authorized to hire another team member. The team busily interviews a number of candidates from inside and outside the company. The other team members agree that one of the candidates (Pat) has truly outstanding credentials. You agree that Pat is a strong candidate, yet you don't want Pat on the team because the two of you were emotionally involved for about a year. You think that working with Pat would disrupt your concentration and bring back hurtful memories. You decide to:

**A.**   tell the group that you have some negative information about Pat's past that would disqualify Pat for the job.

**B.**   telephone Pat and beg that Pat find employment elsewhere.

**C.**   tell the group that you agree Pat is qualified, but explain your concerns about the disruption in concentration and emotional hurt.

**D.**   tell the group that you agree Pat is right for the position, and mention nothing about the past relationship.

**Scoring and Observation:** Scenario 1, about High-Performance Cleaners, raises dozens of ethical questions, including whether humanitarian considerations can outweigh profit concerns. Teams that chose "a" receive 0 points; "b," 20 points; "c," −10 points; "d," 10 points. (Answer "d" is best here because it would not be fair to give the bid to the second-highest bidder. However, you are still finding a way to reward the High-Performance Cleaners for its meritorious work in the community. Answer "c" is the worst because you would be outright lying.)

Scenario 2 raises ethical issues about using company resources. Teams that chose "a" receive 20 points; "b," −10 points; "c," −15 points; "d," 0 points. (Answer "a" is fairest because the company would expect to reimburse you for your roundtrip plus the expenses up through Friday afternoon. Answer "c" is the worst because it would be unjustified for you to be reimbursed for your vacation in New York.)

Scenario 3 raises issues about fairness in making selection decisions. Teams that chose "a" receive −20 points; "b," −10 points; "c," 15 points; "d," 0 points. (Answer "c" is the most ethical because you are being honest with the group about the reason you do not wish to hire Pat. Answer "a" is the most unethical because you are telling lies about Pat. Furthermore, you might be committing the illegal act of libel.)

## CHOOSING BETWEEN TWO RIGHTS: DEALING WITH DEFINING MOMENTS

Ethical decision making usually involves choosing between two options: one we perceive to be right and one we perceive to be wrong. A challenging twist to ethical decision making is to sort through your values when you have to choose between two rights, or two morally sound choices. Joseph L. Badaracco, Jr., uses the term **defining moment** to describe choosing between two or more ideals in which we deeply believe. [12] If you can learn to work through defining moments, your ethical skills will be enhanced. Let's first take a nonwork example to illustrate a defining moment.

■ **Defining moment**
choosing between two or more ideals in which one deeply believes

> *Imagine yourself as a basketball referee in a league for boys 10 years old and younger. Luis, the smallest boy on the team, has a self-confidence problem in general, and he has not scored a basket yet this season. This is the final game of the season. The other team is ahead by 10 points with one minute to go. Luis lets fly with a shot that goes into the basket, but his right heel is on the line. If the goal is allowed, Luis will experience one of the happiest moments in his life, and his self-confidence might increase. You strongly believe in helping people grow and develop. Yet you also strongly believe in following the rules of sports. What should you do?*

You may have recognized that a defining moment is a role conflict in which you have to choose between competing values. A CEO might deeply believe that she has an obligation to the stockholders to make a profit, and at the same time believe in being generous and fair toward employees. However, to make a profit this year she will be forced to lay off several good employees with long seniority. The CEO now faces a moment of truth. Badaracco suggests that the individual can work through a defining moment by discovering "Who am I?" You discover who you are by soul searching answers to three questions:

1. What feelings and intuitions are coming into conflict in this situation?

2. Which of the values that are in conflict are the most deeply rooted in my life?

3. What combinations of expediency and shrewdness, coupled with imagination and boldness, will help me implement my personal understanding of what is right?

Skill-Building Exercise 14-2 gives you an opportunity to deal with defining moments. The three questions just asked could help you find answers, but do not be constrained by these questions.

# Guidelines for Behaving Ethically

Following guidelines for ethical behavior is the heart of being ethical. Although many people behave ethically without studying ethical guidelines, they are usually following guidelines programmed into their minds early in life. The Golden Rule exemplifies a guideline taught by parents, grandparents, and kindergarten teachers. In this section, we approach ethical guidelines from five perspectives: (1) developing virtuousness, (2) following a guide to ethical

## Skill-Building Exercise 14-2

### Dealing with Defining Moments

The toughest ethical choices for many people occur when they have to choose between two rights. The result is a defining moment, because we are challenged to think in a deeper way by choosing between two or more ideals. Working individually or in teams, deal with the two following defining moments. Explain why these scenarios could require choosing between two rights, and explain the reasoning behind your decisions.

**Scenario 1:** You are the manager of a department in a business firm that assigns each department a fixed amount of money for salary increases each year. An average-performing member of the department asks you in advance for an above-average increase. He explains that his mother has developed multiple sclerosis and requires the services of a paid helper from time to time. You are concerned that if you give this man an above-average increase, somebody else in the department will have to receive a below-average increase.

**Scenario 2:** You are the team leader of an e-tailing (retail selling over the Internet) group. In recent months each team member has been working about 60 hours per week, with little prospect of the workload decreasing in the future. Because the e-tailing project is still losing money, higher management insists that one person be dropped from the team. One member of the team, Mildred, is willing to work only 45 hours per week because she spends considerable time volunteering with autistic children. Mildred's work is satisfactory, but her output is the lowest in the group because of her shorter number of working hours. You must make a decision about whether to recommend that Mildred be dismissed.

decision making, (3) developing strong relationships with work associates, (4) using corporate ethics programs, and (5) following an applicable professional code of conduct.

## DEVELOPING VIRTUOUSNESS

A deep-rooted approach to behaving ethically is to have strong moral and ethical principles, or to be virtuous. A person of high virtue has good character, and genuine motivation and intentions. A major problem in becoming virtuous is to agree on what values constitute virtuousness. Management professor Edwin A. Locke has prepared a modern analysis of what values constitute virtue in a business environment. [13] Here we highlight his findings because they are representative of what constitutes virtuousness. Other observers might have a different list of virtuous values.

1. *Rationality* is a principle that leads to being virtuousness. Being rational includes taking reality (facts) seriously, thinking hard, thinking long-range, and thinking of the consequences of one's actions. A rational parachute technician would not ship a defective parachute just because it was close to quitting time and he did not want to work late. And we hope that the manager is rational (and therefore ethical) when writing performance evaluations.

2. *Honesty*, the refusal to fake reality, is a value that contributes directly to ethical behavior. Being dishonest can also be illegal, such as when a company lies to the Internal Revenue Service about expenses it incurred or hides revenue when preparing a tax report. Dishonesty in terms of making false statements about the financial health of an enterprise has been one of the most frequent business frauds. Being caught lying can lead to dismissal at many employers. An example of such a lie would be blaming someone else for a mistake of your own. *Integrity* means loyalty to one's rational convictions, or sticking with one's principles. If you believe that favoritism is immoral, then you would not recommend that the company hire a friend of yours who you know to be unqualified.

3. *Independence* refers to the responsibility of using your own rational judgment rather than relying too heavily on the thinking of others. In personal life being independent means not relying too heavily on others for permanent support. A worker with a strong value of independence would not readily go along with the thinking of the group if he or she had a better idea.

5. *Productivity* means creating, or obtaining through trade, the materials values your life requires. You are therefore virtuous if are productive on the job and contribute enough to be worth of your compensation. Justice refers to looking at the facts of the character and achievements of others and judging them objectively. To be just is to be fair, such as willing to pay somebody what he or she are worth, or pay a fair price for merchandise. When a big company executive "squeezes" a supplier to the point that the supplier can barely make a profit, the executive is not practicing justice.

5. Forgiveness is a virtue providing the breach of morality was not too severe, such as forgiving an employee who ate a sandwich without paying when eating food without paying was not authorized.

6. Pride in the context of virtues refers to working to perfect one's moral character. You would thus be proud because you are virtuous.

These values that contribute to being virtuousness are useful in the study of human relations because they all translate into interpersonal skills, such as knowing how to be productive and treat people justly.

## FOLLOWING A GUIDE TO ETHICAL DECISION MAKING

■ Learning Objective 4

A powerful strategy for behaving ethically is to follow a guide for ethical decision making. Such a guide for making contemplated decisions includes testing ethics. **Ethical screening** refers to running a contemplated decision or action through an ethics test. Such screening makes the most sense when the contemplated

■ **Ethical screening**
running a contemplated decision or action through an ethics test

action or decision is not clearly ethical or unethical. If a sales representative were to take a favorite customer to Pizza Hut for lunch, an ethical screen would not be necessary. Nobody would interpret a "veggie super" to be a serious bribe. Assume, instead, that the sales rep offered to give the customer an under-the-table gift of $1000 for placing a large offer with the rep's firm. The sales representative's behavior would be so blatantly unethical that conducting an ethical screen would be unnecessary.

Several useful ethical screens, or guides, to ethical decision making have been developed. A guide developed by Treviño and Nelson is presented here because it incorporates the basic ideas in other ethical tests. [14] After studying this guide, you will be asked to ethically screen three different scenarios. The eight steps to sound ethical decision making follow.

1. **Gather the facts.** When making an important decision in business, it is necessary to gather relevant facts. Ask yourself the following questions: "Are there any legal issues involved here?" "Is there precedent in our firm with respect to this type of decision?" "Do I have the authority to make this decision?" "Are there company rules and regulations governing such a decision?"

   The manager of a child-care center needed to hire an additional child-care specialist. One of the applicants was a 55-year-old male with experience as a father and grandfather. The manager judged him to be qualified, yet she knew that many parents would not want their preschool children to be cared for by a middle-age male. Many people perceive that a younger woman is better qualified for child care than an older man. The manager therefore had to gather considerable facts about the situation, including facts about job discrimination and precedents in hiring males as child-care specialists.

   Gathering facts is influenced by emotion, with the result that ethical decision making is not an entirely rational process. [15] We tend to interpret facts based upon our biases and preconceived notions. For example, if the child-care center manager has heard negative information about middle-age men who want to engage in child care, the manager might look hard for indicators that this candidate should be disqualified.

2. **Define the ethical issues.** The ethical issues in a given decision are often more complicated than a first glance suggests. When faced with a complex decision, it may be helpful to talk over the ethical issues with another person. The ethical issues might involve character traits such as being kind and caring and treating others with respect. Or the ethical issues might relate to some of the common ethical problems described earlier in the chapter. Among them are facing conflict of interest, dealing with confidential information, and using corporate resources.

   The manager of the child-care center is facing such ethical issues as fairness, job discrimination, and meeting the demands of customers at the expense of job applicants. The manager is also facing a diversity issue: Should the workforce in a child-care center be culturally diverse, or do we hire only young women?

3. **Identify the affected parties.** When faced with a complex ethical decision, it is important to identify all the affected parties. Major corporate decisions

can affect thousands of people. If a company decides to shut down a plant and outsource the manufacturing to a low-wage country, thousands of individuals and many different parties are affected. Workers lose their jobs, suppliers lose their customers, the local government loses out on tax revenues, and local merchants lose many of their customers. You may need to brainstorm with a few others to think of all the parties affected by a given decision.

The parties affected by the decision about hiring or not hiring the 55-year-old male include the applicant himself, the children, the parents, and the board of directors of the child-care center. The government might also be involved if the man were rejected and filed charges of age and sex discrimination.

4. **Identify the consequences.** After you have identified the parties affected by a decision, the next step is to predict the consequences for each party. It may not be necessary to identify every consequence, yet it is important to identify the consequences with the highest probability of occurring and those with the most negative outcomes. The problem is that many people can be harmed by an unethical decision, such as not fully describing the possible side effects of a diet program.

Both short-term and long-term consequences should be specified. A company closing a plant might create considerable short-term turmoil, but in the long-term the company might be healthier. People participating in a diet program might achieve their short-term objective of losing weight. Yet in the long-term, their health might be adversely affected because the diet is not nutritionally balanced.

The symbolic consequences of an action are important. Every action and decision sends a message (the decision is a symbol of something). If a company moves manufacturing out of a community to save on labor costs, it means that the short-term welfare of domestic employees is less important than profit or perhaps the company surviving.

We return to the child-care manager and the job applicant. If the applicant does not get the job, his welfare will be adversely affected. He has been laid off by a large employer and cannot find work in his regular field. His family will also suffer because he will not be able to make a financial contribution to the family. Yet if the man is hired, the child-care center may suffer. Many traditionally minded parents will say, "Absolutely not. I do not want my child cared for by a middle-age man. He could be a child molester." (It may be unethical for people to have vicious stereotypes, yet they still exist.) If the child-care center does hire the man, the act will symbolize that the owners of the center value diversity.

5. **Identify the obligations.** Identify the obligations and the reasons for each obligation when making a complex decision. The manufacturer of automotive brakes has an obligation to produce and sell only brakes that meet high safety standards. The obligation is to the auto manufacturer who purchases the brakes and, more importantly, to the ultimate consumer whose safety depends on effective brakes. The reason for the obligation to make safe brakes is that lives are at stake. The child-care center owner has an obligation to provide for the safety and health of the children at the center.

She must also provide for the peace of mind of the parents and be a good citizen of the community in which the center is located. The decision about hiring the candidate in question must be balanced against all these obligations.

6. **Consider your character and integrity.** A core consideration when faced with an ethical dilemma is how relevant people would judge your character and integrity. What would your family, friends, significant others, teachers, and coworkers think of your actions? To refine this thinking even further, how would you feel if your actions were publicly disclosed in the local newspaper or over e-mail? Would you want the world to know that you gave an under-the-table kickback or that you sexually harassed a frightened teenager working for you? If you would be proud for others to know what decision you made when you faced an ethical dilemma, you are probably making the right decision.

   The child-care center manager might ponder how she would feel if the following information were released in the local newspaper or on the Internet:

   > The manager of Good Times Child Care recently rejected the application of a 55-year-old man for a child-care specialist position. She said that although Mr._____ was well qualified from an experience and personality standpoint, she couldn't hire him. She said that Good Times would lose too much business because many parents would fear that Mr._____ was a child molester or pedophile.

7. **Think creatively about potential actions.** When faced with an ethical dilemma, put yourself in a creative-thinking mode. Stretch your imagination to invent several options rather than thinking you have only two choices—to do or not do something. Creative thinking may point toward a third, and even fourth, alternative. Imagine this ethical dilemma: A purchasing agent is told that if her firm awards a contract to the sales representative's firm, she will find a leather jacket of her choice delivered to her door. The purchasing agent says to herself, "I think we should award the contract to the firm, but I cannot accept the gift. Yet if I turn down the gift, I will be forfeiting a valuable possession that the company simply regards as a cost of doing business."

   The purchasing agent can search for another alternative. She may say to the sales rep, "We will give the contract to your firm because your products fit our requirements. I thank you for the offer of the leather jacket, but instead I would like you to give the jacket to the Salvation Army."

   A creative alternative for the child-care manager might be to offer the applicant the next position that opened for an office manager or maintenance person in the center. In this way she would be offering a qualified applicant a job, but placing him in a position more acceptable to parents. Or do you feel this is a cop-out?

8. **Check your intuition.** So far we have emphasized the rational side of ethical decision making. Another effective way of conducting an ethical screen is to rely on your intuition. How does the contemplated decision

feel? Would you be proud of yourself or would you hate yourself if you made the decision? Imagine how you would feel if you took money from the handbag of a woman sleeping in the park. Would you feel the same way if you took a kickback, sold somebody a defective product, or sold an 80-year-old man an insurance policy he didn't need? How will the manager of the child-care center feel if she turns down the man for the child-care specialist position? In general, experienced workers rely more heavily on intuition when making ethical choices. The reason is that intuition is based largely on experience. [16] Rules for ethical behavior are important, yet often we have to follow our hunches. Experience and rules are not wasted because intuition includes both experience and the study of rules.

You are encouraged to use the guide for ethical decision making when you next face an ethical dilemma of consequence. Skill-Building Exercise 14-3 gives you an opportunity to practice using the eight steps for ethical decision making.

## Skill-Building Exercise 14-3

### Ethical Decision Making

Working in small groups, take one or more of the following ethical dilemmas through the eight steps for screening contemplated decisions. If more than one group chooses the same scenario, compare your answers for the various steps.

**Scenario 1: To Recycle or Not.** Your group is the top management team at a large insurance company. Despite the movement toward digitizing all records, your firm still generates tons of paper each month. Customer payments alone account for truckloads of envelopes each year. The paper recyclers in your area claim they can hardly find a market any longer for used paper, so they will be charging you just to accept your paper for recycling. Your group is wondering whether to recycle.

**Scenario 2: The Hole in the Résumé.** Emily has been working for the family business as an office manager for five years. Because the family business is being sold, Emily has started a job hunt. She also welcomes the opportunity to work in a larger company so she could learn more about how a big company operates. As she begins preparing her job résumé, she ponders how to classify the year of unemployment prior to working at the family business. During that year she worked a total of 10 weeks in entry-level jobs at three fast-food restaurants. Otherwise she filled her time with such activities as walking in the park, watching daytime television shows, surfing the Internet, playing video

*(Continued)*

## Skill-Building Exercise 14-3 (*Continued*)

games, and pursuing her hobby of visiting graveyards. Emily finally decides to tack that year onto the five years in the family business. She indicates on her résumé that she has been working *six* years at the family business. As Emily says, "It's a tight job market for office managers, and I don't want to raise any red flags." Evaluate the ethics of Emily's decision to fill in the year off from work, and perhaps offer her some advice.

**Scenario 3: The High-Profit Toys.** You are a toy company executive starting to plan your holiday season line. You anticipate that the season's hottest item will be Robo-Woman, a battery-operated crime fighter and superheroine. Robo-Woman should wholesale for $25 and retail for $45. Your company figures to earn $15 per unit. You receive a sales call from a manufacturing broker who says he can produce any toy you want for one-third of your present manufacturing cost. He admits that the manufacturer he represents uses prison labor in China, but insists that his business arrangement violates no law. You estimate you can earn $20 per unit if you do business with the manufacturing broker. Your decision is whether to do business with him.

## DEVELOPING STRONG RELATIONSHIPS WITH WORK ASSOCIATES

A provocative explanation of the causes of unethical behavior emphasizes the strength of relationships among people. [17] Assume that two people have close professional ties to each other, such as having worked together for a long time or knowing each other both on and off the job. As a consequence, they are likely to behave ethically toward one another on the job. In contrast, if a weak professional relationship exists between two individuals, either party is more likely to engage in an unethical relationship. The owner of an auto service center is more likely to behave unethically toward a stranger passing through town than toward a long-time customer. The opportunity for unethical behavior between strangers is often minimized because individuals typically do not trust strangers with sensitive information or valuables.

The ethical skill-building consequence of information about personal relationships is that building stronger relationships with people is likely to enhance ethical behavior. If you build strong relationships with work associates, you are likely to behave more ethically toward them. Similarly, your work associates are likely to behave more ethically toward you. The work associates I refer to are all your contacts, both internal and external customers.

## USING CORPORATE ETHICS PROGRAMS

Many organizations have various programs and procedures for promoting ethical behavior. Among them are committees that monitor ethical behavior, training programs in ethics, and vehicles for reporting ethical violations. The presence of these programs is designed to create an atmosphere in which unethical behavior is discouraged and reporting on unethical behavior is encouraged.

Ethics hotlines are one of the best-established programs to help individuals avoid unethical behavior. Should a person be faced with an ethical dilemma, the person calls a toll-free line to speak to a counselor about the dilemma. Sometimes employees ask questions to help interpret a policy, such as, "Is it okay to ask my boss for a date?" or "Are we supposed to give senior citizen discounts to customers who qualify but do not ask for one?" At other times, a more pressing ethical issue might be addressed, such as, "Is it ethical to lay off a worker just five months short of his qualifying for a full pension?"

Human resource professionals contend that no amount of training will ensure that employees will act ethically in every situation, particularly because ethics deals with subtle matters rather than strictly right or wrong. However, Deborah Haliczer, director of employee relations at Northern Illinois University, explains that training is valuable in starting a useful dialogue about right and wrong behavior that employees could remember in murky situations. [18]

Sears Holding Corp. has an ethics hotline the company refers to as an "Assist Line" because very few of the 15,000 calls it receives per year represent crises. Often the six full-time ethics specialists who handle the calls just listen; at other times they intervene to help resolve the problem. The Assist Line is designed to help with the following kinds of calls: guidance about company policy, company code of conduct issues, workplace harassment and discrimination, selling practices, theft, and human resource issues. Employees and managers are able to access information and guidance without feeling they are facing a crisis. The Assist Line is thus a cross between "911" and "411" calls. At times an ethical problem of such high moral intensity is presented that employee confidentiality cannot be maintained. However, the Ethics Office handles the inquiries in as confidential a manner as practical and assigns them case identification numbers for follow-up. [19]

Wells Fargo & Co., a mammoth bank, emphasizes both a code of conduct and ethics training. Its Code of Ethics and Business Conduct specifies policies and standards for employees, covering a variety of topics from maintaining accurate records to participating in civic activities. Each year, employees also participate in ethics training. Any Wells Fargo employee may ask questions or report ethical breaches anonymously using an ethics hotline or dedicated e-mail address. The company will fire violators, dismissing about 100 people a year for misconduct ranging from conflicts of interest to cheating on incentive plans.

Patricia Callahan, executive vice president and director of human resources at the bank, says, "I'm the biggest soft touch in the world. But when someone lies or cheats, you can't have people like that representing us to our customers, whose trust is all we have." [20] The link between the programs just described and individual ethical skills is that these programs assist a worker's skill development. For example, if you become comfortable in asking about ethical issues, or turning in ethical violators, you have become more ethically skilled.

## BEING ENVIRONMENTALLY CONSCIOUS

Another ethical skill is to be *green* or to do your job in helping sustain the physical environment. (*Green* derives from the idea that green vegetation such as trees and forests are a plus for the environment.) The reasoning behind this statement is that it is morally responsible to protect the environment. Do not be concerned with taking sides on the issue of global warming. Whether or not humans and the carbon dioxide emissions they create have contributed to global warming, the physical environment needs your help.

The skill of being environmentally conscious has two major components. The first is to take as many steps as you can individually to help preserve the environment even in such small steps as carrying a reusable cloth bag to the grocery store and not throwing a plastic bottle on a lawn. The second is to be an advocate for the environment by mentioning its importance at work. You might, for example, present data to management about how solar heating can save the company money in the long-run, and how benches and walkways made from recycled tires and plastics are attractive and economical. Figure 14-5 gives you a starting point for contributing to a sustainable environment. You might want to add to this list with suggestions of your own, or those you find in the media and scientific articles.

You may need to use your persuasive communication skills to make an impact on the environment. You will also need to use your positive political skills so you will not be perceived as an environmental, tree-hugging pest.

## FOLLOWING AN APPLICABLE PROFESSIONAL CODE OF CONDUCT

Professional codes of conduct are prescribed for many occupational groups including physicians, nurses, lawyers, paralegals, purchasing managers and agents, and real estate salespeople. A useful ethics guide for members of these groups is to follow the code of conduct for their profession. If the profession or trade is licensed by the state or province, a worker can be punished for deviating from the code of conduct specified by the state. The code of conduct developed by the profession or trade is separate from the legal code, but usually supports the same principles and practices. Some of these codes of conduct developed by the professional associations are 50 and 60 pages long, yet all are guided by the kind of ethical principles implied in the ethical decision-making guide described earlier. Figure 14-6 presents a sampling of provisions from these codes of conduct.

1. Conserve energy by adjusting thermostats to keep working areas cooler during cold months and warmer during warm months.

2. Place a lawn on the roof, which can reduce its surface temperature by 70° F and internal temperatures by 15° F.

3. Carpool to work with at least three coworkers, and provide preferred parking spaces for carpoolers and hybrid or electric cars.

4. Encourage employee use of mass transportation, and provide company shuttle buses from locations convenient to where employees live.

4. Offer employees at least $2,000 toward the purchase of a hybrid vehicle or electric car.

4. Turn off electronic machines when not in use unless starting and stopping them frequently uses more energy than leaving the machines turned on during working hours. Encourage the replacement of incandescent bulbs with fluorescent ones (providing the replacement bulb gives enough light for the purpose).

5. Recycle as many packages as possible and purchase products, such as office furniture and driveways, made from recycled products including vehicle tires. When possible, use old newspapers for packing material instead of new paper and plastic.

6. Use mugs instead of Styrofoam and set up bins to recycle aluminum cans and plastic bottles.

7. When constructing a new building, seek Leadership in Energy and Environmental Design (LEED) certification from the U.S. Green Building Council.

8. Provide bicycle racks and shows that enable employees to bike to work.

9. Construct a system that captures rainwater to be reused for irrigation.

10. Grow as much vegetation on company premises as feasible, including celebrating special events by planting another tree. Use plants that are native to the region because native vegetation does not require as much maintenance, fertilizer, chemical sprays, or water.

11. Drink as much tap water as possible to minimize the use of bottled water, or filter tap water to one's specifications.

12. Combat litter and clutter in your work area and on company premises to help attain a pleasant, environmentally friendly atmosphere. Take such actions as alerting the company to exposed, rusted pipes, broken concrete in the parking lot, peeling paint, and broken fences.

13. Alert influential people to energy-saving and money-saving solar heating systems, such as solar buildings that provide solar hot water and solar heating.

14. Encourage people in your network not to drive at high speeds or sit in an idling vehicle while making phone calls. Encourage safe driving in general because vehicular accidents consume enormous amounts of energy including tow trucks, salvage operations, and life-sustaining hospital stays. Also encourage them to walk to errands instead of driving, whenever feasible.

15. Your own suggestions.

**Figure   14-5**

**Representative Suggestions for Helping a Company Contribute to a Sustainable Environment**

**Source:** Several of the ideas are from Michael Barbaro, "At Wal-Mart, Lessons in Self-Help," *The New York Times* (nytimes.com), April 5, 2007; Matthew Haggan, "Staples to Build Its First 'Green' Store in Miami," *MiamiHerald.com,* September 29, 2007; Kathryn Tyler, "Going Green," *HR Magazine,* October 2006, pp. 99–104; Charles Lockwood, "Building the Green Way," *Harvard Business Review,* June 2006, pp. 129–137.

## BE READY TO EXERT UPWARD LEADERSHIP

A politically delicate situation can arise when a worker wants to behave ethically, yet he or she works for an unethical manager. He or she might worry that being ethical will lead to being reprimanded or job loss. The ethical person working for an unethical boss might feel that his or her values are

| Professional Organization | Sample of Ethical Guidelines and Regulations |
|---|---|
| *Institute of Management Accountants* | 1. Maintain an appropriate level of professional competence by ongoing development of their knowledge and skills.<br>2. Refrain from disclosing confidential information acquired in the course of their work and monitor their activities to assure the maintenance of that confidentiality.<br>3. Actual or apparent conflicts of interest and advise all appropriate parties of any potential conflict. |
| *National Association of Legal Assistants* | 1. A legal assistant (paralegal) must not perform any of the duties that attorneys only may perform nor take any actions that attorneys may not take.<br>2. A legal assistant may perform any task which is properly delegated and supervised by an attorney, as long as the attorney is ultimately responsible to the client, maintains a direct relationship with the client, and assumes professional responsibility for the work product.<br>3. A legal assistant must protect the confidences of a client and must not violate any rule or statute now in effect or hereafter enacted controlling the doctrine of privileged communications between a client and an attorney. |
| *National Association of Purchasing Management* | 1. Avoid the intent and appearance of unethical or compromising practice in relationships, actions, and communications.<br>2. Refrain from any private business or professional activity that would create a conflict between personal interests and the interest of the employer.<br>3. Refrain from soliciting or accepting money, loans, credits, or prejudicial discounts, and the acceptance of gifts, entertainment, favors, or services from present or potential suppliers which might influence, or appear to influence purchasing decisions. |

**Figure   14-6**

**Excerpts from Professional Codes of Conduct**
**Source:** Institute of Management Accountants Code of Ethics; National Association of Legal Assistants Professional Standards; National Association of Purchasing Management Principles and Standards of Purchasing Practice.

■ **Upward ethical leadership**

leadership displayed by individuals who take action to maintain ethical standards although higher-ups engage in questionable behavior

being compromised, such as a virtuous credit-card specialist being told to approve credit cards for people who will probably wind up paying many late fees. **Upward ethical leadership** is leadership displayed by individuals who take action to maintain ethical standards although higher-ups engage in questionable moral behaviors. [21]

At the extreme, an employee might blow the whistle on the boss and report the unethical behavior to top management or a government agency. An example would be telling the Consumer Protection Agency that your company was selling cribs with too much lead paint, after your boss refused to accept your complaint.

The upward leadership approach would be to attempt to resolve the problem before going to the extreme of whistle-blowing. The employee who spots the immoral or unethical behavior would use problem-solving and

## Skill-Building Exercise 14-4

### Confronting the Unethical Boss

One student plays the role of Fred, a manager who makes frequent business trips by airplanes. Fred also likes to fly frequently on vacation, and appreciates accumulating frequent-flyer miles. Company policy allows employees to keep the frequent-flyer miles they accumulate for work, so Fred will often take indirect trips to a destination to accumulate more air miles. For example, to fly to San Francisco, he will fly from Boston to Atlanta, and then to San Francisco. In this instance, he could have made a shorter trip by flying directly from Boston to San Francisco, or from Boston to Chicago to San Francisco. In general, the longer, indirect flights are more expensive.

Another person plays the role of Kelly, the office administrative assistant who sometimes helps Fred prepare his travel vouchers. Kelly, who has good knowledge of geography, notices this strange pattern of Fred taking indirect flights. She is also aware of company policy that permits employees to accumulate frequent-flyer miles that are earned on business trips. Kelly is disturbed about what she perceives to be an inappropriate use of company resources—and therefore an ethical violation.

Kelly decides to discuss this most likely ethical violation with Fred. The role-play takes place in Fred's cubicle, and you can imagine how defensive Fred is going to be.

Observers look to see if Kelly can preserve her sense of ethics while not doing too much damage to her relationship with her boss, Fred.

communication skills, along with conflict-resolution skills. For example, the employee who spotted the lead-paint problem might say to the boss, "I have a problem and I would like to discuss it with you." The employee would therefore be engaging the boss in helping solve the problem. Recognizing that you have less power than your boss does, you would have to be diplomatic and nonaccusatory. It would be important to point to the problem (high levels of lead paint) rather than accusing the boss of being unethical or immoral.

Skill-Building Exercise 14-4 gives you an opportunity to practice upward leadership skills for correcting unethical behavior.

## Self-Assessment Quiz in Overview

One self-assessment quiz was presented in this chapter, The Ethical Reasoning Inventory. Use the quiz as an alert to keep your ethical values in mind whenever faced with an ethical dilemma. Although you may study ethics, and learn to use a guide to ethical decision making, your values will continue to exert a strong influence on your behavior. For example, if a person values the environ-ment, he or she will not empty a car ashtray of cigarette butts onto a parking lot pavement. If you know that your ethical values are in the low range, you will have to work extra hard to be ethical in work and personal life.

# Concept Review and Reinforcement

## Key Terms

Moral intensity, 433

Utilitarian predisposition, 434

Conflict of interest, 437

Defining moment, 441

Ethical screening, 443

Upward ethical leadership, 452

## Summary of Key Concepts

Ethics refers to what is good and bad, right and wrong, just and unjust, and what people should do. Ethics turn values into action. A person's ethical code has a significant impact on his or her interpersonal relationships.

Understanding ethics is important for a variety of reasons. First, people are motivated by self-interest and a desire to be morally right. Second, good ethics can enhance business and avoid illegal acts. Third, having high ethics improves the quality of work life.

Being ethical is not always easy for several reasons, including the complexity of ethical decisions, lack of recognition of the moral issues, poor moral development, and pressures from the work environment. Ethical violations in the form of lying are widespread in the workplace. Another problem is that some people have a utilitarian predisposition that tends toward unethical behavior.

Commonly faced ethical dilemmas include illegally copying software; treating people unfairly, including cronyism; sexually harassing coworkers; facing a conflict of interest; dealing with confidential information; misrepresenting employment history; using corporate resources; and ethically violating computers and IT.

A challenging twist to ethical decision making is to sort through your values when you have to choose between two morally sound choices. A defining moment is when you have to choose between two or more ideals in which you deeply believe.

One strategy for behaving ethically is to develop virtuousness, which includes rationality, honesty, independence, productivity, forgiveness and pride. A key strategy for behaving ethically is to follow the eight steps in making a contemplated decision:

1. Gather the facts.
2. Define the ethical issues.
3. Identify the affected parties.
4. Identify the consequences.
5. Identify the obligations (such as to customers and society).
6. Consider your character and integrity.
7. Think creatively about potential actions.
8. Check your intuition.

Another way to raise the level of ethical behavior is to form strong professional relationships with work associates. This is true because people tend to behave more ethically toward people who are close to them. At times using a corporate program such as an ethics hotline can help a person resolve ethical dilemmas. Being environmentally conscious contributes to ethical behavior. Following an applicable code of professional conduct, such as that for accountants, paralegals, and purchasing specialists, is another guide to behaving ethically. Upward leadership behavior can help you deal with the situation of maintaining ethical standards when the boss engages in questionable moral behavior.

## Check your Understanding

1. The business owner described in the chapter opener contends that people are fundamentally good. What is your opinion about people being fundamentally good?

2. How can behaving ethically improve a person's interpersonal relationships on the job?

3. What would most likely be some of the specific behaviors of a manager who scored 20 points on the ethical reasoning inventory?

4. An animal advocacy group turned up coats with fur from domesticated dogs and from raccoon dogs from Asia. The fur was labeled as "faux" (false or synthetic). What is your opinion of the ethics of these coat manufacturers who used dog fur labeled as faux fur?

5. Give an example from your own experiences or the media in which a business executive did something of significance that was morally right.

6. Provide an example of an action in business that might be unethical but not illegal.

7. Virtually all accountants have studied ethics as part of their education, yet many business scandals involve accountants. What's their problem?

8. Based on your knowledge of human behavior, why do professional codes of conduct—such as those for doctors, paralegals, and realtors—not prevent all unethical behavior on the part of members?

9. Check out the Web site of a couple of major business corporations such as GE and Ford Motor Company. What conclusion do you reach about whether an environmentally conscious (or green) person would fit in those companies?

10. What decision of ethical consequence have you made in the last year that you would not mind having publicly disclosed?

## Web Corner

http://www.ethics.org
(Ethics Resource Center.)

http://trade.gov/index.asp
(Business ethics and anticorruption as presented by the International Trade Administration of the U.S. Department of Commerce.)

http://globalethicsuniversity.com
(An examination of many phases of business ethics.)

### Internet Skill-Builder: Learning from Ethical Role Models

One of the many ways of learning ethical skills is to get good ideas from ethical role models. For example, you might observe a professor who takes the initiative to change a grade upward because she later discovered a calculation error. This Internet skill-builder is more abstract than some others, so you might find it a little frustrating. Search for a few specific ways in which you can learn from an ethical role model. To illustrate, you might learn from a business executive, sports figure, or public servant you admire.

# Developing Your Human Relations Skills

## Interpersonal Relations Case 14–1

### "Where Does My Loyalty Lie?"

As HR (human resources) director, Lauren had fiduciary responsibility for the company's defined contribution retirement plan. (Under this type of plan, the company agrees on how much it will contribute to the pension fund, not how much it will pay.) After the small nonprofit hired a new president, Lauren was instructed to enroll him in the plan immediately and to waive the mandatory one-year waiting period in effect for new employees. She also was ordered to keep quiet about employees who were wrongly classified as exempt (from overtime regulation)—an effort to avoid paying them overtime. When she protested that these actions were illegal and would expose her and the company to liability, an attorney acting for the firm informed her that "you will do what you're told."

But Lauren viewed her duties as an HR professional as "the antithesis of just doing what you are told." She enjoyed using her analytical skills. With a master's degree in business communication and certification in professional human resource management, she had served as president of her local HR organization and had become a "go-to" person for other HR professionals. She also taught HR at the university level.

"I believe HR is the conscience of the organization," says Lauren, so she was "rocked to my core," by the behavior of senior management at her company. "Where does my loyalty lie," she asked herself, "to my company or to my personal and professional ethics? I always felt I walked a tightrope in HR between 'crazy management ideas' and being an advocate for employees."

Following her conscience, Lauren resigned and began a search for a new job. Because Lauren lives in a very small community, job opportunities are scarce. She did eventually find another HR position 75 miles from her home, but the grueling commute became too difficult and she left that job. In addition, says Lauren, she realized that "they hired me because they could pay me $38,000 in an area where the going rate was $90,000." She feels she lost out on other job openings because "I was thought of as a problem" after she explained her reason for leaving her previous employer.

Today, Lauren works part time as a secretary. "I didn't sell out my integrity, and I can hold my head up," she says. But there's a trade-off: "I basically decided to give up my career. My husband and I adjusted our lifestyle downward," she says, "I'm pretty sure my HR days are over."

Even now with the benefit of hindsight, she doesn't see a different course she could have taken. "I have racked by brain for seven years, and I just don't see what else I could have done," says Lauren.

### Case Questions

1. What do you think Lauren could have done to save her career and preserve her sense of ethics at the same time?
2. Does Lauren have a useful message for you and others in your network? Or, is she just a loser who we can forget about?
3. To what extent does it surprise you that a lawyer would ask someone to act unethically?

**Source:** Ann Pomeroy, "The Ethics Squeeze," HR Magazine, March 2006, pp. 51–52, 55.

## Interpersonal Relations Case 14–2

### *The Highly Rated but Expendable Marsha*

Department manager Nicholas had thought for a long time that Marsha, one of his financial analysts, created too many problems. Although Marsha performed her job in a satisfactory manner, she required a lot of supervisory time and attention. She frequently asked for time off when her presence was needed the most because of a heavy workload in the department. Marsha sent Nicholas many long and complicated e-mail messages that required substantial time to read and respond. When Nicholas responded to Marsha's e-mail message, she would typically send another e-mail back asking for clarification.

Marsha's behavior during department meetings irritated Nicholas. She would demand more time than any other participant to explain her point of view on a variety of issues. At a recent meeting she took 10 minutes explaining how the company should be doing more to help the homeless and invest in the development of inner cities.

Nicholas coached Marsha frequently about the problems she was creating, but Marsha strongly disagreed with his criticism and concerns. At one time, Nicholas told Marsha that she was a high-maintenance employee. Yet Marsha perceived herself as a major contributor to the department. She commented once, "Could it be, Nick, that you have a problem with an assertive woman working in your department?"

Nicholas developed a tactic to get Marsha out of the department. He would give her outstanding performance evaluations, emphasizing her creativity and persistence. Marsha would then be entered into the company database as an outstanding employee, thereby making her a strong candidate for transfer or promotion. Within six months, a manager in a new division of the company took the bait. She requested that Marsha be recruited into her department as a senior financial analyst. Nicholas said to the recruiting manager, "I hate to lose a valuable contributor like Marsha, but I do not want to block her career progress."

Two months later, Marsha's new manager telephoned Nicholas, and asked, "What's the problem with Marsha? She's kind of a pill to have working with us. I thought she was an outstanding employee."

Nicholas responded, "Give Marsha some time. She may be having a few problems adjusting to a new environment. Just give her a little constructive feedback. You'll find out what a dynamo she can be."

#### Case Questions

1. How ethical was Nicholas in giving Marsha a high performance evaluation for the purposes of attracting her to other departments?
2. What should the manager do who was hooked by Nicholas's bait of the high performance evaluation?
3. What might the company do to prevent more incidents of inflated performance evaluations for the purpose of transferring an unwanted employee?

## Interpersonal Skills Role-Play 14–1

### *Confronting the Ethical Deviant*

One student plays the role of the manager who transferred Marsha into his or her department. The new manager has become suspicious that Nicholas might have manipulated Marsha's performance evaluations to make her appear like a strong candidate for transfer or promotion. In fact, the new manager thinks she (or he, if a man plays the role) may have caught an ethical deviant. Another student plays the role of Nicholas who wants to defend his reputation as an ethical manager. During the role-play, pay some attention to ethical issues. As usual, other students will provide feedback on the effectiveness of the interaction they observed.

# REFERENCES

1. Mark Henricks, "Well, Honestly!" *Entrepreneur*, December 2006, pp. 103–104.
2. Linda K. Treviño and Katherine A. Nelson, *Managing Business Ethics: Straight Talk About How to Do It Right* (New York: Wiley, 1995), pp. 24–35; O. C. Ferrell, John Fraedrich, and Linda Ferrell, *Business Ethics: Ethical Decision Making and Cases,* 4th ed. (Boston: Houghton Mifflin, 2000) pp. 13–16; Anita Bruzzese, "Tools Take Ethics to the Real World," Gannett News Service, May 16, 2005.
3. Thomas M. Jones, "Ethical Decision Making by Individuals in Organizations: An Issue Contingent Model," *Academy of Management Review*, April 1991, p. 391.
4. Linda Kelbe Treviño, "Managing to Be Ethical: Debunking Five Business Ethics Myths," *Academy of Management Executive*, May 2004, pp. 69–72.
5. Scott J. Reynolds, "Moral Awareness and Ethical Predispositions: Investigating the Role of Individual Differences in the Recognition of Moral Issues," *Journal of Applied Psychology*, January 2006, p. 234.
6. Data from Ethics Resource Center and Kronos, Inc., reported in Sue Shellenbarger, "How and Why We Lie at the Office: From Pilfered Pens to Padded Accounts," *The Wall Street Journal*, March 24, 2005, p. D1.
7. Treviño and Nelson, *Managing Business Ethics,* pp. 47–64.
8. Data reported in "McAfee Anti-Piracy Information," http://www.networkassociates.com/us/antipiracy_policy.htm, accessed May 25, 2005; "Software Piracy," http://blog.ndiyo.org, May 1, 2006.
9. Edmund L. Andrews, "Interior Official Assails Agency for Ethics Slides," *The New York Times* (http://www.nytimes.com, September 14, 2006.
10. Nanette Byrnes, "The Comeback of Consulting," *Business Week*, September 3, 2007, p. 66.
11. "O'Leary Admits Lying, Quits," Associated Press, December 15, 2001.
12. Joseph L. Badaracco, Jr., "The Discipline of Building Character," *Harvard Business Review*, March–April 1998, pp. 114–124.
13. Edwin A. Locke, "Business Ethics: A Way Out of the Morass," *Academy of Management Learning & Education*, September 2006, pp. 328–330.
14. Treviño and Nelson, *Managing Business Ethics*, pp. 71–75.
15. Scott Sonenshein, "The Role of Construction, Intuition, and Justification in Responding to Ethical Issues at Work: The Sensemaking–Intuition Model," *Academy of Management Review*, October 2007, p. 1030.
16. Sonenshein, "The Role of Construction, Intuition," p. 1033.
17. Daniel J. Brass, Kenneth D. Butterfield, and Bruce C. Skaggs, "Relationships and Unethical Behavior: A Social Network Perspective," *Academy of Management Review*, January 1998, pp. 14–31.
18. Cited in Jean Thilmany, "Supporting Ethical Employees," *HR Magazine*, September 2007, p. 106.
19. "Extolling the Virtues of Hot Lines," *Workforce*, June 1998, pp. 125–126; Daryl Koehn, "An Interview with William Griffin," http://www.stthom.edu/cbes/griffin.html (Accessed May 27, 2005).
20. "The Optima Awards: They've Got Game," *Workforce Management*, March 2005, p. 44.
21. Mary Uhl-Bien and Melissa K. Carsten, "Being Ethical When the Boss Is Not," *Organizational Dynamics,"* Issue 2, 2007, p. 197.

# 15

# Communication in the Workplace

## Learning Objectives

After studying the information and doing the exercises in this chapter, you should be able to:

1 Describe the formal channels of communication within organizations.

2 Describe the informal channels of communication within organizations.

3 Identify the challenges to interpersonal communication created by information technology.

4 Be ready to do an effective job of conducting or participating in a business meeting.

## Outline

1 **What Are the Formal Channels of Communication Within Organizations?** **463**
Communication Channels for Managing Crises
Company Blogs as Formal Channels
Communication Directions

2 **What Are the Informal Channels of Communication Within Organizations?** **465**
Networks of Contacts
The Grapevine
Chance Encounters and Management by Walking Around

3 **What Are the Challenges to Interpersonal Communication Created by Information Technology?** **468**
E-Mail and Communication among People
Use Presentation Technology to Your Advantage
Improve Your Telephone, Voice Mail, and Speakerphone Communication Skills
Telecommuting and the Distributed Workforce
The Multitasking Movement

4 **How Does One Do An Effective Job of Conducting or Participating in a Business Meeting?** **475**

The youngest CEO in the National Basketball Association (NBA), Brett Yormark, 39, is arguably the hardest-working too. He has signed 84 new corporate sponsors in slightly more than a year on the job. The East Rutherford, New Jersey, team brought in an estimated $86 million in a recent season. On a typical workday morning, he wakes up at 3:35 A.M. in his Franklin, New Jersey, home after about three hours sleep. He stops at Dunkin' Donuts during his commute. Clad in gym gear, he arrives at Nets' corporate office. At 4:10 A.M. he responds to 60 messages and reads through a thick stack of yesterday's e-mails, which his assistant has printed out for him. After running 3.4 miles on the treadmill downstairs while watching ESPN, he showers and gets dressed. At 7:35 A.M. he has a biweekly direct-report meeting. At 9:25 A.M., over the phone, he placates a disgruntled season ticket holder. At 12:30 P.M. he checks his Blackberry and then has lunch.

*At 1:15 P.M. Yormark has a meeting at NBA headquarters in midtown to brainstorm ways to increase the rate of renewals on season tickers. At 8:40 P.M. he is watching tonight's game against Orlando in the Meadowlands arena. At 9 P.M. he does some work in his basement office, checking more messages. Toward the end of the game he gathers his key team members to have a strategy meeting under the stands. At 10 P.M. he checks his Blackberry at Chill, a night club in Mill Valley. There's an e-mail from a tech staffer working to solve a customer problem. [1]*

The dizzying workday of the energetic CEO described illustrates many aspects of human relations. Of particular relevance here, the story illustrates how communications is such a key part of a businessperson's life, from checking e-mails to resolving conflicts over the phone.

Effective communication contributes to organization success in many ways, such as keeping employees informed as to what needs to be accomplished and identifying problems before they cripple a company. For example, a lab technician might quickly warn her manager that a new food supplement being sold by the company had an unacceptably high level of mercury, thereby avoiding a recall and lawsuits. Another example of the benefit of effective communication is that workers kept up to date about key issues that affect them are much more likely to stay on the job. According to a survey of 2,600 employees by Mercer Human Resources Consulting, only 15 percent of those who enjoy good workplace communication are thinking about finding new employment. In contrast, 41 percent of employees in companies that limit communication are thinking of leaving. [2]

In this chapter we study communication in organizations from several perspectives: formal and informal communication channels, the communication challenges created by information technology, and dealing effectively with meetings.

# What Are the Formal Channels of Communication Within Organizations?

■ **Learning Objective 1**

■ **Formal communication channels**
the official pathways for sending information inside and outside an organization

Messages in organizations are sent over both formal (official) and informal (unofficial) channels. **Formal communication channels** are the official pathways for sending information inside and outside an organization. The primary source of information about formal channels is the organization chart. It indicates the channels the messages are supposed to follow. By carefully following an organization chart, an entry-level worker would know how to transmit a message to someone in the executive suite. Formal communication channels are often bypassed through information technology. Using e-mail, anybody can send a message to anybody else in the organization. During an emergency, workers are also likely to bypass formal channels, such as a technician telephoning the plant manager directly about a chemical spill.

Two relatively recent formal channels of communication are procedures for crisis management and blogs. We also look at communication directions.

## COMMUNICATION CHANNELS FOR MANAGING CRISES

Many companies have developed formal communication channels for managing crises, such as fires and explosions, massive product recalls, financial scandals, and terrorist attacks. One of the most crucial parts of a disaster plan is how to communicate with the company's workforce during a crisis. A key part of the challenge is to locate and reestablish contact with employees who may be scattered in the streets or stranded in airports around the world. Aon Corporation, an international insurance, risk-management, and consulting company, improvised to use its Web site as an official communication channel during the crisis of September 11. A company official said, "With everything else down, we decided to use the company Web site. That seemed like the only option we had." [3]

Web sites have now become the premier formal crisis communication channel. Formal channels during a crisis are necessary for informing employees about a disaster, work assignments, health services and grief counseling, and assistance in returning to work. Other formal communication channels during a crisis include the television or radio.

## COMPANY BLOGS AS FORMAL CHANNELS

The company blog (or more precisely a Web log or journal) is a rapidly growing form of formal communication, paralleling the surging use of blogs in private life. Blogs originated by consumers are often used to complain about products or services and less often to compliment a company. Blogs were first used by business to communicate with customers in a personal, direct manner and perhaps form a bond with them. [4]

The blog communicates business information but with a soft, human touch. For example, a product manager for bicycle helmets might write, "Just the other day, I heard from a mother of a six year old in our housing development. Little Jason complained about having to wear a helmet simply to ride his tricycle around the neighborhood. But then he was hit lightly by a car and thrown five feet. He escaped with a few scratches and bruises but no head injury. I'm so happy for Jason and so thankful to our fine staff who built that bike helmet to get the job done."

A company might also use a blog to communicate its side of the story in response to outside criticism, such as the ***http://blogs.sun.com*** launched by Jonathan Schwartz, president and chief operating officer (COO) of Sun Microsystems. For example, one time he complained about a negative magazine article written about the company and criticism by Intel executives. [5]

The company blog can also be used to communicate with employees in a relaxed, casual tone. Employees, as well as customers, can interact with the Web log by providing comments that can be a source of valuable feedback to management and communicated directly to other visitors to the site.

An individual who establishes a blog on his or her own to chat about the employer creates an *informal* rather than a formal channel—when the blog is not authorized by the company. Bloggers who publish negative information about their employer, or publish unprofessional photos of themselves, are liable to being fired. The rationale behind these firings is that the employee is making unwarranted use of his or her association with the company. To prevent problems of negativity appearing on personal blogs by employees, many companies now establish guidelines, such as "no disclosure of negative information about the company," "no nude photos," or "no profanity."

## COMMUNICATION DIRECTIONS

Another aspect of formal communications in the directions messages follow in the organization. Messages in organizations travel in four primary directions: downward, upward, horizontally, and diagonally. **Downward communication** is the flow of messages from one level to a lower level. It is typified by a middle manager giving orders to a lower-level supervisor or by top management sending announcements to employees. Information is sometimes transmitted from a higher level to a lower one without the sender inviting a response. When this occurs, the feedback built into two-way communication is lost.

**Upward communication** is the transmission of messages from lower to higher levels in an organization. It is the most important channel for keeping management informed about problems within the organization. Simply talking regularly to employees improves upward communication. An **open-door policy** is a more structured upward communication channel that allows employees to bring a gripe to top management's attention without first checking with their manager. Managers who are willing to listen to bad news without becoming upset at the messenger are more likely to receive upward communication. Alan Lafley, the chief executive at Procter & Gamble is recognized for his ability to listen to problems without becoming vindictive. As a result, he often receives early warning of impending problems. Upward communication is more widely used in less bureaucratic firms than in highly bureaucratic firms. Almost all executives contend that they value upward communication, regardless of whether the majority employees agree.

■ **Downward communication**
the transmission of messages from higher to lower levels in an organization

■ **Upward communication**
the transmission of messages from lower to higher levels in an organization

■ **Open-door policy**
communication channel that is structured upward that allows employees to bring a gripe to top management's attention without first checking with the employee's manager

*Horizontal communication* is sending messages among people at the same organization level. It often takes the form of coworkers from the same department talking to one another. Horizontal communication is the basis for cooperation. When coworkers are not sharing information with and responding to one another, they are likely to fall behind schedule. Also, efforts are duplicated and quality suffers. Another type of horizontal communication takes place when managers communicate with other managers at the same level.

*Diagonal communication* is the transmission of messages to higher or lower organizational levels in different departments. Because these pathways are infrequently spelled out on the organization chart, diagonal communication is usually an *informal* channel. A typical diagonal communication event occurs when a manager from one department contacts a lower-ranking person from a department outside of his or her chain of command. Diagonal communication becomes an *informal* pathway.

# What Are the Informal Channels of Communication Within Organizations

**Informal communication channels** are the unofficial network of channels that supplements the formal channels. Most of these informal channels arise out of necessity. For example, people will sometimes depart from the official communication channels to consult with a person with specialized knowledge. Suppose an administrative professional in the inventory control department spoke and wrote fluent German. Employees from other departments would regularly consult her when they were dealing with a customer from Germany. Here we study several aspects of informal communication channels: networks of contacts, the grapevine, rumors, chance encounters, and management by walking around.

■ Learning Objective 2

■ **Informal communication channels** unofficial networks of channels that supplement the formal channels

## NETWORKS OF CONTACTS

Perhaps the most useful aspect of informal communication channels is that they enable workers to accomplish many tasks they would not be able to if they relied exclusively on formal channels. The network of contacts often means in practice that an individual worker might be in touch with people in his or her formal and informal channels to get work accomplished. However, the emphasis is on the informal communication channels.

Some observers believe that the network of contacts explains how work really gets accomplished. According to this viewpoint, all companies have hidden **shadow organizations** where much of the real work gets accomplished. The shadow organization is revealed by *network analysis* which traces who talks to whom. [6] For example, in most firms there are "tech fixers" who supplement—but do not replace—the technical support center. Suppose a worker is stuck with an information technology problem, such as a document being

■ **Shadow organizations** where much of the real work gets accomplished, the shadow organization is revealed by network analysis, which traces who talks to whom

filled with mysterious codes that he or she cannot eliminate. The worker might get in immediate contact with a tech fixer (whose formal job responsibilities do not include solving technical problems outside his or her department) for help with the problem.

Your network of contacts can also extend outside the organization. A real estate developer, for example, might have contacts inside a bank who inform him of upcoming foreclosures. In this way the developer can make an early appraisal of the property to be ready with an effective bid on the foreclosed property. The mortgage specialist in the bank is part of the real estate developer's network of contacts.

At Fannie Mae, a private, shareholder-owned company based in Washington, DC, network analysis is used to enhance collaboration among workers. "We want to break down silos (separate self-contained departments)," says David Flaxman, an executive in charge of eSolutions products and services. "By analyzing their personal networks, employees establish new relationships across the organization. This helps employees to be more effectively share information and solve complex problems." [7] An important output of network analysis is to find an employee working someplace else in the organization who might have skills or knowledge that can help perform your work well. A Fannie Mae specialist who purchases mortgages from banks with many customers with poor credit ratings might need the expertise of someone else at Fannie Mae who has faced this challenge.

The networks under discussion help explain why changes in organizational structure (which specifies the formal communication channels) sometimes do not change the quantity and quality of work that gets accomplished. The same pattern of networks that workers use to accomplish their tasks may not change despite the changes on the organization chart. [8]

## THE GRAPEVINE

■ **Grapevine**

major informal communication channel in organizations; the grapevine refers to the tangled pathways that can distort information

The **grapevine** is the major informal communication channel in organizations. The grapevine refers to the tangled pathways that can distort information. The term referred originally to the snarled telegraph lines on the battlefield during the U.S. Civil War. The grapevine is often thought to be used primarily for passing along negative rumors and negative gossip. Gossips sometimes use the Internet and e-mail as channels for transmitting negative gossip. When left to fester, gossip can cause individuals chagrin and also lead to turnover, conflict, and lawsuits. Gossip often increases when workers are bored or lack ample information about company events. Managers can often stop negative gossip by confronting the source of the gossip, demanding that he or she stop. Positive gossip, however, makes a contribution to the organization because trading information strengthens ties among workers and humanizes the workplace. Gossip can be viewed as the glue that binds social groups together. [9] An example of positive gossip would be, "I heard management is considering adding a paid holiday next year. Everyone with five or more service years gets his or her birthday off from work."

The grapevine is sometimes used purposely to disseminate information along informal lines. For example, top management might want to hint to employees that certain work will be outsourced (sent to another company or outside the country) unless the employees become more productive. Although the plans are still tentative, feeding them into the grapevine may result in improved motivation and productivity.

## Rumors

Rumors are an important informal communication force within organizations, and they tend to thrive in organizations with poor corporate communication, such as a penitentiary. Respondents to a worldwide survey agreed that rumors are an important early source of information. To ensure that rumors are more helpful than harmful, management might do the following:

- Be wary of vague communication, which fosters misinterpretation and anxiety.

- Promote healthy, accurate communication. Encourage employees to discuss rumors with their manager.

- Avoid concealing bad news. Promise employees that they will receive accurate information as soon as it becomes available.

- Correct erroneous communications that relate to organizational policies, practices, and strategic plans. [10]

Consultant and author Tom E. Jones reinforces the importance of open communication to combat rumors. He recommends that unless the company is bound by some legal restriction, top-level management should tell everyone what they know about the facts. "Don't wait until you have all the details. Just get the truth out there fast." [11]

A problem with inaccurate rumors is that they can distract workers, create anxiety, and decrease productivity. A frequent by-product of false rumors about company relocation or a pending merger is that some of the more talented workers leave in the hopes of more stable employment.

## CHANCE ENCOUNTERS AND MANAGEMENT BY WALKING AROUND

Another informal channel of significance is *chance encounters*. Unscheduled informal contact between managers and employees can be an efficient and effective communication channel. John P. Kotter, professor of leadership at Harvard Business School, found that effective managers do not confine their communication to formal meetings. [12] Instead, they collect valuable information during chance encounters. Spontaneous communication events may occur in the cafeteria, near the water fountain, in the halls, and on the elevator. In only two minutes, the manager might obtain the information that would typically be solicited in a 30-minute meeting or through a series of e-mail exchanges. A representative question might be, "What seems to be the buzz on our newest product?"

One important communication channel can be classified as either formal or informal. **Management by walking around** involves managers intermingling freely with workers on the shop floor or in the office, as well as with customers. By spending time in personal contact with employees, the manager

■ **Management by walking around** managers intermingle freely with workers on the shop floor or in the office, as well as with customers; enhances open communication

enhances open communication. During contacts with employees the manager will often ask questions such as, "How are you enjoying your work?" or "What bottlenecks have you encountered today?" Because management by walking around is systematic, it could be considered formal. However, a manager who circulates throughout the company is not following the formal paths prescribed by the organization chart. Management by walking around differs from chance encounters in that the latter are unplanned events; the former occur intentionally.

Another perspective on management walking around is that it is similar to a physician making rounds to visit his or her hospital patients. Instead of visiting patients, the manager drops by to see employees and engages in brief, informal conversations. Sample questions to ask on rounds include, "What is working well today?" "Do you have the tools and equipment you need to do your job?" "Is there anything I could do better?" [13] Recognizing the nature of the rounds, the employees are likely to respond with brief, spontaneous, and useful feedback—assuming the manager making the rounds is trusted!

# What Are the Challenges to Interpersonal Communication Created by Information Technology?

■ Learning Objective 3

Rapid advances in information technology may enable workers to communicate more easily, rapidly, and quickly than they could even a few years ago. Quite often the influence has been positive, but at other times the effectiveness of interpersonal communication has decreased. Five developments that illustrate the impact of information technology on interpersonal communication are e-mail, presentation technology, telephones and voice mail, telecommuting, and multitasking. (The author realizes that telephones are not usually considered part of information technology, but they too are electronic devices that create communication challenges.)

## E-MAIL AND COMMUNICATION AMONG PEOPLE

E-mail is the information technology system with the most dramatic impact on interpersonal communication in the current era. For both work and personal life, e-mail is typically less formal than a letter but more formal than a telephone conversation. The major impact of e-mail on interpersonal communication is that written messages replace many telephone and in-person exchanges. Team members often keep in regular contact with each other without having lengthy meetings or telephone conversations.

E-mail, including instant messaging, has become the dominant form of communication on the job. The same technology is likely to expand into a form of communication that will incorporate not only still drawings and photographs but also audio, video, and chunks of voice mail. The biggest threat to e-mail, however, is that about 50 percent of e-mails are classified as *spam,* or unwanted and uninvited messages, often of a commercial nature. Several potential communication problems that e-mail and instant messaging create should be kept in mind to minimize these problems. [14]

A major problem with e-mail is that it encourages indiscriminate sending of messages Some professional workers receive an average of 300 e-mail messages per day. Some of these workers make cynical comments such as, "My job is answering e-mail" or "I answer e-mail during the day and do my work at night and on weekends." Some workers conduct virtual joke-telling contests over e-mail, with some of the jokes being perceived as offensive by many other workers. The proliferation of electronic junk mail (spam) has prompted some company officials to take corrective action, such as the installation of spam filters.

Although many people contend that they are overloaded with e-mail, one study suggests that e-mail is being used wisely and is under control. As revealed in a survey of close to 2,500 workers, the majority of e-mail users find that it is a manageable part of their job. The typical work user of e-mail spends approximately 30 minutes during the workday processing e-mail, receives about 10 incoming messages, and sends five messages. A subgroup of these e-mailers, labeled power e-mailers, spends two hours or more daily on e-mail. They handle between 30 and 50 messages per day, yet only 11 percent say they feel overwhelmed by processing e-mail. [15]

To minimize feeling overwhelmed by e-mail, it is best to schedule blocks of time for sending and answering e-mail—assuming you have the type of work that allows you to limit e-mail. Many successful people control e-mail, rather than letting it control them. Jeff Bezos, founder and CEO of Amazon.com, is besieged by people sending him e-mails. To protect his creativity and time for interacting with his staff, Bezos reserves part of every Tuesday for reading and responding to e-mail messages. [16] (Of course, the customer service rep does not have this luxury of time blocking.)

The informal style of many e-mail exchanges can lead a person to believe that incorrect spelling, poor grammar, and disconnected thoughts are acceptable in all forms of business communication. The opposite is true. To appear professional and intelligent, writers of business e-mail messages should use correct spelling, grammar, capitalization, and punctuation.

E-mail has become a new tool for office politicians who search for ways to look good themselves and make others look bad. Many office politicians use e-mail to give credit to themselves for their contributions to a project, perhaps using a companywide distribution list. When something goes wrong, such as a failed project, the office politician will inform hundreds of people that it was not his or her fault.

Many supervisors and other workers use e-mail to reprimand others because, by sending a message over the computer, they can avoid face-to-face confrontation. E-mail is well suited for managers who would prefer to avoid face-to-face contact with group members. Harsh messages sent over e-mail create several problems. First, it is shocking to be reprimanded or insulted in writing. Second, the person cannot offer a defense except by writing back an e-mail message explaining his or her position. Third, the recipient, not knowing what to do about the harsh message, may brood and become anxious.

The use of e-mail and instant messaging during negotiations points to the strengths and limitations of this form of communication. E-mail should be used to supplement, not substitute for face-to-face negotiations. Professor Janet Nadler of Northwestern University School of Law conducted a study in which students paired up to negotiate a commercial transaction. Half of the students used e-mail exclusively, and half conducted a brief phone conversation before beginning the negotiation via e-mail. The students who first interacted by phone were four times more likely to reach an agreement than those who relied only on e-mail. The problem highlighted by the experiment is that there are no audio or visual cues (such as facial expressions or voice tone) to establish rapport when using e-mail. [17] Figure 15-1 presents suggestions for good etiquette when using e-mail, including messaging. The good etiquette leads to more productive use of e-mail.

Some business firms have counterattacked the problems associated with e-mail by shifting to related technologies. The major problem counterattacked is the time drain of sending and responding to e-mail messages. Workers at such well known organizations as Disney, Eastman Kodak, and the U.S. military are replacing e-mail with other software tools that function in real time. Among them are private workplace wikis, blogs, instant messaging, RSS, and more elaborate forms of groupware that allow workers to create Web sites for the team's use on a specific project. A *wiki* is a site allows a group of people to comment on and edit each other's work. *RSS* is the acronym for really simple, syndication that enables people to subscribe to the information they need. E-mail will probably remain strong for one-to-one communication, but the tools just mentioned will be relied on more heavily for collaboration. [18]

## USE PRESENTATION TECHNOLOGY TO YOUR ADVANTAGE

Speakers in all types of organizations supplement their talk with computer slides and overhead transparencies and often organize their presentation around them. Many people want presentations reduced to bulleted items and eye-catching graphics. (Have you noticed this tendency among students?) The communication challenge here is that during an oral presentation the predominant means of connection between sender and receiver is eye contact. When an audience is constantly distracted from the presenter by movement on the screen, sounds from the computer, or lavish colors, eye contact suffers, as does the message.

One of the biggest challenges is to learn how to handle equipment and maintain frequent eye and voice contact at all times. Several professionals in the field of business communication offer these sensible suggestions for overcoming the potential communication barrier of using presentation technology inappropriately: [19]

- **Reveal points only as needed.** Project the overhead transparencies or computer slides only when needed and use a cursor, laser pointer, or metal pointer for emphasis.

- **Talk to the audience and not the screen.** A major problem with computer slides is that the presenter as well as the audience is likely to focus continually on the slide. If the presenter minimizes looking at the slide and spends

Observing the following tips will enhance your e-mail etiquette and electronic communication effectiveness.

*Keep it simple.* Each message should have only one piece of information or request for action so that it's easier for the executive to respond. However, avoid sending an e-mail with an attachment without some type of greeting or explanation. Do not allow e-mail threads longer than a football field. E-mail messages longer than one screen often are filed instead of read.

*Include an action step.* Clearly outline what type of reply you're looking for as well as any applicable deadlines.

*Use the subject line to your advantage.* Generic terms such as "details" or "reminder" do not describe the contents of your message or whether it's time sensitive. So the executive may delay opening it. Do not forward a long chain of e-mails without changing the subject; otherwise, you might have a confusing subject line, such as "RE: FW: RE: FW: RE: FW."

*Take care in writing e-mails.* Clearly organize your thoughts; avoid sending e-mails with confusing, incomplete, or missing information. Never use profane or harsh language (referred to as *flaming*). Use business writing style and check carefully for grammatical and typographical errors. (Also, avoid the trend of spelling "I" in lowercase.)

*Be considerate.* Use "please" and "thank you" even in brief messages. Part of being considerate, or at least polite, is to begin you e-mail with a warm salutation, such as "Hello Gina," rather than jumping into the subject with no greeting.

*Don't include confidential information.* E-mail is occasionally forwarded to unintended recipients. If your message is in any way sensitive or confidential, set up a meeting or leave a voice mail in which you request confidentially.

*Do not use e-mail to blast a coworker, and send copies to others.* Criticizing another person with e-mail is equivalent to blasting him or her during a large meeting.

*When in doubt, send plain text e-mail, not HTML.* Not everybody can receive e-mails with fancy formatting, and some receivers dislike nontraditional formatting.

*Ask before sending huge attachments.* Do not clog e-mail systems without permission.

*Avoid passing along chain letters.* Few people believe that if they pass along your e-mail letter to 10 friends, they will ultimately become rich or avoid bad luck. In a work setting, chain letters make the sender appear unprofessional.

Instant messaging requires a few additional considerations for practicing good electronic etiquette:

*Don't be Big Brother.* Some bosses use instant messaging to check up on others, to make sure they are seated at their computer. Never intrude on workers unless it is urgent.

*Lay down the instant messaging law.* Make sure your message has some real value to the recipient before jumping right in front of someone's face. Instant messaging is much like walking into someone's office or cubicle without an appointment or without knocking.

*Take it off-line.* When someone on your buddy list becomes too chatty, don't vent your frustration. By phone, in-person, or through regular e-mail, explain tactfully that you do not have time for processing so many instant messages. Suggest that the two of you might get together for lunch or coffee soon.

*Set limits to avoid frustration.* To avoid constant interruptions, use a polite custom status message, such as "I will be dealing with customers today until 4:40."

**Source:** Todd Grady, "Even via E-Mail, Courtesy Matters," *Rochester Democrat and Chronicle,* May 1, 2000, p. 1F; Andrea C. Poe, "Don't Touch That 'Send' Button!" *HR Magazine*, July 2001, pp. 76, 80; Heinz Tschabitscher, "The Ten Most Important Rules of E-mail Etiquette," available at http://email.about.com/cs/netiquettetips/tp/core_netiquette.htm, retrieved September 9, 2003: Monte Enbysk, "Bosses: Ten Tips for Better E-Mails," *Microsoft Small Business Center,* available at www.microsoft.com/smallbusiness/resources/technology/communications/bosses_10, 2006.

**Figure   15-1**

**E-Mail and Messaging Etiquette**

considerable time looking at the audience, it will be easier to maintain contact with the audience.

- **Keep the slide in view until the audience gets the point.** A presenter will often flash a slide or transparency without giving the audience enough time to comprehend the meaning of the slide. It is also important for presenters to synchronize the slides with their comments.

- **Reduce the text on each page of your PowerPoint presentation to a bare minimum.** Few people can really listen to you and read your slides at the same time, even if they think they are effective at multitasking.

- **Make sure to triple-check your presentation for spelling errors.** A spelling error projected on a screen can quickly become a joke passed around the room.

The point again is not to avoid the new technologies for communication but to use them to your advantage skillfully.

## IMPROVE YOUR TELEPHONE, VOICE MAIL, AND SPEAKERPHONE COMMUNICATION SKILLS

A direct way of overcoming communication barriers is to use effective telephone and voice mail communication skills because these two communication media often create communication problems. Also, many businesses attract and hold on to customers because their representatives interact positively with people through the telephone and voice mail. Many other firms lose money, and non-profit organizations irritate the public because their employees have poor communication and voice mail skills. Furthermore, despite the widespread use of computer networks, a substantial amount of work among employees is still conducted via telephone and voice mail. For example, investment firms, such as Merrill Lynch, do not want to send sensitive financial information by e-mail but instead encourage telephone conversations.

Speakerphones present some of their own communication challenges. Small noises, such as crumpling paper, eating crunchy food, and placing a handset on a hard desk, magnify when broadcast over a speakerphone. If other people are present in the office, advise the person you are telephoning at the beginning of the conversation. [20] Doing so may save a lot of embarrassment, such as the caller making negative comments about your boss or coworker. Most of the previous comments about overcoming communication barriers apply to telephone communications including speakerphones. Keep in mind these three representative suggestions for improving telephone effectiveness:

> "Say your phone number slowly. I can't tell you how many people have zipped through it."
> —Michael Shepley, the owner of a public relations firm in New York City

- Vary your voice tone and inflection to avoid sounding bored or uninterested in your job and the company.

- Smile while speaking on the phone—somehow a smile gets transmitted over the telephone wires or optic fibers!

- Although multitasking has become the mode, when speaking on a telephone do not conduct a conversation with another person simultaneously and do not have a television or radio playing in the background. (The last point is a challenge for people who work from home.) Business callers expect your undivided attention.

# TELECOMMUTING AND THE DISTRIBUTED WORKFORCE

A **telecommuter** is an employee who works at home full time or part time and sends output electronically to a central office. An estimated 22.5 million people in the United States work at home, out of their cars, or from customer premises as corporate employees. Collectively, they are referred to as the distributed workforce. Technology companies rely the most heavily on the distributed workforce. For example, at IBM, 40 percent of employees have no office at the company. [21] The majority of people who work at home do so only a day or two per week at their residence. Also, millions of people work from their homes in self-employment. Concerns about terrorists threats, contagious diseases, and the high cost of gasoline have made working at home even more attractive for many workers in recent years. Some people believe that the pollutants from driving a gasoline-powered vehicle contribute to global warming. Furthermore, some people find workplaces to have too many interruptions and distractions, such as conversations with coworkers, superiors, and meetings.

Telecommuters can communicate abundantly via electronic devices, but they miss out on the face-to-face interactions so vital for dealing with complex problems. Another communication problem telecommuters face is feeling isolated from activities at the main office and missing out on the encouragement and recognition that take place in face-to-face encounters. (Of course, many telecommuters prefer to avoid such contact.) Many telecommuters have another communications problem: Because they have very little face-to-face communication with key people in the organization, they believe they are passed over for promotion. Most telecommuters spend some time in the traditional office, yet they miss the day-by-day contact.

■ **Telecommuter**
employee who works at home full time or part time and sends output electronically to a central office

## Human Relations in Practice

### The Distributed Workforce at Sun Microsystems

Charlie Grantham, a cofounder of Work Design Collaborative LLC, was asked how do workplaces change with distributed workers. He responded as follows:

"Sun Microsystems has a program called iWork, a network of 127 remote work sites around the world. Employees can go to one of these locations for part of the work-week to plug in. Once Sun gave people this opportunity, getting them to come back to their assigned workplace was very difficult. These workplaces look and feel more residential. We're already starting to see housing developments with separate community offices attached in places like suburban Atlanta."

Source: Interview by Christopher Percy Collier, "Workplace 1.5: Managing Teleworkers—At Home, at Work, at Starbucks," *Fast Company*, November 2005, p. 105.

Another communication problem with telecommuting is that it lacks a solid human connection. As one telecommuting marketing consultant put it, face time is critical for building empathy. "It's a human connection. It takes time, and human beings need visual cues, the symbols of being together and caring for one another." [22] The accompanying Human Relations in Practice illustrates how far working away from the traditional office has become integrated into the modern workplace.

## THE MULTITASKING MOVEMENT

A major consequence of electronic communication devises is that they encourage multitasking, for good or for bad. It has become standard communication practice for many workers to read e-mail while speaking on the phone, to surf the Internet while in a business meeting, and to check text messages while listening to a presentation. Some customer contact workers even conduct cell phone conversations with friends while serving customers. Many workers are now using two computer monitors so they can write reports while attending to e-mail. Multitasking has become a way of life for many members of generation Y, who grew up studying while watching television and chatting with their friends on a cell phone.

Advocates of multitasking contend that it increases productivity, such as accomplishing two or more tasks at once. A prime example is Marissa Mayer, vice president, Search Products and User Experience, Google (and a former computer science major). Among the comments she makes in describing the "secrets of her greatness" are as follows:

> I don't feel overwhelmed with information. I really like it. I use Gmail for my personal e-mail—15 to 20 e-mails a day—but on my work e-mail I get as many as 700 to 800 a day, so I need something really fast. I use an e-mail application called Pine, a Linux-based utility I started using in college. . . . I do marathon e-mail catch-up sessions, sometimes on a Saturday or Sunday. I'll just sit down and do e-mail for 10 to 14 hours straight. I almost always have the radio or my TV on. Sometimes it's the news. Sometimes it's a sitcom. I actually like the two streams of information. I guess I'm a typical 25 to 35 year old who's now really embracing the two-screen experience. [23]

Although many workers can multitask successfully, the bulk of scientific evidence is that performing more than one demanding cognitive activity at once lowers accuracy and productivity. Would you want a brain surgeon to operate on a loved one while he or she chatted on the cell phone with an investment consultant? While flying a commercial airline, would you want the pilot to be surfing the Internet? Or to take a less than life-and-death situation, would you want your tax accountant to e-file your return while making calculations on someone else's return?

Decades of research indicate that the quality of mental output and depth of thought deteriorate as a person attends to more than one task simultaneously. One of the problems is that the brain does not handle multitasking well. The brain rapidly toggles (an on-an-off switch effect) among tasks rather than performing true simultaneous processing. The problem is more acute for complex and demanding tasks that require action planning, such as deciding how to respond to a customer complaint or solve an accounting problem. Highly practiced and routine tasks, such as sealing an envelope, suffer less from multitasking.

David E. Meyer, the director of the Brain, Cognition and Action Laboratory at the University of Michigan, notes that when people attempt to perform two or more related tasks at the same time or alternating rapidly—instead of doing them sequentially—two negative consequences occur. Errors increase substantially, and the amount of time required to perform the task may double. [24]

The scientific findings just mentioned support the complaints of many professional and managerial workers that the constant inflow of electronic information hampers their creativity and analytical thinking ability. A practical antidote is to reserve multitasking for routine, well-rehearsed activities and to focus on one tasks at a time for creative and analytical work. Yet this conclusion does not mean that everybody is incapable of multitasking and producing good results.

Whether communication in the workplace is formal or informal, electronic or printed, the human touch should be included for the highest level of effectiveness. Many of the points already made about informal communication illustrate this point. Consider also that an adhesive note (Post-It style) is useful in obtaining a quick response from a colleague. A study by psychology professor Randy Garner at Sam Houston University in Texas examined response rates to a questionnaire. Volunteers who were asked to fill out a survey were more likely to comply, and give more complete answers, if it included a handwritten sticky note. Writing on the survey cover page was not as effective. Garner believes that the sticky note is perceived as a request for a personal favor, even between strangers. [25]

# How Does One Do An Effective Job of Conducting or Participating in a Business Meeting?

■ Learning Objective 4

Much of workplace communication, including group decision making, takes place in meetings. Among the many purposes of meetings are problem solving, including brainstorming; disseminating information; training; and building team spirit. When conducted properly, meetings accomplish the purpose. Yet when conducted poorly, meetings represent a substantial productivity drain. The following suggestions apply to those who conduct physical and electronic meetings, and some are also relevant for participants. Videoconferencing is sometimes used to conduct meetings with people in dispersed locations, as is teleconferencing. The globalization of business is increasing the demand for videoconferencing. [26] By following these nine suggestions, you increase the meeting's effectiveness as a communication vehicle.

1. **Meet only for valid reasons.** Many meetings lead to no decisions because they lacked a valid purpose in the first place. Meetings are necessary only in situations that require coordinated effort and group decision making. Memos can be substituted for meetings when factual information needs to

be disseminated and discussion is unimportant. When looking to meet for valid reasons, be aware of possible cultural differences in the motives for having a meeting. In many cultures, meetings are conducted to build relationships. For example, a key to doing business in Asia is to get to know work associates on a personal level before getting down to problem solving, buying, or selling. [27] So for an Asian manager, conducting a meeting to build personal relationships *is* a valid reason.

2. **Start and stop on time, and offer refreshments.** Meetings appear more professional and action oriented when the leader starts and stops on time. If the leader waits for the last member to show up, much time is lost and late behavior is rewarded. Stopping the meeting on time shows respect for the members' time. Offering refreshments is another tactic for emphasizing the importance of the meeting and also enhances satisfaction with the meeting. Agree in advance on when and if there will be a break to reduce anxiety about when the break will occur.

3. **Keep comments brief and to the point.** A major challenge facing the meeting leader is to keep conversation on track. Verbal rambling by participants creates communication barriers because other people lose interest. An effective way for the leader to keep comments on target is to ask the contributor of a non sequitur, "In what way does your comment relate to the agenda?"

4. **Encourage critical feedback and commentary.** Meetings are more likely to be fully productive when participants are encouraged to be candid with criticism and negative feedback. Openness helps prevent groupthink and also brings important problems to the attention of management.

5. **Strive for wide participation.** One justification for conducting a meeting is to obtain a variety of input. Although not everybody is equally qualified to voice a sound opinion, everyone should be heard. A skillful leader may have to limit the contribution of domineering members and coax reticent members to voice their ideas. Asking participants to bring several questions to the meeting will often spur participation. The meeting leader should not play favorites by encouraging the participation of some members, and ignoring others. If the meeting leader spends the entire time making a PowerPoint presentation, participation will be discouraged. The slides should supplement the meeting and be starting points for discussion.

6. **Solve small issues ahead of time with e-mail.** Meetings can be briefer and less mundane when small issues are resolved ahead of time. E-mail is particularly effective for resolving minor administrative issues and also for collecting agenda items in advance.

7. **Consider "huddling" when quick action is needed.** A huddle is a fast-paced, action-oriented way to bring workers together into brief meetings to discuss critical performance issues. A department store manager might bring together five floor managers 10 minutes before opening to say, "We have a line-up of about 500 customers waiting to get in because of our specials today. Is everybody ready for the rush of excitement? What problems do you anticipate?" The huddle is particularly important when it would be difficult for the workers to attend a long meeting. [28]

8. **Ensure that all follow-up action is assigned and recorded.** All too often, even after a decision has been reached, a meeting lacks tangible output. Distribute a memo summarizing who is responsible for taking what action and by what date.

9. **Minimize distractions during the meeting.** The group should agree on whether meeting participants will be allowed to use laptop computers for purposes other than recording information in the meeting. If handouts are used, allow participants enough time to read them so one person is not presenting while the others are reading. Ensure beforehand that computer-related equipment, such as the projector, is working and that it is compatible with the presenter's software.

# Concept Review and Reinforcement

## Key Terms

Formal communication
  channels, 463
Downward communication, 464
Upward communication, 464

Open-door policy, 464
Informal communication
  channels, 465
Shadow organizations, 465

Grapevine, 466
Management by walking
  around, 467
Telecommuter, 473

## Summary and Review

Messages in organizations are sent over both formal (official) and informal (unofficial) channels. Three key aspects of the formal channels are as follows:

- Many companies have developed formal communication channels for managing crises, such as fires and terrorist attacks.
- The company blog is a rapidly growing type of formal communication. It communicates business information with a soft, human touch.
- Messages in organizations travel in four primary directions: downward, upward, horizontally, and diagonally. An open-door policy facilitates upward communication.

An informal communication channel supplements the formal channel.

- A major informal communication channel is the network of contacts that employees use to accomplish work, sometimes referred to as the shadow organization.
- The grapevine is the major informal communication channel, and it carries rumors and gossip.
- Chance encounters between managers and employees foster informal communication as does management by walking around.

Information technology creates challenges for interpersonal communication, despite all its advantages.

- E-mail has the most dramatic impact on interpersonal communication in organizations. Some workers are overwhelmed by e-mail, whereas others have the system under control.
- E-mail encourages informal, unprofessional communication, and the system is too often used to play office politics.
- E-mail should be used to supplement, not substitute, face-to-face negotiations.
- Some business firms have counterattacked the problems associated with e-mail by shifting to related technologies.

Presentation technology creates challenges of its own, including the need to learn how to handle equipment and maintain eye contact at the same time. It is important to talk to the audience and not the screen and reduce the text on each page to a bare minimum.

Effective telephone and voice mail communication skills are helpful in overcoming communication problems. Remember to vary your voice tone and avoid multitasking while speaking.

Telecommuters are now referred to as the distributed workforce.

- Telecommuters may miss out on the face-to-face interactions necessary for dealing with complex problems.
- Telecommuting is also a challenge because it lacks a solid human connection.

Electronic communication facilitates the multi-tasking that is so popular with generation Y.

- Advocates of multitasking claim it enhances productivity.
- The bulk of scientific evidence is that performing more than one demanding cognitive

activity at once lowers accuracy and productivity. Mental output and depth of thought deteriorate while multitasking.

Much of workplace communication takes place in meetings. Among the many suggestions for productive meetings are:

- Meet only for valid reasons.
- Start and stop on time and offer refreshments.
- Solve small issues ahead of time with e-mail.
- Minimize distractions during the meeting.

## Check your Understanding

1. The CEO of a professional basketball team described in the opening case has somebody print out his e-mail messages so he can read them. What might be his problem?
2. Suppose you thought that the CEO of your company was moving the company in the wrong direction, and you want to tell him or her. Explain which communication channel you would choose to deliver your message.
3. In what ways does diagonal communication make an organization more flexible?
4. In what way might management by walking around undermine the authority of the supervisor?

5. How might an e-mail message contain nonverbal communication?
6. Give three examples of business situations in which telephone conversations still play a key role.
7. Give an example from your own life in which multitasking has enhanced your performance?
8. Give an example from your own life in which multitasking has lowered your performance.
9. Why are face-to-face meetings still so popular even in high-technology companies?
10. Why do people complain so much about meetings on the job?

## Web Corner

*Suggestions for writing better e-mails:*
www.microsoft.com/smallbusiness/resources/technolgy/communication/bosses_10

*How to run an effective business meeting:*
www.allbusiness.com/business_advice/articles/11341.html

*Internet Skill Builder:*
Use your preferred search engine or engines to identify three different negative rumors about business companies. You might even find a Web site or two devoted to combating a particular rumor launched about a company. Attempt to identify how any of these rumors started or whether they had any validity. Do you have any thoughts as to what the companies involved might have done to combat these rumors?

# Developing Your Human Relations Skills

## Applying Human Relations Exercise 15-1

### Designing an Office for a Virtual Customer Agent

Work in a team to design a home office for a virtual customer agent, a worker whose responsibilities are to fill orders for merchandise for three different companies. The agent receives calls through a toll-free number and then uses the computer to enter the order. He or she also processes orders on-line. The office in question will be placed somewhere in a three bedroom house that also has a family room, kitchen, basement, and enclosed porch.

While designing the office, include such factors as the layout of the furniture and equipment, the equipment needed, and any decorations. Keep in mind ergonomic factors that focus on making the equipment easy to use and with low risk for physical problems such as carpal tunnel syndrome and backaches. Because the virtual agent will have to pay for the office setup, derive a tentative budget.

Draw your design on any convenient format including a flip chart, whiteboard, blackboard, or computer screen. Your team leader might be asked to present the design to the rest of the class so class members can compare the effectiveness of each design. Class members evaluating the home office design might use the following evaluation factors in addition to whatever their intuition suggests:

- To what extent does the office design help reduce possible conflict with other people living in the same household?
- How might this design offer productivity advantages over a conventional office?
- When and if customers or company representatives call into this office, how professional the will setup sound?
- How will this office design contribute to job satisfaction?

## Applying Human Relations Exercise 15-2

### Evaluating a Business Meeting

The class organizes into teams of about six students to conduct a meeting to formulate plans for building temporary housing for homeless people downtown in your city or a nearby city. Three other students, or the entire class, will observe the meeting. This exercise should take about 35 minutes; it can be done inside or outside of class. Each team takes on the assignment of formulating plans for building temporary shelters for the homeless. The dwellings you plan to build, for example, might be two-room cottages with electricity and indoor plumbing. During the time allotted to the task, formulate plans for going ahead with Shelters for the Homeless.

Consider dividing up work by assigning certain tasks to each team member. Sketch out tentative answers to the following questions: (1) How will you obtain funding for your venture? (2) Which homeless people will you help? (3) Where will your shelters be? (4) Who will do the actual construction?

After the meeting is completed, the three observers will provide feedback to the team members about the effectiveness of the meeting, using the following criteria:

1. How effective was the teamwork? Support you conclusion with an example of specific behavior.
2. How well did group members stay on track in terms of focusing on their goal?

3. Did the team members make any introductory warm-up comments to help build rapport?

4. To what extent was the participation among team members balanced?

5. Did the team move toward any conclusions or action plans?

6. Choose another criterion you think might be relevant.

## Human Relations Case Study 15-1

### *Can Microsoft Groups Communicate with Each Other?*

In March 2005, Microsoft Corp. consolidated six divisions into three, with each division having its own president, as shown in the accompanying organization chart. The hope of the new structure was that Microsoft will be able to more efficiently deliver products by combining technology from divisions that previously had difficulty in working together because they were in separate organizational units (divisions of the company). Robe Enderle, principal analyst for the research firm the Enderle Group in San Jose, California, said, "The company had become almost unmanageable. In the past two and a half years, it felt like you just couldn't get anything done. The turf wars became more pronounced."

Enderle used the example of the handheld gaming machines. "Microsoft couldn't build one because you have to bring together a bunch of different groups that don't work together," he said. An issue like this is capable of being resolved under the reorganization. One reason is that it aligns different groups that previously were separate divisions. Also, workers now have an approachable throat to choke—in the form of a division president—in case there are collaboration problems among the teams, Enderle said.

"Before you kind of had to go up to CEO Steve Ballmer, and you don't want to go up to him and say people aren't working together because Steve will start picking up bodies and hurling them around. Microsoft has built the company in a way that makes sense," said Enderle.

### Questions

1. In what way is the Microsoft reorganization a way of improving organizational communications?

2. Why will communication among the various groups now likely be better?

3. What suggestions can you offer Microsoft to obtain good communication among the three divisions?

4. Comment on the communication effectiveness of CEO Steve Ballmer.

**Source:** Chart derived from information presented in Robert A. Guth, "Microsoft to Restructure Businesses," *The Wall Street Journal*, September 21, 2005, pp. A3, A5; Elizabeth Montalbano, *IDG New Service*, San Francisco Bureau, September 21, 2005 (redistributed in *IT World.com*) www.microsoft.com; Allison Linn, "Microsoft Realigns Execs as Windows Update Lags," The Associated Press, March 24, 2006. As with any organization chart, the arrangement of people and the names of units are subject to frequent change.

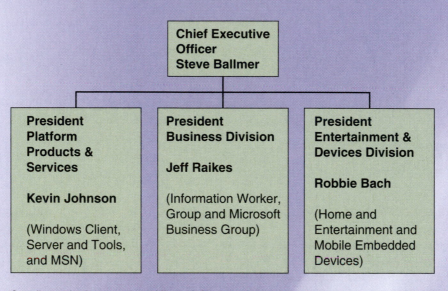

Overall organization structure at Microsoft Corp.

## Human Relations Case Study 15-2

### Is Telecommuting Good for Us?

Susan Lepsch and Russell Stratton, co-owners of Lepsch and Stratton Travel Agency, met for breakfast on the first Monday in July. "Either we take decisive action or we stop complaining about too little office space and too much turnover," said Russ. "We've expanded despite people making their own travel arrangements over the Internet. Our focus on giving advice that you don't get with the on-line travel agencies has helped us grow. We should expand our office from 4,000 to 5,000 square feet. Our volume of business is good, but not good enough to cover that much increase in expenses."

Sue responded, "I've read that one of the best ways to keep good office staff is to give them a work schedule that makes life easy. If we allowed our staff to telecommute, we could get by without the additional space. This would save us a lot of money."

"I'm willing to try the program on a voluntary basis," said Russ. "Who should we start with?"

"The likely candidates are the support specialists and one direct-mail specialists. Those people could do a substantial portion of their work at home if they had the right equipment. Our staff members all have PCs or laptops at home, but they might not have powerful enough equipment to run our software. They would need upgrades." Sue and Russ later identified five volunteers for the telecommuting program.

The telecommuting program was launched September 1. During mid-November, Sue and Russ decided to evaluate the new system. Neither partner had heard of any substantial complaint about the program from the employees or from travel clients because of poor service. If the program were working well, the present space could be retained, thus avoiding the expense and effort of relocation.

Sue began her evaluation of telecommuting by describing her experiences in supervising the work of Kim and Betty. "I was worried about the possibility of Kim not doing her job because she wasted time on the telephone and with e-mail. That proved to be not a problem. Kim did all the work that was required."

Russ spoke to Kristin, the direct-mail specialist, about her experiences as a teleworker. Kristin replied, "My reaction has been mixed. I enjoy being treated like a true professional. Nobody has to watch over me to see that I get my work done. Besides, our work is driven by clients anyway. I like saving commuting time, so I have a little more time for reading the newspaper and taking care of errands."

"What I don't like is being so alienated from the office. I want to move up to supervisor as our agency expands substantially. If you two hardly ever see me, I could easily be passed over for promotion. Another problem I didn't anticipate is the distraction at home. My daughter asks me for rides, and my friends drop by. People simply don't take working at home as seriously as working in an office building."

Sue asked Cindy, one of the support specialists, for her reaction to working at home. With a gleam in her eye and a smile, Cindy replied, "Telecommuting has helped make my life work. My biggest problem before working at home was that I had a latchkey child. Trevor, my son, is too old for child care yet too young to go home unsupervised. He gets home at around 3:15 in the afternoon. When he arrives, he knows that I'm working, but it's better than my not being on the premises. By not worrying so much about Trevor on my working days, I feel much less stressed and better able to concentrate on my work."

Russ interviewed Tony, another support specialist, about his telecommuting experiences. "On a scale of 1 to 10," said Tony, "I would rate teleworking a 5. I like being able to avoid commuting on a day when road conditions are bad. And I like getting home from work at 4:31 after having stopped work at 4:30. The pay is the same so I have no complaints there."

"What reservations do you have?" Russ asked.

"I miss the interaction with the office buddies," said Tony. "I never wanted to be a loner. I like people. I like taking coffee breaks with coworkers. At home, I drink my coffee at my desk. For a break, I take out the garbage. If I'm lucky, I say hello to the mail carrier."

After this round of interviews, Sue and Russ had not made up their minds about the effectiveness of the telecommuting program. Sue mentioned, however, "I don't know how far we will go with telecommuting. But I do know that we will always need somebody around the office to talk to our clients both in person and on the phone."

## Questions

1. What is your opinion of the effectiveness of the telecommuting program at the travel agency so far?
2. What evidence should Sue and Russ be seeking to know if the telecommuting program is beneficial to the travel agency?
3. What recommendations do you have for Tony so his teleworking will become a more positive experience for him?

# REFERENCES

1. Adapted from Secrets of Success: All in a Day's Work," *Fortune*, March 20, 2006, pp. 97–105.
2. "Keep Workers in the Loop or They'll Say Goodbye," *Employee Recruitment & Retention*, Sample Issue, 2004.
3. Patrick Kiger, "Lessons from a Crisis: How Communication Kept a Company Together," *Workforce*, November 2001, p. 28.
4. Michelle Conlin and Andrew Park, "Blogging with the Boss's Blessing," *Business Week*, June 28, 2004, p. 102.
5. "It's Hard to Manage If You Don't Blog," *Fortune*, October 4, 2004, p. 46.
6. Mark Hendricks, "The Shadow Knows," *Entrepreneur*, January 2000, p. 110.
7. Rob Cross and Sally Colella, "Building Vibrant Employee Networks," *HR Magazine*, December 2004, pp. 101–104.
8. Interview with Bob Rosner, "Studying the World Beneath the Org Chart," *Workforce*, September 2001, p. 65.
9. Sameul Greengard, "Gossip Poisons Business: HR Can Stop It," *Workforce*, July 2001, pp. 26–27; Lea Winerman, "Have Your Heard the Latest?" *Monitor on Psychology*, April 2006, pp. 56–57.
10. "Make the Rumor Mill Work for You," *Executive Leadership*, May 2003, p. 7.
11. Anne Fisher, "Psst! Rumors Can Help at Work," *Fortune*, December 12, 2005, p. 202.
12. John P. Kotter, *The General Managers* (New York: Free Press, 1991).
13. "'Making Rounds' Like a Physician," *Manager's Edge*, February 8, 2006. As adapted from Quint Studer, *Hardwiring Excellence* (Gulf Breeze, FL: Fire Starter Publishing, 2005).
14. "Using E-Mail and Voice Mail Effectively," *Business Education Forum*, October 1998, pp. 6–9, 51; Andrew Blackman, "Spam's 'Easy Target,'" *The Wall Street Journal*, August 19, 2003, pp. B1, B4.
15. Survey reported in Carol Monaghan, "Inbox Glutted? Maybe You're a Power E-Mailer," *Chicago Tribune*, December 15, 2002.
16. Letitia Baldrige, "How to Cope with E-mails," Briefings Publishing Group, available at *www.briefings.com*. Retrieved February 15, 2003.
17. Janice Nadler, "Rapport in Legal Negotiation: How Small Talk Can Facilitate Email Dealmaking," *Harvard Negotiation Law Review*, Vol. 9, 2004, pp. 225–253.
18. Michelle Conlin, "E-Mail Is So Five Minutes Ago: It's Being Replaced by Software That Promotes Real-Time Collaboration," *Business Week*, November 28, 2005, pp. 111–112.
19. Jean Mausehund and R. Neil Dortch, "Presentation Skills in the Digital Age," *Business Education Forum*, April 1999, pp. 30–32; Michael Patterson, "The Pitch Coach," *Business Week SmallBiz*, Fall 2005, p. 61.
20. John T. Adams, III, "When You're on a Speakerphone, Don't Make Noise," *HR Magazine*, March 2001, p. 12.
21. Based on U.S. Bureau of Labor statistics and data reported in Michelle Conlin, "The Easiest Commute of All," *Business Week*, December 12, 2005, p. 79.
22. "Work à la Modem," *Business Week*, October 4, 1999, p. 176.
23. "Secrets of Greatness: How I Work," *Fortune*, March 20, 2006, p. 68.
24. The scientific information about multitasking is reviewed in Claudia Wallis, "The Multitasking Generation," *Time*, March 27, 2006, pp. 48–55. See also Joshua Rubinstein, David Meyer, and Jeffrey Evans, "Human Perception and Performance," *Journal of Experimental Psychology*, no 4, 2001.
25. Research reported in "Post-It Persuasion: Read Me Now!" *Psychology Today*, December 2005, p. 32.
26. Martha McKay, "Face-to-Face Meetings Gain Remote Possibilities," *The Bergen, N.J. Record*, March 20, 2006.
27. Ed Frauenheim, "Custom-Fit Communication," *Workforce Management*, November 21, 2005, p. 30.
28. Pamela Babcock, "Sending the Message," *HR Magazine*, November 2003, p. 70.